TEST

MID. I → 87/100

OVER 50 =

A+
A
A-   13
B+   12
B   11
B-   10
C+   9
C   8
C-   7

W9-BNI-379

32

MANAGEMENT

3567   135.95

Exame
31 inent
18 mult. choice
Numer

MANAGEMENT
THIRD EDITION

ROBERT KREITNER
Arizona State University

HOUGHTON MIFFLIN COMPANY BOSTON
Dallas   Geneva, Illinois   Lawrenceville, New Jersey   Palo Alto

Dedicated with love to three very special ladies:
Margaret, Caroline, and Jean (my wife,
my mother, and my mother-in-law).

Cover photography by Martin Paul.

Copyright © 1986 by Houghton Mifflin Company. All Rights Reserved.

No part of this work may be reproduced or transmitted in any form or by any means, electronic or mechanical, including photocopying and recording, or by any information storage or retrieval system, except as may be expressly permitted by the 1976 Copyright Act or in writing by the Publisher. Requests for permission should be addressed to Permissions, Houghton Mifflin Company, One Beacon Street, Boston, Massachusetts 02108.

Printed in the U.S.A.

Library of Congress Catalog Card Number: 85-80157

ISBN: 0-395-35676-8

BCDEFGHIJ-D-89876

Contents

5 Strategic Management: Planning for Long-Term Success 162

8 Organizing

9 Staffing and Human Resource Management

14 Change and Organization Development 491

Part V Controlling 527

15 The Control Function 528

Part VI   Expanding Horizons in Management   651

18   Social Responsibility and Business Ethics   652

Preface

Management, Third Edition, is a comprehensive introduction to management theory and practice. It is intended to help today's students successfully meet the challenge of effectively and efficiently managing society's large or small, profit and not-for-profit organizations. This third edition is organized according to a traditional functional/process approach. It combines important traditional and modern concepts of management theory, in a highly readable writing style, with abundant examples and cases from the real world of management practice.

In order to make *Management,* Third Edition, as complete a teaching and learning tool as possible, careful steps have been taken to achieve balances in topical coverage, approach, and degree of theoretical and practical emphasis. Where appropriate, timely research evidence has been integrated into the discussion to provide valuable insights. Based on feedback from instructors and students who used the first and second editions and from general market surveys, forty-four topics, concepts, and applications that were not discussed in the first two editions have been added. Among the new topics are small business and public sector management, an agenda for improving productivity, organizational cultures, functions of mentors, the personal computer revolution, and *kanban* inventory control. Moreover, twenty-one real-life cases have been added, thus bringing the total case count to thirty-seven. The net result is a relevant, up-to-date, and interesting treatment of all the major approaches to the study and practice of management.

Reflecting AACSB recommendations and emerging trends in the field of management, the following topical areas receive full chapter treatment:

- Strategic management.
- Organizations and organizational cultures.
- Decision making and problem solving (with special emphasis on creativity).
- Information management (with special emphasis on personal computers).
- Operations management.
- Social responsibility and business ethics.
- International management.

Management, Third Edition, is organized according to the traditional functional framework, beginning with the planning function and concluding with the controlling function. Some structural changes have been made in response to feedback from users of the second edition. For example, the third edition has nineteen chapters as opposed to twenty-one in the second edition. This consolidation was achieved by integrating material from second edition Chapters 6 and 19 into third edition Chapter 4 and Appendix B.

In addition to topical updating and structural refinements, a concerted effort has been made to weave fresh, real-life examples into each chapter. The result is a realistic picture of what managers are doing today and are likely to do in the years ahead.

Pedagogical features and real-world examples play a key role in making *Management,* Third Edition, a relevant and instructive teaching and learning tool that will satisfy the needs of professors and students alike. This is evidenced by the following:

- Both within the text and in supporting cases, many references are made to such well-known organizations as Procter & Gamble, K mart, Pan Am, Chrysler, Revlon, Pizza Hut, Sears, and Texaco.
- Because they were received so well in the second edition, this edition includes nineteen chapter-opening cases that capture throught-provoking, real-world situations. At the end of each chapter are stimulating discussion questions that help the reader integrate the opening cases and textual material. Among the organizations treated in brand new chapter-opening cases are People Express, McDonald's, Apple Computer, IBM, and Exxon.
- Chapter objectives at the beginning of each chapter focus the reader's attention on key concepts.
- Key terms listed at the end of each chapter further reinforce important concepts.
- Clear, comprehensive chapter summaries refresh the reader's memory of important material.
- Chapter-closing cases and exercises afford additional opportunities for analyzing and handling real-world management problems. Among the organizations covered in the chapter-closing cases are AT&T, Adolph Coors, Intel, General Motors, Ford, Motorola, Manville, and IBM Japan.
- Ten discussion questions following each chapter enhance understanding by helping the reader personalize the textual material.
- An end-of-text glossary (with chapter annotations) of all key terms provides a handy reference for the study of management.

A comprehensive study guide—*Understanding Management,* Third Edition, by Kreitner and Sova—provides additional review and reinforcement of all topics covered in the text. Each study guide chapter includes a chapter summary, review of chapter objectives, and terms to understand. A chapter self-quiz of true/false, multiple-choice, matching, completion, and discussion questions follows, with complete answers at the end of the study guide. Following each of the six sections is a collection of relevant, informative, and interesting experiential exercises, self-awareness questionnaires, cases, readings, and skill-building exercises. New to this edition are nineteen crossword-review exercises that test the reader's knowledge of key concepts, names, and facts in a challenging but enjoyable manner. Answers to the exercises, cases, and crossword reviews, as well as analyses of the readings, are provided in the back of the study guide for immediate feedback.

Another instructional aid is a computerized management game called *Manager II: A Simulation* prepared by Dr. Jerald R. Smith. This game simulates a business environment in which students act as management teams to produce and market a product. Players experience both positive and negative outcomes of various management decisions.

Literally scores of people, including colleagues, students, and relatives, have contributed in countless ways to the three editions of this book. Whether critical or reinforcing, all of their suggestions and recommendations have been helpful and greatly appreciated. While it is impossible to acknowledge every contributor here, some key people need to be identified and sincerely thanked.

All of my colleagues in the Department of Management at Arizona State University have given generously and unselfishly of their time, talent, and enthusiasm to this project through the years. I particularly appreciate the help of my colleague and good friend Professor Angelo Kinicki. Professors Jack Mendleson, Dick Montanari, Bill Ruch, Frank Shipper, and Peter Hom also deserve thanks for responding so cheerfully and helpfully when I charged into their offices time and again seeking ideas, materials, citations, and support. Thanks also to my brother Clint Kreitner, president of American Information Systems, for reading and commenting on the real-world value of some of the cases.

Warm thanks are also extended to the following colleagues from around the country who have provided valuable input in reviewing the manuscript:

Gerald E. Ridinger
Kent State University

Arlyn J. Melcher
Kent State University

Charles R. Williams
Michigan State University

Leslie E. Munneke
Pan American University

Alonzo J. Strickland
University of Alabama

Thomas P. Verney
Shippensburg State College

Abraham Stein
Hofstra University

Kenneth Lundberg
Rhode Island College

Allen K. Gulezien
Central Washington University

Donald A. Ryktarsyk
Schoolcraft College

Donald S. Tompkins
*Slippery Rock University of
    Pennsylvania*

Harvey Tschirgi
Ohio University

Richard M. Conboy
*University of North Carolina—
    Charlotte*

Arthur L. Darrow
Bowling Green State University

Monique A. Pelletier
San Francisco State University

Jack L. Mendleson
Arizona State University

Ronald W. Clement
Murray State University

Edwin C. Leonard, Jr.
Purdue Univeristy at Fort Wayne

Angelo Kinicki
Arizona State University

Robert I. Kutscher
*California State University—
    Fresno*

William P. Smith
Hofstra University

Robert J. Piersol
*California State University—
    Fresno*

Lance Masters
*California State College at San
    Bernadino*

Jerald W. Young
University of Florida

M. Dean Martin
Western Carolina University

David Abner
Howard University

The discussion of mentoring in Chapter 13 is dedicated once again with respect and appreciation to Coach Don Watchorn and Professor Fred Luthans, two mentors who headed me in constructive directions. For their continuing wise counsel and support, I would like to extend a special thanks to two colleagues and good friends, Professor Keith Davis and Dean Bill Reif. To Margaret, my wife and hiking buddy, go my warmest thanks for another great job on the study guide, for her keen common sense, and most of all, for being herself.

Finally, I would like to thank the hundreds of introductory management students I have had the pleasure of working with through the years for teaching me a great deal about tomorrow's managers. Best wishes for a rewarding career in management.

R.K.

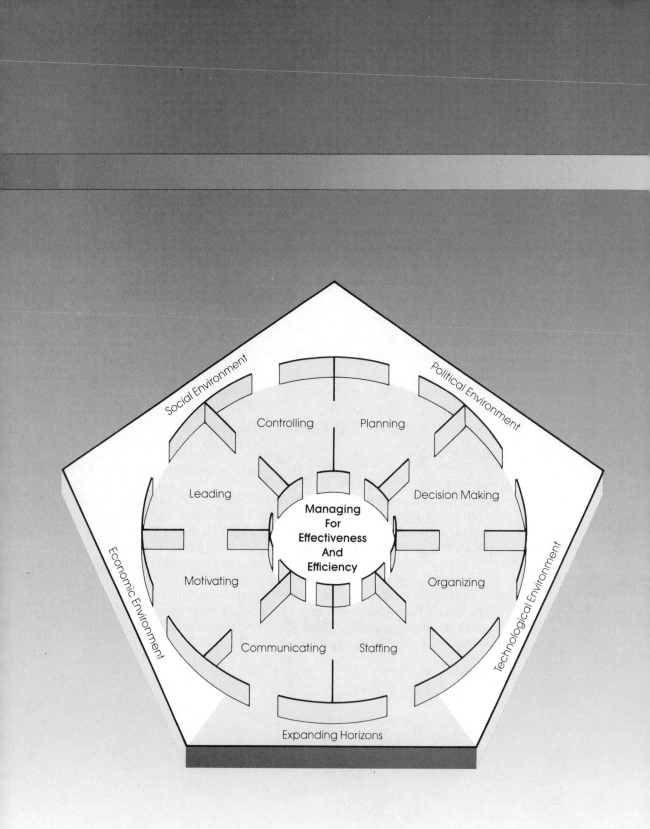

PART ONE

The Management Challenge

Part One provides a background for what lies ahead by defining the management process, reviewing management history, and exploring the changing environment of management. In Chapter 1, the term *management* is formally defined and the practice of management is discussed from different perspectives. A formula for managerial success is provided for those who wish to set their sights on a career in management in large or small businesses or the public sector. Chapter 2 amounts to a brief history of management thought. Modern-day management concepts and approaches make more sense when one appreciates how they have evolved through the years. Since management is not practiced in a vacuum, attention turns in Chapter 3 to the social, political-legal, economic, and technological environments of management. Those managers who anticipate and prepare for inevitable environmental changes will tend to be the more successful ones.

Chapter 1

The Nature of Management

The only choice for an institution is between management and mismanagement. ... Whether it is being done right or not will determine largely whether the enterprise will survive and prosper or decline and ultimately fail.

Peter F. Drucker

Chapter Objectives

When you finish studying this chapter, you should be able to

- Define the term *management* and explain the managerial significance of the terms *effectiveness* and *efficiency*.
- Contrast the functional and role approaches to explaining what managers do.
- Explain the nature of the basic formula for managerial success (S = A × M × O).
- Discuss the unique challenges that managers face in small businesses and public sector organizations.
- Explain why productivity improvement is the central challenge for modern managers.

Opening Case 1.1

Through the Looking Glass—A Manager in Action*

Among the activities at the Center for Creative Leadership in Greensboro, North Carolina, is a simulation called Looking Glass, Inc. "The design of the simulation," says the Center, "recreates accurately the demanding, fast-paced, complex world of a large organization. By studying the behavior of managers participating in Looking Glass, researchers here

*Reprinted by permission of The Conference Board and of the Center for Creative Leadership Newsletter, February, 1980.

hope to answer questions about the relationships between managers and organization." Not long ago the Center sent a member of its Newsletter staff to participate in a simulation session and report. She had the role of Plant Manager, Commercial Glass Division. Here ... [are some excerpts from] her story.

It was 8:00, fully one hour before the day would begin and the switchboard would open. The morning mail had yet to be delivered. Still, my in-basket was already overloaded with memos. I began to read quickly, voraciously, knowing these few moments were precious. Once the day actually began, interruption would follow interruption. The incessant ringing of the phone and the inevitable meetings would preclude reflection and concentrated reading.

As usual, my in-basket was a potpourri of problems and issues that required my attention. Some were serious—a possible shortage of soda ash, an ingredient critical to my glass manufacturing operation; a letter from the EPA [Environmental Protection Agency] threatening to shut down my plant if the emissions from the stacks could not be cleaned up; other problems with equipment and personnel. There were also the seemingly less consequential issues—the invitation to brunch at the V.P.'s home; the request from the local Rotary Club for a speaker at their next meeting, which had been routed to me by my boss, the Director of Manufacturing for the Commercial Glass Division. Since I am ambitious and eager to get ahead, I knew that my responses to these invitations were almost as important to my career as my decisions on the soda ash and emission problems.

I was beginning to feel a little less overwhelmed by 8:45. I had at least glanced at all the memos. I had begun to establish priorities and to think about how to attack the most pressing problems. Then the quiet ended.

I heard the voices of my boss and the other Plant Manager in Commercial Glass. ... I decided to get a cup of coffee and get into the conversation.

"Just the person I wanted to see," my boss said to me as I approached the coffee machine. "We're having a division meeting at 9:30. I'll want to discuss union, EPA, sales figures for the quarter, and the production problems in your plant."

I groaned inwardly. Another meeting, and I really needed to get on the soda ash thing. I smiled. ... My stomach began the familiar tightening. Sales figures, I thought anxiously. They were pretty grim last quarter. Of course, if you're running at 105 percent of capacity, how are you going to sell more? ... I got on the phone and called my purchasing man. Yes, he knew about the pending soda ash problem. What did I want him to do? I resisted the urge to tell him irritably that I was paying *him* to be on top of things and to give *me* suggestions. He was new in the job, and although I prefer to manage people who need virtually no training or supervision, you sometimes have to suit your management style to the situation. I explained what I felt should be done. ...

9:20. The meeting was ten minutes away and I wasn't prepared. But the phone was ringing insistently and my secretary was away. As I answered, my stomach tightened another notch. It was the quality control manager. Something about the new packing suggested by R&D [research and development] and 200,000 bulb casings that had been shattered. Just what we needed when we were running at capacity. I promised to get back after talking to R&D. Good thing I had to go to the meeting. I didn't need to meet the R&D people now. Here I was fighting for renovation dollars, and money was being poured down the tubes to finance their pie-in-the-sky ideas.

I grabbed my notes and memos and dashed to the meeting, my phone jangling behind me.

The meeting seemed interminable. Lots of talk. Not many decisions. My mind kept wandering back to the soda ash [and emission problems]. Then we were talking about sales. I winced when my plant's dismal record was paraded. There were good reasons why we couldn't sell more, although it would take too long to explain them. Fighting back my frustration, I promised to do better. ...

I returned to my desk. There were four phone messages and five more memos. ... The phone rang. A plant manager in the Advanced Products Division was requesting a meeting at 1:00 to discuss tactics for a performance appraisal task force we'd been appointed to. Since I was supposed to chair the committee, I agreed reluctantly to a meeting over lunch. ...

Fatigued with the pressures, I pushed aside the bigger problems, hoping to get a sense of accomplishment by dealing with some smaller ones. I dashed off memos saying "yes" to the brunch and the Rotary Club appearance, approved a raise for my Plant Engineer, and dictated a note to Legal about the EPA predicament.

Then I concentrated on my notes for the luncheon meeting. I made two calls to get information. One source couldn't give me what I needed, and the other's line was busy.

Before I was ready, it was time to meet and eat. My stomach had registered the full shock of a frenetic, demanding, often frustrating Monday morning in the Looking Glass. ...

(Discussion questions linking this case with the material you are about to read can be found at the end of this chapter.)

In our increasingly complex and rapidly changing world, the need for intelligent management is greater than ever before. Many difficult and worrisome problems have emerged in recent years, and they will not go away by themselves. As our opening case illustrates, a modern manager faces a variety of pressures and challenges. Adequately informed and competent managers are needed to help us move ahead by seeing our problems as opportunities rather than obstacles. Exciting and progressive things can happen when managers turn obstacles into constructive and socially responsible opportunities.

Management can be studied from two very different perspectives: one is personal, the other global. From a personal perspective, a working knowledge of management theory and practice helps us understand what makes today's complex profit and not-for-profit organizations tick. More importantly, a basic knowledge of management is a useful steppingstone to productive and gainful employment in a highly organized world in which virtually everything is managed.

From a global perspective, two apparently unrelated events that occurred during your lifetime symbolize the ultimate in successful management and mismanagement.

On July 20, 1969, Neil Armstrong became the first human being to set foot on the moon. The largest television audience ever assembled held its breath as the *Apollo 11* commander spoke those unforgettable words, "One small step for man, one giant leap for mankind," from a distance of a quarter of a million miles. An event that many had considered impossible just a few years earlier had become a reality. Human imagination swelled with visions of how wonderful the world could become through the application of space-age technology and management.

Neil Armstrong's walk on the moon was dramatic testimony to effective management, demonstrating that systematically managed technology and resources could extend our reach to unbelievable limits. For example, the 500,000-mile round trip of *Apollo 11* required eighty-eight major steps. The failure of even a single step could have destroyed the mission or cost the lives of the crew; yet the mission was successful. As the largest peacetime program ever undertaken, it amounted to an incredible investment of talent and money. Construction of the *Apollo* rockets, spacecraft, and support equipment required the efforts of 20,000 industrial contractors and a total of 400,000 people. The final price tag for the *Mercury, Gemini,* and *Apollo* programs was over $25 billion.[1] While reviewing the success of his *Apollo* executive group, made up of the chief executive officers of the U.S. industrial firms that contributed to America's moon-landing effort, Dr. George Mueller saw "no black magic in what they did—only determined management."[2]

Less than one year later, on April 22, 1970, a second significant, but less heralded, event took place: the first Earth Day was observed. Noisy but relatively peaceful demonstrations took place around the world to protest the careless destruction of our natural environment. Human imagination was haunted by visions of a mismanaged, polluted, ugly, and unlivable earth.

If *Apollo 11* was a testimony to effective management, then Earth Day was a recognition of gross mismanagement. Earth Day observers each year point to smog-filled skies, sewage-choked rivers and streams, rapidly depleting water tables, uncontrolled hazardous wastes, and vegetation-stripped land as evidence of the haphazard mismanagement of our natural resources. Since the first Earth Day, many have come to realize that all earthly resources are limited. Even once-abundant and traditionally free resources such as fresh air and clear water have proved to be in short supply. According to editorialist Dael Wolfle, "Earth Day was a day of excitement, indignation, and dedication. That was a start, but the problems Man has given Earth require more than a day; they need permanent attention."[3] That permanent attention means wise management.

Apollo 11 and Earth Day represent the overriding challenge to today's and tomorrow's managers. Specifically, managers need to understand that their day-to-day decisions and actions ultimately have a global impact. Effective management helps promote a better world, but mismanagement squanders our resources and jeopardizes our well-being. Every manager, regardless of his or her level or scope of responsibility, is either part of the solution or part of the problem. The choice is ours, management or mismanagement.

Management Defined

We now need to define management, in order to highlight the importance, relevance, and necessity of studying management.

Management is the process of working with and through others to achieve organizational objectives in a changing environment. Central to this process is the effective and efficient use of limited resources.

Five parts of this definition require closer examination, (1) working with and through others, (2) organizational objectives, (3) effectiveness versus efficiency, (4) limited resources, and (5) changing environment (see Figure 1.1).

Working with and Through Others

Management is, above all else, a social process. For whatever collective purpose that individuals are brought together (for example, to build cars, provide emergency health care, or publish books), managers are responsible for getting things done by working with and through others. Aspiring

Figure 1.1 Key Aspects of the Management Process

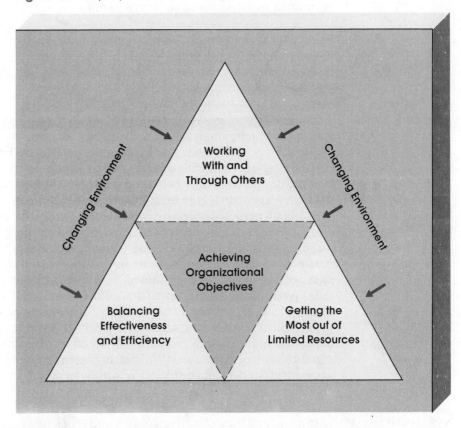

managers who do not interact well with others hamper their careers. A recent study of 20 successful managers and 21 "derailed" managers underscores the importance of being able to work effectively with and through others. In this study, managers were considered to be derailed if they did not live up to what their peers and superiors originally expected of them. In contrast to their successful colleagues, the derailed managers were found to have made these mistakes:

1. Insensitive to others; abrasive, intimidating, bullying style.
2. Cold, aloof, arrogant.
3. Betrayal of trust.
4. Overly ambitious: thinking of next job, playing politics.
5. Specific performance problems with the business.
6. Overmanaging: unable to delegate or build a team.
7. Unable to staff effectively.
8. Unable to think strategically.

9. Unable to adapt to boss with different style.
10. Overdependent on advocate or mentor.[4]

Significantly, only two of these shortcomings, numbers 5 and 8, are not directly related to working effectively with and through others. People—whether superiors, peers, or subordinates—can literally make or break one's career in management.

Organizational Objectives

An objective is a target to be strived for and, one hopes, attained. Organizations, like individuals, are usually more successful when their activities are guided by challenging, yet achievable, objectives. From an individual perspective, the scheduling of a student's course load becomes more systematic and efficient when he or she sets an objective, such as graduating with a specific degree by a given date.

Although personal objectives are typically within the reach of individual effort, organizational objectives require joint or collective action. For example, when McDonald's set an organizational objective to serve every customer in sixty seconds or less, numerous individuals in many different areas of the business contributed to the effort. Equipment had to be redesigned, work rules had to be reformulated, and people had to be retrained. The complexity of collective action necessitates systematic management. Organizational objectives give purpose and direction to the management process. Organizational objectives also serve later as measuring sticks for performance. Without organizational objectives, the management process would be like a trip without a specific destination, aimless and wasteful.

Effectiveness Versus Efficiency

Distinguishing between effectiveness and efficiency is much more than an exercise in semantics. The relationship between these two terms is important, and it presents managers with a never-ending dilemma. **Effectiveness** entails achieving a stated objective. Swinging a sledgehammer against the wall, for example, would be an effective way of killing a bothersome fly. But given the reality of limited resources, effectiveness alone is not enough. **Efficiency** enters the picture when the resources required to achieve an objective are weighed against what was actually accomplished. The more favorable the ratio of benefits to costs, the greater the efficiency. Although a sledgehammer is an effective way of killing flies, it is highly inefficient when the wasted effort and smashed walls are taken into consideration. A fly swatter is both an effective and efficient way of killing a single housefly.

Managers are responsible for balancing effectiveness and efficiency (see Figure 1.2). On the one hand, managers must be effective by getting the job done. But on the other hand, they need to be efficient by containing costs as much as possible and conserving limited resources. *Columbia,* Amer-

Figure 1.2 Balancing Effectiveness and Efficiency

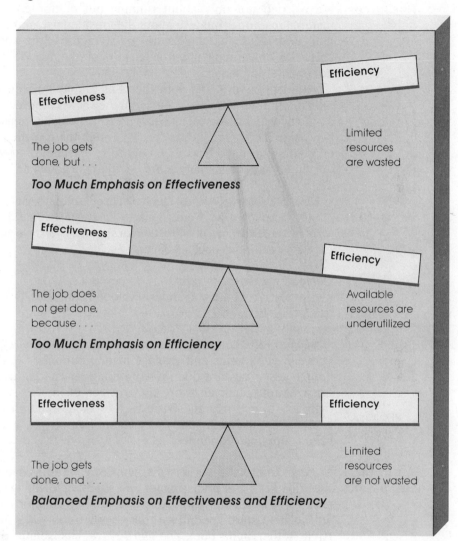

ica's first successful space shuttle, is a prime example of an effective but inefficient program. Though *Columbia* did indeed make the spectacular round trip from earth to space and back without a hitch, a 30 percent cost overrun mushroomed its price tag to $9.9 billion.[5] Too much emphasis in either direction leads to mismanagement. Managers who are too stingy with resources will not get the job done. Managers who waste resources may get the job done but risk bankruptcy in the process.

**Limited
Resources**

We live in a world of scarcity. Those who are concerned with such matters are worried not only about running out of nonrenewable energy and material resources but also about the lopsided use of those resources. The United States, for example, with one-sixteenth of the world's population is currently consuming about one-third of the world's annual output of nonrenewable resources.[6]

Although experts and nonexperts alike may quibble over exactly how long it will take to exhaust our nonrenewable resources or come up with exotic new technological alternatives, one bold fact remains. Our planet is becoming increasingly crowded. Although the growth rate of the world's population dropped from 2 percent to 1.7 percent between 1974 and 1984, our finite planet has many more occupants each year.

> During the past decade, the number of people on earth increased by 770 million, to 4.75 billion. The World Bank estimates that in 2025, a date within the foreseeable lifetime of most Americans under 30, global population could nearly double, to about 8.3 billion.[7]

Considering that approximately 84 percent of those 8.3 billion people will live in relatively poor and underdeveloped countries, developed and industrialized nations will be pressured to divide the limited resource pie more equitably.

Because of a common focus on resources, there is a close relationship between economics and management. Economics is the study of how limited resources are distributed among alternative uses. In productive organizations, managers are the trustees of limited resources, and it is their job to see that the basic factors of production—land, labor, and capital—are used efficiently as well as effectively. Management could be called "applied economics."

**Changing
Environment**

More and more, the world is characterized by rapid change. Managers face the difficult task of preparing for and adapting to change rather than being passively swept along by it. An awareness of the major sources of change is an excellent starting point for today's and tomorrow's managers. Futurist Alvin Toffler, in his book *The Third Wave,* has isolated five major sources of change likely to affect the practice of management:

1. **Physical environment.** A growing world population is stretching the planet's carrying capacity. This stress is demonstrated by resource depletion and pollution. Toffler believes that if managers do not voluntarily shift their environmental impacts from negative to positive, they will be forced by popular public opinion to do so.
2. **Social environment.** Society has fragmented into many well-educated, highly organized, and politically astute special interest groups who

examine and often criticize key managerial decisions. These groups are more interested in business's "social" products, such as unemployment and community disruption, than they are in economic products, such as profits.

3. **Informational environment.** As information becomes an even more vital resource, conflict over the control of information will increase. Huge volumes of information moving through space-age electronic networks will put additional pressures on managers to get the best available information and use it wisely while at the same time protecting the individual's right to privacy.

4. **Political environment.** Since productive organizations unavoidably produce political impacts along with goods and services, managers will increasingly be drawn into local, regional, national, and international politics, and they are being held accountable for their uses and abuses of political power.

5. **Moral environment.** Managers are under strong pressure to behave better. Traditional values such as honesty and integrity will become more important in managerial decision making and conduct. Because of closer public scrutiny, ethical questions will not be easily ignored.[8]

Considering the variety of these sources of change, successful managers will be those who are aware of world events and trends outside their organizations.

What Do Managers Do?

Although nearly all aspects of modern life are touched at least indirectly by the work of managers, many people do not really understand what the management process is. Management is much more, for example, than the familiar activity of telling employees what to do. Management is a complex and dynamic mixture of systematic techniques and common sense. As with any complex process, the key to learning about management lies in dividing it into readily understood subprocesses. Currently, there are two different approaches to dividing the management process for study and discussion. One approach, dating back to the early part of this century, is to separate managerial functions. A second, more recent approach focuses on managerial roles. **Managerial functions** are general administrative duties carried out in virtually all productive organizations. **Managerial roles** are specific categories of managerial behavior. Functions tend to be more general and more encompassing than roles. Because managerial roles are more behaviorally specific than functions, a growing number of

"You know what I'd like to do, Caslow? I'd like to create a far-reaching, innovative program that will open a lot of channels, offer great opportunities, link up with all kinds of things, and enable something or other to happen. Any ideas?"
Source: Drawing by Stevenson; © 1985; The New Yorker Magazine, Inc.

management experts believe that a great deal can be learned about effective and ineffective management by observing the roles managers play in various situations. We shall examine both of these approaches more closely.

Managerial Functions

For more than half a century, the functional view has been the most popular approach to describing what managers do. It has been popular because it characterizes the management process as a sequence of rational steps. Henri Fayol, a French industrialist turned writer, became the father of the functional approach in 1916 when he identified five managerial functions: planning, organizing, command, coordination, and control.[9] Fayol claimed that these five functions were the common denominators of all managerial jobs, whatever the purpose of the organization. Over the years Fayol's original list of managerial functions has been updated and expanded by management scholars. For example, this book is organized around eight different managerial functions: planning, decision making, organizing, staffing, communicating, motivating, leading, and controlling (see Figure 1.3). A brief overview of these eight managerial functions will describe what managers do and preview what lies ahead in this text.

Figure 1.3 Identifiable Functions in the Management Process

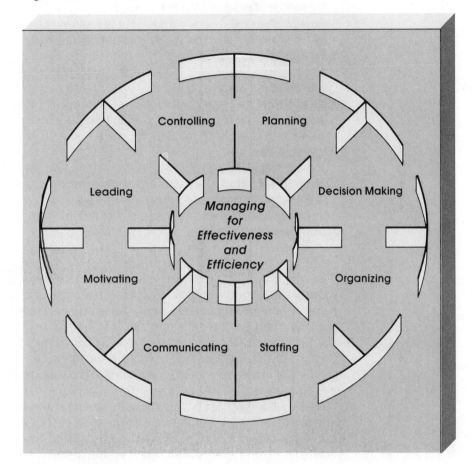

- **Planning.** Commonly referred to as the primary management function, planning is the formulation of future courses of action. Plans and the objectives on which they are based give purpose and direction to the organization, its subunits, and contributing individuals.
- **Decision making.** Managers choose among alternative courses of action when they make decisions. Making the correct decision in today's complex world is a major management challenge.
- **Organizing.** Structural considerations such as the chain of command, division of labor, and assignment of responsibility are part of the organizing function. Careful organizing helps ensure the efficient use of human resources.
- **Staffing.** Organizations are only as good as the people in them. Staffing

consists of recruiting, training, and developing people who can contribute to the organized effort.

- **Communicating.** Today's managers are responsible for communicating to their employees the technical knowledge, instructions, rules, and information required to get the job done. Recognizing that communication is a two-way process, managers should be responsive to feedback and upward communication.
- **Motivating.** An important aspect of management today is motivating individuals to pursue collective objectives by satisfying needs and meeting expectations with meaningful work and valued rewards.
- **Leading.** Managers become inspiring leaders by serving as role models and adapting their management style to the demands of the situation.
- **Controlling.** When managers compare desired results with actual results and take the necessary corrective action, they are keeping things on track through the control function. Deviations from past plans should be considered when formulating new plans.

Managerial Roles

During the 1970s, a researcher named Henry Mintzberg criticized the traditional functional approach as unrealistic. His firsthand observation of managers and similar studies conducted by others led him to conclude that functions "tell us little about what managers actually do. At best they indicate some vague objectives managers have when they work."[10] Because of the longstanding popularity of the traditional functional perspective, Mintzberg's work has stirred a degree of controversy in management circles.

Those who agree with Mintzberg believe that the functional approach portrays the management process as far more systematic and rational and less complex than it really is. Even the most casual observation reveals that managers do not plan on Monday, organize on Tuesday, coordinate on Wednesday, and so on, as the functional approach might lead one to believe. Moreover, according to the Mintzberg view, the average manager is not the reflective planner and precise "orchestra leader" that the functional approach suggests (see Table 1.1 for a nonfunctional profile of managers). Mintzberg characterizes the typical manager in the following way: "The manager is overburdened with obligations; yet he cannot easily delegate his tasks. As a result, he is driven to overwork and is forced to do many tasks superficially. Brevity, fragmentation, and verbal communication characterize his work."[11]

Mintzberg and his followers have suggested that a more fruitful way of studying what managers do is to focus on the key roles they play. Using a method called "structured observation" which entailed recording the activities and correspondence of top-level managers, Mintzberg isolated ten roles that he believes are common to managers at all levels.[12] These ten

Table 1.1 Ten Facts of Managerial Life (from direct observation and diaries)

1. **Managers work long hours.** The number of hours worked tends to increase as one climbs the managerial ladder.
2. **Managers are busy.** The typical manager's day is made up of hundreds of brief incidents or episodes. Activity rates tend to decrease as rank increases.
3. **A manager's work is fragmented; episodes are brief.** Given managers' high activity level, they have little time to devote to any single activity. Interruptions and discontinuity are the rule.
4. **The manager's job is varied.** Managers engage in a variety of activities (paperwork, phone calls, scheduled and unscheduled meetings, and inspection tours/visits), interact with a variety of people, and deal with a variety of content areas.
5. **Managers are "homebodies."** Managers spend most of their time pursuing activities within their own organizations. As managerial rank increases, managers spend proportionately more time outside their work areas and organizations.
6. **The manager's work is primarily oral.** Managers at all levels spend the majority of their time communicating verbally (by personal contact or telephone).
7. **Managers use a lot of contacts.** Consistent with their high level of verbal communication, managers continually exchange information with superiors, peers, subordinates, and outsiders on an ongoing basis.
8. **Managers are not reflective planners.** The typical manager is too busy to find uninterrupted blocks of time for reflective planning.
9. **Information is the basic ingredient of the manager's work.** Managers spend most of their time obtaining, interpreting, and giving information.
10. **Managers don't know how they spend their time.** Managers consistently overestimate the time they spend on production, reading and writing, phone calls, thinking, and calculating and consistently underestimate the time spent on meetings and informal discussions.

SOURCE: Adapted from Morgan W. McCall, Jr., Ann M. Morrison, and Robert L. Hannan, *Studies of Managerial Work: Results and Methods* (Greensboro, N.C.: Center for Creative Leadership, 1978), Technical Report #9, pp. 6–18. Used by permission of the authors.

managerial roles (see Figure 1.4) have been grouped into three major categories: interpersonal roles, informational roles, and decisional roles.

Interpersonal Roles   Because of their formal authority and superior status, managers engage in a good deal of interpersonal contact, especially with subordinates and peers. The three interpersonal roles that managers play are those of figurehead, leader, and liaison.

Informational Roles   Every manager is a clearinghouse for information relating to the task at hand. Informational roles are important because information is the lifeblood of organizations. Typical roles include acting as nerve center, disseminator, and spokesperson.

Figure 1.4 Mintzberg's Managerial Roles

Category	Role	Nature of Role
Interpersonal Roles	1. Figurehead	As a symbol of legal authority, performing certain ceremonial duties (e.g., signing documents and receiving visitors)
	2. Leader	Motivating subordinates to get the job done properly
	3. Liaison	Serving as a link in a horizontal (as well as vertical) chain of communication
Informational Roles	4. Nerve Center	Serving as a focal point for nonroutine information; receiving all types of information
	5. Disseminator	Transmitting selected information to subordinates
	6. Spokesperson	Transmitting selected information to outsiders
Decisional Roles	7. Entrepreneur	Designing and initiating changes within the organization
	8. Disturbance Handler	Taking corrective action in nonroutine situations
	9. Resource Allocator	Deciding exactly who should get what resources
	10. Negotiator	Participating in negotiating sessions with other parties (e.g., vendors and unions) to make sure the organization's interests are adequately represented

SOURCE: Adapted from Henry Mintzberg, "Managerial Work: Analysis from Observation," *Management Science* 18 (October 1971): B97–B110.

Decisional Roles   In their decisional roles, managers balance competing interests and make choices. Through decisional roles, strategies are formulated and put into action. Four decisional roles are those of entrepreneur, disturbance handler, resource allocator, and negotiator.

Merging Functions and Roles   Both the functional approach and the role approach to explaining management are valuable to the student of management. Managerial functions are a useful categorization of a manager's tasks. It is important for future managers to realize that planning and staffing, for example, require different techniques and perspectives. In addition, the role approach injects needed realism by emphasizing that the practice of management is less rational and systematic than the functional approach implies. This book merges the functional and role approaches by explaining how the important roles are played within each functional category.

What Does It Take to Become a Successful Manager?

Successful managers come from a wide variety of backgrounds and possess an equally wide variety of traits and skills. It is impossible to describe precisely those who eventually enjoy the financial rewards of climbing to the top of the managerial ladder (see Table 1.2). But it is possible to isolate at least three key preconditions for achieving success as a manager. They are ability (A), motivation to manage (M), and opportunity (O). Thus the basic formula for managerial success (S) is: $S = A \times M \times O$. Notice that success depends upon a balanced combination of ability, motivation to manage, and opportunity. A total absence of one factor can cancel out strength in the other two. For example, high ability and motivation are useless if there is no opportunity.

Ability   As the term is used here, **managerial ability** is the demonstrated capacity to achieve organizational objectives both effectively and efficiently. Actually, today's successful manager needs a whole package of conceptual, technical, and interpersonal abilities. A leading management consultant has summarized the qualities and abilities that future managers will need as follows:

Any business can be reasonably sure of having effective and well-prepared leaders if it focuses on finding and developing people (1) who possess ... eight basic qualities ... (character; initiative; desire to serve people; intellect; awareness and perception; foresight and vision; open-mindedness and flexibility; and persuasiveness); (2) who are conceptual strategic thinkers; (3) who can lead the business in adjusting to social change; (4) who can help the business

Table 1.2   Financial Rewards of Climbing to the Top of the Managerial Ladder

The rewards are good . . .

Chief Executive Officer	1983 Salary and Bonus	Total 1983 Compensation*
Philip Caldwell, Ford Motor Co.	$1,421,000	$7,313,000
David Tendler, Phibro-Solomon	2,080,000	6,821,000
Thomas S. Murphy, Capital Cities Communications	480,000	6,152,000
Gerard S. Fulham, Pneumo	868,000	5,334,000
Dean L. Buntrock, Waste Management	499,000	5,315,000
William S. Cook, Union Pacific	905,000	4,315,000
Edward R. Telling, Sears, Roebuck	1,425,000	4,251,000
James F. Beré, Borg-Warner	677,000	3,912,000
George A. Strichman, Colt Industries	865,000	3,556,000
George T. Scharffenberger, City Investing	1,124,000	2,940,000

*Includes benefits, deferred compensation, and gains from exercised stock options.

SOURCE: Adapted from "Who Gets the Most Pay," *Forbes* 133 (June 4, 1984): 98–146.

. . . but not everyone is happy . . .

According to a recent Louis Harris public opinion poll, 76 percent of a random sample of Americans believed that top corporate executives are overpaid.

SOURCE: "Top Executive Pay Peeves the Public," *Business Week* No. 2848 (June 25, 1984): 15.

Nonetheless, the business community defends executive compensation practices . . .

"The objective of any pay program, for chief executives or athletes, is for rewards to correlate with results over the long term. Despite the current headlines, there is new evidence that the corporate compensation system works surprisingly well.

[Economists at the University of Rochester] . . . tracked over 300 top-paid chief executives and compared their salaries and bonuses to their companies' stock performance from 1977 through 1980. The link is impressive: When share and dividend gains were among the top 10%, the boss typically went home with a real 9% pay increase, without considering gains from stock options. But when a company meandered along the bottom 10%, the boss averaged a real 4% annual pay cut. . . .

For every *Thriller* album Michael Jackson sells, he gets $2 in royalties. [The 25-year-old entertainer reportedly earned $50 million from the *Thriller* album in 1983, approximately equalling the *combined* compensation of the above-listed top corporate earners.] No one should begrudge a chief executive similar rewards for a job well done."

SOURCE: John A. Byrne, "Worth His Weight," *Forbes* 133 (June 4, 1984): 97.

NOTE: See Closing Case 1.2 for more on the executive pay issue.

cope with governmental regulation; and (5) who can lead the business in managing its human resources effectively.[13]

Figure 1.5 Acquiring the Ability to Manage by Merging Theory and Practice

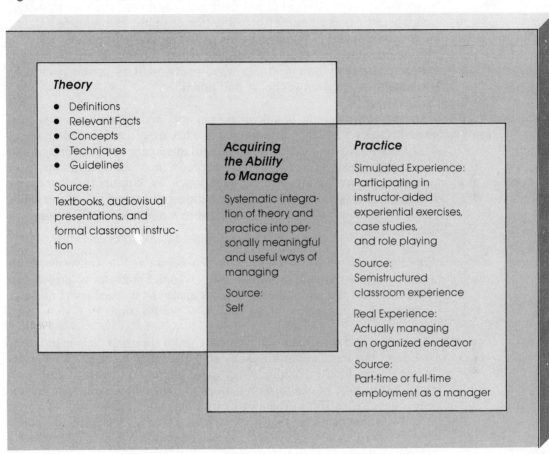

Students of management are left with one overriding question: "How do I acquire the necessary abilities?" This question has stimulated a good deal of debate among those interested in management. What is the key, theory, or practice? Some contend that future managers need a solid background in management theory acquired through formal education. Others argue that managing can be learned only by actually doing it. All things considered, a middle ground is recommended. As indicated in Figure 1.5, one learns to manage by systematically integrating theory and practice. Theory helps one systematically analyze, interpret, and internalize the managerial significance of practical experience.

Ideally, an individual acquires theoretical knowledge and practical experience at the same time, perhaps through work-study programs. Usually, though, full-time students get a lot of theory and little practice. This is when simulated and real experience become important. Serious management students are advised to put their newly acquired theories into practice wherever and whenever possible (for example, in organized sports; positions of leadership in fraternities, sororities, or clubs; and part-time and summer jobs). In regard to learning to manage, the debate over theory versus practice is unimportant; what really matters is the personally meaningful integration of theory and practice.

Motivation to Manage Inspiring stories about handicapped persons and adventurers who succeed despite seemingly insurmountable odds are often summed up in one word: desire. So, too, it is with successful managers. All the ability in the world will not help a future manager succeed if he or she does not possess a persistent desire to move ahead. Frederick W. Smith, the founder of Federal Express Corp., the original nationwide overnight delivery specialist, is a prime example of what desire can do for one's managerial career:

> In 1965, writing a paper for an economics course at Yale University, Smith proposed a new kind of freight service. ... Smith's professor pointed out the futility of the idea, given the regulatory climate and the hostility of the huge, entrenched airlines. He awarded Smith a "C" for his efforts.[14]

Six years later, Smith's Federal Express Corporation was well on its way to becoming the $1.2 billion company that promises to be at our service "when it absolutely, positively has to be there overnight." Until fairly recently, this kind of desire was an intangible trait that could be measured only subjectively. But in the mid-1960s a management researcher named John B. Miner developed a psychometric instrument to measure objectively an individual's motivation to manage. Miner's test, in effect, measures one's desire to be a manager.

The Seven Dimensions of Motivation to Manage. Miner's measure of motivation to manage is anchored to the following seven dimensions:

1. Favorable attitude toward those in positions of authority, such as superiors.
2. Desire to engage in games or sports competition with peers.
3. Desire to engage in occupational or work-related competition with peers.
4. Desire to assert oneself and take charge.
5. Desire to exercise power and authority over others.
6. Desire to behave in a distinctive way, which includes standing out from the crowd.

7. Sense of responsibility in carrying out the routine duties associated with managerial work.[15]

The higher the individual scores on each of these traits, the greater is the motivation to manage. (Although the complete instrument is not given here, the reader can probably gauge his or her own motivation to manage as low, moderate, or high.) Miner's research indicates that this concept can accurately predict how fast one will move up the hierarchy and how effective one will be as a manager.

Motivation to Manage Among Business Students   By tracking motivation to manage scores for business students at two major U.S. universities over a 20-year period, Miner and his colleagues have come to some interesting conclusions.[16] First, although the steady decline of motivation to manage during the 1960s and early 1970s has stopped, students' motivation to manage still remains very low. Generally speaking, students continue to show a distaste for authority, competitiveness, assertiveness, and routine managerial duties. Miner contends that this situation foreshadows a shortage of managerial talent over the next fifteen years. A second conclusion is that female students are no longer lagging behind their male counterparts in motivation to manage.

Other researchers have drawn essentially opposite conclusions after studying different student samples.[17] As a result, a profile of motivation to manage among tomorrow's managers is not yet at hand.

Opportunity   Talented and highly motivated potential managers can be compared to seeds. Fertile ground will foster growth; unfavorable circumstances will prohibit growth. The opportunity for managerial growth has two requirements: the first is to obtain a suitable managerial job, and the second is to have a supportive climate once on the job. In regard to the first requirement, landing a managerial job, the situation looks good. As indicated in Figure 1.6, there has recently been a steadily rising demand in the United States for managerial talent in both the public and private sectors. But, according to the *Occupational Outlook Handbook,* published by the U.S. Bureau of Labor Statistics, opportunities for managers will vary according to industry:

> On the whole, employment of managers and administrators is projected to grow about as fast as the average for all occupations through the 1980s. The growing size and complexity of both private and government enterprise is expected to require increasingly sophisticated management techniques. Therefore, the demand for trained management specialists will increase.
>
> Employment opportunities will be better in some industries than in others,

Figure 1.6   Managers/Administrators in the U.S. Labor Force

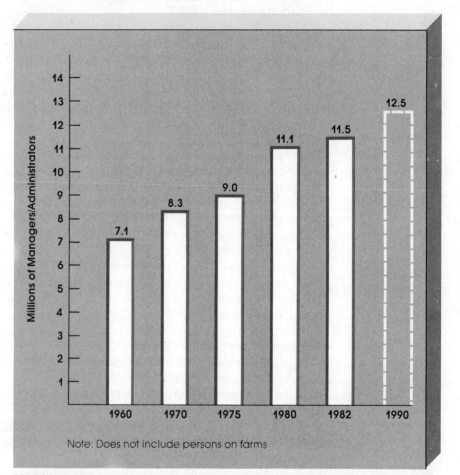

Note: Does not include persons on farms

SOURCE: Historical data from U.S. Bureau of the Census, *Statistical Abstract of the United States:* 1983, p. 417; projected data from Bureau of Labor Statistics, *Occupational Outlook Handbook,* 1980–1981 Edition, p. 22.

however. Little employment growth is foreseen [for administrators] in educational institutions during the 1980s. ... By contrast, projected expansion in the health industry will generate many new managerial and administrative support positions in hospitals, clinics, nursing homes, insurance companies, pharmaceutical and medical supply firms, and other health-related organizations. Employment growth should also be strong in wholesale and retail trade and in manufacturing.

Both the number and proportion of self-employed managers and administrators are expected to decline during the 1980s, as large enterprises and chain operations increasingly dominate business activity.[18]

In regard to the second requirement, finding a supportive climate once on the job, one must periodically reassess any job to see if it is meeting one's expectations. If not, a change may be in order. In short, tomorrow's managers need to start thinking today about how they can best work out their own $S = A \times M \times O$ formula.

Small Business and Public Sector Management: Some Unique Challenges

Although the basic management functions discussed earlier are performed in virtually all organizations, small businesses and government agencies present managers with unique and exciting challenges. A better understanding of what managers can expect in these two areas serves a dual purpose. First, it underscores the point that the practice of management is not restricted to big business. The local family-owned pizza parlor as well as huge government agencies such as the U.S. Air Force and the New York State government need to follow sound management practices too. Second, by briefly discussing the special circumstances of small businesses and public sector organizations, potential managers may acquire valuable background information for use in career planning. Readers who yearn to start and manage their own business can use the following discussion of small business management as a framework for better understanding the concepts and techniques in later chapters. Those readers who aspire to a career in government will find that the public sector presents some unique challenges. Still other readers, who will eventually take managerial positions in large corporations, stand to gain a richer perspective of management as it is practiced in sectors that profoundly affect big businesses.

Small Business Management

Small businesses are an indispensable part of the U.S. economy. In 1984, President Reagan offered the following perspective of small business: "We should be mindful of the important role played by small business in our Nation as employer of our citizens, as job creator, and as innovator."[19] While many experts in the field would agree with this claim, agreement is scarce when it comes to the definition of a small business. Various yardsticks for distinguishing small from large businesses include number of employees, level of annual sales, amount of owner's equity, and total assets. To serve our present purpose, a **small business** is defined as an independently owned and managed profit-seeking enterprise employing fewer than 100 persons.

According to the U.S. Small Business Administration: "In 1982, small enterprises with under 100 employees comprised about 34 percent of employment and 32 percent of sales in the non-government, nonfarm

Figure 1.7 Managerial Role Profiles for Small Versus Large Businesses

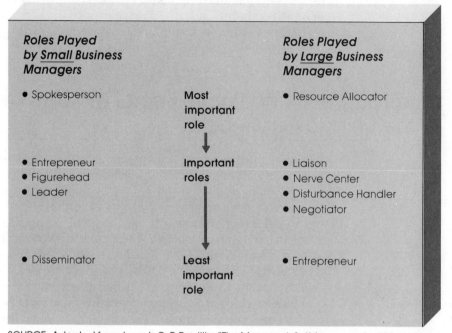

SOURCE: Adapted from Joseph G. P. Paolillo, "The Manager's Self Assessments of Managerial Roles: Small vs. Large Firms," *American Journal of Small Business* 8 (Jan.–Mar. 1984): 58–64.

economy."[20] Moreover, "small enterprises with under 20 employees generated all of the net new jobs in the economy between 1980 and 1982."[21] To a large extent, the health of the nation's economy depends on how well our small businesses are managed. To get a better idea of the challenges small business managers face, we will take a look at the roles they play and the problems they face.

Managerial Roles in Small Versus Large Businesses Does organizational size affect the way management is practiced? Due to a lack of credible research evidence, answers to this question have long been based on speculation and hunch. There is a general saying that small business managers tend to be generalists whereas managers in large businesses tend to be specialists. But beyond that, there has been little hard evidence from which to draw meaningful conclusions. However, a recent study of 178 small companies and 174 large companies, using 300 employees as the dividing point, has provided some instructive evidence in this important area. Managers employed by each of the firms surveyed " ... were asked to indicate the importance of each of Mintzberg's ten managerial roles in the effective performance of their present jobs."[22] (Refer back to those ten roles, listed in Figure 1.4, if necessary.) Analysis of the results has yielded significantly different role profiles for managers in small vs. large businesses (see Figure 1.7).

Starting with the most important role—spokesperson vs. resource allocator—the small business manager is first and foremost a window to the outside world. This implies that the typical small business manager has valuable outside contacts, such as bankers, suppliers, and customers and the ability to influence their behavior. An effective small business manager needs to know not only the technical aspects of his or her business, but also the social/political/economic environment in which he or she operates. In contrast, the typical large business manager's attention is generally directed *inward,* deciding who should get what resources. This distinction appears to reinforce the axiom of the small business generalist and the large business specialist.

Another important distinction between small and large business managers centers on the entrepreneurial role. Small business managers are expected to be innovative, whereas managers in large businesses generally do not see themselves as entrepreneurs. This finding helps explain why large companies are often criticized for stifling entrepreneurs. For example, according to *Business Week,* "Product ideas for ... [new companies] are most often formed while the entrepreneurs are still employed by established companies. Frequently, the idea was rejected or sidelined by the bigger company."[23]

In addition, the small business manager's figurehead and leader roles imply a greater degree of power and influence than the large business manager's essentially facilitative roles of liaison, nerve center, disturbance handler, and negotiator. Future managers need to gauge their abilities and preferences accordingly when deciding to work for a small or large firm.

Problems That Small Business Managers Face   If managers in small businesses have a different managerial role profile than their large business counterparts, then they also face a unique set of problems. Of course, the major threat facing small business managers is business failure. The mortality rate among new businesses is incredibly high. According to one small business expert, "... 50% of new businesses fail within their first seven years."[24] Why do so many small businesses fail? Researchers have uncovered some interesting answers.

One survey of 1002 small business owners and managers from across the United States posed the following question: "What do you think is the primary cause of small business failures in this country?"[25] Twenty-nine percent of the respondents said the major culprit was "lack of management expertise." "High interest rates" came in second with 16 percent. It is interesting to note that "federal regulations" tallied only 4 percent, in spite of grumbling in the small business community about too much government

Table 1.3   Persistent Management Problems for Small Business Managers

Marketing

- Lack of knowledge of target markets.
- Lack of objectives.
- Inadequate market research and planning.
- Poor image and location.
- Misdirected advertising.
- Little appreciation for the role of pricing strategy.
- Lack of promotion and distribution strategies.

Accounting

- Lack of systematic accounting systems.
- Antiquated accounting systems.
- Lack of knowledge of accounting functions (hence, hired accountants are under-utilized).
- Weak accounts receivable collection procedures.
- Mismanaged operating expenses.

Inventory Control

- Low inventory turnover (slow-moving or obsolete goods kept in stock).
- Stockouts of high profit items ("selling from an empty wagon").
- Failure to detect excessively high inventories due to poor accounting procedures.

Cash Flow

- Weak marketing + inadequate accounting procedures + loose inventory control = poor cash flow.
- Lack of cash flow analysis (hence, no early detection of cash shortages).
- Lack of knowledge about alternative borrowing arrangements (for example, other than from commercial banks).

SOURCE: Adapted from M. Riaz Khan and Joseph R. Rocha, Jr., "Recurring Managerial Problems in Small Business," *American Journal of Small Business* 7 (July–Sept. 1982): 50–58.

interference. It appears that small business managers are their own worst enemies when it comes to business failure.

Although the study points in a general direction, it does not reveal *specific* managerial deficiencies. The up-and-down story of a computer entrepreneur provides a good example of what other small business researchers have discovered:

[Adam Osborne] ... chided manufacturers for ignoring the needs of the mass market. When no one listened, he started Osborne Computer Corp. Within just two years it hit $100 million in annual sales of inexpensive portable computers. But the company's smashing success was short-lived. It soon [in 1983] landed in bankruptcy court, with disgruntled investors, who lost $20 million, blaming its flamboyant founder for mismanaged financial controls and marketing tactics.[26]

When a team of researchers analyzed detailed performance reviews of 52 small businesses located in the Northeast, they found four major recurring managerial problem areas: marketing, accounting, inventory control, and cash flow management.[27] As one reviews the specific managerial shortcomings in each of these four areas (see Table 1.3), it is easy to see why the successful small business manager is often characterized as a "jack-of-all-trades."

The risk of failure is great, but the personal satisfaction and financial rewards can be immense for those who are willing to try their hand at small business ownership/management.

Managing in the Public Sector

Like small businesses, public sector organizations touch our lives each day. Experts estimate that 18 million people work for 80,000 governmental agencies in the United States today.[28] That encompasses not only the federal government and the military, but state, county, and municipal governments as well. Sheer size (see Table 1.4) and mounting pressure for greater efficiency in government make the need for talented and motivated public sector managers greater than ever. Managers of tax-funded government organizations face their own unique set of management problems. Public sector managers must cope with a negative stereotype and constraints generally not found in private, profit-seeking businesses.

A Negative Image How often do you hear government employees referred to as "bureaucrats"? Perhaps you have used that label yourself on occasion. The term bureaucrat carries a strong negative connotation involving inefficiency, waste, and red tape. On the other hand, managers in large businesses are rarely, if ever, called bureaucrats. As we will see in Chapter 7, however, virtually all large organizations (whether private or public) are bureaucracies. Trends in public opinion polls indicate that this negative image for government employees is getting worse. For example, "In 1958, 24 percent thought 'there are quite a few crooks' in government; 70 percent thought so in 1980."[29] Is this negative stereotype justified?

In response to a widely held belief that public sector employees tend to be less motivated and creative than their private sector counterparts, an extensive review of the relevant research evidence led a pair of management scholars to conclude:

The negative stereotype of government employees persists despite the evidence from several recent studies that there are *no* significant differences between

Table 1.4   The U.S. Government—The World's Largest Conglomerate

The absence of efficient and effective management practices is compounded by the very size and complexity of the federal bureaucracy, which can best be understood when one considers that the federal government spends in excess of $91 million an hour, 24 hours a day, and handles over $1.7 trillion in receipts and outlays annually. For starters, the federal government:

- employs 2.8 million people;
- purchases over $130 billion annually in goods and services;
- owns one-third of the U.S. land mass—an estimated 744 million acres, equal to all of the states east of the Mississippi River plus Texas;
- occupies 2.6 billion square feet of office space, the equivalent of all the office space in the 10 largest cities in America times four;
- owns and operates 437,000 nonmilitary vehicles;
- provides 95 million subsidized meals a day;
- has over 17,000 computers, 332 accounting systems, and 319 payroll systems;
- issues 4.8 billion publications annually;
- delivers medical care to 47 million people; and
- administers or owns over 50,000 single or multifamily units.

In short, the federal government is the world's largest conglomerate—the largest power producer, insurer, lender, borrower, hospital system operator, and land owner, landlord, holder of grazing land, timber seller, grain owner, warehouse operator, ship owner, and truck fleet operator.

SOURCE: J. Peter Grace, "A Businessman's View of Washington," *The Bureaucrat* 13 (Summer 1984): 15.

managers in the public and private sectors on such critical dimensions as leadership styles, ability, personality, role ambiguity and conflict, motivational orientation, work patterns, time constraints, problem definitions, activities, or job characteristics.[30]

In spite of sensational news stories about government ineffectiveness, inefficiency, and foul ups, there is persuasive evidence that public sector managers are doing a better job than public opinion gives them credit for.

In face-to-face interviews [in a public opinion poll], respondents indicated a median of $52.10 out of every $100 is used for administrative overhead for *social security*. In fact, social security spent $1.6 billion in 1983 for administrative expenses of the regular retirement program. . . . This is large in absolute terms, but only 1.1 percent of benefit payments. (Even the more complex programs have low overhead. For the medicare program it is under 2 percent and for the disability program it is 4 percent.)[31]

The negative image plaguing public sector employees, however misguided or unfounded, hampers the quest for more efficient government.[32] Certainly, some of the talented and highly motivated managers so dearly needed in the public sector are being scared away.

Constraints Facing Public Sector Managers   Although the circumstances in which government managers operate are extremely complex, it is possible to select out four major constraints.[33] Each clearly sets public management apart from business management.

- **Legislated purposes.** In sharp contrast to private businesses, which can pursue any legal and potentially profitable purposes they desire, government agencies are told what to do by law-making bodies. This seriously limits their options. The U.S. Environmental Protection Agency, for instance, cannot suddenly decide to get out of the air quality business because it no longer pays. (U.S. Steel Corp., for example, is putting less emphasis on the steel business and more on the oil business.) To make matters worse, some government agencies are mandated to "take a loss" (for example, those in disaster assistance). Government managers often must stand and face society's typically vague and often contradictory expectations for performance.

- **No competition.** Public sector organizations do not have to pass the test of the competitive marketplace. Says one government executive: "Without this ultimate discipline of the market, there is no automatic weeding out of bad public management."[34] In place of a market test, public sector managers must fall back on difficult and time-consuming cost control programs and program audits to gauge their agencies' effectiveness.

- **Weak incentive systems.** Unlike private businesses, where an impressive array of incentives ranging from cash bonuses to exotic vacations can be used to motivate performance, public sector managers have few "carrots" to dangle in front of their employees. For example, it is against the law for U.S. government agencies to pay for interview trips or moving expenses, both common recruiting techniques in the private sector. Consequently, government agencies have a hard time attracting and retaining first-rate managers.

- **Organizational inflexibility.** Large governmental bureaucracies such as the U.S. Social Security Administration have to be highly structured to provide standard services to millions of clients nationwide. Unfortunately, reams of procedures and regulations can stifle innovation. Public sector managers are constantly challenged to find ways to foster creativity and innovation in spite of an overriding emphasis on predictability and uniformity.

These constraints offer a special managerial challenge to those interested in trying to make government more responsive and efficient.

Our overview of small business and public sector management has been directed more toward identifying problems than offering specific solutions. Our purpose here was to explore alternative contexts for the practice of management. Subsequent chapters provide a rich selection of possible solutions to problems within different managerial contexts.

Productivity Improvement: A Central Challenge

What do the following situations have in common?

- **Auto industry.** Primarily because of new technology, Ford Motor Company reduced the number of hours worked per vehicle by 27 percent between 1980 and 1983.
- **Retailing.** A major goal for K mart is to increase sales per square foot of floor space in its more than 2,100 stores from $155 in 1983 to $200 in 1988.
- **Steel industry.** Allegheny Ludlum, a Pittsburgh firm specializing in stainless steel, turned out 35 percent more tonnage per man-hour in 1984 than in 1980.
- **Research and development.** Engineers working for TRW, Inc. now produce two to four times more drawings with a computerized product design system than they formerly did by hand.[35]

All of the preceding situations have two things in common. First, each deals with *productivity,* a central challenge for managers in all types of organizations. Managers are being asked to get more mileage out of all resources: human, financial, and material. Second, in spite of warnings during the late 1970s and early 1980s of a productivity crisis in America, signs of improvement are now evident. But there is still a long way to go. Managers need to tackle the productivity improvement challenge aggressively and creatively if Japan's impressive record of growth is to be matched. In this section, we examine America's recent productivity growth record, define organizational productivity, briefly highlight Japan's approach, and introduce a topical framework for the rest of this book.

Ragged Productivity Growth in the United States

Annual productivity growth in the United States averaged less than 1 percent during the ten years prior to 1983. Because Japan's productivity grew at about a 7 percent annual rate during the same period, with West Germany and France not far behind, a U.S. productivity crisis was proclaimed and widely discussed. Between the last quarter of 1982 and mid-1984, however, the annual productivity growth rate in the United States rose to 3.3 percent. Although the United States still trails Japan, economic observers believe that the following factors heavily influenced the 1983-84 upswing:

- **A maturing work force.** The post-World War II baby boom generation has aged and is no longer a large, inexperienced segment of the work force.
- **Lower inflation and cheaper energy.** The double-digit inflation rates of the late 1970s and early 1980s that ate into profits and inhibited investment gave way to lower inflation. Lower prices for oil and services in deregulated industries such as transportation and communications have been major contributors to reduced inflation.
- **Technological advancement.** Public and private research and development spending increased from a low of 2.2 percent of the U.S. gross national product in 1977 to 2.6 percent in 1984. This spending has led to technological innovations.
- **Increased labor-management cooperation.** Employee participation techniques such as quality control circles and greater labor-management cooperation, prompted by recessions and foreign competition, have helped eliminate restrictive union work rules. In addition, wage increases have moderated.[36]

If these last three factors remain positive, then productivity growth is likely to continue to climb in the United States. If however, persistently high interest rates prompt increased wage demands, higher prices, and thus higher inflation, productivity could slump once again. Management, for its part, can continue to push for technological advancement and foster additional labor-management cooperation.

**Defining
Organizational
Productivity**

Although national productivity indexes such as those just mentioned are a helpful barometer of overall economic health, organizational productivity is more relevant to the average manager. Regardless of the level of analysis, productivity is difficult to define and measure. From an organizational standpoint, one expert on productivity has offered the following introduction to the concept:

Many think of productivity as being a measure of labor, usually expressed as output per hour. Actually it is a much broader concept than that. Productivity is any output to input ratio. For the firm as a whole, outputs include all goods and services produced during a given time. Inputs include all resources consumed to produce those outputs. Labor is one of the input resources but so too are capital, material, and energy. Virtually all of the resources used by the firm fall in one of these four categories.

... total firm productivity is defined as follows:

$$\text{Productivity} = \frac{\text{output}}{\text{input}} = \frac{\text{goods and services produced}}{\text{labor, capital, materials, and energy}}[37,*]$$

Formally defined, **organizational productivity** is the ratio of an organization's total output to total input, adjusted for inflation, for a specified period of time.

The Japanese Model: More with Less

Despite a recent slowing in its productivity growth rate, Japan's average annual rate of productivity growth is still well ahead of that of other industrialized nations. Japan's success is due in large part to its highly efficient and productive use of limited resources. For example, "... the average Japanese auto worker makes 48 to 50 cars per year, compared with 25 for the U.S. worker. The average Japanese steelworker produces 421 tons vs. 250 in the U.S."[38] Additionally, Japan's productivity is enhanced by its streamlined organizational hierarchies. For example, "At Ford Motor Co., there are 11 layers of management between the factory worker and the chairman, while Toyota Motor Co. makes do with six."[39] In effect, Japan has demonstrated to the rest of the world that it is possible to do more with less.

Time magazine has nicely summed up the Japanese situation by posing the following questions:

> How has an overpopulated island country with less land than California leaped in only three decades from wartime defeat and the status of industrial sweatshop to that of high-technology dynamo? How has a country that imports 100% of its aluminum, 99.8% of its oil, 98.4% of its iron ore and 66.4% of its wood and lumber become a world economic power?[40]

Those who say that Japan's competitive edge is due to lower wage rates and lax occupational safety and pollution control laws would have been right several years ago, but that is no longer the case. Moreover, costly real estate, expensive imported raw materials, and crowded highways make the cost of doing business in Japan very high.[41] According to the authors of the best-selling book, *The Art of Japanese Management,* "... a major reason for the superiority of the Japanese is their managerial skill."[42]

Although there is a good deal of difference between Japan's culture and Western cultures (for example, see Figure 11.9 and Table 19.6), much can be learned from the Japanese success story of doing more with less. The key is

*Reprinted from William A. Ruch, "Productivity Measurements," *Arizona Business* February, 1981, published by the Bureau of Business and Economic Research, College of Business Administration, Arizona State University, Tempe, Arizona.

Figure 1.8 A Topical Framework for the Study and Practice of Management

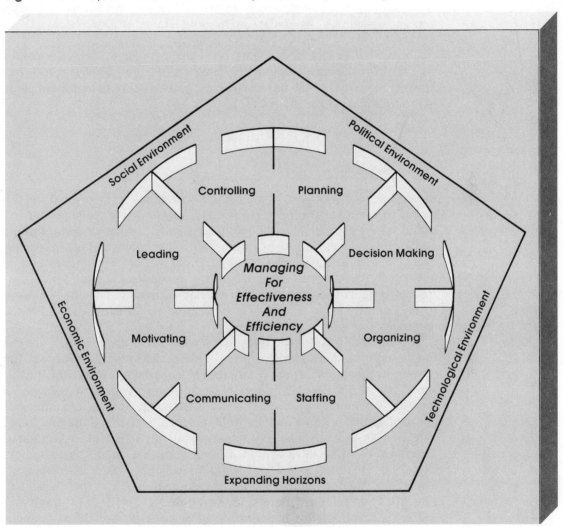

to *adapt,* not blindly imitate or mimic Japanese management techniques,[43] several of which are covered in this text.

Meeting the Challenge More than anyone else, today's and tomorrow's managers need to meet the challenge of improving productivity. Two writers have summarized this idea as follows:

> ... no one can deny that improving productivity is and always has been management's responsibility. If corporations accept the challenge of providing adequate

resources for the production of goods and services, they must also accept the challenge of assuring that these resources—people, money, machines, and materials—are put to efficient use.[44]

Accordingly, the balance of this book is intended to help the reader successfully meet the productivity challenge. Figure 1.8 (on page 33) is a kind of roadmap for what lies ahead, each portion being an important piece in the overall productivity puzzle.

Summary

Management is an important area of study from both the personal and the global perspective. On the personal side, knowledge of management is a useful steppingstone to a good job in our highly organized world. From a global perspective, Neil Armstrong's walk on the moon and the first Earth Day symbolize the extremes of effective and ineffective management.

Formally defined, management is the process of working with and through others to achieve organizational objectives in a changing environment. Central to this process is the effective and efficient use of limited resources.

Two ways to answer the question, "What do managers do?" are the functional approach and role approach. Managerial functions relate to the purposes of managerial action, whereas managerial roles categorize managers' actual behavior. This text is organized around eight managerial functions: planning, decision making, organizing, staffing, communicating, motivating, leading, and controlling. Having criticized the functional approach as unrealistically systematic and rational, Henry Mintzberg concluded from his observation of managers that management is best explained in terms of roles. Three managerial roles, according to Mintzberg, are the interpersonal, the informational, and the decisional. Functions and roles are merged in this book.

The basic formula for managerial success is $S = A \times M \times O$ (managerial success = ability × motivation to manage × opportunity). Managerial ability results when theory and practice are systematically integrated. John Miner identified six dimensions of the motivation to manage that predict success as a manager. A 20-year study of motivation to manage in college business students shows that although the decline in motivation to manage has stopped, it still remains very low. Thus Miner foresees a shortage in managerial talent for the next fifteen years. Because the number of managers/administrators in the U.S. labor force increased from 7.1 million to 11.5 million between 1960 and 1982, there are many opportunities to manage.

Small business and public sector organizations afford managers some unique opportunities and challenges. Research indicates that small business managers have a different managerial role profile than do managers in larger businesses. The axiom of the small business generalist and the large business specialist appears to be valid. "Lack of management expertise" was found by researchers to be the primary cause of the high failure rate in small businesses. In spite of a good deal of evidence to the contrary, public sector managers must cope with a negative image. Many people assume that bureaucrats are incompetent and wasteful. Four major constraints public sector managers must deal with are: legislated purposes, no competition, weak incentives, and organizational inflexibility.

Slumping productivity growth in the United States took an upward swing in 1983–84 largely due to a maturing work force, lower inflation and cheaper energy, technological advancement, and increased labor-management cooperation. Still, there is much room for improvement if the United States is to match Japan's record of productivity growth. It is important for managers to translate the productivity problem into organizational terms. Organizational productivity is the ratio of total input to total output, adjusted for inflation, for a specific period of time. Japan, with the world's highest rate of productivity growth, is an inspiring example of how to do more with less. One of the aims of this book is to help today's and tomorrow's managers successfully meet the challenge of improving productivity.

Terms to Understand

Management	Managerial roles
Effectiveness	Managerial ability
Efficiency	Small business
Managerial functions	Organizational productivity

Questions for Discussion

1. Drawing on your own experience, can you recall any specific examples of effective management and mismanagement?
2. In your opinion, what is the single most important aspect of the definition of management? Why?
3. Think of a person or operation that you have seen recently that did not achieve a workable balance between effectiveness and efficiency. What could have been done to balance the two?

4. Why can a student of management learn from both the functional and role approaches to describing the manager's job?
5. Which factor—ability, motivation to manage, or opportunity—should be most heavily weighted in the basic formula for managerial success?
6. Now that you are familiar with Miner's six dimensions of motivation to manage, how would you rate yourself? Do you feel that this is a valid predictor of your chances to succeed as a manager?
7. Are you interested in owning and managing your own business? Explain why.
8. In view of the negative image problem, why would someone want to be a manager in the public (government) sector?
9. Why is greater labor-management cooperation so important to increased productivity growth?
10. What can an individual manager do to meet the challenge to improve productivity?

Back to the Opening Case

Now that you have read Chapter 1, you should be able to answer the following questions about the Looking Glass, Inc., case:

1. What managerial functions has the manager performed? Cite specific evidence for each function identified.
2. How well do you think Mintzberg's managerial roles approach explains what has taken place in this case? What particular roles can you identify?
3. Do you think that the manager in this case is a good manager? Explain your answer, citing evidence from the case.
4. If you were the manager in this case, what would you have done differently? Why?

Closing Case 1.2

Chrysler's Iacocca: The Most Bang for the Corporate Buck*

Some people might say that Chrysler Corp. Chairman Lee A. Iacocca walks on water. After all, in the 4½ years [as of mid-1984] that the flamboyant and gutsy Iacocca has been calling the shots at Chrysler—once

*Reprinted from the May 7, 1984 issue of *Business Week* by special permission, © 1984 by McGraw-Hill, Inc.

bloated and money-losing, now lean and scrappy—the company has cut its breakeven point [the level of sales at which Chrysler begins to make a profit] by more than half. Its market share has jumped several points, and plants are running at capacity. It repaid its federally backed loans years early. It has just resumed paying common-stock dividends after a five-year hiatus, and it is posting record earnings. "We made more money in the first three months of 1984 than any full year in Chrysler's history," boasts Iacocca of the $706 million profit.

Chrysler shareholders certainly cannot complain about what Iacocca is giving them for his pay. When his compensation and performance are stacked up against those of other executives, Iacocca wins hands down as the top producer. His annual salary plus long-term income over the past three years are worth about $2.6 million. During that same period, shareholder returns—as measured by stock appreciation and dividends—totaled 466.6%.

It could be argued that Iacocca is underpaid. Although in 1983 he received a 30% raise, to $475,000, it was his first since he joined Chrysler in 1978. The lack of bonuses has checked his earning power. But shareholders will soon vote on a new incentive plan that would narrow the gap between Iacocca's pay and that of his peers.

Using restraint. But directors are wary of going overboard. "The industry is still facing problems, and a labor settlement will be negotiated next year" [1985], notes Anthony J. A. Bryan, a member of Chrysler's compensation committee and chief executive of Copperweld Corp. "We felt we should exercise some restraint." To secure Iacocca's commitment to Chrysler, the board recently gave him an option to buy 300,000 shares at about $28 each and an outright grant of 150,000 shares if he stays through 1986. A fourth year would yield more options and grants.

Yet Iacocca's value to Chrysler may be impossible to quantify. Insiders and longtime Chrysler watchers say that the outspoken chairman deserves a lot of the credit for the company's revival. "He steered it through the crisis period," says Douglas A. Fraser, retired president of the United Auto Workers and an outgoing Chrysler director. [In return for wage concessions, a union representative was appointed to Chrysler's board of directors in 1981.] "I don't know if somebody else could have merchandised the K-car as he did." Adds an industry analyst: "If he wasn't there, Chrysler wouldn't be there."

Iacocca, 59, is a consummate salesman with an eye for product and styling—key strengths for a company that was saddled with outdated vehicles. He was instrumental in promoting the compact K-body, which made its debut in 1980 and became the building block for a family of successful new cars.

Iacocca also has credibility and visibility. During the darkest days, he starred in TV commercials, personalizing the company and shoring up consumer confidence. He lobbied for the government-backed loans that kept Chrysler afloat. Today he sounds off on economic and foreign policy. He has become a folk hero, in part because he beat the odds and pulled Chrysler through. The son of immigrants, he has directness, humor, and salty language that appeal to the public.

No less important, Iacocca has attracted scores of motivated young managers, including many from Ford Motor Co., his ex-employer. Associates say he inspires fierce loyalty and a desire to achieve, and he thrives on instinct. "He can smell a weakness in an argument or when you skate past an inconvenient fact," says Richard Goodyear, general counsel and secretary.

But questions still remain about Chrysler's long-term viability. Analysts worry that the company has focused too much on lower-margin small and midsize cars. They also insist that Chrysler needs an international partner. While Iacocca publicly shares that assessment, he has yet to act.

Perhaps the biggest uncertainty is Chrysler without Iacocca. The Office of the Chairman includes three other executives. But none is as charismatic as Iacocca. When he retires or moves on—maybe into government— the gap he leaves will be hard to fill.

For Discussion

1. Which of Mintzberg's managerial roles has Iacocca played in recent years? Which role has proved to be the most important for Chrysler?
2. Why could it be said that Iacocca tackled his job at Chrysler like a small business manager?
3. Taking into consideration both Iacocca's compensation and the executive salaries listed in Table 1.2, are top managers in the United States overpaid? (As mentioned in Chapter 1, this has become a big issue in the business press. For more information on both sides of this issue, see: Arch Patton, "Why So Many Chief Executives Make Too Much," *Business Week* No. 2812 [October 17, 1983]: 24–26; Lisa Miller Mesdag, "Are You Underpaid?" *Fortune* 109 [March 19, 1984]: 20–24; "Executive Pay: The Top Earners," *Business Week* No. 2841 [May 7, 1984]: 88–95; Stephen Koepp, "Those Million-Dollar Salaries," *Time* 123 [May 7, 1984]: 84–85; Bruce A. Jacobs, "Are CEOs Worth $1 Million," *Industry Week* 221 [May 14, 1984]: 43–46; Steven E. Prokesch, "Executive Pay: Who Made the Most," *Business Week* No. 2893 [May 6, 1985]: 78–88.)

References

Opening quotation: Peter F. Drucker, *People and Performance: The Best of Drucker on Management* (New York: Harper & Row, 1977), p. 8.

Opening case: Diana Hawes, "Through the Looking Glass—A Manager in Action," *Across the Board* 17 (October 1980): 57–59.

Closing case: "Chrysler's Iacocca: The Most Bang for the Corporate Buck," *Business Week* No. 2841 (May 7, 1984): 90–91.

1. John Noble Wilford, *We Reach the Moon* (New York: Norton, 1971), p. 19.
2. Evert Clark, "The Moon Program's Business Brain Trust," *Nation's Business* 58 (May 1970): 36.
3. Dael Wolfle, "After Earth Day," *Science* 168 (May 8, 1970): 657.
4. Morgan W. McCall Jr. and Michael M. Lombardo, "What Makes a Top Executive?" *Psychology Today* 17 (February 1983): 28.
5. See Frederic Golden, "Touchdown, Columbia!" *Time* 117 (April 27, 1981): 16–23.
6. Herman Kahn, William Brown, and Leon Martel, *The Next 200 Years* (New York: Morrow, 1976), p. 19.
7. George Russell, "People, People, People," *Time* 124 (August 6, 1984): 24.
8. For more on these five sources of change, see Alvin Toffler, *The Third Wave* (New York: Bantam, 1980), pp. 235–238.
9. See Henri Fayol, *General and Industrial Management,* trans. Constance Storrs (London: Isaac Pitman & Sons, 1949).
10. Henry Mintzberg, "The Manager's Job: Folklore and Fact," *Harvard Business Review* 53 (July–August 1975): 49.
11. Ibid., p. 54.
12. Henry Mintzberg, "Managerial Work: Analysis from Observation," *Management Science* 18 (October 1971): B 97–B 110.
13. Marvin Bower, "Corporate Leaders for the Year 2000," in *Managers for the Year 2000,* ed. William H. Newman (Englewood Cliffs, N.J.: Prentice-Hall, 1978), p. 50.
14. Eugene Linden, "Frederick W. Smith of Federal Express: He Didn't Get There Overnight," *Inc.* 6 (April 1984): 89.
15. More detailed accounts of Miner's motivation to manage research may be found in John B. Miner, *The Human Constraint: The Coming Shortage of Managerial Talent* (Washington, D.C.: Bureau of National Affairs, 1974), pp. 6–7 and John B. Miner and Norman R. Smith, "Decline and Stabilization of Managerial Motivation Over a 20-Year Period," *Journal of Applied Psychology* 67 (June 1982): 297–305.
16. Miner and Smith, "Decline and Stabilization of Managerial Motivation Over a 20-Year Period," 1982.
17. For example, see Kathryn M. Bartol, Carl R. Anderson, and Craig Eric Schneier, "Sex and Ethnic Effects on Motivation to Manage Among College Business Students," *Journal of Applied Psychology* 66 (February 1981): 40–44.
18. Bureau of Labor Statistics, *Occupational Outlook Handbook,* 1982–83 Edition, pp. 22–23.

19. U.S. Small Business Administration, *The State of Small Business: A Report of the President* (Washington, D.C.: U.S. Government Printing Office, 1984), p. x.

20. Ibid., p. 12.

21. Ibid., p. 25.

22. Joseph G. P. Paolillo, "The Manager's Self Assessments of Managerial Roles: Small vs. Large Firms," *American Journal of Small Business,* 8 (Jan.-Mar. 1984): 59.

23. "The New Entrepreneurs," *Business Week* No. 2786 (April 18, 1983): 80.

24. "The Disenchantment of the Middle Class," *Business Week* No. 2787 (April 25, 1983): 86.

25. Robert A. Peterson, George Kozmetsky, and Nancy M. Ridgway, "Perceived Causes of Small Business Failures: A Research Note," *American Journal of Small Business* 8 (July–Sept. 1983): 17.

26. "Adam Osborne Is Back in Computers—With Software," *Business Week* No. 2836 (April 2, 1984): 37.

27. See M. Riaz Khan and Joseph R. Rocha, Jr., "Recurring Managerial Problems in Small Business," *American Journal of Small Business* 7 (July–Sept. 1982): 50–58.

28. See Charles T. Goodsell, *The Case for Bureaucracy* (Chatham, N.J.: Chatham House, 1983), pp. 110–111.

29. David G. Mathiasen, "Rethinking Public Management," *The Bureaucrat* 13 (Summer 1984): 11.

30. Barry Z. Posner and Warren H. Schmidt, "What Kinds of People Enter the Public and Private Sectors? An Updated Comparison of Perceptions, Stereotypes, and Values," *Human Resource Management* 21 (Summer 1982): 35.

31. Mathiasen, "Rethinking Public Management," pp. 10–11.

32. For an interesting discussion of the private sector push for more efficient government, see Peter A. Holmes, "The Saving Grace," *Nation's Business* 72 (March 1984): 33–36.

33. This discussion is based on material found in Mathiasen, "Rethinking Public Management," pp. 9–13; Allen H. Barton, "A Diagnosis of Bureaucratic Maladies," *American Behavioral Scientist* 22 (May–June 1979): 483–492; Laurence E. Lynne, Jr., "Improving Public Sector Management," *California Management Review* 26 (Winter 1984): 112–124.

34. Mathiasen, "Rethinking Public Management," p. 9.

35. These examples of productivity improvement have been drawn from "What's Creating an 'Industrial Miracle at Ford,' " *Business Week* No. 2853 (July 30, 1984): 80–81; "K mart: The No. 2 Retailer Starts to Make an Upscale Move— At Last," *Business Week* (June 4, 1984): 50–51; Bill Saporito, "Allegheny Ludlum Has Steel Figured Out," *Fortune* 109 (June 25, 1984): 40–44; "A Productivity Revolution in the Service Sector," *Business Week* No. 2806 (September 5, 1983): 106–108.

36. Based on material found in John W. Kendrick, "Productivity Gains Will Continue," *Wall Street Journal* 111 (August 29, 1984): 22 and "Rapid Productivity Gains: An Auspicious Omen," *Business Week* No. 2847 (June 18, 1984): 16.

37. William A. Ruch, "Productivity Measurement," *Arizona Business* 28 (February 1981): 20. Published by the Bureau of Business and Economic Research, College of Business Administration, Arizona State University, Tempe, Arizona.

38. Frank A. Weil, "Management's Drag on Productivity," *Business Week* No. 2614 (December 3, 1979): 14.

39. Claudia H. Deutsch, "Trust: The New Ingredient in Management," *Business Week* No. 2695 (July 6, 1981): 104.

40. Christopher Byron, "How Japan Does It," *Time* 117 (March 30, 1981): 55–56.

41. See Richard Tanner Pascale and Anthony G. Athos, *The Art of Japanese Management* (New York: Warner Books, 1981), p. 23.

42. Ibid., p. 24.

43. For interesting discussions of Japanese vs. American management, see Leonard Nadler, "What Japan Learned from the U.S.—That We Forgot to Remember," *California Management Review* 26 (Summer 1984): 46–61 and George S. Odiorne, "The Trouble with Japanese Management Systems," *Business Horizons* 27 (July–Aug. 1984): 17–23.

44. Charles R. Day, Jr., and Perry Pascarella, "Righting the Productivity Balance," *Industry Week* 206 (September 29, 1980): 50, 54.

Chapter 2

The Evolution of
Management Thought

In the renewing society the historian consults the past in the service of the present and the future.
    John W. Gardner

Chapter Objectives

When you finish studying this chapter, you should be able to

- Identify two key assumptions supporting the universal process approach and briefly describe Henri Fayol's contribution.
- Discuss Frederick W. Taylor's approach to improving the practice of industrial management.
- Describe the general aim of the human relations movement and explain the circumstances in which it arose.
- Explain the significance of applying open-system thinking to management.
- Explain the practical significance of adopting a contingency perspective.
- Identify and explain the nature of at least four of Peters' and Waterman's eight attributes of excellence.

Opening Case 2.1

Caterpillar Tractor Tries to Get Back on Track

From 1932 to 1981, Caterpillar Tractor Company had an unbroken string of profitable years. The world's largest manufacturer of heavy construction equipment ran over the competition like one of its familiar yellow bulldozers. But in 1982, they came to a grinding halt. First, the company had to lay off 20,000 employees because of a recession in the construction industry. Next, 20,400 employees who belonged to the United Auto Workers union (UAW) started what was to be a bitter seven-month strike over wage ceilings and stricter job transfer rules. Top management failed in its attempt to convince the UAW that increased competition from Komatsu, an aggressive Japanese price cutter, necessitated deep cost-cutting measures. Consequently, Caterpillar recorded a $180 million loss in 1982 and slid $345 million more into the red in 1983. The firm's sales dropped 41 percent for the same period. Observers asked: How could a company that had an apparently unbeatable "formula for success" wind up in such a mess? A brief overview of Caterpillar's recent history suggests an answer.

An Old-fashioned Formula for Success

During the 1970s, companies throughout the United States competed vigorously to hire MBAs from well-known schools who could introduce and implement the newest management techniques. Caterpillar, however, continued to hire its management trainees primarily from middle-level colleges in the Midwest. While other companies created sophisticated strategic planning departments and complex organizational structures, Caterpillar continued to rely heavily on informal planning, a start-at-the-bottom management development program, and an emphasis on trust rather than rules.

By sticking to basics through the years, Caterpillar became a major force in its three principal markets—earth-moving equipment, materials-handling equipment, and diesel engines. Caterpillar's sincere devotion to identify and satisfy customer needs quickly has helped hold off the challenge of foreign competitors' lower prices. For example, if a customer is unable to get a replacement part for a Caterpillar Tractor (no matter how old) within 48 hours through the firm's extensive distribution system, Caterpillar will supply the part free. Many longstanding Caterpillar customers say the firm's reputation for reliable parts and service is what keeps them coming back, in spite of Caterpillar's comparatively high prices.

A Cohesive Management Team

Caterpillar's long-term approach to virtually all aspects of its operations extends to its executive development program as well. Those who expect rapid promotion do not last long at Caterpillar. In fact, it is common for managers to start at bottom-rung positions on the production floor and slowly work their way up through the ranks. Most of Caterpillar's top managers have been with the company for 25 years or more. Consequently, a climate of mutual trust has evolved among managers who are intensely loyal to the firm.

A good deal of top-level decision making at Caterpillar takes place during informal discussions aimed at generating a consensus. When senior managers meet to discuss a project, no formal minutes are taken and voting is never used to resolve an issue. However, some Caterpillar dealers have complained that it takes too long for decisions to be made at the Peoria, Illinois headquarters. Organizational structure is kept simple to enhance the free interchange of ideas among managers. Unlike most companies its size, Caterpillar has no separate strategic planning function. Strategic considerations are an integral part of all top-level planning.

Labor Relations Problems

Unfortunately, the goodwill that is so important in the managerial ranks has not trickled down to the blue-collar level. Caterpillar and its unionized labor force have been at odds for years. A strike in 1979 put about 40,000 Peoria-area Caterpillar employees out of work for eleven weeks. The seven-month strike in 1982–83 that ended when management finally agreed to most of the UAW's demands only served to worsen what some have called the poorest labor relations in the country. Caterpillar's first progressive attempt to mend management/labor relationships occurred in 1980 when the firm introduced a participative management program called quality control circles. Under this experimental program, assembly-line employees are encouraged to join problem-solving teams to identify and implement solutions that enhance product quality. Caterpillar also agreed to work with the union to install a quality-of-work-life program that would give workers a greater say in things. Caterpillar's internal communications program is in line for attention, too. Management's earlier attempt to use the employee newsletter to warn of the threat of increased foreign competition failed when employees responded with disbelief and the longest strike in UAW history.

The Road Ahead

Komatsu's improving quality, growing U.S. dealer network, erosion of Caterpillar's foreign market shares, and lower prices have Caterpillar's top managers more than a little concerned. In response to Komatsu's pricing pressure, they have set their sights on a 20 percent reduction in costs by 1986 to remain competitive in the long run. Achievement of this goal hinges on the active support of employees at all levels. Industry observers believe Caterpillar will benefit greatly from increased U.S. government spending for bridge and road reconstruction.

(Discussion questions linking this case with the material you are about to read can be found at the end of this chapter.)

In Caterpillar's last half-century of operations we see many of the situations and forces that have shaped the evolution of management thought. The history of management and of management theory can be a fruitful study. Management historians believe that a better knowledge of the past will lead to a more productive future. In fact, they contend that students of management who fail to understand the evolution of management thought are destined to repeat past mistakes.

Historians draw a distinction between history and historical perspective. According to one management scholar:

> Historical perspective is the study of a subject in light of its earliest phases and subsequent evolution. Historical perspective differs from history in that the object of historical perspective is to sharpen one's vision of the present, not the past.[1]

This chapter qualifies as a historical perspective because it is part historical fact and part modern-day interpretation. Various approaches in the evolution of management thought are discussed relative to the lessons each can teach today's managers. The term *evolution* is appropriate here because management practice has developed in bits and pieces through the years. A historical perspective helps put the pieces together to form meaningful evolutionary patterns.

The Practice and Study of Management

Although the practice of management may be traced to the earliest recorded history, the systematic study of management is relatively new. As an area of academic study, management is essentially a product of the twentieth century. Only three universities—Pennsylvania, Chicago, and California—offered business management courses before 1900.[2]

But the actual practice of management has been around for thousands of years. The pyramids of Egypt, for example, stand as tangible evidence of the ancient world's ability to manage. It took more than 100,000 individuals twenty years to construct the great pyramid of Cheops. This remarkable achievement did not come about by luck or accident; it was the result of systematically managed effort. Although the Egyptians' management techniques were crude by modern standards, many of the problems they faced are still around today. They, like today's managers, had to make plans, obtain and mobilize human and material resources, coordinate interdependent jobs, keep records, report their progress, and take corrective action when and where needed.

An Information Explosion

Since the building of the pyramids, entire civilizations have come and gone. In one form or another, management was practiced in each. Sadly, one modern element was missing during those thousands of years of management experience. That missing element was a systematically recorded body of management knowledge. In early cultures, management was something one learned by word of mouth and trial and error, not something one studied in school, read about in textbooks, theorized about, experimented with, or wrote about.

Thanks to modern printing techniques and electronic media, the collective genius of thousands of management theorists and practitioners has been compressed into a veritable mountain of textbooks, periodical journals, research monographs, microfilms, movies, audio tapes, and computer tapes and disks. A walk to the nearest library opens the door to much of this compressed experience. Never before have present and future managers had so much relevant information at their fingertips. As an indication of what is available, a 1975 study uncovered sixty-four management-oriented periodicals.[3] The number had grown to over one hundred by 1985. In fact, there is so much information on management theory and practice today that it is difficult, if not impossible, to keep abreast of all of it. Managers are challenged to draw selectively from the management theory information explosion and not be overwhelmed by it.

The Management Theory Jungle

One of the principal causes of the information explosion in management theory is its interdisciplinary nature. Individuals from many different academic and professional areas have contributed to our knowledge of management. Scholars from several fields—including psychology, sociology, cultural anthropology, mathematics, philosophy, statistics, political science, economics, logistics, computer science, history, and various fields of engineering—have, at one time or another, been interested in management. In addition, administrators in business, government, church, health care, and education all have drawn from and contributed to the study of management. Each group of scholars and practitioners has interpreted and reformulated management according to its own perspective. With each new perspective have come new questions and assumptions, new research techniques, different technical jargon, and new conceptual frameworks. In 1961, management scholar Harold Koontz detected at least six different approaches to explaining the nature and knowledge of managing, thus prompting him to coin the term *management theory jungle*.[4] A reexamination of the field nearly twenty years later led Koontz to conclude:

> The jungle still exists, and, in fact, there are nearly double the approaches to management that were identified nearly two decades ago. At the present time, a total of eleven approaches to the study of management science and theory may be identified. These are: (1) the empirical or case approach, (2) the interpersonal behavior approach, (3) the group behavior approach, (4) the cooperative social system approach, (5) the sociotechnical systems approach, (6) the decision theory approach, (7) the systems approach, (8) the mathematical or "manage-

ment science" approach, (9) the contingency or situational approach, (10) the managerial roles approach, and (11) the operational theory approach.[5]

We can safely state that there is no single theory of management that is universally accepted: management theory does indeed resemble a jungle.[6] To help put different theories in perspective, we shall discuss five conventional approaches and one modern unconventional perspective. Among the five conventional approaches are: (1) the universal process approach; (2) the operational approach; (3) the behavioral approach; (4) the systems approach; and (5) the contingency approach. The unconventional perspective centers on "attributes of excellence," as discussed in the best-selling book, *In Search of Excellence* (see Figure 2.1). An understanding of these general approaches to the theory and practice of management helps one appreciate how management has evolved, where it is today, and where it appears to be headed.

The Universal Process Approach

The universal process approach is the oldest and one of the most popular approaches to management thought. It is also known as the universalist or functional approach. According to the **universal process approach,** the administration of all organizations, public or private or large or small, requires the same rational process. This approach requires two main assumptions. First, although the purpose of an organization may vary (for example, business, government, education, or religion), it is assumed that there is a core management process that remains the same across all organizations. Successful managers, therefore, are interchangeable among organizations of differing purpose. Second, universalists assume that the universal management process can be reduced to a set of separate functions and related principles. Early universal process writers emphasized the specialization of labor (who does what), the chain of command (who reports to whom), and authority (who is ultimately responsible for getting things done).

Henri Fayol's Universal Management Process

In 1916, at the age of seventy-five, Henri Fayol published his now classic book, *Administration Industrielle et Generale,* though it did not become widely known in England and America until an English translation became available in 1949.[7] Despite its belated appearance in the English-speaking world and despite its having to compete with enthusiastic scientific management and human relations movements in the United States, Fayol's work has left a permanent mark on twentieth-century management think-

Figure 2.1 Evolution of Management Thought in the 20th Century

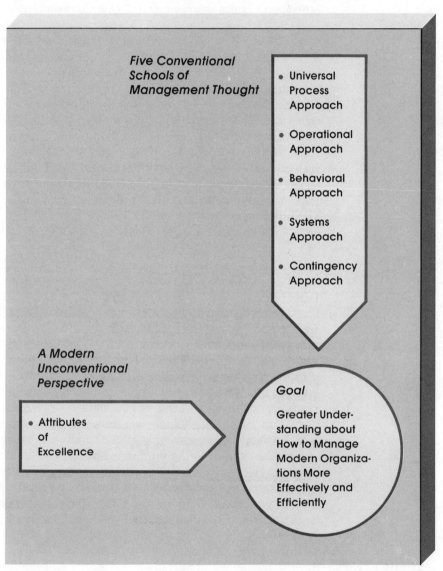

ing. Today Fayol is considered the father of the universal process approach.

Fayol was first an engineer and later a very successful administrator in a large French mining and metallurgical concern, which is perhaps why he did not resort to abstract theory in his pioneering management book.

Rather, Fayol was a manager who attempted to translate his broad administrative experience into practical guidelines for the successful management of all types of organizations.

As we mentioned in the previous chapter, Fayol believed that the manager's job could be divided into five functions, or areas, of managerial responsibility. Fayol viewed these five functions—planning, organizing, command, coordination, and control—as essential to managerial success. His fourteen universal principles of management, as listed in Table 2.1, were intended to show managers how to carry out their functional duties. Fayol's functions and principles have withstood the test of time because of their widespread applicability. In spite of years of reformulation, rewording, expansion, and revision, Fayol's original management functions can still be found in nearly all management texts (including this one).

Lessons from the Universal Process Approach

Fayol's main contribution to management thought was to show how the complex management process can be separated into interdependent areas of responsibility, or functions. Fayol's contention that management is a continuous process beginning with planning and ending with controlling also remains popular today. Contemporary adaptations of Fayol's functions offer students of management a useful framework for analyzing the management process. But as we mentioned in Chapter 1, this sort of rigid functional approach has been criticized for creating the impression that the management process is more rational and orderly than it really is. Fayol's functions, therefore, form a skeleton that needs to be fleshed out with concepts, techniques, and situational refinements from the more modern approaches. The functional approach is useful because it specifies *what* managers do, but the other approaches are needed to explain *how* managers should do their jobs.

The Operational Approach

The term **operational approach** is a convenient description of the production-oriented area of management dedicated to improving efficiency and cutting waste. Since the turn of the century, it has had a number of labels, including scientific management, management science, operations research, and operations management. Underlying this somewhat confusing evolution of terms has been a consistent purpose: to make person-machine systems work as efficiently as possible. Throughout its historical development, the operational approach has been more technical, quantitative, and objectively scientific than the other approaches discussed in this chapter.

Table 2.1 Fayol's Fourteen Universal Principles of Management

1. **Division of work.** Specialization of labor is necessary for organizational success.
2. **Authority.** The right to give orders must accompany responsibility.
3. **Discipline.** Obedience and respect help an organization run smoothly.
4. **Unity of command.** Each employee should receive orders from only one superior.
5. **Unity of direction.** The efforts of everyone in the organization should be coordinated and focused in the same direction.
6. **Subordination of individual interests to the general interest.** Resolving the tug of war between personal and organizational interests in favor of the organization is one of management's greatest difficulties.
7. **Remuneration.** Employees should be paid fairly in accordance with their contribution.
8. **Centralization.** The relationship between centralization and decentralization is a matter of proportion; the optimum balance must be found for each organization.
9. **Scalar chain.** Subordinates should observe the formal chain of command unless expressly authorized by their respective superiors to communicate with each other.
10. **Order.** Both material things and people should be in their proper places.
11. **Equity.** Fairness that results from a combination of kindliness and justice will lead to devoted and loyal service.
12. **Stability and tenure of personnel.** People need time to get to know their jobs.
13. **Initiative.** One of the greatest satisfactions is formulating and carrying out a plan.
14. **Esprit de corps.** Harmonious effort among individuals is the key to organizational success.

SOURCE: Adapted from Henri Fayol, *General and Industrial Management,* trans. Constance Storrs (London: Isaac Pitman & Sons, 1949).

Frederick W. Taylor's Scientific Management

Born in 1856, the son of a Philadelphia lawyer, Frederick Winslow Taylor was the epitome of the self-made man. Because a temporary eye problem kept him from attending Harvard University, Taylor went to work as a common laborer in a small Philadelphia machine shop. In just four years he picked up the trades of pattern maker and machinist.[8] Later, Taylor went to work at Midvale Steel Works, in Philadelphia, where he quickly moved up through the ranks while studying at night for a mechanical engineering degree. As a manager at Midvale, Taylor was appalled at industry's unsystematic practices. He observed little if any cooperation between the managers and the laborers. Inefficiency and waste were rampant. Output restriction among groups of workers, which Taylor called "systematic soldiering," was widespread. Ill-equipped and inadequately trained workers were typically left on their own to determine how to do their jobs. Hence, the father of scientific management committed himself to the

Frederick W. Taylor, 1856–1915
SOURCE: The Bettmann Archive, Inc.

relentless pursuit of "finding a better way."[9] Taylor sought nothing less than what he termed a "mental revolution" in the practice of industrial management.

According to an early definition, **scientific management** is "that kind of management which *conducts* a business or affairs by *standards* established by facts or truths gained through *systematic* observation, experiment, or reasoning."[10] The word *experiment* deserves special emphasis because it was Taylor's trademark. While working at Midvale and later at Bethlehem Steel, Taylor started the scientific management movement in industry in four areas: standardization, time and task study, systematic selection and training, and pay incentives.

Standardization   By closely studying metal-cutting operations, Taylor collected extensive data on the optimum cutting-tool speeds and the rates at which stock should be fed into the machines for each job. The resulting standards were then posted for quick reference by the machine operators. He also systematically catalogued and stored the expensive cutting tools that usually were carelessly thrown aside when a job was completed. Operators could go to the carefully arranged tool room, check out the right tool for the job at hand, and check it back in when finished. Taylor's approach caused productivity to jump and costs to fall.

Time and Task Study   According to the traditional rule-of-thumb approach, there was no "science of shoveling." But Taylor saw things differently. After thousands of observations and stopwatch recordings, he detected a serious flaw in the way various materials were being shoveled— each laborer brought his own shovel to work. Taylor knew that the company was losing rather than saving money when a laborer used the same shovel for both heavy and light materials. A shovel load of iron ore weighed about thirty pounds, according to Taylor's calculations, whereas a shovel load of rice coal weighed only four pounds. Systematic experimentation revealed that a shovel load of twenty-one pounds was optimum (permitted the greatest movement of material in a day). Taylor significantly increased productivity by having the workers use specially sized and shaped shovels provided by the company. Large shovels were used for the lighter materials and smaller ones for the heavier work.

Systematic Selection and Training   Although primitive by modern standards, Taylor's pig iron–handling experiments clearly reveal the intent of this phase of scientific management. The task was to lift a ninety-two-pound block of iron (referred to in the steel trade as a "pig"), carry it up an incline (a total distance of about thirty-six feet), and drop it into an open railroad car. Taylor observed that on the average, a pig iron handler moved about twelve and a half tons in a ten-hour day of constant effort. After careful study, Taylor found that if he selected the strongest men and instructed them in the proper techniques of lifting and carrying the pigs of iron (see Table 2.2), he could get each man to load forty-seven tons in a ten-hour day. Surprisingly, this nearly fourfold increase in output was achieved by having the pig iron handlers spend only 43 percent of their time actually hauling iron. The other 57 percent of the time was spent either walking back empty handed or sitting down. Taylor reported that the laborers liked the new arrangement because they were less fatigued and took home 60 percent more pay.

Pay Incentives   According to Taylor, "What the workmen want from their employers beyond anything else is high wages."[11] This "economic man" assumption led Taylor to believe that piece rates were important to improved productivity. Under traditional piece-rate plans, an individual received a fixed amount of money for each unit of output. Thus the greater the output was, the greater the pay would be. In his determination to find a better way, Taylor attempted to improve the traditional piece-rate scheme with his differential piece-rate plan.

Figure 2.2 illustrates the added incentive effect of Taylor's differential plan. (The amounts are typical rates of pay in Taylor's time.) Under the traditional plan, the worker would receive a fixed amount (for example, 5

Table 2.2 F. W. Taylor in Action

Would this approach work today?

Taylor (talking to Schmidt*): If you are a high-priced man, you will do exactly as this man tells you to-morrow, from morning till night. When he tells you to pick up a pig and walk, you pick it up and you walk, and when he tells you to sit down and rest, you sit down. You do that right straight through the day. And what's more, no back talk.... Now you come on to work here to-morrow morning and I'll know before night whether you are really a high-priced man or not.

*Schmidt was a pseudonym for a very strong Pennsylvania Dutchman who would run more than a mile to and from work every day. After following Taylor's methods, Schmidt's output went from twelve and a half to forty-seven and a half tons per day, and his wages went from $1.15 to $1.85 per day.

SOURCE: Frederick Winslow Taylor, *The Principles of Scientific Management* (New York: Harper & Brothers, 1911), pp. 45–46.

cents) for each unit produced. Seventy-five cents would be received for producing fifteen units and $1.00 for twenty units. In contrast, Taylor's plan required that a time study be carried out to determine the company's idea of a fair day's work. Two piece rates were then put into effect. A low rate would be paid if the worker finished the day below the company's standard, and a high rate would be paid when the day's output met or exceeded the standard. As the lines in Figure 2.2 indicate, a hard worker who produced twenty-five units would earn $1.25 under the traditional plan and $1.50 under Taylor's plan.

Taylor's Followers Among the many who followed in Taylor's footsteps, Frank and Lillian Gilbreth and Henry L. Gantt stand out.

Frank and Lillian Gilbreth Inspired by Taylor's time studies and motivated by a desire to expand human potential, the Gilbreths turned motion study into an exact science. In so doing, they pioneered the use of motion pictures for studying and streamlining work motions. They paved the way for modern work simplification by cataloguing seventeen different hand motions such as "grasp" and "hold." These they called "therbligs" (actually the name Gilbreth spelled backward with the *t* and *h* reversed). Some of their success stories include:

> In laying brick, the motions used in laying a single brick were reduced from eighteen to five—with an increase in output of from one hundred and twenty bricks an hour to three hundred and fifty an hour and with a reduction in the resulting fatigue. In folding cotton cloth, twenty to thirty motions were reduced to ten or twelve, with the result that instead of one hundred and fifty dozen pieces of cloth, four hundred dozen were folded, with no added fatigue.[12]

Figure 2.2 Taylor's Differential Piece-Rate Plan

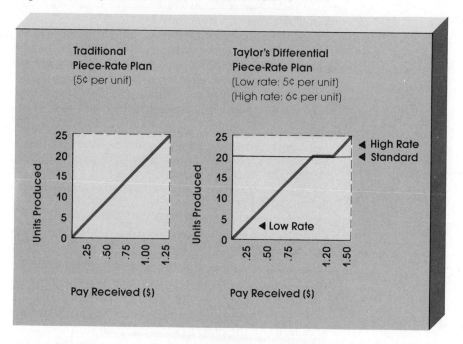

Frank and Lillian Gilbreth were so dedicated to the idea of finding the one best way to do every job that two of their twelve children wrote *Cheaper by the Dozen,* a humorous recollection of scientific management and motion study applied to the Gilbreth household.[13]

Henry L. Gantt   Gantt contributed to scientific management by refining production control and cost control techniques. As illustrated in Chapter 4, variations of Gantt's work-scheduling charts are still in use today. He also humanized Taylor's differential piece-rate system by combining a guaranteed day rate (minimum wage) with an above-standard bonus. Gantt was ahead of his time in emphasizing the importance of the human factor and urging management to concentrate on service rather than profits.[14]

Operations Management   Even though portions of operations management can be traced to Taylor's scientific managment, operations management is essentially a product of the post–World War II era. Operations management, like scientific management, aims at promoting efficiency through systematic observation and experimentation. However, operations management (sometimes called production/operations management) tends to be broader in scope and application than scientific management was.

Whereas scientific management was limited largely to hand labor and

Frank B. Gilbreth, 1868–1924
Lillian M. Gilbreth, 1878–1972
SOURCE: The Bettmann Archive, Inc.

machine shops, operations management specialists apply their expertise
to all types of production operations. For instance, they are concerned with
the purchase and storage of materials, energy use, product design, work
flow, safety, quality control, and data processing. According to one expert
in the field, **operations management** "encompasses the design, implementation, operation, and control of systems made up of men, materials,
capital equipment, information, and money to accomplish some set of
objectives."[15] Operations management specialists attempt to put together
all the pieces of the complex productivity puzzle, often relying on sophisticated models and quantitative techniques. Chapter 17 of this text is devoted
entirely to operations management.

**Lessons from
the
Operational
Approach**

Scientific management often appears rather unscientific to those who live
in a world of miracle drugs, manned moon landings, industrial robots, and
laser technology. *Systematic management* might be a more accurate label.
Nevertheless, within the context of haphazard, turn-of-the-century industrial practices, scientific management was indeed revolutionary, often hav-

Henry L. Gantt, 1861–1919
SOURCE: Historical Pictures Service, Inc., Chicago.

ing dramatic results. Heading the list of lasting contributions from this area is a much-needed emphasis on promoting production efficiency and combating waste. Dedication to finding a better way is more important today than ever in view of uneven productivity growth and diminishing resources. Critics, however, have roundly criticized Taylor and the early scientific management proponents for viewing workers as unidimensional economic beings interested only in more money. They fear that scientific management techniques have dehumanized people by making them act like mindless machines. But, according to one respected management scholar who feels that Taylor's work is widely misunderstood and unfairly criticized, Taylor actually improved working conditions by reducing fatigue and redesigning machines to fit people. A systematic analysis of Taylor's contributions led this same management scholar to conclude:

> Taylor's track record is remarkable. The point is not, as is often claimed, that he was "right in the context of his time" but is now outdated, but that *most of his insights are still valid today.*[16]

More recently, behaviorally oriented management theorists have been critical of the tendency of some operations management specialists to translate everything, including human behavior, into numbers. They argue that people are too multidimensional and unpredictable to have their behavior reduced to abstract models and simplistic mathematical assumptions.

The Behavioral Approach

Like the other approaches to management, the behavioral approach has evolved gradually over many years. Advocates of the behavioral approach to management point out that people deserve to be the central focus of organized activity. They believe that successful management depends largely on one's ability to understand and work with people who have a variety of backgrounds, needs, perceptions, and aspirations. The progress of this humanistic approach from the human relations movement to modern organizational behavior has greatly influenced management theory and practice.

The Human Relations Movement

The **human relations movement** was a concerted effort among theorists and practitioners to make managers more sensitive to their employees' needs. It came into being as a result of special circumstances that occurred during the first half of this century. As illustrated in Figure 2.3, the human relations movement may be compared to the top of a pyramid. Just as the top of a pyramid must be supported, so too the human relations movement was supported by three very different historic influences: (1) unionization, (2) the Hawthorne studies, and (3) the philosophy of industrial humanism.

Unionization To understand why the human relations movement evolved, one needs first to appreciate its sociopolitical background. From the late 1800s to the 1920s, American industry grew by leaps and bounds as it attempted to satisfy the many demands of a rapidly growing population. Cheap labor was readily available, and there was a seller's market for finished goods. Then came the Great Depression in the 1930s, and millions stood in bread lines rather than in pay lines. Many believed that business was somehow responsible for the depression, causing public sympathy to swing from management to labor. Congress consequently began to pass prolabor legislation. When the Wagner Act was passed in 1935, thus legalizing union-management collective bargaining, management began searching for ways to stem the tide of all-out unionization. Early human relations theory proposed an enticing answer; that is, satisfied employees would be less inclined to join unions. Business managers subsequently began adopting morale-boosting human relations techniques as a union-avoidance tactic.

Figure 2.3   The Human Relations Movement Pyramid

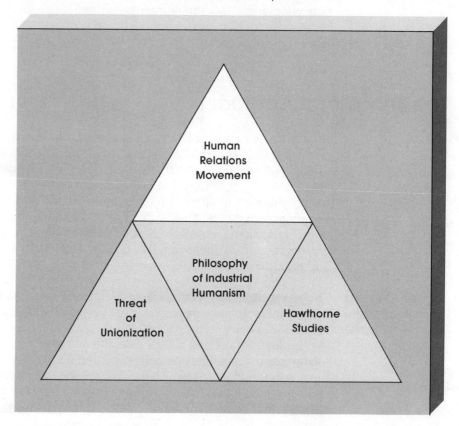

The Hawthorne Studies   As the sociopolitical climate changed, a second development in industry took place. Behavioral scientists from prestigious universities began to conduct on-the-job behavioral studies. They did not study tools and techniques in the scientific management tradition; rather, they focused on people. Practical behavioral research stirred management's interest in the psychological and sociological dynamics of the workplace. The famous Hawthorne studies paved the way for an unprecedented wave of job-related behavioral research.

The Hawthorne studies began in 1924 in a Western Electric plant near Chicago as a small-scale scientific management study of the relationship between light intensity and productivity. Curiously, the performance of a select group of employees tended to improve no matter how the physical surroundings were manipulated. Even when the lights were dimmed to moonlight intensity, productivity continued to climb! Scientific management doctrine could not account for what was taking place, and so a team

Elton Mayo 1880–1949
SOURCE: Courtesy, Harvard University Archives.

of behavioral science researchers headed by Elton Mayo was brought in from Harvard to conduct a more rigorous study. By 1932, when the Hawthorne studies ended, over twenty thousand employees had participated in the studies in one way or another. The human relations lessons learned at Hawthorne were to have a profound impact on the practice of management. Three lessons that had a major influence were:

- Employees have higher morale and work harder under supportive supervision. A supportive supervisor is one who shows sincere concern for subordinates.
- Indirect interviewing is superior to traditional direct-question techniques. Indirect questions (those that require more than just a yes or no answer) make interviewees feel more comfortable and more willing to share their personal thoughts and opinions.
- Employees operating under traditional nonsupportive supervision tend to restrict output systematically by establishing and enforcing their own informal group standards.[17]

These conclusions from the Hawthorne studies inspired similar on-the-job behavioral studies and focused management's attention on the human factor.

The Philosophy of Industrial Humanism Although unionization prompted a search for new management techniques and the Hawthorne studies demonstrated that people were important to productivity, a philosophy of human relations was needed to provide a convincing rationale for treating employees better. Elton Mayo, Mary Parker Follett, and Douglas McGregor, although from very different backgrounds, offered just such a philosophy of human relations.

Born in Australia, Elton Mayo was a Harvard professor specializing in psychology and sociology when he took over the Hawthorne studies. His 1933 book, *The Human Problems of an Industrial Civilization,* inspired by what he had learned at Hawthorne, cautioned managers that emotional factors were a more important determinant of productive efficiency than physical and logical factors were. Claiming that employees create their own unofficial yet powerful workplace culture complete with norms and sanctions, Mayo urged managers to provide work that fostered personal and subjective satisfaction. He called for a new social order designed to stimulate individual cooperation.

Before her death in 1933, Mary Parker Follett's experience as a management consultant and her background in law, political science, and philosophy produced a strong conviction that managers should be aware that each employee is a complex collection of emotions, beliefs, attitudes, and habits. In order to get employees to work harder, she felt that managers had to recognize the motivating desires of the individual. Accordingly, Follett urged managers to motivate performance rather than simply to demand it. Cooperation, a spirit of unity, and coordination of effort were seen by Follett as the keys to both productivity and a democratic way of life.[18]

A third philosophical rallying point for industrial humanism was provided by an American scholar named Douglas McGregor. In his 1960 classic *The Human Side of Enterprise,* McGregor outlined a set of highly optimistic assumptions about human nature. McGregor viewed the typical employee as an energetic and creative individual who could achieve great things if given the opportunity. He labeled the set of assumptions for this optimistic perspective **Theory Y.** McGregor's Theory Y assumptions are listed in Table 2.3 along with what he called the traditional Theory X assumptions. These two sets of assumptions about human nature enabled McGregor to contrast the modern or enlightened view he recommended (Theory Y) with the prevailing traditional view (Theory X), which he criticized for being pessimistic, stifling, and outdated. Because of its relative recency (compared to Mayo's and Follett's work), its catchy labels, and its intuitive appeal, McGregor's Theory X/Y philosophy has left an indelible mark on modern management thinking. Some historians have credited McGregor with launching the field of organizational behavior.

Table 2.3 McGregor's Theories X and Y

Theory X: Some traditional assumptions about people	Theory Y: Some modern assumptions about people
1. Most people dislike work, and they will avoid it when they can.	1. Work is a natural activity, like play or rest.
2. Most people must be coerced and threatened with punishment before they will work. They require close direction.	2. People are capable of self-direction and self-control if they are committed to objectives.
3. Most people prefer to be directed. They avoid responsibility and have little ambition. They are interested only in security.	3. People will become committed to organizational objectives if they are rewarded for doing so.
	4. The average person can learn both to accept and seek responsibility.
	5. Many people in the general population have imagination, ingenuity, and creativity.

Organizational Behavior

Organizational behavior is a modern approach to management that attempts to determine the causes of human work behavior and translate the results into effective management techniques. As such, it is strongly committed to research. Organizational behaviorists have borrowed an assortment of theories and research techniques from psychology, sociology, and cultural anthropology and have applied them to people at work in modern organizations. The result is an interdisciplinary field that is somewhat difficult to define. One organizational behaviorist has tagged the field "a fledgling, schizophrenic, fragmented subject."[19] But in spite of its new and relatively immature state, organizational behavior has had a significant impact on modern management thought by helping explain why employees behave as they do. Because human relations has become a practical how-to-do-it discipline for supervisors, organizational behavior has become a scientific extension of human relations. Many organizational behavior findings will be examined in Part IV.

Lessons from the Behavioral Approach

Above all else, the behavioral approach makes it clear to present and future managers that people are the key to productivity. According to advocates of the behavioral approach, technology, work rules, and standards do not guarantee good job performance. Instead, success depends on motivated individuals who are committed to organizational objectives. Only a manager's sensitivity to individual concerns can foster the cooperation necessary for high productivity. On the negative side, traditional human relations

Mary Parker Follett, 1868–1933
SOURCE: Joan C. Tonn and the Urwick Management Center.

doctrine has been criticized as vague and simplistic. According to these critics, relatively primitive on-the-job behavioral research does not justify such broad conclusions. For instance, critics do not believe that supportive supervision and good human relations will lead automatically to higher morale and hence to better job performance. In fact, recent analyses of the Hawthorne studies, using modern statistical techniques, suggest that many of the Hawthorne researchers' conclusions were probably unjustified.[20]

Fortunately, organizational behavior, as a scientific extension of human relations, promises to fill some of the gaps left by the human relationists while at the same time retaining the emphasis on people. Today, organizational behaviorists are trying to piece together the multiple determinants of effective job performance in various work situations.

The Systems Approach

A **system** is a collection of parts that operate interdependently to achieve a

Douglas McGregor 1906–1964
SOURCE: UPI/Bettman Newsphotos.

common purpose. Working from this definition, the systems approach represents a marked departure from the past; in fact, it requires a completely different style of thinking.

Universal process, scientific management, and human relations theorists studied management by taking things apart. They assumed that the whole is equal to the sum of its parts and that the whole can be explained in terms of its parts. Systems theorists, in contrast, study management by putting things together, and they assume that the whole is greater than the sum of its parts. The difference is analytic versus synthetic thinking. According to one management systems expert, "Analytic thinking is, so to speak, outside-in thinking; synthetic thinking is inside-out. Neither negates the value of the other, but by synthetic thinking we can gain understanding that we cannot obtain through analysis, particularly of collective phenomena."[21]

Systems theorists recommend synthetic thinking because management is not practiced in a vacuum. Managers affect, and in turn are affected by, many other organizational and environmental variables. Systems thinking has presented the field of management with an enormous challenge: to

Figure 2.4 Barnard's Cooperative System

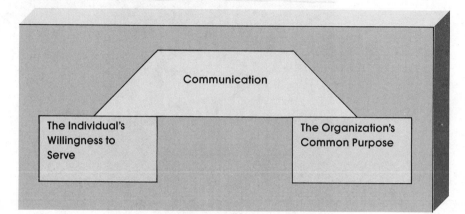

identify all relevant parts of organized activity and to discover how those parts interact. Two management writers have predicted that systems thinking offers "a basis for understanding organizations and their problems which may one day produce a revolution in organizations comparable to the one brought about by Taylor with scientific management."[22]

Chester I. Barnard's Early Systems Perspective

In one sense, Chester I. Barnard followed in the footsteps of Henri Fayol. Like Fayol, Barnard established a new approach to management on the basis of his experience as a top-level manager. But the former president of New Jersey Bell Telephone took an approach that was different from Fayol's. Rather than isolating specific management functions and principles, Barnard devised a more abstract systems approach. In his 1938 classic, *The Functions of the Executive*, Barnard characterized all organizations as cooperative systems: "A cooperative system is a complex of physical, biological, personal, and social components which are in a specific systematic relationship by reason of the cooperation of two or more persons for at least one definite end."[23]

According to Barnard, willingness to serve, common purpose, and communication are the principal elements in an organization (or cooperative system).[24] He felt that an organization did not exist if these three elements were not present and working interdependently. As illustrated in Figure 2.4, Barnard viewed communication as an energizing force that bridges the natural gap between the individual's willingness to serve and the organization's common purpose.

Barnard's early systems perspective has encouraged management and organization theorists to study organizations as complex and dynamic wholes instead of piece by piece. Barnard opened a promising door in the evolution of management thought.

Chester I. Barnard, 1886–1961
SOURCE: Historical Pictures Service, Inc., Chicago.

General Systems Theory

General systems theory is an interdisciplinary area of study based on the assumption that everything is part of a larger, interdependent arrangement. According to Ludwig von Bertalanffy, a biologist and the founder of general systems theory, "In order to understand an organized whole we must know both the parts and the relations between them."[25] This interdisciplinary perspective was eagerly adopted by Barnard's followers because it categorized levels of systems and distinguished between closed and open systems.

Levels of Systems   Envisioning the world as a collection of systems was only the first step for the general systems theorists. One of the more important recent steps has been the identification of hierarchies of systems, ranging from very specific systems to general ones. Identifying systems at various levels has helped translate abstract general systems theory into more concrete terms. A hierarchy of systems relevant to management is the seven-level scheme of living systems shown in Figure 2.5. Notice that each system is a subsystem of the next higher one.

Closed Versus Open Systems   In addition to identifying hierarchies of systems, general systems theorists have distinguished between closed and

Figure 2.5 Levels of Living Systems

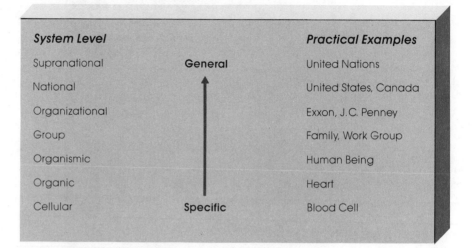

System Level		Practical Examples
Supranational	**General**	United Nations
National		United States, Canada
Organizational		Exxon, J.C. Penney
Group		Family, Work Group
Organismic		Human Being
Organic		Heart
Cellular	**Specific**	Blood Cell

open systems. A **closed system** is a self-sufficient entity, whereas an **open system** is one that depends on the surrounding environment for survival. In reality, these two kinds of systems cannot be completely separated from each other. The key to classifying a system as relatively closed or relatively open is to determine the amount of interaction between the system and its environment. A battery-powered digital watch, for example, is a relatively closed system because once the battery is in place, it runs without help from the outside environment. In contrast, a solar-powered clock is a relatively open system because it cannot operate without a continual supply of outside energy. The human body is a highly open system because life depends on the body's ability to import oxygen and energy and export waste. In other words, the human body is highly dependent on the environment for survival.

Along the same lines, general systems theorists tell us that all organizations are open systems because organizational survival depends on interaction with the surrounding environment. Just as "no man is an island," no organization or organizational subsystem is an island, according to the systems approach.

Lessons from the Systems Approach

Because of the influence of the systems approach, managers have a greater appreciation now than in the past for the importance of seeing the whole picture. Open-systems thinking does not permit the manager to become preoccupied with one aspect of organizational management while ignoring other internal and external realities. For instance, the manager of a business must consider resource availability, technological developments, and market trends when producing and selling a product or service. Another positive aspect of the systems approach is that it tries to make sense of the management theory jungle. Both operations management and organizational behavior, although quite different in emphasis, have been strongly influenced by systems thinking.

There are critics of the systems approach, of course. Some management scholars see systems thinking as long on intellectual appeal and catchy terminology and short on verifiable facts and practical advice. Even two staunch advocates of a management systems perspective are wary: "Recognizing that the social organization is a contrived system cautions us against making an exact analogy between it and physical and biological systems."[26] At the present time, the systems approach is an instructive way of thinking rather than a collection of final answers to managing modern organizations.

The Contingency Approach

A new line of thinking among management theorists has been labeled the contingency approach. Contingency management advocates are attempting to take a step away from universally applicable principles of management and toward situational appropriateness. In the words of one management writer, "The traditional approaches to management were not necessarily wrong, but today they are no longer adequate. The needed breakthrough for management theory and practice can be found in a contingency approach."[27] Formally defined, the **contingency approach** is an effort to determine through research which managerial practices and techniques are appropriate in specific situations. Imagine using Taylor's instructional approach (Table 2.2) with a college-educated computer engineer! Different situations require different managerial responses, according to the contingency approach.

Generally, the term *contingency* refers to the choice of an alternative course of action. For example, a hostess may have a contingency plan to move her party indoors if it rains. Her subsequent actions are said to be contingent (or dependent) on the weather. In a management context, contingency has become synonymous with situational management. According to one contingency theorist, "The effectiveness of a given management pattern is contingent upon multitudinous factors and their interrelationship in a particular situation."[28] This means that the application of various management tools and techniques must be appropriate to the particular situation, because each situation presents the manager with its own problems.

In real-life management, the success of any given technique is dictated by the situation. For example, researchers have found that rigidly structured organizations with many layers of management function best when environmental conditions are relatively stable. Unstable surroundings dictate a more flexible and streamlined organization that can adapt quickly to change. Consequently, traditional principles of management that call for rigidly structured organizations, regardless of the situation, have come into question.

Contingency Characteristics   Some management scholars are attracted to contingency thinking because it is a workable compromise between the systems approach and what can be called a purely situational perspective. Figure 2.6 illustrates this relationship. The systems approach is often criticized for being too general and abstract, although the purely situational view, which assumes that every real-life situation requires a distinctly different approach, has been called hopelessly specific. Contingency advocates have tried to take advantage of common denominators without getting trapped into simplistic generalization. Three characteristics of the contingency approach are (1) an open-system perspective, (2) a practical research orientation, and (3) a multivariate approach.

An Open-System Perspective   Open-system thinking is fundamental to the contingency view. Contingency theorists are not satisfied with focusing on just the internal workings of organizations. They see the need to understand how organizational subsystems combine to interact with outside social, political, and economic systems. Contingency scholar Fred Luthans offered the following open-system perspective:

> In the past, most effort in the theory and practice of management has been devoted to the internal environmental factors. The external environment was either ignored or treated as a given. Only recently with open-system analysis has the external environment been given attention in management literature. ... Contingency management must of course give attention to both the external and internal environments.[29]

A Practical Research Orientation   Practical research is that which ultimately leads to more effective on-the-job management. Contingency researchers are attempting to translate their findings into tools and situational refinements for more effective management.

A Multivariate Approach   Traditional closed-system thinking prompted a search for simple, one-to-one causal relationships. This approach is called bivariate analysis. For example, the traditional human relations assumption that higher morale leads automatically to higher productivity was the result of bivariate analysis. Only one variable, morale, was seen as

Figure 2.6 The Contingency View: A Compromise

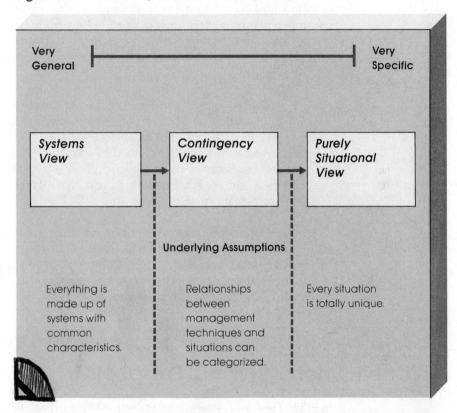

the sole direct cause of changes in a second variable, productivity. Subsequent multivariate analysis has shown that many variables including the employee's personality, the nature of the task, rewards, and job and life satisfaction collectively account for variations in productivity. **Multivariate analysis** is a research technique used to determine how a combination of variables interacts to cause a particular outcome. For example, if an employee's personality is authoritarian, the task highly structured, and the individual highly satisfied with his or her life and job, then analysis might show that productivity could be expected to be high. Contingency management theorists strive to carry out practical and relevant multivariate analyses.

Lessons from the Contingency Approach

Although still not fully developed, the contingency approach is a helpful addition to management thought because it emphasizes situational appropriateness. People, organizations, and problems are too complex to justify rigid adherence to universal principles of management. Too, contingency thinking is a practical extension of the systems approach. Assuming that systems thinking is a unifying, synthetic force in management thought, the contingency approach promises to add practical direction.

The contingency approach, like each of the other conventional approaches, has its share of critics. One has criticized contingency theory on the following two counts:

> ... first, it negates one of the basic attributes of good theory, which is to provide generalizations that are useful. Contingency theory is basically nihilistic; it is anti-theory. And, second, in its most recent deterministic form it overlooks the primary reason why management exists which is, of course, to make a difference for the better in an organization. If the organization is a captive of its environment, the implication is that there is no need for management, because there is nothing it can do.[30]

Whether the contingency management theorists have bitten off more than they can chew remains to be seen. At present they appear to be headed in a constructive direction. But it is good to keep in mind that the contingency approach is a promising beginning rather than the end of the evolution of conventional management thought.

Attributes of Excellence:
A Modern Unconventional Perspective

In 1982, Thomas J. Peters and Robert H. Waterman, Jr., a pair of management consultants, wrote a book that took the management world by storm. It topped the nonfiction best-seller lists for months, was translated into several foreign languages, and later appeared in paperback. Within two years, more than 1.3 million hardcover copies had been sold; only Alex Haley's *Roots* had sold at a faster pace.[31] The book was entitled *In Search of Excellence* and its purpose was to explain what makes America's best-run companies successful. Many respected corporate executives hailed Peters' and Waterman's book as the remedy for America's productivity problems. Certain management scholars, however, called the book simplistic and accused the authors of pandering to management's desire for a quick fix. If for no other reason than its widespread acceptance in the management community, *In Search of Excellence* deserves discussion in any historical perspective of management thought.

Peters' and Waterman's approach to management is unconventional for three reasons. First, they attack conventional management theory and practice for being too conservative, rationalistic, analytical, unemotional,

Thomas J. Peters

inflexible, negative, and preoccupied with bigness. Second, they replace conventional management terminology (such as planning, management by objectives, and control) with catch phrases gleaned from successful managers (for example, "Do it, fix it, try it" and "management by wandering around"). Third, they make their key points with stories and anecdotes rather than with objective, quantified data and facts. All this adds up to a challenge to take a fresh new look at management. In this section we explore that challenge by discussing the eight attributes of excellence uncovered by Peters and Waterman.

Eight Attributes of Excellence

Peters and Waterman employed a combination of subjective and objective screening criteria to identify 62 of the best-managed companies in the United States. Among the final subsample of 36 "excellent" companies that boasted 20-year records of innovation and profitability were such familiar names as Boeing, Caterpillar Tractor, Delta Airlines, Eastman Kodak, IBM, Johnson & Johnson, McDonald's, and 3M. Extensive interviews were conducted at half of these firms while less extensive interviewing took place at the rest.[32] After analyzing the results of their interviews, Peters and Waterman isolated the eight attributes of excellence summarized in Table 2.4. It is important to note that " . . . not all eight attributes were present or conspicuous to the same degree in all of the excellent companies we studied. But in every case at least a preponderance of the eight was clearly visible, quite distinctive."[33]

Robert H. Waterman

Lessons from the Excellence Approach

Certainly more than anything else, Peters and Waterman did a good job of reminding managers to pay closer attention to *basics* such as customers, employees, and new ideas. While reviewing their findings, they noted:

> The project showed, more clearly than could have been hoped for, that the excellent companies were, above all, brilliant on the basics. Tools didn't substitute for thinking. Intellect didn't overpower wisdom. Analysis didn't impede action. Rather, these companies worked hard to keep things simple in a complex world. They persisted. They insisted on top quality. They fawned on their customers. They listened to their employees and treated them like adults. They allowed their innovative product or service "champions" long tethers. They allowed some chaos in return for quick action and regular experimentation.[34]

Although discussion of these basics may strike some as a tedious rehash of the obvious, it is precisely the basics that keep many organizations and individuals from achieving excellence. Students who have failed an important exam because they didn't read the assigned material or forgot to set their alarm will readily attest to the importance of basics.

Despite Peters' and Waterman's flagrantly subjective research methodology, they deserve credit for reminding managers of the importance of on-the-job experimentation. All the planning in the world cannot teach the practical lessons that one can learn by experimentally rearranging things and observing the results, trying an improved approach, observing, and so on.

Table 2.4 Peters' and Waterman's Eight Attributes of Excellence

Attributes of Excellence	Key Indicators
1. A bias for action	● Small scale, easily managed experiments to build knowledge, interest, and commitment. ● Managers stay visible and personally involved in all areas through active, informal communication and spontaneous MBWA ("management by wandering around").
2. Close to the customer	● Customer satisfaction is practically an obsession. ● Input from customers is sought throughout the design/production/marketing cycle.
3. Autonomy and entrepreneurship	● Risk taking is encouraged; failure is tolerated. ● Innovators are encouraged to "champion" their pet projects to see them through to completion. ● Flexible structure permits the formation of "skunk works" (small teams of zealous innovators working on a special project). ● Lots of creative "swings" are encouraged to ensure some "home runs" (successful products).
4. Productivity through people	● Individuals are treated with respect and dignity. ● Enthusiasm, trust, and a family feeling are fostered. ● People are encouraged to have fun while getting something meaningful accomplished. ● Work units are kept small and humane.
5. Hands-on, value-driven	● A clear company philosophy is widely disseminated and followed. ● Personal values are discussed openly, not buried. ● The organization's belief system is reinforced through frequently shared stories, myths, and legends. ● Leaders are positive role models; not "Do-as-I-say, not-as-I-do" authority figures.
6. Stick to the knitting	● Management sticks to the business it knows best. ● Emphasis is on internal growth, not mergers.
7. Simple form, lean staff	● Authority is decentralized as much as possible. ● Headquarters staffs are kept small; talent is pushed out to the field.
8. Simultaneous loose-tight properties	● Tight overall strategic and financial control is counterbalanced by decentralized authority, autonomy, and opportunities for creativity.

SOURCE: Adaptation based on eight attributes from pages 13–15 of *In Search of Excellence: Lessons from America's Best-Run Companies* by Thomas J. Peters and Robert H. Waterman, Jr. Copyright © 1982 by Thomas J. Peters and Robert H. Waterman, Jr. Reprinted by permission of Harper & Row Publishers, Inc.

Nonetheless, critics have taken Peters and Waterman to task for giving managers more questions than answers and relying too heavily on unsupported generalizations. They also criticize them for taking an overly narrow viewpoint of organizational success. According to one skeptical management consultant:

> The authors fail to position management effectiveness among the several non-management variables that are also important to sustained corporate excellence. Technology, finances, government policy, raw materials, and others must be acknowledged, if only to forestall unreasonable expectations of and for management.[35]

In fact, after reviewing research evidence that fourteen of Peters' and Waterman's "excellent" companies had fallen on hard times by 1984, *Business Week* observed:

> One major lesson from all this is that the excellent companies of today will not necessarily be the excellent companies of tomorrow. But the more important lesson is that good management requires much more than following any one set of rules. *In Search of Excellence* was a response to an era when management put too much emphasis on number-crunching. But companies can also get into trouble by overemphasizing Peters' and Waterman's principles.[36]

A concluding comment is in order to help put the foregoing historical overview into proper perspective. The theoretical tidiness of this chapter, while providing a useful conceptual framework for students of management, generally does not carry over to the practice of management. As the excellence approach makes clear, managers are, first and foremost, pragmatists. They use whatever works. Instead of faithfully adhering to a given school of management thought, successful managers tend to use a "mixed bag" approach. This chapter is a good starting point for you to begin building your own personally relevant and useful approach to management by blending theory, the experience and advice of others, and your own experience.

Summary

Management thought has evolved in bits and pieces over the years. Although the practice of management dates back to the earliest recorded history, the systematic study of management is largely a product of the twentieth century. An information explosion in management theory has created a management theory jungle. Five conventional approaches to management are (1) the universal process approach, (2) the operational approach, (3) the behavioral approach, (4) the systems approach, and (5) the contingency approach. A modern unconventional approach centers on Peters' and Waterman's attributes of corporate excellence.

Henri Fayol's universal process approach assumes that all organizations, regardless of purpose or size, require the same management process. Furthermore, it assumes that this rational process can be reduced to separate functions and principles of management. The universal process approach, the oldest of the various approaches, is still popular today.

Dedicated to promoting production efficiency and reducing waste, the operational approach has evolved from scientific management to operations management. Frederick W. Taylor, the father of scientific management, and his followers revolutionized industrial management through the use of standardization, time and motion study, selection and training, and pay incentives. Largely a product of the post–World War II era, operations management has broadened the scientific pursuit of efficiency to include all productive organizations. Operations management specialists often rely on sophisticated models and quantitative techniques.

Management has turned to the human factor in the human relations movement and organizational behavior. Emerging from such factors as unionization, the Hawthorne studies, and the philosophy of industrial humanism, the human relations movement began as a concerted effort to make employees' needs a high management priority. Today, organizational behavior tries to identify the multiple determinants of job performance.

Advocates of the systems approach recommend that modern organizations be viewed as open systems. Open systems depend on the outside environment for survival, whereas closed systems do not. Chester I. Barnard stirred early interest in systems thinking in 1938 by suggesting that organizations are cooperative systems energized by communication. General systems theory, an interdisciplinary field based on the assumption that everything is systematically related, has identified a hierarchy of systems and has differentiated closed and open systems.

A comparatively new approach to management thought is the contingency approach, which stresses situational appropriateness rather than universal principles. The contingency approach is characterized by an open-system perspective, a practical research orientation, and a multivariate approach to research. Contingency thinking is a practical extension of more abstract systems thinking.

In Search of Excellence, Peters' and Waterman's best-selling book, challenged managers to take a fresh, unconventional look at managing. They isolated eight attributes of excellence after studying many of the best-managed and most successful companies in America. Generally, the excellent companies were found to be relatively decentralized and value-driven organizations dedicated to humane treatment of employees, innovation, experimentation, and customer satisfaction.

Terms to Understand

Universal process approach	System
Operational approach	General systems theory
Scientific management	Closed system
Operations management	Open system
Human relations movement	Contingency approach
Theory Y	Multivariate analysis
Organizational behavior	

Questions for Discussion

1. Why is the term *management theory jungle* appropriate?
2. Referring to this book's table of contents, what evidence of Fayol's five functions can you find?
3. In your opinion, which of Fayol's fourteen principles of management are still generally valid? Explain.
4. How did scientific management change industrial management?
5. How did the Gilbreths and Gantt extend Taylor's work?
6. Why could the human relations movement be called a significant turning point in management history? How did McGregor help focus needed attention on the "human factor"?
7. Why is an open-system perspective valuable to managers?
8. Cite your own examples of relatively closed and relatively open systems. How can you tell the difference?
9. What important lesson does the contingency approach teach managers?
10. Which of the attributes of excellence listed in Table 2.4 could end up hurting a company if taken to the extreme?

Back to the Opening Case

Now that you have read Chapter 2, you should be able to answer the following questions about the Caterpillar case:

1. Which of Henri Fayol's fourteen universal principles are clearly evident among Caterpillar's top managers? In your view, how important are these factors to organizational success?
2. What would Frederick W. Taylor probably have to say about the quality circle experiment?

3. How do you suppose Elton Mayo, Mary Parker Follett, and Douglas McGregor would interpret Caterpillar's attempt to improve management/labor relations?
4. Why would Chester I. Barnard probably applaud Caterpillar's efforts to strengthen its internal communication program?
5. Drawing upon the attributes of excellence, what arguments could be made for dropping Caterpillar from Peters' and Waterman's list of excellent companies?

Closing Case 2.2

A Curious Search for Excellence at AT&T

January 1, 1984 was a landmark day for American Telephone & Telegraph (AT&T). On that day the federal government's order to divest its 22 regional Bell telephone companies took effect. "Ma Bell" ceased to exist as the giant regulated monopoly that had touched the lives of generations of Americans. In fact, the courts even prohibited AT&T from using the famous bell symbol. As an unregulated company, AT&T was free to compete with IBM and other computer and telecommunications companies for pieces of huge information processing and transmitting markets. Critical observers said that AT&T's service-oriented corporate culture would make it difficult, if not impossible, to muster the marketing know-how needed to compete successfully with companies such as IBM. Others were skeptical about AT&T's stated intention to speed up its new product development process. AT&T's top management, meanwhile, was busy reorganizing and putting aggressive go-getters in key positions. What follows is the story of one manager who was brought in to turn AT&T around.

A Golden Opportunity

AT&T Information Systems was created in January 1983 to market information processing equipment. Two major subunits were formed. After the divestiture, General Business Systems (GBS) would be responsible for selling a high volume of small systems. Large accounts were to be handled by the 12,000-person National Business Systems unit. A 43-year-old manager, William F. Buehler, was appointed vice president and head of the 3,000-person GBS unit. According to observers, he was given a "free hand" by his boss to shake the old ways. Buehler's 16-hour days convinced everyone right from the start that he was serious about pumping some zest into the old AT&T bureaucracy.

An Unconventional Approach

A self-proclaimed charismatic leader who reportedly likes the limelight and tends to dominate conversations, Buehler made one thing perfectly clear to his people: he wanted results. But he was willing to do whatever was needed to help them get those results. In a style that was totally out of character with the old Ma Bell way of doing things, Buehler implemented lessons he had learned from two readings of Peters' and Waterman's best-seller, *In Search of Excellence*. Through conversations and internal documents he echoed Peters' and Waterman's advice: "bias for action," "keep it simple," "reward results not process," and "the customer is king." He did a lot of MBWA (management by wandering around), visiting all of his unit's 27 branches across the country. Instead of relying on formal presentations to get across *his way* of doing things, he freely crossed once sacred hierarchical lines to reach his people more informally. In one instance, Buehler reportedly chatted with billing personnel in New Jersey while they all lunched on submarine sandwiches. Most branch personnel had never even met an AT&T vice president before.

Not that Buehler was a softy. He established tough sales quotas, making sure that those who met them were handsomely rewarded and those who failed were driven out. In order to take advantage of peer pressure, he posted sales results for all to see. It took a while for his way to catch on, and his unit's sales initially trailed those of the National Business Systems unit. Other AT&T units appeared to enjoy his apparent failure. It was at this critical juncture that his boss, the man responsible for bringing Buehler in from Pacific Telephone Company, left AT&T.

During his first year, over one-third of his sales force either quit, were transferred, or were fired. However, the remaining salespeople responded favorably to Buehler's willingness to streamline bureaucratic forms (for example, reducing four-page standard contracts to one page) and eliminate what he believed to be useless memos, meetings, and planning manuals. In addition, he made decisions much faster than formerly had been the case. Buehler's unconventional action-oriented approach eventually caught on and salespeople began exceeding their quotas and enjoying the healthy commissions (the highest in AT&T's history) he had established.

A Surprise Ending

One would naturally expect that Buehler was destined to become a "crown prince" at AT&T. Unfortunately, such was not to be the case. Barely a year after taking his new position, Buehler was pushed aside into what the *Wall Street Journal* termed "an obscure planning position," though he retained his vice president title. Insiders reported that Buehler's unique style of leadership had ruffled the feathers of top management. Observers were left to ponder if AT&T was thereby stifling the sort of flexibility and competitiveness needed to take on IBM.

For Discussion

1. What aspects of Buehler's approach would F. W. Taylor have endorsed?

2. Why do you suppose Buehler was pushed aside? (*Note:* The discussion of organizational cultures in Chapter 7 should give you some good hints.)

3. What lessons in excellence had Buehler apparently learned from *In Search of Excellence*?

4. Was Buehler's quest for excellence at AT&T doomed right from the start? Explain.

References

Opening quotation: John W. Gardner, *Self-Renewal: The Individual and the Innovative Society* (New York: Harper & Row, 1964), chap. 11.

Opening case: For additional information on Caterpillar, see "Caterpillar: Sticking to the Basics to Stay Competitive," *Business Week* No. 2686 (May 4, 1981): 74–80; Paul Gibson and Barbara Rudolph, "Playing Peoria—To Perfection," *Forbes* 127 (May 11, 1981): 60–65; "What's Pushing Caterpillar to Settle," *Business Week* No. 2781 (March 14, 1983): 28; "A Strike-Weary Caterpillar Knuckles Under," *Business Week* No. 2788 (May 2, 1983): 30–31; Carol J. Loomis, "High Stakes in the Cat Fight," *Fortune* 107 (May 2, 1983): 66–80; Douglas Williams, "CAT Comes Roaring Back!" *Automotive Industries* 164 (April 1984): 39–41; "Betting on a Caterpillar Comeback," *Fortune* 109 (April 30, 1984): 346–348; and "Komatsu Digs Deeper into the U.S.," *Business Week* No. 2862 (October 1, 1984): 53.

Closing case For additional information on American Telephone and Telegraph (AT&T), see "Changing Phone Habits," *Business Week* No. 2806 (September 5, 1983): 68–71; Frank Barbetta, "AT&T Info Sys. Reassigns Small Business User Execs," *Electronic News* 29 (October 10, 1983): 1, 4; W. Brooke Tunstall, "Cultural Transition at AT&T," *Sloan Management Review* 25 (Fall 1983): 15–26; Monica Langley, "AT&T Manager Finds His Efforts to Galvanize Sales Meet Resistance," *Wall Street Journal* 109 (December 16, 1983): 1, 16; Kathleen K. Wiegner, "Prometheus Unbound, and Seeking His Footing," *Forbes* 133 (March 12, 1984): 141–148; and "AT&T Takes Its First Giant Steps into Commercial Computers," *Business Week* No. 2837 (April 9, 1984): 100–102.

1. Barbara S. Lawrence, "Historical Perspective: Using the Past to Study the Present," *Academy of Management Review* 9 (April 1984): 307.

2. For a discussion in this area, see "How Business Schools Began," *Business Week* No. 1781 (October 19, 1963): 114–116.

3. From Charles N. Weaver, "Evaluations of Sixty-four Journals Which Publish

Articles on Management," Working Paper for the Management Education and Development Division of the Academy of Management, 1975, Table 1.

4. See Harold Koontz, "The Management Theory Jungle," *Academy of Management Journal* 4 (December 1961): 174–188.

5. Harold Koontz, "The Management Theory Jungle Revisited," *Academy of Management Review* 5 (April 1980): 176.

6. An interesting call for the reintegration of management theory may be found in Max S. Wortman, Jr., "Reintegrating and Reconceptualizing Management: A Challenge for the Future," *Review of Business and Economic Research* 18 (Spring 1983): 1–8.

7. See Henri Fayol, *General and Industrial Management,* trans. Constance Storrs (London: Isaac Pitman & Sons, 1949).

8. Frank B. Copely, *Frederick W. Taylor: Father of Scientific Management* (New York: Harper & Brothers, 1923), I: 3.

9. For expanded treatment, see Frederick W. Taylor, *The Principles of Scientific Management* (New York: Harper & Brothers, 1911).

10. George D. Babcock, *The Taylor System in Franklin Management,* 2nd ed. (New York: Engineering Magazine Company, 1927), p. 31.

11. Frederick W. Taylor, *Shop Management* (New York: Harper & Brothers, 1911), p. 22.

12. Frank B. Gilbreth and Lillian M. Gilbreth, *Applied Motion Study* (New York: Sturgis & Walton, 1917), p. 42.

13. See Frank B. Gilbreth, Jr., and Ernestine Gilbreth Carey, *Cheaper by the Dozen* (New York: Thomas Y. Crowell, 1948).

14. For detailed coverage of Gantt's contributions, see H. L. Gantt, *Work, Wages, and Profits,* 2nd ed. (New York: Engineering Magazine Company, 1913).

15. Thomas E. Vollmann, *Operations Management: A Systems/Model-Building Approach* (Reading, Mass.: Addison-Wesley, 1973), p. 5.

16. Edwin A. Locke, "The Ideas of Frederick W. Taylor: An Evaluation," *Academy of Management Review* 7 (January 1982): 22–23.

17. The Hawthorne studies are discussed in detail in F. J. Roethlisberger and William J. Dickson, *Management and the Worker* (Cambridge, Mass.: Harvard University Press, 1939).

18. See Henry C. Metcalf and L. Urwick, *Dynamic Administration: The Collected Papers of Mary Parker Follett* (New York: Harper & Brothers, 1942); and Mary Parker Follett, *Freedom and Coordination* (London: Management Publications Trust, 1949).

19. Joe Kelly, *Organizational Behaviour: An Existential-Systems Approach,* rev. ed. (Homewood, Ill.: Irwin, 1974), p. vii.

20. For a statistical interpretation of the Hawthorne studies, see Richard Herbert Franke and James D. Kaul, "The Hawthorne Experiments: First Statistical Interpretation," *American Sociological Review* 43 (October 1978): 623–643.

21. Russell L. Ackoff, "Science in the Systems Age: Beyond IE, OR, and MS," *Operations Research* 21 (May–June 1973): 664.

22. Charles J. Coleman and David D. Palmer, "Organizational Application of Systems Theory," *Business Horizons* 16 (December 1973): 77.

23. Chester I. Barnard, *The Functions of the Executive* (Cambridge, Mass.: Harvard University Press, 1938), p. 65.

24. Ibid., p. 82.

25. Ludwig von Bertalanffy, "The History and Status of General Systems Theory," *Academy of Management Journal* 15 (December 1972): 411.

26. Fremont E. Kast and James E. Rosenzweig, *Organization and Management: A Systems Approach,* 4th ed. (New York: McGraw-Hill, 1985), p. 108.

27. Fred Luthans, *Introduction to Management: A Contingency Approach* (New York: McGraw-Hill, 1976), p. 28. Also see Henry L. Tosi, Jr. and John W. Slocum, Jr., "Contingency Theory: Some Suggested Directions," *Journal of Management* 10 (Spring 1984), pp. 9–26.

28. Y. K. Shetty, "Contingency Management: Current Perspective for Managing Organizations," *Management International Review* 14, no. 6 (1974): 27.

29. Luthans, *Introduction to Management,* p. 30.

30. Joseph W. McGuire, "Management Theory: Retreat to the Academy," *Business Horizons* 25 (July–August 1982): 37.

31. For an interesting update, see Susan Benner, "Three Companies in Search of an Author," *Inc.* 6 (August 1984): 49–55.

32. Information about the sample in this study may be found in Thomas J. Peters and Robert H. Waterman, Jr., *In Search of Excellence* (New York: Harper & Row, 1982), pp. 19–26.

33. Ibid., pp. 16–17.

34. Ibid., p. 13.

35. Daniel T. Carroll, "A Disappointing Search for Excellence," *Harvard Business Review* 61 (November–December 1983): 88.

36. "Who's Excellent Now?" *Business Week* No. 2867 (November 5, 1984), pp. 76–78.

Chapter 3

The Changing Environment of Management

My interest is in the future because I am going to spend the rest of my life there.
    Charles F. Kettering

Chapter Objectives

When you finish studying this chapter, you should be able to

- Explain the managerial significance of transience.
- Identify and briefly highlight the thrust of Naisbitt's ten *megatrends*.
- Summarize the changing attitudes toward work.
- Discuss how the political-legal environment of management is changing.
- Explain why managers need to be particularly knowledgeable about the economic environment.
- Describe managers' problems with the innovation process and the new industrial revolution.

Opening Case 3.1

Innovation: 3M Company's Eleventh Commandment

At Minnesota Mining & Manufacturing (3M) Company, innovation has been a driving force since it began as a small sandpaper manufacturing operation in 1902. Widely known among consumers for its Scotch-brand tapes, the St. Paul, Minnesota, company today enjoys a reputation as a superbly managed organization. Employee and community relations at 3M have been called exemplary. Those familiar with 3M's record of accomplishments were not surprised when the firm was profiled in both *In Search of Excellence* and *The 100 Best Companies to Work for in America*, two recent best sellers. Among its more than 45,000 products are some exotic offerings including a suntan lotion that only washes off with soap and water, a surgical stapler, a chemical that makes grass grow slower, a hearing aid for the totally deaf, and an artificial hip. In spite of a leveling off of sales during the 1982 recession, 3M's profits have grown ten percent annually over the last decade. Forty percent of the firm's sales are made abroad and forty percent of 3M's 87,000 employees work outside the United States.

The basic strategy at 3M involves finding and filling cracks in a wide variety of markets rather than trying to dominate individual markets. Despite the familiarity of the Scotch brand, less than ten percent of the company's sales come from consumer goods. The balance comes from the sales of industrial and commercial products including coating and bonding products, x-ray film, photocopiers, and traffic lights. Historically, 3M has competed on the basis of quality and innovative function rather than on the basis of low prices.

An Organization of Entrepreneurs

3M likes to train its own executives, typically hiring engineers right out of midwestern or southern universities. Due to a desire to be self-sufficient, both upper management and new ideas come strictly from within the company. Turnover among executives is practically nonexistent. In fact, more than 4,000 employees have been with 3M for 25 years or more.

According to *Fortune,* "What keeps them satisfied in St. Paul is the knowledge that anyone who invents a new product, or promotes it when others lose faith, or figures out how to mass-produce it economically has a chance to manage that product as though it were his or her own business and to do so with a minimum of interference from above."[1] Eventually, when several new products are spun off from the original good idea, a separate division may be formed. In fact, 3M now has 40 divisions, each treated essentially as an autonomous profit center with production, marketing, and finance responsibilities.

Pushing Innovation

Top management sets the stage for innovation by requiring all divisions to earn 25 percent of their sales from products that did not exist five years earlier. Behind 3M's apparent love of new and different things is a practical motive. Although government guidelines keep the company from increasing prices on existing products, new products can be priced without interference. Half of the new products are developed in response to specific customer needs, and half come from basic research. A workable blend of innovation and marketing is important at 3M because the company is constantly in search of a market for a product or a product for a market.

Innovative ideas are nurtured at 3M in a number of ways. First and foremost, even the most far-fetched ideas are given a chance to prove themselves. "Thou shalt not kill a new product idea" is the often-voiced Eleventh Commandment at 3M. Researchers at 3M are routinely allowed to spend one day a week tinkering with their pet projects. In addition, the Carlton Award, named for a former 3M president, is given to top innovators as the company's version of the Nobel Prize.

Art Fry, inventor of the yellow "Post-It" note pads found in most offices today, was honored with a Carlton Award. As the story goes " ... Fry found it annoying when the bookmarks fell out of his hymnal at his church in North St. Paul, Minnesota. It would be better, he thought, if he could put in a piece of paper that would adhere to the pages yet be removable to mark other pages."[2] After nearly a year of experimenting with various combinations of semi-adhesives and paper and building interest among his colleagues, Fry had a product that he thought would sell. And indeed it has. The familiar yellow notes that peel off without a trace now generate over $40 million a year in sales for 3M.

Things Sometimes Go Wrong
All is not creative bliss at 3M. For example, 1975 was a disastrous year. After it was revealed that for several years 3M had made illegal campaign contributions, including one for $30,000 to President Nixon's reelection effort in 1972, the chairman and two other high-ranking company executives resigned. Making matters worse, 3M was caught unprepared for skyrocketing oil prices and the subsequent economic recession of the mid-1970s. Earnings dropped sharply because many of 3M's products are derived from petroleum. Additionally, not all of 3M's promising ideas make it to the marketplace. For example, 3M's innovative answer to Johnson & Johnson's highly successful Band-Aid had to be dropped because a cost-competitive manufacturing process could not be developed. Some critics also fault 3M for not taking more aggressive advantage of consumer markets. Meanwhile, however, 3M continues to be a leader in what it does best, innovation.

(Discussion questions linking this case with the material you are about to read can be found at the end of this chapter.)

Through its emphasis on innovation, 3M provides a good example of how one company handles the ramifications of change in modern society. In his best-selling book, *Future Shock,* Alvin Toffler maintains that we are experiencing an unusual form of change today. He applied the term **transience** to the accelerating rate of change that hurls ideas, places, relationships, and technologies at us at an ever faster pace. Using Toffler's language, those who are unprepared to face accelerating change will suffer future shock, a disoriented inability to cope.[3]

Figure 3.1 Managing in a Complex and Changing World

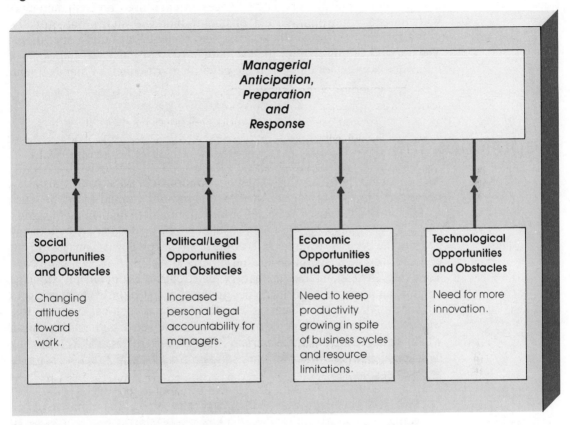

Managers, by the very nature of their work, often experience a great deal of transience. Hence they are prime candidates for future shock. How can managers prepare for an uncertain future? How can they avoid future shock?

The key is for managers to anticipate significant environmental trends and changes and prepare accordingly. Modern managers must keep an ear to the ground, so to speak, as important changes often are preceded by early warning signs. These early warning signs can be detected by alert managers who carefully collect, sort out, and interpret reliable and relevant information about what is going on in the outside world. Anticipation of change is foresighted and helps managers avoid future shock. Mere reaction to change, on the other hand, is hindsighted and thrives on wishful thinking and blind faith in the status quo.

Ignoring the impact of general environmental factors on management makes about as much sense as ignoring the effects of weather and road conditions on high-speed driving. As illustrated in Figure 3.1, the general environment of management includes social, political-legal, economic, and technological dimensions. Changes in each area present managers with unique opportunities and obstacles that will shape not only the organization's strategic direction but also the course of daily operations. The purpose of this chapter then is to identify some early warning signs of important sources of change in the general environment of management.

Megatrends: The General Shape of Things to Come

As a departure point for this chapter, let us consider what John Naisbitt, a respected futurist, foresees. The ten *megatrends* he and his colleagues have identified promise to reshape the environment of management significantly. Interestingly, Naisbitt believes that important trends work their way up from the bottom, whereas fads come from the top down. Thus he did not collect his evidence by interviewing experts in Washington, D.C. and New York City. Instead, he and his team of researchers conducted an extensive content analysis of 6000 local newspapers every month. According to Naisbitt: "After a dozen years of carefully monitoring local events in this way, I have slowly developed what to me is a clear sense of the directions in which we are restructuring America."[4] The arrows for each of the following megatrends indicate what we are moving *away from* and what we seem to be moving *toward*.

1. **Industrial society ⟶ Information society.** Naisbitt summarizes U.S. economic history in three words: farmer ⟶ laborer ⟶ clerk. Over 60 percent of today's employees in America's service-oriented economy have jobs involving the creation, processing, and distribution of information. The economic value of information needs to be more widely recognized, according to Naisbitt. Because of the computer revolution and robotics, a central labor-management issue during the next decade will be the loss of jobs due to automation. Generalists who have the ability to adapt will replace specialists who tend to become obsolete.
2. **Forced technology ⟶ High tech/High touch.** We are searching for a workable *balance* between impersonal technology and the need for meaningful human interaction. For example, contrary to early predictions, people with video-cassette recorders still go to the movies because they desire social contact. In the workplace, increased use of "high tech" robots has been accompanied by "high touch" quality control circles (small problem-solving groups who work to improve quality). Employees are striving also for a new balance between work and leisure.

3. **National economy ⟶ World economy.** There actually are two distinct economies in the United States. In the emerging "sunrise economy," opportunities are exploding in the telecommunications, biotechnology, electronics, alternative energy, and health-care fields. However, in the "sunset economy," opportunities are being lost to foreign competitors in smokestack industries such as automobiles and steel. Trying to average the impacts of these two economies is like comparing oranges and apples. The U.S. economy is no longer self-sufficient; it is part of a highly interdependent global economy. Naisbitt recommends three language skills for the future: English, Spanish, and computer.

4. **Short term ⟶ Long term.** Management's preoccupation with short-term profitability is giving way to preparations for long-term survival. Businesses are redefining their purposes more broadly. Xerox, for example, sees itself in the automated office business, not simply the photo-reproduction business. People are realizing that although pollution is expedient in the short term, it erodes the long-term quality of life.

5. **Centralization ⟶ Decentralization.** A fundamental distrust of centralized power in the United States has paved the way for proportionately more state and local power. A growing number of city dwellers are moving back to the country; small towns and rural areas grew nearly 16 percent faster than cities during the 1970s. Companies are building facilities away from big cities in response to employees' quality-of-life needs.

6. **Institutional help ⟶ Self-help.** A growing disenchantment with institutional help has prompted a return to the traditional value of self-reliance. People are discovering that disease prevention through wellness and exercise are cheaper than hospitalization and cure. There is an entrepreneurial explosion in the United States; 600,000 new businesses were formed in 1980 versus 93,000 in 1950.

7. **Representative democracy ⟶ Participative democracy.** People are increasingly demanding a *direct* say in the decisions that affect their lives, both in government and on the job. Worker participation schemes are growing in popularity. Naisbitt characterizes the new leader as a *facilitator,* not just an order giver.

8. **Hierarchies ⟶ Networking.** The predominantly vertical orientation of traditional bureaucracies is giving way to horizontal linkages based on convenience and need. "Structurally, the most important thing about a network is that each individual is at its center. . . ."[5] Minorities and women have learned the value of networks. The new networks are more egalitarian than the traditional "Old Boy" networks.

9. **North ⟶ South.** According to the 1980 census, more Americans lived in the South and West than in the North and East for the first time

in history. Regarding the claim that Sunbelt states are stealing away Frostbelt companies, Naisbitt has pointed out: "The decline of the North has more to do with the shift from an industrial to an information society than it has to do with any movement of North-based companies to the Sunbelt."[6] Florida, Texas, and California are largely responsible for what Naisbitt calls the Sunbelt mystique.

10. **Either/or ⟶ Multiple option.** Today we live in a "Baskin-Robbins" society where choices and opportunities abound. New options are opening up regarding how we work, live, and play. Gender barriers are breaking down as more women join the work force. As a sign of how much things have changed, only seven percent of American families fit the traditional "Leave It to Beaver" pattern (i.e., father as sole breadwinner, housewife/mother, and two children). With the world's fourth largest Spanish-speaking population, the United States is well on its way to becoming a bilingual country. More choices in life, work, and play mean challenging new responsibilities.

Our own intuitive feel for the course of things seems to validate these megatrends. Whether we like them or not is another matter. An unemployed steelworker in Buffalo, New York is likely to have a different opinion than an electronics engineer in California's Silicon Valley. Nonetheless, progressive managers need to detect early warning signs of change in the social, political-legal, economic, and technological environments of management.

The Social Environment

Some societal observers concentrate only on the cooperative aspects of society, and others are preoccupied with conflict and competition. Realizing that neither extreme adequately describes our complex, contemporary society, modern sociologists have formulated a compromise view, the synthesis perspective. This **synthesis perspective** views society as the product of a constant tug of war between the forces of stability and the forces of change. It is based on the following assumptions:

1. The processes of stability and change are properties of all societies.
2. Societies are organized but the process of organization produces conflict.
3. Societies are dynamic social *systems*.
4. Complementary interests, consensus on cultural values, and coercion hold societies together.

5. Social change may be gradual or abrupt, but all societies experience constant social change.[7]

A synthesis perspective considers both cooperation and competition. It is neither unreasonably optimistic nor unduly pessimistic. Forces of cooperation draw society together, whereas forces of conflict and competition pull it apart. The net result is a rough consensus that gives society its general direction. Operating from this synthesis perspective, we shall discuss three important dimensions of the social environment: demographic shifts, changing attitudes toward work, and egalitarianism.

Demographic Shifts Demographic studies of population size, density, location, and shifts are a valuable planning tool for managers. More specifically, accurate projections of *how* populations are likely to change enable foresighted managers to do a better job of staffing and marketing. For example, management needs to know if the right quantity and quality of job candidates will be available during a given time frame. Companies employing primarily entry-level workers will be profoundly affected by the projected shrinkage of the 18–24 age group during the 1990s.[8] It is no accident that McDonald's has already started hiring women whose children are in school or have left home. The company is grooming a new pool of job applicants (and customers) in anticipation of a reduction in its traditional labor/customer base.

Managers in small and large businesses as well as in government agencies keep their eyes on demographic projections to gauge who their next customers/clients are likely to be, and how they can best be reached. Foresight, not hindsight, is required if demographics are to aid marketing. According to the president of Princeton's Opinion Research Corporation: "The key is to look at your product mix in terms of where the population is going and make the necessary changes in advance of the demographic changes, so you're ready to capitalize on them."[9] Avon Products, for example, failed to anticipate how more women in the work force would impact their door-to-door sales program. "These days, when 'Avon ladies' call, fewer women are home to listen."[10] Two important demographic topics are slower labor-force growth and our aging population.

Slower Growth of the Labor Force As outlined in Table 3.1, the U.S. labor force is expected to undergo some significant changes during the next decade. Heading the list are two key changes: more women and slower overall growth. The U.S. Bureau of Labor Statistics has offered the following projection:

The labor force will continue to grow during the 1980s but at a slower rate than in recent years. By 1990 about 119 million persons will be in the labor force—an

Table 3.1 Demographics Tell Managers an Important Story

- Workers aged 25–44 will constitute more than half the work force by 1990.
- Women will represent more than 47 percent of the work force by 1995, compared with 32 [percent] in 1960.
- The percentage of women in the 25–34 age group who have attended college is already much higher than in the 35-plus group. These better-educated young women are likely to want careers in which they can command higher wages than their predecessors and to resist taking what has traditionally been considered "women's work."
- By 1995, 27 percent of U.S. households will consist of single individuals—30 million of them—constituting a market for goods and services far different than that offered by the standard family unit.
- The ranks of over-65 Americans will increase from 11 percent of the population now to 16 percent by 2020.
- Husband and wife now work in 40 percent of all families, compared with 12 percent in 1959, and the ratio continues to increase. Demographers expect that sometime in the 1990s, the figure will be more than 50 percent.
- Half of all women with children under 6 are in the labor force.

SOURCE: Harry Bacas, "America's Changing Face," *Nation's Business* 72 (July 1984): 18–25. Condensed by permission. Copyright © 1984, Chamber of Commerce of the United States.

18.5 percent increase over the 1978 level. Contributing to this growth will be the expansion of the working age population and the continued rise in the proportion of women who work. The labor force will grow more slowly between 1985 and 1990 than in the early 1980s. This slowdown will result from a drop in the number of young people entering the working age and less rapid growth of the participation rate of women.[11]

The Graying of America   As the postwar baby-boom generation (mainly those born between 1947 and 1957) matures, the average age of the U.S. population will climb. In 1970, the median age in the United States was under 28. It passed 30 in the early 1980s and will reach 35 by the year 2000.[12] Consequently, markets are shifting as the former purchasers of records and blue jeans begin setting up households requiring appliances and insurance policies. An aging population has caused some firms to take some surprising steps to keep up with the market. In 1984, Touchstone Films, a division of Walt Disney Productions, released the adult comedy *Splash*, complete with enough nudity to make Snow White blush.[13] The film was a hit largely because the Disney people had done their demographic homework.

**Changing
Attitudes
Toward Work**

The traditional American dream is based squarely on the work ethic. According to the traditional view, hard work at whatever jobs are available is the pathway to material wealth and hence happiness. Based on the assumption that America's potential for economic growth is unlimited, proponents of the traditional American dream believe that economic security and the self-esteem that goes with it are available to those who are willing to work hard enough. Ronald Reagan vigorously promoted this perspective to inspire citizens during the 1980 and 1984 presidential campaigns. Interestingly, however, sociologists tell us that an updated version of the American dream has evolved. Many people in our labor force today want more than just a job and a paycheck. Although they will work to achieve material wealth, it is not an end in itself. They want more.

Public opinion expert Daniel Yankelovich contends that the updated American dream has the following characteristics:

- Growing acceptance of the idea that there are realistic limits to economic growth.
- Decreasing relative emphasis on material possessions: material well-being does not necessarily equal personal happiness.
- Greater emphasis on leisure in the balance between work and leisure.
- Growing dissatisfaction with dull, monotonous, and unchallenging jobs.
- Greater emphasis on quality of life, physical and mental well-being, and personal growth and satisfaction.
- Emergence of an antiwaste morality.[14]

Is the Work Ethic Dead?   Pointing to increased absenteeism and turnover and decreased job satisfaction among younger workers in recent years, a number of social observers have proclaimed the death of the work ethic. For example, "Turnover among managers out of college less than five years has quintupled since 1960. Today the average corporation can count on losing 50% of its college graduates within five years. ..."[15] But closer analysis shows that the work ethic is not dead among younger workers. Rather, like the more encompassing American dream, it simply has been updated in accordance with emerging values.

One survey of over three thousand persons employed by a variety of companies nationwide identified differing attitudes toward work between younger (aged 17 to 26) and older (aged 40 to 65) workers.[16] Although the younger workers in the study did not value hard work and pride in craftsmanship as highly as did the older workers, the researcher concluded that the work ethic was still very much alive among the younger workers. However, the younger workers did not seem as willing as the older workers to become deeply involved in company and community affairs. And the younger workers were reportedly more committed to friendship ties than were the older workers.

Although younger workers are likely to be less loyal to a single organization, they have not turned their backs on work. For instance, after surveying over 23,000 *Psychology Today* readers, most of whom were young, researchers concluded:

> People seem to believe again in the value of hard work and in developing themselves at the workplace. On the other hand, they are not likely to be easy to satisfy or retain as employees. They are likely to demand a great deal, and, if they don't receive it, will look elsewhere.[17]

Those who embrace the new work ethic want jobs with challenge and meaning, in addition to good pay and generous employee benefits.

More Leisure The orientation toward more leisure is another important feature of the new work ethic. For many, leisure has replaced work as the primary focal point of life. This does not mean that new breed employees do not want to work; they simply derive more meaning from leisure-time activities. It is a matter of shifting proportion, not an all-or-nothing proposition. Today, the balance increasingly tips in favor of leisure, even if it means forgoing some luxury goods in the process.

Egalitarianism **Egalitarianism** is a social philosophy that advocates social, political, and economic equality. An egalitarian ideal is at the heart of the women's rights movement and the civil rights movement. Although women's rights and civil rights demonstrations tend to come and go, the motivation behind them remains strong because of longstanding inequalities such as those documented in Figure 3.2.

As a large and influential minority, women are demanding and getting a fairer share of workplace rewards and opportunities. But the financial gap is still sizable. In 1979, women working full time earned only 60 percent of what men earned, a mere 1 percent above the 1970 figure.[18] Even women with advanced business degrees have found themselves lagging behind their male counterparts. Researchers at Columbia University tracked the careers of 45 males and 45 females who earned their MBA degrees at Columbia between 1969 and 1972. Although the women started at approximately the same level of pay as the men ($14,000), ten years later the women were earning 81 percent of what their male counterparts were earning ($40,022 vs. $49,356).[19] It is still very difficult for women to move all the way up the corporate ladder. Experts have pointed out recently that:

> ... [women] make up about 50% of entry management and 25% of middle management. But although business began recruiting and promoting women in

Figure 3.2   Statistics of Inequality

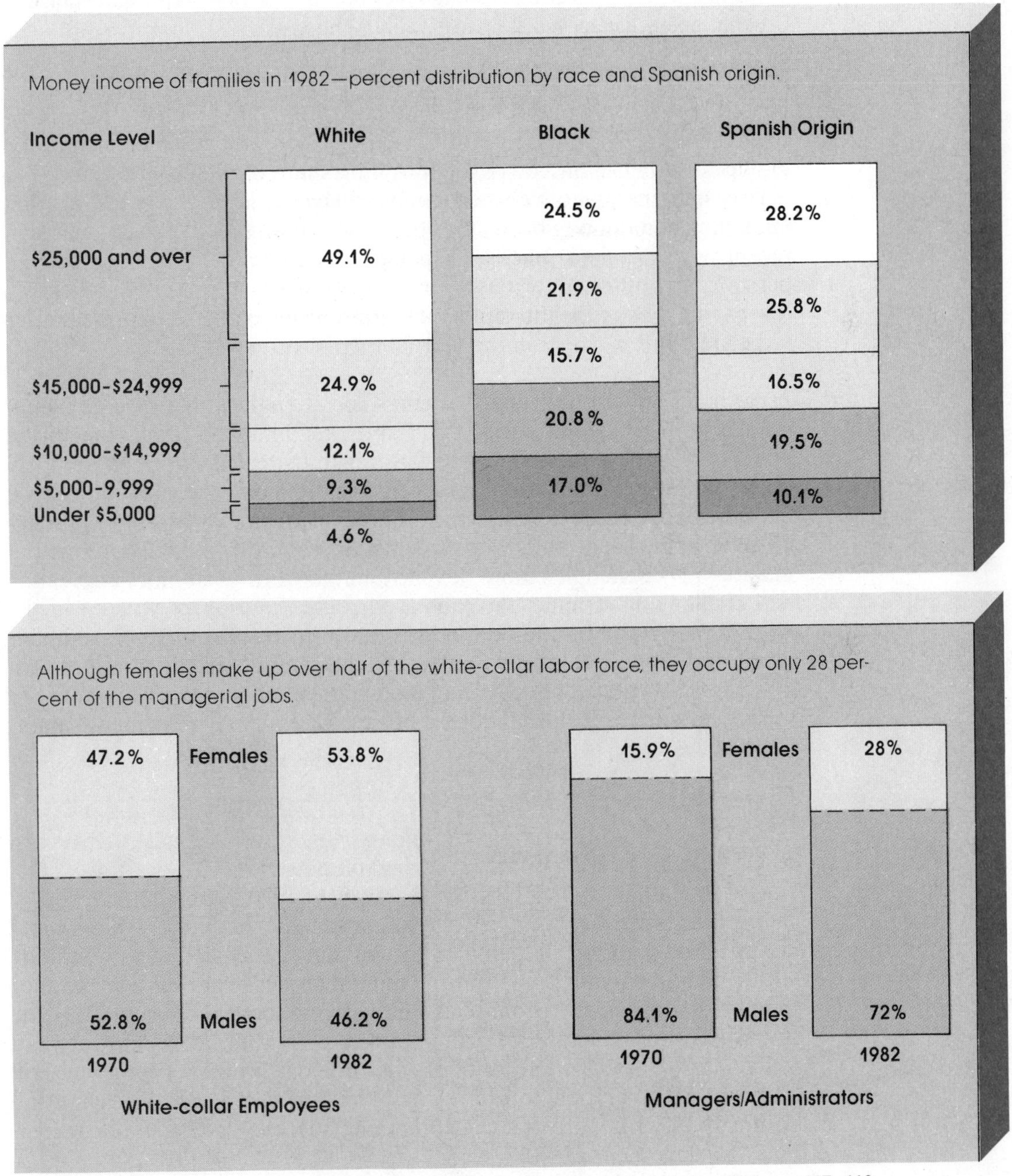

Money income of families in 1982—percent distribution by race and Spanish origin.

Income Level	White	Black	Spanish Origin
$25,000 and over	49.1%	24.5%	28.2%
		21.9%	25.8%
		15.7%	16.5%
$15,000–$24,999	24.9%	20.8%	19.5%
$10,000–$14,999	12.1%	17.0%	10.1%
$5,000–9,999	9.3%		
Under $5,000	4.6%		

Although females make up over half of the white-collar labor force, they occupy only 28 percent of the managerial jobs.

	White-collar Employees			Managers/Administrators
Females	47.2%	53.8%	15.9%	28%
Males	52.8%	46.2%	84.1%	72%
	1970	1982	1970	1982

SOURCE: Data from U.S. Bureau of Census, *Statistical Abstract of the United States:* 1984, pp. 417, 463.

substantial numbers in the early 1970s—far enough back to give them time for considerable career advancement—they account for only a tiny percentage of upper management.[20]

In fact, among the *Fortune* 500 companies, the 500 largest companies in the United States, only one is headed by a woman. "That woman, Katharine Graham of the Washington Post Co. (No. 342), readily admits she got the job because her family owns a controlling share of the corporation."[21]

Persistent inequality between whites and blacks is shown by the fact that unemployment among blacks has been more than twice that for whites in recent years. Women, blacks, Hispanics, American Indians, handicapped persons, and other minorities who are overrepresented in either low-level, low-paying jobs or the unemployment line can be expected to press harder to become full partners in the world of work.

Social Implications for Management

From our discussion of management's social environment, we can summarize how prevailing social conditions are likely to affect the future practice of management. Leisure has begun to replace work as the focal point of modern life. This trend promises to continue. Additionally, a maturing work force dominated by the new work ethic will prompt managers to experiment with work reforms. These reforms will be aimed at making work schedules more flexible and the work itself more interesting and challenging. Finally, the increased representation of women in the work force will put additional pressures on management to erase unfair gender differences in status and pay. Blacks and other ethnic minorities, motivated by persistent economic inequalities, will press management to follow the spirit as well as the letter of existing Equal Employment Opportunity laws.

The Political-Legal Environment

In its broadest terms, politics is the art (or science) of public influence and control. Laws are an outcome of the political process that differentiate good and bad conduct. An orderly political process is necessary because modern society is the product of an evolving consensus among a wide diversity of individuals and groups, often with conflicting interests and objectives. Although the list of special interest groups is long and still growing, not everyone can have his or her own way. This is when the political system tries to balance competing interests in a generally acceptable manner.

Ideally, elected officials pass laws that, when enforced, control individual and collective conduct for the general good. Unfortunately, as we all know, variables such as hollow campaign promises, illegal campaign financing, and voter apathy throw sand into a democracy's political gears. Managers, as both citizens and caretakers of socially, politically, and economically powerful organizations have a large stake in the political-legal environment. Two key pressure points for managers in this area are the politicization of management and their increased personal legal accountability.

The Politicization of Management

Prepared or not and willing or not, today's managers often find themselves embroiled in issues with clear political overtones. According to one government-business relations expert:

> Politicization of corporate strategy, policies, and operations is increasing. Traditional economic objectives of profit, growth, and survival are being supplemented by new socio-political demands in regard to employment, prices, labor benefits, regional development, the environment, domestic ownership, minority rights, conservation, and the like. The traditional roles of top management—supervising operations and strategic planning—are being superseded by political negotiation, a new role that promises in many industries to become a pervasive and over-riding concern.[22]

Government regulations head the list of reasons why managers are becoming more politically oriented. Since 1960, more than fifty important acts affecting business have been passed by the United States Congress. This wave of business-related legislation has created a huge government bureaucracy of commissions and regulatory agencies. Consequently, managers in the profit-making business sector are spending significantly more time and money reporting to government agencies. One large U.S. company, Champion Spark Plug, annually sends more than 500 reports to fifteen federal bureaus and agencies and 2500 reports to state and local agencies across the country.[23] Managers argue that all this takes time, money, and talent that could otherwise be channeled into productive organizational activities. A special task force at Dow Chemical discovered that in 1975 the firm spent $147 million to comply with domestic regulations. Furthermore, after dividing regulatory expenses into three categories—appropriate, questionable, and excessive—the Dow task force concluded that $50 million, or 34 percent of its 1975 regulatory expense, was excessive.[24] Prompted mainly by what they believe to be excessive and counterproductive government regulation, a growing number of managers are becoming active players in the political arena rather than passive bystanders.

General Political Responses   The three general political responses available to management can be plotted on a single continuum, as illustrated in

Figure 3.3 Management's Political Response Continuum

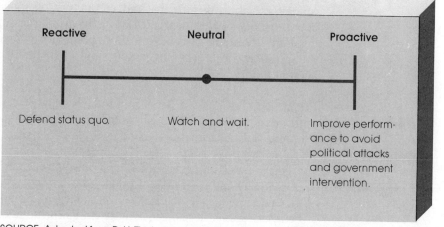

SOURCE: Adapted from D. H. Thain. "Improving Competence to Deal with Politics and Government: The Management Challenge of the 80's," *The Business Quarterly* 45 (Spring 1980): 31–45.

Figure 3.3. Managers who are politically inactive occupy the middle neutral zone and have a "wait and see" attitude. But few managers today can afford the luxury of a neutral political stance. Those on the extreme left of the continuum are politically active in defending the status quo. In contrast, politically active managers on the right end of the continuum try to identify and respond to public wishes before they are forced to do so by government action.

In recent years, business managers have noticeably swung from being reactive to being proactive, from merely reacting to taking positive action. An inspiring example in this area is 3M Company's "Pollution Prevention Pays" program, winner of a special commendation from the U.S. Environmental Protection Agency. Instead of lobbying against government pollution control efforts or waiting for a court order to clean up its operation, 3M Company set up a program "to get personnel to stop thinking about pollution removal and instead stress product reformulation, equipment changes, process modification, and materials recovery."[25] The first nineteen projects in the 3M pollution prevention program not only earned the contributors attractive bonuses, but they also saved the firm approximately $10 million. Moreover, these projects enabled 3M to cut its annual pollution by 73,000 tons of air pollutants, 500 million gallons of waste water, and 2,800 tons of sludge.

Specific Political Strategies   Whether acting reactively or proactively, there are four major political strategies that managers can employ.[26]

1. **Campaign financing.** Although federal law prohibits U.S. corporations from backing a specific candidate or party with the firm's name, funds, or free labor, a legal alternative is available. Corporations can form political action committees (PACs) to solicit volunteer contributions from employees biannually for the support of preferred candidates and parties. Importantly, PACs are registered with the Federal Election Commission and are required to keep detailed and accurate records of receipts and expenditures. Some criticize corporate PACs for having too great an influence over federal politics. But the evidence is to the contrary. In the 1981–82 election year, ". . . the average contribution by a corporate PAC was about $500, or 0.04 percent of the average cost of a successful Senate race. . . ."[27] Moreover, 45 percent of the 500 largest corporations in the United States did not even sponsor a PAC in 1982.

2. **Lobbying.** Historically, lobbying has been management's most popular and successful political strategy. Secret and informal meetings between hired representatives and key legislators in smoke-filled rooms have largely been replaced by a more forthright approach. Today, formal presentations by well-prepared company personnel are the preferred approach to lobbying for political support.

3. **Coalition building.** In a political environment of countless special interest groups, managers are finding that coalitions built around common rallying points are required for political impact. For example, an unlikely coalition of disenchanted blue-collar workers and conservative business leaders suppressed their differences long enough to help elect Ronald Reagan in 1980 and re-elect him in 1984.

4. **Indirect lobbying.** Having learned a lesson from unions, business managers now appreciate the value of grassroots lobbying. Members of legislative bodies tend to be more responsive to the desires of their constituents than to those of individuals who vote in other districts. Likewise, employee and consumer letter-writing campaigns have proved effective. **Advocacy advertising,** the controversial practice of promoting a point of view along with a product or service, is another form of indirect lobbying that has grown in popularity in recent years.

Increased Personal Legal Accountability

How corrupt are business managers? Critics of business contend that the wave of post-Watergate cases involving price fixing, fraud, bribery, payoffs, and illegal campaign contributions confirm their worst suspicions. Pro-business forces, on the other hand, claim that the highly publicized cases of managerial misconduct are the exception rather than the rule. Unfortunately, precise statistics gauging the extent of illegal acts among managers are not available, but a recent study by *Fortune* magazine has shed some light on the issue. In a review of 1043 major American corporations, 117, or 11 percent, were found to have committed at least one major offense during the decade of the 1970s.[28] Whether one sees 11 percent as high or low is a matter of personal values and interpretation. The key points are that some managers do resort to illegal activities and that the public is demanding greater accountability.

Recent changes in the political and legal climate have made it increasingly difficult for managers to take refuge in the bureaucratic shadows when a law has been broken. Managers who make illegal decisions stand a good chance of being held personally accountable in a court of law. For example, consider the following legal decisions. In 1975, the U.S. Supreme Court upheld the conviction of the president of a multibillion dollar grocery chain who was fined personally when his subordinates failed to comply with a law requiring the extermination of rats in a company warehouse.[29] A 1977 U.S. district court decision went a step further. In that case, two firms manufacturing paper bags were fined a record $2 million for price fixing. Two vice presidents who were responsible for the price fixing were fined a total of $70,000 and sentenced to four-month jail terms.[30] In 1984, after an employee at a Chicago-area company died of cyanide poisoning, Illinois State prosecutors indicted the firm's five top managers for murder (three were subsequently convicted). According to this unprecedented indictment, the managers "... were fully aware of the life-threatening dangers posed by the operation but failed to train or equip the workers to ensure their protection."[31] These and other cases indicate that the legal system is showing a clear pattern of holding managers *personally* responsible for the illegal actions of their companies.

Political-Legal Implications for Management

Managers will continue to be forced into becoming more politically astute, whether they like it or not. There appears to be growing support for the idea that managers can and should try to shape the political climate in which they operate. And the vigilant media and a wary public can be expected to keep a close eye on the form and substance of managerial politics to ensure that the public interest is served. Managers who abuse their political power and/or break the law will increasingly be held personally accountable.

The Economic Environment

These are turbulent times for national and world economics. Supposedly tried and true fiscal and monetary policies have been revamped as recessions increase in frequency and record-high interest rates prove difficult to bring down. Conservatives, who believe that the competitive marketplace should be the final arbiter of who gets what, recommend supply-side economics and less government interference. Liberals, who believe the marketplace has been responsible for the growing gap between the rich and the poor, suggest various government interventions ranging from egalitarian legislation to wage and price controls. As stated in Chapter 1, there is a close relationship between economics and management. **Economics** is the study of how scarce resources are used to create wealth and how that wealth is distributed. Managers, as trustees of our resource-consuming productive organizations, perform an essentially economic function.

Four aspects of the economic environment of management that warrant special consideration are business cycles, the global economy, productivity improvement, and resource management.

Coping with Business Cycles

A **business cycle** is the up and down movement of an economy's ability to generate wealth; it has a predictable sequence but variable timing. Historical economic data from industrialized economies show a clear pattern of alternating expansions and recessions. In between have been peaks and troughs of varying magnitude and duration. According to economist Paul Samuelson, the four phases are like the changing seasons: "Each phase passes into the next. Each is characterized by different economic conditions: for example, during expansion we find that employment, production, prices, money, wages, interest rates, and profits are usually rising, with the reverse true in recession."[32]

Cycle-sensitive Decisions   Important decisions are hinged to the ebb and flow of the business cycle (see Figure 3.4). These decisions include ordering inventory, borrowing funds, increasing staff, and spending capital for land, equipment, and energy. Managers attempt to make the right decisions at the right time by responding appropriately to valid economic forecasts. Unfortunately, this is easier said than done.

Benefiting from Economic Forecasts   *Timing* is everything when it comes to making good cycle-sensitive decisions. Just as a baseball batter needs to start his or her swing *before* the ball reaches home plate, managers need to cut back on ordering, borrowing, hiring, and spending prior to the onset of a recession. Failure to do so, in the face of decreasing sales, leads to bloated inventories and idle productive resources, both of which are costly situations (see Table 3.2). On the other hand, managers cannot afford to get caught short during a period of rapid expansion. Prices and wages rise sharply when everyone is purchasing inventories and hiring at the same time. The trick is to stay ahead of the pack. This is where accurate economic forecasts are a necessity.

In view of the fact that economists generally failed to predict the timing and severity of the 1981–82 recession, the worst since the Great Depression, and wrongly predicted rising inflation in 1984, economic forecasting has come under fire lately. As one critic put it: "... economists' predictions

Figure 3.4   Business Cycles Affect Managerial Decisions

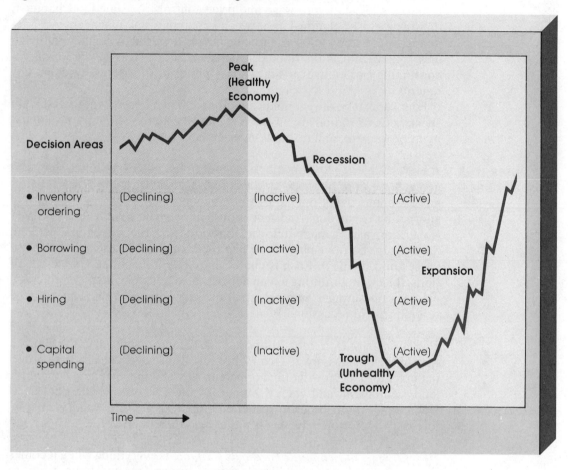

have been so far off lately they make weather forecasters look psychic."[33]
How, then, can managers get some value from the hundreds of economic
forecasts they receive each year?

A pair of respected forecasting experts recommends that managers take
a *consensus approach.*[34] They urge managers to survey a wide variety of
economic forecasts, taking the forecasters' track records into consideration, and look for a consensus or average opinion. Cycle-sensitive decisions are then made accordingly. Slavish adherence to a single forecast is
not recommended. Another sure formula for failure is to naively assume
that the future will simply be a replication of the past. In spite of their
imperfection, professional economic forecasts are better than no forecasts
at all. (Specific forecasting techniques are discussed in Chapter 5 under the
heading of strategic management.)

Table 3.2 The Effects of Misleading Economic Forecasts

Bad forecasts or bad decisions?

Robert Lohr, a Bethlehem Steel executive, blames his firm's $768 million operating losses in 1982–83 partly on 'the investments we made because we believed in the boom of 1981 that an economist promised us.' AMAX, a major metal mining concern (1983 sales: $2.4 billion), dug itself an $879 million hole over the past two years by heeding forecasts of continuing inflation. Those projections led the company to assume that the prices of its copper, molybdenum and other metals would keep rising. Instead, their market value has fallen 50%.

SOURCE: John Greenwald, "The Forecasters Flunk," *Time* (August 27, 1984): 42.

The Challenge of a Global Economy

According to Naisbitt's third megatrend, we are moving from a national economy to a world economy. Evidence is all around us in the form of Japanese cars, French perfumes, German wines, and Italian shoes. "Out of every dollar that Americans now spend, 20¢ goes for imports."[35] Deeper analysis, however, reveals a profound change. According to Harvard economist Robert B. Reich: "In short, the globe is fast becoming a single marketplace. Goods are being made wherever they can be made the cheapest, regardless of national boundaries."[36] The resulting economic interdependency is exceedingly complex (see Table 3.3). Although proponents of economic globalization promise a wider variety of less expensive goods, many Americans are troubled by growing trade imbalances (more imports than exports) and the loss of world leadership in both consumer and industrial markets. For example:

> By 1981 America was importing almost 26 percent of its cars, 25 percent of its steel, 60 percent of its televisions, radios, tape recorders, and phonographs, 43 percent of its calculators, 27 percent of its metal-forming machine tools, 35 percent of its textile machinery, and 53 percent of its numerically controlled machine tools. Twenty years before, imports had accounted for less than 10 percent of the U.S. market for each of these products.[37]

Now that economic globalization is well under way, the key question is: Where do we go from here?

Do we run and hide or stand and compete? Fearing further loss of market share and jobs, nonexporting/nonimporting businesses and organized labor in the United States are calling for trade barriers. Import quotas, protective tariffs, and other trade restrictions are one way of dealing with increased foreign competition. Unfortunately, experience shows that this sort of protectionism can backfire if trade wars break out. One researcher has estimated how much consumers are penalized by protectionism. "A dizzying array of tariffs, quotas, voluntary export restraints, and other nontariff barriers on everything from steel, textiles,

Table 3.3 The Impact of a Global Economy

The United States and Mexico share much more than a 1,500 mile border....

"It is crucial to the U.S. that Mexico succeed [in solving its current economic crisis]. U.S. banks hold $26 billion of the country's debt, and some 2,900 U.S. companies have direct investments in Mexico. In 1981, the year before the crisis, U.S. business sold Mexico more than $17 billion in goods."

SOURCE: "Will Mexico Make It?" *Business Week* No. 2862 (October 1, 1984): 74.

and shoes to motorbikes and machine tools already cost consumers over $50 billion a year."[38]

As an alternative to protectionism, the same researcher recommends that the United States stand its ground and compete. He reasons that only by facing the rigors of stiff foreign competition will U.S. companies and employees generate the hard work and innovation needed to compete successfully in a global economy. Inevitably, the focus shifts once again to the need for greater productivity.

An Agenda for Improving Productivity

We mentioned in Chapter 1 that productivity improvement is management's central challenge. It is the responsibility of managers to improve the ratio of outputs to inputs. Although average annual productivity growth in the United States started to rebound in late 1982, it has trailed other industrialized nations in recent decades. Virtually every major sector of the economy—government, management, unions, and employees in general—has been blamed for low productivity growth in the United States. (See Table 3.4 for a list of factors that inhibit productivity growth.) Some of the productivity hurdles in Table 3.4 are being addressed, but many others persist. Consequently, calls continue to go out for a national agenda for productivity improvement.

In late 1983, productivity began to get the national attention it deserves when the White House Conference on Productivity convened. More than 750 experts on productivity from business, universities, government, and labor attended. They discussed the results of four preparatory conferences that analyzed four dimensions of productivity: capital investment, human resources, government, and private-sector initiatives. Recommendations were made for tax reform and improved capital formation, better employee training and retraining and greater labor-management cooperation, and regulatory reform. Significantly, the fourth topic, private-sector initiatives, prompted the most vigorous discussion. It also generated the most excitement. According to one participant, three themes stood out as particularly significant.

First, participants fully endorsed the assumption of conference planners that the battle for U.S. productivity growth will be won or lost in the private sector.

Table 3.4   Potential Barriers to Productivity Growth in the United States

1. The comparatively low savings rate, which decreases capital spending;
2. The violent economic swings from recession to inflation-induced prosperity which handicap long-range planning and weaken financial structures;
3. The shift from a manufacturing-oriented economy to a service economy, in which it may be argued that productivity gains are more difficult to achieve, or at least to measure;
4. The mandatory capital spending for environmental protection, which has no accompanying measurable growth in goods and services;
5. The OPEC oil price hikes—tariff-like actions which idle much of our energy-intensive productive capital;
6. The antagonistic relationship between labor and management and government, which results in large business expenditures unlikely to improve productivity;
7. Our litigious society, with its tremendous cost in time and money, which is not only not productive, but is counterproductive;
8. New government regulatory laws in a number of areas such as consumer protection and safety, which increase costs without increasing products;
9. A tax system which not only promotes spending rather than saving, but also—at the same time—curbs investment, innovation, and entrepreneurship;
10. A social security system which deters saving for one's old age, a historic source of saving for capital investment;
11. Huge federal deficits caused by runaway government spending preempts productive private-sector capital and uses it for "Robin Hood"-like transfer payments;
12. The short-term outlook of business executives encouraged by compensation based on current results, which promotes operating business on the near-term, "forget the future" basis;
13. Reduced spending for product research and development which has been attributed to a number of different factors, from lack of trained scientists to administration of patent laws;
14. The declining ability of the computer to improve productivity due to the decrease in hardware costs and the increase in software costs, software being much less amenable to productivity improvement;
15. The decline in workers' desire to produce a full day's work for a full day's pay, sometimes, in part, attributed to union-dictated work practices, and other times, to a general decline in the work ethic;
16. Inflation, a predominant force during recent years that eroded savings, hampered long-term planning, and produced discounted cash flows, all of which prohibit long-term investments;
17. The training given future executives by American schools of business which emphasizes graduating MBA consultants who know the financial and theoretical sides of business, but not how to be "hands-on" managers; nor have the schools produced the engineers and scientists necessary for improved business performance;
18. The alleged inefficiency of governmental operations, which take a larger share of resources, while returning a less efficient service;
19. The decline in rigor of education at all levels resulting in lower literacy, employability, and productivity;
20. The large increase in numbers of young unskilled and untrained individuals in the work force, resulting in a lower productivity potential for a skilled work force.

SOURCE: L. William Seidman, "The White House Conference on Productivity," *National Productivity Review* 2 (Autumn 1983): 420–421. Reprinted by permission.

Second, there was overwhelming consensus that management—especially line management—determines productivity. .... Very little real progress can be made toward solving productivity or quality problems until business abandons "quick fix" solutions. Management must be willing to make changes in the methods, systems, attitudes, functions, and style of present managerial behavior.

The third dominant theme was the need to pay more attention to the human side of the enterprise. Participants endorsed the need to encourage "real" employee involvement and stated the importance of a "willingness to change traditional attitudes towards hierarchy, decision making, and sharing of information and rewards." Worker involvement in decision making was widely viewed as the primary means of building commitment and tapping the full potential of every employee. Private- and public-sector managers were instructed to "move towards a less authoritarian and more interactive management style at every organizational level."[39]

The preceding points present a clear and inspiring agenda for managers interested in doing their part to improve productivity. Later chapters discuss many productivity-enhancing ideas that can be implemented to satisfy this agenda. In the long run, managers who innovatively attack productivity problems head-on will accomplish much more than those who spend time trying to pin the blame on others such as government, labor, and foreign competitors.

Managing Limited Resources   Given that material and energy resources are vital factors of production, managers can boost productivity by getting more mileage out of those resources. Thanks to a 1500 percent price increase for crude oil during the 1970s, managers and people in general today tend to be more energy conscious (see Table 3.5). Rapid population growth makes it imperative that we stretch not only our energy resources, but all material resources, through intelligent use. This section focuses on strategic minerals, a 1970s-type energy crisis possibly in the making, and a strategy for managing resources more efficiently.

Strategic Minerals: A Potential Resource Problem   Looking ahead to the late 1980s, the end of the age of cheap oil promises to be the first shock wave in what could become a landslide of resource limitations. Specifically, our current heavy reliance on imported strategic minerals could produce a minerals crisis in the late 1980s and early 1990s. The problem narrows down to this:

... The U.S. appears disturbingly dependent on five minerals that together are the metallurgical Achilles' heel of our civilization. In 1979 we relied on imports for all the titanium used in airframes and missiles; for 98% of our manganese,

Table 3.5 A Straightforward Appraisal of the Energy Situation

A word of caution from Donald Hodel, former U.S. Energy Secretary....

Though the present world oversupply of oil could mean still further price reductions ..., Hodel says, "supplies are subject to interruption at a moment's notice at the hands of any number of persons or events."

The United States is relatively better off than many other industrial nations because of its domestic oil supplies, strategic petroleum reserve and alternative sources of energy, Hodel says, but any significant reduction in world supplies would force up prices to all consuming nations....

[Hodel adds] "... I would not be willing to gamble the long-term future of my company on a reliable, low-cost supply of oil."

SOURCE: Henry Eason, "Energy Supplies: Danger Ahead," *Nation's Business* 72 (April 1984): 70.

essential to steelmaking; 90% of our cobalt, used in cutting tools as well as jet engines; 89% of the metals in the platinum group (emission-control devices for autos and oil refining); and 90% of our chromium, essential for making stainless steel.[40]

Following the pattern of imported oil, a good share of these strategic minerals come from politically unstable countries. Largely inadequate domestic stockpiles, possible cartelization, and Russian adventurism in supplying countries foretell a rough road ahead for strategic minerals. Constructive action is needed immediately if management is to cope successfully with potential energy and mineral resource limitations.

A Strategy for Managing Resources More Efficiently   Rather than getting caught up in the self-defeating argument of exactly which nonrenewable resources (such as oil, coal, natural gas, uranium, and strategic minerals) will run out and precisely when, it is far more productive to concentrate on how to make the most of what remains. Experts on the subject have identified two strategies: (1) conservation and deprivation and (2) conservation and innovation.[41] The latter route, *conservation and innovation,* is desirable if the economy is to regain its productive vitality and to grow. Conservation deserves to be the centerpiece of a resource strategy, as pointed out in a highly regarded Harvard Business School report:

> Conservation may well be the cheapest, safest, most productive energy alternative readily available in large amounts. And conservation is a quality energy source. It does not threaten to undermine the international monetary system, nor does it emit carbon dioxide into the atmosphere, nor does it generate problems comparable to nuclear waste. And contrary to the conventional wisdom, conservation can stimulate innovation, employment, and economic growth.[42]

Figure 3.5 The Three-step Innovation Process

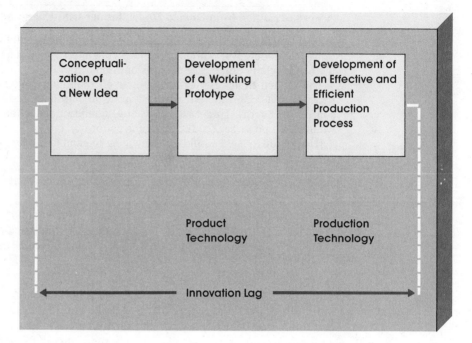

The U.S. Energy Department has estimated that American industry could be just as productive with 50 percent less energy. In fact, the Japanese steel industry produces a ton of steel with half as much energy as American steel producers, largely because of more efficient technology.[43]

For the innovation portion of the conservation and innovation strategy, the following steps are necessary:

- **Increased capitalization for exploration and research and development.** Massive amounts of capital will have to be mobilized to exploit remote sources (such as offshore drilling) and marginally productive resources (such as oil shale) in an environmentally responsible manner. Basic research to develop new technologies for enhanced resource recovery, more efficient applications, and waste reduction will also require a huge capital investment.
- **Increased emphasis on recycling.** It takes less than 10 percent as much energy to recycle aluminum as it does to produce new aluminum from bauxite. Solid waste deserves to be viewed as a valuable resource, not as trash to be discarded.[44] Remanufacturing, the process of restoring worn-out products to working condition, saves energy and materials.[45]
- **Increased use of alternative sources of energy and materials.** Renewable

energy sources, including solar, geothermal, wind, hydroelectric, ocean thermal energy conversion, and hydrogen energy, can supplement fossil fuels and nuclear energy.[46] Laser beams channeled through glass strands are already replacing cumbersome and costly metal telecommunications cables. New microcrystalline iron alloys and space-age plastics are replacing more scarce and costly metals.

Economic Implications for Management

Stubborn economic realities such as business cycles, high interest rates, an increasingly global economy, and periodic resource shortages must prompt innovative responses from managers. Managers can use the growing number of economic forecasting software packages on their personal computers to fine tune forecasts to their specific industry or organization. Progressive managers will view increasing foreign competition positively and take it as a challenge to design, produce, and market products and services more innovatively. Some productivity improvements have already been achieved by replacing the traditional adversary relationship between labor and management with more cooperative and participative programs. Energy audits and sophisticated energy management programs can help management bridge the gap between the present age of nonrenewable energy and the future age of renewable energy.

The Technological Environment

Technology is a term that ignites vigorous debates in many circles these days. Some believe that technology is mainly responsible for environmental and cultural destruction. Others view technology as the keystone of economic and social progress. No doubt, reality is somewhere between these two extremes. For our purposes, **technology** is defined as all the tools and ideas available for extending the natural physical and mental reach of humankind. A central theme in technology is the practical application of new ideas, a theme that is clarified by the following distinction between science and technology: "Science is the quest for more or less abstract knowledge, whereas technology is the application of organized knowledge to help solve problems in our society."[47] Two dimensions of technology with important implications for managers are the innovation process and the new industrial revolution.

The Innovation Process

Technology comes into being through the **innovation process,** defined as the systematic development and practical application of a new idea. A great deal of time-consuming work is necessary to develop a new idea into a marketable product or service. And many otherwise good ideas do not become technologically feasible, let alone marketable and profitable. A better understanding of the innovation process can help raise management's chances of turning new ideas into profitable goods and services.

A Three-step Process The innovation process has three steps (see Figure 3.5 on page 106). First is the conceptualization step, when a new idea occurs to someone. Development of a working prototype is the second step, called **product technology.** This involves actually creating a product that will work as intended. The third and final step is developing a production process to create a profitable quantity-quality-price relationship. This third step is labeled **production technology.** Successful innovation depends on the right combination of new ideas, product technology, and production technology. A missing or deficient step can ruin the innovation process.

Innovation Lag The time it takes for a new idea to be translated into satisfied demand is called **innovation lag.** The longer the innovation lag, the longer society must wait to benefit from a new idea. Over the years, the trend has been toward shorter innovation lags, but the process can still be painfully slow.

One expert has found that the innovation lags for ten major twentieth-century innovations averaged 19 years. For example, the heart pacemaker was conceived in 1928 but not put into general use until 1960—a 32-year innovation lag. The innovation lags for hybrid corn and the video tape recorder were 25 years and 6 years, respectively.[48] Today, many promising products like interferon, a potential cancer-blocking agent, are locked up in innovation lags.

Reducing the innovation lag deserves to be a high-priority goal for modern managers. A step in the right direction is to create an organizational climate in which bright ideas are given an opportunity to blossom into marketable products. Too often management unconsciously sets up needless barriers to creativity. An exciting example of what can be done to encourage creativity is Texas Instruments' IDEA program. Each year the firm hands out $1 million worth of $25,000 grants to employees with promising ideas for a new product or process. This program allows the creative employee to concentrate solely on his or her special project. Many of the IDEA-sponsored projects have paid off handsomely for Texas Instruments. "The $19.95 digital watch that tore apart the market in 1976 got its start as an IDEA program in the Semiconductor Group."[49] It is possible to shorten the innovation lag considerably if this type of positive approach is adopted organizationwide.

The New Industrial Revolution

Announcements in the popular media of technological breakthroughs that will supposedly revolutionize our lives are common today. Consequently, many people have difficulty believing them, or perhaps are even skeptical that they really mean anything. We hear of drugs that delay aging, computers that can think, cars that get 100 miles to the gallon, and superspecies that are genetically engineered, and then silence. But those who are aware of innovation lag in technological development know that product and production technologies are being developed during the period of silence following the announced breakthrough. The period of silence has ended for microelectronic technology, which promises to launch what some have called the new industrial revolution. What was once science fiction is already becoming reality.

Microcomputers and Robots Because of the development of microprocessors, quarter-inch square silicon chips that have the electronic switching capabilities of 100,000 or more old-fashioned vacuum tubes, the age of "smart" machines has arrived. Among the many applications are typewriters, microwave ovens, automobiles, and industrial machines containing microprocessors that can remember and selectively carry out programmed instructions. Two new applications, microcomputers (also known as personal computers or desk-top computers) and industrial robots (see Figure 3.6), are significantly reshaping the workplace. Automated offices and factories are rapidly becoming reality now that dramatically greater computing power is available in a much more compact form and at a significantly lower cost.[50]

Automated Offices and Factories With microcomputers at their fingertips, managers can expedite inventory control, correspondence, accounting transactions, and budget reviews, along with dozens of other applications, at the touch of a few buttons. Managers in automated offices can compose, edit, send, and file letters and memos in minutes at their own computerized work stations without having to rely on costly clerical support. The marriage of microcomputers and modern telecommunications technology also extends managers' informational domain.

In regard to the so-called factory of the future in the United States, annual investment in CAD/CAM (computer-aided design/computer-aided manufacturing) systems is expected to climb sharply during the 1980s. The U.S. industrial robot population is projected to be about 32,000 by the year 1990.[51] **Robots** can be generally defined as reprogrammable machines capable of performing a variety of tasks requiring programmed manipulations of materials and tools. They boost factory productivity by working faster and more reliably than humans do. Chrysler replaced 200 welders with 50 robots in its K-car body assembly line, and output increased nearly 20 percent.[52] Moreover, much to management's pleasure, robots perform to varied and exacting specifications 24 hours a day without complaining, insisting on lunch and coffee breaks, joining a union, or being absent on Fridays and Mondays. To date, robots have been used most extensively for handling hazardous materials and routine assembly-line tasks, jobs that

Figure 3.6 Industrial Robots Look Different from the Science Fiction Versions

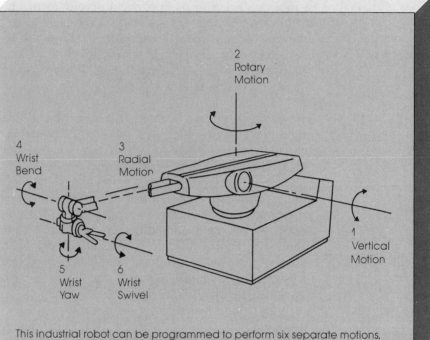

SOURCE: Dan T. Moore, Jr., "Will Robots Save Democracy?" *The Futurist* 15 (August 1981): 17. Reprinted by permission of the publisher, World Future Society, 4916 St. Elmo Avenue, Washington, D.C. 20014.

This industrial robot can be programmed to perform six separate motions, in any sequences its operator desires. Its microprocessor "brain" remembers whatever sequence is in its program, allowing it to learn a task. The robot can be taught to do different jobs around a factory simply by changing its program.

SOURCE: © Lucasfilm Ltd. (LFL) 1980. All rights reserved. *Courtesy of Lucasfilm Ltd.*

"Unfortunately, the unions won't allow us full automation yet.
SOURCE: © Punch/Rothco.

humans do not particularly like anyway. Robots will be perceived as a greater threat to employment when they begin replacing jobs that are more desirable. In the factory of the future, CAD/CAM and robots will increase productivity by cutting manufacturing lead times, reducing human error, simplifying the retooling process, and reducing costly inventories.

Facing the Problem of Technological Displacement   Automation carries with it the dilemma of what to do about those who lose their jobs to machines, a problem called **technological displacement.** Noting that experts believe that 45 percent of all jobs could be affected by office and factory automation before the year 2000, *Business Week* has offered the following perspective of technological displacement in the new industrial revolution:

> The rapidly developing drive toward the workerless factory—and the auto-
> mated but still populated office—will affect American jobs and jobholders on a
> scale unprecedented in modern times. Scholars of automation do not expect this
> rapid substitution of machinery for human labor to increase unemployment,
> assuming healthy economic growth. But they do expect a radical restructuring

of work, including a devaluation of current work skills and the creation of new ones at an ever-increasing rate. This will result in a fundamental change in most workplaces and an often painful adjustment for the workers involved. These changes will require employers to retrain huge numbers of workers. Ultimately, the nation's education system will have to prepare future workers for functioning in an electronic society.[53]

Not surprisingly, automation and job security have become central collective bargaining issues during the 1980s.

The issue of technological displacement requires both objective analysis and compassion for those who suddenly find themselves in the labor market with skills nobody wants to buy. It is estimated that each year for the foreseeable future, between one and two million employees in the United States will be permanently displaced from their jobs because of foreign competition or new technology. Some say the booming "high tech" (high technology) industries such as electronics will more than make up for the lost jobs. Closer analysis, however, suggests that the high-tech solution has been greatly overstated. For example, "While ... robots are expected to create 3,000 to 5,000 jobs, they will replace up to 50,000 auto workers."[54] Unless comprehensive retraining programs are undertaken by government and business, many former smokestack industry employees will have to settle for comparatively low-paying jobs in the fast-growing service sector.

In response to the Reagan administration's call for private-sector initiatives, American companies are dealing with the problem of technological displacement through creative retraining programs. Retraining can take one of two different directions: (1) retrain displaced employees for other jobs within the organization, or (2) retrain laid-off employees for jobs elsewhere. The first option is popular in sunrise industries where net employment is growing. For example, Digital Equipment Corporation, a computer maker, has retrained hundreds of technologically displaced repair technicians and administrative personnel for sales jobs.[55]

Companies in industries with declining employment, such as autos and steel, have had to pursue the second option. Some interesting variations have emerged. For example, Bethlehem Steel opened "career continuation centers" where its laid-off employees could get everything from job-hunting tips to psychological and family counseling for the trauma of unemployment.[56]

**Technological
Implications
for
Management**

In an age of complex and difficult challenges, pressure on managers to immediately provide the innovative goods and services society demands will remain high. Managers who view employee creativity as a vital resource to be nurtured will have a competitive edge. But regardless of how prepared or unprepared managers are, the new industrial revolution, with its sweeping automation of offices and factories, is fast approaching. Relatively high energy and labor costs and microprocessor technology assure that it will arrive soon. New approaches to hiring, training, and retraining employees will have to be developed as labor-intensive jobs are taken over by "smart" machines.

Summary

Since the world of most managers is characterized by transience, or accelerating change, they are potential victims of future shock. They can avoid it by preparing for, rather than passively responding to, changes in the social, political-legal, economic, and technological environment. Naisbitt's ten megatrends are helpful early warning signs of impending changes.

According to the synthesis perspective, society is best described as the result of a constant tug of war between the forces of stability and change. Important aspects of the social environment of management are demographic shifts, changing attitudes toward work, and egalitarianism. The new breed of worker in a growing but aging labor force puts more emphasis on leisure, is more likely to move when dissatisfied, and wants more meaning in his or her work. Contrary to the opinion of some social observers, the work ethic is not dead. The persistence of opportunity and income inequalities among women and other minorities is a strong stimulus for change.

Because of government regulations and sociopolitical demands from a growing list of special interest groups, managers are becoming increasingly politicized. More and more believe that if they are going to be affected by political forces, they should be more active politically. Managers can respond politically in three ways: they can be reactive, neutral, or proactive. Four political strategies that managers have found useful for pursuing active or reactive political goals are campaign financing, lobbying, coalition building, and indirect lobbying. Recent court cases have demonstrated a pattern of holding managers personally accountable for the misdeeds of their organizations.

Managers can make timely decisions about inventory, borrowing, hiring, and capital spending during somewhat unpredictable business cycles by taking a consensus approach to economic forecasts. Business is urged to compete actively and creatively in the emerging global economy instead of passively calling for trade restrictions. Although there are many potential barriers to productivity growth, experts are pinning their hopes for improvement on private-sector initiatives. More employee involvement, greater sharing of information and rewards, and less authoritarian management are key items on management's agenda for productivity improvement. Because more efficient resource use means greater productivity, a general strategy of conservation and innovation is recommended to stretch strategic minerals and energy resources.

In management's technological environment, the innovation process and the new industrial revolution are special concerns. Including conceptualization, product technology, and production technology, a healthy innovation process is vital to technological development. Innovation lags must be shortened. The new industrial revolution, stemming from space-age microelectronic technology, promises to reshape the world of work through automation. Because of high energy and labor costs, microcomputers and robots can be expected to take over many jobs in both offices and factories. Managers and society are challenged to deal fairly with those who are put out of work by these "smart" machines.

Terms to Understand

Transience	Innovation process
Synthesis perspective	Product technology
Egalitarianism	Production technology
Advocacy advertising	Innovation lag
Economics	Robots
Business cycle	Technological displacement
Technology	

Questions for Discussion

1. What evidence of transience can you detect in your life? Have you ever been the victim of future shock? Explain.
2. In your opinion, which of the ten megatrends will have the greatest impact on management? Why?
3. Why are demographic shifts relevant to management?
4. What is your attitude toward work, in terms of your aspirations and expectations? How does it compare with the so-called new work ethic?
5. Why are today's managers having to polish their political skills?
6. What is happening to managers' legal accountability? What is your opinion of this trend?
7. What do you think is the primary barrier to productivity growth in the United States?

8. What evidence do you see in your own community of management doing either a good or bad job of managing resources conservatively and innovatively?
9. Using your imagination and drawing on your personal experience, how do you think management can shorten innovation lags?
10. What signs of the new industrial revolution have you seen lately?

Back to the Opening Case

Now that you have read Chapter 3, you should be able to answer the following questions about the 3M Company case:

1. How many of the various environmental pressures on 3M can you list under each of the following headings: social, political-legal, economic, and technological? Feel free to draw reasonable inferences from the facts of the case.
2. How would the new breed employee probably respond to 3M's organizational climate?
3. In reference to 3M's answer to the Band-Aid, where did the three-step innovation process go wrong? Why is this a particularly serious problem for a firm that thrives on new ideas?

angie

Closing Case 3.2

What About Evelyne Mills?

In 1983, when the economy was recovering from the severe 1981–82 recession, the *Wall Street Journal* reported the following case incident:

Evelyne Mills is one of the long-term jobless for whom the recovery isn't producing much hope. She is angry at the system and at Allied Corp.'s Bendix machine-tool unit, a Cleveland company that laid her off more than a year ago after 10 years of service. Her anger was inflamed early last month when Bendix held a reception and introduced its new computerized machining centers, imported from Japan, right in one of the plants where the company is still making cuts to reduce its 1,700 workers to 600.

As officials demonstrated the machines for guests inside the plant, she and about 25 former workers demonstrated outside, protesting being left behind by imported technology and exported jobs. "I was a skilled worker," she says, "a plant inspector for seven years. It's hard to believe no one wants those skills now." She also found it hard to believe that she would have to go back to school to work again, but she has started an accounting course. "It's the only option I've got," she says.*

For Discussion

1. Based on what you have just read in Chapter 3, what environmental forces came together to put Evelyne Mills in this plight?
2. Assuming you are a manager at Allied's Bendix machine-tool division, how would you justify the company's actions? (*Note:* A good share of Bendix's business involves making parts such as brakes for the auto industry.)
3. What could Bendix have done to improve Evelyne Mills's situation?

References

Opening Quotation: Laurence J. Peter, *Peter's Quotations* (New York: Bantam, 1977), p. 387.

Opening Case: For additional information on 3M, see Lee Smith, "The Lures and Limits of Innovation," *Fortune* 102 (October 20, 1980): 84–94; Thomas J. Peters and Robert H. Waterman, Jr., *In Search of Excellence* (New York: Harper & Row, 1982), pp. 224–234; G. Bruce Knecht, "Three M's Unusual Strategy," *Dun's Business Month* 121 (April 1983): 55–56; Robert Levering, Milton Moskowitz, and Michael Katz, *The 100 Best Companies to Work for in America* (Reading, Mass.: Addison-Wesley, 1984), pp. 221–224; and Cathryn Jakobson, "High-Tech Vision," *Barron's* 64 (May 28, 1984): 14, 16.

Closing Case: Quoted from Geraldine Brooks, "Despite the Recovery, Some Lose Jobs Now, and It's a Hard Blow," *Wall Street Journal* 109 (August 5, 1983): 10.

1. Smith, "The Lures and Limits of Innovation," p. 86.
2. Levering, Moskowitz, and Katz, *The 100 Best Companies to Work for in America,* p. 221.
3. See Alvin Toffler, *Future Shock* (New York: Bantam, 1970).
4. John Naisbitt, *Megatrends* (New York: Warner Books, 1982), p. 8.
5. Ibid., p. 196.
6. Ibid., p. 213.
7. D. Stanley Eitzen, *Social Structure and Social Problems in America* (Boston: Allyn & Bacon, 1974), pp. 12–14.

*Reprinted by permission of the *Wall Street Journal.* © Dow Jones & Company, Inc. 1983. All rights reserved.

8. See "Why Late Retirement Is Getting a Corporate Blessing," *Business Week* No. 2824 (January 16, 1984): 69, 72.

9. Harry Bacas, "America's Changing Face," *Nation's Business* 72 (July 1984): 25.

10. "Avon Tries a New Formula to Restore Its Glow," *Business Week* No. 2849 (July 2, 1984): 46.

11. Bureau of Labor Statistics, *Occupational Outlook Handbook, 1980–81 Edition,* Bulletin 2075 (Washington, D.C., March 1980), p. 17.

12. "The Graying of America," *Newsweek* 89 (February 28, 1977): 50.

13. See "Problems in Walt Disney's Magic Kingdom," *Business Week* No. 2832 (March 12, 1984): 50–51.

14. See Daniel Yankelovich and Bernard Lefkowitz, "The New American Dream," *The Futurist* 14 (August 1980): 14–15; Daniel Yankelovich and Bernard Lefkowitz, "The Public Debate on Growth: Preparing for Resolution," *Technological Forecasting and Social Change* 17 (June 1980): 95–140; and Daniel Yankelovich, "New Rules in American Life: Searching for Self-fulfillment in a World Turned Upside Down," *Psychology Today* 15 (April 1981): 35–91.

15. Roy Rowan, "Rekindling Corporate Loyalty," *Fortune* 103 (February 9, 1981): 54.

16. See David Cherrington, "The Values of Younger Workers," *Business Horizons* 20 (December 1977): 18–30.

17. Patricia A. Renwick, Edward E. Lawler, and the *Psychology Today* staff, "What You Really Want from Your Job," *Psychology Today* 11 (May 1978): 65.

18. Data drawn from U.S. Bureau of the Census, *Statistical Abstract of the United States: 1980,* Washington, D.C., 1980, Table 768, p. 463.

19. See "An Earnings Chasm Separates Female Managers from Males," *Business Week* No. 2833 (March 19, 1984): 16.

20. "You've Come a Long Way, Baby—But Not as Far as You Thought," *Business Week* No. 2862 (October 1, 1984): 126.

21. Susan Fraker, "Why Women Aren't Getting to the Top," *Fortune* 109 (April 16, 1984): 40.

22. D. H. Thain, "Improving Competence to Deal with Politics and Government: The Management Challenge of the 80's," *Business Quarterly* 45 (Spring 1980): 31.

23. See "The Law Closes in on Managers," *Business Week* No. 2431 (May 10, 1976): 110–116.

24. For more, see "Dow Chemical's Catalog of Regulatory Horrors," *Business Week* No. 2477 (April 4, 1977): 50.

25. "3M Gains by Averting Pollution," *Business Week* No. 2459 (November 22, 1976): 72.

26. Drawn from S. Prakash Sethi, "Serving the Public Interest: Corporate Political Action for the 1980s," *Management Review* 70 (March 1981): 8–11.

27. Murray L. Weidenbaum, "Undue Influence from Business PACs? The Record

Shows It Really Isn't That Great," *The Christian Science Monitor* 76 (September 28, 1984): 19.

28. For a complete list of offenders, see Irwin Ross, "How Lawless Are Big Companies?" *Fortune* 102 (December 1, 1980): 56–64.

29. See "The Law Closes in on Managers," p. 111.

30. A brief review of this case can be found in "Paper Bag Price-fixing," *Business Week* No. 2555 (October 9, 1978): 56.

31. "Job Safety Becomes a Murder Issue," *Business Week* No. 2854 (August 6, 1984): 23.

32. Paul A. Samuelson, *Economics,* 10th ed. (New York: McGraw-Hill, 1976): 253.

33. Thomas Hazlett, "The Forecaster's Hazy Art," *Ad Forum* 5 (April 1984): 59.

34. For an informative discussion of the value of economic forecasting, see Peter L. Bernstein and Theodore H. Silbert, "Are Economic Forecasters Worth Listening To?" *Harvard Business Review* 62 (September–October 1984): 32–40.

35. "The Import Invasion: No Industry Has Been Left Untouched," *Business Week* No. 2863 (October 8, 1984): 172.

36. Robert B. Reich, *The Next American Frontier* (New York: Penguin Books, 1983), p. 125.

37. Ibid., pp. 121–122.

38. Peter Navarro, "The Capture of Walter Mondale," *The Christian Science Monitor* 76 (September 27, 1984): 13.

39. Marta Mooney, "A Time for Government Action," *National Productivity Review* 3 (Winter 1983–84): 87.

40. Herbert E. Meyer, "How We're Fixed for Strategic Minerals," *Fortune* 103 (February 9, 1981): 68–69; see also Sumer C. Aggarwal, "Prepare for Continual Materials Shortages," *Harvard Business Review* 60 (May–June 1982): 6–10.

41. For example, see Newt Gingrich, "Innovation or Deprivation," *The Futurist* 15 (August 1981): 31–37.

42. Daniel Yergin, "Conservation: The Key Energy Source," in *Energy Future,* ed. Robert Stobaugh and Daniel Yergin (New York: Ballantine, 1979), p. 168.

43. For a good discussion of the economic impacts of conservation, see "Energy Conservation: Spawning a Billion-dollar Business," *Business Week* No. 2682 (April 6, 1981): 58–69.

44. An interesting discussion of recycling may be found in William U. Chandler, "Converting Garbage to Gold," *The Futurist* 18 (February 1984): 69–77.

45. For more on remanufacturing, see Robert T. Lund, "Remanufacturing," *Technology Review* 87 (February–March 1984): 18–27.

46. A good overview of alternative energy sources is William R. Huss, Cynthia A. Richmond, and Christopher K. Badger, "Alternative Generation Technologies: Can They Compete?" *Public Utilities Fortnightly* 113 (March 15, 1984): 17–24.

47. Jerome B. Wiesner, "Technology and Innovation," in *Technological Innovation and Society,* ed. Dean Morse and Aaron W. Warner (New York: Columbia University Press, 1966), p. 11.

48. See Robert C. Dean, Jr., "The Temporal Mismatch—Innovation's Pace vs Management's Time Horizon," *Research Management* 17 (May 1974): 12–15.

49. "Texas Instruments Shows U.S. Business How to Survive in the 1980s," *Business Week* No. 2552 (September 18, 1978): 84.

50. For complete discussions of microprocessor technology, see Colin Norman, "The New Industrial Revolution: How Microelectronics May Change the Workplace," *The Futurist* 15 (February 1981): 30–42; and Blake M. Cornish, "The Smart Machines of Tomorrow: Implications for Society," *The Futurist* 15 (August 1981): 5–13.

51. An informative discussion of robots may be found in R. L. Eshleman and F. S. Pagano, "What Managers Need to Know When Choosing Robots," *National Productivity Review* 2 (Summer 1983): 242–256; see also Fred K. Foulkes and Jeffery L. Hirsch, "People Make Robots Work," *Harvard Business Review* 62 (January–February 1984): 94–102.

52. See Otto Friedrich, "The Robot Revolution," *Time* 116 (December 8, 1980): 72–83.

53. "Changing 45 Million Jobs," *Business Week* No. 2699 (August 3, 1981): 62.

54. "America Rushes to High Tech for Growth," *Business Week* No. 2783 (March 28, 1983): 87.

55. For more on retraining programs, see Alexander L. Taylor III, "The Growing Gap in Retraining," *Time* 121 (March 28, 1983): 50–51.

56. See John S. DeMott, "After the Mill Shuts Down," *Time* 122 (August 15, 1983): 46.

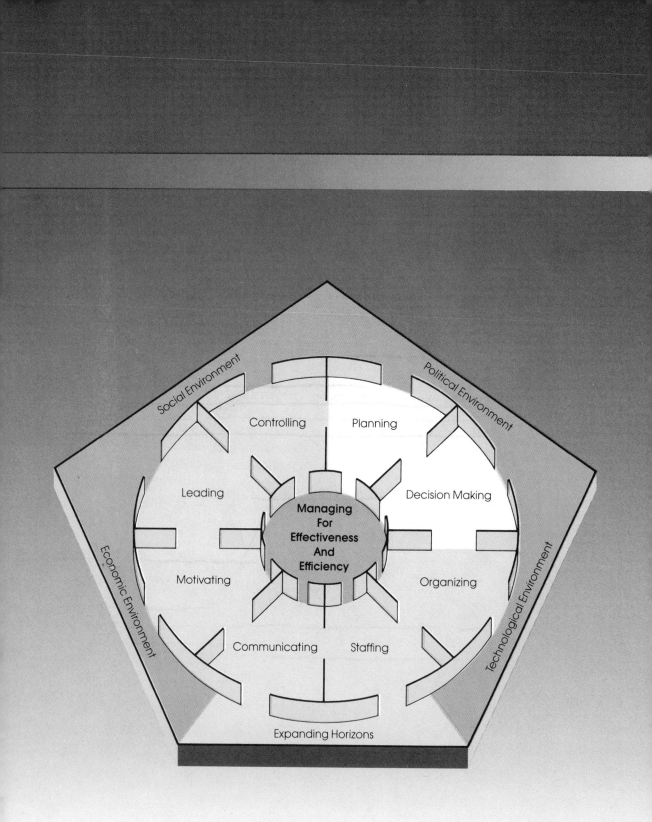

PART TWO

Planning and Decision Making

Part Two focuses on planning and decision making, two fundamental management functions that complement one another. Planning helps managers determine where they want to go, and decision making helps them get there. In Chapter 4, a definitional and conceptual framework for the planning function is presented. Special attention is devoted to management by objectives, a proven planning/control technique. Strategic management is discussed in Chapter 5 to underscore the importance of determining the organization's overall purpose and of planning for long-term success. Concepts and techniques for better decision making and more creative problem solving are covered in Chapter 6. The important role personal values play in decision making is explored along with ways to enhance managerial creativity.

Chapter 4

Planning: The Primary Management Function

Despite the fact that planning is considered the foundation of management, it is still too often the poorest performed task of the managerial job.
Harold Koontz

Chapter Objectives

When you finish studying this chapter, you should be able to

- Explain why limited resources and an uncertain environment make planning particularly important today.
- Write good objectives and discuss the role of objectives in planning.
- Describe the four-step management by objectives (MBO) process and explain how it can foster individual commitment and motivation.
- Compare and contrast flow charts and Gantt charts and discuss the value of PERT networks.
- Explain how break-even points can be calculated.

Opening Case 4.1

People Express Airlines Takes Off in a Big Way*

... By all accounts, People Express is, quite simply, the fastest-growing airline in the history of aviation, a happy fact that flight attendants will sometimes announce at the end of a flight. Says ... [one observer]: "Fantastic is even an understatement. Their growth is a phenomenon all its own."

In one furious acceleration akin to the lift-off thrust of a Boeing 737, People Express rose, in just two and a half years, from relative obscurity to international prominence. From 250 to more than 3,000 full- and part-time employees. From three planes serving 3 cities with 24 flights a day to

*Excerpted with permission from *INC*. magazine, January 1984. Copyright © 1984 by INC. Publishing Company, 38 Commercial Wharf, Boston, MA 02210.

a fleet of 22 Boeing 737s, 10 Boeing 727s, and one 747 making 264 nonstop flights daily to 20 destinations, including London. ... [People Express] reported revenues of $116 million and net income of $6.3 million for the first six months of 1983. People Express has carried some 10 million passengers and is currently the largest single airport operation in the New York metropolitan area. [People Express operates out of Newark International airport.]

And it has done all this despite a severe economic recession, withering price wars, a national air-traffic-controllers strike, and otherwise dismal conditions in the airline industry that have included bankruptcies and widespread operating losses.

"We have a unique problem," president and founder Donald Burr recently told a group of college educators. "We've designed a product which is so popular we can't satisfy the demand for it."

That product is a seat on an aircraft that flies between Newark and some other major city on the East Coast (and London), that is frequently available, and that is, above all, cheap. ... People Express passengers are ticketed on board or pay in advance through a travel agent. They pay to have baggage checked and for snacks and drinks on board. There are no free magazines, either. The most telling measure of the popularity of the Spartan treatment is called the "load factor." The load factor expresses with a percentage that portion of all available seats in any given time period that were actually filled by paying customers. In July [1983], People Express's load factor was a stunning 83.6% compared to an average load factor of 60% for the airline industry. "We believe," Burr says, "that if you respect people and give them a good deal, they'll use the hell out of it."

But Burr also says, "Being a commercial success is not enough. It's a derivative of doing other things well. The whole purpose of creating this enterprise in the first place was to create an environment which would enable and empower employees to release their creative energies." For Burr, the interplay of marketing, scheduling, and cost control has a beauty all its own, but the personal fulfillment of individual employees through the company's "people structure" offers something more. "People," he says, "are the glory and frustration of People Express. ..."

[A Low Break-even Point]

"Our strategy," says Burr, "is to knock the price down so low that it fills the plane." So low, in fact, that flying People Express will often be cheaper than driving or taking a bus. ...

Of course, popularity doesn't necessarily mean profitability. Many a plane has taken off packed to the baggage compartments only to land in red ink. The load factor is just one of three variables that must be handled with surgical dexterity if the airline is to make a profit. The other variables are revenue per passenger mile and costs per available seat mile, both of which resemble the revenue and cost-of-goods-sold components in a manufacturing company. The lower the costs, the less an airline has to charge the customer, and the lower its break-even load factor. In 1982, People Express's cost per available seat mile of 5¢ was the lowest in the industry. Thus, the company could maintain its deep discount pricing, charging travelers as little as 8¢ per passenger mile and still make money. At those levels, only 60% of available seats had to be filled to break even. ...

[A Share-the-Wealth Plan]

Every employee is required to own stock in People Express. Customer-service managers must purchase, as a condition of their employment, 100 shares at prices far below the market. If they aren't able to afford it, the company gives them an interest-free loan. Since additional buying opportunities are made available throughout the year, employees generally end up with a significant investment. ... Each employee owns an average of 2,500 shares worth about $46,000 at today's [January 1984] prices. "We're not sitting around here counting roses," asserts Burr. "This is capitalism. People are getting rich here. There are millionaires walking around here and tons of 24- to 25-year-olds worth $75,000, $100,000, $200,000. Tons of 'em. The only way I know to wealth in the long term is to own a piece of something and build it. ..."

[A Participative Approach]

Although it had existed in the collective mind of the start-up team, People Express's direction wasn't written down until December 1981. Eight months after the first flights, Burr convened a meeting of the [start-up] team. ... He was concerned that the company's objectives might be lost among the daily distractions of a rapidly growing business. The meeting was recalled by everyone involved as a day of intense, argumentative debate. Burr asked each member in turn for his or her idea of what People Express was trying to accomplish. He wrote the answers on large sheets of paper and taped them to the walls. "They worked hard," he says. "I mean they put their blood on those walls." The team emerged with a list of six "precepts" that dedicated the company to "service, growth, and development of people"; becoming the "best provider of air transportation"; the "highest quality of management"; becoming a "role model"; "simplicity"; and the "maximization of profits. ... "

The best method he has yet found to translate the precepts into action is by organizing all the managers into teams of two or three members and by cross-utilization. Everyone in the company, including the managing officers, are members of a team. This design is thought to foster self-management and a highly productive esprit de corps while at the same time eliminating additional layers of supervisory control. Teams also participate in the decision- and policymaking of the company by electing members to advisory and coordinating councils, which meet with Burr, the managing officers, and the general managers. ...

(Discussion questions linking this case with the material you are about to read can be found at the end of this chapter.)

The only thing certain about the future of any organization today is change. Exxon, the American Heart Association, the U.S. Department of Agriculture, the New York Mets, and Smilin' Ed's Used Cars all are sure to change their form and direction as they move into the future. People Express will doubtless make many changes in its unique approach to commercial aviation as circumstances dictate in the years ahead. Managers everywhere face an increasingly fluid social, political, economic, and technological environment, and ignoring or resisting change practically guarantees organizational failure. Effective managers keep informed about what is going on inside and outside their organizations, actively anticipate change, and plan future courses of action accordingly.

Planning is defined as the process of preparing for change and coping with uncertainty by formulating future courses of action. Because planning paves the way for all downstream management functions (see Figure 4.1) by serving as a bridge between the present and the future, it has been called the primary management function.[1]

As a backdrop for what lies ahead, let us briefly examine what 250 executives from America's largest companies had to say in a recent survey about planning during the 1980s. Because of limited growth opportunities and increased competition, the executives identified the following new directions for the planning function:

- Academically trained planning specialists are being replaced by planners with hands-on managerial experience.
- Teamwork and cooperation throughout the planning/control cycle are breaking down the traditional distinction between those who plan and those who carry out plans.
- Canned planning techniques and theories are giving way to customized planning programs based on competitive marketing strategies specific to the organization.
- Plans are becoming more flexible to accommodate greater emphasis on entrepreneurship (risk taking).
- Planners are being asked to translate broad marketing strategies into how-to-do-it plans that can be easily communicated and understood.[2]

With these trends in mind, we shall explain why planning is necessary, highlight five essential aspects of the planning function, and take a close

Primary Management Function

Figure 4.1 Planning: The Primary Management Function

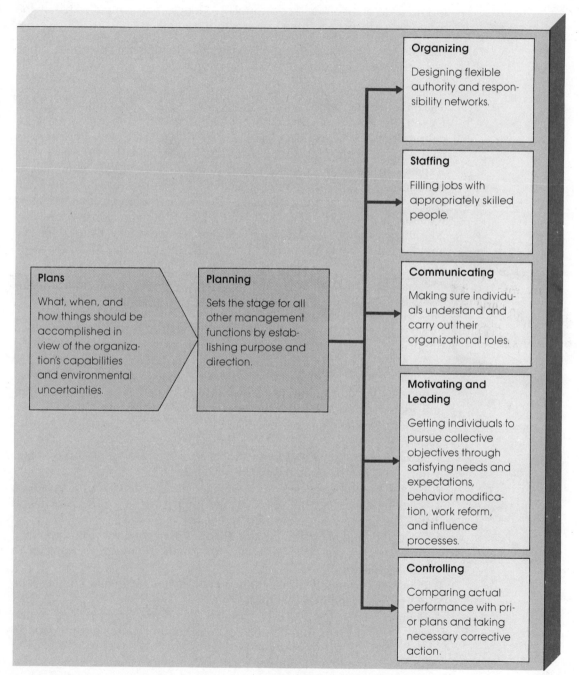

Table 4.1 Two Practicing Managers Answer the Question "Why Plan?"

Douglas B. Gehrman Manager, Compensation Exxon Company U.S.A.	Merritt L. Kastens Editor and Publisher *Food Industry Futures* (formerly a planning director at Union Carbide)
Why plan? ● Increases chances of success by focusing on results, not activities. ● Forces analytical thinking and evaluation of alternatives, thus improving decisions. ● Establishes a framework for decision making consistent with top management's objectives. ● Orients people to action, instead of reaction. ● Modifies style from day-to-day managing to future-focused managing. ● Helps avoid crisis management and provides decision-making flexibility. ● Provides a basis for measuring organizational and individual performance. ● Increases employee involvement and improves communications.	So why do you plan? Not to predict the future—because you're kidding yourself if you think you can. Not to lock yourself into a lot of predetermined actions because that is likely to be as disastrous as persisting in what you have been doing in the past. You plan in order to find out what the hell is going on and because it gives you the only chance of getting a grip on the future success of the enterprise. You plan because you're bruised and bloody from being knocked around by events that you don't understand and from finding yourself in corners when it is too late to do anything about getting out of them. You plan because you're tired of managing from crisis to crisis, of constantly putting out fires—or more likely stumbling around in the hot ashes. You plan, not because it's fun. It's not, but it can be exciting. You plan, not because it's a new management fad. After thirty years it is well beyond that stage. You plan because it's your best chance for survival in a world that is changing as fast as ours is. Furthermore, I'll clue you; if you're going to be a manager, it's a lot more pleasant when you know what you're doing.

SOURCES: Douglas B. Gehrman, "Techniques of Planning in Employee Relations," *Personnel Journal* 58 (November 1979): 762; and Merritt L. Kastens, "The Why and How of Planning," *Managerial Planning* 28 (July–August 1979): 34.

look at management by objectives. We shall also introduce four practical planning tools (flow charts, Gantt charts, PERT networks, and break-even analysis).

Why Plan?

Since the time of Henri Fayol, the necessity of planning has been emphasized by many people in many ways. Both conceptual reasons and practical reasons (see Table 4.1) have been given. Two conceptual reasons supporting systematic planning by managers are limited resources and an uncertain environment. We shall examine each.

Table 4.2 Different Organizational Responses to an Uncertain Environment

Type of Organizational Response to the Environment	Characteristics of Response
1. Defenders	● Highly expert at producing and marketing a few products in a narrowly defined market ● Opportunities beyond present market not sought ● Few adjustments in technology, organization structure, and methods of operation because of narrow focus ● Primary attention devoted to efficiency of current operations
2. Prospectors	● Primary attention devoted to searching for new market opportunities ● Frequent development and testing of new products and services ● Source of change and uncertainty for competitors ● Loss of efficiency because of continual product and market innovation
3. Analyzers	● Simultaneous operations in stable and changing product-market domains ● In relatively stable product/market domain, emphasis on formalized structures and processes to achieve routine and efficient operation ● In changing product/market domain, emphasis on detecting and copying competitors' most promising ideas
4. Reactors	● Frequently unable to respond quickly to perceived changes in environment. Makes adjustments only when finally forced to do so by environmental pressures

SOURCE: Adapted from *Organizational Strategy, Structure, and Process,* by Raymond E. Miles and Charles C. Snow. Copyright © 1978, McGraw-Hill Book Company, p. 29. Used with permission of McGraw-Hill Book Company.

Limited Resources   Resource scarcity is an especially important consideration today because it will be a major factor in our lives for the foreseeable future. At the very least, as two scientific observers have noted, "dwindling supplies of energy and materials resources pose what may be the most significant problem for the United States in the last quarter of the twentieth century."[3] As surprising as it may sound, in view of the worldwide population explosion, even human resources are limited. This is true because an uneducated or untrained person, or one who lives too far away to commute to a particular job, can contribute little to a productive organization or to the economy as a whole.

There would be little need for planning if material, financial, and human resources were unlimited. Waste and inefficiency would not matter if cheap resources were plentiful. But as the smog alerts, water shortages, and energy crunches of the 1970s dramatically demonstrated, even seemingly limitless resources such as fresh air, clean water, and petroleum are subject to supply limitations. Modern planners, in both private industry and government, are challenged to stretch our limited resources through intelligent planning. Otherwise, wasteful inefficiencies will drive up prices, contribute to outright shortages, and promote public dissatisfaction.

Uncertain Environment   It is often remarked that the only sure things in life are death and taxes. Although this is a gloomy prospect, it does capture a key theme of modern life. We are faced with a great deal of uncertainty. Organizations, like individuals, are continually challenged to accomplish something in spite of general uncertainty. Organizations meet this challenge largely through planning. Some organizations do a better job of planning amidst environmental uncertainty than others do, partly because of their differing patterns of response to environmental factors beyond the organization's immediate control. As outlined in Table 4.2, organizations cope with environmental uncertainty by adopting one of four positions vis-à-vis the environment in which they operate. These positions are defenders, prospectors, analyzers, and reactors,[4] each with its own characteristic impact on planning.

Defenders   Organizations that are defenders can be successful as long as their narrowly defined market remains strong. Caterpillar Tractor Company is a good example of a defender because it has stuck to its three basic product lines—earth-moving equipment, diesel engines, and materials-handling devices—and has resisted the trend among its less successful competitors to diversify to other areas.[5] But defenders can become stranded on a dead-end road if their primary market seriously weakens or dissolves.

Prospectors   Organizations that are prospectors are easy to spot because they have a reputation of aggressively making things happen rather than waiting for them to happen. Prospectors enjoy the advantage of getting the edge on the competition by being innovative. At the same time, prospectors suffer the disadvantage of sometimes throwing money away on ideas that fail. Texas Instruments, the Dallas-based electronics giant, exemplifies the prospector's dilemma. It clearly dominates the electronic educational product market with innovations like its popular Speak & Spell. But it reportedly lost $50 to $100 million when it terminated its innovative pursuit of magnetic bubble memories in 1981.[6]

A recent study of 1452 business units shed some light on the comparative effectiveness of these first two strategies. "Specifically, in every type of environment examined, defenders outperformed prospectors in terms of current profitability and cash flow. The costs and risks of product innovation appear significant."[7] Prospectors in the business sector need to pick their opportunities very carefully, selecting those with the best combination of feasibility and profit potential.

Analyzers An essentially conservative strategy of following the leader marks an organization as an analyzer. This response to environmental uncertainty is fine as long as (1) the leader is headed in the right direction, and (2) changes in the leader's direction are detected and properly interpreted. Ford Motor Company, second in size to General Motors among U.S. auto makers, experienced the woes of an analyzer when it failed to follow GM's shift to smaller cars in the late 1970s.

> Ford had been convinced that Americans were still in love with the big-car image, so it deliberately set about reducing fuel consumption while keeping that good ol' gas-guzzler look. As things turned out, consumers came to hunger for the look and feel of fuel efficiency as well as its reality. GM and the imports had it. Ford didn't.[8]

But on the positive side, analyzers can conserve capital by letting prospectors assume the risks of expensive research and development projects and then later copying and developing their most promising ideas.

Reactors The reactor is the exact opposite of the prospector. Reactors wait for adversity, such as declining sales, before taking corrective steps. They are slow to develop new products to supplement their tried-and-true ones. Their strategic responses to changes in the environment are often late. An interesting example in this area is Joseph E. Seagram & Sons, Inc. Seagram grew into the world's largest distiller by specializing in brown liquors such as Seagram's 7 Crown. But drinking habits have changed in recent years. Consequently, white liquors such as Bacardi rum and Smirnoff vodka pushed Seagram's 7 Crown from first place to third. Moreover, with more Americans drinking wine, the public outcry against drunk driving, and higher excise taxes on liquor, Seagram's sales dropped. By the time Seagram reacted by bolstering its wine business in the early 1980s, the wine market was glutted because of European imports and overplanted vineyards in California.[9]

Overall, the planner's job is to gauge the nature and degree of major environmental uncertainties, to assess the organization's response pattern, and to develop appropriate plans. Firm plans can be made for areas of low uncertainty, though areas marked by high uncertainty require flexible plans that can be adjusted to changing conditions. As a general rule, the higher the degree of environmental uncertainty, the greater the need for flexibility in planning.

The Essentials of Planning

Virtually everyone is a planner, at least in the informal sense. We plan leisure activities after school or work; we make career plans. Personal or informal plans give purpose to our lives. In a similar fashion, more formalized plans enable managers to mobilize their intentions to accomplish organizational purposes. According to the head of Alcan Aluminum Corporation, a company with an exemplary planning program, "... plans are truly the working documents by which we manage our business."[10] A **plan** is a specific, documented intention consisting of an objective and an action statement. The objective portion is the end, and the action statement represents the means to that end. Stated another way, objectives give management targets to shoot at, whereas action statements provide the arrows for hitting the targets. Properly conceived plans tell *what, when,* and *how* something is to be done.

In spite of the wide variety of formal planning systems managers encounter on the job, it is possible to identify some essentials of sound planning. Among these common denominators are organizational mission, levels of planning, objectives, priorities, and the planning/control cycle.

Organizational Mission

To some, defining an organization's mission might seem like a waste of time because they believe that an organization would not exist if it did not have a purpose. But exactly the opposite is often true. Some organizations never have a clear mission, and others lose sight of theirs. Or an organization may fulfill its mission and, by doing so, lose its reason for existing. An example of this latter situation is the March of Dimes organization, which had to shift its mission from fighting polio to fighting birth defects when a polio vaccine was developed. General Motors, Ford, Chrysler, and American Motors each have broadened their mission from producing cars to providing transportation. Similarly, some petroleum companies now see themselves in the energy business, not just in the oil and gas business. Periodically redefining an organization's mission is both common and necessary in an era of rapid change.

A clear, formally written, and publicized statement of an organization's mission is the cornerstone of any planning system if it is to be effective at guiding the organization through uncertain times. A good mission statement does more than just express generalities such as making money. Instead, it helps define the organization's special niche in the economy or culture, spelling out the organization's areas of endeavor that differentiate it from other organizations. An example of an effective organizational mission statement is displayed in Table 4.3. Kimberly-Clark Corporation's mission statement gives managers, investors, nonmanagerial employees,

Figure 4.2 Levels of Planning

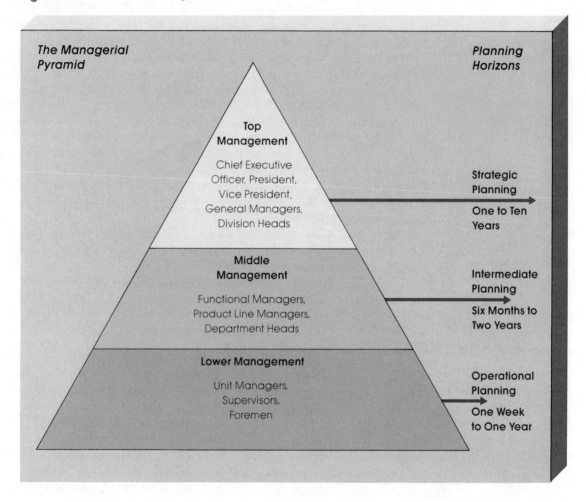

suppliers, customers, and other interested parties a general idea of the nature of its business. Most importantly, it provides a focal point for its entire planning process.

Levels of Planning

To be effective and consistent, planning necessarily begins at the top of the organizational pyramid and filters down. The reason for beginning at the top is clear. It is top management's job to make key assumptions, state the organization's purpose and philosophy, establish priorities, and draw up major policies. After, and only after, these factors are in place can plans with specific objectives and action statements be made.

Successive levels of plans are made by top, middle, and lower manage-

Table 4.3 A Sample Statement of Organizational Mission

Kimberly-Clark Corporation, its consolidated subsidiaries and equity companies are engaged in a single, worldwide business employing advanced technologies in absorbency, fiber-forming, and other fields. The Corporation produces and markets a wide range of products made from natural and synthetic fibers for personal care, health care, and other uses in the home, business, and industry. The Corporation also produces and markets specialty papers requiring specialized technology in development or application as well as traditional paper and related products for newspaper and other communication needs.

SOURCE: Kimberly-Clark Corporation: Annual Report 1983.

ment (refer to Figure 4.2). Top management engages in strategic planning; middle management assumes the task of intermediate planning; and lower management carries out the operational planning. **Strategic planning** is the process of determining how to pursue the organization's long-term goals with the resources expected to be available. **Intermediate planning** is the process of determining the contributions that subunits can make with allocated resources. Finally, **operational planning** is the process of determining how specific tasks can best be accomplished on time with available resources. Each level of planning is vital to the organization's success and cannot effectively stand alone without the support of the other two levels.

Time is the key variable in distinguishing among strategic, intermediate, and operational planning. As illustrated in Figure 4.2, planning horizons vary for the three types of planning. The term **planning horizon** refers to the time that elapses between the formulation and the execution of a planned activity. As the planning process filters down the managerial pyramid, planning horizons shorten, and plans become increasingly specific in accordance with the means-ends chain of objectives. Naturally, management can be more confident, and hence more specific, about the near future than it can for the distant future. Notice, however, that the three planning horizons overlap, their boundaries being elastic rather than rigid. It is not uncommon for top and lower managers to have a hand in formulating intermediate plans, and middle managers often help lower managers draw up operational plans as well.

Objectives Just as a distant port serves as a target or goal for a ship's crew, objectives give organizational members targets to steer toward. Although some theorists draw a fine distinction between goals and objectives, managers typically use the terms interchangeably. A goal or an **objective** is defined as a specific commitment to achieve a measurable result within a given time frame. Many experts view objectives as the single most important feature of the planning process. According to a team of management consultants, "It is very difficult to see how an organization or an individual can even begin to plan until concrete objectives are clearly defined."[11] It is important for present and future managers to be able to write good objectives, to be aware of their importance, and to understand how objectives combine to form a means-ends chain.

Writing Good Objectives An authority on objectives recommends that "as far as possible, objectives are expressed in quantitative, measurable, concrete terms, in the form of a written statement of desired results to be achieved within a given time period."[12] In other words, objectives represent a firm commitment to accomplish something specific. A well-written objective should state what is to be accomplished and when it is to be accomplished. In the following sample objectives, note that the desired results are expressed in quantitative terms such as units of output, dollars, or percentage of change.

● To increase subcompact car production by 240,000 units during the next production year.
● To reduce bad-debt loss by $50,000 during the next six months.
● To achieve an 18 percent increase in Brand X sales by December 31 of the current year.

The following is a handy three-way test to judge how well objectives are written:

● *Test 1:* Does this objective tell me exactly *what* the intended result is?
● *Test 2:* Does this objective specify *when* the intended result is to be accomplished?
● *Test 3:* Can the intended result be *measured?*

Statements of intention that fail one or more of these three tests do not qualify as objectives and will tend to hinder rather than help the planning process.

The Importance of Objectives From the standpoint of planning, carefully prepared objectives benefit managers by serving as targets and measuring sticks, fostering commitment, and enhancing motivation.[13]

● **Targets.** As mentioned earlier, objectives provide managers with specific targets. Without objectives, managers at all levels would find it difficult to make coordinated decisions. People quite naturally tend to pursue their own ends in the absence of formal organizational objectives.
● **Measuring sticks.** An easily overlooked feature of objectives is that they are useful tools for measuring how well an organizational subunit or

Figure 4.3   A Typical Means-Ends Chain of Objectives

Position in Organization	Level of Management	Objective
Corporate President	Top	To increase corporate sales to $250 million by the end of the year.
		End ↑ **Means**
Laundry Products Manager	Middle	To increase market share of 'Soapy Suds' detergent by 5 percent by July 1.
		End ↑ **Means**
Area Field Sales Manager (Boston area)	Lower (supervisory)	To increase unit sales of 'Soapy Suds' detergent in Boston area by 100,000 units by April 1.

individual has performed. This is an after-the-fact feature of objectives. When appraising performance, managers need objectives as an established standard against which they can measure performance. Concrete objectives enable managers to weigh performance objectively on the basis of accomplishment rather than subjectively on the basis of personality or prejudice.

- **Commitment.** The very process of getting an employee to agree to pursue a given objective gives that individual a personal stake in the success of the enterprise. Thus objectives can be helpful in encouraging personal commitment to collective ends. Without individual commitment, even the most well intentioned and carefully conceived organizations are doomed to failure.
- **Motivation.** Since good objectives represent a challenge—something to be reached for—they provide a motivational aspect. People usually feel

good about themselves and what they do when they have successfully achieved a fair and challenging objective. Moreover, objectives give managers a rational basis for rewarding performance. Employees who believe they will be equitably rewarded for achieving a given objective will be motivated to perform well.

The Means-Ends Chain of Objectives   Like the overall planning process, objective setting is a top-to-bottom proposition. Top managers set broader objectives with longer time horizons than do successively lower levels of managers. In effect, this downward flow of objectives creates a means-ends chain. As illustrated in Figure 4.3 (on page 135), supervisory-level objectives provide the means for achieving middle-level objectives (ends) which, in turn, provide the means for achieving top-level objectives (ends).

Of course, the organizational hierarchy in Figure 4.3 has been telescoped and narrowed at the middle and lower levels for illustrative purposes. Usually there would be two or three layers of management between the president and the product-line managers. Another layer or two would separate the product-line managers from the area sales managers. But the telescoping helps point up the fact that lower-level objectives provide the means for accomplishing higher-level ends or objectives.

Priorities   Defined as a ranking of goals or objectives in order of importance, **priorities** play a special role in planning. By listing long-range organizational objectives in order of their priority, top management prepares to make later decisions regarding the allocation of resources. Limited time, financial and material resources, and talent need to be channeled proportionately more into important endeavors and proportionately less into other areas. Priorities determine what is relatively more important. For example, one hospital's principal goal might be high-quality patient care. But another hospital might rank research first. The first hospital will probably devote proportionately more attention and funds to achieving high-quality patient care than the second hospital does, which is mainly interested in advancing medical science. This variance in priorities will take the two hospitals in quite different directions. Along with the organizational mission statement, priorities give both insiders and outsiders answers to the questions "Why does the organization exist?" and "Where is it headed?"

Establishing priorities for the entire organization normally is a highly subjective process subject to social, political, and economic pressures and marked by value conflicts. Although there is no universally acceptable formula for carrying out this important function, the A-B-C priority system outlined in Table 4.4 is helpful in this regard.

Table 4.4   The A-B-C Priority System for Objectives

Priority Code	Description
A	= "Must do" objectives *critical* to successful performance. They may be the result of special demands from higher levels of management or other external sources.
B	= "Should do" objectives *necessary* for improved performance. They are generally vital, but their achievement can be postponed if necessary.
C	= "Nice to do" objectives *desirable* for improved performance, but not critical to survival or improved performance. They can be eliminated or postponed to achieve objectives of higher priority.

SOURCE: Anthony P. Raia, *Managing by Objectives* (Glenview, Ill.: Scott, Foresman, 1974), p. 54.

The Planning/ Control Cycle

To put the planning process in perspective, it is important to show how it is connected with the control function. Figure 4.4 illustrates the cyclical relationship between planning and control. Planning gets things headed in the right direction, and control keeps them headed in the right direction. (Because of the importance of the control function, it is covered in detail in Part Five.) Basically, each of the three levels of planning is a two-step sequence followed by a two-step control sequence.

The initial planning/control cycle begins when top management establishes strategic plans. When those strategic plans are carried out, intermediate and operational plans are formulated, thus setting in motion two more planning/control cycles. As strategic, intermediate, and operational plans are carried out, the control function begins. Corrective action is necessary when either the preliminary or the final results deviate from plans. For planned activities still in progress, this corrective action can get things back on track before it is too late. Deviations between final results and plans, on the other hand, are instructive feedback for the improvement of future plans. Importantly, the dotted lines in Figure 4.4 represent the sort of feedback that makes the planning/control cycle a dynamic and evolving process. Our attention now turns to some practical planning tools.

Management by Objectives

Management by objectives (MBO) is a comprehensive management system based on measurable and participatively set objectives. MBO has

Figure 4.4 The Basic Planning/Control Cycle

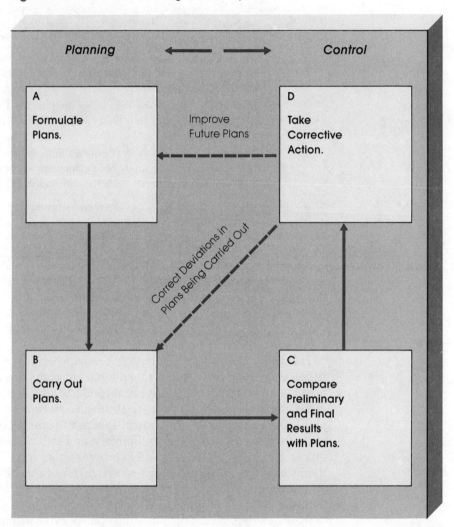

come a long way since it was first suggested by Peter Drucker in 1954 as a way of promoting managerial self-control.[14] In one form or another, and under various labels, MBO has been adopted by many organizations around the world. In fact, it is difficult to find a public or private organization of any significant size that has not tried some variation of the MBO theme. As an indication of the widespread interest in MBO, over 700 books, articles, and technical papers had been written on the subject by the late 1970s.[15]

The common denominator that has made MBO programs so popular in both management theory and practice is the emphasis on objectives that are both *measurable* and *participatively set*. Unfortunately, as pointed out by a management consultant, a gap exists between MBO theory and practice: "Today, MBO is being used as an exploitive, manipulative management control mechanism as often as a liberating, humanistic philosophy of management. It seems to be venerated more by its abuse than for its proper use."[16] Whether properly or improperly applied, MBO is by far the most widely used planning tool among those discussed in this chapter.

A Management System

Originally characterized as a relatively simple performance appraisal technique, MBO evolved into a more complex planning and control tool and eventually into a comprehensive management system. According to one recognized expert on MBO:

> Within the past few years MBO has emerged as a system designed to integrate key management processes and activities in a logical and consistent manner. These include the development of overall organizational goals and strategic plans, problem solving and decision making, performance appraisal, executive compensation, manpower planning, and management training and development.[17]

Proponents claim that when MBO is applied as a comprehensive management system, it becomes an integral part of the manager's job, not just something else to do.

The MBO Cycle

At the heart of MBO is the four-step cycle illustrated in Figure 4.5. Because MBO combines planning and control, the MBO cycle closely follows the planning/control cycle introduced in the previous section. Steps 1 and 2 make up the planning phase of MBO, and steps 3 and 4 are the control phase.

Step 1: Setting Objectives   A hierarchy of challenging, fair, and internally consistent objectives is the necessary starting point for the MBO cycle because it serves as the foundation for all that follows. All objectives, according to MBO theory, should be reduced to writing and put away for later referral during steps 3 and 4. Consistent with what was said earlier about setting objectives, objective setting in MBO begins at the top of the managerial pyramid and filters down, one layer at a time.

MBO's main contribution to the objective-setting process is its emphasis on the participation and involvement of subordinates. In MBO, there is no place for the domineering manager who says, "Here are the objectives I've written for you," nor for the passive manager who says, "I'll go along with whatever objectives you set." Instead, MBO calls for a give-and-take negotiation of objectives between superior and subordinate.

Figure 4.5 The MBO Cycle

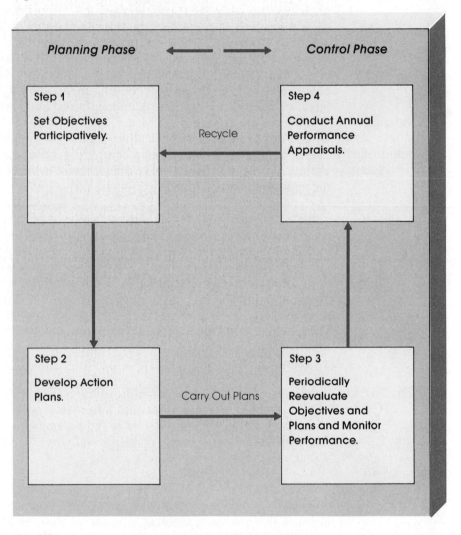

Step 2: Developing Action Plans With the addition of action statements to the participatively set objectives, the planning phase of MBO is complete. Managers at each level develop plans that incorporate the objectives established in step 1. Higher managers are responsible for making sure that their direct subordinates' plans complement one another and do not work at cross-purposes.

Step 3: Periodic Review As plans turn into action, attention turns to step 3, monitoring performance. Advocates of MBO usually recommend face-to-face meetings between superior and subordinate at three-, six-, and nine-month intervals. These periodic checkups permit those who are responsible for a particular set of objectives to reconsider them to see if they are still valid. Sometimes unexpected events such as added duties or the loss of a key assistant can make the objectives obsolete or invalid. If an objective is no longer valid, it is updated accordingly. Otherwise, progress toward valid objectives is assessed. Periodic checkups also give managers an excellent opportunity to give subordinates needed and appreciated feedback.

Step 4: Performance Appraisal   At the end of one complete cycle of MBO, typically one year after the original goals were set, final performance is matched with the previously agreed-upon objectives. The pairs of superior and subordinate managers who mutually set the objectives one year earlier meet face-to-face once again to discuss how things have turned out. MBO calls for emphasis on results, not on personalities or excuses. The control phase of the MBO cycle is completed when success is rewarded with promotion, merit pay, or other suitable benefits and when failure is noted for future corrective action.

When appraising performance during steps 3 and 4, managers are urged to keep the following behavioral principles in mind:

- **Principle of participation.** Motivation tends to increase as participation in decision making and objective setting increases.
- **Principle of feedback.** Motivation tends to increase when employees know where they stand.
- **Principle of reciprocated interest.** Motivation tends to increase when the pursuit of organizational objectives is accompanied by the achievement of personal objectives.
- **Principle of recognition.** Motivation to achieve organizational objectives tends to increase when employees are recognized for their contributions.[18]

After one round of MBO, the cycle repeats itself, with each cycle contributing to the learning process. A common practice in MBO is to start at the top and to introduce a new layer of management to the MBO process each year. Experience has shown that plunging several layers of management into MBO all at once often causes confusion, dissatisfaction, and failure. In fact, it typically takes five or more years for even a moderate-sized organization to evolve a full-blown MBO system that ties together such areas as planning, control, performance appraisal, and the reward system. MBO proponents believe that higher productivity and greater motivation—through the use of realistic objectives, more effective control, and self-control—are the natural by-products of a proper MBO system.

MBO Research

An ironic aspect of MBO is that in spite of its widespread application, research evidence of MBO's effectiveness is sparse. Research conducted to date on actual MBO applications can be characterized as encouraging but inconclusive.[19] One management writer has concluded that "... most organizations have adopted MBO on faith, as the result of questionable studies, or on the basis of unsubstantiated testimonials, many of them in the form of case studies."[20] On-the-job research on MBO is lacking because in complex organizational settings it is very difficult to prove causation between a multidimensional management technique such as MBO and job performance. For instance, improved performance might be due to the state of the economy or new technology rather than to a recently introduced MBO program. Consequently, many MBO researchers have fallen back on either measuring employee attitudes toward MBO or contrived laboratory studies. Attitudinal studies are often deficient because they merely infer rather than prove MBO's effect on actual performance. Laboratory studies of MBO generally are oversimplified and unrealistic.

Without solid, on-the-job evidence proving that MBO improves job performance, could one say that MBO is a useful technique? Judging from a number of behavioral science studies on goal setting, the very heart of MBO, the answer appears to be yes. After examining dozens of research studies on goal setting, two organizational behaviorists concluded:

- Specific goals usually increase performance.
- Difficult goals, if accepted, stimulate greater performance than do easy goals.
- Goal setting is effective at both the managerial and operative levels.
- Both assigned and participatively set goals help improve performance.[21]

With the exception of the last, these findings suggest that the use of challenging yet attainable objectives, as prescribed by MBO advocates, can enhance performance. But the key to success, as indicated in the second finding, is persuading employees to accept difficult objectives. It is on this particular point that MBO theory and goal-setting research diverge. MBO proponents firmly believe that participation by subordinates in setting objectives is necessary for personal commitment. But the research on goal setting suggests that improved performance does not necessarily depend on participation. One possible explanation for this disparity is that not all subordinates are willing and able to accept the added responsibility of participation.

Figure 4.6   Weighing MBO's Strengths and Limitations

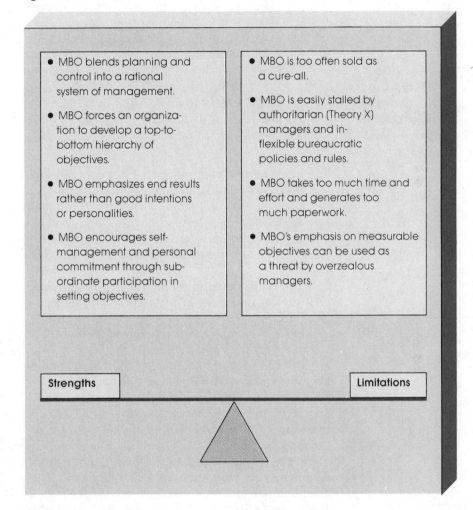

- MBO blends planning and control into a rational system of management.

- MBO forces an organization to develop a top-to-bottom hierarchy of objectives.

- MBO emphasizes end results rather than good intentions or personalities.

- MBO encourages self-management and personal commitment through subordinate participation in setting objectives.

- MBO is too often sold as a cure-all.

- MBO is easily stalled by authoritarian (Theory X) managers and inflexible bureaucratic policies and rules.

- MBO takes too much time and effort and generates too much paperwork.

- MBO's emphasis on measurable objectives can be used as a threat by overzealous managers.

Strengths

Limitations

Balancing MBO's Strengths Against Its Limitations   Any widely used management technique is bound to generate debate about its relative strengths and weaknesses, and MBO is no exception.[22] Four primary strengths of MBO and four common complaints about it are compared in Figure 4.6. Present and future managers are more apt to walk away with realistic expectations about MBO when they are familiar with both sides of this debate. It is important to note, however, that this debate is not likely to be resolved in the near future. Critics of MBO claim that its strengths are merely theoretical and that its limitations are a matter of practical fact. Conversely, MBO advocates are quick to point out that it is the misapplication of MBO that leads to problems and that the MBO concept itself is not to blame. In the final analysis, MBO will probably work when organizational conditions are favorable and will probably fail when those conditions are unfavorable.

Creating a Favorable Climate for MBO

Thanks to the widespread use of MBO, a number of important lessons have been learned about how to make MBO work. Managers thinking of adopting MBO are advised to consider the suitability of their organization in accordance with the following factors:[23,*]

- **Top management commitment.** Firm commitment of top managers to the success of an MBO program is essential because (1) objective setting begins at the top and filters down, and (2) top managers are influential role models for lower-level managers. High-level managers with a "do as I say, not as I do" attitude toward MBO virtually guarantee its failure.
- **A favorable environment for change.** Since MBO itself represents change, key managers should agree that constructive change is necessary if performance is to improve. Strong vested interests opposing change can doom an MBO program to failure before it gets off the ground.
- **A relatively open, nonthreatening environment.** Managers with a nonarbitrary, nonauthoritarian (Theory Y) style have a better chance than authoritarian or punitive managers do of generating the trust so necessary for participative objective setting.
- **Willingness of superior managers to share authority.** When subordinate managers are given the added responsibility of challenging objectives, their superiors must be willing to relinquish the necessary authority to get the job done.
- **Willing and able subordinates.** MBO cannot succeed without subordinate managers who are both willing and able to assume the burden of added responsibility and authority.
- **Willingness of subordinate managers to accept objective measurements of their jobs.** Managers at all levels must be willing to be held accountable for "hard" results. A prevailing attitude of "My job is different, it can't be measured" effectively undermines MBO's objectivity.
- **Willingness to comply with procedural requirements.** Because an MBO program means a net increase in paperwork (for example, formally written, typed, cross-tabulated, and filed objectives), managers need to

*Adapted by permission from Richard Babcock and Peter Sorensen, Jr., "An MBO Checklist: Are Conditions Right for Implementation?" *Management Review*, June 1979 (New York: AMACOM, a division of American Management Associations, 1979), pp. 59–62.

believe that today's added work will pay off in improved performance tomorrow.

- **An environment predictable enough for planning.** Organizations that hang by the thread of unpredictable day-to-day orders are too unstable for MBO's typical one-year planning horizon.

By reviewing these situational factors, it quickly becomes apparent why MBO is not a cure-all. Too many unfavorable factors in the organizational climate can kill an otherwise well-designed and well-intentioned MBO program.

Graphic Planning/Scheduling/Control Tools

Management science specialists have introduced needed precision to the planning/control cycle through graphical analysis. Three graphical tools for planning, scheduling, and controlling operations are flow charts, Gantt charts, and PERT networks.

Sequencing with Flow Charts

Although flow charts achieved their greatest popularity among computer programmers,[24] they are readily adaptable to general management. A **flow chart** is a graphical device for sequencing significant events and yes-or-no decisions. Sequencing simply is arranging events in the order of desired occurrence. For instance, this book had to be purchased before it could be read. Thus the event "purchase book" would come before the event "read book" in a flow chart sequence.

A sample flow chart is given in Figure 4.7. Notice that the chart consists of boxes and diamonds in addition to the start and stop ovals. Each box contains a major event, and each diamond contains a yes-or-no decision.

Managers at all levels and in all specialized areas can identify and properly sequence important events and decisions with flow charts of this kind. In doing so, they are forced to consider all relevant links in a particular endeavor as well as their proper sequence. This is an advantage because it encourages analytical thinking. But flow charts have two disadvantages. First, they do not indicate the time dimension, that is, the varying amounts of time that may be required to complete each step and make each decision. Second, flow charts are not practical for complex situations in which several activities are taking place at once.

Scheduling with Gantt Charts

Scheduling is important to planning. In projects where later steps depend on the successful completion of earlier steps, schedules help managers determine when and where human and material resources are needed. Without schedules, inefficiency creeps in as equipment and people stand

Figure 4.7 A Sample Flow Chart

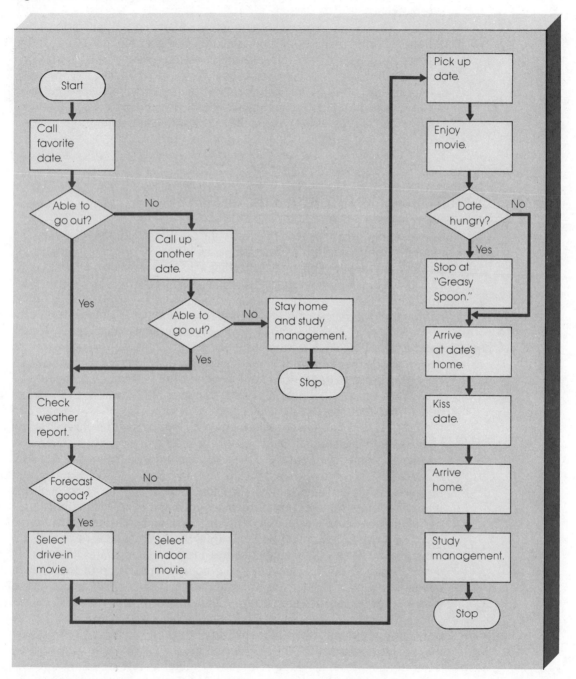

idle. Also, like any type of plan or budget, schedules provide management with a measuring stick for corrective action. Gantt charts, named for Henry L. Gantt who developed the technique, are a convenient scheduling tool for managers.[25] Gantt worked with Frederick W. Taylor at Midvale Steel beginning in 1887 and, as discussed in Chapter 2, helped refine the practice of scientific management. A **Gantt chart** is a graphical scheduling technique typically applied to production operations. According to a management historian, "The [Gantt] chart shows output on one axis with units of time on the other. Nothing could be simpler, yet at the time nothing could have been more revolutionary in the area of production control."[26] Things have changed since the early 1900s, and so have Gantt chart applications. Updated versions of Gantt charts like the one in Figure 4.8 are widely used today for planning and scheduling all sorts of organizational activities.

Figure 4.8 also shows how a Gantt chart can be used for more than just scheduling the important steps of a job. By filling in the time lines, *actual* progress can be compared easily with *planned* progress. Like flow charts, Gantt charts have the advantage of forcing managers to be analytical, since jobs or projects must be reduced to separate steps. Moreover, Gantt charts improve on flow charts by allowing the planner to specify the *time* to be spent on each activity. A disadvantage that Gantt charts share with flow charts is that overly complex situations are difficult to chart.

PERT Networks   The more complex a project, the greater the need for reliable sequencing and scheduling of key activities. Simultaneous sequencing and scheduling amounts to programming, and one of the most popular programming tools used by managers is a technique referred to simply as PERT. An acronym for Program Evaluation and Review Technique, **PERT** is a graphic sequencing and scheduling tool for large, complex, and nonroutine projects.

History of PERT   PERT was developed in 1958 by a team of management consultants for the U.S. Navy Special Projects Office. At the time, the navy was faced with the seemingly insurmountable task of building a missile that could be fired underwater from the deck of a submarine. PERT not only contributed to the development of the Polaris submarine project, but it also was credited with helping bring the sophisticated weapon system to combat readiness nearly two years ahead of schedule. Needless to say, news of this dramatic administrative feat caught the attention of managers around the world. But, as one user of PERT reflected: "No management technique has ever caused so much enthusiasm, controversy, and disappointment as PERT."[27] Realizing that PERT is not a panacea, but rather a specialized planning and control tool that can be appropriately or inappropriately applied, helps managers accept it at face value.

Figure 4.8 A Sample Gantt Chart

Job: Build 3 dozen electric golf carts   Period covered: 8/1 to 8/25

Step	Week #1 1 2 3 4 5	Week #2 8 9 10 11 12	Week #3 15 16 17 18 19	Week #4 22 23 24 25 26
1. Prepare blueprints.	▓			
2. Purchase parts.	▓▓▓			
3. Fabricate fiberglass bodies.	▓▓▓▓▓▓			
4. Fabricate frames.	▓▓			
5. Build drive trains.		▓▓		
6. Assemble carts.			☐☐	
7. Test carts.				☐

Key: Planned ☐   Completed ▓

PERT Terminology Because PERT has its own special language, four key terms need to be defined and understood.

- **Event.** A **PERT event** is a performance milestone representing the start or finish of some activity. Handing in a difficult management exam is an *event*.
- **Activity.** A **PERT activity** represents work in process. Activities are time-consuming jobs that begin and end with an event. Studying for a management exam and taking the exam are *activitites*.
- **PERT time. PERT times** are estimated times for the completion of PERT activities. PERT times are weighted averages of three separate time estimates: (1) *optimistic time* (T_o)—the time an activity should take

under the best of conditions; (2) *most likely time* (T_m)—the time an activity should take under normal conditions; and (3) *pessimistic time* (T_p)—the time an activity should take under the worst possible conditions. The formula for calculating *estimated* PERT time (T_e) is

$$T_e = \frac{T_o + 4T_m + T_p}{6}$$

- **Critical path.** The **critical path** is the most time-consuming chain of activities and events in a PERT network. In other words, the longest path through a PERT network is critical because if any of the activities along it are delayed, the entire project will be delayed accordingly.[28]

PERT in Action   A PERT network is shown in Figure 4.9. The task in this example, the design and construction of three dozen customized golf carts for use by physically disabled adults, is relatively simple for instructional purposes. PERT networks are usually reserved for more complex projects with dozens or even hundreds of activities. PERT events are coded by circled letters, and PERT activities, shown by the lines connecting the PERT events, are coded by number. A PERT time (T_e) has been calculated and recorded for each PERT activity.

See if you can pick out the critical path in the PERT network in Figure 4.9. By calculating which path will take the most time from beginning to end, the critical path turns out to be A-B-C-F-G-H-I. This particular chain of activities and events will require an estimated 21¾ workdays to complete. The overall duration of the project is dictated by the critical path, and a delay in any of the activities along this critical path will delay the entire project.

Positive and Negative Aspects of PERT   During the quarter century that PERT has been used in a wide variety of settings, both its positive and negative aspects have become apparent.

On the plus side, PERT is an excellent scheduling tool for large, non-routine projects, ranging from constructing an electric generation station to planning an organization's move into a new office building. But it is inappropriate for repetitive assembly-line operations in which scheduling is dictated by the pace of machines. PERT is a helpful planning aid because it forces managers to analyze projects in their entirety. It also gives them a tool for predicting resource needs, potential problem areas, and the impact of delays on project completion. If an activity runs over or under its estimated time, its ripple effect of lost or gained time on downstream activities can be calculated. PERT also gives managers an opportunity, through the calculation of optimistic and pessimistic times, to factor in realistic uncertainties about planning horizons.

Figure 4.9 A Sample PERT Network

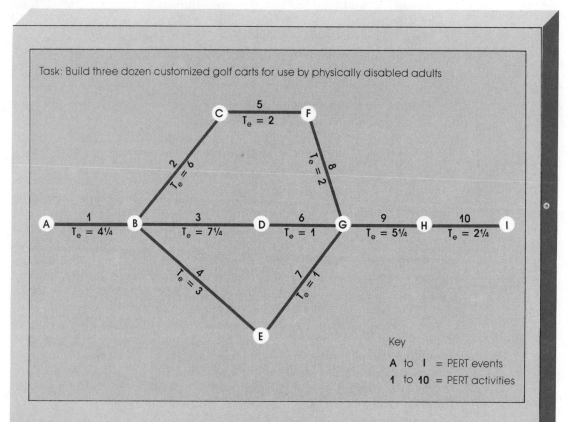

Task: Build three dozen customized golf carts for use by physically disabled adults

Key

A to I = PERT events
1 to 10 = PERT activities

PERT Events

A. Receive contract.
B. Begin construction.
C. Receive parts.
D. Bodies ready for testing.
E. Frames ready for testing.
F. Drive trains ready for testing.
G. Components ready for assembly.
H. Carts assembled.
I. Carts ready for shipment.

PERT Activites and Times

Activities	T_o	T_m	T_p	T_e*
1. Prepare final blueprints.	3	4	6	4¼
2. Purchase parts.	4	5	12	6
3. Fabricate bodies.	5	7½	9	7¼
4. Fabricate frames.	2½	3	4	3
5. Build drive trains.	1½	2	3	2
6. Test bodies.	½	1	1½	1
7. Test frames.	½	1	1½	1
8. Test drive trains.	1	1½	5	2
9. Assemble carts.	3	5	9	5¼
10. Test carts.	1	2	5	2¼

*Rounded to nearest ¼ workday

On the minus side, PERT shares with other planning and decision-making aids the disadvantage of being only as good as its underlying assumptions. In the case of PERT, false assumptions about activities and events and miscalculations of PERT times can render it ineffective. Despite the objective impression of numerical calculations, PERT times are derived rather subjectively. Also, PERT has been criticized for being too time consuming. A complex PERT network prepared by hand may be obsolete by the time it is completed, and frequent updates can tie PERT in knots. Commercially available computerized PERT packages are a must for complex projects, as they can greatly speed the graphic plotting process and update time estimates.[29]

Break-even Analysis

In well-managed businesses, profit is a forethought rather than an afterthought. A widely used tool for projecting profits relative to costs and sales volume is break-even analysis.[30] In fact, break-even analysis is often referred to as cost-volume-profit analysis. By using either the algebraic method or the graphical method, planners can calculate the break-even point. The **break-even point** is the level of sales at which the firm neither suffers a loss nor realizes a profit. In effect, the break-even point is the profit-making threshold. If sales are below that point, the organization loses money. If sales go beyond the break-even point, it makes a profit. Break-even points, as discussed later, are often expressed in units. For example, Chrysler Corporation began to win its battle against bankruptcy in 1982 when severe cost-cutting measures "... lowered Chrysler's North American breakeven point by 50% to 1.1 million vehicles."[31]

From a procedural standpoint, a critical part of break-even analysis is separating fixed costs from variable costs.

Fixed Versus Variable Costs

Some expenses have to be paid even if a firm fails to sell a single unit. Other expenses are incurred only as units are produced and sold. The former are called fixed costs, and the latter are termed variable costs. **Fixed costs** are contractual costs that must be paid regardless of the level of output or sales. Typical examples include rent, utilities, insurance premiums, managerial and professional staff salaries, property taxes, and licenses. **Variable costs** are costs that vary directly with the firm's production and sales. Common variable costs include costs of production (such as labor, materials, and supplies), sales commissions, and product delivery expenses. As output/sales increase, fixed costs remain the same but variable costs accumulate. Looking at it another way, fixed costs are a function of *time,* and variable costs are a function of *volume*. Once these two kinds of costs have been identified, it is possible to calculate the break-even point.

The Algebraic Method

Relying on the following labels,

$$FC = \text{total fixed costs}$$
$$P = \text{price (per unit)}$$
$$VC = \text{variable costs (per unit)}$$
$$BEP = \text{break-even point}$$

the formula for calculating break-even point (in units) is

$$BEP \text{ (in units)} = \frac{FC}{P - VC}$$

The difference between the selling price *P* and per unit variable costs *VC* is referred to as the contribution margin. In other words, the **contribution margin** is the portion of the unit selling price above and beyond the variable costs that can be applied to fixed costs. Above the break-even point, the contribution margin contributes to profits as well as to fixed costs.

Variable costs are normally expressed as a percentage of the unit selling price. As a working example of how the break-even point (in units) can be calculated, assume that a firm has total fixed costs of $30,000, a unit selling price of $7, and variable costs of 57 percent (or $4 in round numbers):

$$BEP \text{ (in units)} = \frac{30,000}{7 - 4} = 10,000$$

This calculation shows that 10,000 units will have to be produced and sold at $7 each if the firm is to break even on this particular product.

Price Planning Break-even analysis is an excellent "what if" tool for planners who want to know what impact price changes will have on profit. For instance, what would the break-even point be if the unit selling price was lowered to match a competitor's price of $6?

$$BEP \text{ (in units)} = \frac{30,000}{6 - 4} = 15,000$$

In this case, a $1 drop in price to $6 means that 15,000 units will have to be produced before a profit can be realized.

Profit Planning It is common practice to set profit objectives and work backward to determine the required level of output. Break-even analysis greatly assists planners in this regard. The modified break-even formula for profit planning is

Figure 4.10   Graphical Break-even Analysis

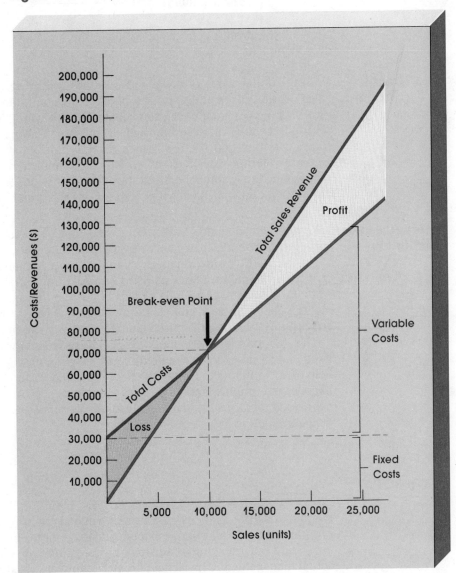

$$BEP \text{ (in units)} = \frac{FC + \text{desired profit}}{P - VC}$$

Assuming that top management has set a profit objective for the year at $30,000 and that the original figures above apply, the following calculation would result:

$$BEP \text{ (in units)} = \frac{30,000 + 30,000}{7 - 4} = 20,000$$

To meet the profit objective of $30,000, the company would need to sell 20,000 units at $7 each.

The Graphical Method

With the dollar value of costs and revenues on the vertical axis and unit sales on the horizontal axis, the break-even point can be calculated by plotting lines for fixed costs, total costs (fixed + variable costs), and total revenue. As illustrated in Figure 4.10, the break-even point is where the total costs line and the total sales revenue line intersect. Although the algebraic method does the same job as the graphical method, some planners prefer the graphical method because it provides a convenient visual aid for detecting various cost-volume-profit relationships at a glance.

Strengths and Limitations of Break-even Analysis

Like the other planning tools discussed in this chapter, break-even analysis is not a cure-all. It has both strengths and limitations.

On the positive side, break-even analysis forces planners to interrelate cost, volume, and profit in a realistic way. All three variables are connected so that a change in one sends ripples of change through the other two. As mentioned, break-even analysis allows planners to ask "what if" questions concerning the impact of price changes and varying profit objectives.

The chief problem with break-even analysis is that the neat separation of fixed and variable costs can be difficult. General managers should get the help of accountants to isolate relevant fixed and variable costs. Moreover, because of complex factors in supply and demand, break-even analysis is not a good tool for setting prices. It serves better as a general planning and decision-making aid.

Summary

Planning has been labeled the primary management function because it sets the stage for all other aspects of management. Recent research has uncovered the following trends in corporate planning: more planners with actual management experience; greater teamwork, customizing, and flexibility; and more translation of broad strategies into how-to-do-it plans. Along with many other practical reasons for planning, two conceptual reasons for planning are limited resources and an uncertain environment. To cope with environmental uncertainty, organizations can respond as defenders, prospectors, analyzers, or reactors.

A properly written plan tells what, when, and how something is to be accomplished. Clearly written organizational mission statements tend to serve as a useful focal point for the planning process. Strategic, intermediate, and operational plans are formulated by top, middle, and lower-level management, respectively. Objectives have been called the single most important feature of the planning process. Well-written objectives spell out in measurable terms what should be accomplished and when it is to be accomplished. Good objectives help managers by serving as targets, acting as measuring sticks, encouraging commitment, and strengthening motivation. Objective setting begins at the top of the organization and filters down, thus forming a means-ends chain. Priorities affect resource allocation by assigning relative importance to objectives. Plans are formulated and executed as part of a more encompassing planning/control cycle.

Management by objectives (MBO) is an approach to planning and controlling that is based on measurable and participatively set objectives. MBO basically consists of four steps: (1) set objectives participatively, (2) develop action plans, (3) periodically reevaluate objectives and plans and monitor performance, and (4) conduct annual performance appraisals. Objective setting in MBO flows from top to bottom. MBO has both strengths and limitations and requires a supportive climate favorable to change, participation, and the sharing of authority.

Flow charts, Gantt charts, and PERT networks are three graphical tools for more effectively planning, scheduling, and controlling operations. Flow charts visually sequence important events and yes-or-no decisions. Gantt charts, named for F. W. Taylor's disciple Henry L. Gantt, are a graphical scheduling technique used in a wide variety of situations. Although both flow charts and Gantt charts have the advantage of forcing managers to be analytical, Gantt charts realistically portray the time dimension, whereas flow charts do not. PERT, which stands for Program Evaluation and Review Technique, is a sequencing and scheduling tool appropriate for large, complex, and nonroutine projects. Weighted PERT times enable management to factor in their uncertainties about time estimates.

Break-even analysis, or cost-volume-profit analysis, can be carried out algebraically or graphically. Either way, it helps planners gauge the potential impact of price changes and profit objectives on sales volume. A major limitation of break-even analysis is that specialized accounting knowledge is required to identify relevant fixed and variable costs.

Terms to Understand

Planning	Strategic planning
Plan	Intermediate planning

Operational planning   PERT event
Planning horizon   PERT activity
Objective   PERT time
Priorities   Critical path
Management by objectives (MBO)   Break-even point
Flow chart   Fixed costs
Gantt chart   Variable costs
PERT   Contribution margin

Questions for Discussion

1. Why is planning the primary management function and why is it particularly important today?
2. What are the advantages and disadvantages of responding to the environment as a defender, a prospector, an analyzer, or a reactor?
3. Can you write five good objectives for things you intend to accomplish in the next six months? Does each pass the three tests of a good objective?
4. Why is it important to establish priorities when planning?
5. What is the relationship between planning and control?
6. What behavioral principles should managers keep in mind when appraising performance under MBO?
7. What does the research on goal setting tell us from the point of view of motivation?
8. What advantage do Gantt charts have over flow charts?
9. How do PERT networks help managers cope with uncertain timing?
10. In pursuing a college degree, what are the student's major fixed and variable costs? (*Note:* Consider the number of credit hours taken as units of output/sales.)

Back to the Opening Case

Now that you have read Chapter 4, you should be able to answer the following questions about the People Express case:

1. Considering the nature of the highly competive commercial airline business, is People Express a defender, prospector, analyzer, or reactor? Explain.
2. What does the ranking of People Express's six precepts say about the firm's priorities? Do you agree with this ranking? Explain.

3. What has Burr done to help ensure that all People Express managers identify with and are committed to the company's objectives?
4. What is People Express's "unit of output" and why is it helpful for management to know where the company's break-even point is?

Closing Case 4.2

Texaco's Turnaround

In the late 1960s, Texaco Inc. was the largest petroleum firm in the United States. It was the most profitable of the major petroleum companies and was among the largest holders of U.S. oil and gas reserves. Operating from an assumption established in the 1950s that there was a virtually limitless supply of cheap crude oil, Texaco's long-term strategy for the 1960s and beyond called for minimal exploration with emphasis on the establishment of a strong nationwide refining and marketing network. Diversification into nonpetroleum-related businesses played no part in this strategy. Texaco's management had a reputation for being centralized, introverted, and inflexible. Augustus C. Long., a strong-willed Texas oilman who reportedly surrounded himself with "yes" men, served as chairman during the 1960s, retiring in 1971. A man with a reputation for being domineering and tightfisted, Long assumed sole responsibility for strategic planning which was carried out on an ad hoc basis.

Texaco's strategy of minimal exploration, heavy emphasis on refining and marketing, and no diversification was dealt a severe blow by the 1973 OPEC oil embargo. It is ironic that rapidly rising oil prices caused Texaco's appraised net worth to increase nearly 12 percent annually during the 1970s, while at the same time the firm dropped to seventh among the majors by 1978. And Texaco's U.S. reserves of oil and gas dropped more sharply during the 1970s than those of all other majors.

Texaco's New Game Plan

A surge in profits resulting from the shutdown of Iranian oil fields and subsequent price increases gave Texaco some breathing room in 1980 to reposition itself. Upon being promoted from president to chairman and chief executive officer in November 1980, John K. McKinley wasted no time implementing Texaco's turnaround strategy. Texaco's new game plan called for broader emphasis on the entire energy business, recognizing that oil was a dying industry because of the eventual depletion of fossil fuels. Doing what its competitors had done five to ten years earlier, Texaco planned to siphon cash from its oil business into high-technology alternative sources of energy. Synthetic fuels were to be Texaco's new thrust for the 1990s and beyond. In the meantime, Texaco planned to devote two-thirds of its capital expenditures to exploration for more oil and gas, thus bolstering its sagging reserves.

To accommodate stepped-up spending for exploration and the development of alternative energy technologies, the company began to prune its marketing network and staff. From 35,500 in 1974, the number of Texaco service stations was cut to 27,000 by late 1980. During the same time period, the marketing staff was reduced by almost 50 percent, from 9548 to 4950 individuals. Plans also were made to withdraw completely from 16 states where Texaco had lost its competitive efficiency. Nationwide marketing emphasis was shifted to a variety of high-volume, self-service outlets, complete with convenience stores and car washes.

A New Organizational Climate

To recover from setbacks attributed largely to its inflexibility, Texaco's new game plan called for a number of administrative and structural changes. Among them were:

- Recognition that plans have to be regularly updated.
- A streamlined decision-making process.
- Open communication among middle managers.
- A decentralization of power and responsibility to make the firm more responsive to economic and political changes.
- Bonuses based primarily on performance rather than strictly on seniority.
- Recruiting of new talent for all levels, instead of just for entry-level jobs.
- Open communication between top managers and the public.
- Rewarding entrepreneurship among staff employees.
- Creation of geographic profit centers to operate as separate yet coordinated businesses.
- Increased emphasis on strategic planning among top management (a planning model was created with a 15-year horizon to forecast the impact on the firm of economic and political changes and alternative strategies).

The result of these changes was that Texaco became a significantly more farsighted company in 1980 than it had been just a decade earlier.

A Bold Stroke

During the early 1980s, evidence of Texaco's new strategic direction and organizational climate began to appear. The drive toward decentralization and greater entrepreneurship paid off in 1982 when a team of local division managers took only four days to put together an $80 million deal involving oil and gas land. Such speed and flexibility simply would not have been possible at the old Texaco. The company's aggressive exploration program yielded mixed results from 1980 to 1983. A 100 million barrel discovery in California's Santa Maria Basin in 1982 was followed in late 1983 by a costly dry test hole in Alaska. Texaco's reserves continued to decline in spite of more aggressive exploration. Meanwhile, the world price for oil dropped as demand slowed.

During a couple of hectic days in January 1984, McKinley shook off what remained of Texaco's longstanding reputation as an inflexible, slow-moving company. In a highly-publicized action, Texaco purchased Getty Oil Co. for over $10 billion. The merger increased Texaco's assets from $27.2 billion to $40.3 billion, a 48 percent increase. More importantly, Texaco doubled its U.S. oil and gas reserves. Proponents of the giant merger claimed the match was perfect for the following reason: Getty had rich reserves but minimal refining capabilities whereas Texaco had shrinking reserves and a strong refining and distribution network. Critics charged that Texaco had paid too much for Getty. Noting that Texaco's cost of finding a barrel of oil had averaged about $12, top management claimed the $5-per-barrel price for Getty's reserves was a good deal. Following the merger, McKinley told *Business Week*: "Our basic strategy is that we're an international, world-wide, integrated oil and gas company."[32]

For Discussion

1. With respect to the categories of defender, prospector, analyzer, and reactor, what kinds of shifts has Texaco made in recent years?
2. What aspects of the new organizational climate instituted in 1980 would enable Texaco to have a good MBO program? Briefly explain why.
3. How did general environmental changes affect Texaco's mission and priorities during the 1970s and early 1980s? Were Texaco's responses appropriate? Explain.

References

Opening Quotation: Harold Koontz, "Making Strategic Planning Work," *Business Horizons* 19 (April 1976): 38.

Opening Case: Excerpted with permission from Lucien Rhodes, "That Daring Young Man and His Flying Machines," *Inc.* 6 (January 1984): 42–52.

Closing Case: For additional information on Texaco, see James Cook, "Rebuilding the House That Long Built," *Forbes* 121 (April 17, 1978): 47–54; "Texaco Restoring Luster to the Star," *Business Week* No. 2668 (December 22, 1980): 54–61; W. David Gibson, "Lighting a Fire Under Texaco," *Barron's* 63 (December 12, 1983): 6–7, 16–17; "Why Texaco Values Getty at $10 Billion,"

Business Week No. 2825 (January 23, 1984): 34–35; and Peter Nulty, "How Texaco Outfoxed Gordon Getty," *Fortune* 109 (February 6, 1984): 106–109.

1. For some interesting and thought-provoking ideas about managerial planning, see Karl E. Weick, "Misconceptions About Managerial Productivity," *Business Horizons* 26 (July-August 1983): 47–52.
2. Adapted from a more extensive list of results found in C. Don Burnett, Dennis P. Yeskey, and David Richardson, "New Roles for Corporate Planners in the 1980s," *The Journal of Business Strategy* 4 (Spring 1984): 64–68.
3. Bill Christiansen and Theodore H. Clark, Jr., "A Western Perspective on Energy: A Plea for Rational Energy Planning," *Science* 194 (November 5, 1976): 578.
4. See Raymond E. Miles and Charles C. Snow, *Organizational Strategy, Structure, and Process* (New York: McGraw-Hill, 1978), p. 29.
5. "Caterpillar: Sticking to Basics to Stay Competitive," *Business Week* No. 2686 (May 4, 1981): 74–80.
6. "When Marketing Failed at Texas Instruments," *Business Week* No. 2693 (June 22, 1981): 91–94.
7. Donald C. Hambrick, "Some Tests of the Effectiveness and Functional Attributes of Miles and Snow's Strategic Types," *Academy of Management Journal* 26 (March 1983): 24.
8. Edward Meadows, "Ford Needs Better Ideas—Fast," *Fortune* 101 (June 16, 1980): 83–84.
9. See "How Seagram is Scrambling to Survive 'The Sobering of America,'" *Business Week* No. 2858 (September 3, 1984): 94–95.
10. Roy A. Gentles, "Alcan's Integration of Management Techniques Raises Their Effectiveness," *Management Review* 73 (April 1984): 33.
11. Charles D. Flory, ed., *Managers for Tomorrow* (New York: NAL, 1965), p. 98.
12. Anthony P. Raia, *Managing by Objectives* (Glenview, Ill.: Scott, Foresman, 1974), p. 24.
13. For a useful summary of research in this area, see Gary P. Latham and Gary A. Yukl, "A Review of Research on the Application of Goal Setting in Organizations," *Academy of Management Journal* 18 (December 1975): 824–845.
14. See Peter F. Drucker, *The Practice of Management* (New York: Harper & Row, 1954).
15. For a brief history of MBO, see George S. Odiorne, "MBO: A Backward Glance," *Business Horizons* 21 (October 1978): 14–24. An excellent collection of readings on MBO may be found in George Odiorne, Heinz Weihrich, and Jack Mendleson, *Executive Skills: A Management by Objectives Approach* (Dubuque, Iowa: Wm. C. Brown, 1980).
16. Jack Bologna, "Why MBO Programs Don't Meet Their Goals," *Management Review* 69 (December 1980): 32.
17. Anthony P. Raia, *Managing by Objectives* (Glenview, Ill.: Scott, Foresman, 1974), p. 15.

18. Adapted from William E. Reif and John W. Newstrom, "Integrating MBO and OBM—A New Perspective," *Management by Objectives* 5, no. 2 (1975): 34–42.

19. For example, see John M. Ivancevich, "Changes in Performance in a Management by Objectives Program," *Administrative Science Quarterly* 19 (December 1974): 563–574. An instructive review of 185 MBO studies may be found in Jack N. Kondrasuk, "Studies in MBO Effectiveness," *Academy of Management Review* 6 (July 1981): 419–430.

20. Jan P. Muczyk, "Dynamics and Hazards of MBO Application," *The Personnel Administrator* 24 (May 1979): 52.

21. Based on Gary P. Latham and Gary A. Yukl: "A Review of Research on the Application of Goal Setting in Organizations," *Academy of Management Journal* 18 (December 1975): 824–845.

22. An interesting study of the positive and negative aspects of MBO may be found in Robert C. Ford and Frank S. McLaughlin, "Avoiding Disappointment in MBO Programs," *Human Resource Management* 21 (Summer 1982): 44–49.

23. Adapted from Richard Babcock and Peter F. Sorensen, Jr., "An MBO Checklist: Are Conditions Right for Implementation?" *Management Review* 68 (June 1979): 59–62.

24. Marilyn Bohl, *Flowcharting Techniques* (Chicago: Science Research Associates, 1971).

25. For examples of early Gantt charts, see H. L. Gantt, *Organizing for Work* (New York: Harcourt, Brace and Howe, 1919), chap. 8.

26. Claude S. George, Jr., *The History of Management Thought,* 2nd ed. (Englewood Cliffs, N.J.: Prentice-Hall, 1972), p. 104.

27. Ivars Avots, "The Management Side of PERT," *California Management Review* 4 (Winter 1962): 16–27.

28. Adapted from John Fertakis and John Moss, "An Introduction to PERT and PERT/Cost Systems," *Managerial Planning* 19 (January-February 1971): 24–31.

29. For a brief description of a computerized PERT package, see "Making Project Management Easy," *Datamation* 24 (April 1978): 47, 50.

30. For interesting and informative reading on the practical application of break-even analysis, see Robert T. Patterson, "Break-Even Analysis: Decision-Making Tool," *Food Service Marketing* 42 (April 1980): 39–42.

31. "The Banks Like Chrysler's Line," *Business Week* No. 2750 (August 2, 1982): 18.

32. "Why Texaco Values Getty at $10 Billion," p. 34.

Chapter 5

Strategic Management: Planning for Long-Term Success

The only limits are, as always, those of vision.
James Broughton

Chapter Objectives

When you finish studying this chapter, you should be able to

- Define the term *strategic management* and explain its relationship to strategic planning.
- Explain how the concept of synergy and product life cycles help managers think strategically.
- Identify and briefly explain the nature of Porter's three generic strategies.
- Identify and highlight the four steps in the strategic management process.
- Identify the three types of forecasts and explain the contibutions that informed judgment, surveys, and trend analysis can make to forecasting.
- Discuss the human dimension of strategic management in terms of logical incrementalism and dominant personalities.

Opening Case 5.1

McDonald's Strategy Chews Up the Competition

McDonald's Corporation epitomizes the fast-food industry. During the last three decades, the Oak Brook, Illinois firm has set the standards for the industry it has come to dominate. By serving nearly 17 million people every day in its 8000 restaurants worldwide, McDonald's recorded sales of $8.7 billion and net income of $343 million in 1983. In early 1984,

McDonald's controlled almost 42 percent of the U.S. fast-food hamburger market. Burger King and Wendy's trailed with 16 percent and 9 percent, respectively. To maintain this scale of operations, McDonald's serves an incredible 10 million pounds of systematically cooked beef patties each week.

Truly, McDonald's has come a long way since 1955 when its founder, the late Ray Kroc, a milkshake-mixer salesman, bought the nationwide rights to Mac and Dick McDonald's efficient little 15¢ hamburger stands in California. Kroc promptly opened his first McDonald's stand in Des Plaines, Illinois; and the rest, as they say, is history. McDonald's owes its present status as fast-food king to Kroc's uncomplicated meat-and-potatoes strategy. That strategy, still central to McDonald's operations, is based on rapid growth, convenient locations, and Kroc's motto: "quality, service, cleanliness, and value." Except for well-researched moves into Egg McMuffins and Chicken McNuggets, top management is still faithful to the meat-and-potatoes part of Kroc's successful strategy.

Not Everyone Is Smiling
In spite of McDonald's resounding success, the firm has its critics. According to *Barron's:*

> Skeptics wonder whether the company has simply become too big to maneuver quickly in the intensely competitive fast-food business. They worry that McDonald's is too timid in introducing new products, that it's locked into a saturated market replete with saturated fats. ...[1]

And *Business Week* has observed: "Critics say ... that the chain's high-quality image is slipping, its advertising is confused, and it has lost touch with the consumer."[2] The fact that members of the now mature baby boom generation are demanding a more diverse diet with less emphasis on red meats is a potential worry for McDonald's. As a sign of changing tastes and eating habits, the fastest growing restaurant segment in 1983 was Mexican foods. Wendy's responded to the call for something other than just hamburgers by adding salad bars and stuffed baked potatoes and by launching its new chain of Sisters Chicken & Biscuits restaurants in 1980. Burger King's management also is said to be contemplating something beyond the hamburger business.

Other observers contend that McDonald's child-oriented facilities and advertising do not lend themselves well to pursuing the expanding adult-dining market. Recent growth in two-paycheck families has increased the demand for a more sophisticated dining experience than a quick hamburger and fries. To complicate matters, increasingly aggressive advertising campaigns by competitors have jostled McDonald's. For example, McDonald's sued Burger King over ads boasting that Burger King broiled its hamburgers whereas McDonald's burgers were fried. After Burger King agreed to tone down its ads in an out-of-court settlement, the No. 2 burger seller reportedly claimed that it received millions of dollars of free publicity from the lawsuit. More recently, Wendy's got into the act by aggressively attacking both McDonald's and Burger King with its popular "Where's the beef?" campaign. McDonald's responded with a serious quality-oriented advertisement featuring stern John Houseman, but the ad was soon withdrawn because it did not mesh well with McDonald's standard "good times and family fun" image.

McDonald's competitors have followed up their aggressive advertising with aggressive growth. Burger King and Wendy's had combined growth of about 500 restaurants in the United States during 1984. Some industry observers believe that this tougher competition will inevitably erode McDonald's market share. However, the fact that McDonald's spends $3 in advertising to every $1 spent by Burger King is a significant plus.

Another stubborn thorn in McDonald's side is the widespread perception that low cost means low quality. Price cuts, such as the one in response to Burger King's 39¢ hamburger promotion, tend to worsen rather than improve this perception.

McDonald's Intends to Stay Number One

Those who criticize McDonald's apparently are unimpressed by the fact that the firm's quarterly profits have grown at a double-digit pace since its stock was first sold publicly in 1965. McDonald's positive cash flow will give it a $1 billion cash reserve by 1990. Moreover, the company's management ranks are experienced, highly motivated people who know a great deal about mass marketing, crew supervision, and real estate acquisition and management. In spite of McDonald's longstanding resistance to diversification, observers believe that the firm's managerial talents would carry over very nicely to a wide range of businesses.

Although many feel that the U.S. fast-food hamburger market is a mature one that has reached the saturation point, McDonald's still intends to grow by 500 restaurants a year. Two keys to maintaining this healthy growth are international markets and captive markets. By 1982, 20 percent of McDonald's sales and 15 percent of its profits were generated outside the United States. Countries targeted by McDonald's for aggressive growth are Canada, Australia, the United Kingdom, West Germany, and Japan. McDonald's plans for captive markets include military bases, universities and schools, hospitals, toll roads, and airports.

Amid complaints about being too conservative and slow to change, McDonald's continues to test market new items and modes of delivery to fine tune its proven formula for success. Several significant changes have in fact been made. Examples include a breakfast menu, Chicken McNuggets, McDonald's Playlands, and drive-thru window service. In spite of pressure from McDonald's franchise owners, management has long resisted "regionalizing" McDonald's menu (for example, offering grits in the Southeast or enchiladas in the Southwest). Industry observers have noted: "... McDonald's can't introduce a raft of new products without diluting its best-in-the-industry service and efficiency record."3 Mc-Donald's is committed to a high national standard of excellence so that the Big Mac served in 60 seconds in St. Louis is virtually the same as those served in 60 seconds in Honolulu or Miami.

(Discussion questions linking this case with the material you are about to read can be found at the end of this chapter.)

Strategic management serves as the cutting edge for the entire management process. Organizations like McDonald's that are guided by a coherent strategic framework tend to execute even the finest details of their mission in a coordinated fashion. For example, by strictly adhering to the rule that burgers left in the warming bin for more than ten minutes should be thrown away, every restaurant manager turns McDonald's strategic emphasis on "quality" into reality. Similarly, the 60-second rule translates McDonald's strategic goal of prompt and efficient service into reality. Without the guidance of a strategic management orientation, organization members tend to work at cross purposes and important things do not get accomplished. Because many people automatically assume that strategy is the exclusive domain of top-level management, something needs to be said about its relevance for those lower in the organization.

Question (from a management student who is ten to twenty years away from a top-level executive position): "If top managers formulate strategies and I'm headed for a supervisory or staff position, why should I care about strategic management?"

Answer: There are really three good reasons why staff specialists and managers at all levels need a general understanding of strategic management. First, in view of widespread criticism that American managers tend to be shortsighted, a strategic orientation encourages farsightedness (see Table 5.1). Second, employees who think in strategic terms tend to understand better how top managers think and why they make the decisions they do. In other words, the rationale behind executive policies and decisions is more apparent when things are put into a strategic perspective. McDonald's 60-second rule makes more sense when explained within the context of the firm's best-in-the-industry service strategy.

A third reason for promoting a broader understanding of strategic management relates to a recent planning trend discussed in the last chapter. Specifically, greater teamwork and cooperation throughout the planning/control cycle is eroding the traditional distinction between those who plan and those who execute plans. Today, more middle and lower-level man-

Table 5.1 Key Dimensions of Strategic Farsightedness

	Shortsighted	**Farsighted**
1. **Organizational strategy**	No formally documented strategies.	A formally written and communicated statement of long-term organizational mission.
2. **Competitive advantage**	"Follow the leader." No attention devoted to long-term competitive edge.	"Be the leader." Emphasis on gaining and holding a strategic competitive edge.
3. **Organizational structure**	Rigid structure emphasizing status quo, downward communication, and predictability.	Flexible structure encouraging change, upward and lateral communication, and adaptability.
4. **Research and development**	Emphasis on applying competitors' good ideas.	Heavy emphasis on developing new products and services and on innovations in production, marketing, and personnel management.
5. **Return**	Emphasis on short-term profits.	Emphasis on increased market share, growth, and future profit potential.
6. **Personnel administration**	Emphasis on stopgap hiring and training. Labor viewed as a commodity. Layoffs common.	Emphasis on long-term development of employees. Labor viewed as a valuable human resource. Layoffs seen as a last resort.
7. **Problem solving**	Emphasis on chasing symptoms and blaming scapegoats.	Emphasis on finding solutions to problems.
8. **Management style**	Emphasis on day-to-day fire fighting, owing to short-term orientation.	Multilevel strategic thinking that encourages managers to consider long-term implications of their actions and decisions.

agers and technical specialists are being asked to play a direct role in both formulating and executing long-term strategies. Consider the following example of how strategy is being taken out of the hands of planning specialists and forced down the line to operating managers who have practical hands-on experience:

At Millipore Corp., a maker of high-tech filtration systems, the planners are noticeably absent: [the] Chairman ... fired the company's six. Instead, "environmental" task forces of operating managers meet every 18 months to two years to brainstorm on what is happening in their markets and where those markets are likely to go in the next 5 to 10 years. This approach has enabled Millipore to keep apace of the increasingly demanding filtration needs of the semiconductor industry by introducing new technology.[4]

Thus, today's management student is not as far away from the strategic domain as he or she may think. The time to start thinking strategically is now.

This chapter defines strategic management, looks at ways to think strategically, explores the strategic management process, discusses forecasting, and examines the human side of strategic management.

Strategic Management = Strategic Planning + Implementation + Control

Strategic management is the ongoing process of ensuring a competitively superior fit between the organization and its ever-changing environment.[5] This particular perspective is the product of a historical evolution including budget control, long-range planning, and strategic planning.[6]

Significantly, strategic management does not do away with earlier, more restricted approaches. Rather, it synthesizes and coordinates all of them in a more systematic fashion. For example, take the relationship between strategic planning, as defined in Chapter 4, and strategic management. Recall that *strategic planning* is the process of determining how to pursue the organization's long-term goals with the resources expected to be available. Notice that nothing is said in this definition about adjustment or control. But, just as astronauts and space scientists need to make midflight corrections to ensure that space shuttles reach their destinations, strategic adjustment and control are necessary. The more encompassing strategic management concept is useful today because it effectively blends strategic planning, implementation, and control.

Given today's competitive pressures, management cannot afford to let ponderous strategic plans sit on the shelf collecting dust, as was too often the case during the 1970s. Managers who adopt a strategic management perspective appreciate that strategic plans are "living documents" that require systematic updating and fine tuning as conditions change (for example, see Table 5.2).

Table 5.2 How Intel Corporation Keeps Its Strategic Plans on Track

Andrew S. Grove, President, Intel Corp., a leading high-tech electronics company:

At Intel, we put ourselves through an annual strategic long-range planning effort in which we examine our future five years off. But what is really being influenced here? It is the *next year*—and only the next year. We will have another chance to replan the second of the five years in the next year's long-range planning meeting, when that year will become the first of the five. So, keep in mind that you implement only that portion of a plan that lies within the time window between you and the next time you go through the exercise. Everything else you can look at again. We should also be careful not to plan too frequently, allowing ourselves time to judge the impact of the decisions we made and to determine whether our decisions were on the right track or not. In other words, we need the feedback that will be indispensable to our planning the next time around.

SOURCE: Andrew S. Grove, *High Output Management* (New York: Random House, 1983), p. 109.

The strategic management process is discussed in detail later in this chapter. But first, we need to consider some practical ways to encourage strategic thinking.

Thinking Strategically

Effective strategic management involves more than just following a few easy steps. It requires managers to think strategically, to develop the ability to see things in motion, and to make sense out of a cloudy and uncertain future by seeing the *interdependency* of key factors. This ability requires more than a passing awareness of significant social, political/legal, economic and technological trends (like those discussed in Chapter 3). Managers who think strategically are able to envision their organizations in the context of world trends and events and to spot important interdependencies. They focus on how their organization should act and react to emerging opportunities and obstacles. As two strategic planning experts have cautioned, "... with diminishing resources, world competition, and rising costs, even the most efficient operations may no longer survive the handicap of operating without a clear, strategic direction. Today's company must formulate a clear strategy from which effective operations flow."[7]

There is also a selfish reason for becoming a better strategic thinker—it can be good for one's managerial career. For example, the chairman of Avon Products Inc. has been quoted as saying: "Those who succeed in thinking strategically and executing strategically are the people who are going to move ahead at this company. ..."[8] Although some people seem to have a special gift for being able to perceive meaningful patterns in complex circumstances, strategic thinking (the ability to identify important organization/environment interdependencies) can be learned through practice. Three helpful tools for strategic thinking are the concepts of synergy and product life cycles and Porter's generic strategies.

Synergy
Although the term *synergy* may not be familiar to many, it is a valuable and well-established concept. **Synergy** occurs when two variables (for example, chemicals, drugs, people, organizations) interact to produce an effect greater than the sum of the effects of the two variables acting independently. Some choose to call this the $2 + 2 = 5$ effect; others prefer to say that with synergy, the whole is greater than the sum of its parts. Whichever definition one prefers is not important as long as one appreciates the significance of interdependency in synergistic relationships. In strategic management, managers are urged to achieve as much *market, cost, technology,* and *management* synergy[9] as possible when making strategically important choices such as those regarding mergers, acquisitions, new products, new technology or production processes, or executive replacement. Each of these four variations of synergy makes its own contribution to both strategic thinking and, ultimately, to organizational health.

Market Synergy   When one product or service fortifies the sales of one or more others, market synergy has been achieved. Sears, Roebuck clearly ranks as one of the masters of market synergy. "In the ultimate one-stop shopping, it is now possible at many Sears stores to buy a house, pick all the needed furniture and appliances and then take out insurance on the whole bundle."[10] And on their way to the hardware department, Sears customers can buy stocks and bonds at stores that have Dean Witter Reynolds Financial Service centers.

Cost Synergy   This second type of synergy can occur in almost every dimension of organized activity. When two or more products can be designed by the same engineers, produced in the same facilities, distributed through the same channels, or sold by the same salespeople, overall costs will be lower than if each product received separate treatment all down the line. In an interesting example of cost synergy, a number of U.S. railroads are making extra dollars by permitting telecommunications companies to lay fiber optics cables along their rights-of-way. "Amtrak, under a 25-year agreement with MCI on the Washington-New York corridor, is getting $4.4 million plus use of the cable for its internal communications."[11] Cost synergy also can be achieved by recycling by-products that would normally be thrown away.

Technological Synergy   The third variety of synergy involves the transfer of technology from one application to another, thus opening up new markets. For example, Alfa-Laval, a Swedish manufacturing company specializing in centrifugal separators, recently broadened its market base through technological synergy.

> ... Alfa designed a separator to remove yeast particles from beer. Brewers were uninterested, but genetic researchers were fascinated: With some modifications, the same equipment is well-suited for preparing cells and harvesting bacteria in genetic research.[12]

Thanks to this sort of technological synergy, profitable new markets can be tapped without the expense of developing totally new products.

Management Synergy   Somewhat parallel to the idea of technological synergy, management synergy requires knowledge transfer. Management synergy would be achieved, for example, if a hospital with a weak accounting department hired a new president with a strong accounting background. Ideally, the new president would be able to transfer his or her technical skills to good advantage.

Considered together, it may be difficult, if not impossible, to take advantage of all four types of synergy when developing new strategies. Nonetheless, strategies are more likely to be realistic and effective if all four types of synergy are given due consideration as early as possible.

**Product Life
Cycles**   Those who advocate a contingency approach to management believe that strategies should be derived from the situation at hand instead of from fixed rules or principles. This is sound advice, considering the acceleration of change in recent years. Product life cycles (PLCs) are a very useful contingency management tool for strategists.[13] In addition to making managers aware of interdependencies among operating areas like research and development, production, finance, and marketing, PLCs force managers to consider the *timing* of their efforts. As time passes, circumstances inside and outside the organization change. Thus strategies need to be updated and reformulated accordingly. PLCs offer management a rational sequencing pattern for strategic updating.

What Is a Product Life Cycle?   A **product life cycle** is a graphic representation of the sequential rise and fall of a product's sales and profit. The PLC in Figure 5.1 is typical, though one should not infer from Figure 5.1 that the four stages of the PLC—introduction, growth, maturity, and decline—all last the same length of time. For instance, IBM's highly successful 360 Series of computers had a growth period of several years following a comparatively shorter introduction period. Also, the overall length of

Figure 5.1 Tying Strategy to the Product Life Cycle

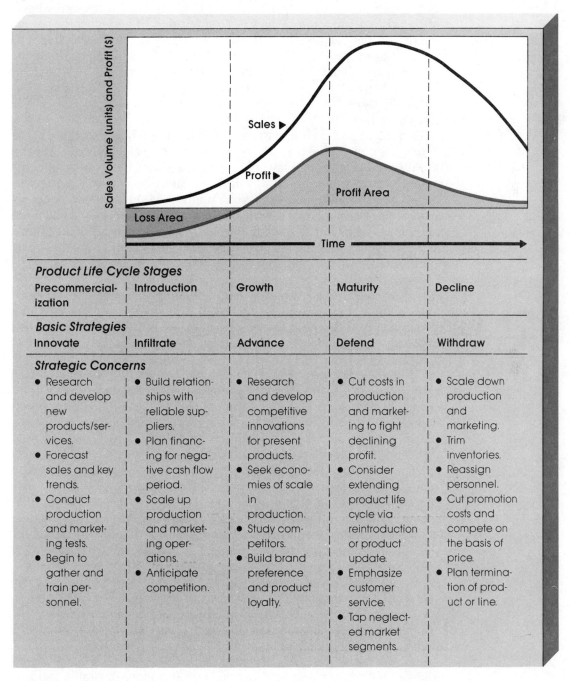

Product Life Cycle Stages				
Precommercial-ization	Introduction	Growth	Maturity	Decline
Basic Strategies				
Innovate	Infiltrate	Advance	Defend	Withdraw
Strategic Concerns				
• Research and develop new products/services. • Forecast sales and key trends. • Conduct production and marketing tests. • Begin to gather and train personnel.	• Build relationships with reliable suppliers. • Plan financing for negative cash flow period. • Scale up production and marketing operations. • Anticipate competition.	• Research and develop competitive innovations for present products. • Seek economies of scale in production. • Study competitors. • Build brand preference and product loyalty.	• Cut costs in production and marketing to fight declining profit. • Consider extending product life cycle via reintroduction or product update. • Emphasize customer service. • Tap neglected market segments.	• Scale down production and marketing. • Trim inventories. • Reassign personnel. • Cut promotion costs and compete on the basis of price. • Plan termination of product or line.

PLCs vary from product to product. Fad items like hula hoops and pet rocks may complete a full product cycle in six months, whereas the cycle for Rolls Royce automobiles may last for decades. PLCs reflect the unique nature and market potential of given products and services. One safe generalization about PLCs is that they probably will speed up in the coming years. Experts attribute this trend to the microelectronics revolution considered in Chapter 3. It has been observed that "except for commodity-type items, mature industries will be forced to march to a faster drummer."[14]

We need to make an important introductory point about the PLC in Figure 5.1, concerning the five categories of strategic concerns. Though they do in fact come into play in the sequence listed, each set of concerns requires advance attention. Lead times for short-cycle goods or services are necessarily short, although a year or more of lead time may be appropriate for a long-cycle item. In other words, a management team that waits for profits to begin heading downward (thus signaling the end of the growth stage) before plotting a defensive strategy for the maturity stage is being shortsighted.

The Precommercialization Dilemma   Although the precommercialization stage is technically not part of the PLC, it deserves special attention here because the research and development (R&D) conducted during this early stage generates the innovation needed for potentially marketable goods and services. After two decades of slumping R&D expenditures in the United States, private-sector spending has been on the increase in recent years. While this trend is generally good news, it presents today's strategists with a troublesome dilemma. On one hand, long-term investments with no immediate or guaranteed payoff are unattractive, given scarce resources and high interest rates. But on the other hand, failure to adequately fund basic research today may mean the loss of future domestic and foreign competitiveness. Strategists are thus faced with a difficult trade-off between short-term costs and long-term benefits.

Strategy During the Product Life Cycle   Many hitherto unknown factors may arise as strategists shift their attention to the PLC's successive stages. The introduction, or infiltration, stage, with its sluggish early sales, is a particularly risky time because large cash outlays for supplies, facilities, and wages are not offset by cash receipts. Compounding the negative cash-flow problem during the PLC's introductory stage is the threat of a product's failure: the rejection of a new product or service in the marketplace can be very costly. Ford Motor Company reportedly lost around $350 million on its Edsel car, which proved a dismal flop in the 1950s.

However, contrary to the popular notion that nine out of ten new products fail, recent research has uncovered a more favorable ratio. A study of 148 medium- and large-sized manufacturers revealed that roughly one out of every three new products introduced during the late 1970s failed.[15] Improved or modified versions of existing products were not included in the study. But even a one-out-of-three risk of new product failure underscores the need for intelligent product introduction strategies.

In the PLC's growth stage, management faces an interesting problem. Large profit margins and limited competition can easily lull management into believing that things will remain the same. But it is precisely during a product's most profitable stage of the PLC that the seeds of its destruction often are sown. Detroit's Big Three auto makers fell into this trap during the mid-1970s when they underestimated the threat of Japanese imports.

Strategy for the maturity stage necessarily focuses on trimming costs and promoting efficiencies because of the erosion of profit margins by the competition. As both sales and profits fall rapidly during the decline stage, withdrawal plans should ensure that the organization is not burdened with unusable raw materials, supplies, or facilities; idle labor; and a large inventory of unmarketable finished goods. All operations are appropriately scaled down during the decline stage, thus making way for new products.

Product life cycles, in spite of their varying time frames, are a helpful tool for encouraging managers at all levels to think strategically. Simply recognizing that the birth, maturation, decline, and death cycle of each product offering is inevitable encourages managers to update their strategies instead of believing that they are dealing with final answers.

**Porter's
Generic
Competitive
Strategies**

According to Michael Porter, a Harvard University economist specializing in strategy, competitive business strategies fall into three basic categories. Porter's three generic strategies are: (1) overall cost leadership, (2) differentiation, and (3) focus.[16] As shown in Figure 5.2, the focus strategy consists of some combination of the first two strategies. But the focus strategy aims at a particular market segment, whereas the overall cost leadership and differentiation strategies are directed industrywide. This straightforward and uncomplicated breakdown is widely accepted among strategic management experts. Like the concepts of synergy and product life cycle, Porter's model helps managers to think strategically; that is, it enables them to see the big picture regarding the organization and its changing environment. Each of Porter's three generic strategies deserves a closer look.

Overall Cost Leadership Strategy   Managers pursuing this strategy have an overriding concern for keeping costs, and therefore prices, lower than those of competitors. Normally, this means extensive production or service facilities with efficient economies of scale (low unit costs of making products or delivering services). Productivity improvement is a high pri-

Figure 5.2 Porter's Generic Competitive Strategies

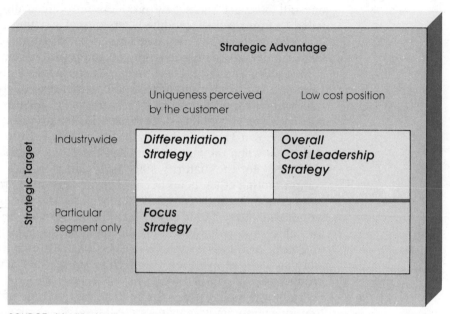

SOURCE: Modified with permission of The Free Press, a division of MacMillan, Inc. from *Competitive Strategy* by Michael Porter. Copyright © 1980 by The Free Press.

ority for managers following the cost leadership strategy. For example, in mid-1983, Apple Computer Inc. made the following cost-cutting move while trying to stay price competitive with IBM.

> Apple Computer ... reduced the number of chips that it needs to assemble its Apple II computer from 110 in the original model to 31 in the Apple IIe—reducing manufacturing costs by 35%, the company claims. Apple can now make the best-selling Apple IIe, which has a suggested list price of $1,395, for about $200 each. ..."[17]

This preoccupation with minimizing costs flows beyond production into virtually all areas such as purchasing, wages, overhead, research and development, advertising, and selling. A relatively large market share is required to accommodate this high volume, low profit margin strategy.

Differentiation Strategy In order for this strategy to succeed, a company's product or service must be perceived to be unique by most of the customers in its industry. The product must stand out from the crowd, so to speak. Specialized design (BMW automobiles), a widely recognized brand (Crest toothpaste), leading-edge technology (Intel Corp.), or reliable service (Caterpillar Tractor Co.) may serve to differentiate a product in the industry. Because customers with brand loyalty are usually willing to spend more for what they perceive to be a superior product, the differentiation strategy can yield larger profit margins than the low cost strategy. It is important to note, however, that cost reduction is not ignored when pursuing the differentiation strategy; it simply is not the highest priority.

Fieldcrest Mills Inc. makes good use of this strategy by attaching its widely-recognized name only to high-grade and higher-priced towels sold strictly in department stores. Because most of Fieldcrest's competitors put their corporate names on the labels of virtually all their products, premium and discount alike, they do not enjoy Fieldcrest's ability to charge more because of brand loyalty.[18]

Focus Strategy   Organizations with a focus strategy attempt to gain a competitive edge in a narrower market through some workable combination of cost cutting and differentiation. The rationale behind the focus strategy is that a narrower market can be served more effectively and efficiently than competing across the board. For example, "Fort Howard Paper focuses on a narrow range of industrial-grade papers, avoiding consumer products vulnerable to advertising battles and rapid introductions of new products."[19] Higher-than-average profits can be achieved with this hybrid strategy if a specific segment of the market is especially well served.

Summarizing, strategic thinking tools such as synergy, the product life cycle, and Porter's generic strategies pave the way for understanding and implementing the strategic management process discussed next.

The Strategic Management Process

Strategic plans are formulated during an evolutionary process that has identifiable steps. In line with the three-level planning pyramid covered in Chapter 4, the strategic management process is more broad and general at the top and filters down to narrower and more specific terms. Figure 5.3 outlines the four major steps of the strategic management process: (1) formulation of a grand strategy, (2) formulation of strategic plans, (3) implementation of strategic plans, and (4) strategic control. Evaluation and corrective action based on feedback take place throughout the entire strategic management process to keep things headed in the right direction. Of course, this model represents an ideal approach. Because of organizational politics, as discussed in Chapter 12, and different planning orientations among managers, a somewhat less systematic process typically results. But for now it is helpful to study the strategic management process

Figure 5.3 The Strategic Management Process

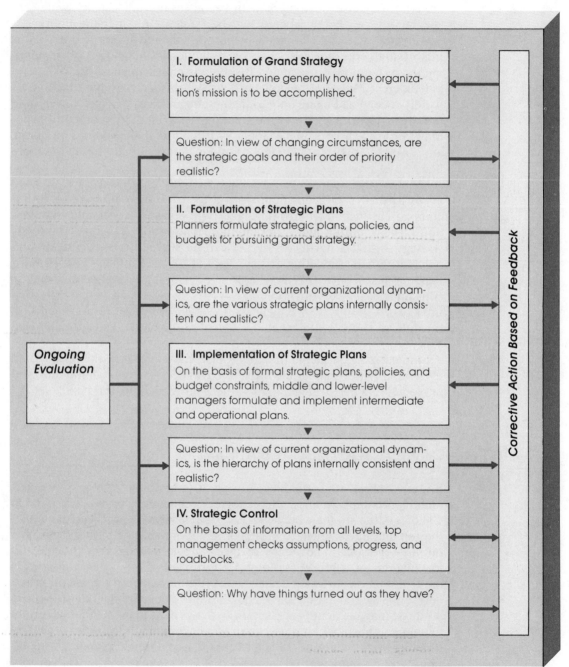

as a systematic and rational sequence to better understand what it involves.

Formulation of a Grand Strategy

As pointed out in the previous chapter, a clear statement of organizational mission serves as a focal point for the entire planning process. People inside and outside the organization are given a general idea of why the organization exists and where it is headed. Working from the mission statement, top management formulates the organization's **grand strategy,** a general explanation of *how* the organization's mission is to be accomplished. Porter's three generic strategies are particularly useful at this point.

As an instructive example, try to identify which of Porter's generic strategies IBM is using as its grand strategy for the 1980s. IBM intends to beat its historical 13 percent annual growth rate by (1) emphasizing low-cost production, (2) building a low-cost distribution network, (3) building a product-oriented organization structure, and (4) pursuing every high-growth market in the computer business.[20] If you believe that IBM is following a grand strategy based on overall low cost leadership, you're right. This answer is based on IBM's strong emphasis on cost control and targeting of the entire computer market.

Grand strategies like IBM's are not drawn out of thin air. They are derived from a careful *situational analysis* of the organization and its environment. Additionally, it helps to center the grand strategy on a *driving force* that gives the organization a competitive edge.

Situational Analysis   A **situational analysis** is a strategic management technique for matching environmental opportunities and obstacles with organizational strengths and weaknesses to determine the organization's right niche (see Figure 5.4). Every organization can conceivably identify the purpose for which it is best suited, though this matching process is more difficult than it may appear at first. Rather than dealing with snapshots of the environment and the organization, top management strategists are faced with a movie of rapidly changing events. One researcher puts it this way: "the task is to find a match between opportunities that are still unfolding and resources that are still being acquired."[21] Forecasting techniques, such as those reviewed later in this chapter, are used during situational analyses.

Strategic planners, whether top managers, key operating managers, or staff planning specialists, have many ways to scan the environment for opportunities and obstacles. They can study telltale shifts in the economy, recent innovations, growth and direction among competitors, market trends, labor availability, and demographic redistributions. Not least among the factors to be considered are current and expected tax rates.

Figure 5.4 Determining Strategic Direction Through Situational Analysis

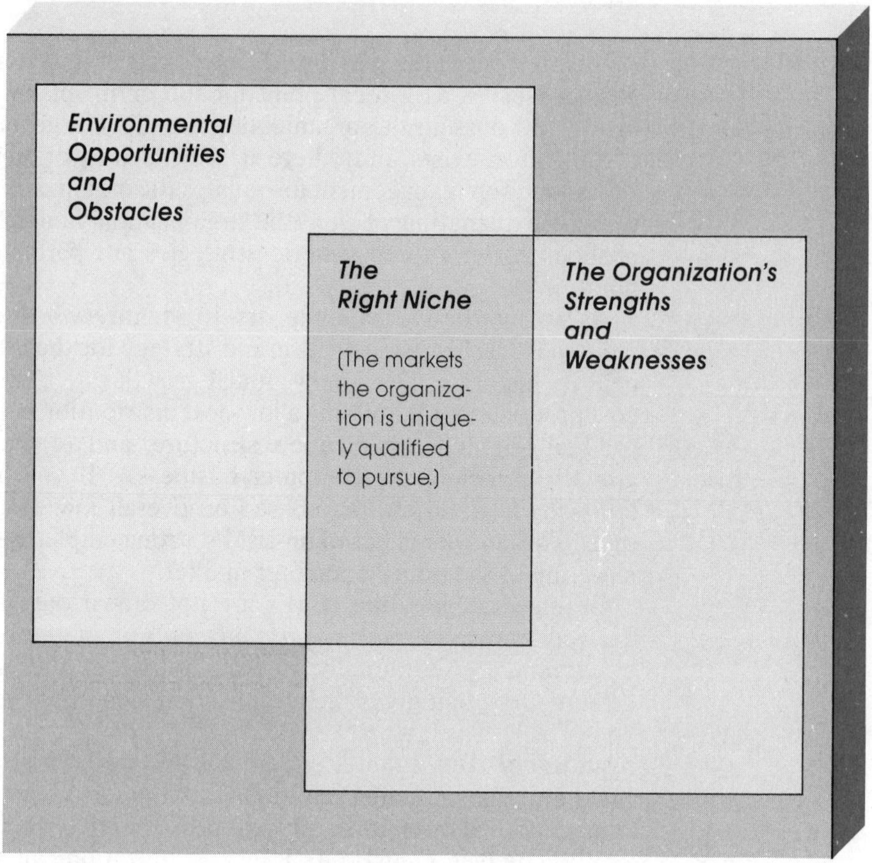

Favorable tax rates in the sun-belt states, for instance, have given many northern companies the opportunity to relocate and prosper.

Environmental opportunities and obstacles need to be sorted out carefully. A perceived obstacle may turn out to be an opportunity, or vice versa. In the late 1970s, a number of cement manufacturers saw the natural gas shortage as a serious obstacle because the cement production process requires extremely high temperatures for proper chemical conversion. As it happened, they switched to coal and ended up saving money with a cheaper and more readily available source of energy. On the other hand, as the case of W. T. Grant Company proves, an apparent opportunity may turn out to be a fatal obstacle. Top managers at Grant saw the trend toward credit-card buying as an excellent opportunity to increase sales. They responded by formulating a marketing strategy with a liberal credit policy

Table 5.3 A Framework for Identifying Organizational Strengths and Weaknesses

General Category	Attributes
Organization	Structure Degree of decentralization Policies and procedures The planning system The control system The communication network
Personnel	Number of employees Employee attitude profile Employee age and skill profiles Union/nonunion status Absenteeism and turnover rates Grievance rate
Marketing	Size of sales force Sales force turnover Knowledge of customers' needs Market share Breadth of product line Channels of distribution Product quality Credit and refund policies Customer service Reputation
Technical	Production facilities Condition of machinery Production techniques Quality control program New product innovation Research program Purchasing system Inventory system
Finance	Financial size Liquidity Return on investment Price-earnings ratio Credit rating Lines of credit Growth record

SOURCE: Based on Howard H. Stevenson, "Defining Corporate Strengths and Weaknesses," *Sloan Management Review* 17 (Spring 1976): 51–68.

to put Grant credit cards into as many hands as possible. Later, Grant discovered that half of its $500 million in credit-card receivables was uncollectable, and so the once-giant, 70-year-old chain of 1100 stores was liquidated by a bankruptcy court in 1976.[22]

After scanning the outside environment for opportunities and obstacles, management's attention turns inward to discover the organization's strengths and weaknesses. This process is sometimes referred to as a capability profile.[23] When tackling this job, the usual question is "Where do we begin?" The list of organizational attributes presented in Table 5.3 is an excellent starting point. By categorizing these organizational dimensions as strengths or weaknesses, strategists have not only a capability profile to match with environmental opportunities and obstacles but also an agenda for organizational improvement.

Driving Forces   A properly conducted situational analysis makes strategists aware of their organization's capabilities. Experts in the field have termed these capabilities "driving forces." Ten major driving forces are:

- Seeking new markets.
- Developing new products and services.
- Improving customer service.
- Developing technology.
- Improving production capability.
- Improving methods of sale.
- Improving methods of distribution.
- Acquiring natural resources.
- Enhancing size and growth.
- Enhancing return on investment and profit.[24]

Any one of the preceding can become a rallying point for an organization's grand strategy. Caterpillar Tractor Company, the well known heavy equipment manufacturer, for example, makes it clear to everyone both inside and outside the firm that improved customer service is its strategic driving force: "To Caterpillar managers, working hard at the business means focusing almost single-mindedly on customer needs and on methods to meet them quickly. The company concentrates on building high-quality, reliable products and on ensuring complete servicing, assuming that market share will take care of itself."[25]

Formulation of Strategic Plans

In the second major step in the strategic management process, general intentions are translated into more concrete and measurable strategic plans, policies, and budget allocations. This translation is the responsibility of top management, though input from staff planning specialists and middle managers is common. Recalling our discussion from the last chapter, a well-written plan consists of both an objective and an action statement. Plans at all levels should specify what, when, and how things are to be accomplished. Many managers prefer to call these specific plans "action plans" to emphasize the need to turn good intentions into action. Even though strategic plans may have a time horizon of one or more years, they need to meet the same criteria as do shorter-run intermediate and operational plans. They should:

1. Develop clear, results-oriented objectives in measurable, time-bounded terms.
2. Identify the particular activities required to accomplish the objectives.
3. Assign specific responsibility and authority to the appropriate personnel.
4. Estimate times to accomplish activities and their appropriate sequencing.
5. Determine resources required to accomplish the activities.
6. Communicate and coordinate the above elements and complete the action plan.[26]

Needless to say, all of this does not happen in a single quick-and-easy session. Specific strategic plans usually evolve over a period of months as top management consults with key managers in all areas to find out their ideas and recommendations and, one hopes, to win their commitment.

Implementation of Strategic Plans

Since planning is a filtering-down process, strategic plans require further translation into successively lower-level plans. Again, the six criteria of good action plans apply. Because a number of months usually pass between the time that strategic plans are formulated and the time that they are translated downward, middle- and lower-level managers deal in shorter time horizons and more specific terms. For example, a strategic plan formulated two years ago to increase home appliance sales by 15 percent and translated into an intermediate plan a year ago to increase washing machine production by 25 percent would set the stage for a production supervisor's operational plan to produce 4000 washing machine parts next month.

Top management strategists can do some groundwork to ensure that the filtering-down process occurs smoothly and efficiently. Specifically, four questions, each tied to a different critical organizational factor, need to be addressed:

- **Organizational structure.** Is the organization structure compatible with the planning process, with new managerial approaches, and with the strategy itself?
- **People.** Are people with the right skills and abilities available for key

assignments, or must attention be given to recruiting, training, management development, and similar programs?

- **Culture.** Is the collective viewpoint on "the right way to do things"
  compatible with strategy, must it be modified to reflect a new perspective, or must top management learn to manage around it?
- **Control systems.** Is the necessary apparatus in place to support the
  implementation of strategy and to permit top management to assess
  performance in meeting strategic objectives?[27]

Strategic plans that pass these four tests have a much greater chance of
helping the organization achieve its intended purpose than those that do
not.

Strategic Control

Strategic plans, like our more casual daily plans, can go astray, but a formal
control system helps keep strategic plans on track. Importantly, strategic
control systems need to be carefully designed ahead of time, not merely
tacked on as an afterthought. Channels for information on progress, problems, and strategic assumptions about the environment or organization
that have proved to be invalid should be set up and tested before strategies
are translated downward. If a new strategy varies significantly from past
ones, new production, financial, or marketing reports will probably have to
be drafted and introduced. The ultimate goal of a strategic control system is
to detect and correct downstream problems to keep strategies updated and
on target.

Ongoing Evaluation

Like strategic control, strategic evaluation is an ongoing process. As
indicated in Figure 5.3, important questions are asked after each of the four
steps in the strategic planning process. First, top management strategists
should regularly ask whether their mission and grand strategy are realistic.
An embargo, strike, natural disaster, or severe economic downturn can
quickly render a strategy invalid, and so strategies need to be updated
accordingly. Next, specific strategic plans need to be reviewed for internal
consistency and realism. Horizontally linked plans are internally consistent if they mesh rather than clash and compete for limited resources and
talent. For example, a plan to double production of a given product should
be accompanied by financial plans to build additional productive capacity.
After the third step, the implementation of strategic plans, strategists
examine the hierarchy of plans to make sure it is internally consistent and
realistic. Finally, after the fourth step, strategists ask, "Why have things
turned out as they have?" Much can be learned about future strategy
through postmortems of past strategies.

**Corrective
Action Based
on Feedback**

As illustrated in Figure 5.3, feedback from each of the four evaluation points and from the final strategic control step provides a basis for corrective action at all four steps. A general rule of thumb here is that negative feedback should prompt corrective action at the step immediately before. Should the problem turn out to be more deeply rooted, then the next earlier step also may require corrective action. The key is to detect problems and initiate corrective action, such as reformulating plans, rewriting policies, making personnel changes, or modifying budget allocations, as soon as possible. In the absence of prompt corrective action, problems can become worse rapidly.

We now shall discuss forecasting. Without the ability to obtain or develop reliable environmental forecasts, managerial strategists have little chance of successfully weaving their way through the strategic management process.

Forecasting

An important aspect of strategic management is anticipating what will happen in the coming months and years. **Forecasts** may be defined as predictions, projections, or estimates of future events or conditions in the environment in which the organization operates.[28] Forecasts may be little more than educated guesses, or they may be the result of highly sophisticated statistical analysis. They vary in reliability (consider the track record of TV weather forecasters!). They may be relatively short run—a few hours to a year—or long run—five or more years. A combination of factors determines the forecast's relative sophistication, time horizon, and reliability. These factors include the type of forecast required, management's knowledge of forecasting techniques, and the money that management is willing to invest.

**Types of
Forecasts**

There are generally three classes of forecasts: (1) event outcome forecasts, (2) event timing forecasts, and (3) time series forecasts.[29] Each type answers a different general question (see Table 5.4). Event outcome forecasts are used when strategists want to predict the outcome of a highly probable future event. Examples are "Who will win the next U.S. presidential election?" or "What will be the first year's sales for a newly launched product?" or "How will an impending strike affect output?" Information bases for reliably answering these three questions could be built by, respectively, polling voters, conducting market tests, and interviewing other strike victims in the industry.

Table 5.4 Types of Forecasts

Type of Forecast	General Question Answered	Example
1. Event outcome forecast	"What will happen when a given event occurs?"	"Who will win the next World Series?"
2. Event timing forecast	"When will a given event occur?"	"When will the United States have a permanently manned space station?"
3. Time series forecast	"What value will a series of periodic data have at a given point in time?"	"What will the closing Dow Jones Industrial Average be on January 5, 1989?"

Event timing forecasts predict when, if ever, a given event will occur. Strategic questions in this area might include "When will the prime interest rate begin to fall?" or "When will our primary competitor introduce a certain product?" Timing questions like these typically can be answered by identifying leading indicators that historically have preceded the events in question. For instance, a declining inflation rate often prompts major banks to lower their prime interest rate, or a competitor may flag the introduction of a new product by conducting market tests or ordering large quantities of a new raw material.

Time series forecasts seek to determine future values in a sequence of values recorded at fixed intervals. As an example, top management strategists may be interested in forecasting future values in a time series of quarterly unemployment data for the region to gauge the availability of labor. Trend analysis, discussed below, helps chart the future course of a time series.

Forecasting Techniques

Modern managers may use one, two, or a combination of three forecasting techniques to forecast future outcomes, timing, and values. These techniques are informed judgment, surveys, and trend analysis.

Informed Judgment Limited time and money often force strategists to rely on their own, intuitive judgment when forecasting. Judgmental forecasts are both fast and inexpensive, but the accuracy of a manager's judgmental forecasts depends greatly on how well informed he or she is. Frequent visits with employees in sales, purchasing, and public relations who regularly tap outside sources of information are a good way of staying informed during the normal course of duties. Also helpful are a broad reading program to stay in touch with current events and industry trends and refresher training through management development programs.

Donald Frey, the chief executive officer of Bell & Howell is a good example of a judgmental forecaster. *Fortune* magazine reports that Frey subscribes to 20 different magazines covering a broad range of topics from foreign affairs to the arts. In addition, he reads one to two books a week. "Frey's intellectual range extends well beyond his own company or industry, and well beyond business in general."[30] Consequently, he has a good reputation for judgmental forecasts. For example, when he was a product-planning manager at Ford Motor Company, Frey fought hard to introduce the Mustang in spite of gloomy market forecasts of only 86,000 units. Frey eventually prevailed. Mustang sales skyrocketed to 418,000 units in 1964, and Frey was promoted to division head.

Surveys   Face-to-face and telephone interviews and mailed questionnaires are excellent survey tools. They can be used to pool expert opinion or fathom consumer tastes, attitudes, and opinions. When carefully constructed and properly administered to representative samples, surveys can give management comprehensive and fresh information. They suffer the disadvantages, however, of being somewhat difficult to construct, time consuming to administer and interpret, and expensive. Although it is true that costs can be trimmed by purchasing an off-the-shelf or "canned" survey, standardized instruments too often do not ask precisely the right questions or ask unnecessary questions.

Trend Analysis   Essentially, a **trend analysis** is the hypothetical extension of a past pattern of events or time series into the future. An underlying assumption of trend analysis is that something's past and present direction will continue into the future. Needless to say, surprise events such as the 1973 OPEC oil embargo can destroy that assumption. But if sufficient valid historical data are readily available and barring disruptive surprise events, trend analysis can be a reasonably accurate, fast, and inexpensive strategic forecasting tool. An unreliable or atypical data base, however, can produce misleading trend projections.

The Human Dimension of Strategic Management

If the difference between textbook models of strategic management and actual practice had to be summed up in a single word, that word would be *people*. Differing perceptions, values, and personalities cause significant variations in people's attitudes toward their work and employing organization. No matter how hard strategic planners may try to be coolly objective and rational, personal emotions and interests will inevitably be included. Does this mean that managers should abandon their attempts to promote rational strategic management? Not at all. An awareness of the so-called invisible war between organizational and individual interests simply alerts managers to consider human factors when formulating and implementing strategic plans. Two human factors that deserve special attention are logical incrementalism and the impact of dominant personalities.

Logical Incrementalism

Strategic management theorists usually belong to one of two main schools of thought regarding the nature of the strategic goal-setting process. One school advocates a rational-analytical approach, and the other prefers a power-behavioral approach. More recently, field research of strategic goal setting in large businesses suggests a third, compromise, approach (see Figure 5.5 for a three-way comparison). This compromise approach has been labeled logical incrementalism. **Logical incrementalism** is a process that top management strategists use to sell the long-range goals that they evolve in a logical but somewhat disjointed fashion. This alternative view is a marked departure from the popular rational-analytical notion that top management formally announces strategic goals as a final integrated package that everyone must somehow endure.

According to the logical incrementalism view, the following pattern of strategic goal formulation is common:

> At first there are simply too many unknowns to specify a cohesive set of new directions for the enterprise. More information is needed. Technical problems must be solved to determine feasibilities. Investments must be made in programs with long lead times. Trends in the market place must crystallize into sufficiently concrete demands or competitive responses to justify risk taking. Various resource bases must be acquired or developed. Different groups' psychological commitments must be diverted from ongoing thrusts toward a new consensus. Lead times for all these events are different. Yet logic dictates that final resource commitments be made as late as possible consistent with the information available—hence incrementalism.
>
> To reshape an organization's accepted culture significantly, an executive must often overcome some potent psychological/political forces. His success will depend on the very group whose perceptions he may want to change. If he moves too precipitously, he can undermine essential strengths of his organization. All too easily he can alienate his people, lose personal credibility, and destroy the power base his future depends on. Unless a crisis intervenes, he cannot change the organization's ethos abruptly. Instead he usually must build commitment—and his own political support—incrementally around specific issues or proposals. The real art is to thoroughly blend these thrusts together, as opportunities permit, into patterns that slowly create a new logical cohesion.[31]

This perspective is useful because it shows how top management strategists can blend rational objectivity with political savvy to achieve their goals.

Figure 5.5 Logical Incrementalism in Strategy Formulation

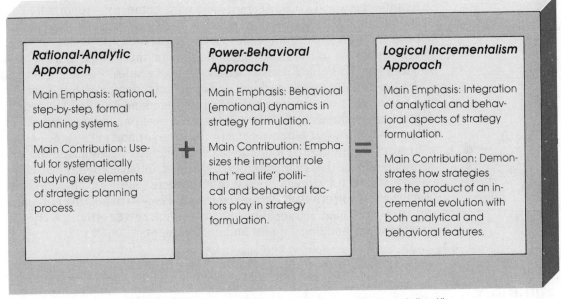

SOURCE: Adapted from James Brian Quinn, "Strategic Change: 'Logical Incrementalism,'"
Sloan Management Review 20 (Fall 1978): 7–21.

Caterpillar's approach to formulating new product strategies clearly illustrates logical incrementalism:

> A product-control department comprised of representatives from manufacturing, marketing, and engineering assesses potential competition and forecasts sales volume for five years. The final decision rests with a committee composed of Chairman Morgan, five executives from his office, and several key vice-presidents. "People begin bouncing ideas off one another, and after a series of meetings, the project finds its way into official status," Morgan says. "I am presumably the guy who makes the decision, but I'm heavily influenced by the consensus."
>
> To arrive at that consensus, Morgan conducts informal discussions that explore all aspects of a project.[32]

The net result of this type of logical incrementalism is a strategy that key managers are more likely to favor because of their personal involvement in its formulation.

The Impact of Dominant Personalities

Strong-willed individuals with dominant personalities are common among the ranks of top management, for it is precisely those characteristics that are often responsible for propelling people to the top. But for formulating strategies, dominant personalities can sometimes mislead an organization. An interesting example is the late Sam Bronfman, who for many years ran Seagram—the world's biggest spirits and wine company—reportedly like a one-man band. It seems that because Mr. Bronfman had a personal distaste for vodka, Seagram only passively pursued the vodka market. Today, vodka far outsells all other liquors in the United States, and Seagram lags far behind its competitors in vodka sales.[33]

The lingering question is "How does one tell a dominant top manager that he or she is on the wrong track without endangering one's career?" Unfortunately, there are no easy answers. The best one can do is to collect an impressive array of supporting facts, rally the support of key colleagues, and present one's case in a nonthreatening manner. Recognizing the tremendous impact that dominant personalities can have on strategy helps managers detect a primary source of misdirected strategy. Of course, as Lee Iacocca's experience at Chrysler amply demonstrates, the combination of a dominant personality and a well-conceived strategy can be valuable when building support and commitment.

Summary

Strategic management sets the stage for virtually all managerial activity. Managers at all levels need to think strategically and be familiar with the strategic management process for three reasons: farsightedness is encouraged, the rationale behind top-level decisions becomes more apparent, and strategy formulation and implementation are more decentralized today. Strategic management is defined as the ongoing process of ensuring a competitively superior fit between the organization and its ever-changing environment. Strategic management effectively merges strategic planning, implementation, and control.

Strategic thinking, the ability to look ahead and spot key organization/environment interdependencies, is necessary for successful strategic management and planning. Three tools that can help managers think strategically are synergy (the $2 + 2 = 5$ effect), product life cycles that trace the life of a product through its introduction, growth, maturity, and decline stages, and Porter's three generic strategies. Porter's three strategies are overall cost leadership, differentiation, and focus.

The strategic management process consists of four major steps: (1) formulation of grand strategy, (2) formulation of strategic plans, (3) implementation of strategic plans, and (4) strategic control. Ongoing evaluation after each of these steps and corrective action based on feedback help keep the strategic management process on track. Strategists formulate the organization's grand strategy by conducting a situational analysis and identifying the driving forces. Results-oriented strategic plans that specify what, when, and how are then formulated and translated downward into more specific and shorter-term intermediate and operational plans. Problems encountered along the way should be detected by the strategic control mechanism or by ongoing evaluation and subjected to corrective action.

Event outcome, event timing, and time series forecasts help strategic planners anticipate and prepare for future environmental circumstances. Popular forecasting techniques among today's managers are informed judgment, surveys, and trend analysis.

Personalities greatly affect the strategic management process because personal emotions and interests can displace cool objectivity. Field research has shown that corporate strategists often blend rational and behavioral-political considerations in a disjointed manner called logical incrementalism. Managers are cautioned to be aware of the impact that dominant personalities can have on the nature of strategies.

Terms to Understand

Strategic management	Situational analysis
Synergy	Forecasts
Product life cycle	Trend analysis
Grand strategy	Logical incrementalism

Questions for Discussion

1. Why is strategic management particularly important today?
2. In reference to a business with which you are familiar, how could it achieve market, cost, technology, or management synergy?
3. Why is the concept of product life cycles useful to strategic planners?
4. How can a company's focus strategy effectively combine both low-cost and differentiation strategies?
5. What takes place during a situational analysis?
6. Relative to taking a strategic perspective of your career, what are your driving forces?
7. Why is it important to conduct ongoing evaluation during the strategic management process?
8. Can you make outcome forecasts for three significant upcoming events? On what did you base these forecasts?

9. Why do you think managers tend to rely heavily on judgmental forecasts? Could it have anything to do with logical incrementalism?
10. Can you see any evidence of logical incrementalism in your personal affairs?

Back to the Opening Case

Now that you have read Chapter 5, you should be able to answer the following questions about the McDonald's case:

1. Which of Porter's three generic strategies is McDonald's pursuing? How can you tell?
2. Based on this case and reasonable assumptions from your own experience with McDonald's, what would a situational analysis of McDonald's tell us about the future direction the firm should take? *Tip:* First arrange your evidence under the four headings: "Environmental opportunities," "Environmental obstacles," "Organizational strengths," and "Organizational weaknesses."
3. What is your judgmental forecast for McDonald's future through 1990?

Closing Case 5.2

Brewing a National Strategy at Adolph Coors Company

Adolph Coors Company traces its roots back to 1868 when Adolph Herman Joseph Coors arrived in the United States as a stowaway. Five years later, he founded the forerunner of Coors's present brewery in Golden, Colorado. Until the late 1970s, Coors adhered to a fairly simple strategy that has been characterized as strictly quality-oriented. It called for brewing a single premium beer at its only brewery and distributing it in a 17-state region in the western United States. A special brewing process that omitted the usual pasteurization step was used to avoid possible deterioration of the beer from heat. Coors's approach to marketing was to rely on its reputation for a quality product and the trademarked claim of "Brewed with Pure Rocky Mountain Spring Water" rather than on expensive mass advertising. Financially, Coors maintained a conservative tradition of generating capital from profits while refusing to borrow money.

A Turn for the Worse
Until the mid-1970s, this simple formula proved profitable, enabling Coors to build the nation's largest brewery as a result of volume increases every

year since the end of Prohibition. During the 1960s and early 1970s, Coors acquired the reputation as the beer that people "bootlegged" to other regions of the country where it was not distributed. The so-called "Coors mystique" was enhanced when a semi-trailer load of Coors played a central role in the Burt Reynolds movie, *Smokey and the Bandit*.

But things began to go sour for Coors when net income dropped from $76 million in 1976 to $40.1 million in 1982, in spite of steadily increasing sales. Significantly, however, even at their low point in 1982, Coors's profits were second only to those for industry leader Anheuser-Busch. One bright spot during this period was Coors Light beer. Introduced in 1978, the company's first new brand soon became the No. 2 light beer in Coors's marketing territory. Still, Coors slipped from fourth in size in the industry to sixth. Along with other regional and local brewers, whose ranks thinned by over 50 independent brewers during the 1970s, Coors was rocked by aggressive competition between Miller Brewing Company and Anheuser-Busch Inc., the industry's giants. Especially worrisome for management was the erosion of Coors's market share in its own backyard. Coors's sales in the western United States declined from 13.2 million barrels (31 gallons per barrel) in 1981 to 11.9 million barrels in 1982.

An Aggressive National Strategy

When profits continued to slip during 1980-1982, top management realized that the key to Coors's survival in the U.S. brewing industry was to go after the national market. As events unfolded, the following features of Coors's new national strategy became apparent:

- **Development and introduction of new products.** A super-premium beer named "Herman Joseph's 1868" was introduced to test markets in six western cities in 1980. (Experts estimate the super-premium share of the U.S. beer market to be about 10 percent.)
- **Eastward market expansion.** In 1983, Coors began distributing its brew in six southeastern states, Washington, D.C., Hawaii, and Alaska. With the addition of West Virginia, Maryland, Kentucky, and four north-central states in 1984, Coors's marketing territory grew to 35 states. However, Coors's reach did not extend to the populous northeast United States.
- **Retention of traditional brewing process.** Coors faithfully maintained its use of all-natural ingredients and its comparatively lengthy 68-day brewing process. As before, the unpasteurized product had to be constantly refrigerated during transportation and storage.
- **Possible construction of an eastern brewery.** With increased sales straining the capacity of its 16-million-barrel-per-year brewery in Golden, Coors considered using internally-generated funds to build a $500 mil-

lion brewery on land in a region of Virginia coincidentally known as Rocky Mountain.

- **Aggressive advertising.** Coors's advertising budget was greatly increased to $88.1 million in 1982, compared to a yearly average of $3 million in the early 1970s.

Some Successes, Some Disappointments

In 1983, Coors's sales grew 21 percent and net income rebounded to $89.3 million. The company's expansion into the southeast, termed "very successful" by a Coors executive, accounted for much of the 1983 turnaround. Meanwhile, the erosion of Coors's market share in the west continued. In late 1984, plans for the Virginia brewery were still on the shelf. Competitors chided Coors about the pitfalls of using eastern water to brew a beer boastfully made from "Pure Rocky Mountain Spring Water." Peter Coors, a marketing executive, told *Forbes* that this is "not a technical problem, but a marketing one."[34]

Coors's super-premium entry, Herman Joseph's 1868, was called a "major disappointment" by Chairman William Coors. In late 1984, the rising costs for corn, aluminum, and advertising caused concern for Coors. Seven-to-eight dollars per barrel rail freight charges for transporting beer from the Colorado brewery to eastern markets, considered potentially damaging by industry observers, were dismissed by Coors as manageable.

For Discussion

1. Using Porter's model, how would you categorize Coors's grand strategy during the early 1980s? What led you to this conclusion?
2. Is Coors relying on a new driving force? If so, what is it?
3. Assume you have been asked to make a presentation on strategy to a panel of Coors executives. How would you sum up the strategic pros and cons of building a second brewery in Virginia? What would be your recommendation?

References

Opening Quotation: James Broughton in M. R. Rosenberg, ed., *Quotations for the New Age* (Secaucus, N.J.: Citadel Press, 1978), p. 100.

Opening Case: For additional information on McDonald's, see "Those Doubts About McDonald's," *Financial World* 152 (June 15, 1983): 38–40; W. David Gibson, "Did McDonald's Deserve a Break?" *Barron's* 63 (September 5, 1983): 6–7, 34; Lawrence D. Maloney, "Recipe for Success in the Fast-food Game," *U.S. News & World Report* 95 (November 21, 1983): 58–59; "The Fast-food War: Big Mac Under

Attack," *Business Week* No. 2826 (January 30, 1984): 44–46; and Stephen Kindel, "Where's the Growth?" *Forbes* 133 (April 23, 1984): 80.

Closing Case: For additional information on Coors, see "Adolph Coors: Brewing Up Plans for an Invasion of the East Coast," *Business Week* No. 2656 (September 29, 1980): 120, 124; Robert Reed, "Coors Charts Path Over a Rocky Road to Growth," *Advertising Age* 54 (July 11, 1983): 4, 59–60; Robert McGough, "A Difference of Perspective," *Forbes* 132 (October 24, 1983): 88; and Jack Liebau, "Coors Country," *Barron's* 64 (April 2, 1984): 57.

1. Gibson, "Did McDonald's Deserve a Break?" p. 6.
2. "The Fast-food War," p. 44.
3. Ibid., p. 45.
4. "The New Breed of Strategic Planner," *Business Week* No. 2860 (September 17, 1984): 68.
5. Based on a definitional framework found in David J. Teece, "Economic Analysis and Strategic Management," *California Management Review* 26 (Spring 1984): 87.
6. For more on the evolution of strategic management, see David A. Aaker, *Developing Business Strategies* (New York: Wiley, 1984), pp. 10–14.
7. Benjamin B. Tregoe and John W. Zimmerman, "Strategic Thinking: Key to Corporate Survival," *Management Review* 68 (February 1979): 10.
8. "The New Breed of Strategic Planner," p. 62.
9. William R. King and David I. Cleland, *Strategic Planning and Policy* (New York: Van Nostrand Reinhold, 1978), pp. 180–183.
10. John S. DeMott, "Sears' Sizzling New Vitality," *Time* 124 (August 1984): 83.
11. "A Ready-Made Track for High-Tech Communications," *Business Week* No. 2807 (September 12, 1983): 43.
12. "Alfa-Laval: Updating Its Knowhow for the Biotechnology Era," *Business Week* No. 2808 (September 19, 1983): 80.
13. See Harold W. Fox, "A Framework for Functional Coordination," *Atlanta Economic Review* 23 (November-December 1973): 8–11; Stephen R. Michael, "Guidelines for Contingency Approach to Planning," *Long Range Planning* 12 (December 1979): 62–69; Ward C. Smith, "Product Life-Cycle Strategy: How to Stay on the Growth Curve," *Management Review* 69 (January 1980): 8–13; and Lester A. Neidell, "Don't Forget the Product Life Cycle for Strategic Planning," *Business* 33 (April-June 1983): 30–35.
14. "Technology Gives the U.S. a Big Edge," *Business Week* No. 2643 (June 30, 1980): 104. Also see Susan Fraker, "High-Speed Management for the High-Tech Age," *Fortune* 109 (March 5, 1984): 62–68.
15. "New Product Success Rate–One Out of Three," *Research Management* 23 (March 1980): 3. For a more detailed study with similar results, see C. Merle Crawford, "New Product Failure Rates–Facts and Fallacies," *Research Management* 22 (September 1979): 9–13.
16. See Michael E. Porter, *Competitive Strategy* (New York: The Free Press,

1980), p. 35; for a more detailed breakdown of strategies, see John A. Pearce II, "Selecting among Alternative Grand Strategies," *California Management Review* 24 (Spring 1982): 23–31.

17. "The Squeeze Begins in Personal Computers," *Business Week* No. 2792 (May 30, 1983): 95.

18. See "Fieldcrest: Saving Its Name for a Luxury Image," *Business Week* No. 2823 (January 9, 1984): 112–113.

19. Porter, *Competitive Strategy*, p. 39.

20. See "No. 1's Awesome Strategy," *Business Week* No. 2691 (June 8, 1981): 84–90.

21. Richard F. Vancil, "Strategy Formulation in Complex Organizations," *Sloan Management Review* 17 (Winter 1976): 18.

22. Rush Loving, Jr., "W. T. Grant's Last Days–As Seen from Store 1192," *Fortune* 93 (April 1976): 108–112, 114.

23. For example, see Howard H. Stevenson, "Defining Corporate Strengths and Weaknesses," *Sloan Management Review* 17 (Spring 1976): 51–68.

24. Adapted from Tregoe and Zimmerman, "Strategic Thinking," p. 13.

25. "Caterpillar: Sticking to Basics to Stay Competitive," *Business Week* No. 2686 (May 4, 1981): 74.

26. Waldron Berry, "Beyond Strategic Planning," *Managerial Planning* 29 (March-April 1981): 14.

27. Charles H. Roush, Jr., and Ben C. Ball, Jr., "Controlling the Implementation of Strategy," *Managerial Planning* 29 (November-December 1980): 4.

28. Based on George A. Steiner, *Top Management Planning* (New York: Macmillan, 1969), p. 17.

29. C. W. J. Granger, *Forecasting in Business and Economics* (New York: Academic Press, 1980), pp. 6–10.

30. Arthur M. Louis, "Donald Frey Had a Hunger for the Whole Thing," *Fortune* 94 (September 1976): 141.

31. James Brian Quinn, "Strategic Goals: Process and Politics," *Sloan Management Review* 19 (Fall 1977): 33–34. For more on this topic, see James Brian Quinn, "Strategic Change: 'Logical Incrementalism,' " *Sloan Management Review* 20 (Fall 1978): 7–21.

32. "Caterpillar: Sticking to the Basics to Stay Competitive," 76.

33. "What Edgar Bronfman Wants at Seagram," *Business Week* No. 2685 (April 27, 1981): 135–142.

34. McGough, "A Difference of Perspective," p. 88.

Chapter 6

Decision Making and Creative Problem Solving

Raising a manager's batting average on decisions by a few percentage points can mean all the difference between the major leagues and the minors.

Charles H. Kepner and Benjamin B. Tregoe

Chapter Objectives

When you finish studying this chapter, you should be able to

- Explain why complexity, uncertainty, and flexible thinking are major challenges for modern decision makers.
- Explain why programmed and nonprogrammed decisions require different decision-making procedures.
- Summarize the positive and negative aspects of group-aided decision making.
- Contrast instrumental and terminal values and discuss why values are important in decision making.
- Identify and briefly describe four of the ten "mental locks" that can inhibit creativity.
- List and explain the four basic steps in the creative problem-solving process.

Opening Case 6.1

Apple Computer Polishes Its Act

Because of its humble beginnings and phenomenal growth, Apple Computer, Inc. has become a Silicon Valley legend. It took the Cupertino, California company only seven years to evolve from a shoestring operation in a computer whiz kid's garage to a spot on *Fortune*'s list of the 500 largest companies in America. In 1975, 21-year-old Steve Jobs and 26-year-old Steve Wozniak took the $1300 they received from the sale of Wozniak's Volkswagen bus and started building personal computers in Jobs' garage. The combination of Jobs' visionary thinking—"computerize the masses"—and Wozniak's technical genius enabled the pair to gather the financial support necessary to launch the company in 1977. Brisk sales of the Apple II personal computer catapulted the young company to $600 million in sales and the *Fortune* 500 by 1982.

A Mission, Not Just a Job

Most of Apple's early employees had two things in common: they were young and they wanted to show the rest of the world that they could make a difference. Spurred on by Steve Jobs' mission to build a "computer for the people," Apple grew up around a strong set of unconventional values. According to observers:

> Because they feel they invented the personal computer, Apple people think they are ideal leaders of the movement. ... a subtle 1960s-style youth culture is pervasive. The average age of employees is 30. Jeans are acceptable attire for corporate vice-presidents.
>
> The counter-corporate culture attitude extends beyond dress. Every new Apple employee is given a sheet that describes "Apple Values." The sheet was the result of a task force of a dozen Apple employees at all levels who spent several months interviewing co-workers regarding their attitudes about working at Apple. ...[1]

As listed in Table 6.1, Apple Values involve much more than a casual dress code. They endorse fundamental beliefs about hard work, service, and teamwork.

A Corporate Shoot Out

In the early days, when Apple was undisputed master of the personal computer market, a youthful shoot-from-the-hip atmosphere pervaded the company. Conflict and lack of coordination were the rules of the day. For example, from 1979 to 1982, two new products, the Lisa and the Macintosh, were designed by different divisions that acted more like separate companies.

The Lisa was destined to become a higher-priced business computer whereas the Macintosh (called simply Mac) was intended for the lower-priced personal computer market. Cofounder Steve Jobs, a vice president at the time, was assigned to head the smaller Mac project because other top executives thought he was too inexperienced and erratic for the larger Lisa project. In his typical enthusiastic and emotional style, Jobs promptly made a $5000 race-to-completion bet with the Lisa division

Table 6.1 The Corporate Values of Apple Computer, Inc.

Apple Values

Achieving our goal is important to us. But we're equally concerned with the WAY we reach it. These are the values that govern our business conduct:

Empathy for Customers/Users—We offer superior products that fill real needs and provide lasting value. We deal fairly with competitors, and meet customers and vendors more than half way. We are genuinely interested in solving customer problems, and will not compromise our ethics or integrity in the name of profit.

Achievement/Aggressiveness—We set aggressive goals, and drive ourselves hard to achieve them. We recognize that this is a unique time, when our products will change the way people work and live. It's an adventure, and we're on it together.

Positive Social Contribution—As a corporate citizen, we wish to be an economic, intellectual, and social asset in communities where we operate. But beyond that, we expect to make this world a better place to live. We build products that extend human capability, freeing people from drudgery and helping them achieve more than they could alone.

Innovation/Vision—We built our company on innovation, providing products that were new and needed. We accept the risks inherent in following our vision, and work to develop leadership products which command the profit margins we strive for.

Individual Performance—We expect individual commitment and performance above the standard for our industry. Only thus will we make the profits that permit us to seek our other corporate objectives. Each employee can and must make a difference; for in the final analysis, INDIVIDUALS determine the character and strength of Apple.

Team Spirit—Teamwork is essential to Apple's success, for the job is too big to be done by any one person. Individuals are encouraged to interact with all levels of management, sharing ideas and suggestions to improve Apple's effectiveness and quality of life. It takes all of us to win. We support each other, and share the victories and rewards together. We're enthusiastic about what we do.

Quality/Excellence—We care about what we do. We build into Apple products a level of quality, performance, and value that will earn the respect and loyalty of our customers.

Individual Reward—We recognize each person's contribution to Apple's success, and we share the financial rewards that flow from high performance. We recognize also that rewards must be psychological as well as financial, and strive for an atmosphere where each individual can share the adventure and excitement of working at Apple.

Good Management—The attitudes of managers toward their people are of primary importance. Employees should be able to trust the motives and integrity of their supervisors. It is the responsibility of management to create a productive environment where Apple values flourish.

SOURCE: Apple Computer, Inc.

head and rushed off to recruit top talent. "… The competition that developed between the divisions sometimes verged on fratricide. At one point a pirate flag flapped above the Mac building as an expression of battle. The Mac team was often condescending about the quality of Lisa. …"2

Although he was working around the clock on the Mac project, Jobs skillfully used parties, stock options, promises of fame and fortune, impulsive deadlines, and bursts of ranting and raving about beating the Lisa division to drive his team on to success. His strong sense of aesthetics and feel for what the average person wanted in a personal computer kept the Mac designers dedicated to building a machine with unprecedented "user friendliness."

Enter: IBM

Although Lisa beat Mac to the marketplace by a year (January 1983 versus January 1984), disappointing Lisa sales made the Mac a much better prospect for future growth. (The Lisa model eventually was discontinued in 1985.) By the end of 1983, Apple had grown to nearly a $1 billion-per-year company. But while Apple's attention was directed inward to the Lisa/Mac product development battle and the hot-selling Apple IIe, IBM was making great inroads into the personal computer market. Because of its highly successful Personal Computer (PC), it took IBM only two years to replace Apple as the No. 1 personal computer company by 1983. Apple's 41 percent share of the U.S. market in 1981 had dropped to 24 percent in two years.

Realizing that Apple was being outmarketed by IBM, Jobs, who had become chairman of the board in 1981, recruited John Sculley from PepsiCo in mid-1983. Characterized as a thorough man who likes to conceptualize things, Sculley "paid his dues" by driving a Pepsi truck and working in a bottling plant in Pittsburgh. He rapidly worked his way up to the presidency of Pepsi-Cola, PepsiCo's U.S. soft-drink division. Most importantly, from Jobs' standpoint, Sculley knew mass marketing inside out.

As the new president of Apple, it didn't take Sculley long to introduce some needed discipline. He reorganized Apple from four to two divisions. This broke up the product cliques and helped give Apple a sense of direction. Sculley also focused on small details such as answering phones promptly and requiring that all memos be no more than one page. Relying on his marketing background, Sculley insisted that Apple product introductions made prior to his arrival be analyzed carefully to discover where mistakes had been made. According to *Fortune*:

Sculley also engendered loyalty through his low-key, unegotistical style and his willingness to roll up his sleeves and work. After the volatile leadership of Jobs, who was known to rave and break into tears while haranguing his troops, Sculley's even temperament was a welcome change. . . .

Exit: Steve Jobs

For nearly two years, Jobs and Sculley were hailed as a model entrepreneur/manager team. But by early 1985, it became apparent that Jobs's erratic style had to be reined in if Apple was to become more disciplined. In May 1985, following Jobs's unsuccessful bid to dump Sculley, a major reorganization engineered by Sculley stripped Jobs of his authority for daily operations. Jobs and Sculley began to quarrel openly. Four months later, Jobs resigned from the company he had co-founded eight years earlier (Wozniak had departed in early 1985). This turn of events, combined with Apple's first losing quarter ever, dealt Apple's self-confidence a severe blow.

(Discussion questions linking this case with the material you are about to read can be found at the end of this chapter.)

Years ago, the story goes, a jack-of-all-trades who had a difficult time staying employed finally landed the perfect job. He excitedly told his best friend that he had found a job sorting potatoes and that he was sure he would never quit. A couple of weeks passed before the two saw each other again. "How's the new job going?" asked the friend. "It was terrible," answered the jack-of-all-trades. "I quit last week." "Why?" asked the friend. "I thought it was easy. In fact, you said you'd never quit." "It was okay for a while," replied the jack-of-all-trades. "All I had to do was put the big potatoes in one bag, the medium in another, and the small in a third, but eventually all that decision making burned me out!"

As this story indicates, decision making is not for the fainthearted. Nevertheless, decision making is one of the primary responsibilities of managers at all levels. The quality of a manager's decisions not only contributes to the success or failure of the organization but greatly affects his or her personal success as well. John Sculley was able to build a solid base of support at Apple Computer because of his decisive management style.

Decision making is the process of identifying and choosing alternative courses of action in a manner appropriate to the demands of the situation. The act of choosing implies that alternative courses of action must be weighed and weeded out. Thus judgment and discretion are fundamental to decision making. This chapter highlights major challenges for decision makers, introduces a general decision-making model, discusses group-aided decision making, explores the role of personal values in decision making, and examines creativity and problem solving.

Challenges for Decision Makers

Though decision making has never been easy, it is especially challenging for today's managers. In an era of accelerating change, the pace of decision making has accelerated. According to Alvin Toffler, "... the very speed of change introduces a new element into management, forcing executives, already nervous in an unfamiliar environment, to make more and more decisions at a faster and faster pace. Response times are honed to a minimum."[4] In addition to having to cope with this acceleration effect, today's decision makers face three other tough challenges: (1) complexity, (2) uncertainty, and (3) the need for flexible thinking.

Dealing with Growing Complexity

For managers, complexity is a self-perpetuating cycle. Increased situational complexity leads to more complex decisions, which in turn make the situation yet more complex. Those who stubbornly resist or naively ignore this cycle of complexity will probably be bowled over by it. A working knowledge of seven intertwined contributors[5] to decision complexity can help decision makers raise their batting averages (see Figure 6.1). They include:

1. **Multiple criteria.** Typically, a decision today must satisfy a number of often conflicting criteria representing the interests of different groups. For example, a decision to install expensive smokestack pollution control equipment may please environmentalists but anger some stockholders because of lower dividends. Identifying interest groups and trading off their conflicting interests is a major challenge for today's decision makers.

2. **Intangibles.** Factors such as customer good will, employee morale, increased bureaucracy, and aesthetic appeal (for example, a billboard on a scenic highway), although difficult to measure, often determine decision alternatives.

3. **Risk and uncertainty.** Along with every decision alternative goes the chance that it will fail to satisfy the relevant criteria. Because of the importance of this particular aspect of decision complexity, we shall devote special attention to it in the next section.

4. **Long-term implications.** Managers are becoming increasingly aware that their decisions have not only intended short-term impact but also unintended long-term impact. For example, Chrysler's management responded to lower sales during the 1974–1975 recession by cutting capital spending and laying off engineers and designers. Although these cost-cutting decisions helped Chrysler reduce its short-run losses, the firm's long-term competitiveness was nearly destroyed because of obsolete facilities and a shortage of creative talent.[6]

Figure 6.1 Sources of Complexity for Today's Managerial Decision Makers

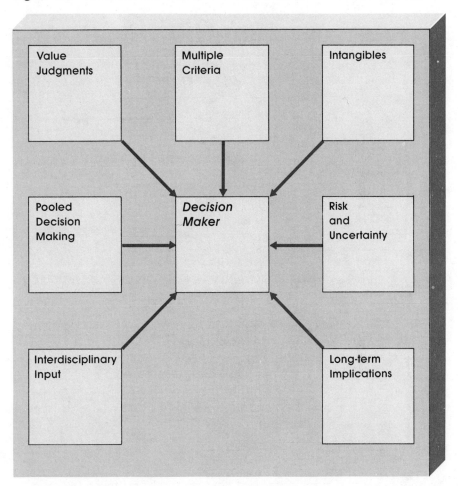

5. **Interdisciplinary input.** Decision complexity is greatly increased when technical specialists such as lawyers, consumer advocates, tax advisers, accountants, engineers, and production and marketing experts are consulted before making a decision. This also is a time-consuming process.

6. **Pooled decision making.** Rarely is a single manager totally responsible for an entire package of decisions. A single decision is usually a link in a chain that is passed from hand to hand. For example, one team of researchers charted the path of a major decision to purchase costly medical equipment in a hospital[7] (see Figure 6.2). Notice how a complex series of recommendations preceded final budget approval by the governing board.

Figure 6.2 Many People Have a Hand in Important Organizational Decisions: A Real-life Example

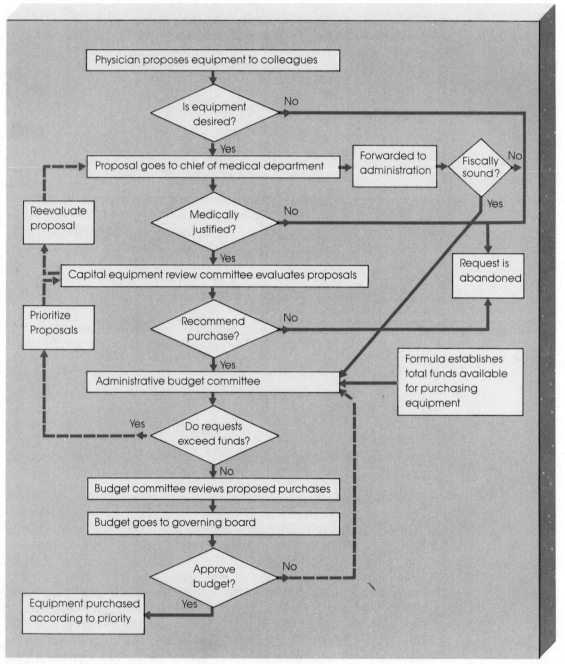

7. **Value judgments.** As long as decisions are made by people with differing backgrounds, perceptions, aspirations, and values, the decision-making process will be marked by disagreement over what is right or wrong and good or bad. We shall say more about the role of values in decision making later in this chapter.

Considering all of the foregoing sources of decision complexity together, it is clear that they are not merely passing problems. Each promises to loom even larger on the decision-making horizon in the years to come.

Coping with Uncertainty

One of the decision theorists' more valuable contributions is the classification of degrees of uncertainty. We are intuitively aware of varying degrees of uncertainty in our daily personal affairs. We attach high degrees of certainty and confidence to the prospect that the sun will rise tomorrow, that our local bank will still have our money next week, and that our favorite TV comic will make us laugh. But our confidence drops when circumstances become more uncertain. Events such as obtaining a loan, getting an A on a final exam, or finding the perfect mate are plagued by doubt and apprehension. Unfortunately, life is filled with uncertainties, and managers are continually asked to make the best decisions they can in spite of uncertainties about both present and future circumstances.

Managers who are familiar with the three primary degrees of uncertainty—certainty, risk, and uncertainty—are able to make more effective decisions. As illustrated in Figure 6.3, there is a negative correlation between uncertainty and the decision maker's confidence in a decision. In other words, the more uncertain a manager is about the principal factors in a decision, the less confident he or she will be about the successful outcome of that decision. The key, of course, lies not in eliminating uncertainty, because it cannot be eliminated, but rather in learning to work within an acceptable range of uncertainty.

Certainty   A **condition of certainty** exists when there is no doubt about the factual basis of a particular decision and its outcome can be predicted accurately. Much like the economic concept of pure competition, the concept of certainty is useful mainly as a theoretical anchor point for a continuum. In a world filled with uncertainties, certainty is relative rather than absolute. For example, the decision to order more rivets for a manufacturing firm's fabrication department is based on the relative certainty that the current rate of use will exhaust the rivet inventory on a specific date. But even in this case, uncertainties about the possible misuse or theft of rivets creep in to reduce confidence. Since nothing is truly certain, conditions of risk and uncertainty are the general rule for managers.

Figure 6.3 The Relationship Between Uncertainty and Confidence

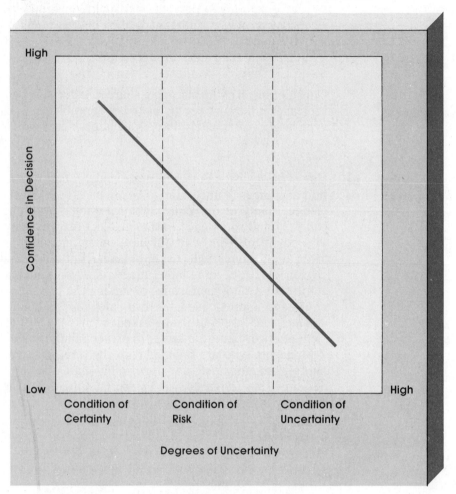

Risk A **condition of risk** is said to exist when a decision must be made on the basis of incomplete but reliable factual information. Incomplete but reliable information helps managers cope with risk by allowing them to calculate the probability that a given event will occur and then to select a decision alternative with favorable odds. There are two basic types of probabilities, objective and subjective. **Objective probabilities** are derived mathematically from reliable historical data, whereas **subjective probabilities** are estimated from past experience or judgment. Decision making based on probabilities is common in all areas of management today. For instance, laundry product manufacturers would not think of launching a new detergent without determining its probability of acceptance with consumer panels and test marketing. A number of inferential statistical techniques can help managers objectively cope with risk.

Uncertainty   A **condition of uncertainty** exists when little or no reliable factual information is available. Although there is no data base from which to calculate objective probabilities, judgmental or subjective probabilities can still be estimated. For example, relevant experience and a good "feel" for the market would allow a retailer to estimate the probable demand for a new line of clothes. If the probability of sufficient demand is favorable, then the decision will be to purchase the new line. Decision confidence is lowest when a condition of uncertainty prevails because decisions are based on educated guesses rather than on hard factual data.

Thinking Flexibly   Thinking is one of those activities we engage in constantly, yet seldom pause to examine systematically. But within the context of managerial decision making and problem solving, it is important that one's thinking does not get into an unproductive rut. The quality of our decisions is a direct reflection of the quality of our thinking.

Researchers have identified three general styles of thinking: right brain thinking, left brain thinking, and integrated thinking.[8] These styles of thinking get their name from the fact that the human brain has right and left hemispheres that process information in distinctly different ways (see Table 6.2). Although scientists do not yet fully understand the mechanisms involved, it is known that some of us become right-hemisphere dominant while others become left-hemisphere dominant. A comparatively small proportion of the population effectively integrates the processing capabilities of both hemispheres of the brain. Quite naturally, difficulties can arise on the job when right brain and left brain thinkers fail to understand or appreciate the way their counterparts view situations and problems. In work organizations, where left brain (verbal, analytical) thinking is said to predominate, right brain (subjective, intuitive, artistic) thinking is typically criticized for being sloppy and imprecise. This is unfortunate because both hemispheres of the brain are needed for good decision making and problem solving.

Those who are not integrated thinkers can take a positive first step by diagnosing their own predominant thinking style. Next, an appreciation for the other style of thinking needs to be cultivated. Eventually, by consciously trying to understand and learn from those with opposite styles, one may develop an integrated thinking style. Skill building exercises also help. For instance, a right brain thinker could take some courses in math or computer programming and polish his or her public speaking ability. Conversely, art classes and science fiction reading can stretch the left brain

Table 6.2 Left and Right Brain Thinking Styles: Which is Your Predominant Style?

Left Brain	Right Brain
• Analyzes details of image.	• Provides overview or spatial thinking.
• Recognizes conceptual similarities but not spatial ones.	• Recognizes spatial similarities but not conceptual ones.
• Is objective and analytical.	• Is subjective, artistic and innovative.
• Views time as continuous and sequential.	• Views time as a series of discrete snapshots of past, present and future.
• Expresses itself best verbally.	• Expresses itself nonverbally—gestures, limited word usage.
• Develops understanding through building up basic concepts.	• Develops understanding through perception, image building.
• Is limited in the amount of detail it can handle.	• Appears almost unlimited in the amount of detail it can handle because of its image-building capability.

SOURCE: Reprinted by permission of the publisher, from "Using the Brain as a Model to Increase Rationality in Organizational Decision Making," by Ramond M. Wilmotte et al., *Management Review*, February 1984, p. 63. Copyright © 1984 AMA Membership Publications Division, American Management Associations, New York. All rights reserved.

thinker's perspective. Experts on the subject also recommend that right brain and left brain thinkers be paired up when assigning decision-making and problem-solving teams.[9]

Making Decisions

It stands to reason that if the degree of uncertainty varies from situation to situation, there can be no single way to make decisions. A second variable with which decision makers must cope is the number of times a particular decision is made. Some decisions are made frequently, perhaps several times a day. Others are made infrequently or just once. Consequently, decision theorists have distinguished between programmed and non-programmed decisions.[10] Each of these two types of decisions requires a different decision-making procedure.

Making Programmed Decisions

Programmed decisions are those that are repetitive and routine. Managers tend to devise fixed procedures for handling these everyday decisions. Examples include hiring decisions in a personnel office, billing decisions in a hospital, supply reorder decisions in a purchasing department, consumer loan decisions in a bank, and pricing decisions in a university bookstore. Most decisions made by the typical manager on a daily basis are of the programmed variety.

At the heart of the programmed decision procedure are decision rules. A **decision rule** is a statement that identifies the situation in which a decision is required and specifies how the decision will be made. Behind decision rules is the idea that standard, recurring problems need to be solved only once. Decision rules permit busy managers to make routine decisions quickly without having to go through comprehensive problem solving over and over again. Generally, decision rules should be stated in "if-then" terms. A decision rule for a consumer loan officer in a bank, for example, might be: "*If* the applicant is employed, has no record of loan default, and can put up 30 percent collateral, *then* a loan not to exceed $4000 can be authorized." Carefully conceived decision rules can streamline the decision-making process by allowing lower-level managers to shoulder the responsibility for programmed decisions and freeing higher-level managers for relatively more important, nonprogrammed decisions.

Making Non-programmed Decisions

Nonprogrammed decisions are those made in complex, important, and nonroutine situations, often under circumstances that are new and largely unfamiliar. This kind of decision is made much less frequently than are programmed decisions. Examples of nonprogrammed decisions include deciding whether or not to merge with another company, deciding how to replace an executive who died unexpectedly, deciding whether a foreign branch should be opened, and deciding how to market an entirely new kind of product or service. According to the president of a *Fortune* 500 company, the following six questions need to be asked prior to making a nonprogrammed decision:

- What decision needs to be made?
- When does it have to be made?
- Who will decide?
- Who will need to be consulted prior to making the decision?
- Who will ratify or veto the decision?
- Who will need to be informed of the decision?[11]

The decision-making process becomes more sharply focused when managers take the time to answer these questions.

One respected decision theorist has described nonprogrammed decisions as follows: "There is no cut-and-dried method for handling the problem because it hasn't arisen before, or because its precise nature and structure are elusive or complex, or because it is so important that it deserves a custom-tailored treatment."[12]

Figure 6.4 A General Decision-making Model

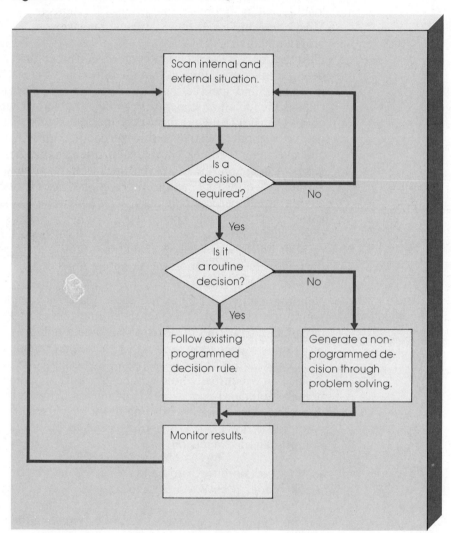

Nonprogrammed decision making calls for creative problem solving. The four-step problem-solving process that we shall examine later in this chapter helps managers make effective and efficient nonprogrammed decisions.

A General Decision-making Model

Although different decision procedures are required for different situations, it is possible to construct a general decision-making model. Figure 6.4 shows a logical sequence of steps that managers can follow when making decisions. Proper handling of each step improves the quality of the final decision.

The first step, a scan of the situation, is important, although it often is underemphasized or ignored altogether in discussions of managerial decision making. Scanning answers the question, "How do I know a decision should be made?" Nearly fifty years ago, Chester I. Barnard gave one of the best answers to this question, stating that "the occasions for decision originate in three distinct fields: (a) from authoritative communications from superiors; (b) from cases referred for decision by subordinates; (c) from cases originating in the initiative of the [manager] concerned."[13] In addition to signaling when a decision is required, alert scanning reveals the degree of uncertainty and provides necessary information for pending decisions.

Once the need for a decision has been established, the manager should determine whether or not the situation is routine. If it is routine and there is an appropriate decision rule, then the rule is applied. But if it turns out to be a new situation demanding a nonprogrammed decision, then comprehensive problem solving begins. In either case, the results of the final decision need to be evaluated to see if any follow-up action is necessary.

Group-aided Decision Making

Decision making, like any other organizational activity, does not take place in a vacuum. Typically, decision making is a highly social activity with committees, study groups, review panels, or task teams contributing in a variety of ways. According to one authority on decision making, at least five aspects of the decision-making process can be assigned to groups:

1. Analyzing the problem.
2. Identifying components of the decision situation.
3. Estimating components of the decision situation [for example, determining probabilities, feasibilities, time estimates, and payoffs].
4. Designing alternatives.
5. Choosing an alternative.[14]

Assuming that two (or more) heads are better than one and that managers can make better use of their time by delegating various decision-making chores, there is a strong case for turning to groups when making decisions. But before bringing others into the decision process, managers need to be aware of the problems of dispersed accountability and consider the trade-off between the advantages and disadvantages of group-aided decision making.

"On the other hand, suppose facts can lie?"
SOURCE: Copyright Ed Arno, Management Review 1983.

The Dilemma of Dispersed Accountability

There is a critical difference between group-aided decision making and group decision making. In the first instance, the group does everything except make the final decision. In the second instance, the group actually makes the final decision. Managers who choose the second route face a dilemma. Although a decision made by a group probably will reflect the collective experience and wisdom of all those involved, personal accountability is lost. Blame for a joint decision that fails is too easily passed on to others.

The traditional formula for resolving this problem is to make sure that a given manager is personally accountable for a decision when the responsibility for it has to be traced. According to this line of reasoning, even when a group is asked to recommend a decision, the responsibility for the final outcome remains with the manager in charge. For managers who want to maintain the integrity of personal accountability, there is no such thing as group decision making; there is only group-*aided* decision making. Three situations in which individual accountability for a decision is necessary are:

- The decision will have a significant impact on the success or failure of the unit or organization.
- The decision has legal ramifications (such as possible prosecution for price-fixing, antitrust, or product safety violations).
- A competitive reward is tied to a successful decision (for example, only one person can get a promotion).

In less critical areas, the group itself may be responsible for actually making decisions.

Table 6.3 Advantages and Disadvantages of Group-aided Decision Making and Problem Solving

Advantages	Disadvantages
1. **Greater pool of knowledge.** A group can bring much more information and experience to bear on a decision or problem than can an individual acting alone.	1. **Social pressure.** Unwillingness to "rock the boat" and pressure to conform may combine to stifle the creativity of individual contributors.
2. **Different perspectives.** Individuals with varied experience and interests help the group see decision situations and problems from different angles.	2. **Minority domination.** Sometimes the quality of group action is reduced when the group gives in to those who talk the loudest and longest.
3. **Greater comprehension.** Those who personally experience the give-and-take of group discussion about alternative courses of action tend to understand the rationale behind the final decision.	3. **Logrolling.** Political wheeling and dealing can displace sound thinking when an individual's pet project or vested interest is at stake.
4. **Increased acceptance.** Those who play an active role in group decision making and problem solving tend to view the outcome as "ours" rather than "theirs."	4. **Goal displacement.** Sometimes secondary considerations such as winning an argument, making a point, or getting back at a rival displace the primary task of making a sound decision or solving a problem.
5. **Training ground.** Less experienced participants in group action learn how to cope with group dynamics by actually being involved.	5. **"Groupthink."** Sometimes cohesive "in-groups" let the desire for unanimity override sound judgment when generating and evaluating alternative courses of action. (Groupthink is discussed in Chapter 12.)

Advantages and Disadvantages of Group-aided Decision Making

Various combinations of positive and negative factors are encountered when a manager brings others into the decision-making process. The main advantages and disadvantages are listed in Table 6.3. If there is a conscious effort to avoid or at least minimize the disadvantages, managers can gain a great deal by sharing the decision-making process with peers, outside consultants, and subordinates. Research has found that individual decision making is faster but that group-aided decisions usually are of higher quality and are more acceptable to those affected. A leading organizational psychologist has summed up the role of groups in decision making and problem solving as follows:

Groups are not a universal solution for all types of problems. They should not be used if the problem does not specifically require a sharing of information and evaluation of alternatives, or if cultural amplification is to be avoided, or if the group climate runs the risk of creating group think by squashing dissent. Most importantly, groups should not be used if the leaders and members are unwilling to invest some time and energy in helping the group to develop into an effective working unit.[15]

Personal Values and Decision Making

Decision-making models generally ignore the decision maker's personal value system. This is a serious oversight, because personal values inevitably affect a manager's choices.[16] Defined broadly, **values** are abstract ideals that shape an individual's thinking and behavior.[17] Contemporary social observers contend that too many managers have turned their backs on socially desirable values such as honesty, responsibility, and integrity. To support their case, they point to the abundant evidence of managerial misconduct in the form of illegal campaign contributions, overseas payoffs, deceptive advertising, and price fixing. Even though these questionable practices may be the exception rather than the rule, they are widespread enough to justify a close look at personal values and their role in decision making.

Instrumental and Terminal Values

Each manager, indeed each living person, values various means and ends in life. Recognizing this means-ends distinction, behavioral scientists have identified two basic types of values. An **instrumental value** is an enduring belief that a certain way of behaving is appropriate in all situations. For example, the time-honored saying, "Honesty is the best policy," represents an instrumental value. A person who truly values honesty will most likely behave in an honest manner. A **terminal value,** on the other hand, is an enduring belief that a certain end-state of existence is worth striving for and attaining.[18] For example, one person may strive for eternal salvation, whereas another may strive for social recognition and admiration. Instrumental values (modes of behavior) help achieve terminal values (desired end-states).

Since a person may hold a number of different instrumental and terminal values in various combinations, it is easy to appreciate that individual value systems are somewhat like fingerprints. Every individual has a unique set.

Table 6.4 The Rokeach Value Survey

Instructions: Study the two lists of values presented below. Then rank the instrumental values in order of importance to you (1 = most important, 18 = least important). Do the same with the list of terminal values.

Instrumental Values	Terminal Values
Rank	*Rank*
_____ Ambitious (hard-working, aspiring)	_____ A comfortable life (a prosperous life)
_____ Broadminded (open-minded)	_____ An exciting life (a stimulating, active life)
_____ Capable (competent, effective)	_____ A sense of accomplishment (lasting contribution)
_____ Cheerful (lighthearted, joyful)	_____ A world at peace (free of war and conflict)
_____ Clean (neat, tidy)	_____ A world of beauty (beauty of nature and the arts)
_____ Courageous (standing up for your beliefs)	_____ Equality (brotherhood, equal opportunity for all)
_____ Forgiving (willing to pardon others)	_____ Family security (taking care of loved ones)
_____ Helpful (working for the welfare of others)	_____ Freedom (independence, free choice)
_____ Honest (sincere, truthful)	_____ Happiness (contentedness)
_____ Imaginative (daring, creative)	_____ Inner harmony (freedom from inner conflict)
_____ Independent (self-sufficient)	_____ Mature love (sexual and spiritual intimacy)
_____ Intellectual (intelligent, reflective)	_____ National security (protection from attack)
_____ Logical (consistent, rational)	_____ Pleasure (an enjoyable, leisurely life)
_____ Loving (affectionate, tender)	_____ Salvation (saved, eternal life)
_____ Obedient (dutiful, respectful)	_____ Self-respect (self-esteem)
_____ Polite (courteous, well-mannered)	_____ Social recognition (respect, admiration)
_____ Responsible (dependable, reliable)	_____ True friendship (close companionship)
_____ Self-controlled (restrained, self-disciplined)	_____ Wisdom (a mature understanding of life)

SOURCE: Copyright, 1967, by Milton Rokeach, and reproduced by permission of Halgren Tests, 873 Persimmon Avenue, Sunnyvale, CA 94087.

**Getting in
Touch with
Your Own
Values**

At this point you may be wondering about your own value system. To help you discover your own set of values, refer to the Rokeach value survey in Table 6.4 (on page 213). (Take a few moments now to complete this survey.)

If you are a bit surprised at how things turned out, it is probably because most of us take our basic values for granted. Seldom do we stop to arrange them consciously according to priority. (As an interesting reliability check between your intentions and your actual behavior, have a close friend or mate evaluate you with the Rokeach survey.)

One of the principal benefits of knowing our values is to see whether there are any serious conflicts among the values in each category or among the values in the two different categories. For instance, some people experience a serious conflict between the instrumental values of ambition and honesty. Honesty has been known to take a back seat for the hard-driving, extremely ambitious person.[19] Likewise, for many there is a conflict between the terminal values of accomplishment and pleasure, particularly with regard to going to work. Someone who works hard to make a lasting contribution at the office may find little time for family, friends, or recreation. Finally, some managers find that their high-priority instrumental values will not help them achieve the terminal values they seek. For instance, imagine the frustration of a manager who values obedience (an instrumental value) while at the same time yearning for freedom (terminal value).

There is another type of value conflict of which present and future managers ought to be aware: the conflict between the individual's values and the values reinforced by the organization's culture. The classic conflict here is the one between the individual's desire for independence and the organization's insistence on obedience. Personal values may clash with those encouraged by the organization in other ways, too. For example, a noncompetitive person who sees nothing pleasurable about physical exercise would have a difficult time at PepsiCo Inc., whose organizational culture has been described as follows:

> Like Marines, Pepsi executives are expected to be physically fit as well as mentally alert: Pepsi employs four physical-fitness instructors at its headquarters, and a former executive says it is an unwritten rule that to get ahead in the company a manager must stay in shape. The company encourages one-on-one sports as well as interdepartmental competition in such games as soccer and basketball. ... In such a culture, less competitive managers are deliberately weeded out.[20]

Of course, judging the wisdom of PepsiCo's approach depends on one's own value system.

Table 6.5   The Erosion of Personal Values

1. Passing blame for errors to an innocent co-worker.
2. Divulging confidential information.
3. Falsifying time/quality/quantity reports.
4. Claiming credit for someone else's work.
5. Padding an expense account over 10 percent.
6. Pilfering company materials and supplies.
7. Accepting gifts/favors in exchange for preferential treatment.
8. Giving gifts/favors in exchange for preferential treatment.
9. Padding an expense account up to 10 percent.
10. Authorizing a subordinate to violate company rules.
11. Calling in sick to take a day off.
12. Concealing one's errors.
13. Taking longer than necessary to do a job.
14. Using company services for personal use.
15. Doing personal business on company time.
16. Taking extra personal time (lunch hour, breaks, early departure, and so forth).
17. Not reporting others' violations of company policies and rules.

SOURCE: John W. Newstrom and William A. Ruch, "The Ethics of Management and the Management of Ethics," *MSU Business Topics* 23 (Winter 1975): 29–37. Reprinted by permission of the publisher, Division of Research, Graduate School of Business Administration, Michigan State University.

The Erosion of Personal Values

Yielding to the pressures of modern life, some employees disregard their personal values and engage in questionable conduct at work. The sale of defective and dangerous products, the misuse of public funds, the illegal dumping of hazardous wastes, deceptive advertising, payoffs, and age, race, and sex discrimination in employment would not be as common as they are today if decision makers at all levels had not compromised their personal values somewhere along the line.

A recent nationwide survey of 1460 managers (90 percent male, 10 percent female) suggests that pressure from above promotes the erosion of personal values. The question posed by the researchers was: "I find that sometimes I must compromise my personal principles to conform to my organization's expectations."[21] Though 20 percent of the top-level managers surveyed agreed with this statement, stronger agreement was found among middle managers (27 percent) and supervisory-level managers (41 percent). Thus, the lower the level of management, the greater the pressure to conform or compromise personal standards.

Compounding the problem of pressure from above is the problem of "creeping erosion." As the list of questionable employee behaviors in Table 6.5 indicates, the erosion of personal values can begin in small ways.

Unfortunately, seemingly minor indiscretions often pave the way for steadily greater abuses. It is easier to compromise the traditional values of honesty, responsibility, courage, and self-control when one is comforted by the notion that "everyone does it." The quality of today's and tomorrow's decisions can only decline unless individual managers adhere to their socially responsible values when generating, evaluating, and selecting decision alternatives. (The related topic of business ethics is discussed in Chapter 18.)

Managerial Creativity

Demands for creativity and innovation make the practice of management endlessly exciting (and sometimes troubling). Nearly all managerial problem solving requires a healthy measure of creativity as managers mentally take things apart, rearrange the pieces in new and potentially productive configurations, and look beyond normal frameworks for new solutions. This process is like turning the kaleidoscope of one's mind. Thomas Edison used to retire to an old couch in his laboratory to do his creative thinking. Henry Ford reportedly sought creative insights by staring at a blank wall in his shop. Although the average manager's attempts at creativity may not be as dramatically fruitful as Edison's or Ford's, workplace creativity needs to be understood and nurtured. As a steppingstone for the next section on creative problem solving, this section defines creativity, discusses the management of creative people, and identifies barriers to creativity.

What Is Creativity? Since creativity is a somewhat mysterious process known chiefly by its results, it is difficult to define. About as close as we can come is to say that **creativity** is the reorganization of experience into new configurations.[22] According to a management consultant specializing in creativity:

> Creativity is a function of *knowledge, imagination,* and *evaluation.** The greater our knowledge, the more ideas, patterns, or combinations we can achieve. But merely having the knowledge does not guarantee the formation of new patterns; the bits and pieces must be shaken up and interrelated in new ways. Then, the embryonic ideas must be evaluated and developed into usable ideas.[23]

Creativity is often subtle and may not be readily apparent to the untrained

*Emphasis added.

eye. But the combination and extension of seemingly insignificant day-to-day breakthroughs lead to organizational progress.

Identifying general types of creativity is easier than defining the basic process. One pioneering writer on the subject isolated three overlapping domains of creativity: art, discovery, and humor.[24] These have been called the "ah!" reaction, the "aha!" reaction, and the "haha!" reaction, respectively.[25]

The discovery ("aha!") variation is the most relevant to management. Staff and patients alike benefited when a hospital administrator said, "Aha! Why don't we realize a savings by sharing our purchasing, laundry, and housekeeping functions with other hospitals in the area?" Similarly, television network profits went up when a network executive said, "Aha! Why don't we start basing our evening programs on the plots of successful movies?" The list of significant "aha's" is endless. Many have made life a little better, thanks to managerial creativity.

Managing the Creative Individual

Creative people present managers with a dilemma. "Creatives" tend to be nonconformists in behavior, dress, and grooming. Attempts to get creatives to conform to rules and regulations may serve to stifle their creativity. Creative individuals often like to get lost in intriguing aspects of the job and resent managerial attempts to get them back on the track. The following account of a highly creative engineer employed at a U.S. naval shipyard, where civilian employees are expected to dress as neatly as the military personnel, demonstrates how creatives sometimes require special consideration.

> In appearance we see a skinny frame whose shoulders under his cape look like a wire coathanger. Yes, cape. It formerly belonged to a Salvation Army lieutenant colonel. Blue jeans, an Aloha shirt, and tennis shoes—no socks—complete his attire. Charlie drives to and from work in a yellow dump truck whose previous owner was the State Highway Department. He lives in a 1952-model house trailer pulled aboard a barge. ... Yes, Admiral Miles winces every time he sees the dump truck come snuffling into the parking lot. Admiral Miles and Charlie don't share too much in the way of a common life style, but Admiral Miles has strong positive feelings toward [Charlie], as well he should. Charlie is one of the yard's most valuable assets.[26]

If organizations are to grow and prosper because of creative ideas, then managers need to be flexible in their handling of creative subordinates. Many creative people dislike close supervision, so the manager may need to serve primarily as a resource person who provides help when it is requested. If creative employees like to work at night or on Sunday, perhaps they can be given a key or special pass to get into the building. If they spend a lot of time staring out the window, it might make sense to measure their productivity by the week or even longer, instead of by the hour. They may be working out their best ideas while apparently daydreaming. Consider, for example, how the Pac-Man concept came into being:

> The idea was born when Toru Iwatami, 27, was daydreaming at his desk just before lunch. As his appetite grew, he visualized little round shapes devouring smaller ones. He took the idea to Namco, his employer [in Tokyo, Japan], and the rest is marketing history.[27]

If Iwatami's creativity had been stifled in some way, Namco would not have collected the more than $15 million in royalties it earned from licensing the Pac-Man concept. Of course, creatives, like all other employees, need to be held accountable for results. Unfortunately, some managers become so preoccupied with superficial aspects of personality, appearance, scheduling, or performance that they end up with a conforming but uncreative employee.

Learning to Be More Creative

Some people naturally seem to be more creative than others. But that does not mean that those who feel the need cannot develop their creative capacity. It does seem clear that creative ability can be learned, in the sense that our creative energies can be released from the bonds of convention, lack of self-confidence, and narrow thinking. We all can learn to be more creative.

The best place to begin is by trying to consciously overcome what one creativity expert calls *mental locks*. The following mental locks are attitudes that get us through our daily activities but tend to stifle our creativity:

1. **Looking for the "right" answer.** Depending on one's perspective, a given problem may have several right answers.
2. **Always trying to be logical.** Logic does not always prevail given human emotions and organizational inconsistencies, ambiguity, and contradictions.
3. **Strictly following the rules.** If things are to be improved, arbitrary limits on thinking and behavior need to be questioned.
4. **Insisting on being practical.** Impractical answers to "what if" questions can become steppingstones to creative insights.
5. **Avoiding ambiguity.** Creativity can be stunted by too much objectivity and specificity.
6. **Fearing and avoiding failure.** Fear of failure can paralyze us into not acting on our good ideas. This is unfortunate because we learn many valuable and lasting lessons from our mistakes.

7. **Forgetting how to play.** The playful experimentation of childhood too often disappears by adulthood.
8. **Becoming too specialized.** Crossfertilization of specialized areas helps in defining problems and generating solutions.
9. **Not wanting to look foolish.** Humor can release tensions and unlock creative energies. Seemingly foolish questions can enhance understanding.
10. **Saying "I'm not creative."** By nurturing small and apparently insignificant ideas we can convince ourselves that we are indeed creative.[28]

If these mental locks are conquered, the creative problem-solving process discussed in the next section can be used to its full potential.

Creative Problem Solving

We are all problem solvers. But this does not mean that all of us are good problem solvers or, for that matter, that we even know how to solve problems systematically. Most daily problem solving is done on a somewhat haphazard, intuitive basis. Some difficulty arises, we quickly look around for an answer, jump at the first workable solution to come along, and move on to other things. In a primitive sense, this sequence of events qualifies as a problem-solving process, and it works quite well for informal daily activities. But in the world of management, a more systematic problem-solving process is required for tackling difficult and unfamiliar nonprogrammed decision situations. In the context of management, **problem solving** is defined as "... the conscious process of reducing the difference between an actual situation and the desired situation."[29] Managerial problem solving consists of a four-step sequence: (1) identifying the problem, (2) generating alternative solutions, (3) selecting a solution, and (4) implementing and evaluating the solution (see Figure 6.5).

Identifying the Problem

As strange as it may seem, the most common problem-solving difficulty is the inadequate identification of problems. Busy managers have a tendency to rush into generating and selecting alternative solutions before they have actually isolated the real problem. According to Peter Drucker, a respected management scholar, "the most common source of mistakes in management decisions is emphasis on finding the right answers rather than the right questions."[30] As problem finders, managers should probe for the right questions.

What Is a Problem? Ask a half-dozen people how they identify problems and you are likely to get as many answers. Consistent with the definition

Figure 6.5 The Problem-solving Process

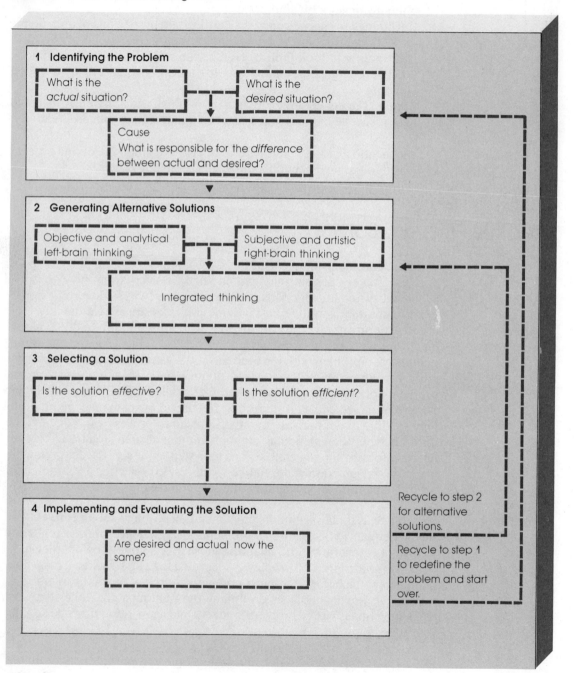

Figure 6.6 Problem Finding

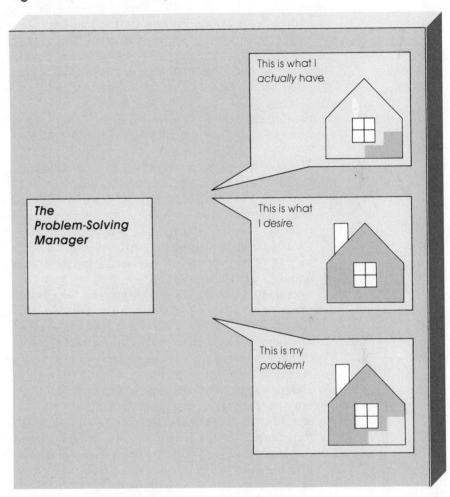

just given for problem solving, a **problem** is defined as the difference between an actual state of affairs and a desired state of affairs. In other words, a problem is the gap between where one is and where one wants to be (see Figure 6.6). Problem solving is meant to close this gap. For example, a person in New York who has to be in San Francisco in 24 hours has a problem. The problem is not being in New York (the actual state of affairs), nor is it being in San Francisco in 24 hours (the desired state of affairs). Instead, the problem is the 2934 miles between New York and San Francisco. Considering the 24-hour time constraint, flying is the only practical way of solving the problem (closing the gap). If more time were available, other modes of transportation could be considered.

Managers need to define problems according to the gaps between the actual and the desired situations. For example, a production manager would be wise to concentrate on the gap between the present level of weekly production and the desired level. This is much more fruitful than complaining about the current low production or wishfully thinking about high production. The challenge is discovering a workable alternative for closing the gap between actual and desired production.

Stumbling Blocks for Problem Finders   There are three common stumbling blocks for those attempting to identify problems:

1. **Defining the problem according to a possible solution.** One should be careful not to rule out alternative solutions in the way one states a problem. For example, a manager in a unit plagued by high absenteeism who says, "We have a problem with low pay," may prevent management from discovering that tedious and boring work is the real cause. By focusing on how to close the gap between actual and desired attendance, instead of simply on low pay, management stands a better chance of finding a workable solution.
2. **Focusing on narrow, low-priority areas.** Successful managers are those who can weed out relatively minor problems and reserve their attention for problems that really make a difference. Formal organizational goals and objectives provide a useful framework for determining the priority of various problems. Why be concerned with waxing the floor when the roof is caving in?
3. **Diagnosing problems in terms of their symptoms.** As a short-run expedient, treating symptoms rather than underlying causes may be appropriate. A bottle of aspirin is cheaper than trying to find a less stressful job, for example. In the longer run, however, symptoms tend to reappear, and problems tend to get worse. There is a simple two-way test for discovering whether one has actually found the cause of a problem: "If I *introduce* this variable, will the problem (the gap) disappear?" or "If I *remove* this variable, will the problem (the gap) disappear?" **Causes** then, are variables that, because of their presence or absence from the situation, are primarily responsible for the difference between the actual and the desired conditions. For example, the absence of a key can cause a problem with a locked door, and the presence of a nail can cause a problem with an inflated tire.[31]

Generating Alternative Solutions   Once the problem and its most probable cause have been identified, attention turns to generating alternative solutions. This is the creative step in problem solving. Unfortunately, as the following statement points out, creativity is often shortchanged.

Table 6.6 Techniques for Generating Creative Alternatives

Brainstorming
An uninhibited approach to ideation, particularly for the purpose of breaking down broadly defined problems into their essential elements. A group approach only.

Free Association
An imaginative approach to idea stimulation based on playing with analogies or symbols in some way related to the problem; a method applied most successfully to develop intangible ideas such as slogans, logos, trade names, acronyms, etc., but also used in Synectics.

Edisonian
An approach to generating ideas based on tedious trial-and-error experimentation; a method best applied when more systematic methods have failed.

Blast! Then Refine
Navy jargon for a cost-cutting or problem-solving method that works this way: the function to be improved upon is completely blasted from one's thoughts; then a complete new approach is devised to meet fully the original objectives.

Attribute Listing
Applied principally to improving tangible objects or things, the technique consists first of listing the parts and the essential features or attributes of the object, then systematically modifying these to improve the object.

Forced Relationship
An approach to developing ideas based on a more structured application of free association: the elements of a problem are identified and listed; then relationships or associations between these elements are systematically sought out to uncover patterns that might lead to new ideas.

Morphological Matrix Analysis
A structured approach to finding combinations of ideas by identifying the problem variables along both axes of a matrix and plotting the interrelationships among the variables in the corresponding squares within the body of the chart.

Operations Research
An approach to finding optimal solutions to problems that relies on the classical concepts of the scientific method, statistics, simulation and logical thinking for developing and testing hypotheses and offering guidance in decision making.

Value Analysis
An orderly approach to finding optimum solutions to problems primarily related to optimizing the performance of a specified function at a minimum cost.

Synectics
A highly structured group approach to problem solving based on the repeated use of various analogies and metaphors that provide unique contexts for seeing the problem from widely divergent points of view. A group approach only.

SOURCE: William G. Hyzer, "First State the Problem," *Industrial Research/Development* 20 (September 1978): p. 144. Used with permission of William G. Hyzer, Consultant in Engineering and Applied Science.

The natural response to a problem seems to be to try to get rid of it by finding an answer—often taking the first answer that occurs and pursuing it because of one's reluctance to spend the time and mental effort needed to conjure up a rich storehouse of alternatives from which to choose.[32]

It takes time, patience, and practice to become a good generator of alternative solutions: a flexible combination of left brain and right thinking is helpful. Several popular and useful techniques for stimulating individual and group creativity are listed in Table 6.6 (on page 223).

Selecting a Solution   Simply stating that the best solution should be selected in step 3 (refer back to Figure 6.5) can be a bit misleading. Because of time and financial constraints and political considerations, "best" is a relative term. Generally, alternative solutions should be screened for the most appealing balance of effectiveness and efficiency, in view of relevant constraints and intangibles. Along more specific lines, Russell Ackoff, a specialist in managerial problem solving, contends that there are three things that can be done about problems: they can be resolved, solved, or dissolved.[33]

Resolving the Problem   When a problem is resolved, a course of action that is good enough to meet the minimum constraints is selected. The term **satisfice** has been applied to the practice of settling for solutions that are good enough rather than the best possible. A badly worn spare tire may satisfice as a replacement for a flat tire for the balance of a trip, although getting the flat repaired is the best possible solution. According to Ackoff, most managers rely on problem resolving. This nonquantitative, subjectively judgmental approach is popular among managers because they claim they do not have the necessary information or time for the other approaches. It is important to note, though, that satisficing has been criticized as a shortsighted and passive technique emphasizing survival instead of improvement and growth.

Solving the Problem   A problem is solved when the best possible solution is selected. Managers are said to **optimize** when they systematically research alternative solutions through scientific observation and quantitative measurement and select the one with the best combination of benefits.

Dissolving the Problem   A problem is dissolved when the situation in which it occurs is changed so that the problem no longer exists. Problem dissolvers are said to **idealize** because they actually change the nature of the system in which a problem resides. Managers who dissolve problems rely on whatever combination of nonquantitative and quantitative tools is needed to get the job done. The replacement of automobile assembly-line welders with robots, for instance, has dissolved the problem of costly absenteeism among people in that job category.

Whatever approach a manager chooses, the following advice from

Ackoff should be kept in mind: "Few if any problems ... are ever perma-nently resolved, solved, or dissolved; every treatment of a problem gener-ates new problems."[34]

Implementing and Evaluating the Solution

Time is the true test of any solution. Until a particular solution has had time to prove its worth, the manager can rely only on his or her judgment concerning its effectiveness and efficiency. Ideally, the solution selected will completely eliminate the difference between the actual and the desired in an efficient and timely manner. Should the gap fail to disappear, two options are open. If management remains convinced that the problem has been correctly identified, then they can recycle to step 2 to try another solution that was identified earlier. This recycling can continue until all feasible solutions have been given a fair chance or until the nature of the problem changes to the extent that the existing solutions are obsolete. If the gap between actual and desired persists in spite of repeated attempts to find a solution, then it is advisable to recycle to step 1 to redefine the problem and engage in a new round of problem solving.

Summary

Decision making is a fundamental part of management because it requires choosing among alternative courses of action. In addition to having to cope with an era of accelerating change, today's decision makers face the challenges of dealing with complexity, uncertainty, and the need for flexible thinking. Seven factors contributing to decision complexity are multiple criteria, intangibles, risk and uncertainty, long-term implications, inter-disciplinary input, pooled decision making, and value judgments. The three major categories of uncertainty are certainty, risk, and uncertainty. Confidence in one's decisions decreases as uncertainty increases. Today's decision maker needs a flexible style of thinking based on the ability to integrate left brain (analytical) and right brain (spatial) thinking patterns.

Two general types of decisions are programmed and nonprogrammed decisions. Because programmed decisions are relatively clear-cut and routinely encountered, fixed decision rules can be formulated for them. Nonprogrammed decisions, on the other hand, require creative problem solving because they are novel and unfamiliar.

Managers may choose to bring other people into virtually every aspect of the decision-making process. However, when the group rather than an individual is responsible for actually making the decision, personal accountability is lost. Dispersed accountability is undesirable in some key decision situations. Group-aided decision making has both advantages and disadvantages.

Publicized accounts of managerial misconduct in recent years have underscored the importance of values in decision making. Both instrumental (means) and terminal (ends) values are vital to the judgmental aspect of decision making. Managers need to be aware of value conflicts within themselves and between themselves and their employing organization. Perceived pressure from above and value erosion appear to be partially responsible for the subordination of traditional, socially responsible values.

Creativity requires the proper combination of knowledge, imagination, and evaluation to reorganize experience into new configurations. Three domains of creativity are art, discovery (the most relevant to management), and humor. Because they tend to be nonconformists, creative employees often require special handling while still being held accountable for results. By consciously overcoming ten mental locks, we can become more creative.

The creative problem-solving process consists of four steps: (1) identifying the problem, (2) generating alternative solutions, (3) selecting a solution, and (4) implementing and evaluating the solution. Inadequate problem finding is common among busy managers. By seeing problems as gaps between an actual situation and a desired situation, managers are in a better position to create more effective and efficient solutions. Depending on the situation, problems can be resolved, solved, or dissolved. It is important to remember that today's solutions often become tomorrow's problems.

Terms to Understand

Decision making
Condition of certainty
Condition of risk
Objective probabilities
Subjective probabilities
Condition of uncertainty
Programmed decisions
Decision rule
Nonprogrammed decisions
Values

Instrumental value
Terminal value
Creativity
Problem solving
Problem
Causes (of problems)
Satisfice
Optimize
Idealize

Questions for Discussion

1. What evidence of the seven sources of decision complexity do you detect in your own life?
2. Are you primarily a right-brain or left-brain thinker? How do you know? How will this help or hinder you as a manager?
3. Can you write a decision rule for a programmed decision at the place you now work or where you have worked in the past?
4. How does knowledge of the difference between programmed and nonprogrammed decisions help a manager?
5. What is wrong with having a group of people make a specific decision?
6. How do you think your personal value system would affect the way you would perform as a manager?
7. What evidence of value erosion do you see around you today?
8. Regarding your own creativity, which mental lock do you find to be the most troublesome? What can you do to overcome it?
9. Why is problem finding especially important?
10. Can you think of a managerial situation in which it would be better to resolve rather than solve or dissolve a problem? How about a situation in which dissolving would be most appropriate?

Back to the Opening Case

Now that you have read Chapter 6, you should be able to answer the following questions about the Apple Computer case:

1. What instrumental values are encouraged by the "Apple Values"?
2. Is Steve Jobs probably left-brain or right-brain dominant? How can you tell? How could this tendency both help and hinder him as a manager?
3. Why were Steve Jobs and John Sculley initially a good decision-making and problem-solving team and later quarrelsome?
4. Why is creativity likely to flourish at Apple Computer?

References

Opening Quotation: Charles H. Kepner and Benjamin B. Tregoe, *The Rational Manager* (New York: McGraw-Hill, 1965), p. 21.

Closing Exercise 6.2

How Creative Are You?

Exercise: Assume that a steel pipe is imbedded in the concrete floor of a bare room as shown below. The inside diameter is .06" larger than the diameter of a ping-pong ball (1.50") which is resting gently at the bottom of the pipe. You are one of a group of six people in the room, along with the following objects:

100' of clothesline	A file
A carpenter's hammer	A wire coat hanger
A chisel	A monkey wrench
A box of Wheaties	A light bulb

List as many ways you can think of (in five minutes) to get the ball out of the pipe without damaging the ball, tube, or floor.

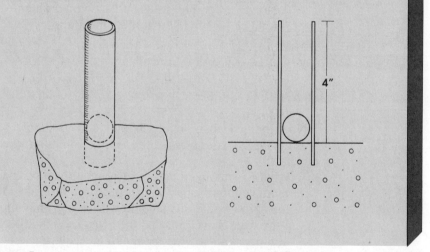

Source: From *Conceptual Blockbusting*. Second Edition, by James L. Adams, by permission of W. W. Norton & Company, Inc. Copyright © 1974, 1976, 1979 by James L. Adams. Originally published as part of The Portable Stanford by the Stanford Alumni Association.

Opening Case: For additional information on Apple, see Erik Larson and Carrie Dolan, "Once All Alone in Field, Apple Computer Girds for Industry Shakeout," *Wall Street Journal* 109 (October 4, 1983): 1, 16; "Apple Computer's Counterattack Against IBM," *Business Week* No. 2824 (January 16, 1984): 78–81; Michael Moritz, "Apple Launches a Mac Attack," *Time* 123 (January 30, 1984): 68–69; Sabin Russell, "Steve Jobs' Mega-Risk," *Venture* 6 (March 1984): 66–72; Robert Levering, Milton Moskowitz, and Michael Katz, *The 100 Best Companies* *to Work for in America* (Reading, Mass.: Addison-Wesley, 1984), pp. 11–14; Joel Dreyfuss, "John Sculley Rises in the West," *Fortune* 110 (July 9, 1984): 180–184; and Barbara Rudolph, "Shaken to the Very Core," *Time* 126 (Sept. 30, 1985): 64–65.

1. Levering, Moskowitz, and Katz, *The 100 Best Companies to Work for in America*, p. 12.
2. Moritz, "Apple Launches a Mac Attack," p. 69.
3. Dreyfuss, "John Sculley Rises in the West," pp. 182–183, 184.
4. Alvin Toffler, *The Third Wave* (New York: Bantam, 1980), p. 229.
5. Adapted from Ralph L. Keeney, "Decision Analysis: How to Cope with Increasing Complexity," *Management Review* 68 (September 1979): 24–40.
6. See Irwin Ross, "Chrysler on the Brink," *Fortune* 103 (February 9, 1981): 38–42.
7. See Alan D. Meyer, "Mingling Decision Making Metaphors," *Academy of Management Review* 9 (January 1984): 6–17.
8. For an informative discussion of the three styles of thinking, see Weston H. Agor, "Using Intuition to Manage Organizations in the Future," *Business Horizons* 27 (July-August 1984): 49–54.
9. For example, see Raymond M. Wilmotte, Philip I. Morgan, and H. Kent Baker, "Using the Brain as a Model to Increase Rationality in Organizational Decision Making," *Management Review* 73 (February 1984): 62–65.
10. For example, see Herbert A. Simon, *The New Science of Management Decision,* rev. ed. (Englewood Cliffs, N.J.: Prentice-Hall, 1977), p. 40.
11. Andrew S. Grove, *High Output Management* (New York: Random House, 1983), p. 98.
12. Simon, *The New Science of Management Decision,* p. 46.
13. Chester I. Barnard, *The Functions of the Executive* (Cambridge, Mass.: Harvard University Press, 1938), p. 190.
14. George P. Huber, *Managerial Decision Making* (Glenview, Ill.: Scott, Foresman, 1980), pp. 141–142.
15. Edgar H. Schein, *Organizational Psychology,* 3rd ed. (Englewood Cliffs, N.J.: Prentice-Hall, 1980), p. 171.
16. For a good management-oriented discussion of values, see Barry Z. Posner and J. Michael Munson, "The Importance of Values in Understanding Organizational Behavior," *Human Resource Management* 18 (Fall 1979): 9–14.
17. For an excellent treatment of values and related concepts, see Milton Rokeach, *Beliefs, Attitudes, and Values* (San Francisco: Jossey-Bass, 1968), p. 124.
18. Ibid.
19. An interesting and candid account of the conflict between ambition and honesty can be found in John Dean, *Blind Ambition* (New York: Simon & Schuster, 1976).
20. "Corporate Culture," *Business Week* No. 2660 (October 27, 1980): 154.
21. Barry Z. Posner and Warren H. Schmidt, "Values and the American Manager:

An Update," *California Management Review* 26 (Spring 1984): 211.

22. Based on discussion in N. R. F. Maier, Mara Julius, and James Thurber, "Studies in Creativity: Individual Differences in the Storing and Utilization of Information," *The American Journal of Psychology* 80 (December 1967): 492–519.

23. Sidney J. Parnes, "Learning Creative Behavior," *The Futurist* 18 (August 1984): 30–31. Additional informative and interesting reading on creativity may be found in Emily T. Smith, "Are You Creative?" *Business Week* No. 2914 (September 30, 1985): 80–84.

24. See Arthur Koestler, *The Act of Creation* (London: Hutchinson, 1969), p. 27.

25. See James L. Adams, *Conceptual Blockbusting* (San Francisco: Freeman, 1974), p. 35.

26. John Senger, "Organizational Problem Solving and Creativity," *Public Personnel Management* 3 (November-December 1974): 541.

27. "E.T. and Friends are Flying High," *Business Week* No. 2772 (January 10, 1983): 77.

28. For a stimulating treatment of creativity, see Roger von Oech, *A Whack on the Side of the Head* (New York: Warner, 1983).

29. Huber, *Managerial Decision Making,* p. 12.

30. Peter F. Drucker, *The Practice of Management* (New York: Harper & Row, 1954), p. 531.

31. Adapted from Huber, *Managerial Decision Making,* pp. 13–15.

32. James L. Adams, *Conceptual Blockbusting* (San Francisco: Freeman, 1974), p. 7.

33. See Russell L. Ackoff, "The Art and Science of Mess Management," *Interfaces* 11 (February 1981): 20–26.

34. Ibid., p. 22.

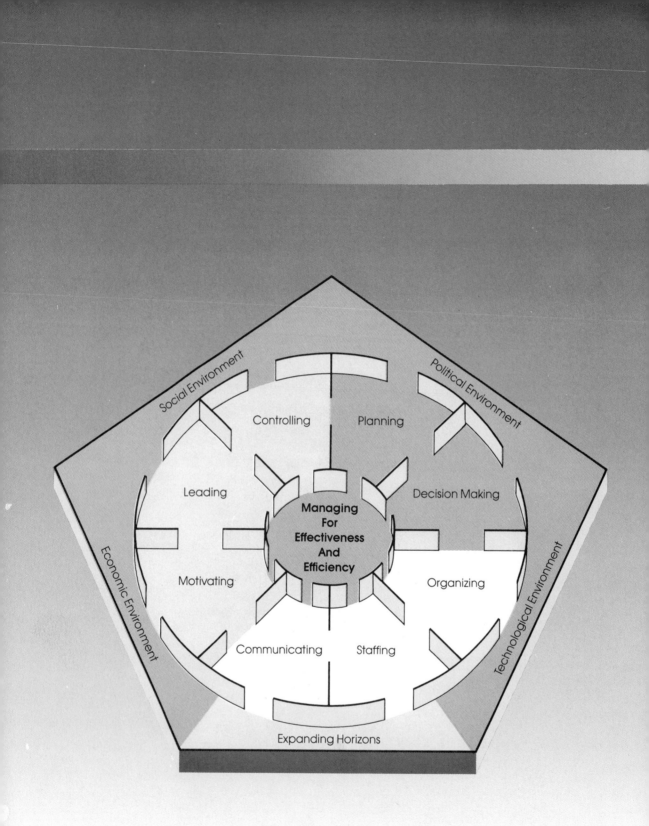

PART THREE

Organizing, Staffing, and Communicating

Part Three looks at organizational structure, the individual-organization matching process, and the linking role of communication. Traditional and modern models of organization are contrasted in Chapter 7, along with a discussion of organizational cultures. Based on the assumption that organizations are dynamic open systems, Chapter 8 focuses on alternative organization design formats within a contingency framework. Delegation is given special attention. In Chapter 9, staffing and human resource management are discussed within the context of getting the right person in the right job at the right time. Attention turns to the communication process, perception, and dynamics of organizational communication in Chapter 10. Practical guidelines are provided for effective listening and writing and for effectively running meetings.

Chapter 7

Organizations and Organizational Cultures

Organizations are social inventions or tools developed ... to accomplish things otherwise not possible.
Joseph A. Litterer

Chapter Objectives

When you finish studying this chapter, you should be able to

- Identify and describe four characteristics common to all organizations.
- Explain how organizations can be classified by purpose and technology.
- Contrast the traditional and modern views of organizations.
- Discuss the bureaucratic paradox.
- Describe a business organization in terms of the open-system model.
- Identify and explain four symptoms of a weak organizational culture.

Opening Case 7.1

IBM: "Big Blue" Rolls On

By any measuring stick, International Business Machines Corporation (IBM) is a huge organization. The Armonk, New York, company earned over $6 *billion* in after-tax profits in 1984, making it the world's most profitable corporation. IBM's 1984 sales were eight times greater than those of its nearest competitor, Digital Equipment Corporation. Big Blue, so-called because of the distinctive blue color of many of its products, reportedly is the market leader in virtually all of the 130 countries where it does business. More than 370,000 IBM employees worldwide manufacture, sell, and service a complete line of data-processing equipment including everything from $800 electric typewriters to giant computer systems costing over $100 million. Thanks to the company's aggressive ad campaign featuring Charlie Chaplin's Little Tramp, IBM's personal computer has become its most widely known product. But because IBM so convincingly dominates other segments of the computer market, the IBM PC accounted for only about 10 percent of the firm's sales in 1984. IBM introduced 600 new hardware and software products in 1983 and controls an estimated one-third of the U.S. data-processing industry.

Pointing to the firm's size and new aggressiveness, observers in the business community consider IBM to be unstoppable:

> Since the Reagan administration in early 1982 dropped a 13-year-old anti-trust suit, IBM has been on a tear. It is entering new markets, pricing more aggressively, suing rivals and buying large chunks of other high-tech firms such as Intel, a major producer of semiconductor chips. Result: Sales and earnings growth have exceeded the industry norms.[1]

IBM's 1988 sales are projected to reach $88 billion with after-tax profits of almost $13 billion. Paradoxically, it is the little things that have enabled IBM to become so big.

The Watson Tradition

Although critics often poke fun at IBM for being an army of white-shirted clones who look, talk, and act alike, the company is proud of its strong culture that has descended from the Watson tradition. Thomas J. Watson ran IBM from 1914 to 1956, until Thomas J. Watson, Jr. took over the reins of the company until 1971.

> Under [the elder] Watson, IBM had rules for practically everything. Employees were told what to wear (dark business suits, white shirts and striped ties) and what to drink (no alcohol, even when off the job), and were urged in signs posted everywhere to THINK. Aspiring executives usually started out in sales and marketing and were transferred so frequently that they took to joking that IBM stood for "I've Been Moved." [Indeed, John Opel, the recently retired chief executive officer of IBM, held 19 different positions after joining the company in 1949.]
>
> … Many Watson-instilled codes remain in effect today, though in a softened form. All IBMers are subject to a 32-page code of business ethics. Sample warning from the blue-covered rulebook: "If IBM is about to build a new facility, you must not invest in land or business near the new site."[2]

IBM expects employees to express their loyalty by spending their entire careers with the company and honoring IBM's strong penchant for secrecy. In return, IBM employees enjoy high wages and generous benefits, comprehensive training, and the protection of a no-layoff policy. If an employee's job is eliminated, he or she is retrained for another position within the company. Fair treatment and respect for individual employees are cherished IBM values. Employees with grievances can take advantage of the company's open-door policy. If necessary, an appeal process leading ultimately to the chairman is available. Significantly, there has never been a union-certification election at an IBM facility in the United States.

A remaining cornerstone of the Watson tradition is a near fanatical devotion to providing customers with the best possible service. Frequently circulated stories about IBMers who went to heroic ends to provide excellent service reinforce the commitment to "go that extra inch" when serving customers. Sales quotas are deliberately set at a level attainable by about 80 percent of the sales force to create lots of self-perceived winners. Those who consistently meet their quotas are honored with membership in the Hundred Percent Club. Formal recognition in company publications, such as one reminiscently entitled *Think,* helps ensure that those who go the extra inch in serving customers are held up as examples and rewarded.

Who Says Elephants Can't Dance?

During the 1970s, when it was preoccupied with fighting the government's antitrust suit, critics claimed that IBM had become too big, too bureaucratic and complex, and too inflexible to respond to rapidly changing markets. However, the IBM PC project proved that "an elephant can dance." In August 1980, a team of 12 was sent to a warehouse in Boca Raton, Florida to develop a personal computer that could compete successfully with the hot-selling Apple II computer. Uncharacteristically, the PC-development team was made an "independent business unit" and allowed to function as an almost separate entrepreneurial business. This arrangement stood in marked contrast to IBM's usual practice of closely controlling all operations from the Armonk headquarters.

Don Estridge, the PC team leader, outlined the advantages of the independent business unit approach for *Inc.* magazine:

> ... he said that he deliberately set out to mimic the culture of the small entrepreneurial companies IBM was up against [such as Apple]. "If you're competing against people who started in a garage," he said, "you have to start in a garage." Among other things, this meant establishing a system that was not going to be confounded by the bureaucracy, that was not going to have checks and balances—"people watching people." Moreover, since they were competing with hungry people, they would have to be staffed by hungry people. He noted that the biggest advantage of his operation was that "people felt it was theirs," and that "the hardest thing we've had to do is let people make mistakes. If they can't make mistakes, it isn't theirs. ..."[3]

Remarkably, for a company the size of IBM, it took the PC team only 13 months to transform the IBM PC from an idea into a market-ready product. After the IBM PC took the market by storm, the PC-development unit was disbanded in favor of a formally structured Entry Systems Division, headed by

Estridge. By 1984, the Entry Systems Division had grown into a 10,000-employee unit capable of producing an IBM PC every seven seconds in its highly automated facilities.

Big Blue Still Has Its Critics

Some observers, particularly IBM's competitors, contend that the huge company dominates the computer industry to the point of stifling competition. On the other hand, many believe that IBM is America's best weapon against the Japanese computer industry. Those concerned with IBM's size say the PC was a lucky accident and that the company is better at marketing than innovating. They cite the disappointing performance of the IBM PCjr, a home computer introduced on the heels of the business-oriented PC. IBM executives are upset by claims that the firm is "... a technological follower rather than a leader."[4] They proudly point out that IBM has been granted 11,000 patents during the last 25 years.

IBM is also criticized for being a clannish organization that stifles individuality. Although recognizing IBM as one of the 100 best employers in the United States, a team of authors observed:

> It appears the rule rather than the exception that IBMers socialize with each other rather than with outsiders. Because of these tendencies, some have compared joining IBM with joining a religious order or going into the military. (One longtime IBM watcher told *Time*, "If you understand the Marines, you can understand IBM.") You must be willing to give up some of your individual identity to survive.[5]

In spite of such criticism, Big Blue truly is an awesome force in the marketplace.

(Discussion questions linking this case with the material you are about to read can be found at the end of this chapter.)

Organizations are an ever-present feature of modern industrial society. We look to organizations for food, clothing, education, employment, entertainment, health care, transportation, and protection of our basic rights. Since nearly every aspect of modern life is influenced in one way or another by organizations, the effective management of organizations is vital to a healthy economy and society.

As IBM's successful experiment with its small PC-development unit demonstrates, the management of organizations is necessarily a creative process. In Chapter 1 we noted that the purpose of the management process is to achieve *organizational* objectives in an effective and efficient manner. Organizations are social entities that enable people to work together to achieve objectives they normally could not achieve working alone. This chapter provides a conceptual foundation for successfully designing and managing organizations. Specifically, this chapter defines the term *organization,* discusses alternative classification schemes for organizations, examines traditional and modern theories of organization, and explores the emerging area of organizational cultures.

What Is an Organization?

In spite of the great number of organizations, the term *organization* is elusive and somewhat difficult to define. This difficulty is pointed up by the fact that a variety of definitions have been suggested by sociologists, psychologists, and organization and management theorists. Chester I. Barnard's definition, though put forth over four decades ago, still remains popular among organization and management theorists. Barnard defined an **organization** as "a system of consciously coordinated activities or forces of two or more persons."[6] In other words, when people gather together and formally agree to combine their efforts for a common purpose, an organization is the result.

There are exceptions, of course, as when two individuals agree to push a car out of a ditch. In this case the task is a one-time affair based on temporary expediency. But if the same two people decide to pool their resources and push cars out of ditches for a living, an organization would be created. The conscious coordination that Barnard referred to, which implies a degree of formal planning and division of labor, is present in the second instance but not in the first.

Although Barnard's statement is a good general definition, it is necessary to go a step farther and identify some important common denominators of organizations. According to Edgar Schein, a prominent organizational psychologist, there are four characteristics common to all organizations: (1) coordination of effort, (2) common goal or purpose, (3) division of labor, and (4) hierarchy of authority.[7]

Coordination of Effort As the old saying goes, "Two heads are better than one." When individuals join together and coordinate their mental and/or physical efforts, great and exciting things can be accomplished. Building the great pyramids, conquering polio, sending manned flights to the moon—all of these far exceeded the talents and abilities of any single individual. Coordination of effort multiplies individual contributions.

Common Goal or Purpose Coordination of effort cannot take place unless those who have joined together agree to strive for something of mutual interest. A common goal or purpose gives organization members a rallying point. For example,

Nucor, a small but highly successful steel company, prints the name of every Nucor employee on the front and back pages of its annual report. This lets everyone know that each of Nucor's 3285 employees has a personal stake in the company.[8]

Division of Labor

By systematically dividing complex tasks into specialized jobs, an organization can efficiently use its human resources. Division of labor permits each organization member to become more proficient by repeatedly doing the same specialized task. (Of course, as is discussed later in Chapter 11, overspecialized jobs can cause boredom and alienation.)

The advantages of dividing labor have been known for a long time. One of its early proponents was the pioneering economist Adam Smith. While touring an eighteenth-century pin-manufacturing plant, Smith observed that a group of specialized laborers could produce 48,000 pins a day. This was an astounding figure, considering that each laborer could produce only 20 pins a day when working alone.[9]

Hierarchy of Authority

According to traditional organization theory, if anything is to be accomplished through formal collective effort, someone should be given the authority to see that the intended goals are carried out effectively and efficiently. Organization theorists have defined **authority** as the right to direct the actions of others. Without a recognized hierarchy of authority, coordination of effort is difficult, if not impossible, to achieve. Some refer to this hierarchy of authority as the chain of command. For instance, a grocery store manager has authority over the assistant manager who has authority over the produce department head who, in turn, has authority over the employees in the produce department. Without such a chain of command, the store manager would have the impossible task of directly overseeing the work of every employee in the store.

Putting All the Pieces Together

All four of the foregoing characteristics are necessary before an organization can be said to exist. Through the years, many well-intentioned attempts to create organizations have failed because something was missing. In 1896 Frederick Strauss, a boyhood friend of Henry Ford, helped Ford set up a machine shop, supposedly to produce gasoline-powered engines. But while Strauss was busy carrying out his end of the bargain by machining needed parts, Ford was secretly building a horseless carriage in a workshop behind his house.[10] Their "organization" never got off the ground. Although Henry Ford eventually went on to become an automobile-industry giant, his first attempt at organization failed because not all of the pieces of an organization were in place. Ford's and his partner's efforts were not coordinated, they worked at cross-purposes, their labor was vaguely divided, and they had no hierarchy of authority. In short, they had organizational intentions, but not an organization.

Source: © 1984 M. Twohy. Management Review.

Classifying Organizations

Classifications are natural to many different areas of study. For example, epidemiologists have made great contributions to world health by systematically isolating and classifying contagious diseases. Like epidemiologists, organization theorists feel that a classification system can provide convenient labels for systematic analysis, study, and discussion. But as one organization theorist has pointed out, a universally accepted classification of organizations is not at hand: "The study of organizational classification is at such a primitive stage that there is not even agreement about terms, let alone agreement about a theory of classification."[11] Recognizing that there is no universally accepted classification scheme for today's organizations, we shall instead consider two alternative approaches. They are based on two important organizational dimensions, purpose and technology.

Classifying Organizations by Purpose

An organization's purpose is, in effect, its reason for being. By carrying out a wide range of purposes, organizations enable society as a whole to function. The four-way classification by organizational purpose discussed

Table 7.1 Classifying Organizations by Purpose

Purpose	Primary Beneficiary	Common Examples	Overriding Management Problem
Business	Owners	Computer manufacturers Newspaper publishers Railroads Fast-food restaurant chains	Must make a profit
Not-for-profit service	Clients	Universities Welfare agencies Church schools Hospitals	Must selectively screen large numbers of potential clients
Mutual benefit	Members	Unions Clubs Political parties Trade associations	Must satisfy members' needs
Commonweal	Public at large	U.S. Postal Service Police departments Fire departments Public schools	Must provide standardized services to large groups of people

here includes business, not-for-profit service, mutual benefit, and commonweal organizations.[12] Because some of today's large and complex organizations overlap categories, the ability to classify organizations by their purpose helps explain the variety of roles that organizations play in society (see Table 7.1). And organizations with similar purposes usually have similar kinds of problems.

Business Organizations   Business organizations like IBM, United Airlines, and the *Washington Post* all have one underlying purpose, to make a profit in a socially acceptable manner. Businesses cannot survive, let alone grow, without earning a profit, and profits are earned by efficiently satisfying demand for products and services. This economic production function is so important to society that many think immediately of business when the word management is mentioned.

Not-for-profit Service Organizations   But unlike businesses, many organizations survive, and even grow, without making any profits at all. They need to be solvent, of course, but they measure their success not in dollars and cents but by how well they provide a specific service for some segment of society. The American Heart Association, Notre Dame University, and

Massachusetts General Hospital are examples of not-for-profit service organizations. Since their services are usually in great demand, one of their biggest problems is screening large numbers of applicants to determine who qualifies for service and who does not. Another problem for most not-for-profit service organizations is securing a reliable stream of funds through donations, grants, or appropriations. Because of today's limited resources, not-for-profit service organizations are under pressure to operate more efficiently.

Mutual Benefit Organizations Often, as in the case of labor unions or political parties, individuals join together strictly to pursue their own self-interests. Occasionally, as in the case of the National Association of Manufacturers, organizations also feel compelled to join together in a blanket organization. Like all other types of organizations, mutual benefit organizations must be effectively and efficiently managed if they are to survive. Survival, in this instance, depends on satisfying the needs of the members.

Commonweal Organizations Like not-for-profit service organizations, commonweal organizations offer public services. But, unlike not-for-profit service organizations, a **commonweal organization** offers standardized service to all members of a given population. The U.S. Army, for example, protects all Americans, not just a select few. The same can be said for local police and fire departments. Commonweal organizations generally are very large, and their great size makes them unwieldy and difficult to manage.

Classifying Organizations by Technology Although the classification of organizations by purpose is useful, it does not reveal how the various purposes are carried out. Thus a second classification scheme based on the organization's dominant technology further aids analysis and study. Organization theorist James D. Thompson, in his often-cited *Organizations in Action,* has suggested a three-way classification of organizations by technology. Included in his classification scheme are long-linked, mediating, and intensive technologies.[13]

Long-linked Technology This variation of technology involves the serial interdependence of work. In other words, work flows from person A to person B to person C and so on. Assembly lines are the classic example of **long-linked technology.** In a washing-machine assembly line, jobs are oriented to the piece-by-piece building of the finished product. An individual working on an assembly line performs a highly specialized task over and over again. Assembly-line conveyors, not the people working on them, dictate the work pace.

Heading the list of long-linked technology's strengths is speed. Some multiline automobile assembly plants today are capable of turning out one hundred vehicles per hour. The main weakness of long-linked technology is inflexibility. For instance, absenteeism, mechanical problems, and major changes in product design can freeze an assembly line.

Mediating Technology   Many organizations today provide a standard service to large numbers of individuals who want to exchange something such as information, money, or property. These organizations rely on **mediating technologies** that link together otherwise unassociated individuals in some mutually beneficial fashion. Commercial banks, insurance companies, and telephone companies mediate on behalf of their clients or customers. As used here, the term *mediate* also covers the broker's role of go-between for potential buyers and sellers of real estate.

Standardization is necessary in organizations based on mediating technology. According to Thompson, "Standardization makes possible the operation of the mediating technology over time and through space by assuring each segment of the organization that other segments are operating in compatible ways."[14] Imagine how difficult it would be to process claims in the U.S. Social Security Administration if each regional office used a different set of criteria for screening claims. Standardization permits the giant organization, which is based on mediating technology, to handle large numbers of clients efficiently and equitably. On the other hand, mediating technology organizations have a tendency to become overly bureaucratic (bureaucracy is discussed later in this chapter).

Intensive Technology   **Intensive technology** has been called a custom technology. Organizations based on intensive technology can, so to speak, custom-build their product or service to fit each customer's particular set of needs. To accomplish this, the organization must have on hand several technologies to mix and match as the situation dictates.

Consider the case of a general hospital. Not every patient admitted needs an appendectomy. Hospitals therefore rely on a wide variety of specialists and techniques to diagnose each patient's problem so that the right combination of technologies (for example, x ray, nutrition, surgery, and so on) can be applied. In effect, hospitals provide a customized service. The major strength of intensive technology is flexibility, and its major weakness is a lack of cost effectiveness. Intensive technologies are not very cost effective because expensive talent and equipment often sit idle between unpredictable spurts of demand.

In summary, the classification of organizations by purpose and/or technology is helpful because it highlights comparative advantages and disadvantages. We now shall examine the more general traditional and modern theories of organization.

Contrasting Theories of Organization

Biblical and classical references to organizational structure notwith-standing, the study of organization theory is largely a twentieth-century development. As one organization theorist philosophically observed, "The study of organizations has a history but not a pedigree."[15] This observation helps make the point that the history of organization theory is marked by disagreement rather than uniformity of thinking. A useful way of approaching the study of organization theory is to contrast the traditional view with a modern view, two very different ways of thinking about organizations.

In the traditional view, the organization is characterized by closed-system thinking. It assumes that the surrounding environment is fairly predictable and that uncertainty within the organization can be eliminated through proper planning and strict control. According to the traditional view, an organization's primary goal is economic efficiency. A dominant modern view, on the other hand, characterizes the organization as an open system that interacts continuously with an uncertain environment. In this view, both the organization and its surrounding environment are filled with variables that are difficult to predict or control. As the open-system theorists see it, the organization's principal goal is survival in an environment of uncertainty and surprise. These contrasting approaches are summarized in Table 7.2.

The Traditional View

Traditional organization theory has a diverse background, with contributions from practicing managers and academics from both sides of the Atlantic. Among them were the early management writers and Max Weber.

The Early Management Writers

Early contributors to the management literature, such as Henri Fayol and Frederick W. Taylor, treated organizing as a subfield of management. In fact, organizing, you will recall, was among Fayol's five universal functions of management. Taylor's narrow task definitions and strict work rules implied a tightly structured approach to organization design.

In general, Fayol and the other pioneering management writers who followed in his footsteps endorsed closely controlled authoritarian organizations. For instance, managers were advised to have no more than six immediate subordinates. Close supervision and obedience were the order of the day. The emphasis in these organizations was on the unrestricted downward flow of authority in the form of orders and rules. Four traditional principles of organization that emerged were (1) a well-defined hierarchy

Table 7.2 Contrasting Theories of Organization

	Traditional View	**Modern View**
General perspective	Closed-system thinking	Open-system thinking
Primary goal of organization	Economic efficiency	Survival in an environment of uncertainty and surprise
Assumption about surrounding environment	Predictable	Generally uncertain
Assumptions about organizations	All causal, goal-directed variables are known and controllable. Uncertainty can be eliminated through planning and controlling.	The organizational system has more variables than can be comprehended at one time. Variables often are subject to influences that cannot be controlled or predicted.

SOURCE: Adapted, by permission, from James D. Thompson, *Organizations in Action* (New York: McGraw-Hill, 1967), pp. 4–7.

of authority, (2) unity of command, (3) authority equal to responsibility, and (4) downward delegation of authority, but not of responsibility (see Table 7.3).

Max Weber's Bureaucracy

Writing around the turn of the century, a German sociologist named Max Weber described what he considered to be the most rationally efficient form of organization, to which he affixed the label *bureaucracy*. It is important to realize that Weber's ideas about organizations were shaped by prevailing circumstances. Before the turn of the century, Germany was a semifeudal state struggling to meet the pressures of the Industrial Revolution. Weber was appalled at the way public administrators relied on subjective judgment, emotion, fear tactics, and nepotism (the prejudicial hiring and promotion of one's relatives) rather than on sound management practices.[16] He used the widely respected and highly efficient Prussian army as a model for his bureaucratic form of organization.

Weber's bureaucracy, in theory, was supposedly the epitome of efficiency. Bureaucracies, as Weber saw them, should have a specific purpose, with the efforts of all the organization's members directed toward that purpose. Accordingly, each member should perform in a rational and predictable manner to contribute as much as possible to the achievement of the overall purpose. According to James D. Thompson, "The rational model of an organization results in everything being functional—making a positive, indeed an optimum, contribution to the overall result. All resources are appropriate resources, and their allocation fits a master plan. All action is appropriate action, and its outcomes are predictable."[17]

Table 7.3 Traditional Principles of Organization

1. **A well-defined hierarchy of authority.** This principle was intended to ensure the coordinated pursuit of organizational goals by contributing individuals.

2. **Unity of command.** It was believed that the possibility of conflicting orders, a serious threat to the smooth flow of authority, could be avoided by making sure that each individual answered to only one superior.

3. **Equal authority and responsibility.** *Authority* was defined as the right to get subordinates to accomplish something. *Responsibility* was defined as the obligation to accomplish something. The traditionalists cautioned against holding individuals ultimately accountable for getting something done unless they were given formal authority to get it done.

4. **Downward delegation of authority, but not of responsibility.** Although a superior with equal authority and responsibility can pass along the *right* to get something accomplished to subordinates, the *obligation* for getting it done remains with the superior. This arrangement was intended to eliminate the practice of "passing the buck."

Weber's intention was for bureaucracies to be run like well-oiled machines.

Among the several characteristics of **bureaucracy** mentioned by Weber, four stand out as significant:[18] (1) division of labor, (2) hierarchy of authority, (3) a framework of rules, and (4) impersonality.

Division of Labor   Weber held that organizations can most efficiently achieve their purposes if individuals perform the same specialized task over and over. In this manner, according to Weber, every individual can become an expert.

Hierarchy of Authority   Weber believed there should be no doubt about who gives and who takes orders. He saw authority as flowing down the organizational pyramid, with the greatest amount of authority being retained at the top. Two organization theorists have summed up this arrangement as follows:

> Each supervisory office is under the control of a higher one. Each official is accountable to his superior for his and his subordinates' job-related actions and decisions. All are accountable to the highest official at the top of the pyramidal hierarchy. Thus the entire operation is organized into an unbroken, ordered, and clearly defined hierarchy.[19]

A Framework of Rules   Generally speaking, rules are simply behavioral specifications. When an employee follows a rule, he or she is behaving in a manner prescribed by the organization. Weber maintained that if organizational members are to behave in necessarily predictable ways, the organization must carefully conceive and enforce a framework of rules. Members of Weberian bureaucracies know exactly what they are expected to do because the rules tell them precisely.

Impersonality Weber was firmly committed to the idea that people should be hired and promoted on the basis of *what* they know, not *who* they know. Rational bureaucratic managers, according to Weberian doctrine, are supposed to be impersonal when deciding who should be hired and who should be promoted. Weber felt that greater impersonality would serve to eliminate the rampant and counterproductive favoritism he observed in the organizations he studied. If Weber were alive today, he would probably label bureaucratic managers as professionals. Professionals, by definition, are impersonal because they concentrate strictly on the technical task at hand and avoid emotional involvement.[20]

The Bureaucratic Paradox A paradox is said to exist when something has apparently contradicting qualities. Bureaucracy qualifies as a paradox because of the contradiction between Weber's conceptualization and everyday experience. As we stated, Weber characterized bureaucracies as the most rationally efficient form of organization. But experience with bureaucracies has shown that they can tie people up in knots of red tape. In fact, the term *bureaucracy* today has a strongly negative connotation. Are bureaucracies to be applauded for promoting efficiency or feared for their tendency to dehumanize and befuddle?

Bureaucracy: A Critical Appraisal In his thoughtful book *The Bureaucratic Experience,* Ralph Hummel takes bureaucracies to task on several accounts. He is mainly concerned with how efficiency is emphasized in bureaucracies to the point of creating emotionless bureaucrats and frustration among clients who resent being shuffled around like numbers. He sees bureaucracy as a strange new world complete with its own social, cultural, psychological, linguistic, and political dimensions (see Table 7.4). Hummel has offered the following critical appraisal of why he believes otherwise efficient bureaucracies appear to clients and other outsiders to be so hopelessly tangled up:

> Bureaucracy is an efficient means for handling large numbers of people. "Efficient" in its own terms. It would be impossible to handle large numbers of people in their full depth and complexity. Bureaucracy is a tool for ferreting out what is "relevant" to the task for which the bureaucracy was established. As a result, only those facts in the complex lives of individuals that are relevant to the task need be communicated between the individual and the bureaucracy.[21]

Anyone who has tried to have a computer error corrected on a utility bill

Table 7.4 A Critic's View of Bureaucracy

Misunderstandings	Understandings
Socially	
Bureaucrats deal with people.	Bureaucrats deal with cases.
Culturally	
Bureaucrats care about the same things we do: justice, freedom, violence, oppression, illness, death, victory, defeat, love, hate, salvation, and damnation.	Bureaucrats care about control and efficiency.
Psychologically	
Bureaucrats are people like us.	Bureaucrats are a new personality type, headless and soulless.
Linguistically	
Communication with bureaucrats is possible: we all speak the same language.	Bureaucrats find it in their interest to define how and when communication shall take place: they create their own secret languages.
Politically	
Public bureaucracies are service institutions.	Public bureaucracies are control institutions.

SOURCE: Ralph P. Hummel, *The Bureaucratic Experience* (New York: St. Martin's Press, © 1977), p. 3. Reprinted by permission of the publisher.

knows what Hummel means. What may in fact be a bureaucracy's well-oiled efficiency is often perceived as inefficiency by clients and customers who see their cases passed from one coldly impersonal specialist to another.

A Matter of Degree Every systematically managed organization, regardless of its size or purpose, is to some extent a bureaucracy. Bureaucratic characteristics are simply more pronounced or advanced in some organizations than in others. Bureaucracy is a matter of degree. As Table 7.5 indicates, a moderate degree of bureaucratization can enhance organizational efficiency. But taken too far, each dimension of bureaucracy can hinder efficiency. By learning to read and retreat from the symptoms of dysfunctional bureaucracy, managers can reap the benefits of functional bureaucracy.

Aiding managers in the fight against dysfunctional bureaucracy are contemporary societal forces borne out of the 1960s. These societal forces have been summed up as follows:

The continuing demand for equality has its organizational counterpart in some-

Table 7.5 Functional Versus Dysfunctional Bureaucracy: A Matter of Degree

	Indications of Functional Bureaucracy	**Symptoms of Dysfunctional Bureaucracy**
Degree of bureaucratization	Moderate	High
Division of labor	More work, of higher quality, can be completed faster because complex tasks are separated into more readily mastered jobs.	Grievances, absenteeism, and turnover increase as a result of overly fragmented jobs that people find boring and dehumanizing. Poor quality performance leads to customer complaints.
Hierarchy of authority	A generally accepted chain of command serves to direct individuals' efforts toward organizational goal accomplishment.	Motivated by a fear of termination, a climate of blind obedience to authority, whether right or wrong, exists.
Framework of rules	Individual contributions to the collective effort are directed and coordinated by rules that answer important procedural questions.	Pursuit of the organization's mission is displaced by the practice of formulating and enforcing self-serving rules that protect, create unnecessary work, hide, or disperse accountability.
Impersonality	Hiring, promotion, and other personnel decisions are made on the basis of objective merit rather than favoritism or prejudice.	Subordinates and clients complain about being treated like numbers by bureaucrats who fail to respond to the full range of human needs.

what utopian designs for organizations without hierarchy, oligarchy, and even specialization. The transformation of the merit principle brought by the demands of minorities and women for a redress of ancient grievances provides a new departure. Demands for greater participation by those in the lower reaches of the bureaucratic world are similarly germane. Finally, the expanding tolerance for individual autonomy, and even deviance, in American society has probably made some inroads upon the stereotypical behaviors traditionally seen inside big organizations.[22]

Since modern organizations cannot avoid bureaucracy, calls for its elimination are futile. The overriding challenge for both management and society is to keep bureaucratic characteristics within functional limits.

Challenges to the Traditional View

Because the traditionalists' rigid recommendations for organizing and managing did not apply in some situations, the validity of those recommendations was eventually challenged. Prescriptions for machinelike efficiency that looked good on paper and worked in simple shop operations often failed to work in complex organizations. It turned out that Fayol's universal functions and principles were no guarantee of success. Similarly, experience proved that there was more to organizing than just strict obedience to authority, as Taylor had emphasized. In spite of Weber's rationally efficient organizational formula, in practice bureaucracy often became the epitome of inefficiency. In addition to these revelations, there were challenges to traditional thinking about organizations from two other sources.

Bottom-up Authority
Traditionalists left no doubt about the origin of authority in their organizational models. They believed that authority was inextricably tied to property ownership, and so it naturally flowed from the top of the organization to the bottom. In businesses, those farthest removed from the ownership of stock were entitled to the least amount of authority. Of course, this notion appealed strongly to those interested in maintaining the power base of society's more fortunate members. But when Chester I. Barnard described organizations as cooperative systems, he questioned the traditional assumption about the automatic downward flow of authority. Instead, he proposed a more democratic **acceptance theory of authority.** According to Barnard's acceptance theory, a leader's authority is determined by his or her subordinates' willingness to comply with it. Barnard believed that a subordinate recognizes a communication from above as being authoritative and decides to comply with it only when the following four conditions are met:

1. He can and does understand the communication.
2. At the time of his decision he believes that it is not inconsistent with the purpose of the organization.
3. At the time of his decision he believes it to be compatible with his personal interest as a whole.
4. He is able mentally and physically to comply with it.[23]

Barnard's acceptance theory of authority opened the door for a whole host of ideas, such as upward communication and the informal organization that is based on friendship rather than work rules. Prior to Barnard's contribution, these concepts had been discussed only by human relationists. In effect, Barnard humanized organization theory by characterizing subordinates as active controllers of authority rather than as mere passive recipients.

Environmental Complexity and Uncertainty

Although traditionalists liked to believe that rigid structure and rational management were important to organizational effectiveness and efficiency, environmental complexity and uncertainty often intervened to upset them. As Charles Perrow observed in writing about the history of organization theory, "The increasing complexity of markets, variability of products, increasing number of branch plants, and changes in technology all required more adaptive organizations."[24] Plans usually have to be made on the basis of incomplete or imperfect information, and consequently, not everything always works out according to plan. Similarly, many of the traditional principles of organization, such as how many people a manager can effectively manage, have proved to be naive.

The net result of these and other challenges to traditional thinking was a desire to look at organizations in new ways. When open-systems thinking appeared on the management horizon, as discussed in Chapter 2, it was eagerly embraced by many organization theorists because it emphasized the need for flexibility and adaptability in organization structure.

A Modern View: Organizations as Systems

Proponents of the systems approach to management have suggested that it is useful to study organizations as open systems. Open-system thinking permits a more realistic view of the interaction between an organization and the environment. Traditional closed-system perspectives, such as Fayol's universal process approach, scientific management, and bureaucracy, effectively ignored environmental influences. For example, it is scarcely realistic to assume that a computer-manufacturing firm's plans or authoritarian structure can eliminate uncertainty, because technological breakthroughs are a regular occurrence in the computer industry.

Organizations are systems made up of interacting subsystems. Organizations are themselves subsystems that interact with larger social, political-legal, and economic systems. Those who take an open-system perspective realize that system-to-system interactions are often as important as the systems themselves. For instance, we study movements of people in and out of the labor force (for example, unemployment), movements of capital (for example, stock exchanges and corporate borrowing), and movements of goods and services (for example, international trade). A highly organized and vigorously interactive world needs realistically dynamic models, and this is where open-system thinking can make a contribution to organization theory.

Some Open-System Characteristics

According to general systems theory, regardless of the system under study—the human body, an organization, a society, or the solar system—they all share certain characteristics. But at the same time, the theory recognizes that there are also significant differences among the various kinds of open systems. Two respected management scholars have qualified the analogy between natural and artificial systems:

> Social organizations are not natural like physical and biological systems, they are contrived. They have structure, but it is the structure of events rather than of physical components, and it cannot be separated from the processes of the system. The fact that social organizations are contrived by human beings suggests that they can be established for an infinite variety of objectives and do not follow the same life-cycle pattern of birth, maturity, and death as biological systems.[25]

With these cautionary words in mind, we list the four characteristics that emphasize the adaptive and dynamic nature of all open systems: (1) interaction with the environment, (2) synergy, (3) dynamic equilibrium, and (4) equifinality.

Interaction with the Environment   Open systems have permeable boundaries, whereas closed systems do not. Open systems, like the human body, are not self-sufficient. Life-sustaining oxygen, nutrients, and water must be imported from the surrounding environment, and waste must be exported. Similarly, in business organizations, materials, energy, capital, and ideas are imported, processed into marketable goods or services, and exported back out into the environment. Negative feedback from the environment (for example, unsold goods) signals the need for corrective action, whereas positive feedback (for example, growing demand) indicates that things are on the right track.

Synergy   As discussed in Chapter 5, synergy is the 2 + 2 = 5 effect. In other words, an open system adds up to more than the sum of its parts. A winning athletic team is more than its players, coaches, plays, and equipment. Only when all the parts are in place and working in concert can the winning edge be achieved. Likewise, a successful business is more than the factors of production—land, labor, and capital. Synergistic thinking emphasizes that a firm's competitive edge is dictated as much by how the factors of production are mobilized as by what those factors are.

Dynamic Equilibrium   In regard to the functioning of open systems, **dynamic equilibrium** is the process of maintaining the internal balance necessary for survival by importing needed resources from the environment. Proper blood chemistry in the human body is maintained through dynamic equilibrium. When a person's blood sugar drops below normal, a craving for sugar prompts the ingestion of something sweet, thus increasing the blood-sugar level. Chrysler's battle to stay in business is an organizational example of dynamic equilibrium. Slumping sales for the big cars it produced threatened to drive Chrysler out of business through bankruptcy (a loss of dynamic equilibrium). But the government's $1.5 billion loan guarantee gave the firm a second chance to remain in business (regain dynamic equilibrium). In order to regain its dynamic equilibrium, Chrysler was forced to switch its emphasis from large to small cars and to cut its payroll in half.[26]

Equifinality Open systems are made up of more than fixed cause-and-effect linkages. **Equifinality** means reaching the same result by different means. In organizations, "the concept of equifinality suggests that the manager can utilize a varying bundle of inputs into the organization, can transform them in a variety of ways, and can achieve satisfactory output."[27] For example, Nucor, the small but highly profitable steel producer mentioned earlier, is almost completely different from the major steel companies. Nucor builds its own mills, makes steel from scrap rather than ore, uses the latest energy-saving technology, and ties its nonunion employees' weekly bonuses to productivity.[28] Although America's steel giants have been losing money at a record pace, Nucor has thrived because of equifinality (a different way of getting the job done).

Developing an Open-System Model

An appreciation of the principal characteristics of an open system is helpful because it forces a break with traditional closed-system thinking. An open-system model of organizations encourages managers to think globally (the whole picture). Because organizations are shaped and molded by the surrounding environment, it is naive to treat them as closed systems. A good example of the shaping influence of environmental factors on a business is the situation in which the *New York Times* found itself in the mid-1970s. Management at the *Times* faced a classic profit squeeze, with costs rising and revenues declining. *Business Week* described what was taking place at the time:

> Some of the problems at the *Times* are the same ones worrying virtually all big-city newspapers. Costs of production, paper, and distribution are skyrocketing at the same time that television and other competing media are grabbing a growing chunk of advertising budgets. As an added worry, suburban newspapers are stealing a growing number of readers and advertisers from big-city dailies.[29]

As a direct consequence of these environmental influences, a massive

Figure 7.1 The Organization as a Black Box

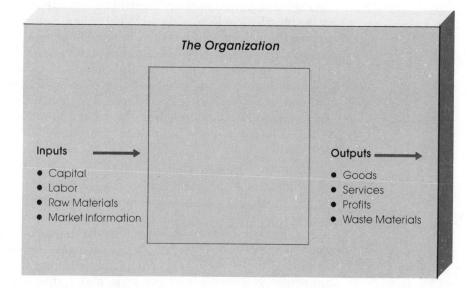

reorganization effort was launched to streamline the *Times*'s organization so that it could regain its competitive equilibrium and survive.

An open-system model helps existing and future managers understand the highly interactive nature of organizations. Our open-system model, although descriptive of a business organization, readily generalizes to all types of organizations.

The Organization as a Black Box   The basic open-system model is the so-called black box. As illustrated in Figure 7.1, the black-box model reveals nothing of what goes on inside the organization; it merely identifies what goes in and what comes out. A business must acquire various inputs: capital, either through selling stock or borrowing; labor, through hiring people; raw materials, through purchases; and market information, through research. On the output side of the black box, goods and services are marketed, profits (or losses) are realized, and waste materials are discarded (if not recycled).

Even though the black-box model tells nothing of the internal workings of the organization, it clearly demonstrates the ongoing interaction between the organization and the surrounding environment. Now, for a look inside the black box.

Organizational Subsystems   By using the open-system premise that systems are made up of interacting subsystems, we can identify three prominent organizational subsystems: technical, boundary-spanning, and

Figure 7.2 Looking Inside the Organizational Black Box

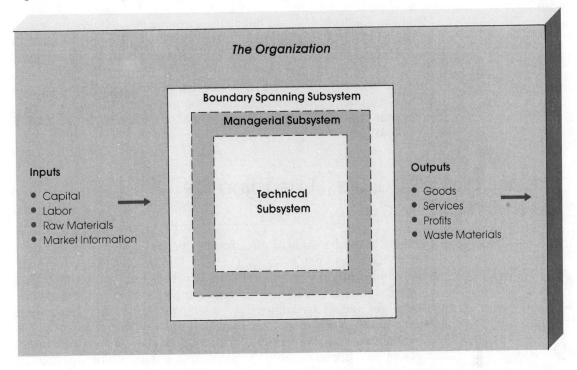

The Organization

Boundary Spanning Subsystem

Managerial Subsystem

Technical Subsystem

Inputs

- Capital
- Labor
- Raw Materials
- Market Information

Outputs

- Goods
- Services
- Profits
- Waste Materials

managerial. Figure 7.2 shows how these three subsystems fill the organizational black box.

Sometimes called the production function, the technical subsystem physically transforms raw materials into finished goods and services. But the ability to turn out a product does not in itself guarantee organizational survival. Other supporting subsystems are needed as well.

Whereas technical subsystems may be viewed as being at an organization's very core, boundary-spanning subsystems are directed outward toward the general environment. Most boundary-spanning jobs, or interface functions, as they are sometimes called, are easily identified by their titles. Purchasing agents are responsible for making sure that the organization has a steady and reliable flow of raw materials and subcomponents. Public relations staff are in charge of developing and maintaining a favorable public image of the organization. Long-range (or strategic) planners have the responsibility of surveying the general environment for actual or potential opportunities and obstacles. Sales personnel probe the environment for buyers for the organization's goods or services. Purchasing agents, public relations staff, long-range planners, and sales personnel all have one thing in common: they all facilitate the organization's interaction with its environment. Each, so to speak, has one foot inside the organization and one foot outside.

Although the technical and boundary-spanning subsystems are important and necessary, one additional subsystem is needed to tie the organization together. As Figure 7.2 indicates, the managerial subsystem serves as a bridge between the other two subsystems. Managerial subsystems "comprise the organized activities for controlling, coordinating, and directing the many subsystems of the structure."[30] It is within this subsystem that the subject matter of this book is practiced as a blend of science and art.

Organizational Cultures: Extending the Open-System Model

As we have seen, the study of organizations becomes more realistic when they are viewed as open systems. Open-system thinking helps us to appreciate more fully the dynamic interaction between organizations and their environments. Recently, however, the open-system model has been criticized for failing to address the *time dimension* of organizations adequately. A more encompassing *cultural* perspective has been recommended—one that realistically intertwines past, present, and future aspects of the organization.[31] Your present behavior, for instance, is affected by your past (family and cultural history) and your future (goals and aspirations). So, too, organizational actions result from a dynamic interaction between past experience, present capabilities, and future goals. Although the traditional planning/control cycle embraces the present and future dimensions, the organization's past is too often ignored by those who study organizations. By studying organizations as distinct cultures, the powerful influence of past actions, people, and events on organizational processes becomes more apparent.

In this section, we define organizational culture and present a conceptual framework that attempts to extend rather than replace the open-system model.

What Does Organizational Culture Involve?

The notion of organizational culture is rooted in anthropology. **Organizational culture** is the collection of shared (stated or implied) beliefs, values, rituals, stories and legends, myths, and specialized language that fosters a feeling of community among organization members.[32] Some prefer the term *corporate* culture when discussion is limited to profit-making businesses. But the broader term *organizational* culture is used here to underscore the point that distinct cultures also may be found in not-for-profit service, mutual benefit, and commonweal organizations.

Table 7.6 Organizational Cultures Vary in Strength

A Strong Culture at Hallmark Cards*	A Weak Culture at Atari†
They [employees] say Hallmark is like "a family," and they speak of "how people care for each other."... They talk with pride about what it means to become a "Hallmarker." Just being hired by the company isn't enough to make someone a Hallmarker. Employees have to internalize Hallmark's sense of quality. It may be hard to define what makes a Hallmark card, but press operators will refuse to print cards they think don't meet Hallmark's standards. They may disagree with the content or tone of the message, or think the artwork doesn't look right. Whatever the reason, they can expect to be patted on the back rather than reprimanded, even if their objections cost time and money. True Hallmarkers care about their product.	A marketing manager who worked at Atari before it got new management recalls: "You can't imagine how much time and energy around here went into politics. You had to determine who was on first base this month in order to figure out how to obtain what you needed to get the job done. There were no rules. There were no clear values. Two of the men at the top stood for diametrically opposite things. Your bosses were constantly changing. All this meant that you never had time to develop a routine way for getting things done at the interface between your job and the next guy's. Without rules for working with one another, a lot of people got hurt, got burned out, and were never taught the "Atari way" of doing things because there wasn't an Atari way.

SOURCE: *Robert Levering, Milton Moskowitz, and Michael Katz, *The 100 Best Companies to Work for in America* (Reading, Mass: Addison-Wesley, 1984), p. 132. †Richard Pascale, "Fitting New Employees into the Company Culture," *Fortune* 109 (May 28, 1984): 40.

Although the cultural factors listed in our definition are largely taken for granted by members of the organization and thus "invisible," they exert a powerful influence on behavior. As one might suspect, organizational cultures vary in strength; they can be strong or weak (see Table 7.6). But, according to the authors of the best-selling book, *Corporate Cultures,* "... a strong culture has almost always been the driving force behind continuing success in American business."[33] A strong organizational culture performs four important functions:

1. It gives organizational members a sense of identity.
2. It encourages commitment to the organization's mission.
3. It promotes organizational stability.
4. It influences behavior by helping individuals to make sense of their surroundings.[34]

Organizations with weak cultures do not enjoy the advantages of these four functions.

The Organizational Socialization Process

Organizational socialization is the process through which outsiders are transformed into accepted insiders.[35] In effect, the socialization process shapes newcomers to fit the organizational culture. According to one expert on the subject:

> The culture asserts itself when the taken-for-granted cultural assumptions are in some way violated by the uninitiated and provoke a response. As the uninitiated bump into one after another taken-for-granted assumption, more acculturated employees respond in a variety of ways (tell stories, offer advice, ridicule, lecture, shun, and so forth) that serve to mold the way in which the newcomer thinks about his or her role and about "how things are done around here."[36]

Stories deserve special attention here because they are a central feature of organizational socialization and culture. Company stories about heroic or inspiring deeds let newcomers know what "really counts." For example, 3M's eleventh commandment—"Thou shalt not kill a new product idea"— has been ingrained into new employees through one inspiring story about the employee who invented transparent cellophane tape.

> According to the story, an employee accidentally discovered the tape but was unable to get his superiors to buy the idea. Marketing studies predicted a relatively small demand for the new material. Undaunted, the employee found a way to sneak into the board room and tape down the minutes of board members with his transparent tape. The board was impressed enough with the novelty to give it a try and experienced incredible success.[37]

Upon hearing this story, a 3M newcomer has believable, concrete evidence that innovation and persistence pay off at 3M. It has been said that stories are social road maps for employees, telling them where to go and where not to go and what will happen when they get there. Moreover, stories are remembered longer than abstract facts or rules and regulations. How many times have you recalled a professor's colorful story but forgotten the rest of the lecture?

Diagnosing Organizational Cultures

If one is to gain a realistic picture of an organization, both open-system thinking and a cultural diagnosis are needed. Cultural diagnoses are useful for (1) those about to join an organization and (2) those desiring to change an organization in some significant way. (Change and organization development are covered in detail in Chapter 14.) Whatever the reason for diagnosing an organization's culture, it is good to keep in mind that:

> ... reading a culture is an interpretive, subjective activity. There are no exact answers, and two observers may come up with somewhat different descriptions of the same culture. The validity of the diagnosis must be judged by the utility of the insights it provides, not by its "correctness" as determined by some objective criteria.[38]

Figure 7.3 A Framework for Diagnosing an Organization's Culture

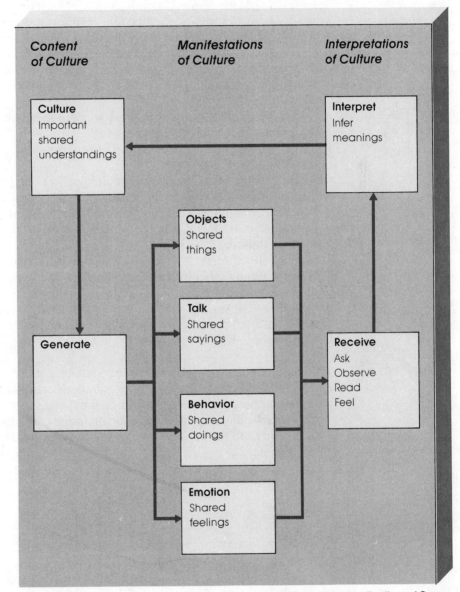

SOURCE: Reprinted, by permission of the publisher, from "Some Action Implications of Corporate Culture: A Manager's Guide to Action," by Vijay Sathe, *Organizational Dynamics* 12 (Autumn 1983) p. 8. © 1983 Periodicals Division, American Management Associations, New York. All rights reserved.

A framework for diagnosing organizational cultures is illustrated in Figure 7.3. Notice that the observer needs to "ask," "observe," "read," and "feel" when gathering information on the four manifestations of culture: objects, talk, behavior, and emotion. It is instructive and important to compare intentions with actual behavior. Taken-for-granted beliefs and values generally need to be inferred from behavior. Symptoms of a weak organizational culture include:

- **Inward focus.** Has internal politics become more important than real-world problems and the marketplace?
- **Short-term focus.** Is too much time and energy spent on achieving short-term results?
- **Morale problems.** Is there chronic unhappiness and high turnover?
- **Fragmentation/Inconsistency.** Is there a lack of "fit" in the way people behave, communicate, and perceive problems and opportunities?
- **Emotional outbursts.** Does emotionalism override sound judgment and rational thinking?
- **Ingrown subcultures.** Is there a lack of communication among subunits?
- **Warfare among subcultures.** Has constructive competition given way to destructive conflict?
- **Subculture elitism.** Have organizational units become exclusive "clubs" with restricted entry? Have subcultural values become more important than the organization's values?[39]

Evidence of these symptoms may encourage a potential recruit to look elsewhere. Each of these symptoms of a weak organizational culture can be a formidable barrier to organizational change.

Now that we have a solid foundation of organization theory in place, our attention turns in the next chapter to designing organizations that fit their environment.

Summary

Organizations need to be understood and intelligently managed because they are an ever-present feature of modern life. All organizations, whatever their purpose, have four characteristics: (1) coordination of effort, (2) common goal or purpose, (3) division of labor, and (4) hierarchy of authority. If even one of these characteristics is absent, an organization does not exist.

Organizational classifications aid the systematic analysis and study of organizations. There is no universally accepted classification scheme among organization theorists. Two useful ways of classifying organizations are by purpose and technology. In regard to purpose, organizations can be classified as business, not-for-profit service, mutual benefit, or commonweal. In regard to technology, there are long-linked, mediating, and intensive technologies. Each of these technologies has characteristic strengths and weaknesses.

There are both traditional and modern views of organizations. Traditionalists such as Fayol, Taylor, and Weber subscribed to closed-system thinking by ignoring the impact of environmental forces. Modern organization theorists tend to prefer open-system thinking because it realistically incorporates organizations' environmental dependency. Early management writers proposed tightly controlled authoritarian organizations. Max Weber, a German sociologist, applied the label bureaucracy to his formula for the most rationally efficient type of organization. Bureaucracies are characterized by their division of labor, hierarchy of authority, framework of rules, and impersonality. Unfortunately, in actual practice, bureaucracy has become a synonym for red tape and inefficiency. The answer to this bureaucratic paradox is to understand that bureaucracy is a matter of degree. When bureaucratic characteristics, which are present in all organizations, are carried to an extreme, efficiency gives way to inefficiency.

Chester I. Barnard's acceptance theory of authority and growing environmental complexity and uncertainty questioned traditional organization theory. Open-system thinking became a promising alternative because it was useful in explaining the necessity of creating flexible and adaptable rather than rigid organizations. Although the analogy between natural systems and human social systems (organizations) is an imperfect one, there are important parallels. Organizations, like all open systems, are unique because of their (1) interaction with the environment, (2) synergy, (3) dynamic equilibrium, and (4) equifinality. In open-system terms, business organizations are made up of interdependent technical, boundary-spanning, and managerial subsystems.

Viewing organizations as cultures serves to realistically connect their past, present, and future dimensions. Successful organizations tend to have strong organizational cultures in which there are widely shared values and a sense of community. Diverse outsiders are transformed into accepted insiders through the process of organizational socialization. Stories about company heroes are a powerful and lasting socialization technique. Systematic diagnosis can reveal symptoms of a weak organizational culture. The cultural perspective extends rather than replaces the open-system model of organizations.

Terms to Understand

Organization	Bureaucracy
Authority	Acceptance theory of authority
Commonweal organization	Dynamic equilibrium
Long-linked technology	Equifinality
Mediating technology	Organizational culture
Intensive technology	Organizational socialization

Questions for Discussion

1. Is the audience in a movie theater an organization? Explain. What about an individual writing a novel? How about two people playing a friendly round of golf?
2. Why do you suppose not-for-profit service organizations are considered to be a particularly difficult challenge for managers today?
3. What are the relative strengths and weaknesses of long-linked, mediating, and intensive technology organizations?
4. Why is the modern open-system view of organizations more realistic than the traditional view?
5. In your opinion, how applicable today are the four traditional principles of organization (refer back to Table 7.3)? Explain your reasoning.
6. What recent experiences have you had with dysfunctional bureaucracy? What should the organization do to correct the situation?
7. How did Chester I. Barnard's ideas about authority question the traditional view of organizations?
8. How can equifinality help you get a college degree?
9. Why do you think successful organizations tend to have strong cultures?
10. Thinking of the organization where you work (or worked in the past), does it have a strong or weak organizational culture? How do you know?

Back to the Opening Case

Now that you have read Chapter 7, you should be able to answer the following questions about the IBM case:

1. What kind of technology does IBM use to produce its personal computers (PCs)? What are the comparative strengths and weaknesses of this technology?

2. How has IBM tried to avoid dysfunctional bureaucracy?
3. Viewing IBM as an open system, what sources of environmental uncertainty has it encountered?
4. What kinds of steps does IBM take to maintain a strong organizational culture?
5. Considering the rapid growth of the Entry Systems Division due to the IBM PC's success, what do you suppose happened to the entrepreneurial spirit in the small PC-development unit?

Closing Case 7.2

Intel's Battle Against Bureaucracy

Intel Corporation, the Santa Clara, California-based microprocessor manufacturer, has earned a reputation over the years as an innovative and well-run company. In fact, the microprocessor was invented by Intel. Although success has proved temporary for most companies in the fast-paced computer electronics business, Intel has remained a formidable competitor. In recent years, however, competition has become even stiffer. In 1980, the price of a 16-K programmable memory computer chip declined from $25 to under $7. Slowed growth in demand further pinched Intel's profit margins.

In the process of devising ways to become more efficient, top management realized that administrative costs had gotten out of hand. In 1979, 64 percent of Intel's 10,000 American employees worked in nonproduction jobs. In spite of rapid growth in administrative staff and costs, complaints from customers and creditors were on the rise. There were internal signs of inefficiency as well. For example, it took twelve pieces of paper and ninety-five administrative steps just to order a $2.79 mechanical pencil. Recognizing that the company's usual solution of hiring still more administrative staff simply wasn't working, management decided to initiate a unique white-collar productivity improvement program.

Working Smarter, Not Harder

After experimenting with outside consultants, management decided it would be best to tailor-make their own productivity program. A work simplification specialist was hired, and Intel's four-step program began to take shape. Step 1 was to obtain a valid base-line measure of productivity. For example, during the second quarter of 1980, 71 employees in accounts payable processed a monthly average of 33,000 vouchers (one every 23 minutes). Step 2, goal setting, established a goal of 16 minutes per voucher with no decline in quality. The actual process of work simplification took place in step 3. This was accomplished by having employees draw out detailed step-by-step flow charts (see Chapter 4) of administrative procedures and weed out unnecessary steps. The procedure for handling expense accounts was cut from 25 steps to 14. In the personnel area, the number of steps required to hire a new employee was cut from 364 to 250. Finally, in step 4, an "after" measure of productivity was taken to assess the impact of the work simplification. Referring once again to the accounts payable department, the streamlining of a dozen procedures to achieve the goal of sixteen minutes per voucher was accomplished by using 20 fewer employees.

After the productivity improvement program had been in force for four and a half years, Intel's corporate manager for administrative productivity reported:

> Our cost reductions to date exceed $15 million annually, or the equivalent of $88.35 million in pretax revenues. We believe that we can attain a 30 percent improvement across the company that will be worth $60 million in annual direct cost reductions or the equivalent of a $277 million boost in annual sales.[40]

Overcoming Resistance to Change

Because of Intel's commitment to participative management, a number of steps were taken to overcome possible opposition to the productivity improvement program:

- From the very beginning, management promised not to fire permanent employees whose jobs might be eliminated.
- All employees were assured that working smarter did not necessarily mean working harder.
- Humorous touches were integrated into the program. For example, when an employee used the excuse "But we've always done it this way" to defend an existing procedure, he or she received a "working dumber" ticket from the productivity manager.
- All work simplification was conducted by those who actually performed the job in question on a daily basis.

Although most Intel employees reportedly were enthusiastic about the program because it made their work more satisfying by eliminating tedious busy work, there was some turnover.

For Discussion

1. Which of the four basic characteristics of bureaucracy was getting out of control at Intel? Explain.
2. Do you feel that Intel's management was correct in paying so much attention to overcoming resistance to the productivity program? Explain your reasons.

3. In your opinion, what aspect of Intel's program probably accounted for most of its success? What could have been done to make it even more successful?

References

Opening Quotation: Joseph A. Litterer, *The Analysis of Organizations,* 2nd ed. (New York: Wiley, 1973), p. 5.

Opening Case: For additional information on IBM, see John Greenwald, "The Colossus That Works," *Time* 122 (July 11, 1983): 44–54; Marc G. Schulman, "Big Blue's Big Bucks," *Datamation* 30 (February 1984): 131–136; Robert Levering, Milton Moskowitz, and Michael Katz, *The 100 Best Companies to Work for in America* (Reading, Mass.: Addison-Wesley, 1984): 156–160; Eugene Linden, "Let a Thousand Flowers Bloom," *Inc.* 6 (April 1984): 64–76; Manuel Schiffres, "IBM: Setting Out to be No. 1 in U.S. Business," *U.S. News & World Report* 96 (June 18, 1984): 61–63; and "How the IBM Juggernaut Will Keep Rolling," *Business Week* No. 2851 (July 16, 1984): 105–106.

Closing Case: For additional information on Intel, see Jeremy Main, "How to Battle Your Own Bureaucracy," *Fortune* 103 (June 29, 1981): 54–58; Keith A. Bolte, "Intel's War for White-Collar Productivity," *National Productivity Review* 3 (Winter 1983-84): 46–53; Robert Levering, Milton Moskowitz, and Michael Katz, *The 100 Best Companies to Work for in America* (Reading, Mass.: Addison-Wesley, 1984), pp. 152–155; and "Is the Semiconductor Boom Too Much of a Good Thing for Intel?" *Business Week* No. 2839 (April 23, 1984): 114–116.

1. Schiffres, "IBM: Setting Out to be No. 1 in U.S. Business," p. 61.
2. Greenwald, "The Colossus That Works," p. 46.
3. Linden, "Let a Thousand Flowers Bloom," p. 70.
4. Schiffres, "IBM: Setting Out to be No. 1 in U.S. Business," p. 63.
5. Levering, Moskowitz, and Katz, *The 100 Best Companies to Work for in America,* p. 159.
6. Chester I. Barnard, *The Functions of the Executive* (Cambridge, Mass.: Harvard University Press, 1938), p. 73.
7. Adapted from Edgar H. Schein, *Organizational Psychology,* 3rd ed. (Englewood Cliffs, N.J.: Prentice-Hall, 1980), pp. 12–15.
8. See Richard I. Kirkland, Jr., "Pilgrims' Profits at Nucor," *Fortune* 103 (April 6, 1981): 43–46.
9. See Adam Smith, *The Wealth of Nations* (New York: Modern Library, 1937), p. 7.
10. For an interesting biography of Henry Ford, see Ann Jardim, *The First Henry Ford: A Study in Personality and Business Leadership* (Cambridge, Mass.: MIT Press, 1970), p. 40.

11. Bill McKelvey, "Guidelines for the Empirical Classification of Organizations," *Administrative Science Quarterly* 20 (December 1975): 509. For a good overview of organizational classification theories, see William B. Carper and William E. Snizek, "The Nature and Types of Organizational Taxonomies: An Overview," *Academy of Management Review* 5 (January 1980): 65–75.

12. This classification scheme is adapted from Peter M. Blau and William R. Scott, *Formal Organizations* (San Francisco: Chandler, 1962).

13. For an expanded treatment, see James D. Thompson, *Organizations in Action* (New York: McGraw-Hill, 1967), pp. 15–18.

14. Ibid., p. 17.

15. James G. March, *Handbook of Organizations* (Chicago: Rand McNally, 1965), p. ix.

16. For a more detailed discussion, consult Warren G. Bennis, *Changing Organizations* (New York: McGraw-Hill, 1966), pp. 4–5.

17. Thompson, *Organizations in Action,* p. 6.

18. Drawn from Max Weber, *The Theory of Social and Economic Organization,* trans. A.M. Henderson and Talcott Parsons (New York: Oxford University Press, 1947). An interesting critique, based on the claim that Weber's work was mistranslated, can be found in Richard M. Weiss, "Weber on Bureaucracy: Management Consultant or Political Theorist?" *Academy of Management Review* 8 (April 1983): 242–248.

19. Herbert Hicks and C. Ray Gullett, *Organizations: Theory and Behavior* (New York: McGraw-Hill, 1975), p. 129.

20. See Harold L. Wilensky, "The Professionalization of Everyone?" *American Journal of Sociology* 70 (September 1964): 137–158.

21. Ralph P. Hummel, *The Bureaucratic Experience* (New York: St. Martin's Press, 1977), p. 24.

22. Robert Presthus, *The Organizational Society,* rev. ed. (New York: St. Martin's Press, 1978), p. 3.

23. Barnard, *The Functions of the Executive,* p. 165.

24. Charles Perrow, "The Short and Glorious History of Organizational Theory," *Organizational Dynamics* 2 (Summer 1973): 4.

25. Fremont E. Kast and James E. Rosenzweig, *Organization and Management: A Systems and Contingency Approach,* 3rd ed. (New York: McGraw-Hill, 1979), p. 103. An excellent glossary of open-system terms can be found on page 102 of this source.

26. Irwin Ross, "Chrysler on the Brink," *Fortune* 103 (February 9, 1981): 38–42.

27. Kast and Rosenzweig, *Organization and Management: A Systems and Contingency Approach,* p. 103.

28. See Kirkland, "Pilgrims' Profits at Nucor."

29. "Behind the Profit Squeeze at the New York Times," *Business Week* No. 2447 (August 30, 1976): 42.

30. Daniel Katz and Robert L. Kahn, *The Social Psychology of Organizations,* 2nd ed. (New York: Wiley, 1978), p. 55.

31. For a complete discussion, see Andrew M. Pettigrew, "On Studying Organizational Cultures," *Administrative Science Quarterly* 24 (December 1979): 570–581.

32. This definition is based in part on material found in Linda Smircich, "Concepts of Culture and Organizational Analysis," *Administrative Science Quarterly* 28 (September 1983): 339–358.

33. Terrence E. Deal and Allan A. Kennedy, *Corporate Cultures* (Reading, Mass.: Addison-Wesley, 1982), p. 5.

34. Adapted from Smircich, "Concepts of Culture and Organizational Analysis."

35. An instructive model of organizational socialization may be found in Daniel Charles Feldman, "The Multiple Socialization of Organization Members," *Academy of Management Review* 6 (April 1981): 309–318.

36. Alan L. Wilkins, "The Culture Audit: A Tool for Understanding Organizations," *Organizational Dynamics* 12 (Autumn 1983): 34–35.

37. Alan L. Wilkins, "The Creation of Company Cultures: The Role of Stories and Human Resource Systems," *Human Resource Management* 23 (Spring 1984): 43.

38. Vijay Sathe, "Implications of Corporate Culture: A Manager's Guide to Action," *Organizational Dynamics* 12 (Autumn 1983): 6–7.

39. Adapted from Deal and Kennedy, *Corporate Cultures,* pp. 136–139.

40. Bolte, "Intel's War for White-Collar Productivity," p. 52.

Chapter 8

Organizing

There is no one way of doing things.
Anant R. Negandhi

Chapter Objectives

When you finish studying this chapter, you should be able to

- Identify the two dimensions of an organization chart and explain the nature of each.
- Explain the contributions of Burns and Stalker's and Lawrence and Lorsch's studies to contingency design theory.
- Identify and briefly describe the four basic departmentalization formats.
- Describe how a highly centralized organization differs from a highly decentralized one.
- Define the term *delegation* and list at least five common barriers to delegation.

Opening Case 8.1

General Motors Streamlines for Efficiency

General Motors (GM), the well-known Detroit auto maker, recorded its best year ever in 1983 earning $3.7 billion in profits on $76.5 billion in sales. Roger Smith, the chairman of the board, was awarded a $1 million bonus. To casual observers, GM appeared to have found an unbeatable formula for success. GM's top management, however, was worried. In spite of 1983's record performance, the organization had become bloated and sluggish. *Business Week* chronicled GM's problems:

> The auto giant has been embarrassed over the past few years by poky J-cars, locking X-car brakes, faulty diesel engines, and delays in introducing front-wheel-drive replacements for its biggest cars. Worse, GM's five car divisions have been saddled with look-alike models that have confused consumers and have contributed to a drop in GM's market share.[1]

The crux of this whole scenario was that GM was not as efficient as its Japanese competitors.

Recognizing that GM needed serious reorganization, Smith announced his plan in January 1984. At the time of the announcement, Chairman Smith contended that the reorganization would be a more sweeping change than anything he had experienced during his 35 years with the company. An estimated 300,000 GM employees would be affected by the reorganization that was projected to take three to five years to fully implement. The newly appointed executive vice president for North American passenger car operations, Alexander A. Cunningham, spelled out GM's motives for the reorganization by saying: "... if we don't learn to do things more efficiently and be more effective about it with this new organization, and if we can't be better than the Japanese in getting a product to market at the right cost, we're going to be in trouble."[2]

The reorganization was particularly dramatic because it scrapped an organization structure GM had faithfully adhered to since the 1920s.

Heading for Saturn

General Motors was formed in 1910 when a visionary businessman named William C. Durant bought up a number of small automobile companies. Because of Durant's free-wheeling management style and the fierce independence of his acquisitions, the loosely knit GM almost went under during the post-World War I depression. But thanks to the organizational genius of Alfred P. Sloan, Jr., who led the company from 1921 to 1955, GM reversed its fortunes to become the largest automobile company in the world. A central feature of Sloan's turnaround strategy was a unique organizational structure based on the centralized control of decentralized operations. Although headquarters coordinated planning and finances, GM divisions such as Chevrolet, Pontiac, and Buick acted like independent businesses, even to the extent of competing with each other in the marketplace. Each division engineered, manufactured, and marketed its own distinctly different brand of automobile.[3] This highly decentralized model was hailed in management circles as the prototype of the future. And indeed, GM was without peer until the early 1970s.

As Japanese competition stiffened during the late 1970s and early 1980s, GM's half-century-old decentralized structure began to show signs of rust. A bold new venture code named the Saturn Project was formulated to get GM back into the thick of the automobile business. The strategy behind the Saturn Project involved using state-of-the-art product design and manufacturing techniques to produce a subcompact car that would be price competitive with Japanese models by the late 1980s (see Opening Case 17.1 for details). Top management came to realize, however, that the Saturn Project could not be achieved without significant reorganization. Sloan's structure, appropriate for a company producing a handful of clearly distinguishable models, became obsolete when GM grew into a giant manufacturer of 34 lines of look-alike cars. GM's flexibility and innovation were being crushed under the weight of a complex bureaucracy that had evolved since the Sloan era.

An Internal Merger

Outside consultants interviewed 500 GM executives to discover what they needed in the way of organizational restructuring to do a better job. Armed with the data from these interviews, top management consolidated the eight GM divisions into two product groups, one for small cars and one for large cars (see Figure 8.1). Observers called the reorganization the equivalent of an internal merger. A new position, the executive vice president for North American passenger car operations, was created to oversee the two car groups. Following the reorganization announcement, an industry observer outlined the new relationship between the groups and the divisions: "The car divisions essentially are reduced to marketing arms of the new groups, each of which will have its own fully integrated engineering, product-planning, manufacturing and assembly operations."[4] Under the former GM structure, engineering, product development, and manufacturing had been scattered throughout the various car divisions. Top management hopes that the new alignment will help GM cut new product development time from four years to three.

By consolidating GM's operations, Smith believed headquarters could do a better job of pushing decision-making authority down to people who knew the nuts and bolts of making cars. Smith told *Fortune*: "We sat down and increased almost every authorization limit we had on what individual managers and supervisors could approve. ... And that means salaries, projects, and almost everything else. We made a desperate effort to get rid of all those reports."[5]

Some Lingering Questions

Employees and GM car dealers were understandably concerned about how the reorganization would affect their particular interests. Admitting that plant closures and staff cuts were inevitable, Cunningham emphasized the firm's commitment to retraining. Still, many employees held their breath in a wait-and-see fashion. GM's 10,000 new car dealers were assured that they would be practically unaffected by the changes. Meanwhile, critics pointed out that GM had not drawn a clear enough distinction between large and small cars, thus possibly blurring the product domains of the two car groups. Moreover, in view of the high probability that the reorganization would not reduce any layers of management,

Figure 8.1 The Restructuring of General Motors

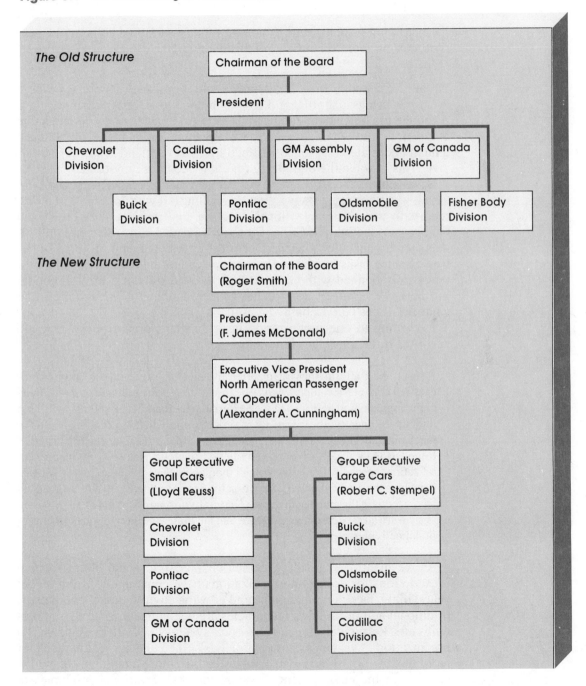

observers were left to wonder if a streamlined GM would in fact be fast enough to catch the Japanese.

(Discussion questions linking this case with the material you are about to read can be found at the end of this chapter.)

We all are familiar with disorganized situations such as picnics where everyone brings a bottle of ketchup but no one brings the mustard. Although too much of one thing and too little of another may be laughable at a picnic, it can spell disaster for an organization that needs to manage human and material resources effectively and efficiently in order to survive. This is when the organizing function becomes important.

Organizing is the structuring of a coordinated system of authority relationships and task responsibilities. By spelling out who does what and who reports to whom, organizational structure can translate strategy into an ongoing productive operation. Structure always follows strategy in well-managed organizations, as we saw in the case of General Motors. This is true because tasks and interrelationships cannot be realistically and systematically defined without regard for the enterprise's overall direction. Furthermore, strategy determines what technologies are required and what resources will probably be available.

According to one organization design expert, organization structure performs three important functions:

> First of all, it affords the organization the mechanisms with which to *reduce* external and internal *uncertainty*. The forecasting, research, and planning units in the organization help it to reduce external uncertainty. The control units help it to reduce uncertainty arising out of variable, unpredictable, random human or mechanical behavior within the organization. Next, it enables the organization to undertake a wide variety of activities through devices such as departmentalization, specialization, division of labor, and delegation of authority. Finally, it enables the organization to keep its activities *coordinated,* to pursue goals, to have a focus in the midst of diversity. Hierarchy, formal committees, information system are all aspects of the structure that facilitates the integration of organizational activities.[6]

As we mentioned in the previous chapter, traditional closed-system prescriptions for designing organizations have come under fire in recent years. In the face of rapid change and growing environmental complexity, traditional authoritarian bureaucracies are becoming unwieldy structural dinosaurs. Fortunately, the modern open-system view with its emphasis on organization-environment interaction has helped underscore the need for more flexible organization structures that are more adaptable to sudden changes in the environment. Recognizing that traditional principles of organization are severely bent or broken when designing flexible and adaptive organizations, managers need new formulas for designing new organizations. This is where the contingency approach enters the picture. The contingency approach permits the custom tailoring of organizations to meet unique external and internal situational demands.

In this chapter we introduce and discuss organizational design alternatives that enhance situational appropriateness and, hence, organizational effectiveness. First, we examine organization charts, since they are the principal visual aid in structuring organizations.

Organization Charts

An **organization chart** is a diagram of an organization's official positions and formal lines of authority. In effect, an organization chart is a visual display of an organization's structural skeleton. These charts (called tables by some), with their familiar pattern of boxes and connecting lines, are a useful management tool because they are an organizational blueprint for deploying human resources. They are common in both profit and not-for-profit organizations.

Every organization chart has two dimensions, one representing vertical hierarchy and one representing horizontal specialization. Vertical hierarchy establishes the chain of command, or who reports to whom. Horizontal specialization establishes the division of labor. A short case tracing the evolution of a new organization helps demonstrate the relationship between vertical hierarchy and horizontal specialization.

For years, George Terrell was an avid trout fisherman. The sight of George loading up his old sedan with expensive fly-casting gear and heading out to the nearest trout stream was familiar to his family and neighbors. About six years ago, George tried his hand at the difficult task of tying his own trout flies. Being a creative individual and a bit of a handyman, George soon created a fly that trout seemingly fought over to bite. Word about what came to be known as George's Super Fly spread rapidly among local and regional fishing enthusiasts. Within weeks he was swamped with orders. Three dollars turned out to be a reasonable price for his newly patented Super Flies. What had started out as a casual hobby turned into a lucrative business bringing in roughly $300 per week. George no longer found any time to fish; all his time was taken up tying and selling Super Flies. An organization chart at that point would have looked like the one in Figure 8.2A. Since George was the entire operation, an organization technically did not exist. There was no vertical hierarchy or horizontal specialization at that early stage.

George soon found it impossible to tie more than a hundred flies a week

Figure 8.2   The Evolution of an Organization Chart

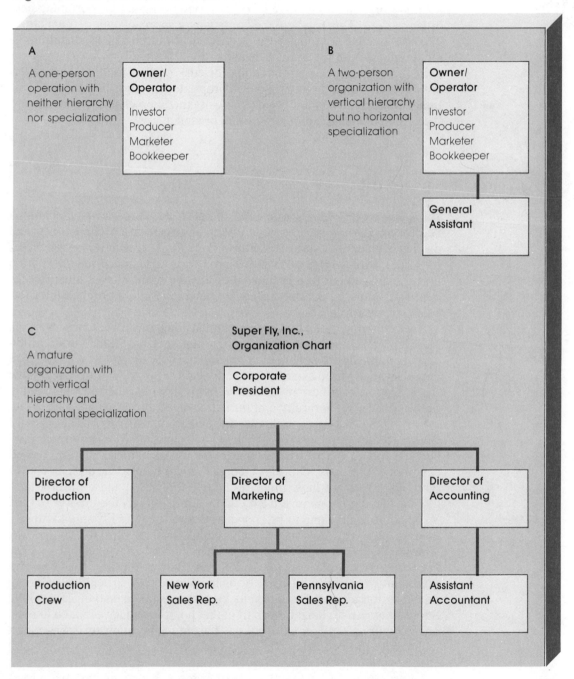

and still get out to visit fishing-tackle retailers who might carry his Super Flies. To free some of his time, George hired and trained a family friend named Amy to help him run the operation in a small building he had leased. Although George still did not have an organization chart, one could have been drawn up because an organization came into existence once an assistant was hired. (Remember from the last chapter that it takes at least two people to make an organization.) A chart at that point would have resembled the one in Figure 8.2B. Vertical hierarchy had been introduced, since Amy was George's subordinate. However, there still was no horizontal specialization, because Amy did a lot of different things to help out.

As business picked up in the following months, George had to hire and train four full-time employees to work under Amy tying flies. He also hired Fred, a sharp salesman and an old fishing buddy, to head up the marketing operation and recruit and train two regional sales representatives. Shortly afterward, an accountant was brought into the organization to set up and keep the books. Today, Super Fly, Inc., is recording annual sales in excess of $850,000. George has finally gotten around to formally organizing the company he built in patchwork fashion through the years. His organization chart is displayed in Figure 8.2C.

Notice that the company now has three layers in the vertical hierarchy and three distinct forms of horizontal specialization. The three specialized directors now do separately what George used to do all by himself. One can readily see how George's job of general management will become progressively more difficult as additional vertical layers and horizontal specialists are added. Coordination is essential; the "right hand" must operate in concert with the "left hand." Generally, specialization is achieved at the expense of coordination when designing organizations. A workable balance between specialization and coordination can be achieved through contingency design.

Contingency Design

As we discussed in Chapter 2, contingency thinking amounts to situational thinking. Specifically, the contingency approach to organizing involves taking special steps to make sure that the organization fits the demands of the situation. In direct contrast to traditional bureaucratic thinking, contingency design is based on the assumption that there is no single best way to structure an organization. **Contingency design** is the process of determining the degree of environmental uncertainty and adapting the organization and its subunits to that environment. This does not necessarily mean that all contingency organizations are different from each other. Instead, it means that managers who take a contingency approach select from a

Table 8.1 Determining the Degree of Environmental Uncertainty

	Degree of Environmental Uncertainty		
	Low	*Moderate*	*High*
1. How strong are social, political, and economic pressures on the organization?	Minimal	Moderate	Intense
2. How frequent are technological breakthroughs in the industry?	Infrequent	Occasional	Frequent
3. How reliable are resources and supplies?	Reliable	Occasional, predictable shortages	Unreliable
4. How stable is the demand for the organization's product or service?	Highly stable	Moderately stable	Unstable

number of design alternatives to create the most situationally effective organization possible. Contingency managers typically start with the same basic collection of design alternatives but end up with unique combinations of them as dictated by situational demands.

The contingency approach to designing organizations boils down to two questions: (1) How much environmental uncertainty is there? (See Table 8.1 for a handy way to answer this question.) (2) What combination of structural characteristics is most appropriate? We will examine two somewhat different contingency models to establish the validity of the contingency approach. Each of the models presents a scheme for systematically matching structural characteristics with environmental demands.

The Burns and Stalker Model

Tom Burns and G. M. Stalker, both British behavioral scientists, have proposed a useful typology for categorizing organizations by structural design.[7] They have distinguished between mechanistic and organic organizations. **Mechanistic organizations** tend to be rigid in design and have strong bureaucratic qualities. In contrast, **organic organizations** tend to be quite fluid and flexible in structure. Actually, these two organizational types are the extreme ends of a single continuum. Pure types are difficult to find, but it is fairly easy to check off the characteristics listed in Table 8.2 to determine whether a particular organization (or subunit) is relatively mechanistic or relatively organic.

The following excerpts from interviews by Studs Terkel, the Chicago radio personality, come very close to describing pure examples of, respectively, mechanistic and organic organizations.

Table 8.2 Mechanistic Versus Organic Organizations

Characteristic	Mechanistic Organizations	Organic Organizations
1. Task definition for individual contributors	Narrow and precise	Broad and general
2. Relationship between individual contribution and organization purpose	Vague	Clear
3. Task flexibility	Low	High
4. Definition of rights, obligations, and techniques	Clear	Vague
5. Reliance on hierarchical control	High	Low (reliance on self-control)
6. Primary direction of communication	Vertical (top to bottom)	Lateral (between peers)
7. Reliance on instructions and decisions from superior	High	Low (superior offers information and advice)
8. Emphasis on loyalty and obedience	High	Low
9. Type of knowledge required	Narrow, technical, and task-specific	Broad and professional

SOURCE: Adapted from Tom Burns and G. M. Stalker, *The Management of Innovation* (London: Tavistock, 1961), pp. 119–125.

A long-distance telephone operator: You're in a room about the size of a gymnasium, talking to people thousands of miles away. You come in contact with at least thirty-five an hour. ...

You have a number—mine's 407. They put your number on your tickets, so if you make a mistake they'll know who did it. You're just an instrument. You're there to dial a number. ...

You've got a clock next to you that times every second. When the light goes off, you see the party has answered, you have to write down the hour, the minute, and the second. ... When the light goes on, they disconnect and you've got to take the card out again and time down the hour, the minute, and the second—plus keeping on taking other calls. It's hectic.[8]

A director of a bakery cooperative: I'm the director. It has no owner. Originally I owned it. We're a nonprofit corporation 'cause we give our leftover bread away, give it to anyone who would be hungry.

> We have men and women, we all do the same kind of work. Everyone does everything. It's not as chaotic as it sounds. Different people take responsibility for different jobs. ...
>
> We try to have a compromise between doing things efficiently and doing things in a human way. Our bread has to taste the same way every day, but you don't have to be machines.[9]

It is important to interpret these examples carefully. Employees are not necessarily unhappy in mechanistic organizations or happy in organic ones. Furthermore, profit-making organizations as well as not-for-profit organizations may be organic in design. Recognizing the difference between the two types depends on identifying characteristics such as task definition and flexibility, hierarchical control, and knowledge requirements.

Burns and Stalker's research uncovered distinct organization-environment patterns indicating the relative appropriateness of both mechanistic and organic organizations. They discovered that *successful organizations in relatively stable and certain environments tended to be mechanistic.* Conversely, they also discovered that *relatively organic organizations tended to be the successful ones when the environment was unstable and uncertain.*

For practical application, this means that mechanistic design is appropriate for environmental stability, and organic design is appropriate for high environmental uncertainty. Imagine the difficulty that a cumbersome mechanistic organization such as the U.S. Postal Service would have adjusting to the rapid change that computer manufacturers must cope with. To create a uniform and reliable nationwide mail service, however, a large and stable bureaucracy is appropriate for the postal service. In contrast, computer companies need to be more organic so that they can respond rapidly to changing technology and emerging markets.

Since Burns and Stalker's pioneering study, several different contingency models have been proposed. Some, such as Joan Woodward's study of the relationship between technology and structure, focused on a single environmental variable rather than on general environmental certainty-uncertainty. Applying her own scale of technological complexity to one hundred British firms, Woodward found distinctly different patterns of structure as technological complexity increased from low to moderate to high.[10] In spite of criticism of weak methodology, Woodward's study added to the case against the traditional notion of a universally applicable organization design.

The Lawrence and Lorsch Model

Paul R. Lawrence and Jay W. Lorsch, researchers from Harvard University, made a valuable contribution to contingency design theory by documenting the relationship between two opposing structural forces and

Figure 8.3   Differentiation and Integration: Opposing Organizational Forces

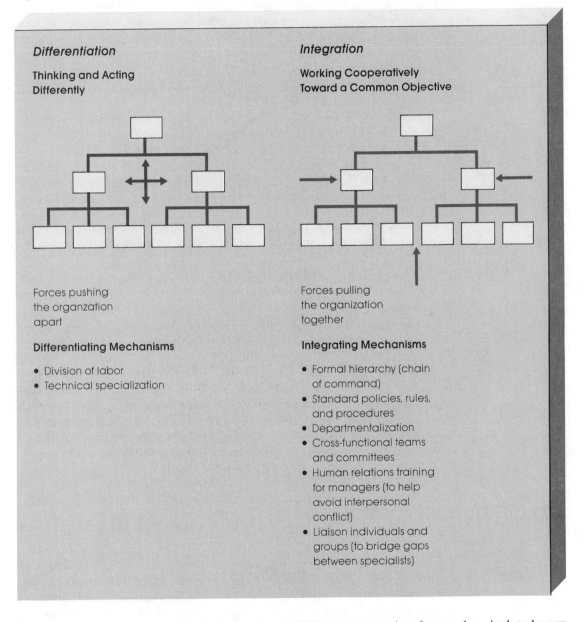

Differentiation

**Thinking and Acting
Differently**

Forces pushing
the organzation
apart

Differentiating Mechanisms

- Division of labor
- Technical specialization

Integration

**Working Cooperatively
Toward a Common Objective**

Forces pulling
the organization
together

Integrating Mechanisms

- Formal hierarchy (chain
  of command)
- Standard policies, rules,
  and procedures
- Departmentalization
- Cross-functional teams
  and committees
- Human relations training
  for managers (to help
  avoid interpersonal
  conflict)
- Liaison individuals and
  groups (to bridge gaps
  between specialists)

environmental complexity. The two opposing forces they isolated were labeled differentiation and integration. **Differentiation** is the tendency among specialists to think and act differently. This structural force is achieved through division of labor and technical specialization. Differentiation tends to fragment and disperse the organization (see Figure 8.3). **Integration,** in direct opposition to differentiation, is the collaboration among specialists that is needed to achieve a common purpose.[11] Integration can be partially achieved through a number of mechanisms, including hierarchical control, policies and procedures, departmentalization, cross-functional committees and teams, better human relations, and liaison individuals and groups. As illustrated in Figure 8.3, integration is a unifying and coordinating force.

According to Lawrence and Lorsch, every organization requires an appropriate *dynamic equilibrium* (applying an open-system term) between the two opposing structural forces of differentiation and integration. In fact, by contrasting successful and unsuccessful firms in three different industries, they discovered that in the successful firms *both differentiation and integration increased as environmental complexity increased.* Significantly, their findings not only applied to the overall organization but also to organizational subunits (for example, departments). But they also found that "the more differentiated an organization, the more difficult it is to achieve integration."[12] This suggests that organizational failure in the face of environmental complexity is probably due to a combination of high differentiation and inadequate integration. Hence specialists in different areas work at cross-purposes and get embroiled in counterproductive jurisdictional conflicts. Constructive steps can be taken to achieve needed coordination, however, as the case of Dun & Bradstreet demonstrates (see Table 8.3).

Although contingency design models may differ in perspective and language, two conclusions stand out. First, research has proved time and again that there is no single best organization design. Second, research generally supports the idea that the more uncertain the environment, the more flexible and adaptable the organization structure must be.[13] With this contingency perspective in mind, we now consider four structural formats.

Basic Structural Formats

As we noted earlier, differentiation occurs through division of labor. When labor is divided, complex processes are reduced to distinct and less complex jobs. But because differentiation tends to fragment the organization, some sort of integration needs to be introduced to achieve the necessary coordination. Aside from the hierarchical chain of command, one of the most common forms of integration is departmentalization. It is through **departmentalization** that related jobs, activities, or processes are grouped into major organizational subunits. For example, all jobs involving staffing activities like recruitment, hiring, and training are often

Table 8.3 Striking a Balance Between Differentiation and Integration

Dun & Bradstreet, the highly successful and well-known financial information company, is a good example of how an imaginative balance of differentiation and integration can help a company grow and prosper amid rapidly changing conditions. In order to stay competitive, 130 profit centers were created in the firm's product-centered divisions during the 1970s to stimulate the entrepreneurial abilities of managers. While this differentiation was taking place, a vast computerization program was installed to improve the speed and quality of service. Coordination between various divisions and among the many profit centers was achieved through the following forms of integration:

- Managers were regularly rotated to other divisions to break emotional ties with single product lines.
- In an unprecedented meeting, 140 senior managers were brought together to exchange ideas on a personal basis and brainstorm new product ideas.
- Frequent interdisciplinary meetings were encouraged among managers in different product areas to identify common problems, interests, and potential joint ventures.
- To help improve interdepartmental communication, managers received crash courses in computer technology and listening skills from an in-house staff of 70 trainers.
- Although managerial compensation was based on individual profit center performance, top management made sure that bonuses were not eroded by cooperative programs (thus encouraging cooperation).

SOURCE: Adapted from "How D&B Organizes for a New-Product Blitz," *Business Week* No. 2714 (November 16, 1981): 87, 90.

grouped into a personnel department. Grouping jobs through the formation of departments, according to James D. Thompson, "permits coordination to be handled in the least costly manner."[14] A degree of coordination is achieved through departmentalization because all those in a separate department work on interrelated tasks, obey the same departmental rules, and report to the same department head. It is important to note that although the term *departmentalization* is used here, it does not always literally apply; the term *division* is commonly used in large organizations.

Four basic types of departmentalization are functional departments, product-service departments, geographic location departments, and customer classification departments.

Functional Departments

Functional departments categorize jobs according to the activity performed. Among profit-making businesses, variations of the functional production-finance-marketing arrangement in Figure 8.4A are the most common form of departmentalization. Functional departmentalization is popular because it permits those with similar technical expertise to work in a coordinated subunit. On the other hand, functional departmentalization has been criticized because it creates "technical ghettos" in which departmental concerns tend to override more important organizational concerns. For example, production specialists may overlook financial concerns about cost containment or marketing concerns about competitive prices. Of course, functional departmentalization is not restricted to profit-making businesses. Functional departments in a not-for-profit hospital might be administration, nursing, housekeeping, food service, laboratory and x ray, admission and records, and accounting and billing.

Product-Service Departments

Because functional departmentalization has been faulted for encouraging differentiation at the expense of integration, a somewhat more organic alternative has evolved. It is called product-service departmentalization because a product (or service) is the unifying theme rather than a functional category of work. As diagramed in Figure 8.4B, the product-service approach permits each of, say, two products to be managed as semi-autonomous businesses. Some organizations render a service instead of turning out a tangible product, and they might find it advantageous to organize around service categories. For example, a janitorial company could have a rug-cleaning department and an office-cleaning department. In effect, the product (or service) managers are responsible for managing their own minibusinesses. Ideally, those working in a product-service department have a broad "business" orientation rather than a narrow functional orientation. It is the president's job to ensure that these minibusinesses work in a complementary fashion.

This design format was used successfully by General Motors for over half a century (see Opening Case 8.1). The head of its Pontiac Division competed for resources and sales not only with other General Motors divisions, such as Buick, but also with other auto makers, such as Ford and Chrysler. Management believed that if Pontiac could stand on its own two feet it would make a greater contribution to the overall objectives of General Motors. One danger of the product-service approach, as General Motors discovered prior to its recent reorganization, is inefficient and costly duplication of effort. In addition, departments or business units with overlapping markets may resort to destructive competition.

Geographic Location Departments

Sometimes, as in the case of organizations with nationwide or worldwide markets, geography dictates structural format (see Figure 8.4C). Geographic dispersion of resources (for example, mining companies), facilities (for example, railroads), or customers (for example, chain supermarkets) may encourage the use of a geographic format to put administrators "closer to the action." For example, drilling engineers in a Houston-based petroleum firm would be better able to get a job done in Alaska if they actually went up there. Similarly, a department-store marketing manager

Figure 8.4   Alternative Departmentalization Formats

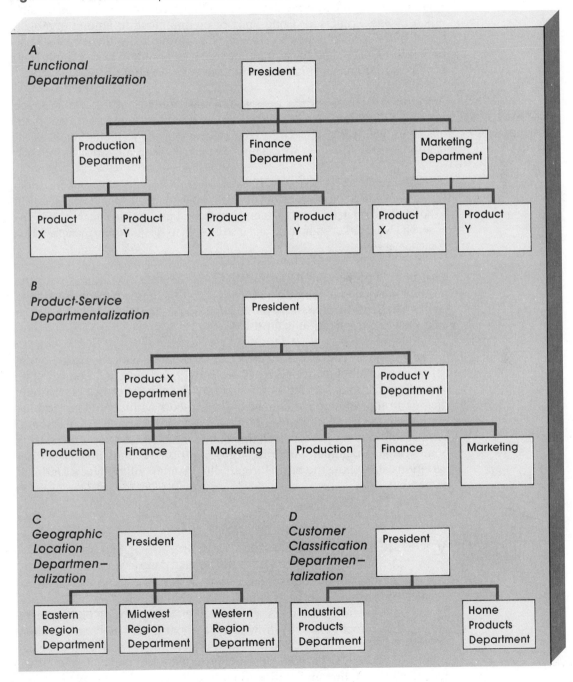

would be in a better position to judge consumer tastes among New Englanders if working out of a regional office in Boston rather than a home office in San Francisco. Long lines of communication among organizational units is an obvious limitation of geographically dispersed operations. But space-age telecommunication technology (see Chapter 16) promises to diminish this problem in the years to come.

Customer Classification Departments

A fourth structural format centers on various customer categories (see Figure 8.4D). When Hewlett-Packard Co., a well-managed computer manufacturer, wanted to serve a wider market it turned to a customer classification format. *Business Week* summed up HP's reorganization as follows:

> Its new structure ... regroups HP's dozens of product divisions under sectors that are focused on markets rather than product lines. Two major sectors will now sell computers: One will concentrate on business customers, while the second will market computers and instruments to scientific and manufacturing customers.[15]

Customer classification departmentalization shares a weakness with the product-service and geographic location approaches: all three can create costly duplication of personnel and facilities. Functional design is the answer when duplication is a problem.

Each of the preceding design formats is presented in its pure form, but in actual practice, hybrid versions are commonly encountered. For example, large organizations serving broad markets may find it useful to combine their central production and finance departments with several geographic marketing departments instead of having a single marketing department. From a contingency perspective, the four design formats are useful starting points rather than final blueprints for organizers. A number of structural variations show how the basic formats can be adapted to meet situational demands.

Contingency Design Alternatives

Contingency design requires managers to select from a number of situationally appropriate alternatives instead of blindly following fixed principles of organization. Managers who face a relatively certain environment can enhance effectiveness by drawing on comparatively mechanistic alternatives. Those who must cope with high uncertainty are advised to select organic alternatives. Variable design alternatives include span of control, decentralization, line and staff, and matrix design.

Figure 8.5 Narrow and Wide Spans of Control

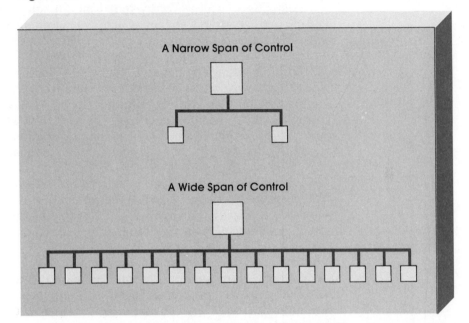

A Narrow Span of Control

A Wide Span of Control

Span of Control The number of people who report directly to a manager is that manager's **span of control.** Some management scholars prefer the term *span of management*. Managers with a narrow span of control oversee the work of few people, whereas those with a wide span of control have many people reporting to them (see Figure 8.5). Generally, narrow spans of control foster tall organizations (many levels in the hierarchy). In contrast, flat organizations (few hierarchical levels) have wide spans of control. Everything else being equal, it stands to reason that an organization with narrow spans of control needs more managers than one with wide spans. Management theorists and practitioners have devoted a good deal of time and energy through the years attempting to answer the question "What is the ideal span of control?"[16] Ideally, the right span of control strikes an efficient balance between too little and too much supervision.

Is There an Ideal Span of Control? Early management theorists confidently specified exactly how many individuals there should be in a manager's span of control. In the words of one early management scholar, "No superior can supervise directly the work of more than five or, at the most, six subordinates whose work interlocks."[17]

As time went by and research results began to push aside strictly intuitive judgments, evidence supporting wider spans of control emerged. James C. Worthy, a vice president of Sears, Roebuck, reported that his

No optimum

company had gotten good results with spans of control far in excess of six individuals. Specifically, Worthy found morale and effectiveness to be higher in one department store in which 36 department managers reported to a single manager than in a second store in which the span of control averaged only five.[18]

Given the present emphasis on contingency organization design and evidence that wide spans of control can be effective, the question of an ideal span has become obsolete. Rather than asking how wide spans of control *should* be, the relevant question now is "How wide *can* one's span of control be?" Wider spans of control mean less administrative overhead and more self-management, both popular notions today.

The Contingency Approach to Spans of Control   Both overly narrow and overly wide spans of control are counterproductive. Overly narrow spans have been criticized for creating unnecessarily tall organizations plagued by such problems as oversupervision; long lines of communication; slow, multilevel decision making; limited initiative due to minimal delegation of authority; restricted development among managers who devote most of their time to direct supervision; and increased administrative costs.[19] Overly wide spans, on the other hand, can erode efficiency and inflate costs through lack of training, behavioral problems among inadequately supervised subordinates, and lack of coordination. Clearly, a rationale is needed for striking a workable balance. Situational factors such as those listed in Figure 8.6 are a useful starting point. The narrow, moderate, and wide span of control ranges in Figure 8.6 are intended to be illustrative bench marks rather than rigid limits. On-the-job experimentation is required. The ideal span simply does not exist.

Centralization and Decentralization

Where are the important decisions made in an organization? Are they made strictly by top management or by middle- and lower-level managers? These questions are at the very heart of the decentralization design alternative. Decentralization actually is at one end of a continuum; at the other end is centralization. **Centralization** and **decentralization** are defined according to the relative retention or delegation of decision-making authority by top management. Almost all decision-making authority is retained by top management in highly centralized organizations. In contrast, decentralization increases as the degree, importance, and range of lower-level decision making *increases* and the amount of checking up by top management *decreases* (see Figure 8.7).

Centralization and decentralization are best discussed in relative terms, similar to the manner in which we usually discuss outdoor temperature. When we say it's a cold day, we mean it is relatively cold for a particular time of year, not that it is absolute zero (–459.69° F). Whenever we speak of

Figure 8.6 Situational Determinants of Span of Control

	Wide Span of Control Appropriate (10 or more)	Moderate Span of Control Appropriate (5 to 9)	Narrow Span of Control Appropriate (2 to 4)
1. Similarity of work performed by subordinates	Identical		Distinctly Different
2. Dispersion of subordinates	Same Work Area		Geographically Dispersed
3. Complexity of work performed by subordinates	Simple and Repetitive		Highly Complex and Varied
4. Direction and control required by subordinates	Little and/or Infrequent		Intensive and/or Constant
5. Time spent coordinating with other managers	Little		A Great Deal
6. Time required for planning	Little		A Great Deal

SOURCE: Adapted from C. W. Barkdull, "Span of Control—A Method of Evaluation," *Michigan Business Review* 15 (May 1963): 25–32.

centralization or decentralization, it is a matter of comparative degree, not absolutes. For example, in the closing case for this chapter, contrast the $200,000 spending limit, monthly reports, and quarterly meetings at Mark Controls Corporation with the situation at Houston's Sysco Corporation, the largest distributor of food to restaurants and institutions in the United States:

> Subsidiary company presidents cannot borrow money; corporate headquarters arranges all lines of credit. And except for replacing equipment, any manager wishing to spend more than $2,500 on anything must submit a full return-on-investment analysis to Houston.
> Each week, the subsidiary heads are required to submit a full profit-and-loss

Figure 8.7   Factors in Relative Centralization/Decentralization

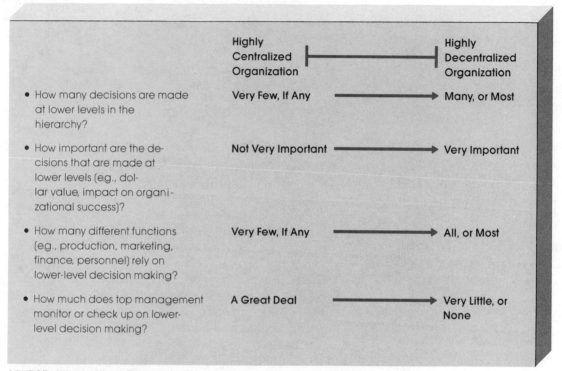

SOURCE: Adapted from Ernest Dale, *Planning and Developing the Company Organization Structure*, Research Report 20 (New York: American Management Association, 1952), p. 118.

statement and to report changes in working capital. Moreover, as part of the weekly report, the local company must explain in writing what happened when any customer's order was not met with at least 98% accuracy.[20]

Mark Controls is relatively decentralized, whereas Sysco is highly centralized.

Decentralization Through Strategic Business Units   Due to their growing popularity, particularly among very large businesses attempting to become more entrepreneurial, strategic business units deserve special mention here. A **strategic business unit** (SBU) is an organizational subunit that acts like an independent business in all major respects, including the formulation of its own strategic plans. In order for an organizational unit to qualify as a full-fledged SBU it must meet the following four criteria:

1. It must serve a specific market outside the parent organization, rather than being simply an internal supplier.
2. It must be faced with outside competitors.
3. It should be in a position of controlling its own destiny, especially through strategic planning and new product development. However, SBUs may choose to share the parent organization's resources such as manufacturing facilities or sales personnel. The key here is that the SBU makes the key choices, not the parent organization.
4. It should be a profit center with its effectiveness measured in terms of profit/loss.[21]

Units that do not meet all of these criteria often are called SBUs also. Like the underlying concept of decentralization, SBUs vary in degree. A true SBU is highly decentralized.

In addition to encouraging organizational units to engage in greater entrepreneurial risk taking, SBUs can speed up the new product development process. For example, in response to a sharp drop in market share for plain-paper copiers, Xerox Corporation reorganized its copier business into four SBUs. One direct result was that a sophisticated new copier (a $130,000 unit designed to compete with printing machines) was developed in only three years, not the usual five.[22] Within Xerox's SBU framework, "... small engineering teams compete for the opportunity to take an idea from the concept stage to a feasibility model."[23] This way, unworkable product ideas can be weeded out quickly. Prior to turning to the SBU format, Xerox too often wasted valuable resources on products that eventually turned out to be unworkable.

Turning to the dark side of SBUs, interference by the parent organization is the surest way to render them ineffective. Ironically, if SBUs are to succeed, they need the freedom to fail.

The Case for Decentralization   As the following statement by James C. Worthy, an early advocate of the concept, points out, decentralization appeals to a democratic society:

> Flatter, less complex structures, with a maximum of administrative decentralization, tend to create a potential for improved attitudes, more effective supervision, and greater individual responsibility and initiative among employees. Moreover, arrangements of this type encourage the development of individual self-expression and creativity, which are so necessary to the personal satisfaction of employees and which are an essential ingredient of the democratic way of life.[24]

Proponents of decentralization assume that middle- and lower-level managers are both willing and able to shoulder the added decision-making authority. But realistically, this assumption is not always valid.

The Case Against Decentralization   One word sums up the major argument against decentralization: *control*. For example, *Business Week* reported one advocate of tightly centralized management as saying, "One way to know the company is to have the problems on our hands all the time. We were not sitting in an ivory tower waiting for all the results to come in every month."[25] It is this desire to know exactly what is going on at all times that makes centralization attractive to top managers, even though subordinate managers often complain about being stifled and not trusted. Otherwise, the argument goes, things will get out of control because managers at lower levels will make conflicting decisions and top management won't find out until the damage has already been done.

Centralization is popular among top managers for another reason as well. It supposedly streamlines the organization by eliminating inefficient duplication of effort. For example, Studebaker-Worthington abandoned its decentralized design when it discovered that several of its subsidiaries were selling similar products to the same customers.[26] Along the same lines, IBM centralized its three sales divisions into one that could market and service all the company's products. "Even though IBM tried to coordinate the sales calls of its three divisions, customers were often confused— especially as rapidly evolving technology made product offerings of the three divisions appear similar."[27] IBM now presents a "single face" to its customers.

As with span of control, there is no magic formula for achieving an optimum degree of centralization or decentralization. Centralization, because of its mechanistic nature, generally works best for organizations in relatively stable environmental conditions. A more organic, decentralized approach is appropriate for firms in complex and changing conditions.

Line and Staff   Through the years, managers of large mechanistic organizations have struggled to strike a balance between technical specialization and unity of command. Remember that unity of command was emphasized by traditional management theorists. According to the unity-of-command principle, people should have only one immediate superior in order to avoid receiving conflicting orders. Unfortunately, in highly differentiated organizations there is often a mismatch between technical expertise and authority. For example, a production manager with the appropriate authority to take constructive action may not perceive sloppy inventory control as the source of runaway production costs. But an assistant accounting manager who has the technical expertise to identify and solve the inventory problem does not have the authority to take direct action in the production area. Line and staff organization design helps management apply technical expertise where it is most needed while maintaining relative unity of command.

Line Versus Staff   Briefly, in a **line and staff organization,** a distinction is made between line positions, those in the formal chain of command, and staff positions, those serving in an advisory capacity outside the formal chain of command. Line managers have the authority to make decisions and give orders to subordinates in the chain of command. In contrast, those who occupy staff positions merely advise and support line managers. Staff authority is normally restricted to immediate assistants. This distinction is relatively clear-cut in mechanistic organizations but tends to get blurred in organic organizations.

Personal Versus Specialized Staff   There are two general types of staff, personal and specialized.[28] Personal staff are individuals who are assigned to a specific manager to provide research support, specialized technical expertise, and counsel. For example, in Figure 8.8, the strategic planning specialist and legal counsel are on the president's personal staff. But, unlike the president who has line authority over all functions, the authority of personal staff is normally limited to those working in their technical areas. Specialized staff, on the other hand, are "a reservoir of special knowledge, skills, and experience which the entire organization can use."[29] For example, because the organization in Figure 8.8 is primarily a manufacturing firm, manufacturing is a line function, whereas research and development, marketing, finance-accounting, and personnel are specialized staff functions. This means that each of the four specialized staff functions supports but does not directly control the manufacturing function.

Functional Authority   Strict distinctions between line and staff tend to disappear in relatively organic organizations. A device called functional authority helps prevent the collapse of unity of command. **Functional authority** is an organic design alternative that gives staff personnel temporary, limited line authority for specified tasks. For example, the president's personal legal counsel in Figure 8.8 may be given functional authority for negotiating a new union contract with factory personnel. When acting in that capacity, the legal counsel's authority would override that of cooperating line managers (for example, the manufacturing and personnel directors). Functional authority can cut out a great deal of bureaucratic red tape while enhancing organizational flexibility by giving knowledgeable staff the direct authority to get something done.[30]

Figure 8.8 A Line and Staff Organization

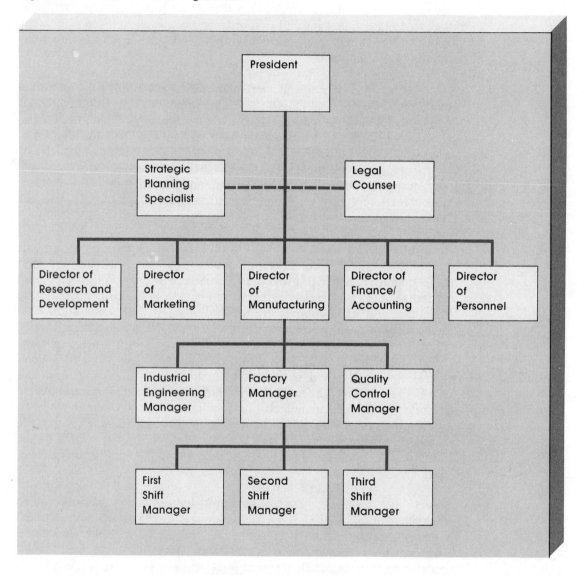

Matrix This last design alternative is sometimes called project management.[31] The term **matrix** refers to an organization structure in which vertical and horizontal lines of authority are combined. In checkerboard fashion, authority flows both down and across in a matrix organization.

Matrix design originally became popular in the construction and aerospace industries. Imagine how difficult it would be for a construction firm to complete, simultaneously and in a cost-effective manner, several huge projects such as hydroelectric dams. Because each major project has its own situational and technical demands, mechanistic bureaucracies have not worked out well as principal contractors of dams and other large projects. A more organic alternative had to be found. Likewise, aerospace giants such as Lockheed, Grumman, and General Dynamics have had to turn to a more organic structure in order to build complex weapons systems and space vehicles for the federal government. Consequently, the matrix format evolved.

Take a moment to study the matrix organization chart in Figure 8.9. Notice the checkerboard configuration. In effect, the project managers borrow specialists from the line managers in charge of engineering, manufacturing, and contract administration. Technical needs dictate how many specialists will be borrowed from a given functional area at a given time. It is important to note that project managers have only limited (project-related) authority over the specialists who otherwise report to their line managers. Matrix design has both strengths and weaknesses.

Strengths   Increased coordination is the principal strength of matrix design. The matrix format places a project manager in a good position to coordinate the many interrelated aspects of a particular project, both inside and outside the organization.[32] In mechanistic bureaucracies, the various aspects of a project normally would be handled in a somewhat fragmented fashion by functional units, such as production and marketing, with no single person being in charge of the project.

A second strength, control, stems from the first. It stands to reason that greater coordination leads to greater control over both personnel and costs. Increased flexibility is a third strength. A project manager may need five engineers one month and sixteen the next. A typical mechanistic organization would have difficulty absorbing the surplus personnel during slack periods, but a matrix organization with several major projects active at once can move specialists from one project to another as the situation requires. This approach reduces the need for short-term layoffs and the problem of costly idle talent.

Weaknesses   First and foremost, matrix design flagrantly violates the traditional unity-of-command principle. A glance at Figure 8.9 reveals that an engineer, for instance, actually has two supervisors at the same time. This special arrangement can and sometimes does cause conflicts of interest. Only frequent and comprehensive communication between functional and project managers (integration) can minimize unity-of-command problems.

A second weakness has been labeled the "authority gap." This problem is due largely to the fact that project managers are responsible for getting their projects accomplished in spite of a lack of formal line authority.

Figure 8.9   A Simplified Matrix Organization Chart

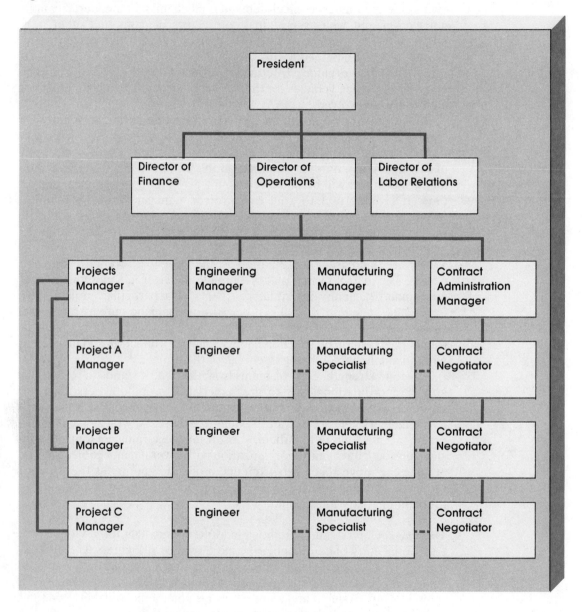

Research has shown that project managers tend to use negotiation, persuasive ability, technical competence, and the exchange of favors to compensate for their authority gap.[33]

A third weakness centers on the delicate balance that the project manager must achieve between a project's technical and administrative aspects.[34] It is not always easy to get highly technical engineers and scientists to realize that costs must be kept within reasonable bounds. Once again, the project manager needs to rely on polished interpersonal skills.

Finally, matrix organizations have turned out to be too complex and cumbersome for some organizations. After years of serving as a model for matrix design, Texas Instruments Incorporated scrapped its complex matrix structure in favor of a more decentralized arrangement approximating strategic business units.[35]

Effective Delegation

Delegation is an important common denominator that runs through virtually all relatively organic design alternatives. It is vital to successful decentralization. Formally defined, **delegation** is the process of assigning various degrees of decision-making authority to subordinates. As this definition implies, delegation is not an all-or-nothing proposition. There are at least five different degrees of delegation (see Figure 8.10).

A word of caution about delegation is necessary because there is one thing it does not include. Former President Harry Truman is said to have had a little sign on his White House desk that read, "The Buck Stops Here!" Managers who delegate should keep this idea in mind, because although *authority* may be passed along to subordinates, *ultimate responsibility* cannot be passed along. For example, a personnel manager may delegate to an assistant the task of recruiting minorities. Even though the personnel manager may hold the assistant accountable for successful minority recruiting, the personnel manager is still ultimately responsible for reaching minority recruiting goals. Thus delegation is the sharing of authority, not the abdication of responsibility.

The Advantages of Delegation

Managers stand to gain a great deal by adopting the habit of delegating. By passing along well-defined tasks to subordinates, managers can free more of their time for important chores like planning. Regarding the question of exactly *what* should be delegated, Intel's President, Andrew S. Grove, has made the following recommendation: "Because it is easier to monitor something with which you are familiar, if you have a choice you should delegate those activities you know best."[36] But Grove cautions that delegators who follow his advice will experience some psychological discomfort because they will quite naturally want to continue doing what they know best.

In addition to freeing up valuable managerial time, delegation is also a

Figure 8.10 The Delegation Continuum

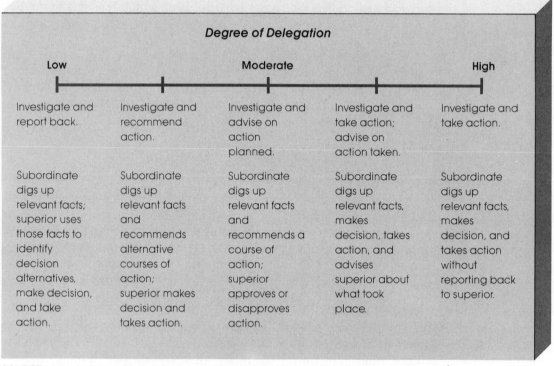

SOURCE: Adapted from Marion E. Haynes, "Delegation: There's More To It Than Letting Someone Else Do It!" *Supervisory Management* 25 (January 1980): 9–15.

helpful management training and development tool. Moreover, subordinates who desire more challenge generally become more committed and satisfied when they are given the opportunity to tackle significant problems. Conversely, a lack of delegation can stifle initiative. Consider the situation of a California home builder:

[The founder and chairman] personally negotiates every land deal. Visiting every construction site repeatedly, he is critical even of details of cabinet construction. "The building business is an entrepreneurial business," he says. "Yes, you can send out people. But you better follow them. You have to manage your managers."

Says one former ... executive: "The turnover there's tremendous. He hires bright and talented people, but then he makes them eunuchs. He never lets them make any decisions."[37]

"B.D. has a little problem delegating."
SOURCE: © 1984 M. Twohy. Management Review.

Perfectionist managers who avoid delegation have problems in the long run when they become overwhelmed by minute details.[38]

Barriers to Delegation

There are several reasons why managers generally do not delegate as much as they should:

- Belief in the fallacy "If you want it done right, do it yourself."
- Lack of confidence and trust in subordinates.
- Low self-confidence.
- Fear of being called lazy.
- Vague job definition.
- Fear of competition from subordinates.
- Reluctance to take the risks involved in depending on others.
- Lack of controls that provide early warning of problems with delegated duties.
- Poor example set by superiors who do not delegate.[39]

Managers can go a long way toward effective delegation by recognizing and correcting these tendencies both in themselves and their fellow managers. Since successful delegation is habit forming, the first step usually is the hardest. Properly trained and motivated subordinates who respond favorably to challenging work generally reward a manager's trust with a job well done.

Summary

Organizing is an important managerial function that translates strategy into a systematic structure of authority relationships and task responsibilities. Contingency organization design has grown in popularity as environmental complexity has increased. Organization charts are helpful visual aids for organizers. Representing the organization's structural skeleton, organization charts delineate vertical hierarchy and horizontal specialization.

The idea behind contingency design is to structure the organization to fit situational demands. Consequently, contingency advocates contend that there is no one best organizational setup for all situations. Diagnosing the degree of environmental uncertainty is an important first step in contingency design. Field studies have validated the assumption that organization structure should vary according to the situation. Burns and Stalker discovered that mechanistic (rigid) organizations are effective when the environment is relatively stable and that organic (flexible) organizations are best when unstable conditions prevail. Lawrence and Lorsch found that differentiation (division of labor) and integration (cooperation among specialists) increased in successful organizations as environmental complexity increased.

There are four basic departmentalization formats, each with its own combination of advantages and disadvantages. Functional departmentalization is the most common approach. The others are product-service, geographic location, and customer classification departmentalization. In actual practice, these pure types of departmentalization usually are combined.

Design variables available to organizers are span of control, decentralization, line and staff, and matrix. As organizers have come to realize that situational factors dictate how many people a manager can directly supervise, the notion of an ideal span of control has become obsolete. Decentralization, the delegation of decision authority to lower-level managers, has been praised as being democratic and criticized for reducing top management's control. Strategic business units foster a high degree of decentralization. Line and staff organization helps balance specialization and unity of command. Functional authority serves to make line and staff organization more organic by giving staff specialists temporary and limited line authority. Matrix organizations are highly organic because they combine vertical and horizontal lines of authority to achieve coordinated control over complex projects.

Delegation of authority, although generally resisted for a variety of reasons, is crucial to decentralization. Effective delegation permits managers to tackle higher-priority duties while helping train and develop lower-level managers. Although delegation varies in degree, it never means abdicating primary responsibility.

Terms to Understand

Organizing	Span of control
Organization chart	Centralization
Contingency design	Decentralization
Mechanistic organizations	Strategic business unit (SBU)
Organic organizations	Line and staff organization
Differentiation	Functional authority
Integration	Matrix
Departmentalization	Delegation

Questions for Discussion

1. Why is organizing an important management function?
2. Why does an organization need both vertical hierarchy and horizontal specialization?
3. Would you rather work in a mechanistic organization or an organic organization? Why?
4. In your own terms, how would increased differentiation and integration help an organization face environmental complexity and uncertainty?
5. Why would a product-service department manager be better qualified than a functional department manager to assume the top position in an organization?
6. What has happened to the search for the ideal span of control? How should a manager proceed in this area?
7. What type of decentralization could take place on a college campus? For the administrators and instructors, what would be the relative advantages and disadvantages of campus decentralization?

8. If you were a project manager in a matrix organization, what would you do about closing your authority gap?
9. Would you be a good delegator or a poor delegator? How would this affect your performance as a manager?
10. If you were a new manager, how could working for a person who likes to delegate help or hinder your career?

Back to the Opening Case

Now that you have read Chapter 8, you should be able to answer the following questions about the General Motors case:

1. Has General Motors effectively linked strategy and structure? Explain.
2. Will the reorganization make General Motors more differentiated or more integrated? How can you tell?
3. What is your interpretation of the reorganization from a centralization/ decentralization point of view?
4. If General Motors wants the "small cars" and "large cars" groups to act as full-fledged strategic business units, what steps will have to be taken?

Closing Case 8.2

Thinking Small Pays Off at Mark Controls

When Gary E. MacDougal became the chairman of Mark Controls Corporation in 1969, the tiny manufacturer of valves recorded an unimpressive $320,000 profit on $17 million in sales. That performance earned Mark Controls the fortieth-place ranking in its industry. Although the company's 1980 profit performance was still nothing to brag about on Wall Street ($7.8 million profit on $264 million in sales), Mark Controls had moved up to number five among valve manufacturers. The firm has found a strategic niche in computerized valves, used for controlling energy consumption in commercial buildings. This line of sophisticated valves is appealing not only for its potential growth but also for its comparatively good profit margins. The growth and strategic positioning of Mark Controls has resulted in large measure from MacDougal's philosophy of management.

Convinced that excessive emphasis on short-term results is a major management evil, MacDougal encourages his managers to take calculated risks and run their "own shows." When considering managers for promotion, MacDougal gives greatest consideration to entrepreneurial ability. He has carefully structured an organization in which the entrepreneurial spirit flourishes. MacDougal is always open to new ideas that promise to be profitable in the long run. He pushes decision making down the hierarchy by keeping operating units small, and he steadfastly avoids breathing down the division managers' necks. Not all managers are ready to accept a greater share of the decision-making burden, however. For example, replacements had to be found for over half of the 45 branch managers in one unit between 1977 and 1981.

Bite-size Units

Entrepreneurial ability will emerge, according to MacDougal's philosophy, only if unit managers can get their arms around their operations. Consequently, when a subsidiary's sales exceed $30 million, he splits it up into self-contained businesses organized around product lines. To ensure that headquarters doesn't get too involved in divisional operations, corporate staff is kept lean. In fact, in 1981, the entire corporate staff, including secretaries and data-processing specialists, totaled only 50 people.

Room to Make Mistakes

MacDougal is resigned to the fact that creativity and risk taking have their price. Sometimes his relatively young group of self-directed managers (average age: 41) make mistakes, and sometimes those mistakes are costly. For example, in 1978, MacDougal acquired Hoyt, a water tank manufacturer, largely on the recommendation of James E. Crawford, director of corporate development. Practically before the ink was dry on the acquisition, Mark Controls was saddled with $1 million in warranty claims because of design flaws in tanks previously manufactured by Hoyt. A quarter of Mark Controls' earnings was lost that year as a result of the warranty claims. Crawford would have been out the door at most companies for not doing his homework. But because of MacDougal's attitude toward risk taking among his subordinates, Crawford was not fired. In fact, he has had two promotions since the Hoyt affair. But, naturally, having learned from the Hoyt experience, MacDougal makes sure that his prospective acquisitions are adequately researched.

Financial Controls and Incentives

Even though MacDougal gives his division managers room to make mistakes, he keeps them on track with a carefully conceived system of financial controls and incentives. He personally reviews division managers' spending requests that exceed $200,000. In addition to submitting detailed financial and progress-on-objectives reports each month, all division heads meet quarterly at the firm's Evanston, Illinois, headquarters for forecasting and goal setting. Each division head is given strategic autonomy within this framework of financial controls. And in regard to incentives, a liberal stock-option plan is tied to the success of the overall corporation to encourage teamwork. Yet entrepreneurial risk taking is simultaneously encouraged by a bonus plan that ties 75 percent of each division head's annual bonus to the performance of his or her unit.

For Discussion

1. Is Mark Controls relatively mechanistic or relatively organic? Explain your evidence.
2. How has MacDougal struck a workable balance between the forces of differentiation and integration?
3. What are the positive and negative aspects of decentralization at Mark Controls?
4. How does MacDougal's incentive plan reinforce his organization design?

References

Opening Quotation: Anant R. Negandhi, "Comparative Management and Organization Theory: A Marriage Needed," *Academy of Management Journal* 18 (June 1975): 334.

Opening Case: For additional information on General Motors, see John K. Teahen, Jr., "GM Reorganizes for Greater Efficiency," *Automotive News* 59 (January 16, 1984): 1, 57; "Can GM Solve Its Identity Crisis?" *Business Week* No. 2825 (January 23, 1984): 32–33; David C. Smith, "GM's Reorganization Is 'Off the Wall,' " *Ward's Auto World* 20 (February 1984): 50, 61; John McElroy, "GM's Reorganization: Streamlining For the Future," *Automotive Industries* 164 (February 1984): 21–22; Anne B. Fisher, "GM's Unlikely Revolutionist," *Fortune* 109 (March 19, 1984): 106–112; and Joseph M. Callahan, "Cunningham Describes His Reorganization," *Automotive Industries* 164 (June 1984): 9.

Closing Case: For additional information on Mark Controls, see "Flow of Profits: Mark Controls Isn't Expecting a Shut-Off," *Barron's* 60 (August 4, 1980): 38–39; and "Mark Controls: Where Small Is Beautiful," *Business Week* No. 2703 (August 31, 1981): 104–105.

1. "Can GM Solve Its Identity Crisis?" pp. 32–33.
2. Callahan, "Cunningham Describes His Reorganization," p. 9.
3. The classic text on General Motors' early structure is Peter F. Drucker, *The Concept of the Corporation* (New York: NAL, 1964).
4. Smith, "GM's Reorganization Is 'Off the Wall,' " p. 50.
5. Fisher, "GM's Unlikely Revolutionist," p. 110.

6. Pradip N. Khandwalla, *The Design of Organizations* (New York: Harcourt Brace Jovanovich, 1977), p. 483.

7. See Tom Burns and G. M. Stalker, *The Management of Innovation* (London: Tavistock, 1961), chap. 5.

8. Studs Terkel, *Working* (New York: Random House, 1974), pp. 36–37.

9. Ibid., pp. 467, 470.

10. For a complete summary of Woodward's findings, see Joan Woodward, *Industrial Organization: Theory and Practice* (London: Oxford University Press, 1965), chap. 4.

11. Adapted from Paul R. Lawrence and Jay W. Lorsch, *Organization and Environment* (Homewood, Ill.: Richard D. Irwin, 1967), p. 11.

12. Ibid., p. 157.

13. For a detailed description of contingency design in action in a U.S. Air Force facility, see Thomas J. Von der Embse and William H. Toliver, "Contingency Organization Design: What It Is and How It Works," *Research Management* 22 (September 1979): 31–36.

14. James D. Thompson, *Organizations in Action* (New York: McGraw-Hill, 1967), p. 59.

15. "Why Hewlett-Packard Overhauled Its Management," *Business Week* No. 2853 (July 30, 1984): 111.

16. For an extensive bibliography on this subject, see David D. Van Fleet and Arthur G. Bedeian, "A History of the Span of Management," *Academy of Management Review* 2 (July 1977): 356–372.

17. L. Urwick, *The Elements of Administration* (New York: Harper & Row, 1944), pp. 52–53.

18. For details of this study, see James C. Worthy, "Organizational Structure and Employee Morale," *American Sociological Review* 15 (April 1950): 169–179.

19. Drawn from C. W. Barkdull, "Span of Control—A Method of Evaluation," *Michigan Business Review* 15 (May 1963): 25–32.

20. "Sysco: Swallowing Its Competitors to Grow in Food Distribution," *Business Week* No. 2701 (August 17, 1981): 116–117.

21. Based on material found in William E. Rothschild, "How to Ensure the Continued Growth of Strategic Planning," *The Journal of Business Strategy* 1 (Summer 1980): 11–18.

22. See "How Xerox Speeds Up the Birth of New Products," *Business Week* No. 2833 (March 19, 1984): 58–59.

23. "Big Business Tries to Imitate the Entrepreneurial Spirit," *Business Week* No. 2786 (April 18, 1983): 84.

24. Worthy, "Organizational Structure and Employee Morale," p. 179.

25. "General Dynamics: Winning in the Aerospace Game," *Business Week* No. 2430 (May 3, 1976): 88.

26. See "If 'Satellization' Fails, Try Centralization," *Business Week* No. 2443 (August 2, 1976): 20–21.

27. "An Overhaul That Will Strengthen IBM's hand," *Business Week* No. 2710

(October 19, 1981): 46; also see "Bundling: IBM Merges Its Sales Force," *Fortune* 104 (November 2, 1981): 13.

28. See Louis A. Allen, "The Line-Staff Relationship," *Management Record* 17 (September 1955): 346–349, 374–376.

29. Ibid., p. 348.

30. For additional suggestions for making the best use of staff, see Edward C. Schleh, "Using Central Staff to Boost Line Initiative," *Management Review* 65 (May 1976): 17–23.

31. See David I. Cleland, "Why Project Management?" *Business Horizons* 7 (Winter 1964): 81–88. For a discussion of how project management has evolved into matrix management, see David I. Cleland, "The Cultural Ambience of the Matrix Organization," *Management Review* 70 (November 1981): 24–28, 37–39; and David I. Cleland, "Matrix Management (Part II): A Kaleidoscope of Organizational Systems," *Management Review* 70 (December 1981): 48–56.

32. An interesting and informative description of a successful matrix organization may be found in Ellen Kolton, "Team Players," *Inc.* 6 (September 1984): 140–144.

33. Drawn from Richard M. Hodgetts, "Leadership Techniques in the Project Organization," *Academy of Management Journal* 11 (June 1968): 211–219.

34. For an extensive discussion of problems in this area, see David L. Wilemon and John P. Cicero, "The Project Manager—Anomalies and Ambiguities," *Academy of Management Journal* 13 (September 1970): 269–282.

35. See "An About-face in TI's Culture," *Business Week* No. 2746 (July 5, 1982): 77.

36. Andrew S. Grove, *High Output Management* (New York: Random House, 1983), p. 60.

37. "How Conservatism Wins in the Hottest Market," *Business Week* No. 2466 (January 17, 1977): 43.

38. For a revealing case study of a top-level manager who lost his job because he could not delegate effectively, see "A 'Nuts-and-Bolts Guy' Is Out at Borg-Warner," *Business Week* No. 2821 (December 19, 1983): 108, 110.

39. Adapted from William H. Newman, "Overcoming Obstacles to Effective Delegation," *Management Review* 45 (January 1956): 36–41; and from Eugene Raudsepp, "Why Supervisors Don't Delegate," *Supervision* 41 (May 1979): 12–15.

Chapter 9

Staffing and Human Resource Management

People are the common denominator of progress. ...
John Kenneth Galbraith

Chapter Objectives

When you finish studying this chapter, you should be able to

- Explain the roles of psychological contracts and incongruency in the relationship between individual and organization.
- Explain what staffing involves and outline the human resource management process.
- Draw a distinction between equal employment opportunity and affirmative action.
- Discuss how performance appraisals can be made legally defensible.
- Compare and contrast the ingredients of good training programs for skill and factual learning.

Opening Case 9.1

Everybody's No. 1 at Exxon*

Exxon is for people who have what Tom Wolfe called "the big-league complex." Wolfe was talking about the Big Apple, but Exxon is the Big Apple of Big Business. Number one on the *Fortune* 500, the largest industrial company in the world, Exxon has a long reach—62 refineries in 33 countries, 14,000 oil wells worldwide, subsidiaries in 100 countries. As one 20-year Exxon employee explained, "There's instant prestige when you say you work for Exxon."

Exxon has more to offer than prestige. Its remarkable management development program can be traced to former president Walter Teagle.

*From Levering, Moskowitz, and Katz, *The 100 Best Companies to Work for in America*, pp. 108–109. © 1984, Addison-Wesley, Reading, Massachusetts. Reprinted with permission.

In 1929 Teagle laid down the law that identifying and training a successor is the first priority of any manager. Today every Exxon manager must develop a systematic succession plan for himself and for all who report to him. It's all part of the company's view that the organization should, as much as possible, consist of interchangeable parts and not rely on exceptional personalities.

Exxon wants team players, but it insists that everyone be extremely well trained. Its management training program is one of the marvels of American business. *New York Times* reporter Anthony J. Parisi said: "Exxon likes to say its strength is its people. So does just about every other company. But few come close to matching Exxon's amazing attention to nurturing new leaders."

The process starts at Exxon's world headquarters in New York's Rockefeller Center. On Monday afternoons, Exxon's top management committee—composed of the company's chairman, president, and six senior vice-presidents—meets to review the professional progress of the top 500 or so managers, as well as the pay of the next 3,000. The goal, according to Parisi, is "to spot talent early and nurture it."

Exxon doesn't rely on intuition or hit-and-miss methods to spot talent. It's incredibly methodical. Each of the company's 175,000 worldwide employees is rated once a year. The company tries to make it as objective and impersonal as possible. Each person is evaluated by several superiors rather than just by his or her immediate supervisor.

The six-page "appraisal review" form contains 21 different categories, from the quality of somebody's work to creativity and leadership. The review even includes an E.E.O. (equal employment opportunity) category, where Exxon employees are rated according to their "sensitivity to the needs of minorities, females, and other protected groups." In each category, supervisors rate employees from 1.0 for "outstanding" to 4.0 for "inadequate."

Other firms evaluate employees regularly. What makes Exxon's system unique is that everyone is then compared with his or her peers. Supervisors send the results of the appraisal reviews to a departmental committee composed of senior managers. The committee prepares a list of all employees at the same level within the department and asks the supervisors to rank them from best to worst. This is done on a bell curve; if more than 10 percent are rated as "outstanding," the departmental committee reduces a few to the next category. Based on detailed comparisons, Exxon establishes succession plans for each job in the firm. The management committee spends one full day a year reviewing the replacement schedules for all top managerial posts. As *Dun's Review* wrote, "Perhaps the company most totally committed to succession planning as a way of corporate life is Exxon."

Exxon employees seem to embrace the process. But it has its drawbacks. As one former employee told *Dun's Review,* "From the individual's viewpoint, the consensus approach at least guarantees that he will always be treated fairly. The only trouble is that no individual is indispensable under the system, and some people may find that unsettling."

With all the effort to seek out the best from within, it's no wonder Exxon rarely hires a manager from outside the firm. Most of the top people in Exxon started as engineers. The company takes great pains to "round off" managers and top technical people, especially the "high po's"— those considered to have the potential to go far. The ideal "Exxon man" serves the company in a variety of locations, including overseas. Managers used to be transferred an average of once every three years. The pace has slowed recently for economic reasons.

Exxon rewards employees for loyalty. Most people who work here consider themselves "womb-to-tombers." The company believes in job security. It avoided layoffs during the recession of 1981-82 with its Special Program of Severance Allowance, or SPOSA (called "Disposal" by some more irreverent Exxon employees). SPOSA encouraged older employees to retire early.

(Discussion questions linking this case with the material you are about to read can be found at the end of this chapter.)

An emphasis on long-term association and loyalty like that at Exxon is found in many, but not all, organizations. In our highly organized society most of us begin joining organizations at an early age. As youngsters we are encouraged by parents, friends, and teachers to join clubs, athletic teams, scout troops, and so on. To the maturing adolescent it becomes clear that taking part in organized activity is more rewarding than relying strictly on one's own resources. Sometimes, as in going to grade school, one is forced to join an organization. But membership in most organizations, including those that offer us jobs, is voluntary. With the exception of painters, sculptors, writers, and other artisans who ply their craft in isolation, getting a job usually means joining an organization.

When an individual and a work organization interact, dramatically different things can happen. Both can prosper because of a mutually beneficial relationship, or alternatively, counterproductive disharmony may result.[1] This chapter examines problems and solutions in the systematic individual-organization matching process.

An Analysis of Individual-
Organization Interaction

Managers need to understand the synergistic relationship between individuals and the organizations in which they work. A person and a job add

Table 9.1 The Relative Advantages of Working for an Organization

Drawbacks of Individual Effort	Organizational Strengths	What Organizations Can Offer Individuals
Economic insecurity	Economies of scale	Economic security
Isolation	Social setting	Social support
Limited opportunity	Larger resource base	Greater opportunity

up to much more than one plus one. For example, money seems to be the obvious reason for getting a job. But much more than money is involved. In addition to achieving some sort of economic security, most people also enjoy needed social support and greater opportunity when they are part of an organized effort (see Table 9.1). Three significant dimensions of individual-organization interaction are students' concerns about organizational life, psychological contracts, and incongruency.

College Students' Concerns About Organizational Life

What kinds of concerns do business students have about their future organizational lives? This question prompted one pair of researchers to survey the opinions of 1082 business students at eight different universities across the United States.[2] The sample was predominantly male (56 percent), white (93 percent), and middle class (50 percent). Respondents were asked to express their degree of concern about aspects of organizational life that had been identified through preliminary interviews. Results of the survey are shown in Table 9.2. Although concerns about money were high on the list, the number one fear involved the quality of supervision. Significant concerns about recognition and opportunities also surfaced.

Are these fears realistic? Though a precise answer to this question is unavailable, the students' concerns probably are overstated. We all tend to have unrealistic fears of the unknown. However, once a college graduate joins a work organization, threatening "unknowns" give way to *real* tasks, people, opportunities, problems, and paychecks. With the help of some rationalization (such as: "My pay isn't so great, but I earn more than some of my friends."), many managers come to fairly agreeable terms with organizational life. Evidence that most American managers are satisfied with their jobs tends to reinforce the notion that the fears expressed in Table 9.2 are overly pessimistic. In fact, in one nationwide survey of job satisfaction among managers, 84 percent responded "very much" to the question, "How do you like your job?"[3]

Even though business students' fears about organizations may be overstated, the existence of those fears cannot be ignored. An understanding of psychological contracts and potential sources of individual-organization mismatch can help us better understand and manage unrealistic fears

Table 9.2 Fears College Students Have About Organizational Life

Fears or Concerns About Organizational Future	Percent of Respondents Expressing Strong to Extreme Concern
1. I will find myself working under superiors who I will not respect or be able to follow with real commitment.	73%
2. I will not be able to earn enough income to live at an appropriate standard of living.	67%
3. I will have to work in an organization I do not really like just so I can make enough money to live adequately.	66%
4. No one will recognize my real worth and I will never be able to show my true abilities and be recognized or rewarded for what I am truly capable of doing.	61%
5. I will give up and become a part of the system I do not really like.	57%
6. I will live and die working in an organization, and my life will not have made any real contribution to anything.	56%
7. I will get lost in the shuffle and become a nameless, faceless number.	55%
8. The organization will not have any decent program or procedure for helping me grow, develop, and become a more useful, productive person.	55%

SOURCE: Adapted, by permission of the publisher, from "The *M*A*S*H* Generation: Implications for Future Organizational Values," by William G. Dyer and Jeffrey H. Dyer, *Organizational Dynamics*, Summer 1984, p. 72 © 1984 Periodicals Division, American Management Associations, New York. All rights reserved.

about organizational life. Individuals and organizations alike can take constructive steps to make work organizations more humane and supportive of individual expression.

Psychological Contracts

An employment contract is created when someone agrees to work for an organization. Although employment contracts vary in degree of detail and often are verbal rather than written, they serve to formalize the individual's desire to work and the organization's willingness to pay a certain rate for that work. Employment contracts are exchange agreements. But no matter how specific the terms of an employment contract may be, both the individual and the organization must do some reading between the lines. What kind of promotion opportunities are there? How diligently will the

"I pledge allegiance to the Drooly Burger and to the company for which it stands—one corporation, indivisible, with employment and profit for all."
SOURCE: Drawing by Dean Vietor.

person work? As indicated in Figure 9.1, the exchange between employer and employee includes many factors. Behavioral scientists have applied the term **psychological contract** to the reciprocal expectations that employees and employers have of one another.[4] Although some of these reciprocal expectations may be openly discussed during the hiring process, most of them are only implied. The result is a gray area of understanding between the individual and the organization. A great deal of conflict and dissatisfaction occurs because of misunderstandings about this gray area.

All too often the terms of psychological contracts are vague and left to chance. For instance, an employee may expect the company to offer frequent promotions. Although nothing in the employment contract specifically supports this expectation, the employee works very hard to earn a promotion. When the expected promotion does not materialize, dissatisfaction sets in and performance declines. Eventually, the situation may deteriorate to the point where the employee quits or is let go.

Employing organizations can take steps to clarify the psychological contracts between themselves and their employees. At the time of hire, for example, the supervisor and the new employee can sit down and discuss mutual expectations. That is the time for management to paint a realistic picture of promotion opportunities and other factors important to the individual. Employees tend to be much more receptive to bad news at the

Figure 9.1 The Individual-Organization Exchange

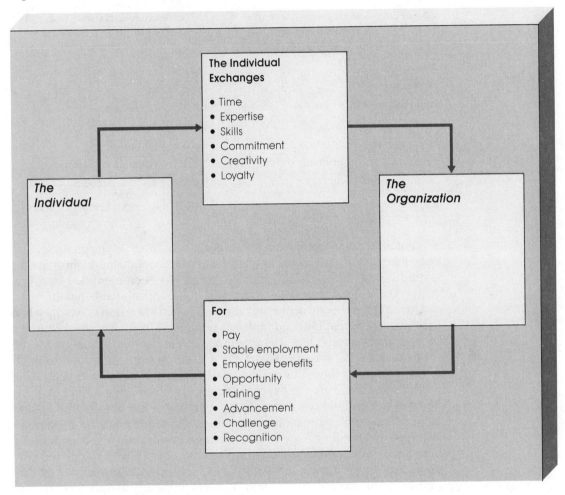

time of hire than they are after working hard to achieve what turns out to be a false hope. A whole range of topics, including duties, privileges, obligations, and rights, come under the umbrella of psychological contracts. Both employer and employee stand to gain by bringing reciprocal expectations out in the open as early as possible so that progress can be made toward resolving areas of misunderstanding or disagreement.

Incongruency   We are all familiar with situations in which square-peg individuals simply do not fit into round-hole organizations. Considering the wide variety of personalities in the labor force and the many different types of organizations in today's society, it is no wonder that individual-organization

Table 9.3 Argyris's Incongruency Thesis

The Typical Organization Forces the Individual to Be Psychologically Immature	The Average Individual Naturally Strives to Be Psychologically Mature
Passive	Active
Dependent	Independent
Limited range of behavior	Broad range of behavior
Shallow interests	Deep interests
Here-and-now orientation	Future orientation
Satisfied with subordinate status	Need for equal or superior status
Limited self-awareness	Developed self-awareness

SOURCE: Chris Argyris, *Personality and Organization* (New York: Harper & Row, 1957), chap. 2. Reprinted by permission of the publisher.

mismatches occasionally occur. A certain number of mismatches are unavoidable, but a growing number of individual-organization mismatches should be cause for concern. Such a trend has been identified by Chris Argyris, a respected scholar in the field of organizational behavior.

Two things are said to be incongruent when they don't match, when they are incompatible and not harmonious. Chris Argyris, with his incongruency thesis, has attempted to stimulate corrective action for the fundamental incongruency he detects in modern work situations. In brief, his **incongruency thesis** states that the demands of the typical organization are incongruent with the psychological needs of the individual. Argyris believes that individuals naturally strive to be mature but that the organizations that employ them often encourage immature behavior. It is important to note here that Argyris uses the term *maturity* in a special way. He draws a distinction between chronological maturity (one's age) and psychological maturity. Since psychological maturity relates to personality development, a young person may be psychologically mature and an older person may be psychologically immature. In other words, these two types of maturity vary independently.

In the following statement, Argyris shows that the typical organization limits rather than enhances psychological maturity:

If the principles of formal organization [division of labor, hierarchy, and close supervision] are used as ideally defined, employees will tend to work in an environment where (1) they are provided minimal control over their workaday world, (2) they are expected to be passive, dependent, and subordinate, (3) they are expected to have a short time perspective, (4) they are induced to perfect and value the frequent use of a few skin-surface shallow abilities, and (5) they are expected to produce under conditions leading to psychological failure.[5]

The heart of Argyris's incongruency thesis is shown in Table 9.3. Notice that each pair of characteristics represents polar extremes. Since individuals generally fall somewhere in between on each of the seven pairs of extremes, there are countless possible combinations of characteristics. Conceivably, each individual has a unique profile. Returning to Argyris's main point, he believes that modern organizational life is pulling most of us toward the psychologically immature end of all seven scales.

To anyone who has personally endured an overly structured and boring job, the specter of Argyris's thesis is convincing. Fortunately, as we will see in Chapter 11, job redesign and other quality-of-work-life innovations can be used to make organizational life more challenging and participative.

The Staffing and Human Resource Management Function

Staffing has long been an integral part of the management process. Like other traditional management functions, such as planning and organizing, the domain of staffing has grown through the years. This growth reflects increasing environmental complexity and greater organizational sophistication. Early definitions of staffing focused narrowly on hiring people for vacant positions. Today, **staffing** is defined more broadly as human resource planning, acquisition, and development aimed at providing the talent necessary for organizational success. This broader definition underscores the point that people are valuable *resources* requiring careful nurturing. In fact, many personnel departments are now called human resource departments. The day has long since passed when management could view labor simply as a commodity to be bought, exploited to exhaustion, and discarded when convenient.

Progressive and successful organizations treat all employees as valuable human resources. For example, according to the authors of the best seller, *In Search of Excellence*: "... if you want productivity and the financial reward that goes with it, you must treat your workers as your most important asset."[6] Honda has an interesting way of emphasizing that each employee at its Marysville, Ohio automobile manufacturing complex is a valuable resource. At the time of hire, each employee goes through the ritual of planting a pine tree on the company's property.[7] A tag with the employee's name is attached to the trunk of his or her tree. Growth of the trees, numbering 1300 by early 1984, symbolizes growth of the employees who planted them. Moreover, the trees are a tangible symbol of Honda's longlasting commitment to each of its employees.

A particularly promising development in the staffing area is the linkage of the human resource perspective with strategic management. Two experts have noted:

> ... human resources specialists have begun to stake a claim on the strategic planning process, arguing that participation in the "front end" of business planning is essential to meeting the long-run needs of the enterprise. Human resources planners have started to learn the language and techniques of strategic planning, have assumed a more proactive stance in promoting strategic thinking in the human resources area, and have extended the personnel function well beyond the limits of its traditional activities.[8]

A model for the balance of this chapter that reflects this strategic orientation is presented in Figure 9.2. Notice how a logical sequence of staffing activities—human resource planning, selection, performance appraisal, and training—all derive from organizational strategy and structure. Without a strategic orientation, the staffing function becomes haphazardly inefficient and ineffective.

Human Resource Planning

Planning enables managers to cope better with an uncertain environment and allocate scarce resources more efficiently. In recent years, management scholars have begun to emphasize the need to plan the human side of organized endeavor: "There continues to be in organizations a failure, particularly on the part of line managers and functional managers in areas other than personnel, to recognize the true importance of planning for and managing human resources."[9]

Human resource planning, sometimes referred to as manpower planning when applied to all employees or management succession planning[10] when applied strictly to managerial employees, helps management find the right people for the right jobs at the right time. Formally defined, **human resource planning** is the development of a comprehensive staffing strategy for meeting the organization's future human resource needs.

A Systems Perspective

Human resource planning requires a systematic approach to staffing.[11] Traditionally, staffing has suffered from a lack of continuity. People are often hired and trained on an "as needed" basis, which is hindsighted and therefore inadequate amid today's rapidly changing conditions. What is needed is a foresighted, systematic approach that provides specific answers to the following questions:

Figure 9.2   A General Model for Human Resource Management

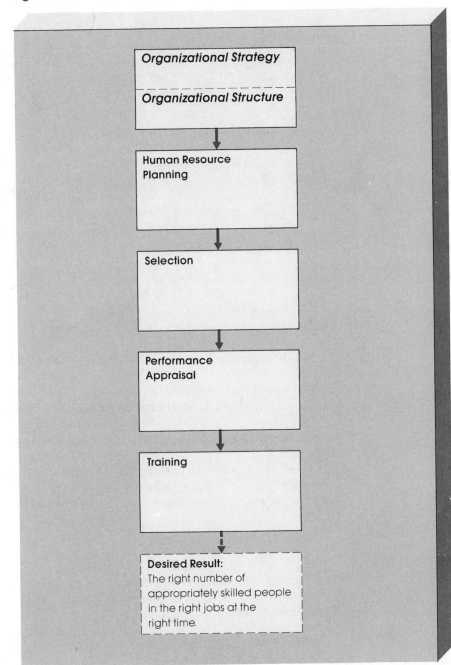

Figure 9.3 A Basic Model for Human Resource Planning Systems

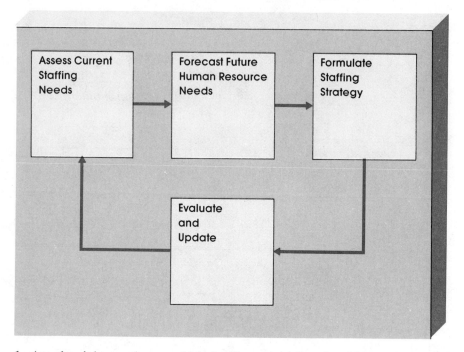

1. Are the right numbers and kinds of people doing the things we need to have done?
2. Are we properly utilizing our people?
3. Do we have the people we need to satisfy our future needs?[12]

Answers to these questions can be obtained through a systematic approach like the one in Figure 9.3. First, current staffing needs are assessed. Next, future needs of human resources are forecasted. Third, a comprehensive staffing strategy is formulated. Finally, evaluation and updating of the system are achieved by continually recycling through the process.

Assessing Current Needs

There cannot be any meaningful forecasting and formulation of staffing strategies until management has a clear picture of the organization's current staffing situation. A time-consuming procedure called job analysis comes into play here. **Job analysis** is the process of determining the fundamental elements of jobs through systematic observation and analysis. Usually, a team of trained specialists isolates specific jobs by analyzing work flows, tracking the procedures for accomplishing subunit objectives, and interviewing individuals about what their jobs entail. If job descriptions exist, they are updated. If not, they are written. A **job description** is a

Table 9.4 Factors to Consider in Forecasting the Demand for and Supply of Human Resources

Forecast demand	• Expected growth of the organization
	• Budget constraints
	• Turnover due to resignations, terminations, transfers, retirement, and death
	• Introduction of new technology
	• Minority-hiring goals
Forecast supply	• Number of employees willing and able to be trained
	• Promotable employees
	• Availability of required talent in local, regional, and national labor markets
	• Competition for talent within the industry and in general
	• Demographic trends (such as movement of families in the United States from the Northeast to the Southwest)
	• Enrollment trends in government training programs, trade schools, and colleges and universities

clear and concise summary of the duties of a specific job and the qualifications for holding it (see Figure 9.4).[13] Job descriptions are a useful staffing tool for achieving productive individual-organization matches.

By comparing updated job descriptions with the qualifications and duties of the individuals currently holding those jobs, management can determine whether the organization is appropriately staffed. Overstaffing can be wastefully expensive, but understaffing can block the achievement of organizational objectives. An appropriately staffed organization has the right number of people working in jobs best suited to their talents.

A growing number of organizations are finding computerized personnel inventories useful. This type of data bank can be compiled most conveniently during the initial assessment of human resources. By keying each present employee's name and biographical summary into the computer along with such pertinent data as seniority, pay status, promotion record, and training experience, a time-saving staffing decision tool is created. For example, in a matter of seconds, a manager can obtain a print-out of the age distribution among upper-level managers to use as an objective basis for predicting where replacements will be needed as older managers retire.

Forecasting Future Needs

This second phase of the human resource planning cycle compares projected demand and projected supply. Many environmental and organizational factors need to be considered (see Table 9.4).[14] It is often helpful for managers to envision human resources as flowing into, through, and out of the organization. Like any other resource, human resources are subject to subtle erosion; that is, employees leave the organization for a wide

Figure 9.4   A Sample Job Description

Job Title: *Service and Safety Supervisor*

Division:	Plastics	**D.O.T. Code:**	889.133-010*
Department:	Manufacturing	**EEO-1/AAP Categories:**	½**
Source(s):	John Doe	**Wage Category:**	Exempt
Job Analyst:	John Smith	**Verified By:**	Bill Johnson
Data Analyzed:	5/26/83	**Date Verified:**	6/5/83

Job Summary

The Service and Safety Supervisor works under the direction of the Impregnating & Laminating Manager: schedules labor pool employees; supervises the work of gardeners, cleaners, waste disposal and plant security personnel; coordinates plant safety programs; maintains daily records on personnel, equipment, and scrap.

Job Duties and Responsibilities

1. Schedules labor pool employees to provide relief personnel for all manufacturing departments: prepares assignment schedules and assigns individuals to departments based on routine as well as special needs in order to maintain adequate labor levels throughout the plant; notifies Industrial Relations Department weekly about vacation and layoff status of labor pool employees, contractual disputes, and other employment-related developments.
2. Supervises the work of gardeners, cleaners, waste disposal and plant security personnel: plans yard, clean-up, and security activities based on weekly determination of needs; assigns tasks and responsibilities to employees on a daily basis; monitors progress or status of assigned tasks; disciplines employees as necessary in accordance with labor contracts.
3. Coordinates plant safety programs: teaches basic first-aid procedures to security, supervisory, and lead personnel in order to maintain adequate coverage of medical emergencies; trains employees in fire fighting and hazardous materials handling procedures; verifies plant compliance with new or changing OSHA regulations; represents division during company-wide safety programs and meetings.
4. Maintains daily records on personnel, equipment, and scrap: reports amount of waste and scrap to cost accounting department; updates personnel records as necessary; reviews maintenance checklists for towmotors.
5. Performs other miscellaneous duties as assigned.

*Standard job classification code number found in *The Dictionary of Occupational Titles,* a U.S. Department of Labor publication available in most reference libraries.
**Equal Employment Opportunity (EEO) and Affirmative Action Program (AAP) code numbers.
SOURCE: "Job Descriptions Made Easy," by Mark A. Jones, copyright May, 1984. Reprinted with the permission of *Personnel Journal,* Costa Mesa, California; all rights reserved.

variety of reasons, and they must be replaced. Both internal and external sources of supply should be explored. One important element is prevailing trends in education. For instance, if enough people are studying computer

Figure 9.4 (cont.)

Job Requirements
1. Ability to apply basic principles and techniques of supervision.
   a) Knowledge of principles and techniques of supervision.
   b) Ability to plan and organize the activities of others.
   c) Ability to get ideas accepted and to guide a group or individual to accomplish a task.
   d) Ability to modify leadership style and management approach to reach a goal.
2. Ability to express ideas clearly both in written and oral communications.
3. Knowledge of current Red Cross first-aid procedures.
4. Knowledge of OSHA regulations as they affect plant operations.
5. Knowledge of labor pool jobs, company policies, and labor contracts.

Minimum Qualifications
Twelve years of general education or equivalent; and one year supervisory experience; and first-aid instructor's certification.

OR

Substitute 45 hours classroom supervisory training for supervisory experience.

Job Specifications
1. Knowledge: Knowledge of supervisory principles/techniques; knowledge of first-aid procedures sufficient to teach others; familiarity with federal safety regulations.
2. Mental Application: Applies effective principles of supervision to direct and motivate employees.
3. Accountability: Directly supervises the work of up to 25 laborers and security personnel; responsible for insuring proper towmotor maintenance.

programming in schools and colleges, data-processing firms may not need to train so many of their own computer programmers in the future.

The net result of human resource demand and supply forecasting is a detailed list of future staffing requirements. This list will tell management how many people and of what kind will be needed at specific future points in time.

Formulating a Staffing Strategy

To satisfy future staffing requirements, two sets of options are open to management. First, management can rely on current employees or hire new ones. Second, employees can be trained or not trained. When these two sets of options are combined, four staffing strategies emerge: (1) do not train current employees, (2) train current employees, (3) hire but do not train outsiders, and (4) hire and train outsiders. Most often in today's larger organizations all four staffing strategies are used simultaneously, according to situational demands.

**Evaluation
and Update**
Like many other systems, human resource planning requires a feedback loop, or a means of monitoring the system. By comparing the actual performance of the system with previously formulated plans, necessary corrections can be made. Unexpected shortages or excesses of qualified people signal a defect in the planning system. Sometimes management discovers that it has overlooked critical demand or supply considerations. Whatever the problem, prompt corrective action will help the human resource planning cycle work more smoothly and effectively each time it is repeated.[15]

Selection

Management finds qualified people to fill available jobs through the employee selection process. In a manner of speaking, employee selection serves as the organization's human resource gatekeeper. Today's managers are challenged to find the best available talent without unfairly discriminating against any segment of society.

In the first step in the selection process, except for job openings at the lowest entry level, managers need to choose between inside and outside talent.

**Promote or
Hire?**
Outsiders are naturally hired for bottom-rung positions in the organizational hierarchy. But what about the many positions above the lowest entry level, whether newly created or recently vacated? Management can promote a current employee from the same geographic location, transfer in a current employee from another location, or hire an outsider. In our comparison of the relative advantages of insiders and outsiders, both transfers and new hires are considered outsiders.

Advantages of Promoting an Insider Three advantages of promoting an insider are (1) promotion from within is less expensive than transferring or hiring; (2) promotable insiders are proven performers; and (3) promotion from within can have a positive motivational effect.

In recent years, both inflationary pressure and more complicated hiring practices have caused hiring and transfer costs to skyrocket. Employment agency fees, recruitment, advertising, testing, interviewing, reference checks, medical exams, reimbursement of relocation expenses, and orientation pile up expenses quickly. For example, in 1981 the average cost of hiring, moving, and training a computer programmer was $60,000.[16] In regard to within-company transfers, by 1981 the average cost of moving home-owning employees had mushroomed to $30,000.[17] Avoiding these hiring and transfer costs has become a powerful incentive to find and promote qualified insiders.

Whenever an outsider is transferred in or hired, management runs the risk that someone who looks good on paper may not be able to handle a new job in an unfamiliar location. To a certain extent, promotable insiders have proved themselves. Evidence of an insider's worth comes from direct observation, whereas management can use only secondhand impressions in evaluating an outsider.

Experience has shown that people tend to work harder when they believe they have a good chance of being promoted. Moreover, a modeling effect occurs when employees see that deserving coworkers are promoted to better-paying, higher-status jobs. Dead-end jobs, on the other hand, tend to stifle motivation and commitment. Promotions from within, when regularly and fairly used, can be a potent motivational tool.

Advantages of Bringing in an Outsider   Countering the benefits of promoting an insider are three advantages of transferring in or hiring an outsider: (1) bringing in outsiders helps prevent social inbreeding; (2) training costs are reduced when a qualified outsider is hired; and (3) new people tend to introduce new perspectives.

Undesirable social inbreeding occurs when people are promoted on the basis of who they know rather than what they know. Bringing in someone new can interrupt any automatic cycle of favoritism that may exist.

Resorting to transfer or hiring also tends to keep down training costs. An insider who lacks the skills necessary for a higher position must be trained before promotion is possible. Consequently, there is a strong economic argument for bringing in someone who already possesses the necessary skills.

New people can be an infusion of new blood into an organization. They bring new perspectives, new ideas, and probing questions that can stimulate thinking among present employees. Newcomers can introduce a healthy questioning attitude about an organization's assumptions and can motivate present employees to develop their own abilities.

After balancing these considerations, if management does decide to hire someone from outside, then it must screen recruits systematically.[18]

Screening   Just because someone has applied for a particular job does not mean that he or she is qualified. Thus a screening mechanism is required to separate those who are qualified from those who are not. Personnel management experts commonly compare the screening process to a hurdle race. Typical hurdles that job applicants have to clear are psychological tests, work sampling tests, reference checks, interviews, and physical examinations. In recent years, federal Equal Employment Opportunity (EEO) legislation has severely constrained what managers in the United States can and cannot do when screening job applicants. As indicated in Figure 9.5, there

Figure 9.5 Adverse Impact of Screening Techniques on Minorities

	Blacks	Females	Elderly	Handicapped
Intelligence and Verbal Tests	✓✓	+	✓	?
Work Sampling Tests	+	NE	NE	NE
Interview	+	✓✓	✓	✓
Educational Requirements	✓✓	+	✓	?
Physical Tests (height, weight, etc.)	+	✓✓	?	✓✓

Key

✓✓ = Fairly established evidence of adverse impact

✓ = Some evidence of adverse impact

? = No data which bears direct evidence of adverse impact, but seems likely depending on type of handicap or type of test

NE = No or little evidence to indicate one way or the other

+ = Evidence indicates that particular minority group does as well as or even better than majority members

SOURCE: Richard D. Arvey, *Fairness in Selecting Employees*, © 1979, Addison-Wesley, Reading, Massachusetts. P. 236, Fig. 9.1. Reprinted with permission.

is no perfect screening device; each has the potential for adversely affecting one or more protected minorities.

Equal Employment Opportunity   Although earlier legislation selectively applies, the landmark law in the EEO area is Title VII of the Civil Rights Act of 1964. Subsequent amendments, presidential executive orders, and related laws have expanded EEO's coverage. The EEO law now provides a broad umbrella of employment protection for traditionally disadvantaged individuals:

> The result of this legislation has been that in virtually all aspects of employment, it is unlawful to discriminate on the basis of race, color, sex, religion, age, national origin, handicapped status, being a disabled veteran, or being a veteran of the Vietnam Era.[19]

What all this means is that managers cannot refuse to hire, promote, train, or transfer employees simply on the basis of the characteristics listed above. Nor can they lay off or discharge employees on these grounds. Selection and all other personnel decisions are to be made solely on the basis of objective criteria such as ability to perform or seniority.

A more rigorous refinement of EEO legislation is affirmative action. An **affirmative action program** (AAP) is a plan for actively seeking out, employing, and developing the talents of those groups traditionally discriminated against in employment. Affirmative action amounts to a concerted effort to make up for *past* discrimination. EEO, in contrast, is aimed at preventing *future* discrimination. Typical AAPs attack employment discrimination on the following four fronts: (1) *active* recruitment of women and minorities; (2) elimination of prejudicial questions on employment application forms; (3) establishment of specific goals and timetables for minority hiring; and (4) statistical validation of employment testing procedures.

Like any public domain policy with legal ramifications, the EEO/AAP area has become a legal jungle.[20] Varying political and legal interpretations and inconsistent court decisions have left many managers frustrated and confused. Although some organizations have used this state of affairs as an excuse to do nothing until confronted with a court order (see Table 9.5), others have taken progressive steps to follow the "spirit" of EEO law and AAP guidelines.

For example, Merck & Co., Inc., a large health products firm, won an award from the U.S. Department of Labor in 1983 for its innovative affirmative action training program. One hundred trainers taught 1000 Merck managers how to lead discussion sessions about affirmative action issues. Groups of 10 to 15 employees then met to watch movies and discuss misconceptions about handicapped employees, women, and minorities. By the time the program was completed, 16,000 Merck employees in 61 locations across the United States had participated. Specific achievements included a session in which

> ... a seemingly uncommunicative woman admitted she had a hearing impairment and had to read lips.
> Her discussion leader, who was also her supervisor, was obviously surprised. Once the secret was out, ... the woman became more outgoing, her co-workers responded to her more, and she ultimately earned a promotion.[21]

Merck is a better company for *all* its employees because it creatively translated EEO/AAP laws and guidelines into concrete action.

Employment Selection Tests   Federal EEO guidelines have broadened the definition of an **employment selection test** to include any procedure used as

Table 9.5 Equal Employment Opportunity Legislation Has Had an Impact: A Case Study

An interesting and instructive case study of EEO in action is that of American Telephone & Telegraph (AT&T). In 1973, AT&T signed a consent decree with the federal government to correct racial and gender imbalances allegedly caused by discriminatory hiring and promotion policies. AT&T's case was intended to serve as a warning to other companies. The settlement included the immediate payment of $18 million in back wages to women who had been receiving unequal pay for equal work. Since that time, AT&T's 750-person EEO staff has changed the face of the nation's largest private employer. The number of women in middle- and upper-level management ranks rose from 9 percent in 1972 to 17 percent in 1978. During the same period, the company's employment of minority females rose from 79,000 to 96,000 and minority males from 31,000 to 43,000. Females are now working in traditionally male crafts, and males are now working as operators and clerks, jobs traditionally reserved for females. However, as noted in *Fortune* magazine, these changes have had their price:

> The favoring of women and minorities that is required by the decree has necessarily also required some lowering of employment standards, and this combination has produced bruising side effects. The rules have embittered many of A.T.&T.'s white male employees, spawned procedures that have infuriated its unions, and arguably hurt operating efficiency.[22]

One can readily see why EEO remains an emotional topic among managers. But as has been pointed out, "Equal employment opportunity isn't just a good idea, it's the *law.*"

a basis for an employment decision. This means that in addition to traditional pencil-and-paper tests, unscored application forms, informal and formal interviews, performance tests, and physical, educational, or experience requirements all qualify as tests.[23] This all-encompassing definition of an employment test takes on added significance when one realizes that the federal government requires all employment tests to be statistically valid and reliable predictors of job success. Historically, women and minorities have been victimized by invalid, unreliable, and prejudicial employment selection procedures.

Effective Interviewing Interviewing warrants special attention here because it has been pointed out that "the interview is probably the most widely used personnel technique, particularly in the selection procedure. Surveys show that almost all personnel managers use this method at some stage in the selection procedure."[24] Additionally, it is common for line managers at all levels to be asked to interview candidates for job openings and promotions. Nearly all managers should be aware of the weaknesses of the traditional unstructured interview, one with no fixed question format

Table 9.6 Types of Structured Interview Questions

Type of Question	Method	Information Sought	Sample Question
Situational	Oral	Can the applicant handle difficult situations likely to be encountered on the job?	"What would you do if you saw two of your immediate subordinates arguing loudly in the work area?"
Job knowledge	Oral or written	Does the applicant possess the knowledge required for successful job performance?	"Do you know the computer languages COBOL and BASIC?"
Job sample-simulation	Observation of actual or simulated performance	Can the applicant actually do essential aspects of the job?	"Can you show us how to prepare a letter on this word processor?"
Worker requirements	Oral	Is the applicant willing to cope with job demands such as travel, relocation, or hard physical labor?	"Are you willing to spend 25 percent of your time on the road?"

SOURCE: Adapted from Elliott D. Pursell, Michael A. Campion, and Sarah R. Gaylord, "Structured Interviewing: Avoiding Selection Problems," *Personnel Journal* 59 (November 1980): 907–912.

or systematic scoring procedure. The traditional unstructured, or informal, interview has been criticized because:

- It is highly susceptible to distortion and bias.
- It is highly susceptible to legal attack.
- It is usually indefensible if legally contested.
- It may have apparent validity, but no real validity.
- It is rarely totally job-related and may incorporate personal items that infringe on privacy.
- It is the most flexible selection technique, thereby being highly inconsistent.
- There is a tendency for the interviewer to look for qualities that he or she prefers, and then justify the hiring decision based on these qualities.
- Often, the interviewer does not hear about the selection mistakes.
- There is an unsubstantiated confidence in the traditional interview.[25]

Structured interviews are the recommended alternative to traditional unstructured or informal interviews. "A **structured interview** may be defined as a series of job-related questions with predetermined answers that are consistently applied across all interviews for a particular job."[26] Structured interviews are constructed, conducted, and scored by a committee of three to six members to try to eliminate individual bias. Because of their structured format and scoring, structured interviews remove each of the weaknesses (listed above) of unstructured interviews. Four types of questions typically found in structured interviews are (1) situational questions, (2) job knowledge questions, (3) job sample-simulation questions, and (4) worker requirements questions (see Table 9.6).

Performance Appraisal

Although formal performance appraisal systems are considered to be essential in today's organizations, they all too often are a source of dissatisfaction. For example, in a survey of 589 personnel administrators, 87 percent reportedly used formal performance appraisal systems. Yet only 56 percent of those with formal appraisal systems were satisfied with them.[27] Like virtually all aspects of management, performance appraisal can be effective and satisfying if haphazard methods are replaced by systematically developed and implemented techniques. For our purposes, **performance appraisal** is defined as the process of evaluating individual job performance as a basis for making objective personnel decisions. This definition intentionally excludes day-to-day coaching in which a supervisor casually checks an employee's work and gives immediate feedback. Although personal coaching is fundamental to good management, formally documented appraisals are also needed to (1) ensure equitable distribution of opportunities and rewards and (2) avoid prejudicial treatment of protected minorities.[28]

A recent survey of nearly 600 organizations belonging to the American Management Associations (AMA) found that managers use performance appraisal results as follows:

The appraisals are used for compensation (85.6 percent), counseling (65.1 percent), training and development (64.3 percent), promotion (45.3 percent), manpower planning (43.1 percent), retention/discharge (30.3 percent), and validation of a selection technique (17.2 percent).[29]

In this section, we will examine four important aspects of performance appraisal: (1) legal defensibility; (2) general approaches; (3) alternative techniques; and (4) the evaluation-versus-development dilemma.

Making Performance Appraisals Legally Defensible

Scores of lawsuits involving the legality of specific performance appraisal systems and resulting personnel actions have sharpened management's concern about legal defensibility (see Table 9.7). With growing frequency, human resource managers are asking themselves: "Will my organization's performance appraisal system stand up in court?" From the standpoint of limiting legal exposure, it is better to ask this question when designing formal appraisal systems rather than after they have been implemented. Managers need specific criteria for legally defensible performance appraisal systems. Fortunately, researchers have detected some instructive patterns in recent court decisions.

After studying the verdicts in 66 employment discrimination cases in the United States, one pair of researchers found four factors that enabled employers to successfully defend their appraisal systems. Those four factors were:

1. A *job analysis* was used to develop the performance appraisal system.
2. The appraisal system was *behavior-oriented,* not trait-oriented.
3. Performance evaluators followed *specific written instructions* when conducting appraisals.
4. Evaluators *reviewed the results* of the appraisals with the ratees.[30]

Each of these factors has a clear legal rationale. Job analysis, discussed earlier relative to human resource planning, anchors the appraisal process to specific job duties, not personalities. Behavior-oriented appraisals properly focus management's attention on *how* the individual actually performed his or her job. Performance appraisers who follow specific written instructions are less likely to be plagued by vague performance standards and/or personal bias. Finally, by reviewing performance appraisal results with those who have been evaluated, managers provide the feedback necessary for learning and improvement. Managers who keep these criteria for legal defensibility in mind are better equipped to select a sound appraisal system from among alternative approaches and techniques.

General Approaches to Appraising Job Performance

There are three general approaches to determining who has done a good job and who has not. They are the trait-oriented approach, the behavior-oriented approach, and the outcome-oriented approach. Respectively, these approaches focus on *who* did the job, *how* the job was done, and *what* was accomplished. Each of these general approaches deserves a closer look.

Trait-oriented Appraisals This approach enjoys the dubious distinction of being both one of the most widely used as well as one of the weakest approaches. Two performance appraisal experts have summed up the case against trait-oriented appraisals by saying:

> If the purpose of the appraisal is to evaluate past *performance,* then an evaluation of simple personality traits such as ... [initiative, dependability, ambition, loyalty] hardly fits the bill. Personality traits are not in and of themselves measures of either behavior or performance. In fact, a great deal of research indicates that traits are unstable within individuals and across situations. In

Table 9.7 Zayre Corporation Toughens Its Performance Appraisal System

In an era of increasing employer-employee litigation, appraisals that settle for generalities such as "needs improvement" or "is well-liked by peers" will not suffice. Companies are responding by building specificity into appraisal forms.

Zayre Corporation, the discount department store chain, is a case in point. The company revamped its rather standard performance evaluation form into a 17-page management booklet that: (1) forces the evaluator to set performance objectives with subordinates; (2) provides for periodic progress reviews; and (3) assigns an elaborate rating system to various employee skills. Zayre has also speeded up the traditionally annual employee-manager performance review. The two now meet several times throughout the year to discuss and modify performance objectives.

SOURCE: "Performance Appraisals—Reappraised," *Management Review* 72 (November 1983): 5.

other words, the extent to which a person possesses "initiative" differs as a function of the situation. Most trait-rating approaches pay little or no attention to the context of behavior.[31]

Consequently, trait-oriented appraisals tend to be unfair and do not stand up well in court.

Behavior-oriented Appraisals Performance appraisals that focus on specific job-related behavior are strongly recommended by experts in the field. The rationale is that behavior, not personality traits or abilities, is ultimately responsible for job success or failure. Legal defensibility is greatly enhanced when a performance appraisal system is tied to specific job behavior.

Outcome-oriented Appraisals If the trait approach focuses on *who* and the behavioral approach on *how,* the outcome approach directs the appraiser's attention to *what* was actually accomplished. The most popular outcome-oriented approach to performance appraisal is management by objectives (MBO). As you may recall from our discussion in Chapter 4, managers who rely on MBO assess performance in terms of how well employees meet measurable and participatively set goals. It is important to note, however, that MBO and other outcome-oriented approaches have a major shortcoming. Because goals are individualized, comparisons between two or more people are difficult if not impossible. As a result, MBO is said to be a poor vehicle for making decisions about promotions or merit pay that require employees to be ranked.[32]

Alternative The list of alternative performance appraisal techniques is long and grow-
Performance ing. Unfortunately, many are simplistic, invalid, and unreliable. In general
Appraisal terms, an *invalid* appraisal instrument does not accurately measure what it
Techniques is supposed to measure. *Unreliable* instruments do not measure criteria in
a consistent manner. Many other performance appraisal techniques are so
complex that they are impractical and burdensome to use. But armed with
a working knowledge of the most popular appraisal techniques, a good
manager can distinguish the strong from the weak. Once again, the
strength of an appraisal technique is gauged by its conformity to the
criteria for legal defensibility discussed above. Six different techniques are
discussed here in diminishing order of popularity, as determined in the
AMA study cited earlier.

- **Goal Setting.** Typically within a management by objectives framework,
  performance is evaluated in terms of formal objectives set at an earlier
  date. This is a comparatively strong technique if desired outcomes are
  clearly linked to specific behaviors. For example, a product design
  engineer's "output" could be measured in terms of the number of product specifications submitted per month.
- **Written Essays.** Managers describe the performance of subordinates in
  narrative form, either offhand or in response to predetermined questions. Evaluators often criticize this technique for being too time consuming. The strength of written essays is also limited by the fact that
  some managers have difficulty expressing themselves in writing.
- **Critical Incidents.** Specific instances of inferior and superior performance are documented by the supervisor when they occur. Accumulated
  incidents then provide an objective basis for evaluations at appraisal
  time. The strength of critical incidents is enhanced when evaluators
  document specific behaviors in specific situations and ignore personality traits.
- **Graphic Rating Scales.** Various traits or behaviors are rated on incremental scales. For example "initiative" could be rated on a 1 (=low)—
  2—3—4—5 (=high) scale. This technique is among the weakest when
  personality traits are employed. However, **behaviorally-anchored rating
  scales** (BARS), defined as performance rating scales divided into increments of observable job behavior determined through job analysis, are
  considered to be one of the strongest performance appraisal techniques
  (see Figure 9.6).
- **Weighted Checklists.** Evaluators check appropriate adjectives or behavioral descriptions that have predetermined weights. The weights,
  which gauge the relative importance of the randomly mixed items on the
  checklist, are usually unknown to the evaluator. Following the evalua-

Figure 9.6   A Sample Behaviorally-anchored Rating Scale for a College Professor

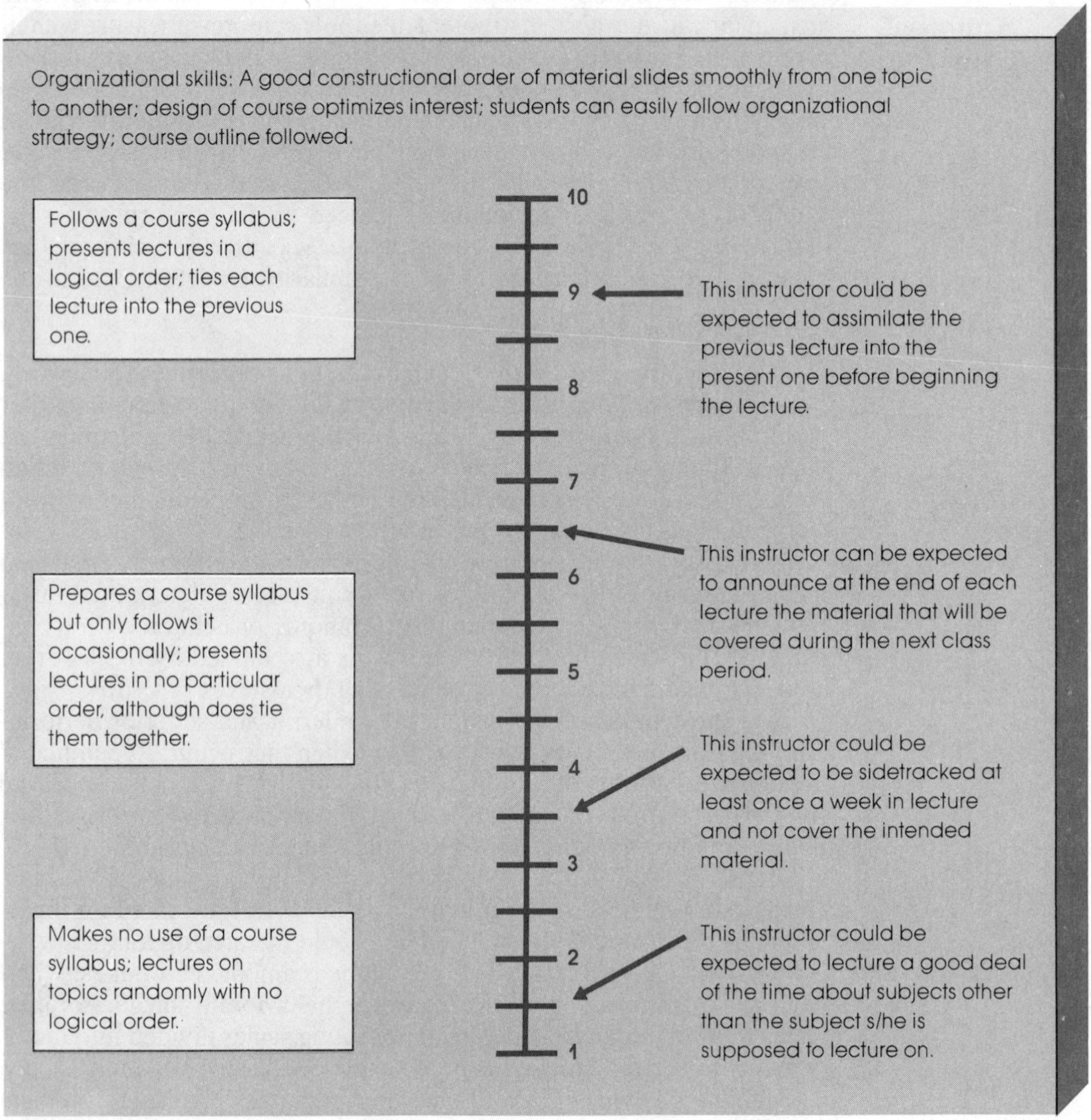

Organizational skills: A good constructional order of material slides smoothly from one topic to another; design of course optimizes interest; students can easily follow organizational strategy; course outline followed.

Follows a course syllabus; presents lectures in a logical order; ties each lecture into the previous one.

— 10

— 9   This instructor could be expected to assimilate the previous lecture into the present one before beginning the lecture.

— 8

— 7

Prepares a course syllabus but only follows it occasionally; presents lectures in no particular order, although does tie them together.

— 6   This instructor can be expected to announce at the end of each lecture the material that will be covered during the next class period.

— 5

This instructor could be expected to be sidetracked at least once a week in lecture and not cover the intended material.

— 4

— 3

Makes no use of a course syllabus; lectures on topics randomly with no logical order.

— 2   This instructor could be expected to lecture a good deal of the time about subjects other than the subject s/he is supposed to lecture on.

— 1

SOURCE: From H. John Bernardin and Richard W. Beatty, *Performance Appraisal: Assessing Human Behavior at Work* (Boston: Kent Publishing Company, 1983), p. 84. © 1984 by Wadsworth, Inc. Reprinted by permission of Kent Publishing Company, a division of Wadsworth, Inc.

tion, the weights of the checked items are added or averaged to permit interpersonal comparisons. As with the other techniques, the degree of behavioral specificity largely determines the strength of weighted checklists.

● **Rankings/Comparisons.** Coworkers in a subunit are ranked or compared in head-to-head fashion according to specified accomplishments or job behaviors. A major shortcoming of this technique is that the absolute distance between ratees is unknown. For example, the No. 1 ranked employee may be five times as effective as No. 2 who in turn is only slightly more effective than No. 3. Rankings/comparisons are also criticized for causing resentment among lower-ranked, but adequately performing, coworkers. This technique can be strengthened by combining it with a more behavioral technique such as critical incidents or BARS.

Regarding the frequency of performance appraisals, a study of 293 U.S. corporations of varying industry and size discovered that 90 percent of the firms surveyed conducted formal appraisals of their managers annually. Although immediate supervisors performed 95 percent of the appraisals at the middle- and lower-management levels, the study concluded "that most supervisors dislike 'playing God' and that many try to avoid responsibility for providing subordinates with feedback of unflattering appraisal information."[33] But how can managers who provide inadequate feedback hope to improve subordinates' performance? In short, they cannot, without first resolving the following dilemma.

Evaluation Versus Development: A Dilemma

Ideally, performance appraisal occurs in three phases:

Phase 1. Objective evaluation of job performance for a specified period of time.
Phase 2. Evaluation feedback interview.
Phase 3. Developmental interview.

All too often, unfortunately, subjective bias contaminates the evaluation, feedback is vague or absent, and development is shortchanged. Worse yet, busy managers sometimes confuse and frustrate their subordinates by trying to accomplish all three phases in one brief sitting. These problems result from a failure to resolve the conflict between being both an evaluator and a developer of subordinates (see Figure 9.7). Objective evaluation calls for "hard-nosed" analysis of an individual's performance, free of political and emotional considerations. Conversely, employee development can occur only in a climate of mutual trust, understanding, teamwork, and honest communication.

Experts suggest that the best way to resolve this dilemma is to play the evaluator role in one face-to-face interview and the developer role in a later interview.[34] Each meeting should have its own, appropriate tone. When time and other factors preclude separate evaluation and developmental

Figure 9.7 The Performance Appraisal Dilemma

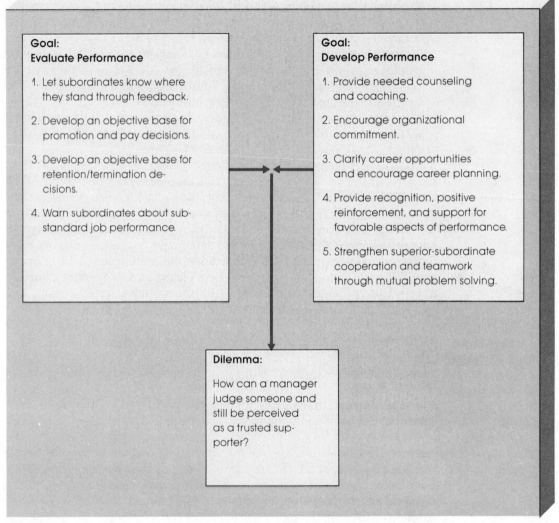

SOURCE: Based on data from Michael Beer, "Performance Appraisal: Dilemmas and Possibilities," *Organizational Dynamics* 9 (Winter 1981): 25.

meetings, as is often the case, a single interview with the following format can be used:

Begin interview ...

1. Open-ended discussion and exploration of problems, in which the subordinate leads and the supervisor listens.

2. Problem-solving discussion, in which the subordinate leads, but supervisor takes somewhat stronger role.
3. Agreement between supervisor and subordinate on performance problems and a plan for improvements.
4. Closing evaluation, in which the supervisor gives his or her views and final evaluation if the subordinate has not dealt with important issues.[35]

... interview ends.

Assuming that the subordinate is told ahead of time what to expect, evaluation and development can occur simultaneously. *Self-evaluation* is the key to success here because it encourages candor and honesty without betraying trust or driving the subordinate into a passive or defensive posture.

Training

There is often a gap between what employees do know and what they should know. Filling this knowledge gap by means of training has become big business. Public and private sector employers in the United States annually spend more than $30 billion on training. This figure equates to roughly half the annual cost of all higher education. In 1980, 30,000 AT&T employees received training through 12,000 courses at 1300 training sites. The cost to AT&T, $1.7 billion, amounted to twice the total budget of the Massachusetts Institute of Technology.[36] As the term is used here, **training** is the process of changing employee behavior, attitudes, or opinions through some type of guided experience.

In this final section, we discuss approaches to training, identify the ingredients of a good training program, and draw an important distinction between skill and factual learning.

Approaches to Training

Given variables such as interpersonal differences, budget limitations, and instructor capabilities, it is safe to say that there is no one best training technique. Trainers have both praised and criticized alternative training techniques, including the traditional lecture-discussion method, case studies, on-the-job training, coaching, role playing, and simulations.[37] Fortunately, studies designed to determine the most appropriate training approaches for various instructional situations offer constructive direction. One study polled a sample of management professors, *Fortune* 500 training directors, and mid-level managers throughout the United States to find out which training approaches they recommended for 20 different instructional areas for management trainees (see Figure 9.8). Actual practice ("doing it") turned out to be the most popular technique for teaching

Figure 9.8 Preferred Training Approaches

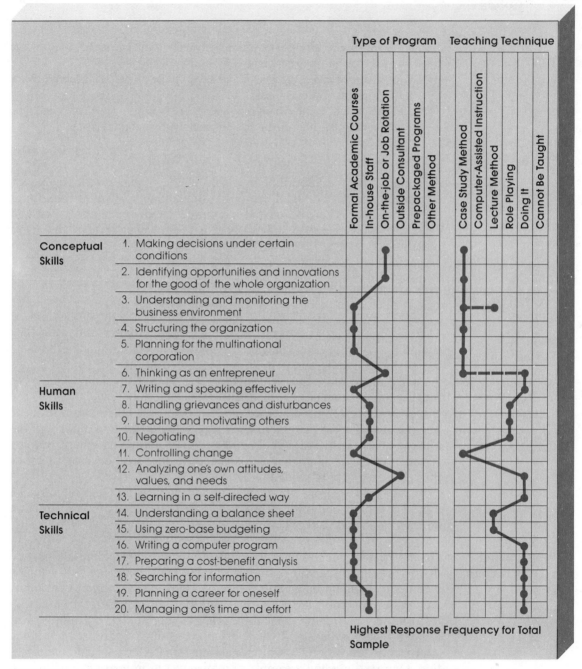

SOURCE: Paul J. Guglielmino, "Developing the Top-Level Executive for the 1980s and Beyond," *Training and Development Journal* 33 (April 1979): 13. Copyright 1979. *Training and Development Journal,* American Society for Training and Development. Used with permission. All rights reserved.

basic management skills. Next came the case study method, and the lecture method and role playing tied for third place. In regard to general types of training programs, formal academic courses headed the list. A practical blend of formal academic courses and hands-on experience appears to be the preferred training approach for basic conceptual, human, and technical management skills.

The Ingredients of a Good Training Program

Although training needs and approaches vary, managers can get the most out of their training budgets by following a few guidelines. According to two training experts, every training program should be designed along the following lines to maximize retention and transfer learning to the job:

1. Maximize the similarity between the training situation and the job situation.
2. Provide as much experience as possible with the task being taught.
3. Provide for a variety of examples when teaching concepts or skills.
4. Label or identify important features of a task.
5. Make sure that general principles are understood before expecting much transfer.
6. Make sure that the trained behaviors and ideas are rewarded in the job situation.
7. Design the training content so that the trainees can see its applicability.
8. Use adjunct questions to guide the trainee's attention.[38]

Skill Versus Factual Learning

The ingredients of a good training program vary somewhat according to whether skill learning or factual learning is needed. It has been pointed out that

> ... effective skill learning should incorporate four essential ingredients: (1) goal setting, (2) modeling, (3) practice, and (4) feedback. Let's take as an example the task of training someone to ride horseback. How would you do it? It basically must entail telling someone specifically what you want them to do (goal setting), showing them how you want them to do it (modeling), giving them the opportunity to try out what you have told them and shown them (practice), and then telling them what they are doing correctly or incorrectly (feedback).[39]

When factual learning is involved, the same sequence is used, except that in step 2, "meaningful presentation of the material" is substituted for modeling. Keep in mind that the object of training is *learning*. Learning requires thoughtful preparation, carefully guided exposure to new ideas or behavior, and motivational support.

Summary

A synergistic relationship exists between individuals and their employing organizations. But students have strong concerns about their future organizational life, especially about the quality of supervision they will experience. Apart from the formal employment contract, an informal and often unspoken psychological contract exists between employee and employer. Serious dissatisfaction can set in when the terms of an individual's psychological contract are not met. According to Argyris's incongruency thesis, the principles of formal organization tend to encourage psychological immaturity in the average employee.

Within the context of strategic human resource management, staffing encompasses human resource planning, acquisition, and development. Four key staffing activities necessarily linked to organizational strategy and structure are: (1) human resource planning, (2) selection, (3) performance appraisal, and (4) training. A systems approach to human resource planning will help management devise staffing strategies for future human resource needs. As the organization's gatekeeper for vital human resources, employee selection should be more than a haphazard process of looking around for people to fill vacancies. There are relative advantages to promoting an insider as opposed to transferring in or hiring an outsider. Federal Equal Employment Opportunity laws require managers to make hiring and other personnel decisions on the basis of ability to perform rather than personal prejudice. Because interviews are the most popular employee screening device, experts recommend structured rather than traditional, informal interviews.

Legally defensible performance appraisals enable managers to make objective personnel decisions. Of the three general approaches to performance appraisal—trait, behavior, and outcome—the behavior-oriented approach is most strongly recommended. Listed in declining order of popularity, six common performance appraisal techniques are goal setting, written essays, critical incidents, graphic rating scales, weighted checklists, and rankings/comparisons. Managers are challenged both to evaluate performance and to develop human potential during the performance appraisal process. This dilemma can be partially resolved by encouraging subordinates to engage in self-evaluation before offering constructive feedback on performance.

Today, training is a huge business in itself. Managers can ensure that their training investment pays off by using techniques appropriate to the situation. Training programs should be designed with an eye toward maximizing the retention and transfer of learning to the job. Successful skill learning and factual learning both depend on goal setting, practice, and feedback. But skills should be modeled, whereas factual information should be presented in a logical and meaningful manner.

Terms to Understand

Psychological contract	Affirmative action program (AAP)
Incongruency thesis	Employment selection test
Staffing	Structured interview
Human resource planning	Performance appraisal
Job analysis	Behaviorally-anchored rating scales (BARS)
Job description	Training

Questions for Discussion

1. What concerns do you have about your future organizational work life? Is it possible they are unrealistically negative?
2. In regard to the psychological contract you have with your present employer (or instructor), what do you expect? Is the other party aware of these expectations?
3. Have you ever personally experienced incongruency? Explain the circumstances and your feelings at the time.
4. In your own view, why is the staffing function a key determinant of organizational success?
5. Why is each portion of the human resource planning system important to effective staffing?
6. Given the choice between a qualified and trusted insider and a qualified outsider to fill a position as your key assistant, which selection option would you probably prefer? Why?
7. What is the essential difference between equal employment opportunity and affirmative action? What is your personal experience with these programs?
8. In reference to a specific job that you can think of, what structured interview questions should be asked of an applicant for that job?
9. What has been your experience with performance appraisals (including student evaluations of teacher effectiveness)? Would the instruments you have used meet the four legal defensibility criteria?
10. What could be done to promote the transfer of learning from the course(s) you are currently taking to your future employment as a manager?

Back to the Opening Case

Now that you have read Chapter 9, you should be able to answer the following questions about the Exxon case:

1. Would you like to work for Exxon? Why?
2. What significant factors can you find for each side of the individual-organization exchange? From the employee's standpoint, is it a *fair* exchange?
3. From an equal employment opportunity/affirmative action perspective, do you find anything wrong about the term "ideal Exxon man"?
4. What aspects of Exxon's performance appraisal system make it strong (or weak)?

Closing Case 9.2

Filling the Top Spots at General Motors

As discussed in opening case 8.1, General Motors (GM) is significantly reshaping itself to compete more effectively in the future. Inconsistent profitability is its prime motivating force for change. For example, GM tallied a $763 million loss in 1980, the company's first losing year since 1921. Just three years later, in 1983, GM recorded its most profitable year ever. One factor that will help GM reorganize for more stable profitability is the high quality of its executive personnel.

GM's top management is proud of its close-knit executive group, its record of hiring fewer executives from outside than other major U.S. companies do, and its low executive turnover. Two-thirds of the auto giant's executives reportedly have worked only for GM. It has been estimated, on the basis of executive turnover during 1980, that less than 1 percent of GM's 6000 highest executives will ever leave the company. GM admirers claim that the firm has a stable corporate culture and a Japanese-like organization in which loyalty is highly valued and rewarded. Critics have called GM a corporate hive of organization people in which innovation and risk taking are often in short supply.

No "Instant Executives" at GM
Most GM managers come from small towns and cities in the Upper Midwest where the traditional work ethic, respect for authority, and institutional loyalty have long been entrenched values. Managers who patiently work their way up through the ranks at GM usually develop strong loyalty based on the assumption that if they do a good job they will be appropriately rewarded. And in fact, GM is large and diverse enough to reward loyalty with job security.

Yet observers claim that outsiders are needed to bring vision and innovative leadership to GM. According to *Fortune* magazine, GM "probably would not have too much trouble in attracting a capable visionary to be, say, its president. But such an appointment from outside would have a devastating psychological effect and perhaps cripple the entire management system."[40]

GM's promote-from-within policy is not ironclad. Through the years, several vice presidents have been hired from outside to take charge of changing areas, such as personnel, in which new ideas were needed.

An Inventory of Executive Talent

GM's present staffing philosophy can be traced back to Alfred Sloan, the man originally responsible for GM's climb to dominance. Sloan believed that his most important job was finding the right people for the right jobs. Relying on what GM management calls its executive-personnel inventory, the executive committee and group vice presidents hold week-long progression and succession meetings twice a year. GM's executive-personnel inventory details the strengths and weaknesses, along with other relevant notations about promotability, of about 10,000 GM managers. Steps are taken to ensure that an individual manager's inventory entry contains the comments of more than just an immediate superior, that observations from other managers and peers are included as well. Ideally, these precautions help management avoid the problem of promoting or holding back an individual solely on the word of one person.

For Discussion
1. How might GM's executive staffing policy of promoting primarily from within end up hurting the firm?
2. In your view, what kind of reception would a newly hired executive with innovative ideas probably get in an organization like GM in which loyalty is highly valued?
3. If you were a manager moving up through the ranks at GM, what would be the relative advantages and disadvantages of GM's executive staffing program?

References

Opening Quotation: John Kenneth Galbraith, *Economic Development*, in M. R. Rosenberg, ed., *Quotations for the New Age* (Secaucus, N.J.: Citadel Press, 1978), p. 120.

Opening Case: Robert Levering, Milton Moskowitz, and Michael Katz, *The 100 Best Companies to Work for in America* (Reading, Mass.: Addison-Wesley, 1984), pp. 108–109.

Closing Case: For additional information on General Motors, see Neal Goff,

"The Case for General Motors," *Financial World* 149 (August 1, 1980): 18–22; Allan Sloan and Christine Miles, "GM's Chance of a Lifetime?" *Forbes* 126 (September 1, 1980): 110–112; "A Tried and True Model for GM," *Fortune* 102 (October 6, 1980): 15–16; and Charles G. Burck, "How GM Stays Ahead," *Fortune* 103 (March 9, 1981): 48–56.

1. An excellent critical appraisal of organizational life may be found in William G. Scott and David K. Hart, *Organizational America* (Boston: Houghton Mifflin, 1979).

2. See William G. Dyer and Jeffrey H. Dyer, "The *M*A*S*H* Generation: Implications for Future Organizational Values," *Organizational Dynamics* 13 (Summer 1984): 66–79.

3. Job satisfaction data drawn from "Discontent is Growing Among Middle Managers," *Training and Development Journal* 35 (April 1981): 8–9.

4. For more on psychological contracts, see Edgar H. Schein, *Organizational Psychology,* 3rd ed. (Englewood Cliffs, N.J.: Prentice-Hall, 1980), pp. 22–24; John Paul Kotter, "The Psychological Contract: Managing the Joining-Up Process," *California Management Review* 15 (Spring 1973): 91–99; and Robert W. Goddard, "The Psychological Contract," *Management World* 13 (August 1984): 12–14, 35.

5. Chris Argyris, *Personality and Organization* (New York: Harper & Row, 1957), p. 66.

6. Thomas J. Peters and Robert H. Waterman, Jr., *In Search of Excellence* (New York: Harper & Row, 1982), p. 238.

7. See Michael Cieply, "Meanwhile, Back in Marysville," *Forbes* 133 (March 12, 1984): 127.

8. Raymond E. Miles and Charles C. Snow, "Designing Strategic Human Resources Systems," *Organizational Dynamics* 13 (Summer 1984): 36–37.

9. Edgar H. Schein, "Increasing Organizational Effectiveness Through Better Human Resource Planning and Development," *Sloan Management Review* 19 (Fall 1977): 1.

10. See James W. Walker and Robert Armes, "Implementing Management Succession Planning in Diversified Companies," *Human Resource Planning* 2, no. 2 (1979): 123–133.

11. An instructive discussion of an actual human resource planning system may be found in David R. Leigh, "Business Planning Is People Planning," *Personnel Journal* 63 (May 1984): 44–54.

12. James W. Walker, "Human Resource Planning: Managerial Concerns and Practices," *Business Horizons* 19 (June 1976): 56.

13. For practical tips on writing good job descriptions, see James Evered, "How to Write a Good Job Description," *Supervisory Management* 26 (April 1981): 14–19 and Mark A. Jones, "Job Descriptions Made Easy," *Personnel Journal* 63 (May 1984): 31–34.

14. For an excellent discussion of human resource forecasting, see James W.

Walker, "Forecasting Manpower Needs," *Harvard Business Review* 47 (March-April 1969): 152–164.

15. A helpful collection of readings dealing with all phases of human resource planning may be found in Elmer H. Burack and James W. Walker, eds., *Manpower Planning and Programming* (Boston: Allyn & Bacon, 1972).

16. See "U.S. Job Security in the Japanese Style," *Business Week* No. 2684 (April 20, 1981): 36.

17. For an interesting discussion of related problems, see "America's New Immobile Society," *Business Week* No. 2698 (July 27, 1981): 58–62.

18. Recruitment is discussed in Donn L. Dennis, "Are Recruitment Efforts Designed to Fail?" *Personnel Journal* 63 (September 1984): 60–67.

19. David A. Brookmire and Amy A. Burton, "A Format for Packaging Your Affirmative Action Program," *Personnel Journal* 57 (June 1978): 294.

20. Useful background information on EEO law can be found in Ann Weaver Hart, "Intent vs. Effect: Title VII Case Law That Could Affect You (Part I)," *Personnel Journal* 63 (March 1984): 31–47; Ann Weaver Hart, "Intent vs. Effect: Title VII Case Law That Could Affect You (Part II)," *Personnel Journal* 63 (April 1984): 50–58; "A Ruling That Could Roll Back Affirmative Action," *Business Week* No. 2849 (July 2, 1984): 31; and Anna Cifelli, "Quotas Live On," *Fortune* 110 (July 23, 1984): 95–96.

21. "16,000 Merck Employees Break Down Affirmative Action Stereotypes," *Personnel Journal* 63 (July 1984): 15, 17.

22. Carol J. Loomis, "A.T.&T. in the Throes of 'Equal Employment'" *Fortune* 99 (January 15, 1979): 45.

23. See Kenneth J. McCulloch, *Selecting Employees Safely Under the Law* (Englewood Cliffs, N.J.: Prentice-Hall, 1981), pp. 24–25 and Dale Yoder and Paul D. Staudohar, "Testing and EEO: Getting Down to Cases," *Personnel Administrator* 29 (February 1984): 67–74.

24. Leon C. Megginson, *Personnel and Human Resources Administration,* 3rd ed. (Homewood, Ill.: Irwin, 1977), p. 232.

25. Elliott D. Pursell, Michael A. Campion, and Sarah R. Gaylord, "Structured Interviewing: Avoiding Selection Problems," *Personnel Journal* 59 (November 1980): 908.

26. Ibid. (Emphasis added)

27. See Barry C. Campbell and Cynthia L. Barron, "How Extensively Are HRM Practices Being Utilized by the Practitioners?" *Personnel Administrator* 27 (May 1982): 67–71.

28. For instructive reading on performance appraisal, see John D. McMillan and Hoyt W. Doyel, "Performance Appraisal: Match the Tool to the Task," *Personnel* 57 (July-August 1980): 12–20; N. B. Winstanley, "Legal and Ethical Issues

in Performance Appraisals," *Harvard Business Review* 58 (November-December 1980): 186, 188, 192; Milan Moravec, "How Performance Appraisal Can Tie Communication to Productivity," *Personnel Administrator* 26 (January 1981): 51–54; Ed Yager, "A Critique of Performance Appraisal Systems," *Personnel Journal* 60 (February 1981): 129–133; and H. John Bernardin and Richard W. Beatty, *Performance Appraisal: Assessing Human Behavior at Work* (Boston: Kent, 1984).

29. "Performance Appraisal: Current Practices and Techniques," *Personnel* 61 (May-June 1984): 57.

30. Adapted from Hubert S. Field and William H. Holley, "The Relationship of Performance Appraisal System Characteristics to Verdicts in Selected Employment Discrimination Cases," *Academy of Management Journal* 25 (June 1982): 392–406. See also Ronald G. Wells, "Guidelines for Effective and Defensible Performance Appraisal Systems," *Personnel Journal* 61 (October 1982): 776–782.

31. Bernardin and Beatty, *Performance Appraisal: Assessing Human Behavior at Work*, p. 64.

32. See Ibid., pp. 116–124.

33. Robert I. Lazer and Walter S. Wikstrom, *Appraising Managerial Performance: Current Practices and Future Directions,* Report 723 (New York: The Conference Board, 1977), p. 26.

34. An excellent discussion of the two-interview performance appraisal format may be found in H. Kent Baker and Philip I. Morgan, "Two Goals in Every Performance Appraisal," *Personnel Journal* 63 (September 1984): 74–78.

35. Michael Beer, "Performance Appraisal: Dilemmas and Possibilities," *Organizational Dynamics* 9 (Winter 1981): 33.

36. Drawn from "Worker-Training Cost Tops $30 Billion," *Arizona Republic* No. 43 (June 28, 1981): c-9.

37. For an interesting discussion of a realistic management simulation, see Peter Petre, "Games That Teach You to Manage," *Fortune* 110 (October 29, 1984): 65–72.

38. Kenneth N. Wexley and Gary P. Latham, *Developing and Training Human Resources in Organizations* (Glenview, Ill.: Scott, Foresman, 1981), pp. 75–77.

39. Ibid., p. 77.

40. Burck, "How GM Stays Ahead," p. 54.

Chapter 10

Communicating

It is a luxury to be understood.
Ralph Waldo Emerson

Chapter Objectives

When you finish studying this chapter, you should be able to

- Identify each major link in the communication process.
- Describe the roles of selectivity, organization, and interpretation in perception.
- Discuss why it is important for managers to know about grapevine, nonverbal, and upward communication.
- Identify and briefly describe four different barriers to communication.
- List at least three practical tips for improving each of the following communication skills: listening, writing, and running a meeting.

Opening Case 10.1

Keeping in Touch at Tandem Computers

Headquartered in Cupertino, California, Tandem Computers Inc. gets its name from its unique "fail-safe" computer systems. Large on-line computer users such as banks and airlines can be devastated by untimely computer breakdowns and data base contamination. By harnessing computers so that they run in tandem, with each being able to pick up the load if the other fails, a Tandem Computer frees its user from worry about costly computer "crashes."

Tandem was founded in 1974 by James G. Treybig (pronounced Tri-big). Since that time, Tandem has grown from a one-office, four-person operation into a $500 million per year company employing over 5000 people worldwide. In 1984, Treybig, now serving as Tandem's president and chief executive officer, was honored with *Industry Week's* Excellence in Management Award. In addition, Tandem was profiled in the 1984 best-seller, *The 100 Best Companies to Work for in America.* All this suggests that Treybig and Tandem must be doing something right. Indeed, Treybig's philosophy of open communication has helped create an organizational climate widely admired in the business community.

An In-house TV Network

Thanks to Treybig's farsightedness and a $1 million investment in facilities, Tandem has its own private television network. Satellite earth stations installed at most of the firm's offices in the United States and Canada enable the home office to communicate simultaneously with about half its employees. Only 30 minutes notice is required to get the network in operation. Marilyn Lawrence, the network's chief engineer, told *Inc.* magazine: "Once you've set up the network, you can reach everyone in the company for the cost of a single air fare to the East Coast. If that isn't cheap, timely, effective communications, I don't know what is."[1]

Although there have been some problems with long-range scheduling, camera-shy managers, and inadequate lead times, Tandem's TV network has proved quite useful. Market presentations, divisional teleconferences, and a variety of training programs are aired regularly. Tandem's TV network even has its own talk show. Once a month, Treybig hosts "Tandem Talk," a two-hour show devoted to important company issues. Employees are encouraged to call in and ask questions while the show is on the air. Like its major network counterparts, "Tandem Talk" has had its problems with ratings. Complaints from employees that early shows were too technical prompted Treybig and the network staff to revamp "Tandem Talk" to include interviews and other features with broader interest. The ratings have since gone up.

Since anyone with a satellite dish can tune in to Tandem's broadcasts, plans to install encoding devices are helping to allay fears that competitors will learn company secrets.

A Computer Terminal on Every Desk

Most of Tandem's employees have computer terminals on their desks that are connected to the company's mainframe computer. Thus, an "electronic mail" system links virtually every desk and work station throughout the company.

Unlike many companies in which only management or a development team can use electronic mail, everyone at Tandem can send electronic messages. "A person can say 'help' to 5,000 people," notes Mr. Treybig. "And, instantly, everyone knows what the problem is—and that kind of joint experience will call up a lot of possible solutions."

It can also put a crimp in a new management plan. A new vice president recently sent out a new company policy via electronic mail and, that very same day, received over 400 messages—all against it. "He said he believed in our 'people philosophy,' " laughs Mr. Treybig, "but it would take awhile to adjust to this democracy."[2]

Employees seem to enjoy fewer traditional memos and less frequent meetings, owing to the electronic mail system.

Thank Goodness It's Friday

Another one of Treybig's communication devices has become legendary in the computer industry. Each Friday afternoon, at the company's headquarters, employees from the president on down to product assembly personnel take time out for a "popcorn party." Free beer and popcorn grease the wheels of informal conversation as employees from all functional areas and various administrative levels freely interact. There is no formal agenda for these meetings; they are strictly social. Key customers are frequently invited to the popcorn parties to find out what makes Tandem tick. Treybig is often collared at the Friday afternoon gatherings to hear an employee's complaint, suggestion, or opinion. Considering the 50 cents-per-person cost for the beer and popcorn, Treybig feels the company reaps a huge return in creativity and goodwill.

(Discussion questions linking this case with the material you are about to read can be found at the end of this chapter.)

One of the most challenging and difficult aspects of management is to get individuals to understand and voluntarily pursue organizational objectives. Effective communication, as at Tandem Computers, is vital to meeting this challenge. Organizational communication takes in a great deal of territory, as virtually every management function and activity can be considered communication in one way or another. Planning and controlling generally require a good deal of communicating, as do organization design and development, decision making and problem solving, leadership, and staffing. Studies have shown that overall organizational performance correlates directly with the quality of managerial communication.[3] Not surprisingly, research has demonstrated that the average manager spends more time communicating than doing anything else.

A work-sampling study of the work habits of 136 managers at three different levels in a large research and development organization precisely measured the nature and extent of managerial communication. The managers who were studied spent between 74 and 87 percent of their workday communicating (see Figure 10.1). Each successively higher level of management spent proportionately more time communicating. Interestingly, for all three levels of management, the predominant category of communication was listening and speaking. Since the managers spent an average of

Figure 10.1 Managers Spend Most of Their Time Communicating

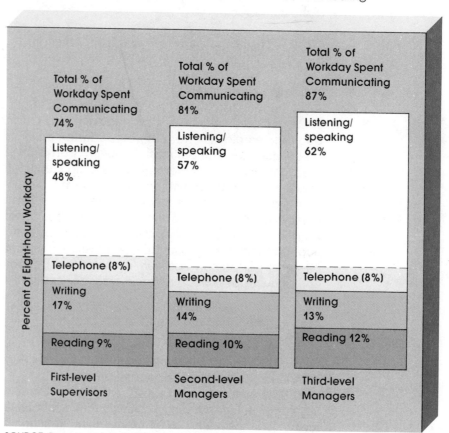

SOURCE: Data from John R. Hinrichs, "Communications Activity of Industrial Research Personnel," *Personnel Psychology* 17 (Summer 1964): 199.

only 8 percent of their day on the telephone, it was clear that most of their listening and speaking was done face to face. As a matter of fact, most of their total communication time was spent in face-to-face listening and speaking.[4]

Just because managers spend most of their time communicating does not necessarily mean that they are effective communicators. One indication that managers believe this area should be improved is the continuing popularity of communication seminars in management development programs. One management writer summed up the state of managerial communication with this somewhat harsh appraisal: "Talk is cheap, so we spend it recklessly, overloading our message systems and thereby depreciating their contents. With so much garbage in the system, much of it will inevitably be sent out."[5] Before managers, or anyone else for that matter, can become more effective communicators they need to appreciate that communication is a complex process subject to a great deal of perceptual distortion and many problems. This is especially true for the apparently simple activity of communicating face to face.

The Communication Process

Well-known management scholar Keith Davis has defined **communication** as "the transfer of information and understanding from one person to another person."[6] Communication is a social process.[7] Whether one communicates face to face with a single person or with a group of people via television, it is still a social activity involving two or more people. By analyzing the communication process, one discovers that it is a chain made up of identifiable links (see Figure 10.2). The essential purpose of this chainlike process is to send an idea from one person to another in such a way that it is understood by the receiver. Like any other chain, the communication chain is only as strong as its weakest link.

Encoding Thinking is an exclusively personal process. It takes place within the human brain and is greatly affected by how one perceives the surrounding environment. But when we want to pass along a thought to someone else, an entirely different process begins. This second process, communication, requires the sender to package the idea for understandable transmission. Encoding starts at this point. The purpose of encoding is to translate internal thought patterns into a language or code that the intended receiver of the message is likely to understand.

Managers usually rely on words, gestures, or other symbols for encoding. Their choice of symbols depends on several factors, one of which is the nature of the message itself. Is it technical or nontechnical, emotional or factual? Perhaps it could be expressed better with numbers than with words, as in the case of a budget report. To express skepticism, merely a shrug might be enough.

The purpose of the message also is important. Is it intended to convey specific information needed for the completion of a job? Or is it intended to persuade, to change attitudes, or to indicate general direction? There are as many purposes as there are situations, and it is important to consider what the message is supposed to accomplish. If a manager wants to propose a bold new program to his or her superiors, for example, then a dry technical report would probably not have the needed persuasive impact. Broad generalizations with a certain emotional appeal for motivational purposes would be a more productive approach; technical details could be communicated later.

Figure 10.2 The Basic Communication Process

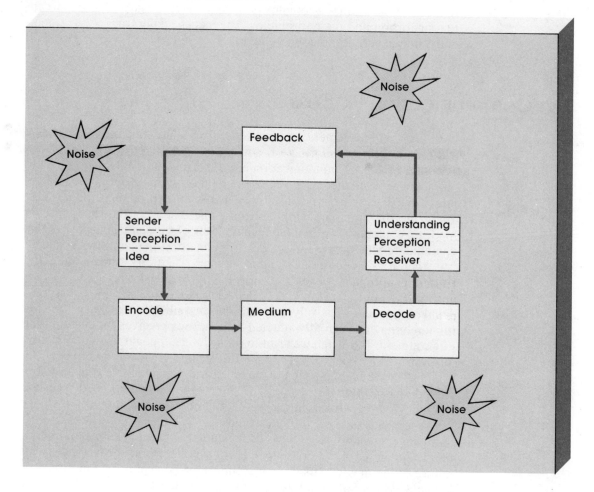

Another important factor is deciding how to encode a message—that is, deciding what physical form it will take. A manager would certainly use different language for a phone call than for a telegram. The number of people to be addressed is also important. Usually, the greater the number of receivers, the more formal the language should be. In talking face to face with a colleague, a manager can be more informal than when speaking to a hundred. The perceived characteristics of the receiver enter into the encoding decision. A manager would speak to a secretary familiar with all the department's activities in a much different way than to an angry superior or a prospective customer.

Selecting a Medium   Managers can choose among a number of media. They should consider the same factors that influenced the encoding decision. The nature of the message, its intended purpose, the number of receivers, and their characteristics all enter into the selection of a medium. Possible media include face-to-face conversation, telephone calls, memos, letters, computers, photographs, bulletin boards, meetings, and organizational publications. Communicating with those outside the organization opens up further possibilities, such as news releases, press conferences, and advertising on television and radio or in magazines and newspapers.

Each particular medium has its own advantages and disadvantages. Telephones, for example, are a quick and easy way to give someone a verbal message, but they do not allow for the valuable nonverbal feedback that is so much a part of face-to-face communication. Computers can handle a vast amount of detailed information but cannot transmit a manager's enthusiasm for a project. Letters and memos, although relatively time consuming to prepare, have the advantage of giving the communicating parties a permanent record of the exchange.

Decoding   Even the most expertly fashioned message will not accomplish its purpose unless it is understood. After physically receiving the message, the receiver must comprehend the symbols and detect shades of meaning. If the message has been properly encoded, decoding will take place rather routinely. But perfect encoding is nearly impossible to achieve in an imperfect world. The receiver's willingness to receive the message is a principal prerequisite for successful decoding. The chances of successful decoding are greatly enhanced if the receiver knows the language and terminology used in the message. It helps too if the receiver understands the sender's purpose and background situation. Effective listening is given special attention later in this chapter.

Feedback   Some sort of feedback, verbal or nonverbal, from the receiver to the sender is required to complete the communication process. Appropriate forms of feedback are determined by the same factors that govern the sender's encoding decision. Without feedback, senders have no way of knowing whether their ideas have been accurately understood. Knowing whether or not others understand us significantly affects both the form and content of our follow-up communication.

Noise   Noise is not an integral part of the chainlike communication process, but it may influence the process at any or all points. As the term is used here, **noise** is any interference with the normal flow of understanding from one person to another. This is a relatively broad definition. Thus, a speech impairment, garbled technical transmission, negative attitudes, misperception, illegible print or pictures, telephone static, partial loss of hearing, and poor eyesight all qualify as noise. Understanding tends to diminish as noise increases. In general, there are two ways to improve the effectiveness of organizational communication. Steps can be taken to maximize the understandability of verbal and written messages. At the same time, noise can be minimized by foreseeing and neutralizing potential sources of interference.

Perception: A Vital Link in Communication

Perception has been defined as "the process by which an individual gives meaning to his environment."[8] Although perception often is regarded as "seeing" things, we perceive with all our senses. Perception is essential to communication, as it helps senders interpret the circumstances on which ideas and messages are based. Receivers, in turn, rely on perception to interpret the messages they receive. With highly personalized perceptual filters operating at both ends of the communication chain, it is no wonder that messages often fail to have their intended impact. For example, in 1977, the worst air disaster in history occurred in the Canary Islands when a jet airliner that was taking off collided with one that was taxiing on the runway. According to the investigation, the pilot of the plane that was taking off had perceived the tower's command to "stand by for take off" as the go-ahead to "take off." Twenty seconds later 583 people lost their lives.[9] Although perception may not be a life-and-death matter for the average manager, an understanding of perception is essential to effective communication.

A general model of the perceptual process is displayed in Figure 10.3. Three subprocesses of perception are selectivity, organization, and interpretation. Each serves as a potential obstacle between environmental stimuli such as communicated messages from others and eventual understanding. Misperception is said to have occurred when the appropriate understanding is not forthcoming.

Selectivity

Selectivity is a sensory screening process that allows one to sort out and mentally process only certain details in one's surroundings. Each of us is constantly bombarded by environmental stimuli, all competing for our attention. These stimuli may be verbal or written messages, noises, lights, symbols, signs, or the nonverbal behavior of others. We would literally go mad if we did not have some mental faculty for sorting out and screening these competing stimuli. Fortunately, we have the ability to select only

Figure 10.3 The Perceptual Process

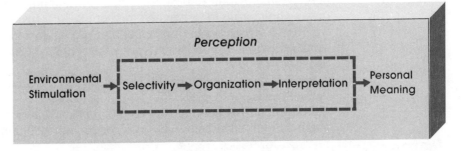

certain environmental inputs. This selectivity occurs in two ways, through perceptual defense and through perceptual set, both of which can help or hinder the communication process.

Perceptual Defense How many times have you seen someone study with the radio or television going full blast? Those who can retain what they read in spite of competing stimuli have highly developed perceptual defenses. **Perceptual defense** is the screening out of environmental stimuli. A training director's perceptual defense to criticisms of his or her department's work may effectively block critical communication from other managers.

One can readily see that perceptual defense has both a good side and a bad side. On the good side, busy managers cannot hope to be effective if they give their fullest attention to every fact, detail, problem, bit of information, criticism, and question that they encounter during a typical day. Managers must be selective to keep from being swamped by endless details. It is this need for selective perception that makes the establishment of priorities so important. Once again, priorities are a ranking of a manager's concerns in order of their importance. Important matters receive attention first, and matters of less importance are put off until later or ignored altogether.

As for the negative side of perceptual defense, blinders may help horses stay on the road, but they do little to promote managerial effectiveness. In other words, a manager may become too restricted in screening out important situational variables. For example, managers in nonunion organizations who ignore rumors about growing pay dissatisfaction among hourly personnel may end up bargaining with a union.

Perceptual Set In direct contrast to perceptual defense, which is a screening-out process, **perceptual set** is a screening-in process. Perceptual set commonly occurs when someone bases a conclusion on a hastily gathered first impression. For example, research has demonstrated that when people have been told to expect a new acquaintance to be "warm," they in fact perceive the person to be warm, intelligent, and generally likable.[10] The reverse holds true for a negative perceptual set. Just as the term implies, we often become set in our perception of people and the messages they send. Jokes told by good friends somehow tend to be funnier than the same ones told by adversaries.

Perceptual set, like perceptual defense, has its advantages and disadvantages. A certain degree of perceptual set allows one to have an eye for relevant detail without getting tangled up in irrelevant minutiae. But too much perceptual set paves the way for prejudice and inflexibility.

Organization

Selectivity is only the first hurdle in the overall perception process. Once something has been selected from among competing stimuli, the subprocess of organization takes over. Through **perceptual organization,** one arranges otherwise meaningless or disorganized stimuli into meaningful patterns. Organization takes place in three ways: grouping, figure-ground, and closure. Many entertaining optical illusions like the ones in Figure 10.4 play havoc with perceptual organization.

Grouping   Look at image 1 in Figure 10.4 and follow the instructions (look now before reading on). If you look very closely, the sentence contains the word *the* twice. But because we normally group words line by line, a duplication in wording between two lines tends to be overlooked. So, too, managers may overlook subtle individual differences by grouping people. On the positive side, grouping helps us quickly and efficiently sort out unusual stimuli, such as defective products when testing for quality.

Figure-ground   Take a quick look at image 2 in Figure 10.4 (look now before reading on). What do you see? Did you first see dark T-shaped blocks (one right side up, the other upside down)? Or did you see a light capital letter H against a dark background? What you saw depended on what you perceived as the figure and what you perceived as the background. In the same fashion people often reverse figure-ground relationships in their surroundings. In an organizational setting, one may initially perceive the recruiter as the principal figure and others in the organization as the undifferentiated background. Eventually, though, the recruiter fades into the background as supervisors, new friends, and others emerge as personally important figures. Similarly, important problems and communications often get lost in a background of trivial matters.

Closure   Now take a fast glance at image 3 in Figure 10.4 (look now before reading on). What do you see? If you see a commercial jet airliner flying toward you from left to right you have relied on the perceptual process of closure. In effect, closure means mentally filling in the blanks of an

Figure 10.4   "What You See Isn't Always What You Get!"

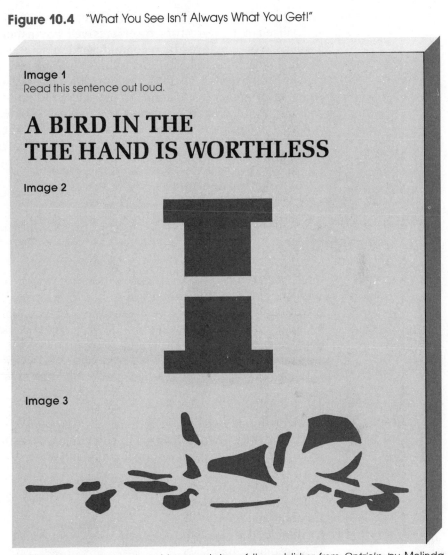

Image 1
Read this sentence out loud.

A BIRD IN THE
THE HAND IS WORTHLESS

Image 2

Image 3

SOURCE: Image 1 reproduced by permission of the publisher from *Optricks,* by Melinda Wentzell and D. K. Holland, © 1973. Troubador Press, 385 Fremont Street, San Francisco, CA 94105.

incomplete whole. Since you are accustomed to seeing complete pictures of airplanes, you perceptually complete an incomplete picture. We are all familiar with the tendency of people to fill in the blanks when they hear only part of a story. Rumors are started this way. But closure can be extremely helpful when one is trying to identify and solve a complex problem with only limited information.

Interpretation
Managers often interpret situations differently because they have highly specialized and thus restricted perspectives. For instance, an engineer and a salesperson employed by a computer manufacturer may come out of a meeting with a customer with very different interpretations of what lies ahead. Suppose the customer wants additional software for an already complex computer installation. To the salesperson this means more sales revenue; to the engineer it means working out significant technical difficulties. The salesperson interprets the situation as an opportunity, but the engineer interprets it as a problem. They can be expected to react quite differently to the situation.

Dynamics of Organizational Communication

It has been pointed out that "civilization is based on human cooperation, and without communication, no effective cooperation can develop."[11] Accordingly, effective communication is essential for cooperation within productive organizations. At least four dynamics of organizational communication—structural considerations, the grapevine, nonverbal communication, and upward communication—largely determine the difference between effectiveness and ineffectiveness in this important area.

Organizing for Coordinated Communication
As we mentioned earlier, the term *organizational communication* takes in a lot of territory. Research on major companies has identified the following seven categories of organizational communication:

1. Advertising and promotion.
2. Employee communications.
3. Media relations.
4. Shareholder relations.
5. Consumer affairs.
6. Community relations.
7. Government relations.

In terms of organization structure, the same study revealed a trend toward greater centralization of the communication function. More and more firms are showing a preference for a separate corporate communications department headed by an executive-level manager, who may be called the director of communications, director of public affairs, or director of public relations. Behind this drive toward greater centralization of the communications function is a desire to support and coordinate companywide communications through a central source. Once specific communications programs were developed at the corporate level, however, there was a tendency among the firms studied to administer those programs at the divisional or local levels.[12]

The Grapevine In every organization, large or small, there are actually two communication systems. One is formal, and the other is informal. Sometimes they complement and reinforce one another; at other times they come into direct conflict. Although theorists have found it convenient to separate the two, distinguishing one from the other in real life can be difficult. Information required to accomplish official objectives is channeled throughout the organization via the formal system. Official or formal communication, by definition, flows in accordance with established lines of authority and structural boundaries. Media for official communication include everything from memos and letters to the telephone, bulletin boards, and in-house publications. But superimposed on this formal network is the infamous **grapevine,** the unofficial and informal communication system. The term *grapevine* can be traced back to Civil War days when vinelike telegraph wires were strung from tree to tree across battlefields.

Grapevine Patterns An authority on grapevine communication has offered the following vivid description:

> The grapevine operates fast and furiously in almost any work organization. It moves with impunity across departmental lines and easily bypasses superiors in chains of command. It flows around water coolers, down hallways, through lunch rooms, and wherever people get together in groups. It performs best in informal social contacts, but it can operate almost as effectively as a sideline to official meetings. Wherever people congregate, there is no getting rid of the grapevine. No matter how management feels about it, it is here to stay.[13]

Contrary to what one might suspect, grapevine communication is not a formless, haphazard process: close study has uncovered definite orderly patterns (see Figure 10.5). Among the alternative grapevine patterns, the cluster configuration is the most common. When the cluster pattern is operating, only select individuals repeat what they hear; others do not.[14] Those who consistently pass along what they hear to others serve as grapevine liaisons or gatekeepers.

> About 10 percent of the employees on an average grapevine will be highly active participants. They serve as liaisons with the rest of the staff members who receive information but spread it to only a few other people. Usually these liaisons are friendly, outgoing people who are in positions that allow them to

cross departmental lines. For example, secretaries tend to be liaisons because they can communicate with the top executive, the janitor, and everyone in between without raising eyebrows.[15]

Alert managers can keep abreast of grapevine communication by regularly conversing with known liaisons.

Managerial Attitudes Toward the Grapevine   One survey of 341 participants in a management development seminar uncovered predominantly negative feelings among managers toward the grapevine. Moreover, first-line supervisors perceived the grapevine to be more influential than did middle managers. This second finding led the researchers to conclude that "apparently the grapevine is more prevalent, or at least more visible at lower levels of the managerial hierarchy where supervisors can readily feel its impact."[16] Finally, the survey found that employees of relatively small organizations (less than 50 people) viewed the grapevine as less influential than did those from larger organizations (over 100 people). A logical explanation for this last finding is that smaller organizations are usually more informal to begin with.

In spite of the negative attitude that many managers have toward it, the grapevine does have a positive side. In fact, experts estimate that grapevine communication is about 75 percent accurate.[17] Though the grapevine has a reputation among managers as a bothersome source of inaccurate information and gossip, it also serves as an emotional outlet for employee fears and apprehensions, helps satisfy a natural desire to know what is really going on, and gives employees a sense of belonging. Grapevine communication can carry useful information through the organization with amazing speed. Moreover, grapevine communication can help management learn how employees truly feel about policies and programs.

Coping with the Grapevine   Considering that the grapevine can be an influential and sometimes negative force, what can management do about it? First and foremost, the grapevine *cannot* be extinguished. In fact, attempts to stifle grapevine communication may serve instead to stimulate it. A policy of subtly monitoring the grapevine and officially correcting or countering any potentially damaging misinformation is about all any management team can do. "Management by wandering around," as discussed in Chapter 2, is an excellent way to monitor the grapevine in a nonthreatening manner. Some managers selectively feed information into the grapevine. For example, a health care administrator has admitted:

"Sure, I use the grapevine. Why not? The employees sure use it. It's fast, reaches everyone, and employees believe it—no matter how preposterous. I limit its use, though."[18]

Figure 10.5 Grapevine Patterns

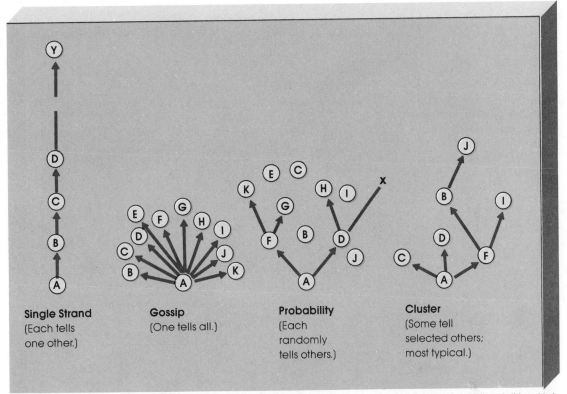

SOURCE: Keith Davis and John W. Newstrom, *Human Behavior at Work: Organizational Behavior,* 7th ed. (New York: McGraw-Hill, 1985), p. 317. Used with permission.

Rumor-control hot lines have proven useful for neutralizing disruptive and inaccurate grapevine communication.

Nonverbal Communication

Sometimes, as we all know, communication is a "damned if you do and damned if you don't" proposition. If we speak our mind, we may offend. If we keep our mouth shut, we may be accused of holding out. Complicating this dilemma, the facial expressions and body movements that accompany our words can also cause problems. This nonverbal communication, sometimes referred to as **body language,** is an important part of the communication process. In fact, one expert contends that only 7 percent of the impact of our face-to-face communication comes from the words we utter; the other 93 percent comes from our vocal intonations, facial expressions, and posture.[19] As the old romantic line goes, "Your words may say no, but your eyes say yes, yes, yes."

Figure 10.6   How Well Do You Read Body Language?

How Well Do You Read Body Language?

Take this quick test to find out. Circle the phrase that you believe best communicates what is being said in each picture. You'll find the correct answers below, printed upside down.

1. a. "I can handle this easily."
— b. "Let me think about it for a while."
c. "That will never work."

2. a. "Look, it's out of my league. Sorry."
b. "I'll do anything I can to help."
c. "You've got to be kidding!"

3. a. "This meeting is making me very tense."
— b. "Don't bore me with details—get to the point."
c. "I'm frustrated that we can't agree."

(see Table 10.1 for explanations.)
Answers: 1.a; 2.b; 3.a; 4.c; 5.c

4. a. "Can it wait until later?"
b. "I'm ready to negotiate."
— c. "I'm much better at my job than you are."

5. a. "I've finally come to a conclusion."
— b. "That's worth considering."
c. "I can't believe I just said that."

Photos: Aboud Dwek

SOURCE: Reprinted with permission from the June 1984 issue of *Association Management* magazine. Copyright 1984 by the American Society of Association Executives. 1575 Eye St. N.W., Washington, D.C. 20005. (202) 626–2722. Photos by Aboud Dweck.

Types of Body Language   There are three kinds of body language: facial, gestural, and postural.[20] Without the speaker or listener consciously thinking about it, seemingly insignificant changes in facial expression, gestures, and posture send various messages (see Figure 10.6). For example, a speaker can tell that a listener is interested through a combination of nonverbal cues, including an attentive gaze, an upright posture, and confirming or agreeing gestures. Negative nonverbal cues let speakers know that they are off course with the listener. For example, consider the following situation:

> A project director in a huge aerospace company called a meeting of higher management people who supported his research project. Consonant with the oft-expressed company policy of commercially exploiting advanced research work, he wanted them to fund development of a new product internally. Early in the meeting, as he began to outline the sizable costs involved, he sensed their disapproval from facial expressions and body postures. His intuition told him that if they were asked to make an explicit decision on the project, it would be negative. So he changed his line of argument and began stressing the possibilities for external rather than internal funding of the project. And he assiduously avoided asking for a funding decision at that time.[21]

Unfortunately, many people in positions of responsibility, such as parents, teachers, and managers, ignore or misread nonverbal feedback. When they do, they become ineffective communicators.

Receiving Nonverbal Communication   Like any other interpersonal skill, sensitivity to nonverbal cues can be learned (see Table 10.1). Listeners need to be especially aware of subtleties. There is a fine distinction between an attentive gaze and a glaring stare, between an upright posture and a stiff one. Knowing how to interpret a nod, a grimace, or a grin can be invaluable to managers. If at any time the response seems inappropriate to what one is saying, it is time to back off and reassess one's approach. It may be necessary to explain things more clearly, adopt a more patient manner, or make other adjustments.

Giving Nonverbal Feedback   What about the nonverbal feedback that managers give rather than receive? A research study carried out in Great Britain suggests that nonverbal feedback from authority figures significantly affects subordinate behavior. Among the people who were interviewed, those who received nonverbal approval from the interviewers in the form of smiles, positive head nods, and eye contact behaved quite differently from those who received nonverbal disapproval through frowns, head shaking, and avoidance of eye contact. Those receiving positive nonverbal feedback were judged by neutral observers to be signifi-

Table 10.1 Reading Body Language

Unspoken Message	Behavior
"I want to be helpful."	• Uncrossing legs. • Unbuttoning coat or jacket. • Unclasping hands. • Moving closer to other person. • Smiling face. • Removing hands from pockets. • Unfolding arms from across chest.
"I'm confident."	• Avoiding hand-to-face gestures and head scratching. • Maintaining an erect stance. • Keeping steady eye contact. • Steepling fingertips below chin.
"I'm nervous."	• Clearing throat. • Expelling air (such as "Whew!"). • Placing hand over mouth while speaking. • Hurried cigarette smoking.
"I'm superior to you."	• Peering over tops of eyeglasses. • Pointing a finger. • Standing behind a desk and leaning palms down on it. • Holding jacket lapels while speaking.

SOURCE: Adapted from William Friend, "Reading Between the Lines," *Association Management* 36 (June 1984): 94–100. Reprinted by permission of the publisher.

cantly more relaxed, more friendly, more talkative, and more successful in creating a good impression.[22] Positive nonverbal feedback from managers is a basic building block of good interpersonal relations. A well-timed wink, nod of the head, or pat on the back tells the individual that he or she is on the right track and to keep up the good work.

Upward Communication

As used here, the term **upward communication** refers to a process of systematically encouraging subordinates to share with management their feelings and ideas.[23] Upward communication has become increasingly important in recent years as employees have demanded—and received—a greater say in their work lives. Yet recent research suggests that improvement is needed in this area. A survey of members of the American Society for Training and Development (ASTD) led to the following conclusion:

Nearly 43% of the respondents indicated that management does "little" or "very little" to encourage upward communication. ... bad news, in particular, does not move upward. Despite the proliferation of participative management strategies—quality circles, project-management teams, communications training, reward systems for suggestions, etc.—the old "shoot-the-bearer-of-bad-news" mentality still dominates most organizations.[24]

At least seven different options are open to managers who want to improve upward communication.

Formal Grievance Procedures   When unions represent rank-and-file employees, provisions for upward communication are usually spelled out in the collective bargaining agreement. Typically, unionized employees have a formal grievance procedure for contesting managerial actions and oversights. Grievance procedures usually consist of a number of progressively more rigorous steps. For example, union members who have been fired may talk with their supervisor in the presence of the union steward. If the issue is not resolved at that level, the next step may be a meeting with the department head. Sometimes the formal grievance process includes as many as five or six steps, with a third-party arbitrator being the last resort. Formal grievance procedures are also found in non-union situations.[25]

Employee Attitude and Opinion Surveys   Both in-house and commercially prepared surveys can bring employee attitudes and feelings to the surface. But statistical analysis and interpretation by hired consultants drive up costs significantly. Employees usually will complete surveys if they are convinced that meaningful changes will result. Surveys with no feedback or follow-up action tend to alienate employees who feel they are just wasting their time.

Suggestion Boxes   Provided that those who submit suggestions receive prompt feedback and appropriate monetary incentives for good ideas, suggestion boxes can be a valuable tool.

Open-door Policy   The open-door approach to upward communication has been both praised and criticized. Proponents say that when managers keep their doors open and subordinates feel free to walk in any time and talk with them, problems can be nipped in the bud. But critics contend that an open-door policy encourages subordinates to leapfrog the formal chain of command. They argue further that it is an open invitation to annoying interruptions when managers can least afford them. A limited open-door policy—afternoons only, for example—can effectively remedy this last objection.

Informal Gripe Sessions   Employees may feel free to air their feelings if they are confident that management will not criticize or penalize them for being frank. But the term *gripe session* seems to encourage only negative communication, and so a more positive label is recommended. One Honeywell division with which this writer is familiar holds regular, informal "coffee talks" to stimulate upward communication.

Task Forces　In spite of its limited use, a task-force approach to upward communication has excellent potential. A task force is a team of management and nonmanagement personnel assigned to a specific problem or issue. Task forces generally are fact-finding and advisory panels with no final decision-making authority. Multilevel participation in a task force encourages better working relationships between managers and subordinates, enhances creativity, and develops interpersonal skills.

Exit Interviews　An employee leaving the organization, for whatever reason, no longer fears possible recrimination from superiors and so can offer unusually frank and honest feedback, obtained in a brief, structured, exit interview. On the other hand, exit interviews have been criticized for eliciting artificially negative feedback, because the employee may have a sour-grapes attitude toward the organization.

In general, attempts to promote upward communication will be successful only if subordinates truly believe that their contributions will have a favorable impact on their employment. Halfhearted or insincere attempts to get subordinates to open up and become involved will do more harm than good.

Communication Problems

Because communication is a complex, give-and-take process, there will naturally be problems. Managers who are aware of common barriers to communication and sensitive, too, to the problem of sexist communication are more likely to be effective communicators.

Barriers to Communication　Earlier in this chapter, the concept of noise was introduced. Noise is common, but it varies in degree. On the low end of the scale, noise such as radio static is a minor irritant that hampers but does not completely block the transfer of understanding. But at the high end of the scale, noise can become an impenetrable barrier to communication. There are four types of communication barriers that represent extreme forms of noise: (1) process barriers, (2) physical barriers, (3) semantic barriers, and (4) psychosocial barriers.

Process Barriers   Every step in the communication process is necessary for effective communication. Blocked steps become barriers. Consider the following situations:

- **Sender barrier.** A management trainee with an unusual new idea fails to speak up at a meeting for fear of criticism.
- **Encoding barrier.** A Spanish-speaking factory worker cannot get an English-speaking supervisor to understand a grievance about working conditions.
- **Medium barrier.** After getting no answer three times and a busy signal twice, a customer concludes that a store's consumer hot line is a waste of time.
- **Decoding barrier.** An older manager is not sure what a young supervisor means when she refers to an employee as "spaced out."
- **Receiver barrier.** A manager who is preoccupied with the preparation of a budget asks a subordinate to repeat an earlier statement.
- **Feedback barrier.** During on-the-job training, the failure of the trainee to ask any questions causes a manager to wonder if there is any real understanding.

The complexity of the communication process itself is a potentially formidable barrier to communication. Malfunctions anywhere along the line can singly or collectively block the transfer of understanding.

Physical Barriers   Sometimes a physical object blocks effective communication. For example, a riveter who wears ear protectors probably cannot hear someone yell fire. Distance is another physical barrier. The 3000 miles between New York and Los Angeles and the time-zone differences can complicate coast-to-coast communication in a nationwide organization. People often take physical barriers for granted, but sometimes they can be removed. For example, an inconveniently positioned wall in an office can be torn out. An appropriate choice of media is especially important in overcoming physical barriers. A manager with a soft voice can reach hundreds of people by using a sound system.

Semantic Barriers   Formally defined, **semantics** is the study of meaning in words. Words are an indispensable feature of everyday life, though unfortunately, words can sometimes cause a great deal of trouble. In a well-worn army story, a growling drill sergeant once ordered a frightened recruit to go out and paint his entire jeep. Later, the sergeant was shocked to find that the private had painted his *entire* jeep, including the headlights, windshield, seats, and dashboard gauges. Obviously, the word *entire* meant something different to the recruit than it did to the sergeant.

In today's highly specialized world, managers in fields such as accounting, computer science, or advertising may become so accustomed to their own technical language that they forget that people outside their field may not understand them. Unexpected reactions or behavior by others may signal a semantic barrier. It may become necessary to reencode the message using more generally used terms. Sometimes, if the relationship among specialists in different technical fields is an ongoing one, remedial steps can be taken. For example, hospital administrators often take a special course in medical terminology so that they can better understand the medical staff.

Psychosocial Barriers Psychological and social barriers are probably responsible for more blocked communication than any other type of barrier. This is true because of people's differing backgrounds, perceptions, values, biases, needs, and expectations. Childhood experiences may result in negative feelings toward authority figures (such as supervisors), racial prejudice, distrust of the opposite sex, or lack of self-confidence. Family and personal problems, including poor health, alcoholism, and emotional strain, may be so upsetting that an employee is unable to concentrate on work. Experience on present or past jobs may have created anger, distrust, and resentment that speak more loudly in the employee's mind than any work-related communication. Sincere sensitivity to the receiver's needs and personal circumstances goes a long way toward overcoming psychosocial barriers to communication.[26]

Sexist Communication In recent years the English language has been increasingly criticized for being sexist.[27] Words like *he, chairman, brotherhood, mankind,* and the like have been commonly used in reference to both men and women. The traditional argument is that everyone understands that these words refer to both sexes, and it is simpler to use the masculine form. Critics, on the other hand, maintain that strictly masculine wording subtly denies women a place and image worthy of their equal status and importance in society.[28] This criticism is largely based on psychological and sociological considerations. Calling the human race *mankind,* for instance, is seldom a real barrier to understanding. But, a Stanford University researcher found that "males appear to use 'he' in response to male-related imagery, rather than in response to abstract or generic notions of humanity."[29] In other words, *he* is commonly interpreted to mean literally *he* (a man), not *they* (men and women). Progressive male and female managers are weeding sexist language out of their vocabularies so as not to subordinate or demean women inadvertently. Selected warning signs of sexist communication are presented in Table 10.2.

Table 10.2   Some Warning Signs of Sexist Communication

How often do you engage in verbal or nonverbal sexist communication? (Women as well as men contribute to this problem.)

1. Do you use the salutation "Gentlemen" in business letters?
2. Do you ever use the term "girls" or "gals" to refer to women in the office?
3. In written information, do you use the pronoun "he" when writing about what a person does/thinks/etc.?
4. Do you use occupational terms which end in "man"—businessman, salesman, chairman, etc.?
5. Do you make it a point to open the door for business women?
6. Do you ever feel awkward if a woman pays for a business meal?
7. If a woman is at the back of the elevator, do you ever cause exit problems by trying to let her out first?
8. Do you support the tradition of having the secretary address the boss by using a courtesy title and having the boss address the secretary by using a first name?
9. Do you think it is ungentlemanly not to light a woman's cigarette?
10. In traveling with a business woman, do you pay the tips for baggage handling and the limousine fee?

SOURCE: Christine B. Steigler, "The Art of Non-Sexist Communication," *Management World* 9, no. 6 (June 1980): 15. Reprinted with permission from the Administrative Management Society, Willow Grove, PA. 19090.

Becoming a Better Communicator

Three communication skills that are especially important in today's highly organized world are listening, writing, and running meetings. Managers who master these skills usually have fewer interpersonal relations problems. Moreover, effective communicators tend to move up the hierarchy faster than poor ones do.

Effective Listening   Almost all training in oral communication in high school, college, and management development programs is in effective speaking. But what about listening, the other half of the communication equation? Listening is the forgotten stepchild in communication skills training. This is unfortunate, because the most glowing oration is a waste of time if it is not heard. Listening takes place at two steps in the communication process. First, the receiver must listen in order to decode and understand the original message. Then the sender becomes a listener when attempting to decode and understand subsequent feedback. Identical listening skills come into play at both ends.

We can hear and process information much more quickly than the normal speaker can talk. Consequently, listeners have some slack time, even though it may be only microseconds, during which they alternatively can daydream or analyze the information received and plan a response. Effective listeners know how to put that slack time to good use. Here are some practical tips for more effective listening.

- Tolerate silence. Listeners who rush to fill momentary silences cease being listeners.
- Ask stimulating open-ended questions, ones that require more than merely a yes or no answer.
- Encourage the speaker with attentive eye contact, alert posture, and verbal encouragers such as "um-hmm," "yes," and "I see." Occasionally repeating the speaker's last few words also helps.
- Paraphrase. Periodically restate in your own words what you have just heard.
- Reflect emotion and feelings to show that you are a sympathetic listener.
- Know your biases and prejudices and attempt to correct for them.
- Avoid premature judgments about what is being said.
- Summarize. Briefly highlight what the speaker has just finished saying to bring out possible misunderstandings.[30]

Effective Writing One of management's main complaints about today's college graduates is that they are poor writers. A survey of personnel executives revealed that recent graduates have considerable difficulty in four areas of writing.[31] Those areas are (1) being concise, (2) making meaning clear, (3) making the message accomplish its purpose, and (4) spelling (see Figure 10.7). These deficiencies in writing stem from an educational system that requires students to do less and less writing. Essay tests have given way in many classes to the multiple-choice variety, and formal term papers are being pushed aside by team activities and projects. As a learned skill, effective writing is the product of regular practice.[32] Students who do not get the necessary writing practice in school are handicapped when they step onto the managerial firing line.

Good writing is clearly part of the encoding step in the basic communication process. If it is done skillfully, potentially troublesome semantic and psychosocial barriers can be surmounted. Caterpillar Tractor Company's publications editor has offered four helpful reminders.

1. **Keep words simple.** Simplifying the words you use will help reduce your thoughts to essentials, keep your readers from being "turned off" by the complexity of your letter, memo, or report, and make it more understandable.

Figure 10.7   Managers' View on the Writing Ability of College Graduates

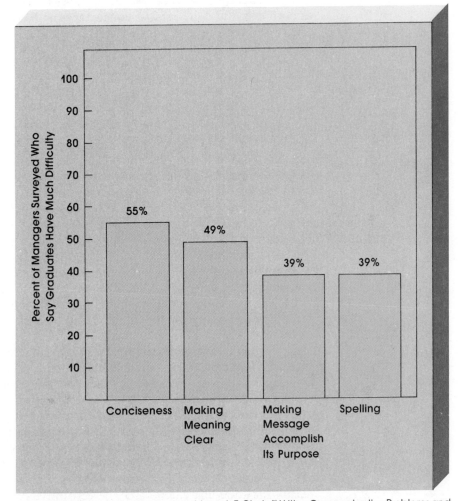

SOURCE: Data from Hilda F. Allred and Joseph F. Clark, "Written Communication Problems and Priorities," *Journal of Business Communication* 15 (Winter 1978): 32.

2. **Don't sacrifice communication for rules of composition.** ... Most of us who were sensitized to the rules of grammar and composition in our schools never quite recovered from the process. As proof, we keep trying to make our writing conform to rigid rules and custom without regard to style or the ultimate purpose of the communication. [Of course, managers need to be sensitive to the stylistic preferences of their bosses.]

3. **Write concisely.** This means express your thoughts, opinions, and ideas in the fewest number of words consistent with composition and smoothness. But don't confuse conciseness with brevity; you may write briefly without being clear or complete.
4. **Be specific.** Vagueness is one of the most serious flaws in written communication because it destroys accuracy and clarity, leaving the reader to wonder about your meaning or intent.[33]

Forewarned is forearmed, as the saying goes. The time to start a writing-improvement program is while you are still in school, not on your first day on the job. One staunch supporter of good writing offers the following advice to college students: "Be sure that every course you take requires written assignments and that grades will penalize bad writing."[34] Unfortunately, precisely the opposite is too often the case.

Running a Meeting

Meetings are an ever-present feature of modern organizational life. Whether they are convened to find facts, devise alternatives, or pass along information, meetings typically occupy a good deal of a manager's time. They are the principal format for committee action. Whatever the reason for a meeting, managers who chair meetings owe it to themselves and the organization to use everyone's time and talent efficiently. Some useful pointers for conducting successful meetings include:

1. **Make certain a meeting is necessary.** Don't call a meeting if the same result can be achieved by personal visit, memo, phone call, etc.
2. **Develop an agenda** and send it out in advance. The agenda should clearly indicate the item(s) to be covered, appropriate supporting materials, time and place of the meeting, approximate time the meeting will require, and some indication of what is expected in the way of participation from the members, e.g., to give advice or make a decision.
3. **Give careful consideration to those being invited to the meeting.** Invite only those people who need to attend. Inviting individuals who have no reason for attending can actually be disruptive or counterproductive, especially if they are vocal.
4. **Give the meeting your undivided attention.** Hold the meeting where distractions and interruptions can be held to a minimum.
5. **Be prepared.** There is no substitute for adequate preparation. Know what it is you want to accomplish and do your homework in such a way that all necessary information is available. Anticipate questions and issues that may arise.
6. If participation by members is important, be prepared to **ask the right questions to stimulate discussion.** Encourage everyone to get involved. Avoid questions which stifle discussion. Reserve personal opinions and judgments until later in the discussion; otherwise the members might

be unduly biased by your comments and fail to provide the type of input really desired. Don't allow one or a few members to monopolize the conversation.

7. **Keep to the agenda.** Encourage members to express themselves, but don't permit them to wander off the subject or waste time with long-winded dissertations.

8. **Conclude the meeting by summarizing the highlights,** including action to be taken as a result of the discussion. Follow up the meeting with a set of accurate and detailed minutes, distributing them to all present.[35,*]

With practice, these guidelines will become second nature. Running a meeting brings into focus all the components of the communication process, including coping with noise and barriers. Effective meetings are important to organizational communication and, ultimately, to organizational success.

Summary

Observational research indicates that managers at all levels spend the majority of their workday communicating. Communication is a social process involving the transfer of information and understanding. Links in the communication process include sender, encode, medium, decode, receiver, and feedback. Noise is any source of interference.

Perception is important to communication because it helps senders and receivers give meanings to environmental stimuli, including messages. Three perceptual subprocesses are selectivity, organization, and interpretation. Perceptual defense enables one to screen out irrelevant stimuli, and perceptual set does the opposite. Grouping, figure-ground, and closure help people perceptually organize otherwise meaningless stimuli. Specialists often interpret situations differently because of their restricted perspectives.

Four dynamics of organizational communication are structural considerations, the grapevine, nonverbal communication, and upward communication. Research suggests a trend toward greater centralization of the overall communication function. The unofficial and informal communication system that sometimes complements and sometimes disrupts the formal communication system has been labeled the grapevine. A sample of managers surveyed had predominantly negative feelings toward it. Recognizing that the grapevine cannot be extinguished, managers are advised to monitor it constructively. Nonverbal communication, including facial,

*From "Conducting a Successful Meeting," by Larry G. McDougle, copyright January 1981. Reprinted with permission of *Personnel Journal,* Costa Mesa, California; all rights reserved.

gestural, and postural body language, accounts for most of the impact of face-to-face communication. Managers can become more effective communicators by doing a better job of receiving and giving nonverbal communication. Upward communication can be stimulated by using formal grievance procedures, employee attitude and opinion surveys, suggestion boxes, an open-door policy, informal gripe sessions, task forces, and exit interviews.

Process, physical, semantic, and psychosocial barriers and sexist communication are common organizational communication problems. Awareness of the various barriers and a sincere effort to eliminate sexist language can improve communication effectiveness. Constructive steps also can be taken to become a better listener, writer, and meeting chairperson.

Terms to Understand

Communication	Perceptual organization
Noise	Grapevine
Perception	Body language
Selectivity	Upward communication
Perceptual defense	Semantics
Perceptual set	

Questions for Discussion

1. In your daily face-to-face communication, which link in the communication process tends to be the weakest? Why? What corrective action could you take?
2. What kinds of noise do you typically have problems with?
3. In what situations would perceptual set be a serious communication problem for a manager?
4. Can you explain the role of perception in a disagreement between you and friend, coworker, or relative?
5. Have you ever been victimized by the grapevine? Explain. What could have been done to prevent this?
6. Why is it important for managers to be well versed in body language?
7. What kind of process barriers can block the transfer of understanding in the classroom?
8. What forms of verbal or nonverbal sexist communication have you observed lately? Do you believe that the elimination of sexist com-

munication is a legitimate concern for managers? Explain your position.

9. In regard to any poor listening habits you may have, how can you become a better listener?

10. In your experience, what do people often do wrong when running a meeting? Give examples.

Back to the Opening Case

Now that you have read Chapter 10, you should be able to answer the following questions about the Tandem Computer case:

1. Is Treybig doing a good job of implementing his philosophy of open communication?

2. What are the relative advantages and disadvantages of Tandem's tele-conferences (meetings via satellite TV), as opposed to traditional face-to-face meetings?

3. How would you answer a manager who says: "Tandem's Friday afternoon 'popcorn parties' officially encourage employees to slack off and be disrespectful to top managers by telling them how to do their jobs. It would be more profitable for Tandem if everyone worked hard at his or her job right up until quitting time on Friday."

Closing Case 10.2

The Case of the Errant Messenger*

[*The following case study has been reported by Robert I. Stevens, a systems consultant and writer.*]

Whenever anyone on the executive floor wanted to tease Henry Reeves, they would ask him, "Are you sure you don't have any messages for me from the president?" Hank would become somewhat flustered and ignore the question. This by-play, which lasted for a year or so, was the result of the following incident—known by many, but not including the president.

The president of the company was a grizzled, dour army veteran who ran the operation as if he was still commanding a unit in the service. He made all major decisions and was almost always right in his judgment. I had seen him join a meeting of top staff just after a policy decision had been reached

*Reprinted by permission of the author.

and ask a few big questions that resulted in a complete reversal of the original decision. The only executive who contested the president, usually at meetings where the president was not present, was vice president James Dubler who was almost always wrong.

The president believed in "seeing what the troops were doing" and spent a good portion of his time visiting the many dispersed locations of the company. During these trips, whenever the president wanted to inform an officer of the company who was not present of a decision, request for information, or at times a reprimand, he would turn to a member of his traveling party and give him an oral message to deliver to the appropriate person. Usually, the selected messenger was Henry Reeves, a shy, introvertive recently hired MBA.

On one trip that I attended just before Reeves was hired, a situation developed that displeased the president. He turned to me and said "You tell Jim Dubler, he better get this problem corrected before it blows up in his face." Although I was only a senior analyst, it would never have occurred to me to question the president's order to deliver such a message to a vice president.

When I delivered the president's message to Mr. Dubler, he became very agitated and gave me the type of verbal thrashing that a vice president can give an analyst. I finally blurted out "Mr. Dubler, I'm only the messenger." He immediately calmed down and told me to leave.

From what we pieced together later, the first time Hank Reeves delivered a message to Mr. Dubler, he received the same type tongue lashing from Dubler without being able to withdraw from the confrontation. Evidently, the occasion so traumatized Reeves that when the president gave him other messages to be relayed to Dubler, he never delivered them. The situation of Reeves not delivering the president's messages to Dubler went on for several months without Reeves telling anyone about his problem. During that time, the president was heard to grumble about Dubler not reacting too fast to various situations.

Then one Friday afternoon the president asked Reeves to get Dubler to prepare a report over the week-end that he wanted on his desk Monday morning. Reeves again did not deliver the message. Monday morning, when the president arrived at his office and no report was present, he checked with his secretary if Dubler had left a message as to why he had not finished the report. He muttered to me (I had just entered his office as requested), "Well, this is the last straw." He then called the personnel officer on the phone and said "Fire Dubler. Give him whatever severance benefits you think he should have, but get him off the property—and I don't want him coming up to see me."

As in most corporations, such situations become common knowledge in short order—and that's why Reeves was asked occasionally if he had any messages to deliver from the president.

For Discussion

1. Who is primarily to blame for Dubler's unfortunate firing, the president, Reeves, or Dubler himself? Why?
2. Did the grapevine have a positive or negative impact in this case? Explain.
3. Considering what you now know about organizational communication, what advice would you give the president? Reeves? Dubler?

References

Opening Quotation: Laurence J. Peter, *Peter's Quotations* (New York: Bantam, 1977), p. 100.

Opening Case: For additional information on Tandem Computers, see Myron Magnet, "Managing by Mystique at Tandem Computers," *Fortune* 105 (June 28, 1982): 84–91; "An Acid Test for Tandem's Growth," *Business Week* No. 2779 (February 28, 1983): 64, 66; "Prime Time at Tandem," *Inc.* 5 (June 1983): 37–38; Robert Levering, Milton Moskowitz, and Michael Katz, *The 100 Best Companies to Work for in America* (Reading, Mass.: Addison-Wesley, 1984), pp. 330–332; and "James G. Treybig," *Industry Week* 223 (October 15, 1984): 50–51.

Closing Case: Robert I. Stevens, "The Case of the Errant Messenger," *Journal of Systems Management* 35 (July 1984): 42.

1. "Prime Time at Tandem," p. 38.
2. "James G. Treybig," p. 51.
3. For example, see Robert A. Snyder and James H. Morris, "Organizational Communication and Performance," *Journal of Applied Psychology* 69 (August 1984): 461–465.
4. For more details on this study, see John R. Hinrichs, "Communications Activity of Industrial Research Personnel," *Personnel Psychology* 17 (Summer 1964): 193–204.
5. David S. Brown, "Barriers to Successful Communication: Part I. Macrobarriers," *Management Review* 64 (December 1975): 28.
6. Keith Davis, *Human Behavior at Work: Organizational Behavior,* 6th ed. (New York: McGraw-Hill, 1981), p. 399.
7. A manager's view of the communication process may be found in Michael L. Peters, "How Important Is Interpersonal Communication?" *Personnel Journal* 62 (July 1983): 554–560.
8. Walter R. Nord, *Concepts and Controversy in Organizational Behavior,* 2nd ed. (Santa Monica: Goodyear, 1976), p. 22.
9. For an interesting report of this accident and its behavioral aspects, see "Spaniards Analyze Tenerife Accident," *Aviation Week & Space Technology* 109 (November 20, 1978): 113–121.

10. For a typical example of this research, see H. H. Kelley, "The Warm-Cold Variable in First Impressions of Persons," *Journal of Personality* 18 (1950): 431–439.

11. Frank Snowden Hopkins, "Communication: The Civilizing Force," *The Futurist* 15 (April 1981): 39.

12. See "Communications Patterns," *Management Review* 66 (August 1977): 4.

13. Keith Davis, "Grapevine Communication Among Lower and Middle Managers," *Personnel Journal* 48 (April 1969): 269.

14. For more extensive discussion, see Keith Davis, "Management Communication and the Grapevine," *Harvard Business Review* 31 (September-October 1953): 43–49.

15. Hugh B. Vickery III, "Tapping Into the Employee Grapevine," *Association Management* 36 (January 1984): 59–60.

16. John W. Newstrom, Robert E. Monczka, and William E. Reif, "Perceptions of the Grapevine: Its Value and Influence," *Journal of Business Communication* 11 (Spring 1974): 12–20.

17. See Roy Rowan, "Where Did *That* Rumor Come From?" *Fortune* 100 (August 13, 1979): 130–137.

18. "Executives Favor Plucking the Fruits From Employee Grapevine," *Association Management* 36 (April 1984): 105.

19. See Albert Mehrabian, "Communication Without Words," *Psychology Today* 2 (September 1968): 53–55.

20. This three-way breakdown comes from Dale G. Leathers, *Nonverbal Communication Systems* (Boston: Allyn & Bacon, 1976), chap. 2.

21. Michael B. McCaskey, "The Hidden Messages Managers Send," *Harvard Business Review* 57 (November-December 1979): 145.

22. See A. Keenan, "Effects of the Non-Verbal Behaviour of Interviewers on Candidates' Performance," *Journal of Occupational Psychology* 49, no. 3 (1976): 171–175.

23. For an instructive and interesting discussion of upward communication, see John B. McMaster, "Getting the Word to the Top," *Management Review* 68 (February 1979): 62–65.

24. "Trainers Gauge Organizational Communication," *Training* 21 (June 1984): 72.

25. See Mary P. Rowe and Michael Baker, "Are You Hearing Enough Employee Concerns?" *Harvard Business Review* 62 (May-June 1984): 127–135.

26. Practical tips on overcoming barriers to communication may be found in Paul R. Timm, "Driving Out the Devils of Communication," *Management World* 13 (July 1984): 27–29 and Cheryl L. McKenzie and Carol J. Qazi, "Communication Barriers in the Workplace," *Business Horizons* 26 (March-April 1983): 70–72.

27. For example, see Bobbye Persing, "Sticks and Stones *and* Words: Women in the Language," *Journal of Business Communication* 14 (Winter 1977): 11–19.

28. For a brief discussion of male-versus-female communication styles, see

Cynthia Berryman-Fink, "Changing Sex-Role Stereotypes," *Personnel Journal* 62 (June 1983): 502, 504.

29. Wendy Martyna, "What Does 'He' Mean? Use of the Generic Masculine," *Journal of Communication* 28 (Winter 1978): 138.

30. This list has been adapted from John F. Kikoski, "Communication: Understanding It, Improving It," *Personnel Journal* 59 (February 1980): 126–131; and John L. DiGaetani, "The Business of Listening," *Business Horizons* 23 (October 1980): 40–46.

31. See Hilda F. Allred and Joseph F. Clark, "Written Communication Problems and Priorities," *Journal of Business Communication* 15 (Winter 1978): 31–35.

32. Several instructive pointers for more readable writing may be found in Arn Tibbetts, "Ten Rules for Writing *Readably*," *Journal of Business Communication* 18 (Fall 1981): 53–62. Also see John S. Fielden and Ronald E. Dulek, "How to Use Bottom-Line Writing in Corporate Communications," *Business Horizons* 27 (July-August 1984): 24–30.

33. Robert F. DeGise, "Writing: Don't Let the Mechanics Obscure the Message," *Supervisory Management* 21 (April 1976): 26–28.

34. Richard Mitchell, "Let's Hear It for Good English," *Across the Board* 15 (May 1978): 4.

35. "Conducting a Successful Meeting," by Larry McDougle, copyright January 1981. Reprinted with permission from *Personnel Journal,* Costa Mesa, California; all rights reserved. Other practical tips on running a meeting may be found in Antony Jay, "How to Run a Meeting," *Harvard Business Review* 54 (March-April 1976): 43–57; Andrew S. Grove, "How (and Why) to Run a Meeting," *Fortune* 108 (July 11, 1983): 132–140; and Glenn W. Soden, "Avoid Meetings or Make Them Work," *Business Horizons* 27 (March-April 1984): 47–49.

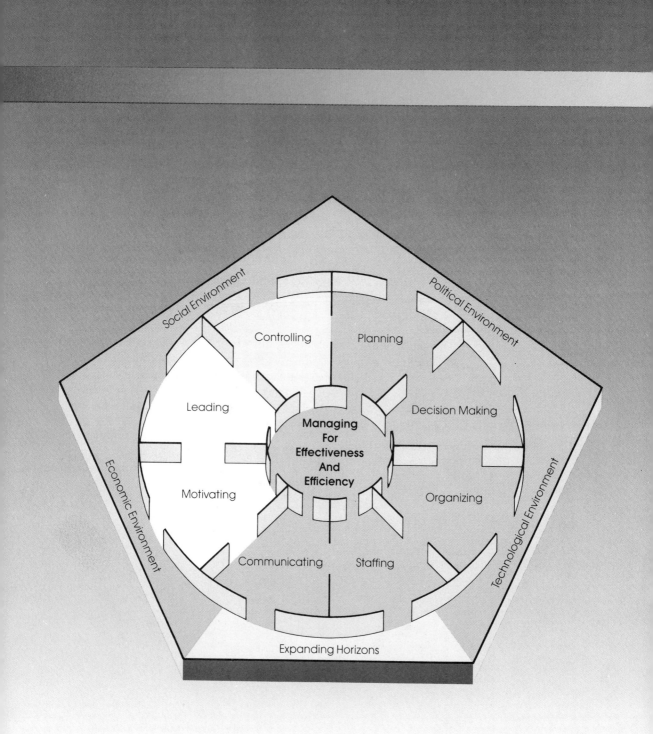

PART FOUR

Motivating and Leading

Part Four focuses on the process of getting individuals to contribute effectively and efficiently to organizational objectives. Like any other valuable resource, people can be used appropriately and to full capacity, or they can be wastefully depleted. In Chapter 11, a basic introduction to motivation theory is used as a springboard for a discussion of rewards and quality-of-work-life-innovations such as participative management. Important group dynamics including trust, organizational politics, conformity, and conflict are explored in Chapter 12 because management is essentially a social process. Chapter 13 examines how managers can more effectively influence employees through power, leadership, and behavior modification. And in Chapter 14, the problem of overcoming resistance to change is discussed within the context of organization development, a systematic approach to planned change.

Chapter 11

Motivating Job Performance

There are no simple, cookbook formulas for working with people.
Keith Davis

Chapter Objectives

When you finish studying this chapter, you should be able to

- Discuss the faulty assumptions that managers often make about what employees want from their jobs.
- Explain the motivational lessons taught by Maslow's theory, Herzberg's theory, and expectancy theory.
- Explain how job enrichment can be used to enhance the motivating potential of jobs.
- Distinguish extrinsic rewards from intrinsic rewards and list four rules for administering extrinsic rewards effectively.
- Identify three quality-of-work-life innovations and discuss how they can improve work motivation.

Opening Case 11.1

Westinghouse Goes Japanese

Heading into the 1980s, Westinghouse Electric Corporation's top management team in Pittsburgh was primed and ready for new ideas to improve the firm's performance. The 1970s had been rough years for Westinghouse. Problems during that period included a highly publicized bribery case, a string of unprofitable acquisitions, and a great loss on the sale of its consumer appliances business. Additionally, rising uranium prices threatened to saddle Westinghouse with a nearly $1 billion debt because the company had signed fixed-price contracts to supply its nuclear reactor customers with uranium.

Finally, like many U.S. companies, Westinghouse was facing a stiff challenge from the Japanese. The challenge was answered in 1979 when an *ad hoc* executive committee was given $20 million to explore alternative ways to increase productivity. *Fortune* magazine quoted the head of this committee in regard to what had to be done: "... we had better concentrate on things we can influence. We are going to have to do more with less—fewer people, less money, less time, less space, fewer resources in general—and I think that's probably a pretty good definition of productivity."[1]

A Cultural Revolution in the Construction Group

Among the promising productivity enhancement strategies identified by the *ad hoc* committee was William Ouchi's Theory Z participative management. Ouchi, an American management professor familiar with the Japanese style of management, formulated his so-called Theory Z to demonstrate how proven Japanese participative management techniques could be successfully interwoven with prevailing American management practices. After consulting with Ouchi, top management decided to experiment with a modified version of Japanese management in the construction group. Westinghouse's construction group, which produced such products as elevators, heating and cooling systems, and rapid-transit equipment, represented about 7 percent of the firm's work force. According to *Fortune* magazine, Westinghouse's adoption of participative management was indeed revolutionary: "... to see it [participative management] seep into a hierarchical old industrial company like Westinghouse, with its established chain of command and staff of tradition-minded engineers, is a bit like watching the U.S. Marines parade in blue jeans, long-haired and unshaven."[2]

Participative management was introduced to the construction group with the help of dozens of outside consultants who conducted seminars and gave lectures on team building and sensitivity training. Selected employees were trained to be "facilitators" (team leaders) for participative councils and committees made up of employees from all levels, not just management. Westinghouse believed that it too, like its Japanese competitors, could build trust, tap creativity, generate motivation, and improve productivity through teamwork.

Turning Adversaries into Team Players

Eventually, the influence of greater participation in the construction group began to be felt. Instead of simply issuing orders, managers became accustomed to discussing pending decisions with their people in order to achieve consensus. For example, the usual practice for allocating capital among the various construction group units was to have each unit manager submit his or her request for funds to the group head who would then decide which units would get what. After Theory Z participative management had been installed, all the unit managers got together to discuss their capital needs. Unit managers subsequently abandoned the usual practice of blindly defending their own needs without regard for the needs of the overall construction group. They discovered they were part of a team, whereas before they had acted as adversaries. Workable funding tradeoffs were achieved through give-and-take discussion ending in consensus on capital funding. Some of the unit managers willingly accepted cuts in their areas when they realized that in the long run such a move would help the group. Formerly, the group head had to resort to forcing any funding cuts on resentful unit managers.

Mistakes, Lessons, and Benefits

Westinghouse had started out on the wrong foot by trying to install participative management from the shop floor up. Ouchi persuaded the firm to switch to a top-to-bottom approach because there was little chance that lower-level participation would work if top management did not believe in and actually practice participation.

One of the important lessons that Westinghouse learned from the construction group experiment was that managers must learn when to step back and let the forces of participation work and when to step in and take decisive action. Some of the participation teams floundered in disagreement or became sidetracked on irrelevant issues. Line managers occasionally had to give their teams a nonauthoritarian nudge to point them in a productive direction. Another valuable lesson learned was that participation takes up a lot of time. But, as the group head observed, the early investment of time paid off later: "We spend a lot of time trying to get consensus, but once you get it, the implementation is instantaneous. We don't have to fight any negative feelings."[3] A third lesson was that some middle- and lower-level managers felt threatened by a perceived loss of power.

Although Westinghouse recognized that the full benefits of its experiment with participative management would take up to ten years to unfold, shorter-term benefits were realized in the form of lower grievance and absenteeism rates and higher productivity.

(Discussion questions linking this case with the material you are about to read can be found at the end of this chapter.)

Westinghouse's experiment in participative management highlights one of the key aspects of the management process, *working with and through others* to achieve organizational objectives. It stands to reason that the better a manager understands people and the way they act on the job, the greater will be his or her chances of success. But as we all know, people are not always easy to understand. For example, we often hear people complaining about having to work so hard. They would gladly opt for a two-hour workday. Curiously, this is how a staff writer for a publishing company reacted to just such an opportunity:

> I have my own office. I have a secretary. If I want a book case, I get a book case. If I want a file, I get a file. If I want to stay home, I stay home. If I want to go shopping, I go shopping. This is the first comfortable job I've ever had in my life and it is absolutely despicable.[4]

If you were this individual's manager, you would probably scratch your head and say, "This doesn't make any sense. I can't figure this person out." At first glance, perhaps this behavior does not make any sense. But after becoming acquainted with the various motivation theories and techniques discussed in this chapter, a number of reasonable explanations will become apparent.

Motivation: An Overview

Managers and management scholars alike have long been intrigued by the fact that some employees consistently work harder than others who are equally talented and qualified. The study of motivation helps managers understand this kind of variance in performance. More importantly, a working knowledge of what motivates people enables managers to take constructive steps to improve their employees' job performance.

The term *motivation* derives from the Latin word *movere,* meaning "to move." It is virtually impossible to determine a person's motivation until that person behaves or literally moves. By observing what someone says or does in a given situation, one can draw reasonable inferences about his or her underlying motivation. As it is used here, the term **motivation** refers to the psychological process that gives behavior purpose and direction.[5] By appealing to this psychological process, managers attempt to get individuals to willingly pursue organizational objectives. Motivation theories are generalizations about the "what" and "how" of purposive behavior.[6]

Before describing specific motivation theories and related applications, we shall examine three important background factors. First, motivation occurs amid complexity, not in isolation. Second, managers often make faulty assumptions about what employees want from their jobs. Third, social change is eroding the usefulness of traditional motivational tools.

Only One Piece of the Performance Puzzle

Human behavior is immensely complicated. This is due to internal psychological processes that we do not fully understand and to external influences that have uncertain impact. One expert on the subject has put job motivation into proper perspective by noting:

> Obviously, other factors besides motivation affect performance. The individual worker's job skills and knowledge, health, emotional state, and other personal factors bear on today's performance and tomorrow's growth potential. Also involved are the many factors of management and organization that are used to promote organizational predictability: equipment and facilities, job designs, organizational structure, policies and procedures, managerial style, and other such matters. It is important for the manager to realize that these factors which bear directly on performance also affect the individual worker's motivational state and may thus have a double impact on performance.[7]

Motivation is simply one of many explanations of human behavior, in general, and of job performance, in particular.

Faulty Assumptions About Employee Needs

Managers often are tempted to make highly subjective assumptions about what their subordinates want from their jobs. Consequently, motivational programs often miss the mark. A study of over 200 employees and their supervisors documented a significant perceptual mismatch in this area.[8] In this study, subordinates were asked to rank their personal preferences among ten job factors that had motivational appeal. Their supervisors were then asked to rank the same items as they believed their subordinates would. The idea was to determine how accurately the supervisors perceived the needs of their subordinates.

As shown in Table 11.1, "interesting work" ended up with the highest average ranking among the subordinate respondents. "Full appreciation of work done" and "feeling of being in on things" came in second and third, respectively. But for the supervisors' responses, there was a very different ranking. "Good wages," although ranked only fifth by the subordinates, was ranked highest by the supervisors. "Job security" and "promotion and growth in the organization" were ranked second and third by the supervisors (but fourth and sixth, respectively, by the subordinates). It is significant that the subordinates' top three choices were ranked fifth, eighth, and tenth by their supervisors.

Because the rankings in this study reflect statistical means, one should take care not to assume a strict uniformity of opinion among each of the two groups. Not every employee values interesting work more than job security and good wages, for example. Nonetheless, the results indicate that the supervisors, on the average, seriously misjudged what their subordinates wanted from their jobs. Thus, it behooves managers to go beyond

Table 11.1 Managerial Misperception of Employee Wants

Employee Ranking	What People Want from Their Work	Supervisor Ranking
1	Interesting work	5
2	Full appreciation of work done	8
3	Feeling of being in on things	10
4	Job security	2
5	Good wages	1
6	Promotion and growth in the organization	3
7	Good working conditions	4
8	Personal loyalty to employees	7
9	Sympathetic help with personal problems	9
10	Tactful discipline	6

SOURCE: Reprinted, by permission of the publisher, from "Why Motivational Theories Don't Work," by Kenneth A. Kovach, *SAM, Advanced Management Journal,* Spring 1980, © 1980 by Society for Advancement of Management, p. 57. All rights reserved.

simple common sense when attempting to motivate job performance. Regarding this point, Philip Caldwell, the former head of Ford Motor Company, summed it up nicely when he said recently: "Although there is a place for the 'seat of the pants' manager, many only end up with shiny suits."[9]

Times Have Changed

As we discussed in Chapter 3 in reference to changing attitudes toward work, leisure is gradually pushing aside work as life's focal point for a growing number of today's employees. Again, being careful not to paint all employees with the same descriptive brush, traditional motivational tools for getting people to work harder are diminishing in effectiveness in some quarters. Respected pollster and social commentator Daniel Yankelovich made the following observation:

> I can sum up what is happening in the American workforce today in a single phrase: a growing mismatch between incentives and motivations. The incentive system does not work as well as it used to. Formerly, management had the tools for motivating people adequately enough to insure ever-increasing productivity. This is no longer true. People's values and attitudes have changed faster than the incentive system—creating a mismatch.[10]

As Yankelovich sees it, the four traditional motivation tools—fear of unemployment, strict supervision, money, and reliance on the work ethic—are inappropriate for nearly half (44 percent) of the work force (see Figure 11.1). In regard to money, Yankelovich asserted, "The desire for

Figure 11.1   Different Incentives Appeal to Different People

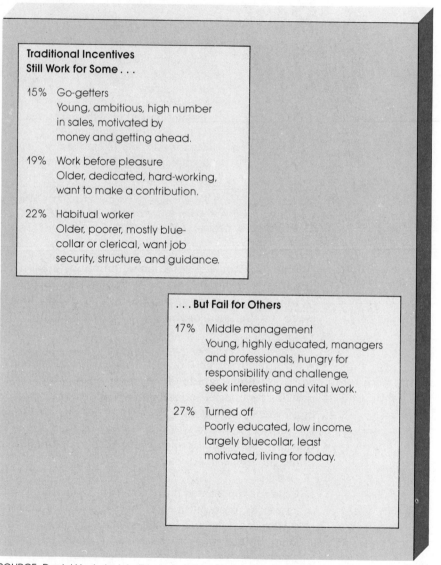

**Traditional Incentives
Still Work for Some . . .**

15%   Go-getters
Young, ambitious, high number
in sales, motivated by
money and getting ahead.

19%   Work before pleasure
Older, dedicated, hard-working,
want to make a contribution.

22%   Habitual worker
Older, poorer, mostly blue-
collar or clerical, want job
security, structure, and guidance.

. . . But Fail for Others

17%   Middle management
Young, highly educated, managers
and professionals, hungry for
responsibility and challenge,
seek interesting and vital work.

27%   Turned off
Poorly educated, low income,
largely bluecollar, least
motivated, living for today.

SOURCE: Daniel Yankelovich, "Yankelovich on Today's Workers: We Need New Motivational Tools," *Industry Week* 202 (August 6, 1979): 63.

more money does not necessarily mean that those who get it are going to work any harder, and yet money continues to be thought of as an incentive for making people work harder."[11]

Among the new incentives that Yankelovich recommends to replace inoperative traditional ones are flexible work schedules, opportunities to develop one's mind and body, personalized feedback mechanisms, broader distribution of symbolic amenities and privileges, integration of lifestyle and workstyle, and job enrichment. We shall consider a number of these promising alternatives.

Motivation Theories

Although there are dozens of different theories of motivation, three have emerged as the most popular: Maslow's needs hierarchy theory, Herzberg's two-factor theory, and expectancy theory. Each theory approaches the motivation process from a different angle, each has supporters and detractors, and each teaches important lessons about the motivation to work.

Maslow's Needs Hierarchy Theory   In 1943, a psychologist by the name of Abraham Maslow proposed that people are motivated by a predictable five-step hierarchy of needs.[12] Little did he realize at the time that his tentative proposal, based on an extremely limited clinical study of neurotic patients, would become one of the most influential concepts in the field of management.[13] Perhaps it is because Maslow's theory is so straightforward and intuitively appealing that it has so strongly influenced those interested in work behavior. Maslow's message was simply this: people always have needs, and when one need is relatively fulfilled, others emerge in a predictable sequence to take its place. From bottom to top, Maslow's need hierarchy includes physiological, safety, love, esteem, and self-actualization needs (see Figure 11.2). According to Maslow, most individuals are not consciously aware of these needs; yet we all supposedly proceed up the hierarchy of needs, one level at a time.

Physiological Needs   At the bottom of the needs hierarchy are physical drives. These include the need for food, water, sleep, and sex. Fulfillment of these lowest-level needs enables the individual to survive, and nothing else is important when these bodily needs have not been satisfied. As Maslow observed, "It is quite true that man lives by bread alone—when there is no bread."[14] But today the average employee experiences little serious deprivation of physiological needs. Figuratively speaking, the prospect of eating more bread is not motivating when one has plenty of bread to eat.

Safety Needs   Maslow's theory contends that once our basic physiological needs are relatively well satisfied, we next become concerned

Figure 11.2 Maslow's Hierarchy of Needs Theory

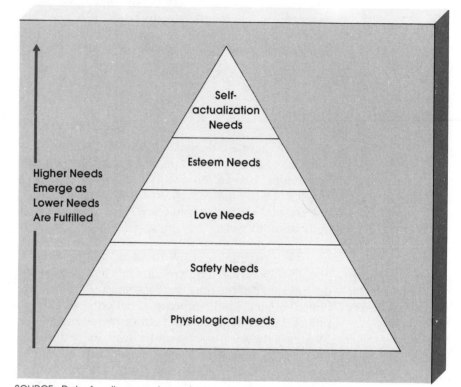

SOURCE: Data for diagram drawn from A. H. Maslow, "A Theory of Human Motivation," *Psychological Review* 50 (July 1943): 370–396.

about our safety from the elements, enemies, and other threats. Most modern employees achieve a high degree of fulfillment in this area by earning a living or collecting unemployment assistance if necessary. According to Maslow, prolonged deprivation of physiological and safety needs will create a seriously maladjusted individual.

Love Needs A physiologically satisfied and secure person focuses next on satisfying needs for love and affection. This category of needs is a powerful motivator of human behavior. People typically strive hard to achieve a sense of belonging with others. As with the first two levels of needs, relative satisfaction of love needs paves the way for the emergence of the next higher level.

Esteem Needs People who perceive themselves as worthwhile individuals are said to possess high self-esteem. Self-respect is the key to esteem needs. Much of our self-respect and hence esteem comes from being accepted and respected by others. It is important for those who are expected to help achieve organizational objectives to have their esteem needs relatively well fulfilled. But according to Maslow's theory, esteem needs cannot emerge if lower-level needs go unattended.

Self-actualization Needs   At the top of Maslow's hierarchy is an open-ended category that he labeled *self-actualization needs*. It is open-ended because it relates to the need "to become more and more what one is, to become everything that one is capable of becoming."[15] One may self-actualize by striving to become a better homemaker, a better plumber, a better rock singer, or a better manager. According to one management writer, the self-actualizing manager possesses the following characteristics:

1. Has warmth, closeness, and sympathy.
2. Recognizes and shares negative information and feelings.
3. Exhibits trust, openness, and candor.
4. Does not achieve goals by power, deception, or manipulation.
5. Does not project own feelings, motivations, or blame onto others.
6. Does not limit horizons; uses and develops body, mind, and senses.
7. Is not rationalistic; can think in unconventional ways.
8. Is not conforming; regulates behavior from within.[16]

Granted, this is a rather tall order to fill. It has been pointed out that "a truly self-actualized individual is more of an exception than the rule in the organizational context."[17] Whether or not productive organizations need more self-actualized individuals is subject to debate. On the positive side, self-actualized employees might help break down the barriers to creativity and steer the organization in exciting new directions. On the negative side, too many unconventional nonconformists could wreak havoc with the typical administrative setup dedicated to predictability.

Relevance of Maslow's Theory for Managers   Behavioral scientists who have attempted to test Maslow's theory in real life claim that it has some deficiencies.[18] Even Maslow's hierarchical arrangement has been questioned. Practical evidence points toward a two-level rather than a five-level hierarchy. In this competing view, the physiological and safety needs are arranged in hierarchical fashion, as Maslow's theory contends. But beyond that point, any one of a number of needs may emerge as the single most important one, depending on the particular individual. Edward Lawler, a leading motivation researcher, has observed, "Which higher-order needs come into play after the lower ones are satisfied and in which order they come into play cannot be predicted. If anything, it seems that most people are simultaneously motivated by several of the same-level needs."[19]

Although Maslow's theory has not stood up well under actual testing, it teaches managers one important lesson: a fulfilled need does not motivate an individual. For example, the promise of unemployment benefits may partially fulfill an employee's need for economic security (safety need). But the chances are that the added security of additional unemployment benefits will not motivate fully employed individuals to work any harder. Effective managers try to accurately anticipate each employee's personal need profile and provide opportunities to fulfill emerging needs. Realizing that challenging and worthwhile jobs and meaningful recognition tend to enhance self-esteem, the esteem level presents managers with the greatest opportunity to motivate better performance.

Herzberg's Two-Factor Theory

During the 1950s, Frederick Herzberg proposed a theory of employee motivation based on satisfaction.[20] His theory implied that a satisfied employee is motivated from within to work harder and that a dissatisfied employee is not self-motivated. Herzberg's research uncovered two classes of factors associated with employee satisfaction and dissatisfaction (see Table 11.2), and so his concept has come to be called Herzberg's two-factor theory.

Dissatisfiers and Satisfiers   Herzberg composed his list of dissatisfiers by asking a sample of about 200 accountants and engineers to describe job situations in which they felt exceptionally bad about their jobs. An analysis of their responses revealed a consistent pattern. Dissatisfaction tended to be associated with complaints about the job context or factors in the immediate work environment.

Herzberg then drew up his list of satisfiers, factors responsible for self-motivation, by asking the same accountants and engineers to describe job situations in which they had felt exceptionally good about their jobs. Again, a consistent pattern of response was noted, but this time, different factors were described. The opportunity to experience achievement, receive recognition, work on an interesting job, take responsibility, and experience advancement and growth were mentioned. Herzberg observed that these satisfiers centered on the nature of the task itself. In other words, employees appeared to be motivated by job content, that is, what they actually did all day long. Consequently, Herzberg concluded that enriched jobs were the key to self-motivation. In other words, the work itself, rather than pay, supervision, or other environmental factors, was the key to satisfaction and hence motivation.

Practical Lessons from Herzberg's Theory   By insisting that satisfaction is not the opposite of dissatisfaction, Herzberg encouraged managers to

Table 11.2 Herzberg's Two-Factor Theory of Motivation

Dissatisfiers: Factors Mentioned Most Often by Dissatisfied Employees	Satisfiers: Factors Mentioned Most Often by Satisfied Employees
1. Company policy and administration	1. Achievement
2. Supervision	2. Recognition
3. Relationship with supervisor	3. Work itself
4. Work conditions	4. Responsibility
5. Salary	5. Advancement
6. Relationship with peers	6. Growth
7. Personal life	
8. Relationship with subordinates	
9. Status	
10. Security	

SOURCE: Reprinted by permission of the *Harvard Business Review.* An exhibit from "One More Time: How Do You Motivate Employees?" by Frederick Herzberg (January-February 1968) copyright © 1968 by the President and Fellows of Harvard College; all rights reserved.

think carefully about what actually motivates employees. According to Herzberg, "the opposite of job satisfaction is not job dissatisfaction but, rather *no* job satisfaction; and similarly, the opposite of job dissatisfaction is not job satisfaction, but *no* dissatisfaction."[21] Rather, the dissatisfaction-satisfaction continuum contains a zero midpoint at which there is a lack of both dissatisfaction and satisfaction. An employee stuck on this midpoint, though not dissatisfied with pay and working conditions, is not particularly motivated to work hard because the job itself lacks challenge. Herzberg believes that the most that managers can hope for when attempting to motivate employees with pay, status, working conditions, and other contextual factors is to reach the zero midpoint. But the elimination of dissatisfaction, according to Herzberg, is not the same as truly motivating someone. An additional step is required. He feels that it takes meaningful, interesting, and challenging work to satisfy and motivate employees. Herzberg is convinced that money is a weak motivational tool because the best it can do is eliminate dissatisfaction.

Like Maslow, Herzberg has triggered lively debate among motivation theorists. His assumption that job performance improves as satisfaction increases has been criticized for having a weak empirical basis. For example, one researcher, after reviewing 20 studies that tested this particular notion, concluded that the relationship, though positive, was too weak to have any theoretical or practical significance.[22] Others have found that one person's dissatisfier may be another's satisfier (for example, money).[23] Nonetheless, Herzberg has made a useful contribution to motivation theory by emphasizing the motivating potential of enriched work. (Job enrichment is discussed in detail in the next section.)

Expectancy Theory

Both Maslow's and Herzberg's motivation theories have been criticized for making unsubstantiated generalizations about what motivates people. Practical experience tells us that the same people are motivated by different things at different times and that different people are motivated by different things at the same time. Fortunately, expectancy theory, which is based largely on Victor H. Vroom's 1964 classic, *Work and Motivation,* effectively deals with the highly personalized rational choices that individuals make when faced with the prospect of having to work to achieve rewards. Individual perception, though secondary in the Maslow and Herzberg models, is central to expectancy theory. Accordingly, **expectancy theory** is a motivation model based on the assumption that motivational strength is determined by perceived probabilities of success. The term **expectancy,** as it is used here, refers to the subjective probability that one thing will lead to another. Work-related expectancies, like all other expectancies, are shaped by ongoing personal experience. For instance, an employee's expectation for a raise, diminished after being turned down, later rebounds when the supervisor indicates a willingness to reconsider the matter.

A Basic Expectancy Model Although Vroom and other expectancy theorists have developed their models in somewhat complex mathematical terms, the descriptive model in Figure 11.3 is helpful for basic understanding. According to this model, one's motivational strength increases as one's perceived effort-performance and performance-reward probabilities increase. All this is not as complicated as it sounds. For example, how strong would be your motivation to study if you expected to do poorly on a quiz no matter how hard you studied (low effort-performance probability) and you knew that the quiz would not be graded (low performance-reward probability)? On the other hand, your motivation to study would increase if you believed that you could do well on the quiz with minimal study (high effort-performance probability) and that by doing well on the quiz your course grade would significantly improve (high performance-reward probability). Employees, like students, are motivated to expend effort when they believe it will ultimately lead to personally valued rewards. This expectancy approach not only appeals strongly to common sense; it has also received encouraging empirical support from researchers.[24]

Relevance of Expectancy Theory for Managers Assuming that employee contributions are dictated by their expectancies, managers can take constructive steps to foster favorable expectations among employees. People will work long and hard when they believe that they stand a good chance of successfully completing the job and subsequently receiving personally

Figure 11.3 A Basic Expectancy Model

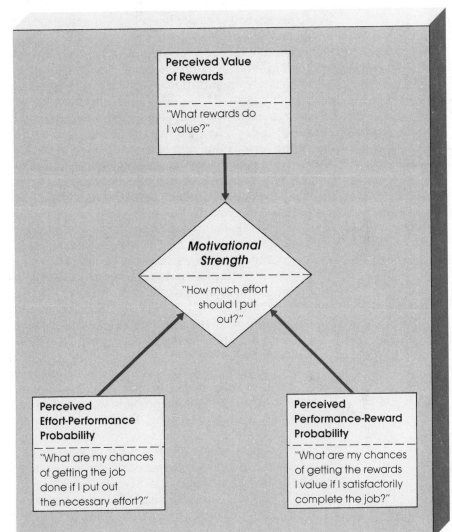

valued rewards. Managers with polished listening skills can readily discover what particular rewards specific individuals value. A combination of training and challenging yet attainable objectives can serve to increase an employee's chances of successfully completing the job. Guided experience is an excellent teacher and developer of favorable expectations.

Motivation Through Job Design

A job serves two separate but related functions. It is a productive unit for the organization and a career unit for the individual. Thus **job design,** the delineation of task responsibilities as dictated by organizational strategy, technology, and structure, is a key determinant of individual motivation and ultimately organizational success. Considering that the average adult spends about half of his or her waking life at work, jobs are a central feature of modern existence. A challenging and interesting job can add zest and meaning to one's life. Boring and tedious jobs, on the other hand, can become a serious threat to one's motivation to work hard, not to mention the effect on one's physical and mental health. Concern about uneven productivity growth, eroded product quality, and declining employee satisfaction have persuaded managers to take a fresh look at job design.

Specialization of Labor: A Dilemma

Frederick W. Taylor's scientific management movement created an undying faith in the notion that increased specialization of labor was the key to greater productivity. Work that was divided and subdivided enabled relatively unskilled employees to achieve record levels of output. Less waste and more predictable performance also resulted. As the years went by, employees in factories and offices performed steadily more fragmented and repetitive jobs. In recent years, however, the practice of creating ever more specialized jobs has been challenged. The basis of this challenge is the "human factor."

Costly tardiness, absenteeism, grievances, turnover, strikes, and even sabotage eventually began to offset the traditional economies of specialization. These behavioral problems are emotional reactions to tedious, boring, and monotonous jobs. Per-unit cost of production declines as specialization increases, but only to a point. As plotted in Figure 11.4, excessive specialization of labor eventually drives up unit costs. The point at which behavioral problems such as the absenteeism and turnover caused by overspecialized jobs drive up the cost of producing each unit of output is called the **boredom and alienation barrier.**

There are two basic motivational strategies for coping with overspecialized jobs.[25] One, managers can fit the individual to the job. Two, the job can be fit to the individual. We now examine each of these motivational strategies.

Strategy One: Fitting People to Jobs

For technological or economic reasons, management is sometimes locked into relying on highly specialized jobs. Nevertheless, some constructive steps can be taken to avoid chronic dissatisfaction and bolster motivation. Three alternatives with proven track records include realistic job previews, job rotation, and limited exposure. Each alternative involves adjusting the

Figure 11.4   The Relationship Between Specialization of Labor and Unit Cost

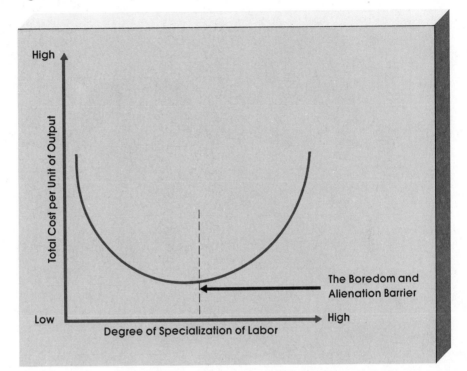

person rather than the job in the person-job match. Hence each entails creating a more compatible fit between the individual and a highly specialized or fragmented job. (In line with this is the use of mentally handicapped workers, often in sheltered workshops.)

Realistic Job Previews   Unrealized expectations are a major cause of job dissatisfaction and low motivation. Managers commonly create unrealistically high expectations in recruits to entice them to accept a position. This circumstance has proved particularly troublesome with regard to routine tasks. Dissatisfaction too often sets in when lofty expectations are brought down to earth by dull or tedious work. **Realistic job previews,** honest explanations of what a job actually entails, have been useful in this area. On-the-job research has demonstrated the practical value of giving a realistic preview of both positive and negative aspects to applicants for highly specialized jobs. For example, telephone operators who saw a realistic job preview film before being hired had fewer thoughts of resigning and in fact accounted for fewer resignations than did a similar group of operators who viewed a traditional "good news only" recruiting film.[26]

SOURCE: © Leo Cullum, 1985.

Though the evidence is clear that realistic job previews can reduce turn-over, their ability to improve job performance has been implied but not conclusively proved.[27]

Job Rotation   As the term is used here, **job rotation** is periodically moving people from one specialized job to another. Doing this prevents stagnation. If highly specialized jobs are unavoidable, then job rotation can help neutralize the boredom and alienation barrier discussed earlier by introducing a modest degree of novelty. Of course, a balance needs to be achieved between rotating people often enough to fight boredom but not so often that they feel unfairly manipulated or disoriented.

Limited Exposure   Still another way of coping with a highly fragmented and tedious job is to limit the individual's exposure to it. A number of organizations have achieved high productivity among routine-task personnel by allowing them to earn an early quitting time.[28] This technique, called **contingent time off** (CTO), involves establishing a challenging yet fair daily performance standard or quota, and letting employees go home when it is reached. The following CTO plan was implemented at a large manufacturing plant where the employees were producing about 160 units a day with 10 percent rejects:

> ... if the group produced at 200 units with three additional good units for each defective unit, then they could leave the work site for the rest of the day. Within a week of implementing this CTO intervention, the group was producing 200+ units with an average of 1.5 percent rejects. These employees, who had formerly *put in* an 8-hour day, were now *working* an average of 6½ hours per day and, importantly, they increased their performance by 25 percent.[29]

Some employees find the opportunity to earn eight hours worth of pay for six hours of steady effort extremely motivating.

Strategy Two: Fitting Jobs to People   This second job design strategy calls for managers to consider changing jobs instead of people. Two job redesign experts have proposed that managers address the question, "How can we achieve a fit between persons and their jobs that fosters *both* high work productivity and a high-quality organizational experience for the people who do the work?"[30] Two techniques for moving in this direction are job enlargement and job enrichment.

Job Enlargement   As the term is used here, **job enlargement** is the process of combining two or more specialized tasks in a work flow sequence into a single job. For example, a clerk in an insurance claims department who normally types only the client's name and address on the claim form may be asked to type in the claim description and disposition as well. A moderate degree of complexity and novelty can be introduced in this manner. But critics claim that two or more potentially boring tasks do not necessarily make a challenging job. Also, organized labor has criticized job enlargement as a devious ploy for getting more work for the same amount of money. But if pay and performance are kept in balance, the boredom and alienation barrier can be pushed aside a bit by job enlargement.

Job Enrichment   In general terms, **job enrichment** is redesigning a job to increase its motivating potential. Job enrichment increases the challenge of one's work by reversing the trend toward greater specialization. Unlike job enlargement, which merely combines equally simple tasks, job enrichment builds more complexity and depth into jobs by introducing planning and decision-making responsibility normally carried out at higher levels (see Table 11.3). Thus, enriched jobs are *vertically* loaded, whereas enlarged jobs are *horizontally* loaded.

According to experts in the field, jobs can be enriched by upgrading five core dimensions of work: (1) skill variety, (2) task identity, (3) task signifi-

Table 11.3 A Workable Combination of Job Rotation and Job Enrichment at General Motors' Packard Electric Division

In a sense, Antoinette Smith and Dominick P. Peters are their own bosses. They are part of a 22-member team that operates a "self-managed" assembly line at Packard Electric's Austintown (Ohio) plant. To avoid the tedium of working at the same station day after day, workers rotate line jobs and—most important—get to work off the line several times a month to handle material and repairs. The team members also perform many of the foreman's functions: setting the line speed, ordering material, establishing rules for handling disputes, checking quality, and doing paperwork. Each day a different worker serves as the "coordinator," the person who makes decisions.

"It's the whole atmosphere that I like," Smith says. "There's not a lot of tension, your mind is exercised, and we all try to keep the department working well." Peters, 33, likes working on the line because "it gives you a feeling of authority." He thinks workers today want more responsibility on the job. "People are finding that you have to bend and stretch a little to keep your job," he says. "If we aren't productive, there's nothing to stop the company from sending 3000 jobs to Mexico."

SOURCE: Reprinted from the August 29, 1983 issue of *Business Week* by special permission, © 1983 by McGraw-Hill, Inc.

cance, (4) autonomy, and (5) job feedback. Each of these core dimensions deserves a closer look.

- **Skill variety.** The degree to which a job requires a variety of different activities in carrying out the work, involving the use of a number of different skills and talents of the person.
- **Task identity.** The degree to which a job requires completion of a "whole" and identifiable piece of work, that is, doing a job from beginning to end with a visible outcome.
- **Task significance.** The degree to which the job has a substantial impact on the lives of other people, whether those people are in the immediate organization or in the world at large.
- **Autonomy.** The degree to which the job provides substantial freedom, independence, and discretion to the individual in scheduling the work and in determining the procedures to be used in carrying it out.
- **Job feedback.** The degree to which carrying out the work activities required by the job provides the individual with direct and clear information about the effectiveness of his or her performance.[31]

Figure 11.5 shows the theoretical connection between enriched core job dimensions and high motivation and satisfaction. At the heart of this job enrichment model are three psychological needs that highly specialized

Figure 11.5 How Job Enrichment Works

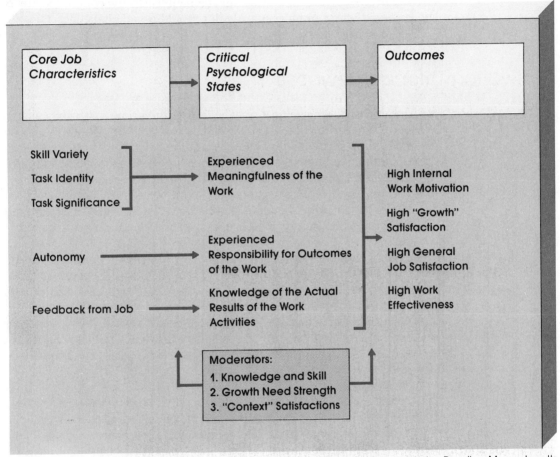

SOURCE: J. Richard Hackman and Greg R. Oldham, *Work Redesign*, © 1980, Addison-Wesley, Reading, Massachusetts.
P. 90, Fig. 4.6. Reprinted with permission.

jobs usually do not satisfy. These are meaningfulness, responsibility, and knowledge of results.

It is important to note that not all employees will respond favorably to enriched jobs. Personal traits and motives influence the connection between core job characteristics and desired outcomes. Only those with the necessary knowledge and skills plus a desire for personal growth will be motivated by enriched work.[32] Furthermore, as we learned from Herzberg's two-factor theory, dissatisfaction with factors such as pay, physical working conditions, or supervision can neutralize enrichment efforts. Researchers have reported that fear of failure, lack of confidence, and lack of trust in management's intentions can stand in the way of effective job enrichment.[33] But job enrichment can and does work when it is carefully thought out, when management is firmly committed to its success, and when employees truly desire additional challenge.

Motivation Through Rewards

All workers, including volunteers who donate their time to worthy causes, expect to be rewarded in some way for their contributions. **Rewards** may be defined broadly as the material and psychological payoffs for doing something. These payoffs can have an immense impact on how long and hard someone works. A person who is pleased with the consequences of work is likely to put forth more effort than someone who feels shortchanged or cheated in some way. Managers have found that job performance and satisfaction can be improved by properly administered rewards.

Extrinsic Versus Intrinsic Rewards

There are two different categories of rewards. **Extrinsic rewards** are payoffs granted to the individual by other people. Examples include money, employee benefits, promotions, recognition, status symbols, and praise. The second category is called **intrinsic rewards,** which are self-granted and internally experienced payoffs. Among intrinsic rewards are a sense of accomplishment, self-esteem, and self-actualization. The following statement by a Chicago supermart owner captures the essence of intrinsic rewards:

> If a chain tried to buy me out, I'd tell them to go to hell. Even a terrific deal. I don't like the idea of somebody else calling the shots. You're better off if you can stay on your own two feet and not depend on these conglomerates or any of the b.s. they give you about how big they're gonna make you. I don't think money is the whole reward. It's the satisfaction of knowing you've done it.[34]

Usually, on-the-job extrinsic and intrinsic rewards are intermingled. For instance, employees often experience a psychological lift when they complete a big project, in addition to reaping material benefits.

Improving Performance with Rewards

Extrinsic rewards, if they are to motivate job performance effectively, need to be administered in ways that (1) satisfy operative needs, (2) foster positive expectations, (3) ensure equitable distribution, and (4) reward results. Let us see how these four criteria can be met.

Rewards Must Satisfy Individual Needs   Whether it is a pay raise or a pat on the back, there is no motivational impact unless the reward satisfies an operative need. Not all people need the same things, and one individual

Table 11.4   Innovative Pay Plans

Type of Pay Plan	Major Advantages	Major Disadvantages	Favorable Situational Factors
All-salary (Both managerial and non-managerial employees are paid an annual salary.)	Climate of trust; increased satisfaction and job attraction.	Possible higher costs and higher absenteeism.	Supervisors who will deal with absenteeism problems; a participative climate; an involved, responsible work force; well-designed jobs.
Skill-based evaluation (Pay is based on degree(s) earned or skills demonstrated.)	More flexible and skilled work force; increased satisfaction; climate of growth.	Cost of training; higher salaries.	Employees who want to develop themselves; jobs that are interdependent.
Lump-sum salary increases (Employee chooses when to receive annual pay increase.)	Increased pay satisfaction; greater visibility of pay increases.	Cost of administration.	Fair pay rates; pay related to performance.
Cafeteria benefits (Employee selects personalized combination of fringe benefits.)	Increased pay satisfaction; greater attraction.	Cost of administration.	Well-educated, heterogeneous work force; large organization; good data processing.

SOURCE: Edward E. Lawler, *Pay and Organization Development*, © 1981, Addison-Wesley, Reading, Massachusetts, pg. 77 (Table 5.1) (adapted material). Reprinted with permission.

may need different things at different times. Money is a powerful motivator for those who seek security through material wealth. But the promise of more money may mean little to a financially secure person who seeks ego stimulation from challenging work. People's needs concerning when and how they want to be paid also vary. Motivation expert Edward Lawler has identified four innovative and flexible pay plans capable of improving the match between individual needs and extrinsic rewards (see Table 11.4).

Because cafeteria compensation is rather special and particularly promising, we shall examine it more closely. **Cafeteria compensation** is a plan for allowing each employee to determine the make-up of his or her benefit package. Realizing that today's employee benefits sometimes range as high as 50 percent of one's total compensation, the motivating potential of such a privilege can be sizable. According to *Business Week*:

Under these plans, employers provide minimal "core" coverage in life and health insurance, vacations, and pensions. The employee buys additional benefits to suit his own needs, using credits based on salary, service, and age.

The elderly bachelor, for instance, may pass up the maternity coverage he would receive, willy-nilly, under conventional plans and "buy" additional pension contributions instead. The mother whose children are covered by her husband's employee health insurance policy may choose legal and dental care insurance instead.[35]

Although some organizations have balked at installing cafeteria compensation because of added bookkeeping expense, the number of programs in effect in the United States has grown from eight in 1980 to over 150 by 1984.[36] Cafeteria compensation represents a revolutionary step toward fitting rewards to people, rather than vice versa.

One Must Believe That Effort Will Lead to Reward According to the expectancy theory of motivation, an employee will not try to attain an attractive reward unless it is perceived as attainable. For example, the promise of an expense-paid trip to Hawaii for being the leading salesperson will prompt only those who feel they have a decent chance of winning to go out and sell more. Those who perceive little chance of winning will not be motivated to try any harder than usual.

Rewards Must Be Equitable Something is equitable if people perceive it to be fair and just. Each of us carries a pair of equity scales in our heads with which we weigh equity balances and imbalances. Figure 11.6 shows one scale for personal equity and another for social equity. The personal equity scale tests the relationship between effort expended and rewards received. The social equity scale, in contrast, compares our own effort-reward ratio with that of someone else in the same situation. We are motivated to seek personal and social equity and avoid inequity. Interestingly, research has demonstrated that inequity is perceived by those who are overpaid as well as those who are underpaid.[37] Since perceived inequity is associated with feelings of dissatisfaction and anger, jealousy, or guilt, inequitable reward schemes tend to be counterproductive.

Rewards Must Be Linked to Performance Ideally, there should be an if-then relationship between work and extrinsic rewards. Managers can strengthen motivation to work by making sure that those who give a little extra get a little extra. In addition to traditional piece-rate and sales commission plans, profit-sharing, an annual bonus, and stock-purchase plans are popular ways of linking pay and performance. Merit pay can be used to give salaried personnel an incentive to go that extra mile.

Figure 11.6   Personal and Social Equity

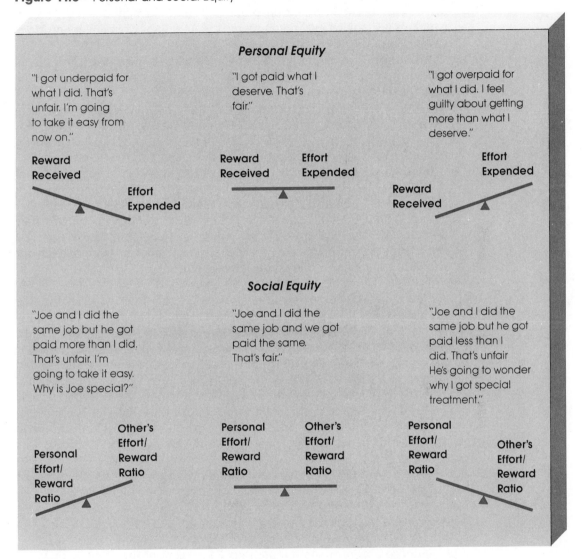

Motivation Through Quality-of-Work-Life Innovations

In recent years, a movement that promises to reshape the workaday world significantly has been steadily gathering force. It has been alternatively labeled the quality-of-work-life movement, the work humanization movement, and the work reform movement. Whatever label is applied, the basic theme remains the same: greater individual say in the nature, conditions, and scheduling of one's work. The *individual's* role is emphasized here to distinguish this new thrust from organized labor or traditional trade unionism. Unions may or may not embrace the quality-of-work-life innovations discussed in this section.

An authority on the subject has defined **quality-of-work-life** (QWL) as "a *process* by which an organization attempts to unlock the creative potential of its people by involving them in decisions affecting their work lives."[38] According to the Work in America Institute, an organization founded in 1975 to serve as a clearinghouse for QWL innovations, the domain of QWL includes pay, employee benefits, job security, alternative work schedules, occupational stress, participation, and democracy in the workplace.[39]

In other words, QWL programs touch virtually every significant aspect of modern work experience. Three major categories of QWL programs are flexible work schedules, participative management, and workplace democracy. The common denominator of these three approaches is that they give employees a greater than usual degree of control over their work lives. QWL proponents claim that greater personal control over one's work situation translates into greater motivation to do a good job.

Flexible Work Schedules
As leisure continues to push aside work as the focal point of life, the standard 8 A.M. to 5 P.M., 40-hour workweek has come under fire. Taking its place is **flexitime,** a work-scheduling plan that allows employees to determine their own arrival and departure times within specified limits.[40] All employees must be present during a fixed core time (see the shaded portion of Figure 11.7). If an eight-hour day is required, as in Figure 11.7, an early bird can put in the required eight hours by arriving at 7:00 A.M., taking a half-hour for lunch, and departing at 3:30 P.M. Alternatively, someone who is a late starter can come in at 9:00 A.M. and leave at 5:30 P.M.

Benefits Researchers have drawn the following conclusions regarding the benefits of flexitime after surveying adopters in the United States:

- Almost always raised employee morale.
- Reduced tardiness in 84 percent of the cases.
- Reduced absenteeism in more than 75 percent of the organizations.
- Reduced turnover more than 50 percent of the time.
- Cut employee commuting time more than 75 percent of the time.
- Increased productivity in almost 50 percent of the companies using flexitime.[41]

Of course, flexitime is not a panacea. Problems reported by adopters include greater administrative expense, supervisory resistance, and inadequate coverage of jobs.

Figure 11.7 Flexitime in Action

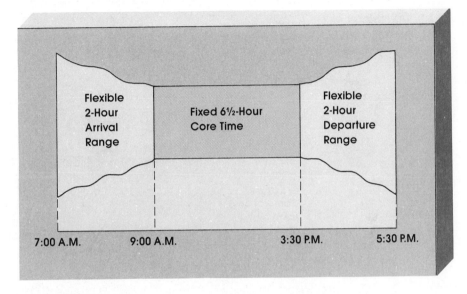

| Flexible 2-Hour Arrival Range | Fixed 6½-Hour Core Time | Flexible 2-Hour Departure Range |

7:00 A.M.   9:00 A.M.   3:30 P.M.   5:30 P.M.

Alternatives Other work-scheduling innovations include compressed workweeks (40 hours in less than five days) and permanent part time (less than 40-hour workweeks). Job sharing (complementary scheduling that allows two or more part timers to share a single full-time job), yet another work-scheduling innovation, is growing in popularity among employers of working mothers. "At First National Bank of Atlanta, for instance, ... [two] mothers of young children ... split an attorney's job between them. Each works three days a week, sharing Thursday, when they coordinate their activities."[42]

Considering that the standard 40-hour, five-day workweek has been a prominent feature on the American workscape for more than four decades, these alternative work schedules represent a significant accommodation to individual needs and circumstances. Naturally, employers expect a motivational return for this sort of accommodation.

Participative Management While noting that the term participation has become a "stewpot" into which every conceivable kind of management fad has been tossed, one management scholar has helpfully identified four key areas of participative management. Employees may participate in (1) setting goals, (2) making decisions, (3) solving problems, and (4) designing and implementing organizational changes.[43] By being personally and meaningfully involved in one or more of these overlapping areas, employee motivation and performance are said to improve via the process illustrated in Figure 11.8. Notice the individual, organizational, and environmental contingency fac-

Figure 11.8   How Participative Management Works

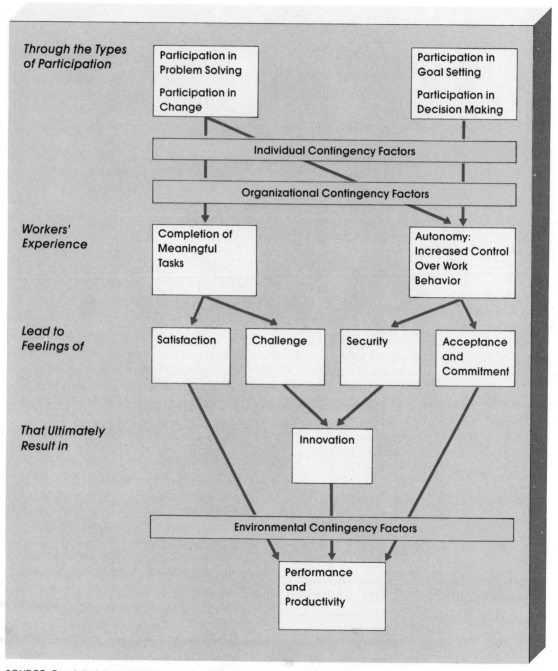

SOURCE: Reprinted, by permission of the publisher, from "Participative Management is an Ethical Imperative," by Marshall Sashkin, *Organizational Dynamics* 12 (Spring 1984): 12 © 1984 Periodicals Division, American Management Associations, New York. All rights reserved.

tors. Participation will not work if individual values and attitudes are not in tune with it. Organizational factors such as job design and culture can also help or hinder the process. Finally, environmental factors like technological change and competition affect the participation process.

A Theory Z Climate for Participation   The work of William Ouchi, a UCLA management scholar, has shed considerable light on the type of organizational culture or climate necessary if participation is to thrive. After identifying contrasting characteristics of Japanese and American companies, Ouchi discovered that a select group of American organizations effectively combined Japanese and American characteristics, a combination he named Theory Z (see Figure 11.9). Among the hybrid companies that Ouchi has labeled Theory Z are IBM, Intel, Hewlett-Packard, Eastman Kodak, and Eli Lilly. Significantly, each of these firms ranks among the most consistently successful companies in the United States. Long before American managers became intrigued by Japanese management techniques, each of these Theory Z organizations evolved a company philosophy that effectively combined the best of both worlds.

At the heart of the Theory Z culture is *consensual, participative decision making*. According to Ouchi, "This participative process is one of the mechanisms that provides for the broad dissemination of information and of values within the organization, and it also serves the symbolic role of signaling in an unmistakable way the cooperative intent of the firm."[44] The informal and egalitarian atmosphere in Theory Z organizations tends to blur the distinction between those who wear the title "manager" and those who do not. In Theory Z organizations, it is "we" rather than "us versus them." Theory Z managers commonly view their organization as a family. Consequently, according to Ouchi, trust is built that in turn motivates all organization members to do their best to achieve shared objectives.[45]

Barriers to Participative Management   Among the more popular formats for participative management are quality control circles (discussed in Chapter 17), labor-management participation teams,[46] multilevel task teams,[47] and management by objectives (discussed in Chapter 4). In whatever form participative management is practiced, significant barriers need to be overcome if it is to succeed. Among those barriers are:

- Top, middle, and/or lower-level managers may resist participation because they do not believe in its underlying philosophy.
- A belief that the short-run costs outweigh the long-term benefits can kill a program before it has started.
- A fear on the part of management that participation threatens conventional authority and power can erode support for participation programs.

Figure 11.9 The Evolution of Theory Z Organizations

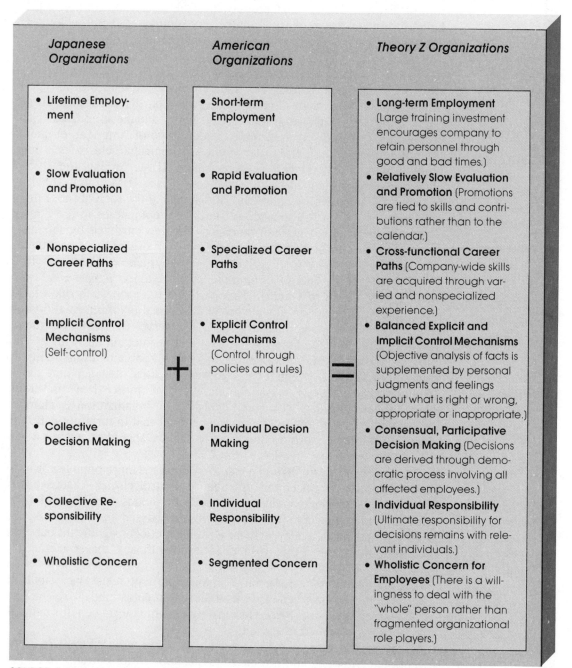

Japanese Organizations	American Organizations	Theory Z Organizations
• Lifetime Employment	• Short-term Employment	• **Long-term Employment** (Large training investment encourages company to retain personnel through good and bad times.)
• Slow Evaluation and Promotion	• Rapid Evaluation and Promotion	• **Relatively Slow Evaluation and Promotion** (Promotions are tied to skills and contributions rather than to the calendar.)
• Nonspecialized Career Paths	• Specialized Career Paths	• **Cross-functional Career Paths** (Company-wide skills are acquired through varied and nonspecialized experience.)
• Implicit Control Mechanisms (Self-control)	• Explicit Control Mechanisms (Control through policies and rules)	• **Balanced Explicit and Implicit Control Mechanisms** (Objective analysis of facts is supplemented by personal judgments and feelings about what is right or wrong, appropriate or inappropriate.)
• Collective Decision Making	• Individual Decision Making	• **Consensual, Participative Decision Making** (Decisions are derived through democratic process involving all affected employees.)
• Collective Responsibility	• Individual Responsibility	• **Individual Responsibility** (Ultimate responsibility for decisions remains with relevant individuals.)
• Wholistic Concern	• Segmented Concern	• **Wholistic Concern for Employees** (There is a willingness to deal with the "whole" person rather than fragmented organizational role players.)

(Columns joined by **+** and **=** symbols between them.)

SOURCE: Adapted from William G. Ouchi, *Theory Z*, © 1981, Addison-Wesley, Reading, Massachusetts. Pp. 58, 71, 72, 78 and 79 (adapted material). Reprinted with permission.

- Labor leaders may harbor suspicions that the participative process will be used to circumvent or weaken the union.
- Managers who lack experience with consensual decision making may fight or compromise the process.
- Unrealistic expectations about short-run economic payoffs can bring participative programs to a premature end.[48]

Participative management involves more than simply announcing a new program such as quality control circles. A good deal of background work often needs to be done to make sure a supportive climate exists. (Organizational change is discussed in Chapter 14.) Participative management needs to be sold, but not oversold, to those involved.

Gainsharing One variation of participative management deserves special attention here because it effectively links performance and rewards, a practice recommended earlier. "**Gainsharing plans** share the responsibility and rewards for organizational improvements among all employees."[49] Types of gainsharing plans include the Scanlon Plan, Improshare, and generic profit-sharing plans. The common element of these different approaches is that employees get cash bonuses based on how well the organization performs. Stated another way, good ideas and hard work translate into extra cash in the pockets of those who contribute to the success of the organization.

An inspiring example in this area is Lincoln Electric Company, the Euclid, Ohio, manufacturer of arc-welding equipment. Generous profit-sharing bonuses have helped the company remain a leader in its field for over half a century. In 1982, the average Lincoln Electric employee received a year-end bonus of $15,640, almost as much as the average annual salary that year! "Since 1934, the company has paid more in annual bonuses than in regular wages."[50] Lincoln Electric enjoys high productivity because it ties significant bonuses directly to quantity and quality improvements and cost-saving ideas. Although researchers have not determined precisely how the motivational mechanisms operate, gainsharing can be a powerful motivational tool.

Workplace Democracy Like the term quality-of-work-life, *workplace* (or industrial) *democracy* has taken on a number of meanings. Generally, **workplace democracy** encompasses all efforts to increase employee self-determination. There are two major variations on the workplace democracy theme: (1) employee-owned companies and (2) workers' self-management.

Employee-owned Companies Employees at all levels are eligible to own a piece of the business through either a co-op arrangement or an Employee Stock Ownership Plan (ESOP). By 1984, there were more than 5000

ESOPs in the United States. The amount of employee ownership in these ESOPs typically ranges from 15 to 35 percent of the outstanding stock.[51] Some companies, such as the 8700-employee Weirton Steel Corporation, are 100 percent employee owned. Except for a handful of ESOP companies such as Chrysler Corporation, Eastern Air Lines Inc., and Weirton Steel Corporation that have employee representatives sitting on the corporate board, employee stockholders generally surrender their power to elect board members to management or trustees.

Contrary to the impression created in the popular press, employee ownership does not mean employee *control*. ESOP employees take orders from professional managers in the traditional fashion. Yet, as stockholders, ESOP employees have a direct economic stake in the profitability of their company. The harder (and smarter) they work, the greater their stock dividends will be.

Workers' Self-management This involves a radical departure from the traditional corporate arrangement. According to an expert on the subject:

> Real workers' control stands the traditional corporate power structure on its head: Management does not grant the workers a few expanded powers on the shop floor, and the workers do not simply put some certificates of stock ownership in their bureau drawers. In worker-controlled firms, workers and their elected representatives control the corporation, period.[52]

Although this second option has made limited inroads in a few European countries, it has met with strong resistance in the United States. Critics believe that employees lack the willingness and ability to manage themselves effectively and responsibly. But self-management advocates argue that American employees will continue to lack the motivation to be fully productive as long as the democratic privileges they enjoy outside of work are not extended to the workplace. Lively debate can be expected on this topic in the years ahead as employees strive for more control over their work lives.

Summary

Motivation is an important area of study for managers because it helps them better understand our most valuable resource, people. (Realistically, motivation is just one of many explanations of work behavior, such as one's knowledge and emotional state and organizational factors.) Even though the employees in one study ranked "interesting work" the highest among the things they wanted from their jobs, their supervisors believed that they wanted "good wages" above all else. This type of misperception of employees' needs can cripple a motivation program. Pollster Daniel Yankelovich contends that traditional motivational tools such as fear, money, strict supervision, and the work ethic are inappropriate for nearly half of today's labor force in the United States.

Among alternative motivation theories, Maslow's needs hierarchy theory, Herzberg's two-factor theory, and expectancy theory stand out as particularly relevant for managers. Maslow's five-level needs hierarchy, although empirically criticized, makes it clear to managers that people are motivated by emerging rather than fulfilled needs. Assuming that job satisfaction and performance are positively related, Herzberg believes that the most that wages and working conditions can do is eliminate sources of dissatisfaction. According to Herzberg, the key to true satisfaction and hence motivation is an enriched job that provides an opportunity for achievement, responsibility, and personal growth. Expectancy theory is based on the idea that the strength of one's motivation to work is the product of perceived probabilities of acquiring personally valued rewards. Both effort-performance and performance-reward probabilities are important to expectancy theory.

Depending on how it is designed, a job can either hamper or promote personal growth and satisfaction. Although historically a key to higher productivity, specialization of labor has been associated with costly human problems in recent years. Managers have the options of fitting people to jobs or fitting jobs to people when attempting to counter the specialization-of-labor dilemma. The first option includes realistic job previews, job rotation, and limited exposure. Managers who pursue the second option, fitting jobs to people, can either enlarge or enrich jobs. Job enrichment vertically loads jobs to meet individual needs for meaningfulness, responsibility, and knowledge of results. Personal desire for growth and a supportive climate are required for successful job enrichment.

Both extrinsic (externally granted) and intrinsic (self-granted) rewards, when properly administered, can have a positive impact on performance and satisfaction. The following rules can help managers maximize the motivational impact of extrinsic rewards: (1) rewards must satisfy individual needs, (2) one must believe that effort will lead to reward, (3) rewards must be equitable, and (4) rewards must be linked with performance.

Quality-of-work-life programs have emerged in recent years in response to employee demands for greater control of their work lives. Flexitime, a flexible work-scheduling scheme that allows employees to choose their own arrival and departure times, has been effective in boosting productivity while reducing tardiness, absenteeism, and turnover. Participative management programs foster direct employee involvement in one or more of the following areas: goal setting, decision making, problem solving, and change implementation. Theory Z organizations are highly participative because they effectively combine Japanese and American organizational characteristics. Barriers to participation, such as management and union resistance, need to be overcome. Gainsharing ensures that those who actively participate toward an organization's success are appropriately rewarded through bonuses. Two major forms of workplace democracy are employee-owned companies and workers' self-management. The latter, although more democratic than the former, has been strongly resisted in the United States.

Terms to Understand

Motivation
Expectancy theory *vrom*
Expectancy
Job design
Boredom and alienation barrier
Realistic job previews
Job rotation
Contingent time off (CTO)
Job enlargement *2 or more tasks combined*

Futp →J

Job enrichment
Rewards
Extrinsic rewards *out*
Intrinsic rewards *in*
Cafeteria compensation
Quality-of-work-life (QWL)
Flexitime
Gainsharing plans
Workplace democracy

Questions for Discussion

1. In reference to the list of ten motivating factors in Table 11.1, what do you want most from a job? Explain. How would you rank the remaining factors?
2. How could self-actualization get one into trouble at work?
3. What things did you like most about the best job you ever had? Does your answer conform to Herzberg's theory? Explain.
4. Which motivation theory—Maslow's, Herzberg's, or expectancy—do you feel has the most practical value for today's managers?
5. Why would job enrichment probably be more appealing to you than job enlargement?
6. In your opinion, which of the innovative pay plans in Table 11.4 has the greatest motivating potential? Why?
7. Why is equity an important consideration when developing a reward plan?
8. Why do you think some organizations would not adopt flexitime?

9. Would you like to work in a Theory Z organization? Why?
10. Do you think gainsharing has a bright future in this country? Why? What about the future of workers' self-management?

Back to the Opening Case

Now that you have read Chapter 11, you should be able to answer the following questions about the Westinghouse case:

1. What role does Maslow's concept of the need for self-esteem play in this case?
2. Why would it be helpful if the team facilitators were familiar with Herzberg's two-factor theory as well as with job design?
3. How do intrinsic rewards enter into this case?
4. What factors could cause Westinghouse's participative management experiment to fail in the longer term?

Closing Case 11.2

Participation + Union/Management Cooperation = Improved Quality at Ford

Considering that a new car is made up of 15,000 different parts, quality control can be a nightmare in automobile assembly operations. During the 1970s, Ford Motor Company's reputation for producing quality products slipped badly. Sagging sales, costly product recalls, and customer complaints plagued the No. 2 auto maker. Making matters worse were complaints about boredom from assembly-line workers with job cycles of less than one minute. The traditional adversarial relationship between management and labor had worsened to a state of mutual distrust and constant infighting over contract "rights." A time-honored response on management's behalf would have been to adopt a "get tougher" policy with the union and hire more quality control inspectors. But it had become abundantly clear to all parties involved that fundamental improvements in labor/management relations were needed if Ford were to remain a viable contender in the automobile industry. During the 1979 contract talks between Ford and the United Auto Workers (UAW) the foundation was built for what the business press now calls Ford's "industrial miracle."

The Birth of EI

By the time the 1979 contract negotiations had ended, Ford and the UAW had agreed to cooperate fully in a participative management program called Employee Involvement (EI). According to Philip Caldwell, Ford's recently retired chief executive officer:

> In its simplest terms, EI allows employees voluntarily to play an important role in shaping the future of the company. Through EI, employees participate in day-to-day decisions about the work environment, the products, and the manufacturing process.[53]

Ford's EI has been put into practice in the form of teams made up of a supervisor and several of his or her workers. After they are voluntarily formed, participation teams meet once a week to identify and solve problems involving quality and other workplace matters. By late 1984, thousands of EI teams were operating at 86 out of 91 Ford facilities. An estimated 20 to 30 percent of Ford's hourly work force—20,000 to 34,000 people—had become directly involved in the EI program.

Stop the Line!

One of the most dramatic EI changes implemented at Ford was the installation in 1982 of "stop buttons" at each work station at the Edison, New Jersey, plant. In keeping with Ford's slogan, "Quality Is Job One," assembly line workers who come across an unsolvable quality problem have the authority to push the stop button.

> "... the workers themselves often halt the line 10 to 20 times a day when a problem prevents them from doing their jobs. A foreman hurries to the trouble area, helps the worker correct a malfunctioning machine or a defect in the car, and usually within 30 seconds the line is moving again."[54]

Under the old ways, dating back to Henry Ford, uninterrupted movement of the assembly line always took precedence over individual problems. The net result: many defects were built right into the finished product only to crop up later after the car had been sold. By giving line workers the authority to catch quality problems at the source, Ford has significantly improved its quality record. In fact, prior to installation of the stop buttons, the Edison plant turned out cars with an average of 17 defects each. That figure dropped to less than one within four months of the stop buttons being installed. Moreover, Ford claims that the stop buttons have also cut absenteeism and improved labor relations.

Although Ford has not attempted to measure precisely the cost-benefit relationship for its EI program, Caldwell has cited some positive impacts:

A survey last year [1983] of more than 750 EI participants at seven facilities found that a full 82 percent felt they now had a chance to accomplish something worthwhile, compared with only 27 percent before EI was initiated. ...

Independent research shows that the quality of our 1983 models is 10 percent better than GM's and 36 percent better than Chrysler's. It is also better than many of the major Japanese and European imports.[55]

Improved Job Security

The spirit of EI was evident when the members of UAW Local 898 ratified an unprecedented agreement with Ford's Rawsonville, Michigan, parts factory in 1983. Terms of the agreement called for the consolidation of skilled trades, which reduced the number of groups from 24 to 14. In return for this cost-cutting move and other changes such as the creation of production teams, Ford guaranteed Rawsonville's 2582 full-time, unionized employees at least 32-hour workweeks for a period of three years. Layoffs of full-time personnel were avoided by hiring part-timers during production peaks. This sort of comprehensive job guarantee was previously unheard of in the U.S. auto industry. Everyone involved seemed to like the new arrangement. The employees received improved job security and Ford was given some leeway to improve efficiency and competitiveness. The spirit of EI has grown. By 1984, 90 EI teams were in operation at Rawsonville.

Some Doubters

Predictably, not everyone has been happy with EI. Some traditional foremen feel threatened with participation because it forces them to realize that hourly people may know more than they do. On the other side of the bargaining table, some union officials fear that EI will undermine the union's relationship with its members. However, *Business Week* has quoted Earl Nail, president of the Edison plant's UAW Local 980, as saying: "Ford has discovered that to build a good car, they've got to have harmony. ... Now it's like we're all one family."[56]

For Discussion

1. How does Maslow's theory help explain the motivational value of the Rawsonville job security agreement?
2. Regarding the enrichment of assembly-line work at the Edison plant, what core job characteristics were enhanced and how was employee motivation probably improved?
3. How can you explain the apparent success of Ford's participative management program?
4. What would a proponent of gainsharing have to say about Ford's EI program?

References

Opening Quotation: Keith Davis, *Human Behavior at Work: Organizational Behavior,* 6th ed. (New York: McGraw-Hill, 1981), p. 2.

Opening Case: For additional information on Westinghouse, see Bruce A. Jacobs, "Does Westinghouse Have the Productivity Answer?" *Industry Week* 208 (March 23, 1981): 95–96, 98; Jeremy Main, "Westinghouse's Cultural Revolution," *Fortune* 103 (June 15, 1981): 74–93; and Steven S. Anreder, "Switch at Westinghouse: Its Efforts to Turn Its Business Around Are Paying Off," *Barron's* 61 (September 21, 1981): 49, 50.

Closing Case: For additional information on Ford, see "The Old Foreman Is On the Way Out, and the New One Will Be More Important," *Business Week* No. 2787 (April 25, 1983): 74–75; Philip Caldwell, "Cultivating Human Potential at Ford," *The Journal of Business Strategy* 4 (Spring 1984): 74–77; and "What's Creating an 'Industrial Miracle' at Ford?" *Business Week* No. 2853 (July 30, 1984): 80–81.

1. Jeremy Main, "Westinghouse's Cultural Revolution," p. 76.
2. Ibid., p. 74.
3. Ibid., p. 93.
4. Studs Terkel, *Working* (New York: Pantheon, 1974), p. 522.
5. A very good overview of motivation theory may be found in Terence R. Mitchell, "Motivation: New Directions for Theory, Research, and Practice," *Academy of Management Review* 7 (January 1982): 80–88.
6. For an excellent historical and conceptual treatment of basic motivation theory, see Richard M. Steers and Lyman W. Porter, *Motivation and Work Behavior* (New York: McGraw-Hill, 1975), chap. 1.
7. Curtis W. Cook, "Guidelines for Managing Motivation," *Business Horizons* 23 (April 1980): 62.
8. See Kenneth A. Kovach, "Why Motivational Theories Don't Work," *S.A.M. Advanced Management Journal* 45 (Spring 1980): 54–59.
9. Caldwell, "Cultivating Human Potential at Ford," p. 76.
10. Daniel Yankelovich, "Yankelovich on Today's Workers: We Need New Motivational Tools," *Industry Week* 202 (August 6, 1979): 62.
11. Ibid., p. 64.
12. See A. H. Maslow, "A Theory of Human Motivation," *Psychological Review* 50 (July 1943): 370–396.
13. For a revealing study of what managers think about management theory, see M. T. Matteson, "Some Reported Thoughts on Significant Management Literature," *Academy of Management Journal* 17 (1974): 386–389.
14. Maslow, "A Theory of Human Motivation," p. 375.
15. Ibid., p. 382.
16. George W. Cherry, "The Serendipity of the Fully Functioning Manager," *Sloan Management Review* 17 (Spring 1976): 73.
17. Vance F. Mitchell and Pravin Moudgill, "Measurement of Maslow's Need

Hierarchy," *Organizational Behavior and Human Performance* 16 (August 1976): 348.

18. For example, see Douglas T. Hall and Khalil E. Nougaim, "An Examination of Maslow's Need Hierarchy in an Organizational Setting," *Organizational Behavior and Human Performance* 3 (February 1968): 12–35.

19. Edward E. Lawler, *Motivation in Work Organizations* (Monterey, Calif.: Brooks/Cole, 1973), p. 34.

20. See Frederick Herzberg, Bernard Mausner, and Barbara Bloch Snyderman, *The Motivation to Work,* 2nd ed. (New York: Wiley, 1959).

21. Frederick Herzberg, "One More Time: How Do You Motivate Employees?" *Harvard Business Review* 46 (January-February 1968): 56.

22. For details, see Victor H. Vroom, *Work and Motivation* (New York: Wiley, 1964), p. 186.

23. See Robert J. House and Lawrence A. Wigdor, "Herzberg's Dual-Factor Theory of Job Satisfaction and Motivation: A Review of the Evidence and a Criticism," *Personnel Psychology* 20 (1967): 369–389.

24. For example, see J. Richard Hackman and Lyman W. Porter, "Expectancy Theory Predictions of Work Effectiveness," *Organizational Behavior and Human Performance* 3 (November 1968): 417–426.

25. Adapted from J. Richard Hackman, "The Design of Work in the 1980s," *Organizational Dynamics* 7 (Summer 1978): 3–17.

26. For more details, see John P. Wanous, "Effects of a Realistic Job Preview on Job Acceptance, Job Attitudes, and Job Survival," *Journal of Applied Psychology* 58 (December 1973): 327–332.

27. For discussion, see John P. Wanous, "Realistic Job Previews: Can a Procedure to Reduce Turnover Also Influence the Relationship Between Abilities and Performance?" *Personnel Psychology* 31 (Summer 1978): 249–258 and James A. Breaugh, "Realistic Job Previews: A Critical Appraisal and Future Research Directions," *Academy of Management Review* 8 (October 1983): 612–619.

28. See M. A. Howell, "Time Off as a Reward for Productivity," *Personnel Administration* 34 (November-December 1971): 48–51.

29. Fred Luthans and Robert Kreitner, *Organizational Behavior Modification and Beyond: An Operant and Social Learning Approach* (Glenview, Ill.: Scott, Foresman, 1985), p. 192.

30. J. Richard Hackman and Greg R. Oldham, *Work Redesign* (Reading, Mass.: Addison-Wesley, 1980), p. 20.

31. Ibid., pp. 78–80.

32. Two classic job enrichment success stories may be found in Robert N. Ford, "Job Enrichment Lessons from A.T.&T.," *Harvard Business Review* 51 (January-February 1973): 96–106 and Pehr G Gyllenhammar, "How Volvo Adapts Work to People," *Harvard Business Review* 55 (July-August 1977): 102–113.

33. Informative critiques of job enrichment may be found in William E. Reif and Fred Luthans, "Does Job Enrichment Really Pay Off?" *California Manage-*

ment Review 15 (Fall 1972): 30–37; and Mitchell Fein, "Job Enrichment: A Reevaluation," *Sloan Management Review* 16 (Winter 1974): 69–88.

34. Studs Terkel, *American Dreams: Lost and Found* (New York: Ballantine, 1980), p. 31.

35. "Companies Offer Benefits Cafeteria-Style," *Business Week* No. 2560 (November 13, 1978): 116. For a review of the theory behind flexible compensation, see William B. Werther, Jr., "Flexible Compensation Evaluated," *California Management Review* 19 (Fall 1976): 40–46.

36. See Dale Gifford, "The Status of Flexible Compensation," *Personnel Administrator* 29 (May 1984): 19–25.

37. See J. Stacy Adams and Patricia R. Jacobsen, "Effects of Wage Inequities on Work Quality," *Journal of Abnormal and Social Psychology* 69 (1964): 19–25 and Jerald Greenberg and Suzyn Ornstein, "High Status Job Title as Compensation for Underpayment: A Test of Equity Theory," *Journal of Applied Psychology* 68 (May 1983): 285–297.

38. Robert H. Guest, "Quality of Work Life—Learning from Tarrytown," *Harvard Business Review* 57 (July-August 1979): 76–77.

39. Jerome M. Rosow, "Quality-of-Work-Life Issues for the 1980s," in *Work in America: The Decade Ahead,* ed. Clark Kerr and Jerome M. Rosow (New York: Van Nostrand, 1979), pp. 157–158.

40. For an extensive treatment of flexitime and other work scheduling alternatives, see Allan R. Cohen and Herman Gadon, *Alternative Work Schedules: Integrating Individual and Organizational Needs* (Reading, Mass.: Addison-Wesley, 1978).

41. Donald J. Petersen, "Flexitime in the United States: The Lessons of Experience," *Personnel* 57 (January-February 1980): 22; also see Stanley D. Nollen, "Does Flexitime Improve Productivity?" *Harvard Business Review* 57 (September-October 1979): 12–22 and V. K. Narayanan and Raghu Nath, "A Field Test of Some Attitudinal and Behavioral Consequences of Flexitime," *Journal of Applied Psychology* 67 (April 1982): 214–218.

42. "Companies Start to Meet Executive Mothers Halfway," *Business Week* No. 2812 (October 17, 1983): 191.

43. See Marshall Sashkin, "Participative Management Is an Ethical Imperative," *Organizational Dynamics* 12 (Spring 1984): 4–22.

44. William G. Ouchi, *Theory Z: How American Business Can Meet the Japanese Challenge* (Reading, Mass.: Addison-Wesley, 1981), p. 78.

45. An interesting critical review of Theory Z can be found in Jeremiah J. Sullivan, "A Critique of Theory Z," *Academy of Management Review* 8 (January 1983): 132–142.

46. See "Steel Listens to Workers and Likes What It Hears," *Business Week* No. 2821 (December 19, 1983): 92, 94–95.

47. An informative discussion of Honeywell's participative management program may be found in Richard J. Boyle, "Wrestling with Jellyfish," *Harvard Business Review* 62 (January-February 1984): 74–83.

48. Based in part on material found in Rosow, "Quality-of-Work-Life Issues for the 1980s," pp. 177–178.

49. R. J. Bullock and Edward E. Lawler, "Gainsharing: A Few Questions, and Fewer Answers," *Human Resource Management* 23 (Spring 1984): 37.

50. Charles Hillinger, "Big Bonuses at Lincoln Electric Get Big Results," *Professional Trainer* 3 (Winter 1983): 1.

51. See "Labor's Voice on Corporate Boards: Good or Bad?" *Business Week* No. 2841 (May 7, 1984): 151–153. An excellent update on ESOPs may be found in John Hoerr, "ESOPs: Revolution or Ripoff?" *Business Week* No. 2890 (April 15, 1985): 94–108.

52. Daniel Zwerdling, "Workplace Democracy: A Strategy for Survival," *The Progressive* 42 (August 1978): 21. Also see Henry P. Guzda, "Industrial Democracy: Made in the U.S.A.," *Monthly Labor Review* 107 (May 1984): 26–33.

53. Caldwell, "Cultivating Human Potential at Ford," p. 75.

54. "What's Creating an 'Industrial Miracle' at Ford," p. 80.

55. Caldwell, "Cultivating Human Potential at Ford," p. 75.

56. "The Old Foreman Is on the Way Out, and the New One Will Be More Important," p. 75.

Chapter 12

Group Dynamics: Trust, Politics, Conformity, and Conflict

Organizations are composed of [many] small groups that have a similar influence on behavior. They inculcate majority values in their members; they reward compliance and punish those who resist their demands.
Robert Presthus

Chapter Objectives

When you finish studying this chapter, you should be able to

- Define the term *group* and explain the significance of cohesiveness, roles, and ostracism in regard to the behavior of group members.
- Identify and briefly describe the six stages of group development.
- Explain why trust is the key to work group effectiveness and discuss what management can do to minimize mistrust.
- Explain how groupthink can lead to blind conformity.
- Identify and generally describe the nature of the five major conflict resolution techniques.

Opening Case 12.1

Turmoil at Pan Am

As airline industry profits nose-dived during the 1980–1981 recession, Pan American World Airways (Pan Am) found itself in particularly dire straits. Financial pressures were immense because stiffer competition had made fare increases difficult in spite of the soaring cost of fuel. Even the company's sale of its landmark Pan Am building in New York City, although profitable, was viewed by critics as an act of desperation. The firm's airline division lost $248 million in 1980 and $240 million in just the first six months of 1981.

Behind these record losses was an iceberg of internal dissension, political back-stabbing, turmoil over strategic policy, and high-level firings and resignations. In fact, out of a 1979 roster of 53 executive-level managers, only 28 were still with Pan Am by mid-1981. Casualties of this wave of turnovers included the company's president, Dan Colussy, eight vice presidents, and a member of the board of directors, James Maloon, a former Pan Am executive vice president. This exodus of managers, compounded by a series of ill-conceived reorganizations, further disrupted the organization by prompting a great many transfers. One vice president found himself moving from New York to San Francisco, back to New York, and back once again to San Francisco in a three-year period. Consequently, competing airlines had little trouble hiring disenchanted Pan Am managers.

The Chairman's Heavy Hand

William Seawell, a man reportedly with a fierce temper of legendary proportions and a penchant for political gamesmanship, was Pan Am's chairman during these troubled times. Critics claimed that the former Air Force general, who became chairman in 1972, had brought instability to the firm through his unwillingness to share power and his deliberate tactics for keeping other Pan Am executives off balance. Seawell created a "shadow organization" of personal confidants and outside consultants that was often in conflict with Pan Am's executives. For example, Seawell promptly hired back a consultant who had been fired by James Maloon when the latter was still Pan Am's executive vice president for finance.

Before Colussy's departure, he and Seawell had some bitter battles over the direction of Pan Am. Colussy, alarmed by the firm's financial problems, attempted to launch a vigorous cost-cutting campaign that included an unpopular early-retirement program to reduce managerial overhead. In direct opposition, Seawell plunged ahead with plans to acquire several 727-200 jetliners from Braniff. Seawell's plan was ultimately unsuccessful because of Pan Am's financial difficulties. Seawell and Colussy reportedly were not even on speaking terms for two days following their last major clash.

At the November 4, 1980, board meeting, after dismissing Maloon as a director because the two had been feuding for a long time, Seawell told the outside directors that he also wanted to fire Colussy. Soon after, Seawell confronted Colussy, and after the standard "You're fired" — "No, I quit" exchange, Colussy resigned as Pan Am's president. Subsequently, a hit list of Colussy's supporters led to the prompt firing of a vice president. Eventually, despite his being transferred from New York to Miami by a supportive boss to "hide," a second vice president who had sided with Colussy was fired.

A Troubled Merger

Pan Am bought National Airlines in 1980 in hopes of building its domestic business. As pointed out by the *Wall Street Journal* shortly thereafter, the marriage was not made in heaven:

> Melding the two organizations triggered even more dislocations, transfers and disruption. Moreover, the two organizations didn't fit together well. With its major base in Miami, Fla., National had a small, tightly knit management. Based in New York, but with operations around the world, Pan Am was heavy with bureaucracy. "If we had a problem," a National manager says, "we used to walk into a guy's office and settle it in five minutes, but at Pan Am we had to set up a committee and then study it for months. It took forever, and you never got a decision."[1]

Not surprisingly, many National managers jumped ship. In fact, a year after the merger, only two executives formerly with National held high positions in the Pan Am organization.

(Discussion questions linking this case with the material you are about to read can be found at the end of this chapter.)

Pan Am's management problems present a vivid picture of group dynamics gone sour. In the early 1980s, issues of trust, politics, and conflict seemed to dominate that company's high-level decision making.

It helps to remember that people are at the same time individuals and social beings. This sometimes frustrating combination—a central fact in any discussion of group dynamics—was thoughtfully explored by Henry David Thoreau, a nineteenth-century American philosopher. Thoreau's two-year experiment with solitary living in the woods near Walden Pond is chronicled in his classic book *Walden*. Only by removing himself from the distractions of life in town could Thoreau reevaluate his relationship with society. He found that he was never truly alone, even though no one else was around, because he was the product of society. Everything Thoreau thought and did was social in origin. He was first and foremost a social being.

Although most of us will never have the opportunity to contemplate our relationship with society by living alone in the woods for a few years, each of us is challenged daily to resolve the inevitable conflict between the demands of individuality and society. It helps to have a working understanding of the social forces that constantly shape and redirect our lives. Such an understanding is particularly important for managers because the practice of management is fundamentally social in nature.

Fundamental Group Dynamics

According to one organization theorist, "all groups may be collections of individuals, but all collections of individuals are not groups."[2] More than a tricky play on words is involved here. It is important to understand that mere togetherness does not automatically create a group. Consider, for example, this situation. A half-dozen people who worked for different companies in the same building often shared the same elevator in the morning. As time passed, they introduced themselves and exchanged pleasantries. Eventually, four of the elevator riders discovered that they all lived in the same suburb. Arrangements for a car pool were made, and they began to take turns picking up and delivering one another. According to commonly accepted definitions of the term *group,* a group did not come into existence until the car pool was formed. The collection of unacquainted individuals who happened to share the same elevator was technically not a group. In regard to the sociological definition, other factors had to be present before this collection of individuals could be called a group.

What Is a Group?

A **group** may be defined as two or more freely interacting individuals who share a common identity and purpose.[3] Careful analysis of this definition reveals four important dimensions (see Figure 12.1). First, a group must be made up of two or more people if it is to be considered a social unit. Second, the individuals must freely interact in some manner. An organization may simultaneously qualify as a sociological group if it is small and personal enough to permit all its members to interact regularly with each other. Generally, however, larger organizations with bureaucratic tendencies are made up of many overlapping groups. Third, the interacting individuals must share a common identity. Each must recognize himself or herself as a member of the group. Fourth, interacting individuals who have a common identity must also have a common purpose. That is, there must be at least a rough consensus on why the group exists.

Types of Groups

Human beings belong to groups for many different reasons. Some people join a group as an end in itself. For example, an accountant may enjoy the socializing that goes along with exercising with a group of friends at a local health spa. On the other hand, that same accountant's membership in a work group in association with paid employment is a means to an end. Both the exercise group and the work group satisfy the sociological definition of a group, but they fulfill very different needs. The former is an informal group, and the latter is a formal group.

Informal Groups As Maslow pointed out, a feeling of belonging is a powerful motivator. People generally have a great need to fit in, to be liked,

Figure 12.1   What Does It Take to Make a Group?

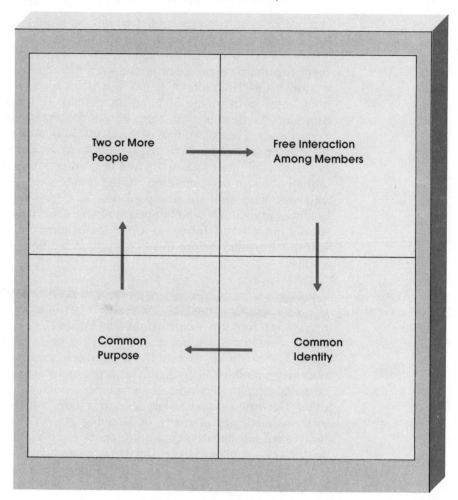

to be one of the gang. Whether the group meets at work or during leisure time, it is still an **informal group** if the principal reason for belonging is friendship. Informal groups usually evolve spontaneously. They serve to satisfy esteem needs because one develops a better self-image when accepted, recognized, and liked by others. Sometimes, as in the case of a group of friends forming a service club, an informal group may evolve into a formal one.

Interestingly, as the experience of William Hewitt proves, informal groups can have unexpected payoffs. A very active social life paved the way for young Hewitt to meet and later marry the great-great-granddaughter of

John Deere. Eventually Hewitt became the chief executive officer of Deere & Company.[4] Although belonging to informal groups doesn't guarantee that one will become the head of a multibillion dollar corporation, it's often easier to get by with a little help from our friends.

Formal Groups   A **formal group** is a group created for the purpose of doing productive work. It may be called a team, a committee, or simply a work group. Whatever its name, a formal group is usually formed for the purpose of contributing to the success of a more encompassing organization. Formal groups tend to be more rationally structured and less fluid than informal groups. Rather than joining formal task groups, people are assigned to them according to their talents and the organization's needs. One person normally is granted formal leadership responsibility to ensure that the formal group's members carry out their assigned duties. Informal friendship groups, in contrast, generally do not have officially appointed leaders, although informal leaders often emerge by popular demand. For the individual, the formal group and an informal group at the place of employment may or may not overlap. In other words, one may or may not be friends with one's coworkers.

Attraction to Groups   What attracts a person to one group but not to another? And why do some group members stay while others leave? Managers who know the answers to these questions can take steps to strengthen the motivation to join and remain a member of a formal work group. Individual commitment to either an informal or formal group hinges on two factors. The first is attractiveness, the outside-looking-in view. A nonmember will want to join a group if it is attractive and will shy away from unattractive groups. The second factor is **cohesiveness,** which may be defined as the tendency of group members to follow the group and resist outside influences. This is the inside-looking-out view. In a highly cohesive group, individual members tend to see themselves as "we" rather than "I." One might say that cohesive group members literally stick together.

Factors that either enhance or destroy group attractiveness and cohesiveness are listed in Table 12.1. It is important to note that each factor is a matter of degree. For example, a group may offer the individual little, moderate, or great opportunity for prestige and status. Similarly, group demands on the individual may range from somewhat disagreeable to highly disagreeable. What all this means is that the decision to join a group and the decision to continue being a member both depend on a net balance of the factors in Table 12.1. Naturally, the resulting balance is colored by one's perception and frame of reference. For example, consider the case of Richard Dale, a former manager of distribution at Commodore International, during his first meeting with the company's founder, Jack Tramiel:

Table 12.1 Factors That Enhance or Destroy Group Attractiveness and Cohesiveness

Factors That Enhance Attractiveness and Cohesiveness	**Factors That Destroy Attractiveness and Cohesiveness**
1. Prestige and status. 2. Cooperative relationship. 3. High degree of interaction. 4. Relatively small size. 5. Similarity of members. 6. Superior public image of group. 7. A common threat in the environment.	1. Unreasonable or disagreeable demands on the individual. 2. Disagreement over procedures, activities, rules, and the like. 3. Unpleasant experience with the group. 4. Competition between the group's demands and preferred outside activities. 5. Unfavorable public image of group. 6. Competition for membership by other groups.

SOURCE: Adapted from pp. 78–86 in *Group Dynamics: Research and Theory*, Second Edition, edited by Dorwin Cartwright and Alvin Zander. Copyright 1953, 1960 by Harper & Row, Publishers, Inc. Reprinted by permission of the publisher.

Dale's first meeting with Tramiel began with a summons to appear at Tramiel's office. Dale flew from his office in Los Angeles to Santa Clara ... , only to find that Tramiel had decided to visit him instead.

Terrified, Dale caught a plane back to find his secretary shaking in her shoes and the burly Tramiel sitting at his desk. For an hour Tramiel grilled Dale on his philosophy of business, pronounced it all wrong, and suggested a tour of the warehouse. When they passed boxes of Commodore Vic-20s and Pets waiting for shipment, recalls Dale, Tramiel seemed to "go crazy," pounding the boxes with his fists and yelling, "Do you think this is bourbon? Do you think it gets better with age?"[5]

Dale's departure within a few months of this episode is not surprising in view of the fact that Tramiel's conduct destroyed group attractiveness and cohesiveness.

Roles According to Shakespeare, "All the world's a stage, and all the men and women merely players. ..." In fact, Shakespeare's analogy between life and play-acting can be carried a step further—to organizations and their component formal work groups. Although employees do not have script books, they do have formal positions in the organizational hierarchy, and they are expected to adhere to company policies and rules. Furthermore, job descriptions and procedure manuals spell out how jobs are to be done. In short, every employee has one or more organizational roles to play. If the organization is properly structured and if everyone plays his or her role(s) properly, then there is a greater chance for organizational success.

A social psychologist has described the concept of role as follows:

> The term role is used to refer to (1) a set of expectations concerning what a person in a given position must, must not, or may do, and (2) the actual behavior of the person who occupies the position. A central idea is that any person occupying a position and filling a role behaves similarly to anyone else who could be in that position.[6]

A **role,** then, is a socially determined prescription for behavior in a specific position. Roles evolve out of the tendency for social units to perpetuate themselves, and they are socially enforced. Through social institutions and groups, society rewards those who play their roles properly and punishes those who deviate from prescribed modes of behavior. The experience of former President Richard M. Nixon attests to the speed with which popular social support can evaporate when society's role expectations are not met.

Norms   Norms are said to define "degrees of acceptability and unacceptability."[7] More precisely, **norms** are general standards of conduct that help individuals judge what is right or wrong or good or bad in a given social setting (for example, work, home, play, or church). Norms have a broader influence than do roles, which focus on a specific position. Although usually unwritten, norms influence behavior enormously.

Every mature group, whether informal or formal, generates its own pattern of norms that constrains and directs the behavior of its members. According to one researcher, norms are enforced for at least four different reasons:

1. To facilitate survival of the group.
2. To simplify or clarify role expectations.
3. To help group members avoid embarrassing situations (protect self-images).
4. To express key group values and enhance the group's unique identity.[8]

As illustrated in Figure 12.2, norms tend to go above and beyond formal rules and written policies. Compliance is shaped with social reinforcement in the form of attention, recognition, and acceptance. Those who fail to comply with the norm may be criticized, ridiculed, or even ostracized. **Ostracism,** or rejection from the group, is figuratively the capital punishment of group dynamics. Informal groups derive much of their power over individuals through the ever-present threat of ostracism.

Figure 12.2   Norms Are Enforced for Different Reasons

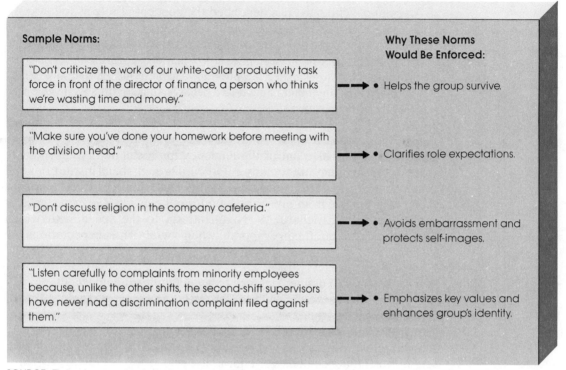

Sample Norms:

"Don't criticize the work of our white-collar productivity task force in front of the director of finance, a person who thinks we're wasting time and money."

"Make sure you've done your homework before meeting with the division head."

"Don't discuss religion in the company cafeteria."

"Listen carefully to complaints from minority employees because, unlike the other shifts, the second-shift supervisors have never had a discrimination complaint filed against them."

Why These Norms
Would Be Enforced:

• Helps the group survive.

• Clarifies role expectations.

• Avoids embarrassment and protects self-images.

• Emphasizes key values and enhances group's identity.

SOURCE: These four reasons have been adapted from Daniel C. Feldman, "The Development and Enforcement of Group Norms," *Academy of Management Review* 9 (January 1984): 47–53.

Norms have an important relationship with cohesiveness. In a highly cohesive group, there is consensus on what the relevant norms are. Disagreement over group norms tends to tear apart cohesiveness. For example, a management advisory committee made up of department heads may establish and enforce a norm that encourages each department head to carry a fair share of the workload. Deviations from this norm will diminish cohesiveness within the group and subsequently undermine its effectiveness.

Group Development

Like inept youngsters who mature into talented adults, groups undergo a maturation process before becoming effective. We have all experienced the uneasiness associated with the first meeting of a new group, be it a sorority or fraternity pledge class, a club, or committee. Initially, there is little mutual understanding, trust, and commitment among the new group members, and their uncertainty over objectives, roles, and leadership doesn't help. The prospect of cooperative action seems unlikely in view of defensive behavior and differences of opinion about who should do what. Someone steps forward to assume a leadership role, and the group is off and running toward eventual maturity (or perhaps premature death). A working knowledge of the characteristics of a mature group can help the manager systematically manage group development, instead of leaving this vital process to chance.

Characteristics of a Mature Group

If and when a group takes on the following characteristics, it can be called a mature group:

1. Members are aware of their own and each other's assets and liabilities vis-à-vis the group's task.
2. These individual differences are accepted without being labeled as good or bad.
3. The group has developed authority and interpersonal relationships that are recognized and accepted by the members.
4. Group decisions are made through rational discussion. Minority opinions and/or dissension is recognized and encouraged. Attempts are not made to force decisions or a false unanimity.
5. Conflict is over substantive group issues such as group goals and the effectiveness and efficiency of various means for achieving those goals. Conflict over emotional issues regarding group structure, processes, or interpersonal relationships is at a minimum.
6. Members are aware of the group's processes and their own roles in them.[9]

A hidden but nonetheless significant benefit of group maturity is that individuality is strengthened and not extinguished, as one might suspect. Protecting the individual's right to dissent is particularly important in regard to the problem of blind obedience, which we shall consider later in this chapter.

Six Stages of Group Development

Experts have identified six distinct stages in the group development process[10] (see Figure 12.3). During stages 1 through 3, attempts are made to overcome the obstacle of uncertainty over power and authority. Once this first obstacle has been surmounted, a second obstacle of uncertainty over interpersonal relations becomes the challenge. This second obstacle must be cleared during stages 4 through 6 if the group is to achieve maturity. Each stage confronts the group's leader and contributing members with a unique combination of problems and opportunities.

Figure 12.3   Group Development from Formation to Maturity

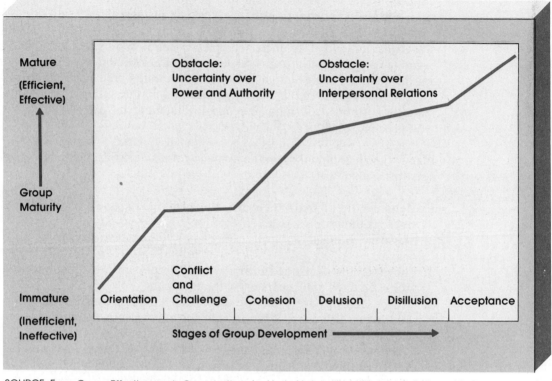

SOURCE: From *Group Effectiveness in Organizations,* by Linda N. Jewell and H. Joseph Reitz, p. 20. Copyright © 1981, Scott, Foresman and Company. Used with permission.

Stage 1: Orientation   Attempts are made to "break the ice." Uncertainty about goals, power, and interpersonal relationships is high. Members generally want and accept any leadership at this point. Emergent leaders often misinterpret this "honeymoon period" as a mandate for permanent control.

Stage 2: Conflict and Challenge   As the emergent leader's philosophy, objectives, and policies become apparent, individuals or subgroups advocating alternative courses of action struggle for control. This second stage may be prolonged while members strive to clarify and reconcile their roles as part of a complete redistribution of power and authority. Many groups never continue past stage 2 because they get bogged down in emotionalism and political infighting. Committees have become the brunt of jokes (for example, a camel is a horse designed by a committee) because they often fail to mature beyond stage 2.

Stage 3: Cohesion   The shifts in power started in stage 2 are completed, under a new leader or the original leader, with a new consensus on authority, structure, and procedures. A "we" feeling becomes apparent as everyone becomes truly involved. Any lingering differences over power and authority are resolved quickly. Stage 3 is usually of relatively short duration. If not, the group is likely to stall.

Stage 4: Delusion   A feeling of "having been through the worst of it" prevails after passing rather rapidly through stage 3. Issues and problems that threaten to break this spell of relief are dismissed or treated lightly. Members seem committed to fostering harmony at all costs. Participation and camaraderie run high, as members believe that all the difficult emotional problems have been solved.

Stage 5: Disillusion   Subgroups tend to form as the delusion of unlimited goodwill wears off, and there is a growing disenchantment with how things are turning out. Those with unrealized expectations challenge the group to perform better and are prepared to reveal their personal strengths and weaknesses if necessary. Others hold back. Tardiness and absenteeism are symptomatic of diminishing cohesiveness and commitment.

Stage 6: Acceptance   It usually takes a trusted and influential group member who is concerned about the group to step forward and help the group move from conflict to cohesion. This individual, acting as the group catalyst, is usually someone other than the leader. Members are encouraged to test their self-perceptions against the reality of how others perceive them. Greater personal and mutual understanding helps members adapt to situations without causing problems. Members' expectations are more realistic than ever before. Since the authority structure is generally accepted, subgroups can pursue different matters without threatening group cohesiveness. Consequently, stage 6 groups tend to be highly effective and efficient.

Time-wasting problems and inefficiencies can be minimized if group members are consciously aware of this developmental process. Just as it is impossible for a child to skip being a teen-ager on the way to adulthood, committees and other work groups will find that there are no short cuts to group maturity. Some emotional lumps are inevitable along the way.

Trust: The Key to Group Effectiveness

Trust, a belief in the integrity, character, or ability of others, is essential if people are to achieve anything together in the long run. Quality-of-work-life programs that encourage participation are particularly dependent on trust. Sadly, trust is not one of the hallmarks of current American management. In contrast, observers have noted the administrative benefits of the trust evident in Japanese management.

Japanese managers trust not only their workers but also their peers and superiors.

The existence of that all-encompassing trust leads to a simplified organization structure that has helped many Japanese companies become low-cost producers. Because Japanese companies assume that personnel at all levels are competent—and, above all, trustworthy enough to have the company's best interests in mind—they do not employ highly paid executives whose only jobs are to review and pass on the work of other highly paid executives. They do not write job descriptions giving managers authority for specific fiefdoms and putting them into conflict with managers of rival fiefdoms. Instead, their operations are lean at the staff level and rich at the line level—where profits are made.[11]

To a greater extent than they may initially suspect, managers determine the level of trust in the organization and its component work groups. This section clarifies the role of trust in work group dynamics and identifies some common sources of mistrust.

Trust is not a free-floating group variable. It affects, and in turn is affected by, other group processes. Dale Zand's model of work group interaction does an excellent job of putting trust into proper perspective (see Figure 12.4). Zand believes that trust is the key to establishing productive interpersonal relationships.[12]

Creating a Climate of Trust

Primary responsibility for creating a climate of trust falls on the manager. Group members usually look to the manager, who enjoys hierarchical advantage and greater access to key information, to set the tone for interpersonal dealings. Threatening or intimidating actions by the manager are likely to encourage the group to bind together in cohesive resistance. Therefore, trust needs to be developed right from the beginning, when group members are still receptive to positive managerial influence.

Trust is initially encouraged by the manager's being open and honest. Trusting managers talk *with* their people rather than *at* them. A trusting manager demonstrates a willingness to be influenced by others and to change if the facts show that a change is appropriate. Furthermore, mutual

Figure 12.4   Trust and Effective Group Interaction

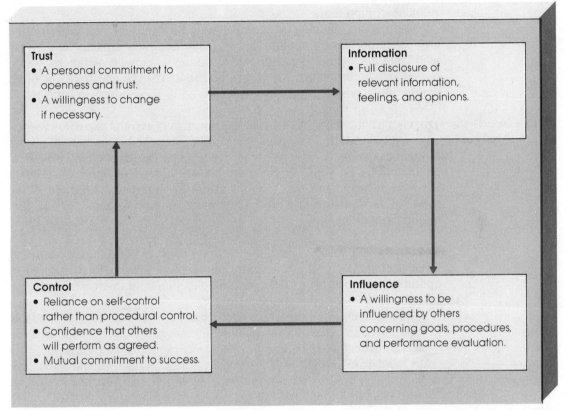

Trust
- A personal commitment to openness and trust.
- A willingness to change if necessary.

Information
- Full disclosure of relevant information, feelings, and opinions.

Control
- Reliance on self-control rather than procedural control.
- Confidence that others will perform as agreed.
- Mutual commitment to success.

Influence
- A willingness to be influenced by others concerning goals, procedures, and performance evaluation.

SOURCE: Adapted from Dale E. Zand, "Trust and Managerial Problem Solving," *Administrative Science Quarterly* 17, no. 2 (June 1972): 231 by permission of *The Administrative Science Quarterly* © 1972 by Cornell University.

trust between a manager and group members encourages self-control, as opposed to control through direct supervision. Hewlett-Packard (HP), the computer company with a reputation for excellent management, has carefully nurtured an organizational culture based on trust. According to the authors of *In Search of Excellence*:

> The faith that HP has in its people is conspicuously in evidence in the corporate "open lab stock" policy. ... The lab stock area is where the electrical and mechanical components are kept. The open lab stock policy means that not only do the engineers have free access to this equipment, but they are actually encouraged to *take it home for their personal use!*[13]

HP's rationale for this trusting policy is that the company will reap innovative returns no matter how the engineers choose to work with the valuable components.

Paradoxically, managerial control actually expands when committed group members enjoy greater freedom in pursuing consensual goals. Those who trust each other generally avoid taking advantage of others' weaknesses or shortcomings. Managers find that trust begets trust; in other words, those who feel they are trusted tend to trust others in return.

The Seeds of Mistrust

Trust is a fragile thing. As most of us know from personal experience, trust grows at a painfully slow pace, yet can be destroyed in an instant with a thoughtless remark. Mistrust can erode the long-term effectiveness of organizations. Fortunately, there are constructive steps that management can take to avoid mistrust. Before discussing these constructive steps, however, we shall look at three managerial assumptions that tend to disrupt organizational life.

Faulty Assumptions According to one expert on organizational trust, three seemingly harmless assumptions about organizational life, when operating in concert, virtually guarantee a climate of mistrust.

> The three assumptions are, first, that important issues naturally fall into two opposing camps, exemplified by either/or thinking; second, that hard data and facts are better than what appear to be soft ideas and speculation, exemplified in the "hard drives out soft" rule; and finally, that the world in general is an unsafe place, exemplified by a person's having a pervasive mistrust of the universe around him or her.[14]

Constructive Steps Managers who find themselves being victimized by these traps can turn things around by fostering "and-also" thinking in lieu of "either/or" thinking. And-also thinking encourages contributors to search for creative options. Either/or thinking, on the other hand, encourages emotional battles between "good guys" and "bad guys." Additionally, a workable blend of hard facts and soft feelings will help management avoid the trap of "damn the long-term consequences, let's get the job done." Finally, by resisting the notion that it is nothing but a dog-eat-dog world, management gives cooperation and trust some room in which to grow.

Organizational Politics

Only recently has the topic of organizational politics (also known as office politics) begun to receive serious attention from management theorists and researchers. But as we all know from practical experience, organizational life is often highly charged with political wheeling and dealing. A corporate executive has underscored this point by asking:

> Have you ever done a very satisfactory piece of work only to have it lost in the organizational shuffle? Have you ever come up with a new idea only to have your boss take credit for it? Have you ever faced a situation where someone else made a serious mistake and somehow engineered it so you got the blame?[15]

Whether politically motivated or not, managers need to be knowledgeable about organizational politics because their careers will be affected by it.

What Does Organizational Politics Involve?
As the term implies, self-interest is central to organizational politics. In fact, **organizational politics** has been defined as "the pursuit of self-interest at work in the face of real or imagined opposition."[16] According to one expert on the subject, political maneuvering encompasses all self-serving behavior above and beyond competence, hard work, and luck.[17] Although the term organizational politics has a negative connotation, researchers have identified both positive and negative aspects:

> Political behaviors widely accepted as legitimate would certainly include exchanging favors, "touching bases," forming coalitions, and seeking sponsors at upper levels. Less legitimate behaviors would include whistle-blowing, revolutionary coalitions, threats, and sabotage.[18]

Whistle-blowing, the practice of reporting the wrongdoings of one's superiors to the media or outside agencies, is discussed in detail in Chapter 18.

Employees resort to political behavior when they are unwilling to trust their career to competence, hard work, or luck. One might say that organizational politicians help luck along by relying on one or more political tactics. Whether or not employees fall back on political tactics has a lot to do with an organization's climate or culture. For example, imagine yourself trying to climb the managerial ladder at PepsiCo Inc., where political maneuvering is said to be active amid a climate of "creative tension":

> Managers are pitted against each other to grab more market share, to work harder, and to wring more profits out of their businesses. Because winning is the key value at Pepsi, losing has its penalties. Consistent runners-up find their jobs gone. Employees know they must win merely to stay in place—and must devastate the competition to get ahead. ...
>
> Kendall [the chairman] himself sets a constant example. He once resorted to using a snowmobile to get to work in a blizzard, demonstrating the ingenuity and

dedication to work he expects from his staff. This type of pressure has pushed many managers out. But a recent survey shows that others thrive under such conditions.[19]

One can only speculate about what this highly political climate will do for PepsiCo in the long term. In view of Pepsi's steady increase in market share in recent years, it appears to be paying off in the short term. Of course, those who were forced out or had their toes stepped on might have a different view.

Research on Organizational Politics

Researchers in one widely cited study of organizational politics conducted structured interviews with 87 managers employed by 30 electronics firms in southern California. Included in the sample were 30 chief executive officers, 28 middle managers, and 29 supervisors. Significant results included:

- The higher the level of management, the greater the perceived amount of political activity.
- The larger the organization, the greater the perceived amount of political activity.
- Personnel in staff positions were viewed as more political than those in line positions.
- People in marketing were the most political; those in production were the least political.
- "Reorganization changes" reportedly prompted the most political activity.
- A majority (61 percent) of those interviewed believed organizational politics helps advance one's career.
- Forty-five percent believed that organizational politics distracts from organizational goals; another 45 percent did not.[20]

Regarding the last two findings, it was clear that political activities were seen as helpful to the individual. On the other hand, the interviewed managers were split down the middle on the question of the value of politics to the organization. Managers who believed political behavior had a positive impact on the organization cited the following reasons: "gaining visibility for ideas, improving coordination and communication, developing teams and groups, and increasing *esprit de corps*. ..."[21]

Political Tactics

As defined above, organizational politics takes in a lot of behavioral territory. The following six political tactics are common expressions of politics in the workplace:

- **Posturing.** Those who use this tactic look for situations in which they can make a good impression. "One upmanship" and taking credit for other people's work are included in this category.
- **Empire building.** Gaining and keeping control over human and material resources is the principal motivation behind this tactic. Those with large budgets usually feel more safely entrenched in their positions and believe they have more influence over peers and superiors.
- **Making the supervisor look good.** Traditionally referred to as "apple polishing," this political strategy is prompted by a desire to favorably influence those who control one's career ascent. Anyone with an oversized ego is an easy target for this tactic.
- **Collecting and using social IOUs.** Reciprocal exchange of political favors can be done in two ways: (1) by helping someone look good or (2) by preventing someone from looking bad by ignoring or covering up a mistake. Those who rely on this tactic feel that all favors are coins of exchange rather than expressions of altruism or unselfishness.
- **Creating power and loyalty cliques.** Based on the adage that there is power in numbers, the idea here is to face superiors and competitors as a cohesive group rather than alone.
- **Destructive competition.** As a last-ditch effort, some people will resort to character assassination through suggestive remarks, vindictive gossip, or outright lies. This tactic also includes sabotaging the work of a perceived competitor.[22]

Obvious illegalities notwithstanding, one's own values and ethics and organizational sanctions are the final arbiters of whether or not using these tactics is acceptable. (See Table 12.2 for a practicing manager's advice on how to win at office politics.)

Antidotes to Political Behavior

Each of the foregoing political tactics varies in degree. The average individual would be hard pressed to claim complete innocence on all counts. But excessive political maneuvering can become a serious threat to productivity when self-interests clearly override the interests of the group or organization. Organizational politics can be kept within reasonable bounds by applying the following five tips:

1. Strive for a climate of openness and trust.
2. Measure performance according to results rather than personalities.
3. Encourage top management to refrain from exhibiting political behavior that will be imitated by subordinates.
4. Strive to integrate individual and organizational goals through meaningful work and career planning.
5. Practice job rotation to encourage broader perspectives and understanding of the problems of others.[23]

Table 12.2   One Manager's Rules for Winning at Office Politics

1. Find out what the boss expects.
2. Build an information network. Knowledge is power. Identify the people who have power and the extent and direction of it. Title doesn't necessarily reflect actual influence. Find out how the grapevine works. Develop good internal public relations for yourself.
3. Find a mentor. This is a trusted counselor who can be honest with you and help train and guide you to improve your ability and effectiveness as a manager.
4. Don't make enemies without a very good reason.
5. Avoid cliques. Keep circulating in the office.
6. If you must fight, fight over something that is really worth it. Don't lose ground over minor matters or petty differences.
7. Gain power through allies. Build ties that bind. Create IOUs, obligations, and loyalties. Do not be afraid to enlist help from above.
8. Maintain control. Don't misuse your cohorts. Maintain the status and integrity of your allies.
9. Mobilize your forces when necessary. Don't commit your friends without their approval. Be a gracious winner when you do win.
10. Never hire a family member or a close friend.

SOURCE: Adapted from David E. Hall, "Winning at Office Politics," *Credit & Financial Management* 86 (April 1984): 23. Reprinted with permission from *Credit & Financial Management*, Copyright April 1984, published by the National Association of Credit Management, 475 Park Avenue South, New York, NY 10016.

The Issue of Conformity

Much is accomplished in this world because people conform to accepted standards of behavior. Imagine how chaotic it would be if all automobile drivers suddenly stopped conforming to traffic laws: our chances of arriving alive would greatly diminish. The same holds true for norms, rules, and regulations at work. Relatively strict conformity is necessary to ensure the efficient accomplishment of organizational objectives.

As it is used here, the term **conformity** means complying with the role expectations and norms perceived by the majority to be associated with a particular situation. Conformity enhances predictability, generally thought to be good for rational planning and productive enterprise. How can anything be accomplished if people cannot be counted on to perform their assigned duties? But, on the other hand, why do so many employees actively participate in or passively condone illegal and unethical organizational practices involving discrimination, environmental degradation, and unfair competition? The answers to these questions lie along a continuum with anarchy at one end and blind conformity at the other. Socially responsible management is anchored to a point somewhere between them.

Figure 12.5   The Asch Line Experiment

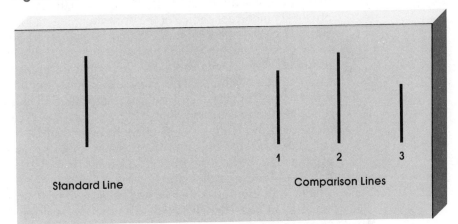

Standard Line   Comparison Lines

Research on Conformity   Social psychologists have discovered much about human behavior by studying individuals and groups in controlled laboratory settings. One classic laboratory study was conducted by Solomon Asch.[24] His study was designed to answer the question, How often will an individual take a stand against a unanimous majority that is obviously wrong? Asch's results were both intriguing and unsettling.

The Hot Seat   Asch began his study by assembling groups of seven to nine college students, supposedly to work on a perceptual problem. Actually, though, Asch was studying conformity. All but one member of each group were Asch's confederates, and Asch told them exactly how to behave and what to say. The experiment was really concerned with the reactions of the remaining student—called the naive subject—who didn't know what was going on.

All the students in each group were shown cards with lines similar to those in Figure 12.5. They were instructed to match the line on the left with the one on the right that was closest to it in length. The differences in length among the lines on the right were obvious. Each group went through 12 rounds of the matching process, with a different set of lines for every round. The experimenter asked one group member at a time to state aloud to the group his or her choice. Things proceeded normally for the first two rounds as each group member voiced an opinion. Agreement was unanimous. Suddenly, on the third round only one individual, the naive subject, chose the correct pair of lines. All the other group members chose a different (and obviously wrong) pair. During the rounds in which there was disagreement, all of Asch's confederates conspired to select an incorrect pair of lines. It was the individual versus the rest of the group.

Following the Immoral Majority Each of the naive subjects was faced with a personal dilemma. Should he or she fight the group or give in to the obviously incorrect choice of the overwhelming majority? Among 31 naive subjects who made a total of 217 judgments, two-thirds of the judgments were correct. The other one-third were incorrect; that is, they were consistent with the majority opinion. Individual differences were great, with some subjects yielding to the incorrect majority opinion more readily than others. Only 20 percent of the naive subjects remained entirely independent. All the rest turned their backs on their own perceptions and went along with the group at least once. In other words, 80 percent of Asch's subjects knuckled under to the pressure of group opinion at least once, even though the majority was dead wrong. (It is instructive to ponder how one would act in such a situation.)

One limitation of Asch's study, because it was a contrived laboratory experiment, was that it failed to probe the relationship between cohesiveness and conformity. Asch's naive subjects were outsiders. But recent research on "groupthink" has shown how a cohesive group of insiders can fall victim to blind conformity.

Groupthink After carefully studying the records of several successful and unsuccessful American foreign-policy decisions, psychologist Irving Janis uncovered an undesirable by-product of group cohesiveness. He labeled this problem **groupthink** and defined it as "a mode of thinking that people engage in when they are deeply involved in a cohesive in-group, when the members' strivings for unanimity override their motivation to realistically appraise alternative courses of action."[25] Groupthink helps explain how otherwise intelligent policy makers, in both government and business, can sometimes make incredibly stupid decisions.

For example, according to Janis's interpretation, President John F. Kennedy and his team of strategic advisers in 1961 approved a Central Intelligence Agency plan for the invasion of Fidel Castro's Cuba by a force of about 1400 Cuban exiles. When the ill-fated Bay of Pigs invasion collapsed in utter failure three days after it was launched, Kennedy realized that he and his advisers had unwittingly rubber-stamped a plan based on nothing but false assumptions. Critical thinking, reality testing, and moral judgment had been temporarily shelved as the Bay of Pigs decision was enthusiastically railroaded through. Although Janis acknowledges that cohesive groups are not inevitably victimized by groupthink, he warns group decision makers to be alert for the symptoms of groupthink because the risk is always there.

Symptoms of Groupthink According to Janis, the onset of groupthink is foreshadowed by a definite pattern of symptoms. Among the early warning signs of groupthink are excessive optimism, an assumption of inherent morality, suppression of dissent, and an almost desperate quest for unanimity.[26] Given such a decision-making climate, the probability of a poor decision is high. Managers face a curious dilemma here. While a group is still in stage 1 or stage 2 of development, its cohesiveness is too low to get much accomplished because of emotional and time-consuming power struggles. But by the time the group achieves enough cohesiveness in stage 3 to make decisions promptly, the risk of groupthink is high. The trick is to achieve needed cohesiveness without going to the extreme of groupthink.

Preventing Groupthink   High on the list of preventive measures, according to Janis, is to have one of the group members periodically ask, "Are we allowing ourselves to become victims of groupthink?"[27] More fundamental preventive measures include

- Avoiding the use of groups to rubber-stamp decisions that have already been made by higher management.
- Urging each group member to be a critical evaluator.
- Bringing in outside experts for fresh perspectives.
- Assigning to someone the role of devil's advocate to challenge assumptions and alternatives.[28]
- Taking time to consider possible side effects and consequences of alternative courses of action.[29]

Ideally, decision quality will improve when these preventive steps are practiced to the point of becoming second nature in cohesive groups. For example, Intel's president, Andrew Grove, effectively prevents groupthink with the following confrontational technique: "I get a much better understanding of an issue with which I am not familiar by listening to two people with opposing views discuss it than I do by listening to one side only."[30] Managers who cannot imagine themselves being victimized by blind conformity are prime candidates for groupthink.

Managerial Implications   Like other elements of group dynamics, conformity has both a good side and a bad side. When the work group identifies with the organization's overall direction, and when that direction is socially responsible, great things can be accomplished. Conformity, in this context, is a positive force. But, as one authority pointed out, "The group has a potential to produce blind loyalty, abject submission, and total obedience, and such conditions have invariably been dehumanizing in the end."[31] Conformity becomes a negative force when it encourages group members to deny their personal convictions, better judgment, or ethical values for fear of group reprisal.

Clearly, one of the difficult challenges facing today's managers is to make sure that they and their peers and subordinates can tell the difference between productive conformity and blind, ultimately destructive conformity.

Managing Conflict

Conflict is an inevitable by-product of interpersonal dealings.[32] This is particularly true of work groups because they generally are expediently assembled collections of individuals with differing backgrounds, perceptions, attitudes, and values. **Conflict,** as defined by an expert in the field, "refers to all kinds of opposition or antagonistic interaction. It is based on scarcity of power, resources or social position, and differing value structures."[33] But one should be careful not to assume that all conflict is bad. Conflict has two faces, one functional (or constructive) and the other dysfunctional (or destructive). According to one expert who emphasizes the positive side of conflict:

> Constructive conflict is crucial for organizations. Without an effective means of handling it, conflict can tear relationships apart and interfere with the exchange of ideas, information and resources in groups and between departments. Well-managed conflict, on the other hand, helps workers anticipate and solve problems, feel confident, strengthen their relationships and be committed to the organization.[34]

Two Faces of Conflict
An organizational perspective is required when distinguishing between functional and dysfunctional conflict. The organizational benefits of functional conflict are increased effort and improved performance, enhanced creativity, and personal development and growth (see Table 12.3). In contrast, the symptoms of dysfunctional conflict include indecision, resistance to change, emotional outbursts, apathy, and increased political maneuvering. By monitoring these various signs and symptoms, management can decide when it is appropriate to encourage conflict and when it is time to step in and attempt to resolve or neutralize it. There are two sets of tools available for managing conflict. The first is called conflict triggers, which stimulate conflict, and the second involves conflict resolution techniques, which are used when functional conflict deteriorates into dysfunctional conflict.

Conflict Triggers
A **conflict trigger** is a circumstance that increases the chances of intergroup or interpersonal conflict. It can stimulate either functional or dysfunctional conflict. As long as a conflict trigger appears to stimulate constructive conflict, it can be allowed to continue. But as soon as the

Table 12.3   Constructive Conflict in Action

"I just don't understand how your new way of measuring things around here will help us at all," the plant manager said, grimacing. Others at the meeting merely looked puzzled. The vice president of manufacturing, the plant manager's direct superior, had just finished vigorously urging the use of a particular statistical indicator to determine whether the company's plants were delivering products on time. Faced with the plant manager's incredulity, the vice president redoubled his efforts, trying again to win over everyone in the room.

The plant manager remained unconvinced. His colleagues then jumped into the fray. Arguments generated rebuttals, numbers collided with other numbers. New ideas began to surface, most of them to be immediately rejected, until eventually the heated exchanges dissipated. The still-animated group of people in the room suddenly realized, with considerable satisfaction, that they had now come up with the right statistical measure.

As the meeting ended, the vice president shook his head in mock dismay. "It's too bad," he said, "that you people are so reticent." He put away his papers somewhat ruefully—his hours of preparation for the meeting had not resulted in his proposal being adopted. But he also knew that what had finally been agreed upon was better than his original idea.

SOURCE: Excerpted from Andrew S. Grove, "How to Make Confrontation Work For You," *Fortune* 110 (July 23, 1984): 73–74. © 1984 Time Inc. All rights reserved.

symptoms of destructive conflict become apparent, steps should be taken to remove or correct the offending conflict trigger. Major conflict triggers include

- **Ambiguous or overlapping jurisdictions.** Unclear job boundaries often create competition for resources and control. Reorganization can clarify job boundaries if destructive conflict becomes a problem (refer to the organization design alternatives discussed in Chapter 8).
- **Competition for scarce resources.** As the term is used here, resources include funds, personnel, authority, power, and valuable information. In other words, anything of value in an organizational setting can become a competitively sought-after scarce resource. Sometimes, as in the cases of money and people, destructive competition for scarce resources can be avoided by enlarging the resource base (such as increasing competing managers' budgets or hiring additional personnel).
- **Communication breakdowns.** As we discussed in Chapter 10, communication is a complex process beset by many barriers. These barriers often provoke conflict. It is easy to misunderstand another person or group of people if two-way communication is hampered in some way. The battle for clear communication never ends.
- **Time pressure.** Deadlines and other forms of time pressure can either stimulate prompt performance or trigger destructive emotional reac-

tions. Managers should consider individuals' coping ability when imposing deadlines.

- **Unreasonable standards, rules, policies, or procedures.** These conflict triggers generally lead to dysfunctional conflict between managers and their subordinates. The best remedy is for the manager to tune into employees' perceptions of fair play and correct extremely unpopular situations before they mushroom.

- **Personality clashes.** Psychologists tell us that it is very difficult to change one's personality on the job. Therefore the most practical remedy for serious personality clashes is to separate the antagonistic parties by reassigning one or both to a new job.

- **Status differentials.** As long as productive organizations continue to be arranged hierarchically, this conflict trigger is unavoidable. But managers can minimize dysfunctional conflict by showing a genuine concern for the ideas, feelings, and values of subordinates.

- **Unrealized expectations.** As pointed out in our discussion of psychological contracts in Chapter 9, dissatisfaction grows when one's expectations are not met. Conflict is another by-product of unrealized expectations. Destructive conflict can be avoided in this area by taking time to discover, through frank discussion, what subordinates expect from their employment. Unrealistic expectations can be countered before they become a trigger for dysfunctional conflict.[35]

Managers who prepare for these conflict triggers will be in a much better position to manage conflict in a systematic and rational fashion. Those who passively wait for things to explode before reacting will find conflict managing them.

Resolving Conflict   Even the best managers sometimes find themselves in the middle of dysfunctional conflict, whether it is due to inattention or to circumstances beyond their control. In these situations, they may choose to do nothing, called an *avoidance* strategy by some, or try one or more of the following conflict resolution techniques.

Problem Solving   When conflicting parties take the time to identify and correct the source of their conflict, they are engaging in problem solving. This approach is based on the assumption that causes must be rooted out and attacked if anything is really to change. Problem solving (refer to our discussion of creative problem solving in Chapter 6) encourages managers to focus their attention on causes, factual information, and promising alternatives rather than strictly on personalities or scapegoats. The major shortcoming of the problem-solving approach is that it takes time, but the investment of extra time can pay off handsomely when the problem is corrected instead of ignored and allowed to worsen.

SOURCE: © Leo Cullum, 1985.

Superordinate Goals   "Superordinate goals are highly valued, unattainable by any one group [or individual] alone, and commonly sought."[36] When a manager relies on superordinate goals to resolve dysfunctional conflict, he or she brings the conflicting parties together and, in effect, says, "Look, we're all in this together. Let's forget our differences so we can get the job done." For example, a company president might remind the production and marketing department heads who have been arguing about product design that the competition is breathing down their necks. Although this technique often works in the short run, the underlying problem typically crops up later to cause friction once again.

Compromise   This technique generally appeals to those living in a democracy. Proponents of this approach claim that everybody wins because it is based on negotiation, or give and take. But everyone also loses something in a compromise. Something must be given up if anything is to be gained. Like problem solving, compromise takes time that management may or may not be able to afford. But, unlike problem solving, the problem is worked around rather than solved.

Forcing   Sometimes, especially when time is important, management must simply step into a conflict and order the conflicting parties to handle the situation in a certain manner. Reliance on formal authority and power of superior position are at the heart of forcing. As one might suspect, forcing does not resolve the personal conflict and, in fact, may serve to compound it by hurting feelings and/or fostering resentment and mistrust.

Smoothing   A manager who relies on smoothing says to the conflicting parties something like "Settle down. Don't rock the boat. Things will work out by themselves." This approach may tone down conflict in the short run, but it does not solve the underlying problem. As with each of the other conflict resolution techniques, smoothing has its place. It can be useful when management is attempting to hold things together until a critical project is completed or when there is no time for problem solving or compromise and forcing is deemed inappropriate.

When one puts things into perspective, problem solving is the only approach that removes the actual sources of conflict. It is the only resolution technique that helps improve things in the long run. All the other approaches amount to short-run, stopgap measures. And managers who fall back on an avoidance strategy are simply running away from the problem. Nonetheless, as mentioned, problem solving can take up valuable time, time that management may not be willing or able to spend at that particular moment. When this is the case, management may choose to fall back on superordinate goals, compromise, forcing, or smoothing, whichever seems most suitable.

Summary

Managers need a working understanding of group dynamics because groups are the basic social building blocks of organizations. Both informal (friendship) and formal (work) groups are made up of two or more freely interacting individuals who have a common identity and purpose. After someone has been attracted to a group, cohesiveness—a "we" feeling—encourages continued membership. Roles are social expectations for behavior in a specific position, whereas norms are more general standards for conduct in a given social setting. Norms are enforced because they help the group survive, clarify role expectations, protect self-images, and enhance the group's identity by emphasizing key values. Compliance with role expectations and norms is rewarded with social reinforcement; non-compliance is punished by criticism, ridicule, and ostracism.

Mature groups that are characterized by mutual acceptance, encouragement of minority opinion, and minimal emotional conflict are the product of a developmental process with identifiable stages. During the first three stages—orientation, conflict and challenge, and cohesion—power and authority problems are resolved. Groups are faced with the obstacle of uncertainty over interpersonal relations during the last three stages—delusion, disillusion, and acceptance. Committees have a widespread reputation for inefficiency and ineffectiveness because they tend to get stalled in an early stage of group development.

Trust is a key ingredient of effective group action that is clearly evident in Japanese management but often underutilized by American managers. When work group members trust one another, there will be a more active exchange of information, more interpersonal influence, and hence greater self-control. Managers who prefer either/or thinking, rely solely on hard data, and envision the world as basically an unsafe place foster a climate of mistrust. Political tactics such as posturing, empire building, making the boss look good, collecting and using social IOUs, creating power and loyalty cliques, and destructive competition need to be kept in check if a healthy degree of trust is to be achieved.

Although a fairly high degree of conformity is necessary if organizations and society in general are to function properly, blind conformity is ultimately dehumanizing and destructive. Research shows that individuals have a strong tendency to bend to the will of the majority, even if the majority is clearly wrong. Cohesive decision-making groups can be victimized by groupthink when unanimity becomes more important than critically evaluating alternative courses of action.

Conflict is inevitable in organized settings. Recognizing that conflict can be either functional or dysfunctional, managers can enhance effort, performance, and creativity by permitting conflict triggers to continue until the symptoms of dysfunctional conflict appear. Dysfunctional conflict can be resolved through problem solving, superordinate goals, compromise, forcing, or smoothing.

Terms to Understand

Group	Trust
Informal group	Organizational politics
Formal group	Conformity
Cohesiveness	Groupthink
Role	Conflict
Norms	Conflict trigger
Ostracism	

Questions for Discussion

1. Applying the sociological definition of "group," how many groups do you belong to at this time? What positive and negative influences do they have on your behavior?
2. What unwritten norms are there for student behavior in the classroom? How are they communicated and enforced?
3. In reference to a particular group you belong to, in what stage of development is it? How do you know?
4. According to your own experience, why do many committees fail to achieve stage 6 maturity?
5. What does it take for you to trust someone? Is this likely to help or hinder you as a manager? Why?
6. What positive and/or negative experiences have you had with organizational politics?
7. Have you ever been a victim of blind conformity? Explain the circumstances.
8. As a member of a committee, what steps could you personally take to help the group avoid groupthink?
9. What kind(s) of functional conflict have you experienced recently?
10. Why is it naive to think that on-the-job dysfunctional conflict can be completely avoided today?

Back to the Opening Case

Now that you have read Chapter 12, you should be able to answer the following questions about the Pan Am case:

1. Why were mistrust and political maneuvering unavoidable at Pan Am?
2. Why was Pan Am's board of directors during the Seawell era a likely candidate for groupthink?
3. What evidence of dysfunctional conflict can you find in this case?
4. Why was the merger with National doomed to problems from the start?

Closing Case 12.2*

Can Larry Fit In?

You are the manager of an auditing team for a major accounting firm. You are sitting in your office reading some complicated new reporting pro-

*From *Developing Management Skills* by David A. Whetten and Kim S. Cameron. Copyright © 1984 by Scott, Foresman and Company. Reprinted by permission.

cedures that have just arrived from the home office. Your concentration is suddenly interrupted by a loud knock on your door. Without waiting for an invitation to enter, Larry, one of your auditors, bursts into your office. He is obviously very upset and it is not difficult for you to surmise why he is in such a nasty mood. You have just posted the audit assignments for the next month and you scheduled Larry for a job you knew he wouldn't like. Larry is one of your senior auditors and the company norm is that they get the better assignments. This particular job will require him to spend two weeks away from home, in a remote town, working with a company whose records are notorious for being a mess.

Unfortunately, you have had to assign several of these less desirable audits to Larry recently because you are short of personnel. But that's not the only reason. You have received several complaints from the junior staff members recently about Larry's treating them in an obnoxious manner. They feel he is always looking for an opportunity to boss them around, as if he were their supervisor instead of a member of the audit team. As a result, your whole operation works smoothly when you can send Larry out of town on a solo project for several days. It keeps him from coming into your office telling you how to do your job, and the morale of the rest of the auditing staff is significantly higher.

Larry slams the door and proceeds to express his anger over this assignment. He says you are deliberately trying to undermine his status in the group by giving him all the dirty assignments. He accuses you of being insensitive to his feelings and says that if things don't change, he is going to register a formal complaint with your boss.

For Discussion
1. Are Larry's coworkers likely to enforce the company norm that senior auditors get the better assignments? Why?
2. What conflict triggers can you identify in this case? How do you know they are present?
3. How have you (Larry's manager) handled the conflict surrounding Larry so far? What are the positive and negative aspects of this approach?
4. How can you (Larry's manager) turn this present confrontation into functional conflict?

References

Opening Quotation: Robert Presthus, *The Organizational Society,* rev. ed. (New York: St. Martin's Press, 1978), p. 113.

Opening Case: For additional information on Pan Am, see William M. Carley,

"Pan Am Turmoil Laid to Deficits, Shake-ups and National Merger," *Wall Street Journal* (August 3, 1981): 1, 6; "No Automatic Pilot: Pan Am's Ed Acker Has Strong Ideas on How to Run an Airline," *Barron's* 61 (November 16, 1981): 4–5, 16–20, 64; Louis Kraar, "Putting Pan Am Back Together Again," *Fortune* 104 (December 28, 1981): 42–47; Geoffrey Smith, "Tail Wind at Pan Am," *Forbes* 132 (July 4, 1983): 42–45; and "A Recovered Pan Am Faces Tomorrow's Hurdles," *Business Week* No. 2845 (June 4, 1984): 60, 65–68.

Closing Case: David A. Whetten and Kim S. Cameron, *Developing Management Skills* (Glenview, Ill.: Scott, Foresman, 1984), p. 444.

1. Carley, "Pan Am Turmoil," p. 6.
2. Joseph A. Litterer, *The Analysis of Organizations,* 2nd ed. (New York: Wiley, 1973), p. 231.
3. For an excellent elaboration of this definition, see David Horton Smith, "A Parsimonious Definition of 'Group': Toward Conceptual Clarity and Scientific Utility," *Sociological Inquiry* 37 (Spring 1967): 141–167.
4. See Charles G. Burck, "For William Hewitt It Was an Easy Ascent," *Fortune* 94 (August 1976): 166–170.
5. Peter Nulty, "Cool Heads Are Trying to Keep Commodore Hot," *Fortune* 110 (July 23, 1984): 38, 40.
6. Albert A. Harrison, *Individuals and Groups: Understanding Social Behavior* (Monterey, Calif.: Brooks/Cole, 1976), p. 16.
7. Ibid., p. 401.
8. Adapted from material found in Daniel C. Feldman, "The Development and Enforcement of Group Norms," *Academy of Management Review* 9 (January 1984): 47–53.
9. From *Group Effectiveness in Organizations* by Linda N. Jewell and H. Joseph Reitz. Copyright © 1981 Scott, Foresman and Company, pp. 14–15. Reprinted by permission.
10. The following discussion of the six stages of group development is adapted from *Group Effectiveness in Organizations* by Linda N. Jewell and H. Joseph Reitz. Copyright © 1981 Scott, Foresman and Company, pp. 15–20. Reprinted by permission. For earlier research in this area, see Warren G. Bennis and Herbert A. Shepard, "A Theory of Group Development," *Human Relations* 9 (1956): 415–437.
11. Claudia H. Deutsch, "Trust: The New Ingredient in Management," *Business Week* No. 2695 (July 6, 1981): 104.
12. See Dale E. Zand, "Trust and Managerial Problem Solving," *Administrative Science Quarterly* 17 (June 1972): 229–239.
13. Thomas J. Peters and Robert H. Waterman, Jr., *In Search of Excellence* (New York: Harper & Row, 1982), p. 245.
14. Louis B. Barnes, "Managing the Paradox of Organizational Trust," *Harvard Business Review* 59 (March-April 1981): 108.

15. David E. Hall, "Winning at Office Politics," *Credit & Financial Management* 86 (April 1984): 20.
16. Victor Murray and Jeffrey Gandz, "Games Executives Play: Politics at Work," *Business Horizons* 23 (December 1980): 16.
17. Andrew J. DuBrin, *Fundamentals of Organizational Behavior: An Applied Perspective,* 2nd ed. (Elmsford, N.Y.: Pergamon Press, 1978), p. 154.
18. Dan Farrell and James C. Petersen, "Patterns of Political Behavior in Organizations," *Academy of Management Review* 7 (July 1982): 407.
19. "Corporate Culture," *Business Week* No. 2660 (October 27, 1980): 148, 154.
20. Adapted from Dan L. Madison, Robert W. Allen, Lyman W. Porter, Patricia A. Renwick, and Bronston T. Mayes, "Organizational Politics: An Exploration of Managers' Perceptions," *Human Relations* 33 (February 1980): 79–100.
21. Ibid., p. 97.
22. These six political tactics have been adapted from a more extensive list found in DuBrin, *Fundamentals of Organizational Behavior,* pp. 158–170.
23. These tips have been adapted from DuBrin, *Fundamentals of Organizational Behavior,* pp. 179–182.
24. See Solomon E. Asch, *Social Psychology* (Englewood Cliffs, N.J.: Prentice-Hall, 1952), chap. 16.
25. Irving L. Janis, *Groupthink,* 2nd ed. (Boston: Houghton Mifflin, 1982), p. 9. See also Gregory Moorhead, "Groupthink: Hypothesis in Need of Testing," *Group & Organization Studies* 7 (December 1982): 429–444.
26. These symptoms of groupthink have been adapted from a list of eight symptoms discussed in Janis, *Groupthink,* pp. 174–175.
27. Ibid., p. 275.
28. For an excellent discussion of the devil's advocate role, see Charles R. Schwenk, "Devil's Advocacy in Managerial Decision Making," *Journal of Management Studies* 21 (April 1984): 153–168.
29. Adapted from a list of nine preventive measures discussed in Janis, *Groupthink,* pp. 262–271.
30. Andrew S. Grove, *High Output Management* (New York: Random House, 1983), p. 79.
31. Andrew Malcolm, *The Tyranny of the Group* (Toronto: Clarke, Irwin, 1973), p. 4.
32. A special, six-article section on conflict and the collaborative ethic may be found in *California Management Review* 21 (Winter 1978): 56–95. Other instructive material on conflict may be found in M. Afzalur Rahim, "A Measure of Styles of Handling Interpersonal Conflict," *Academy of Management Journal* 26 (June 1983): 368–376; Lois B. Hart, "Test Your Ability to Handle Conflict," *Association Management* 35 (August 1983): 70–73; and Rosemary S. Caffarella, "Managing Conflict: An Analytical Tool," *Training and Development Journal* 38 (February 1984): 34–38.
33. Stephen P. Robbins, *Managing Organizational Conflict: A Nontraditional Approach* (Englewood Cliffs, N.J.: Prentice-Hall, 1974), p. 23.

34. Dean Tjosvold, "Making Conflict Productive," *Personnel Administrator* 29 (June 1984): 121.

35. For an alternative list of conditions that tend to precipitate conflict, see Alan C. Filley, *Interpersonal Conflict Resolution* (Glenview, Ill.: Scott, Foresman, 1975), pp. 9–12.

36. Robbins, *Managing Organizational Conflict: A Nontraditional Approach,* p. 62.

Chapter 13

Influence Processes: Power, Leadership, and Behavior Modification

We have not yet seen what man can make of man.
B. F. Skinner

Chapter Objectives

When you finish studying this chapter, you should be able to

- Identify eight general influence tactics and briefly explain why influence is an important part of management.
- Define the term *power*, relate power and authority, and identify the five bases of power.
- Summarize what the Ohio State model and the Managerial Grid® have taught managers about leadership.
- Describe the path-goal theory of leadership and explain how it is based on an assumption different from that on which Fiedler's contingency theory is based.
- Identify the two key functions that mentors perform and explain how a mentor can help develop a young manager's leadership skills.
- Explain the role of the $A \rightarrow B \rightarrow C$ relationship in behavior modification.

Opening Case 13.1

"How to Earn 'Well Pay' "*

The woman in blue jeans and a logger's shirt looks up from the production line and says grimly: "I can't miss work today. It's almost the end of the month, and I'm going to earn that 'well pay' if it kills me."

*Reprinted from the June 12, 1978 issue of *Business Week* by special permission, © 1978 by McGraw-Hill, Inc.

At Parsons Pine Products Inc. in Ashland, Ore., "well pay" is the opposite of sick pay. It is an extra eight hours' wages that the company gives workers who are neither absent nor late for a full month. It is also one of four incentives that owner James W. Parsons has built into a "positive reinforcement plan" for workers: well pay, retro pay, safety pay, and profit-sharing pay.

Beating the Tax Man

The formula, Parsons says, enables him and his wife to beat the combination of federal and state income taxes that leaves them only 14% of any increase in earnings; it allows them to pass along much of the potential tax money to the workers. Under the Parsons system, an employee earning $10,000 a year can add as much as $3,500 to his income by helping the plant operate economically.

Parsons Pine employs some 100 workers to cut lumber into specialty items—primarily louver slats for shutters, bifold doors, and blinds, and bases for rat traps. It is reportedly the U.S.'s biggest producer of these items, with sales last year [1977] of $2.5 million.

The company began handing out "well pay" in January, 1977. "We had a problem with lateness," Parsons explains. "Just before the 7 a.m. starting time, the foreman in a department would take a head count and assign three people to this machine and six over there. Then a few minutes later someone else comes in and he has to recalculate and reshuffle. Or he may be so short as to leave a machine idle."

"Well pay" brought lateness down to almost zero and cut absenteeism more than Parsons wanted it reduced, because some workers came to work even when they were sick. He dealt with this awkwardness by reminding them of "retro pay." Says Parsons: "I'd say, 'By being here while not feeling well, you may have a costly accident, and that will not only cause you pain and suffering, but it will also affect the retro plan, which could cost you a lot more than one day's well pay.' "

Reducing Accidents

The retro plan offers a bonus based on any reductions in premiums received from the state's industrial accident insurance fund. Before the retro plan went into effect in 1976, Parsons Pine had a high accident rate, 86% above the statewide base, and paid the fund accordingly. Parsons told his workers that if the plant cut its accident rate, the retroactive refund would be distributed to them. The upshot was a 1977 accident bill of $2,500 compared to a 1976 bill of $28,500. After deducting administrative expenses, the state will return $89,000 of a $100,000 premium, some $900 per employee.

The retro plan did not improve the accident rate unaided, Parsons concedes. "We showed films and introduced every safety program the state has," he says. "But no matter what you do, it doesn't really make a dent until the people themselves see that they are going to lose a dollar by not being safe. When management puts on the pressure, they say, 'He's just trying to make a buck for himself,' but when fellow workers say, 'Let's work safe,' that means a lot."

The "Little Hurts"
Employees can also earn safety pay—two hours' wages—by remaining accident-free for a month. "Six hours a quarter isn't such a great incentive," says Parsons, "but it helps. When it didn't cost them anything, workers would go to the doctor for every little thing. Now they take care of the little hurts themselves."

As its most substantial incentive, the company offers a profit-sharing bonus—everything the business earns over 4% after taxes, which is Parsons' idea of a fair profit. Each supervisor rates his employees in four categories of excellence, with a worker's bonus figured as a percentage of his wages multiplied by his category. Top-ranked employees generally receive bonuses of 8% to 10%. One year they got 16½%. Two-thirds of the bonus is paid in cash and the rest goes into the retirement fund.

To illustrate how workers can contribute to profits, and profit-sharing bonuses, Parsons presents a dramatic display that has a modest fame in Ashland. Inviting the work force to lunch, he sets up a pyramid of 250 rat trap bases, each representing $10,000 in sales. Then he knocks 100 onto the floor, saying: "That's for raw materials. See why it is important not to waste?" Then he pushes over 100 more, adding: "That's for wages." And pointing to the 50 left, he says: "Out of this little pile we have to do all the other things—maintenance, repairs, supplies, taxes. With so many blocks gone, that doesn't leave much for either you or me."

A Vote for Work
The lunch guests apparently find the display persuasive. Says one nine-year veteran: "We get the most we can out of every piece of wood after seeing that. When new employees come, we work with them to cut down waste."

The message also lingered at the last Christmas luncheon, when, after distribution of checks, someone said: "Hey, how about the afternoon off?" Parsons replied: "O.K., our production is on schedule and the customers won't be hurt. But you know where the cost comes from." Parsons recalls that someone asked him, "How much?" and he replied that the loss would be about $3,000.

"There was a bit of chatter and we took a vote," he says. "Only two hands were raised for the afternoon off. That was because they knew it was not just my money. It was their money, too."

(Discussion questions linking this case with the material you are about to read can be found at the end of this chapter.)

What do the following situations have in common?

- An employee praises her supervisor's new outfit immediately before asking for the afternoon off.
- A milling-machine operator tells a friend that he will return the favor if his friend will watch out for the supervisor while he takes an unauthorized smoke break.
- An office manager attempts to head off opposition to a computerized filing system by carefully explaining how the new system will make everyone's job easier.

Aside from the fact that all of these situations take place on the job, the common denominator is "influence." In each case, someone is trying to get his or her own way by influencing someone else's behavior. Parsons's innovative incentive schemes and his colorful demonstration with 250 rat trap bases had the same overriding goal: influence over others. **Influence is any attempt by an employee to change the behavior of superiors, peers, or subordinates.**[1] Influence is not inherently good or bad. As the foregoing situations illustrate, influence can be used for purely selfish reasons, to subvert organizational objectives, or to enhance organizational effectiveness.

Recent research has identified specific kinds of influence. After factor-analyzing the responses of 165 employees (25 percent female and 75 percent male) to the question "How do you get your boss, coworker, or subordinate to do something you want?" eight different influence tactics were isolated:

1. **Assertiveness.** Issuing an order or making a demand; continually checking up on someone; bawling someone out.
2. **Ingratiation.** Making someone feel important or good before making a request; acting humbly or friendly before making a request.
3. **Rationality.** Trying to convince someone by relying on a detailed plan, supporting information, reasoning, or logic.
4. **Sanctions.** Giving or preventing pay increases; basing promises or threats on pay raises, job security, or promotions.
5. **Exchange.** Offering an exchange of favors; reminding someone of a past favor; offering to make a personal sacrifice.

6. **Upward appeal.** Obtaining formal or informal support of higher-ups; filing a report about someone with a higher-up; sending someone to see the supervisor.
7. **Blocking.** Backing up a request with a threat to notify an outside agency; threatening to stop working with someone, engaging in a work slowdown, or ignoring or not being friendly with someone until they give in.
8. **Coalitions.** Getting coworkers to back up a request; having someone attend a formal conference at which a request is made.[2]

Interestingly, the researchers found that the same tactics were used by both male and female employees to influence both male and female superiors. In other words, there were no male tactics and female tactics. With this review of influence tactics as a foundation, we shall now examine managerial influence (getting individuals to pursue organizational objectives).

Managerial Influence

The term *managerial influence* takes in a great deal of territory. It is a useful generic label embracing a whole host of managerial practices, including motivation, power, leadership, and behavior modification. But, although the end result may be the same, each of these various influence processes works in a different way. As an example, consider the actions of C. Edward Acker, the man who succeeded William T. Seawell as the chairman of Pan Am. When Acker took over in September 1981, Pan Am was losing over $1 million a day. *Fortune* magazine followed the action:

> Hacking away at some of the highest overhead costs in the industry, Acker has persuaded employees to accept a 10% wage cut and freeze until January 1983— in return for promises of stock and possibly (like Chrysler) a union representative on the board. Acker is trimming over 10% of the work force—halving the legal and public-relations departments, chopping layers of supervisory personnel. Acker warns the remaining employees that their jobs depend on raising productivity and "making the passenger feel he is really welcome."[3]

In terms of the eight influence tactics just discussed, Acker relied on exchange, assertiveness, and sanctions while attempting to turn things around at Pan Am. Motivation, power, leadership, and behavior modification theory help translate these broad influence tactics into more specific explanations (see Figure 13.1). One might rightly ask why so many different perspectives of influence are necessary. The answer is simply that, because influence is such a fundamental part of effective management, the more

Figure 13.1   Four Perspectives of Influence in Action

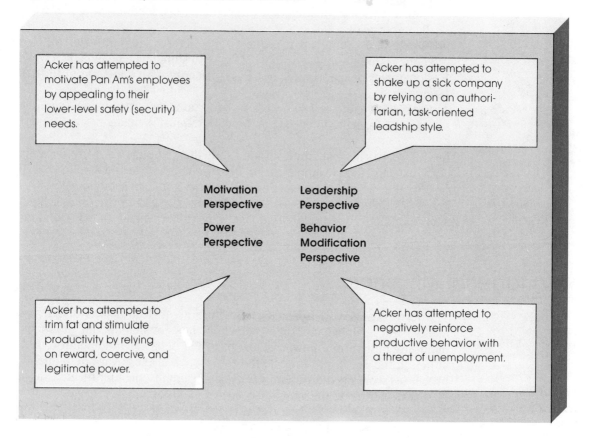

Acker has attempted to motivate Pan Am's employees by appealing to their lower-level safety (security) needs.

Acker has attempted to shake up a sick company by relying on an authoritarian, task-oriented leadship style.

Motivation Perspective

Leadership Perspective

Power Perspective

Behavior Modification Perspective

Acker has attempted to trim fat and stimulate productivity by relying on reward, coercive, and legitimate power.

Acker has attempted to negatively reinforce productive behavior with a threat of unemployment.

influence techniques that managers have in their repertoire, the better the results are likely to be.

An instructive departure point for a discussion of power, leadership, and behavior modification (recall that motivation was treated in Chapter 11) is the model in Figure 13.2. This particular model is based on expectancy theory. In reference to Chapter 11, motivation to perform increases when one perceives that there is a good chance that one's effort will lead to personally valued rewards. Employee expectancies are shaped in four different ways: (1) the types of power used by the leader (power), (2) the leader's influence attempts (leadership), (3) the consequences of behavior (behavior modification), and (4) the needs of subordinates (motivation). This chapter focuses on the use of the first three—power, leadership, and behavior modification—to influence employees to contribute to organizational ends.

Figure 13.2 An Expectancy Model of Managerial Influence

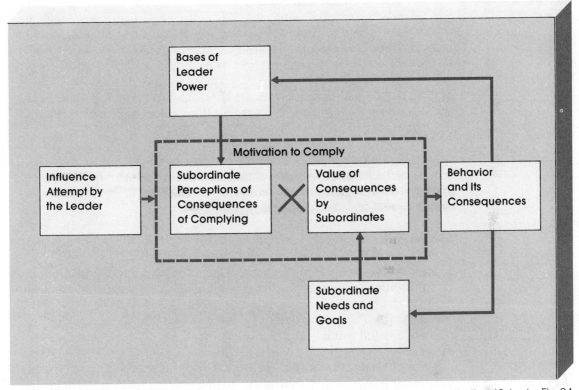

SOURCE: From David A. Nadler, J. Richard Hackman, and Edward E. Lawler III, *Managing Organizational Behavior,* Fig. 9.1. Copyright © 1979 by David A. Nadler, J. Richard Hackman, and Edward E. Lawler III. By permission of the publisher, Little, Brown and Company.

Power

Power, as a subject for popular discussion, has had its ups and downs in recent years. Watergate, President Nixon's resignation, the jailing of a former U.S. attorney general, and corporate bribery scandals during the 1970s drove home the danger of abused power. On the other hand, best-selling books with titles like *Power! How to Get It, How to Use It* emphasize the positive side of power with statements like: "It is not enough to want power, or even to *have* it. It must be used creatively. And it must be enjoyed."[4] Dismal accounts and pop psychology aside for the moment, power is inevitable in modern organizations. According to one advocate of the positive and constructive use of power:

Power must be used because managers must influence those they depend on. Power also is crucial in the development of managers' self-confidence and willingness to support subordinates. From this perspective, power should be accepted as a natural part of any organization. Managers should recognize and develop their own power to coordinate and support the work of subordinates; it is powerlessness, not power, that undermines organizational effectiveness.[5]

Managers who understand power, its bases, and its responsible use enjoy an advantageous position for getting things accomplished with and through others.

What Is Power?

After reviewing the literature on power in organizations, one management scholar defined **power** as "the ability to marshal the human, informational, and material resources to get something done."[6] Power affects organizational members in the following three ways:

1. **Decisions.** A packaging engineer decides to take on a difficult new assignment after hearing her boss's recommendations.
2. **Behavior.** A hospital lab technician achieves a month of perfect attendance after receiving a written warning about absenteeism from his supervisor.
3. **Situations.** The productivity of a product design group increases dramatically following the purchase of computerized work stations.[7]

By emphasizing the word *ability* in our definition of power, it is possible to contrast power with authority. As defined in Chapter 7, authority is the "right" to direct the activities of others. Authority is an officially sanctioned privilege that may or may not get results; power, on the other hand, is the demonstrated ability to get results. As illustrated in Figure 13.3, one may alternatively possess authority but have no power, possess no authority yet have power, or possess both authority and power. The first situation, authority but no power, occurred in Vietnam when American soldiers refused to follow their officers into battle. Power but no authority can occur, for example, when employees respond to the wishes of the supervisor's spouse. Finally, a manager who gets his or her subordinates to work hard on an important project has both authority and power.

The Five Bases of Power

Essential to the successful use of power in organizations is an understanding of the various bases of power. One widely cited classification of power bases identifies five types: (1) reward power, (2) coercive power, (3) legitimate power, (4) referent power, and (5) expert power.[8]

Reward Power This type of power is tied to one's ability to grant rewards to those who comply with a command or request. Management's reward

Figure 13.3 The Relationship Between Authority and Power

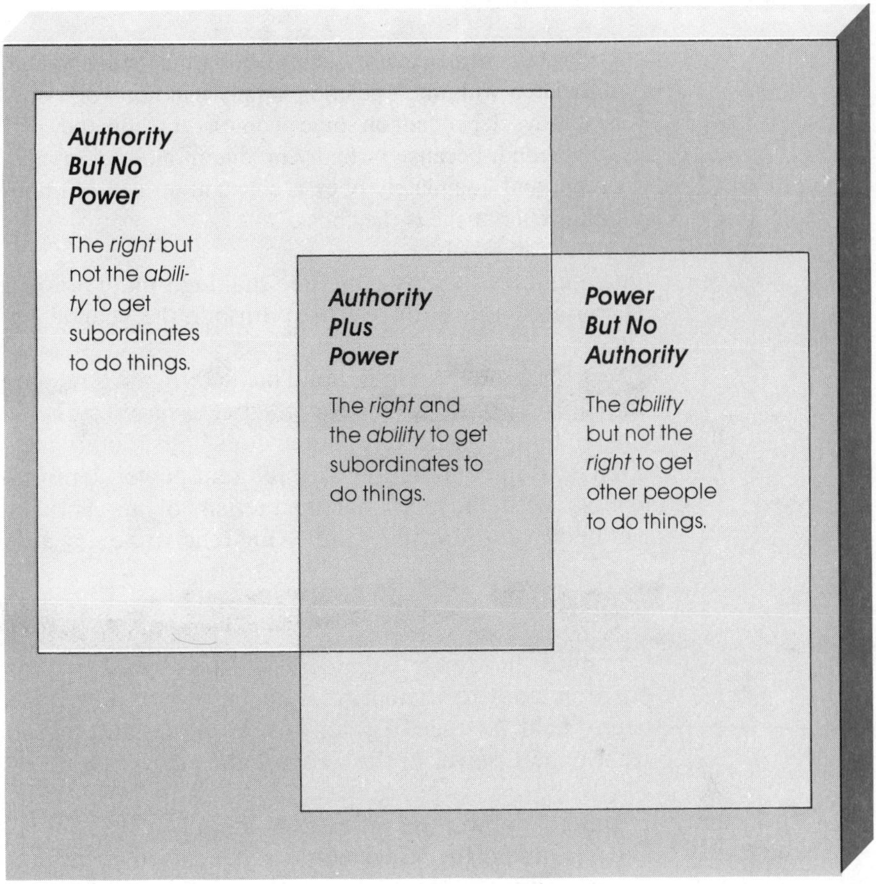

**Authority
But No
Power**

The *right* but
not the *abili-
ty* to get
subordinates
to do things.

**Authority
Plus
Power**

The *right* and
the *ability* to get
subordinates to
do things.

**Power
But No
Authority**

The *ability*
but not the
right to get
other people
to do things.

power can be strengthened by linking pay raises, merit pay, and promotions to job performance. Sought-after expressions of friendship or trust also enhance reward power.

Coercive Power   Rooted in fear, coercive power is based on threatened or actual punishment. For example, a manager might warn a habitually tardy employee that he or she will be demoted if late one more time.

Legitimate Power   Legitimate power is achieved when a person's superior position alone prompts another person to act in a desired manner. This type of power closely parallels formal authority, as discussed above. Parents, teachers, religious leaders, and managers who demand obedience by virtue of their superior social position are attempting to exercise legitimate power. A Harvard scholar has offered the following warning about legitimate power:

> Trying to control others solely by directing them and on the basis of the power associated with one's position simply will not work—first, because managers are always dependent on some people over whom they have no formal authority, and second, because virtually no one in modern organizations will passively accept and completely obey a constant stream of orders from someone just because he or she is the "boss."[9]

One might reasonably conclude that legitimate power has been eroded by its frequent abuse (or overuse) through the years.

Referent Power An individual has referent power over those who identify with him or her if they comply on that basis alone. Personal attraction is an elusive thing to define, let alone consciously cultivate. Charisma is a term often used in conjunction with referent power. Unfortunately, charismatic leaders with the personal magnetism of an Abraham Lincoln, a John Kennedy, or a Martin Luther King tend to be few and far between.

Expert Power Those who possess and can dispense valued information generally exercise expert power over those in need of such information. Computer hardware engineers and programmers, for instance, are in a position today to wield a great deal of expert power. Anyone who has ever been "held hostage" by an unscrupulous automobile mechanic knows what expert power in the wrong hands can mean.

Using Power Responsibly Experts on power are quick to point out that power is neutral. It is a tool, like a hammer. Just as a hammer can be used either constructively to build a house or destructively to smash someone's skull, power also can be used in a positive or negative manner. David C. McClelland, a respected researcher on the power motive, has defined the responsible use of power as it applies to leadership:

> An effective leader is an educator. One leads by helping them set their goals, by communicating widely throughout the group, and by taking initiative in formulating means of achieving the goals, and finally, by inspiring the members of the group to feel strong enough to work hard for those goals. Such an image of the exercise of power and influence in a leadership role should not frighten anybody and should convince more people that power exercised in this way is not only not dangerous but of the greatest possible use to society.[10]

Power for power's sake, on the other hand, can be dangerous and of little use to society.

Leadership

Leadership has fascinated people in all walks of life since the dawn of recorded history. Many references to both good and bad leadership can be found in the literature of every age. A relentless search for good leaders has been one of the common threads running through human civilization. In view of recent research evidence that effective leadership is indeed associated with organizational improvement and success, the search for ways to identify (or develop) good leaders needs to continue.[11]

Leadership Defined

A great deal of research has been done on leadership, and, as might be expected, many definitions have been proposed. Much of the variance among these definitions is semantic; the definition offered here is a workable compromise. **Leadership** is "a social influence process in which the leader seeks the voluntary participation of subordinates in an effort to reach organizational objectives."[12] *Voluntary* is the operative term in this definition. To encourage voluntary participation, leaders supplement any authority and power they may possess with their personal attributes and social skills. As a wit once observed, a good leader is someone who can tell you to go to hell and make you look forward to the trip!

Formal Versus Informal Leaders

Experts on leadership have distinguished between formal and informal leadership. **Formal leadership** is influencing relevant others to pursue official organizational objectives. **Informal leadership,** in contrast, is influencing others to pursue unofficial objectives that may or may not serve the organization's interests. Formal leaders generally have a measure of legitimate power because of their formal authority, whereas informal leaders typically lack formal authority. Beyond that, both types rely on expedient combinations of reward, coercive, referent, and expert power. Informal leaders who identify with the job to be done are a valuable asset to an organization. Conversely, an organization can be brought to its knees by informal leaders who turn cohesive work groups against the organization.

Like the study of management, the study of leadership has been an evolutionary process. Leadership theories have been developed and refined by successive generations of researchers. Something useful has been learned at each stage of development. We now turn to significant milestones in the evolution of leadership theory.

Trait Theory

During most of recorded history the prevailing assumption was that leaders are born and not made. Famous leaders such as Alexander the Great, Napoleon Bonaparte, and George Washington were said to have been blessed with an inborn ability to lead. This so-called great-man approach to leadership eventually gave way to trait theory. According to one observer, "under the influence of the behavioristic school of psychological thought, the fact was accepted that leadership traits are not completely inborn but can also be acquired through learning and experience. Attention turned to the search for universal traits possessed by leaders."[13]

As the popularity of the trait approach mushroomed during the second quarter of the twentieth century, literally hundreds of physical, mental, and personality traits were said to be the key determinants of successful leadership. Unfortunately, there was little agreement over what the most important traits of a good leader were. The predictive value of trait theory was severely limited because traits tend to be a chicken-and-egg proposition: Was George Washington a good leader because he had self-confidence, or did he have self-confidence because he was thrust into a leadership role at a young age? In spite of inherent problems, trait profiles provide a useful framework for what it takes to be a good leader.

An Early Trait Profile   It was not until 1948 that a comprehensive review of competing trait theories was conducted. After comparing over 100 studies of leader traits and characteristics, the reviewer uncovered moderate agreement on only five traits. In the reviewer's words, "the average person who occupies a position of leadership exceeds the average member of his group in the following respects: (1) intelligence, (2) scholarship, (3) dependability in exercising responsibilities, (4) activity and social participation, and (5) socio-economic status."[14]

A Contemporary Trait Profile   With one notable exception, the trait approach has generally been out of favor with leadership researchers in recent years. Convinced that successful leaders do in fact share some common traits, Warren Bennis, a respected management consultant, interviewed 90 highly successful leaders. The sample included both corporate and public-sector executives. Six females and six black males were included. Although Bennis concluded that his sample of successful leaders was an extremely diverse group, he was able to identify the following four common competencies (or traits).

1. **Management of attention.** A combination of vision and strong personal commitment attracts others and inspires them to seek new heights.
2. **Management of meaning.** Successful leaders possess exceptional communication skills that serve to align others with their cause.
3. **Management of trust.** A clear and constant focus on a central purpose builds trust by letting others know where the leader stands.
4. **Management of self.** Successful leaders nurture their strengths and learn from their mistakes. They generally reject the idea of failure.[15]

Aspiring leaders can find helpful hints in this trait profile.

Table 13.1   The Three Classic Styles of Leadership

	Authoritarian	Democratic	Laissez-faire
Nature	Leader retains all authority and responsibility.	Leader delegates a great deal of authority while retaining ultimate responsibility.	Leader denies responsibility and abdicates authority to group.
	Leader assigns people to clearly defined tasks.	Work is divided and assigned on the basis of participatory decision making.	Group members are told to work things out themselves and do the best they can.
	Primarily a downward flow of communication.	Active two-way flow of upward and downward communication.	Primarily horizontal communication among peers.
Primary strength	Stresses prompt, orderly, and predictable performance.	Enhances personal commitment through participation.	Permits self-starters to do things as they see fit without leader interference.
Primary weakness	Approach tends to stifle individual initiative.	Democratic process is time consuming.	Group may drift aimlessly in the absence of direction from leader.

Behavioral Styles Theory   During World War II, the study of leadership took on a significant new twist. Rather than concentrating on the personal traits of successful leaders, researchers began turning their attention to patterns of leader behavior (called leadership styles). In other words, attention turned from who the leader was to how the leader actually behaved. One early laboratory study of leader behavior demonstrated that followers overwhelmingly preferred managers who had a democratic style to those with an authoritarian style or a laissez-faire (hands-off) style.[16] An updated review of these three classic leadership styles can be found in Table 13.1.

For a number of years, theorists and managers hailed democratic leadership as the key to productive and happy employees. Eventually, however, their enthusiasm was dampened when critics pointed out that the original study relied on children as subjects and virtually ignored productivity. Although there is general agreement that these basic styles exist, debate has been vigorous over their relative value and appropriateness. Practical experience has shown, for example, that the democratic style does not always stimulate better performance. Some employees prefer to be told what to do rather than to participate in decision making.

The Ohio State Model   While the democratic style of leadership was receiving attention, a slightly different behavioral approach to leadership

Figure 13.4 Basic Leadership Styles from the Ohio State Study

	Low →	**High**
High Structure, Consideration ↑	**Low Structure, High Consideration** Leader strives to promote group harmony and social need satisfaction.	**High Structure, High Consideration** Leader strives to achieve a productive balance between getting the job done and maintaining a cohesive, friendly work group.
Low	**Low Structure, Low Consideration** Leader retreats to a generally passive role of allowing the situation to take care of itself.	**High Structure, Low Consideration** Leader devotes primary attention to getting the job done. Personal concerns are strictly secondary.

Initiating Structure

emerged. This second approach began in the late 1940s when a team of Ohio State University researchers defined two independent dimensions of leader behavior.[17] One dimension was the leader's efforts to get things organized and get the job done, called "initiating structure." The second dimension was the degree of trust, friendship, respect, and warmth that the leader extended to subordinates, labeled "consideration." By making a matrix out of these two independent dimensions of leader behavior, the Ohio State researchers identified four styles of leadership (see Figure 13.4).

This particular scheme proved to be fertile ground for leadership theorists, and variations of the original Ohio State approach soon appeared.[18]

Leadership theorists began a search for the "one best style" of leadership. The high-structure, high-consideration style was generally hailed as the best all-around style. This "high-high" style has intuitive appeal because it embraces the best of both categories of leader behavior. But one researcher cautioned in 1966 that although there seemed to be a positive relationship between consideration and subordinate satisfaction, a positive link between the high-high style and work group performance had not been proven conclusively.[19]

The Managerial Grid® Developed by Robert R. Blake and Jane S. Mouton, the Managerial Grid® is a trademarked and widely recognized typology of leadership styles.[20] Today, amid the growing popularity of situational leadership theories, Blake and Mouton remain convinced that there is one best style of leadership.

As illustrated in Figure 13.5, the Managerial Grid® has "concern for production" on the horizontal axis and "concern for people" on the vertical axis. Concern for production involves a desire to achieve greater output, cost effectiveness, and profits in profit-seeking organizations. Concern for people involves promoting friendship, helping coworkers get the job done, and attending to things that matter to people, like pay and working conditions. By scaling each axis from 1 to 9, Blake and Mouton created a grid highlighted by five major styles:

9,1 style: primary concern for production; people secondary.
1,9 style: primary concern for people; production secondary.
1,1 style: minimal concern for either production or people.
5,5 style: moderate concern for both production and people to maintain the status quo.
9,9 style: high concern for both production and people as evidenced by personal commitment, mutual trust, and teamwork.

Although they stress that managers and leaders need to be versatile enough to select the courses of action appropriate to the situation, Blake and Mouton contend that a 9,9 style correlates positively with better results, better mental and physical health, and effective conflict resolution. They believe the conclusion that there is no one best leadership style is false because, as they see it, the true 9,9 style has never been adequately tested by the situationalists. In a recent study by Blake and Mouton, 100 experienced managers overwhelmingly preferred the 9,9 style, regardless of how the situation varied.[21] Consequently, they have devised management training and organization development programs to help individuals and entire organizations move into the 9,9 portion of the Managerial Grid®.

Figure 13.5 Blake and Mouton's Managerial Grid®

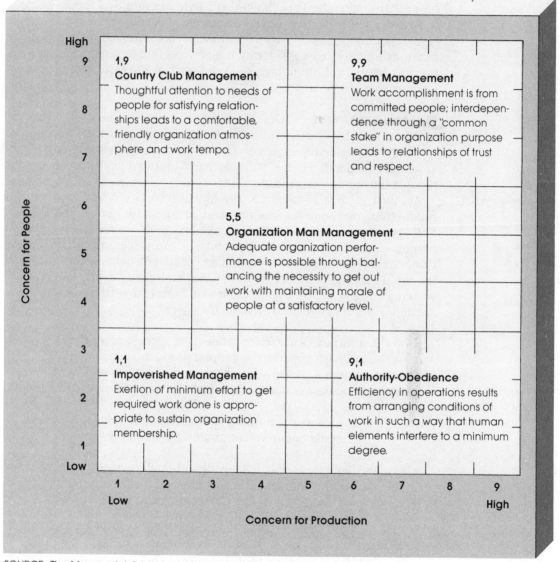

SOURCE: The Managerial Grid® figure from *The Managerial Grid III*, by Robert R. Blake and Jane Srygley Mouton. Houston: Gulf Publishing Company. Copyright © 1985, page 12. Reproduced by permission.

Situational Theory   Convinced that a one best style of leadership simply does not exist, a growing number of management scholars are advocating situational or contingency thinking. Although a number of different situational-leadership theories have been developed, they all share one fundamental assumption: *successful leadership occurs when the leader's style matches the situation*. Situational-leadership theorists stress the need for flexibility and reject the notion of a universally applicable style. Research is under way to determine precisely when and where various styles of leadership are appropriate. Fiedler's contingency theory, the path-goal theory, and Vroom and Yetton's decision-making model are introduced and discussed here because they represent distinctly different approaches to situational leadership.

Fiedler's Contingency Theory of Leadership   Among the various leadership theories proposed so far, Fiedler's is the most thoroughly tested. It is the product of more than thirty years of research by Fred E. Fiedler and his associates. Fiedler's contingency theory of leadership gets its name from the following assumption:

> The performance of a leader depends on two interrelated factors: (1) the degree to which the situation gives the leader control and influence—that is, the likelihood that he can successfully accomplish the job; and (2) the leader's basic motivation—that is, whether his self-esteem depends primarily on accomplishing the task or on having close supportive relations with others.[22]

Regarding the second factor, the leader's basic motivation, Fiedler believes that leaders are either task motivated or relationship motivated. These two motivational profiles are roughly equivalent to initiating structure (or concern for production) and consideration (or concern for people).

A consistent pattern has emerged from the many studies of effective leaders carried out by Fiedler and others.[23] As illustrated in Figure 13.6, task-motivated leaders seem to be effective in extreme situations when they have either very little control or a great deal of control over situational variables. But in moderately favorable situations, relationship-motivated leaders tend to be more effective. Consequently, Fiedler and one of his colleagues have summed up their findings by noting that "everything points to the conclusions that there is no such thing as an ideal leader."[24] There are leaders, and there are situations. The challenge, according to Fiedler, is to analyze a leader's basic motivation and then match him or her with a suitable situation to form a productive combination. He believes that it is more efficient to move leaders to a suitable situation than to tamper with their personalities by trying to get task-motivated leaders to become relationship motivated, or vice versa.

Path-Goal Leadership Theory   A relatively new leadership theory is the path-goal theory, a derivative of expectancy motivation theory (see Chapter 11). This theory gets its name from the assumption that effective leaders

Figure 13.6 Fiedler's Contingency Theory of Leadership

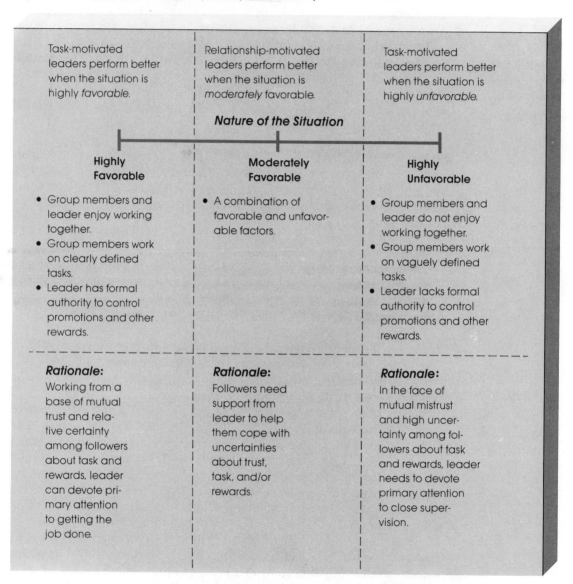

Task-motivated leaders perform better when the situation is highly *favorable*.

Relationship-motivated leaders perform better when the situation is *moderately* favorable.

Task-motivated leaders perform better when the situation is highly *unfavorable*.

Nature of the Situation

Highly Favorable

Moderately Favorable

Highly Unfavorable

- Group members and leader enjoy working together.
- Group members work on clearly defined tasks.
- Leader has formal authority to control promotions and other rewards.

- A combination of favorable and unfavorable factors.

- Group members and leader do not enjoy working together.
- Group members work on vaguely defined tasks.
- Leader lacks formal authority to control promotions and other rewards.

Rationale:
Working from a base of mutual trust and relative certainty among followers about task and rewards, leader can devote primary attention to getting the job done.

Rationale:
Followers need support from leader to help them cope with uncertainties about trust, task, and/or rewards.

Rationale:
In the face of mutual mistrust and high uncertainty among followers about task and rewards, leader needs to devote primary attention to close supervision.

can enhance subordinate motivation by (1) clarifying the subordinate's perception of work goals, (2) linking meaningful rewards with goal attainment, and (3) explaining how goals and desired rewards can be achieved. In short, the idea is for leaders to motivate their followers by providing clear goals and meaningful incentives for reaching them. Path-goal theorists believe that motivation is essential to effective leadership.

According to two path-goal theorists, leaders can enhance motivation by "increasing the number and kinds of personal payoffs to subordinates for work-goal attainment and making paths to these payoffs easier to travel by clarifying the paths, reducing road blocks and pitfalls and increasing the opportunities for personal satisfaction en route."[25] The personal characteristics of subordinates, environmental pressures, and the demands on subordinates all may vary from situation to situation. Thus path-goal proponents believe that managers need to rely contingently on four different leadership styles:

- **Directive leadership.** Tell people what is expected of them and provide specific guidance, schedules, rules, regulations, and standards.
- **Supportive leadership.** Treat subordinates as equals in a friendly manner while striving to improve their well-being.
- **Participative leadership.** Consult with subordinates to seek their suggestions and then seriously consider those suggestions when making decisions.
- **Achievement-oriented leadership.** Set challenging goals, emphasize excellence, and seek continuous improvement while maintaining a high degree of confidence that subordinates will meet difficult challenges in a responsible manner.[26]

This assumption that managers can and do shift situationally from style to style clearly sets path-goal theory apart from Fiedler's model. Fiedler, once again, claims that managers cannot and do not change their basic leadership styles in the way that one would change hats.

Since path-goal theory is relatively new, it has been only partially tested. So far, though, some enlightening contingency relationships have been identified (see Table 13.2). Path-goal leadership theory has a particularly promising future because it effectively weaves together two important influence processes, motivation and leadership.

The Vroom/Yetton Decision-making Model   Thanks to the way in which the path-goal theorists have combined motivation and leadership theory, we gain additional insights about the mechanics of successful leadership. A model put forth by Victor H. Vroom and Philip W. Yetton takes leadership theory a step further by matching leadership with yet another important administrative process.[27] Vroom and Yetton characterize leadership in terms of *decision-making* styles. Their model qualifies as a situational leadership theory because they prescribe different styles for varying situations that managers encounter.

The Vroom-Yetton model identifies five distinct decision-making styles (see Figure 13.7), each of which requires a different degree of subordinate participation. In addition, it suggests what styles are appropriate in four-

Table 13.2   Contingency Relationships in Path-Goal Leadership Model

Leadership Style	Situation in Which Appropriate
Directive	Positively affects satisfaction and expectancies of subordinates working on ambiguous tasks.
	Negatively affects satisfaction and expectancies of subordinates working on clearly defined tasks.
Supportive	Positively affects satisfaction of subordinates working on dissatisfying, stressful, or frustrating tasks.
Participative	Positively affects satisfaction of subordinates who are ego involved with nonrepetitive tasks.
Achievement-oriented	Positively affects confidence that effort will lead to effective performance of subordinates working on ambiguous and nonrepetitive tasks.

SOURCE: From *Managerial Process and Organizational Behavior*, by Alan C. Filley, Robert J. House, and Steven Kerr. Copyright © 1976 Scott, Foresman and Company. Reprinted by permission of the publisher.

teen different situations. The situation is determined by asking a series of seven diagnostic questions (see questions A through G at the top of Figure 13.8). When contemplating exactly how subordinates should be brought in, the leader analyzes the situation by answering questions A through G. One of five basic styles is recommended for each of the fourteen different decision situations that leaders often encounter (see Figure 13.8). For example, a *no* answer to question A, a *yes* answer to question D, and a *no* answer to question E would lead to situation 3, for which decision-making style 5 is recommended. Alternatively, a *yes* answer to A, a *no* to B, a *no* to C, a *yes* to D, a *no* to E, and a *no* to F would lead to situation 13, for which style 4 is recommended.

Vroom and Yetton's model may appear overly complex at first glance, but a closer look reveals a good deal of practical significance. For example, it reminds managers to ask important questions such as: "Who has the needed information?" "How will my people respond?" "Do I need their support during implementation?" "Will my decision cause conflict?" By taking time to answer Vroom and Yetton's diagnostic questions, and responding with the appropriate style, decision makers are more likely to earn the distinction of being good leaders.

Figure 13.7   Vroom and Yetton's Alternative Decision-making Styles

Degree of Subordinate Participation	Decision-making Styles
None	1. You solve the problem or make the decision yourself, using information available to you at that time.
Low	2. You obtain the necessary information from your subordinate(s), then decide on the solution to the problem yourself. You may not tell your subordinates what the problem is in getting the information from them. The role played by your subordinates in making the decision is clearly one of providing the necessary information to you, rather than generating or evaluating alternative solutions.
Moderate	3. You share the problem with relevant subordinates individually, getting their ideas and suggestions without bringing them together as a group. Then you make a decision that may or may not reflect your subordinates' influence.
Moderate	4. You share the problem with your subordinates as a group, collectively obtaining their ideas and suggestions. Then you make the decision that may or may not reflect your subordinates' influence.
High	5. You share a problem with your subordinates as a group. Together you generate and evaluate alternatives and attempt to reach agreement (consensus) on a solution. Your role is much like that of a chairman. You do not try to influence the group to adopt "your" solution and you are willing to accept and implement any solution that has the support of the entire group.

SOURCE: Adapted, by permission of the publisher, from "A New Look at Managerial Decision Making," by Victor H. Vroom, *Organizational Dynamics*, Spring 1973, p. 67. © 1973 AMACOM, a division of American Management Associations, New York. All rights reserved.

Figure 13.8   The Vroom/Yetton Decision-making Model

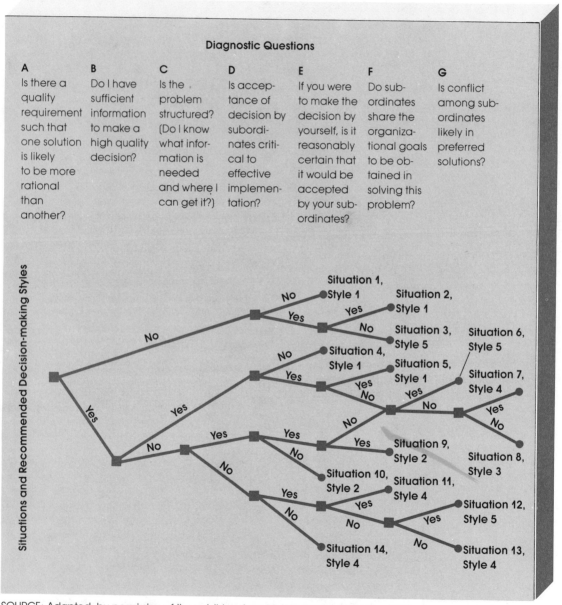

SOURCE: Adapted, by permission of the publisher, from "A New Look at Managerial Decision Making," by Victor H. Vroom, *Organizational Dynamics*, Spring 1973, p. 70. © 1973 AMACOM, a division of American Management Associations, New York. All rights reserved.

Table 13.3 Keys to Effective Leadership

It Helps for the Leader to Have	It Helps for the Followers to Be
• Appropriate technical expertise supported by a strong foundation of general knowledge. • A mastery of the language. • A desire to get things accomplished through people rather than in spite of them. • A willingness to be flexible when dealing with individuals. • A *mentor* who can urge, direct, and coach in addition to providing necessary feedback. • An ability to step back from a disorderly array of details and see things in perspective. • A knack for being in the right place at the right time.	• A cohesive group of individuals who identify with the job to be done. • Knowledgeable people who are still eager to learn. • People who view a difficult task as a challenge rather than a threat. • People who accept and learn through feedback.

It Helps for the Task to Be	It Helps for the Administrative Setting to Have
• Meaningful work demanding responsibility. • Work that offers continuing challenge.	• Clear, challenging, yet attainable objectives. • Policies and rules that support rather than undermine effective leadership. • Clear lines of formal authority that support rather than undermine effective leadership.

Becoming an Effective Leader: A Mentor Can Help

What if you weren't born with the name Rockefeller or Kennedy but you still want to become a leader? Although it may sound a bit unscientific, a strong and unwavering *desire* to grasp the reins of leadership is a prime prerequisite. Such a desire, coupled with appropriate expertise and opportunity, can fuel the drive to achieve needed leadership skills.

We still know relatively little about how to actually develop leaders. In spite of mountains of research on the subject, much remains to be learned. However, it is possible to list a number of variables (see Table 13.3) that appear to set the stage for effective leadership. Aspiring leaders need to be aware of both enabling factors and potential barriers. One particular item, a *mentor*, warrants special attention here.

Learning from a Mentor

Because of the many obstacles and barriers that block the way to successful leadership, it is easy to understand why there is no simple cookbook formula for developing leaders. Abraham Zaleznik, a widely respected sociologist, insists that leaders must be nurtured under the wise tutelage of a mentor. A **mentor** is an individual who systematically

Table 13.4 Mentors Fulfill Two Important Functions

Career Functions[a]	Psychosocial Functions[b]
Sponsorship	Role modeling
Exposure-and-visibility	Acceptance-and-confirmation
Coaching	Counseling
Protection	Friendship
Challenging assignments	

SOURCE: Kathy E. Kram, "Phases of the Mentor Relationship," *Academy of Management Journal* 26 (December 1983), Exhibit 1, p. 614. Reprinted by permission.
[a]Career functions are those aspects of the relationship that primarily enhance career advancement.
[b]Psychosocial functions are those aspects of the relationship that primarily enhance sense of competence, clarity of identity, and effectiveness in the managerial role.

develops a subordinate's abilities through intensive tutoring, coaching, and guidance.[28] Zaleznik explains the nature of this special relationship:

> Psychological biographies of gifted people repeatedly demonstrate the important part a mentor plays in developing an individual. Andrew Carnegie owed much to his senior, Thomas A. Scott. As head of the Western Division of the Pennsylvania Railroad, Scott recognized talent and the desire to learn in the young telegrapher assigned to him. By giving Carnegie increasing responsibility and by providing him with the opportunity to learn through close personal observation, Scott added to Carnegie's self-confidence and sense of achievement. Because of his own personal strength and achievement, Scott did not fear Carnegie's aggressiveness. Rather, he gave it full play in encouraging Carnegie's initiative.
>
>   Mentors take risks with people. They bet initially on talent they perceive in younger people. Mentors also risk emotional involvement in working closely with their juniors. The risks do not always pay off, but the willingness to take them appears crucial in developing leaders.[29]

Research suggests that *informal* mentor relationships that arise naturally work better than formally structured pairings.[30]

Dynamics of Mentoring

According to one researcher who conducted intensive biographical interviews with both members in 18 different senior manager–junior manager mentor relationships, mentoring fulfills two important functions: (1) a career enhancement function and (2) a psychosocial support function (see Table 13.4). Mentor relationships were found to average about five years in length.[31] Thus a manager could conceivably have a series of mentors during the course of an organizational career. Interestingly, the junior member of a mentor relationship is not the only one to benefit. Mentors often derive great intrinsic pleasure from seeing their protégés move up through the ranks and conquer difficult challenges. Moreover, mentors, by passing along their values and technical and leadership skills to promising junior managers, can wield considerable power. As one might suspect, mentor relationships can turn sour. A mentor can become threatened by a protégé who surpasses him or her. Also, cross-gender[32] and cross-racial mentor relationships can be victimized by bias and social pressures.

Finding ways to practice leadership off the job can also help present and future managers develop their abilities. Serving in campus, community, or church organizations, for example, gives one the opportunity to experiment with different leadership styles in a variety of situations.

Behavior Modification

Claiming to be disappointed with the results of the search for the internal causes of job performance, a growing number of management theorists and practicing managers have turned to applied learning theory. This perspective can be traced to two psychologists, John B. Watson and Edward L. Thorndike, who did their work during the early twentieth century. From Watson came the advice to concentrate on observable behavior rather than internal states. Accordingly, the philosophy of **behaviorism** holds that observable behavior is more important than hypothetical inner states such as needs, motives, or expectancies. From Thorndike came an appreciation of the way in which consequences control behavior. According to Thorndike's classic law of effect, favorable consequences encourage behavior, whereas unfavorable consequences discourage behavior.[33] However, it remained for B. F. Skinner, the noted Harvard psychologist, to integrate Watson's and Thorndike's contributions into a precise technology of behavior change.

What Is Behavior Modification? Skinner is the father of **operant conditioning**, the science of how behavior is controlled by the surrounding environment.[34] Although some find Skinner's substitution of environmental control for self-control to be repulsive and dehumanizing, few deny that operant conditioning actually occurs. Indeed, much of our behavior is the product of environmental shaping. Rather, the debate centers on whether or not natural shaping processes should be systematically managed to alter the course of everyday behavior. Advocates of behavior modification believe that they should be.

Behavior modification (B. Mod.) is the practical application of Skinnerian operant conditioning techniques to everyday behavior problems. The purpose of behavior modification is to manage environmental factors systematically to get people to do the right things more often and the wrong things less often. This is accomplished by managing the antecedents (prior events) and/or consequences of observable behavior. If one is to understand B. Mod., one must first understand the dynamic relationship between environmental antecedents and consequences and behavior.

**The ABCs of
Behavior
Modification**

If we see a coworker come in late every time the supervisor is out of town on business, we might conclude that he or she has a bad attitude or is dissatisfied because of unfulfilled needs. Or we might label the individual as inherently lazy, sneaky, or unethical. But from a B. Mod. perspective, these explanations are not adequate, because each contains a hypothesis about what is going on inside the person, and unobservable internal states can be difficult to measure or change. Instead, B. Mod. calls for an analysis of the interaction between the individual's observable behavior and the surrounding environment. More precisely, it calls for the identification of *Antecedent* (A) → *Behavior* (B) → *Consequence* (C) relationships.

Antecedents   An **antecedent** is an environmental cue that prompts an individual to behave in a given manner. Antecedents do not automatically cause an individual to behave in a predictable manner, as when a hot stove causes you to withdraw your hand reflexively when you touch it. Rather, through experience we learn to read antecedents as signals telling us that it is time to behave in a certain way to get what we want or to avoid what we do not want. In our example of the tardy coworker, the antecedent for coming in late is the supervisor's absence. If the supervisor is scheduled to be out of town, this particular employee is prompted to report in late. Thus the antecedent may be said to control (but not cause) the tardy behavior.

Behavior   The B portion of the A → B → C relationship stands for observable behavior. Instead of focusing on the individual's personality, a B. Mod. practitioner pinpoints a specific observable behavior. There is little room for subjective interpretations of objective behavior in this approach. In the case of the tardy employee, he or she is either on time or late, period. Many managers who are accustomed to using terms such as *need* and *purpose* or various unflattering labels have a difficult time simply looking at behavior. But according to one behaviorist: "No matter how we look at it, management is getting other people to do things that have to be done. It is clearly a practice that implies we are going to have to manage other people's *behavior.*"[35]

Consequences   Again, in line with Thorndike's law of effect, consequences are subsequent events that either encourage or discourage behavior. Completing our A → B → C analysis of the tardy employee, the consequence is favorable because the employee has gotten away with

Figure 13.9 Antecedents and Consequences Determine Future Behavior

Antecedent ⟶	Behavior ⟶	Consequence	Behavioral Outcome
"I suppose you don't have the Jones report completed yet."	"No way, I'm swamped with work."	"That's OK, don't worry about it."	Employee continues to make excuses rather than getting the job done on time.
"How are you coming on the Jones report?"	"Here it is, a whole day early."	"All right. Now you can finish Mary's project."	Employee stops handing work in early because it does not pay.
"How are you coming on the Jones report?"	"Here it is, a whole day early."	"Good work! I know you enjoy working on the new accounts. Why don't you spend the rest of the day doing that?"	Employee continues to complete work early because it leads to praise and preferred assignments.

coming in late (so far, at least). This obviously favorable consequence simply encourages the employee to come in late the next time the supervisor is scheduled to be out of town (antecedent). Now if the supervisor unexpectedly cancels a trip and docks the employee's pay when he or she is found coming in late, this comfortable but unproductive A → B → C relationship would be upset. The employee would think twice about coming in late next time the supervisor was scheduled to be out of town.

Once accustomed to viewing job performance in A → B → C terms, managers are in a position to begin to improve performance through behavior modification (see Figure 13.9).

Managing Antecedents and Consequences

Although often overlooked, the management of antecedents is a practical and relatively simple way of encouraging good performance. As Table 13.5 indicates, there are two ways to manage antecedents. Barriers can be removed, and helpful aids can be offered. These steps simply ensure that the path to good performance is clearly marked and free of obstacles (this meshes nicely with the path-goal theory of leadership).

Managing the consequences of job performance is more complex than dealing strictly with antecedents. This is because there are four different classes of consequences, each of which is part of a different process. Positive reinforcement and negative reinforcement encourage behavior. Extinction and punishment discourage behavior. These terms need to be

Table 13.5 Managing Antecedents

Barriers: Remove barriers that prevent or hinder the completion of a good job	Aids: Provide helpful aids that enhance the opportunity to do a good job
• Unrealistic objectives, plans, schedules, or deadlines • Uncooperative or distracting coworkers • Training deficiencies • Contradictory or confusing rules • Inadequate or inappropriate tools • Conflicting orders from two or more superiors	• Challenging, yet obtainable objectives • Clear and realistic plans • Understandable instructions • Constructive suggestions, hints, or tips • Clear and generally acceptable work rules • Realistic schedules and deadlines • Friendly reminders • Posters or signs with helpful tips • Easy-to-use forms • Nonthreatening questions about progress

defined because they have precise meanings that are often confused by casual observers.

Positive Reinforcement **Positive reinforcement** is the encouragement of a specific behavior by immediately following it with a consequence that the individual finds pleasing. For example, a machine operator who maintains a clean work area because he or she is praised for doing so has responded to positive reinforcement. As the term implies, positive reinforcement reinforces or builds behavior in a positive manner.

Negative Reinforcement **Negative reinforcement** is the encouragement of a specific behavior by immediately withdrawing or terminating something the individual finds displeasing. For example, children learn the power of negative reinforcement early in life when they discover that the quickest way to get something from their parents is to cry and scream until they get what they want. In effect, the parents are *negatively* reinforced for complying with the child's demand by the *termination* of the crying and screaming. In other words, the termination or withdrawal of an undesirable state of affairs (for example, the threat of being fired) has an incentive effect. In a social context, negative reinforcement amounts to blackmail. "Do what I want, or I will continue to make your life miserable" is the byword of the person who relies on negative reinforcement to influence behavior.

Extinction **Extinction** is the discouragement of a specific behavior by ignoring it. For example, managers sometimes find that the best way to keep subordinates from asking redundant questions is to simply not answer them. Just as a plant will wither and die without water, behavior will fade away without occasional reinforcement.

Punishment **Punishment** is the discouragement of a specific behavior by either immediately presenting an undesirable consequence or immediately removing something desirable. For example, a manager may punish a tardy employee by either assigning the individual to a dirty job or docking the individual's pay.

It is very important to remember that positive and negative reinforcement, extinction, and punishment all entail the manipulation of the *direct consequences* of a desired or undesired behavior. If action is taken before the behavior, behavior control is unlikely. For instance, if a manager gives an employee a cash bonus *before* a difficult task is completed, the probability of the task being swiftly and effectively completed drops. Where is the incentive effect? In regard to using consequences, behavior modification works only when there is a contingent ("if ... then") relationship between a specific behavior and a given consequence.

Guidelines for Successful Behavior Modification

For two very good reasons, there are no guarantees of success with B. Mod. programs. First, human behavior is highly variable, and workable A → B → C relationships vary from person to person. We are not all under the control of the same antecedents and consequences. Second, managers simply do not control all the antecedents and consequences that dictate the nature of job behavior. For example, attention and laughter from coworkers reinforce counterproductive clowning. The trick is to link highly desired consequences to working, so that the employee learns that working pays off better than clowning. In effect, the manager attempts to win a reinforcement tug of war with the employee's coworkers. Despite these limitations, managers can enhance the effectiveness of their B. Mod. programs by following three guidelines: (1) focus on what is right about job performance, (2) use positive reinforcement whenever possible, and (3) schedule positive reinforcement appropriately.

Focusing on What Is Right About Job Performance Behavior modification proponents prefer to build up desirable behaviors rather than tear down undesirable ones. Like the two sides of a coin, every undesirable behavior has a desirable counterpart that can be reinforced. Because productive behaviors should be encouraged, managers are advised to focus on the positive aspects of job performance when arranging productive A → B → C matches. This positive approach is a central theme in the best-selling book, *The One Minute Manager,* that extols the virtues of "catching people doing something *right*. ... "[36]

This stance is preferred because it creates a healthy, positive work climate rather than an unhealthy "Aha, I caught you, now you're going to get it!" climate. "In an arbitrarily punitive supervisory climate, subordinates are forced into an immature posture of constantly looking over their shoulders for signs of the boss. Subordinates in a positive supervisory

Table 13.6 Behavior Modification in Action

By following a relatively simple, four-step B. Mod. program, Emery Air Freight was able to save $3 million in three years in its warehouse operations.

1. **Pinpoint key performance-related behaviors.** A performance audit at Emery found that the air freight–container utilization rate was only 45 percent of capacity. This rate came as quite a surprise to the managers, who had subjectively assumed the rate to be around 90 percent. Clearly, there was plenty of room for improvement in loading containers more fully before putting them on board the planes. (Air carriers charged Emery a fixed fee, regardless of whether the containers were partially or completely full.)

2. **Establish a realistic output objective.** After careful studies of the container-loading operation, managers at Emery established an overall utilization-rate objective of 95 percent. More modest objectives were formulated for those with very poor performance records.

3. **Provide for self-feedback.** Emery dock workers were given a specially prepared feedback form for keeping track of their personal container-utilization rates. When their daily rate rose above 45 percent, they were the first ones to know that they were on the right track. This feedback form permitted self-reinforcement and self-management.

4. **Positively reinforce improvement.** Emery managers monitored the dock workers' feedback sheets and positively reinforced any improvement with praise and other desired consequences. As a result, the 95 percent utilization objective was achieved in a matter of days with considerable savings to the company.

climate, in marked contrast, actively pursue stated objectives in a mature manner."[37] A positive supervisory climate is created by making it clear what behaviors are required to get the job done and supporting those productive behaviors with helpful antecedents and positive reinforcement.

Emery Air Freight's experience, as highlighted in Table 13.6, clearly demonstrates the power of a positive supervisory climate.[38] A brief A → B → C analysis illustrates the significant elements of Emery Air Freight's very successful behavior modification program. Both the realistic objectives and the feedback forms were antecedents pointing the way to improved performance. Loading the air freight containers more fully was the specific behavior. Finally, the performance improvement documented on the feedback forms and supervisory praise and recognition were the positive consequences. This particular arrangement certainly proved to be a productive one for Emery Air Freight.

Using Positive Reinforcement Whenever Possible Behaviorists claim that in the long run, positive reinforcement is the most effective way of modifying behavior. Extinction is criticized for working too slowly. Negative reinforcement and punishment, although they may produce rapid behavior change, often are accompanied by undesirable side effects. Among those side effects are:

1. **Inadvertent permanent damage to behavior.** For example, a manager who thoughtlessly laughs at a new employee's "bright idea" in front of others may effectively kill future contributions.
2. **Temporary suppression of undesirable behavior.** As the old saying goes, "when the cat's away, the mice will play." This problem plagues managers who insist on using punishment and negative reinforcement to get things done. Since the manager's presence becomes an antecedent signaling the threat of negative consequences, employees work only when the manager rides herd on them. But things usually fall apart when punitive managers turn their backs.
3. **Emotional outbursts.** People generally resent the coercive nature of negative reinforcement and punishment. Consequently, punitive managers must cope with unproductive fear, resentment, and possible retaliation.[39]

A positive incentive effect is achieved by relying on positive reinforcement whenever possible. Table 13.7 suggests many positive consequences that can be used as part of a positive reinforcement strategy. Realizing that the reinforcing effect can wear off, managers need to use their imagination when arranging productive A → B → C relationships.

Scheduling Positive Reinforcement Appropriately   Both the type and the timing of consequences are important in successful B. Mod. When a productive behavior is first tried out by an employee, a continuous schedule of reinforcement is appropriate. Under **continuous reinforcement** every instance of the desired behavior is reinforced. For example, a bank manager who is training a new loan officer to handle a difficult type of account should praise the loan officer after every successful transaction until the behavior is firmly established. Once the loan officer seems able to handle the transaction, the bank manager can switch to a schedule of intermittent reinforcement. As the term implies, **intermittent reinforcement** calls for reinforcing some, rather than all, of the desired responses. The more unpredictable the payoff schedule is, the better the results will be. One way to appreciate the power of intermittent reinforcement is to think of the enthusiasm with which people play slot machines; these gambling devices pay off on an unpredictable intermittent schedule. In the same way, occasional reinforcement of established productive behaviors with meaningful positive consequences is an extremely effective management technique.

Table 13.7 Positive Consequences That May Be Used for Positive Reinforcement

Monetary	Social	
Pay raise	Praise	Compliment
Cash bonus	Friendly greeting	Feedback on performance
Company stock	Recognition	
Employee benefits	Request for suggestions	Invitation to coffee or lunch
Paid vacations		
Paid personal holiday (e.g., birthday)	Pat on the back	Coaching
Profit sharing	Smiles and other nonverbal recognition	Recognition in company publication
Coupons redeemable at local stores	"Bull sessions" about family, hobbies, etc.	Discussion of satisfactory work progress
Movie or dinner theater passes	Discussion of favorite topics (sports, etc.)	Request for advice
Sporting event tickets or season passes		Request for informal recommendations
	Expression of appreciation in front of superiors, peers	Explanation of company or unit mission
		Notes of thanks
	Discussion of anticipated problems	

Summary

Influence is fundamental to management because individuals must be influenced to pursue collective objectives. In addition to motivation, three important influence processes are power, leadership, and behavior modification. Recent research has identified eight different influence tactics that often are used on the job: assertiveness, ingratiation, rationality, sanctions, exchange, upward appeal, blocking, and coalitions.

Authority is defined as the right to seek compliance, whereas power is the demonstrated ability to obtain compliance. A manager may have authority, but not necessarily power. Organizationally, power affects decisions, behavior, and situations. The five types of power are reward, coercive, legitimate, referent, and expert. Power in itself is a neutral tool. It becomes good or bad only through responsible or irresponsible application.

Formal leadership is influencing relevant others to voluntarily pursue organizational objectives. Informal leadership can work for or against the organization. Leadership theory has evolved through three major stages:

Table 13.7 Positive Consequences (cont.)

Status symbols	Opportunity
Formal recognition as employee of the year, month, or week	Job with more responsibility
	Job rotation
Special commendation	Opportunity to explain "great" ideas
Promotion	Early time off with pay
Wall plaque	Extended breaks
Desk accessories	Extended lunch period
Private parking space	Opportunity to participate in important discussions, decisions
Special training	
Private office or improved work area	Opportunity to work on personal project on company time
Rings, trophy, watch	Opportunity to use company tools or facilities for personal project
Personal computer	Use of company recreation facilities
	Time off with pay to work on community projects
	Time for job-related creative expression
	Time off for physical fitness programs

SOURCE: Portions of this table are adapted from Fred Luthans and Robert Kreitner, *Organizational Behavior Modification and Beyond: An Operant and Social Learning Approach* (Glenview, Ill.: Scott, Foresman, 1985), p. 127. Reprinted by permission of the publisher.

trait theory, behavioral styles theory, and situational theory. Trait theory is limited in that personal traits generally have poor predictive value. Researchers who differentiated authoritarian, democratic, and laissez-faire styles concentrated on leader behavior rather than personality traits. Leadership studies at Ohio State University isolated four styles of leadership based on two categories of leader behavior: initiating structure and consideration. According to Blake and Mouton, a 9,9 style (high concern for both production and people) is the best overall style.

Situational leadership theorists believe there is no single best leadership style; rather, different situations require different styles. Many years of study led Fiedler to conclude that task-motivated leaders are more effective in either very favorable or very unfavorable situations, whereas relationship-motivated leaders are better suited to moderately favorable situations. The favorableness of a situation is dictated by the degree of the leader's control and influence in getting the job done. Path-goal leadership theory, an expectancy perspective, assumes that leaders are effective to the extent that they can motivate followers by clarifying goals and clearing the paths to achieving those goals and valued rewards. Unlike Fiedler, path-goal theorists believe that managers can and should adapt their leadership style to the situation. A third situational leadership model has been put forth by Vroom and Yetton. It matches five decision-making styles with 14 different situations. The Vroom/Yetton model calls for greater subordinate participation in situations where the manager has incomplete information and requires subordinate support for implementation.

Mentors can help develop younger managers' leadership skills by providing career and psychosocial guidance. Aspiring leaders are also urged to practice leadership off the job in school, church, or community organizations.

Behavior modification (B. Mod.) is the practical application of Skinnerian operant conditioning. B. Mod. occurs when the antecedent and consequence portions of the A → B → C relationship are rearranged to strengthen desirable behavior and weaken undesirable behavior. Proponents of B. Mod. prefer to shape behavior positively through positive reinforcement in lieu of negative reinforcement, extinction, and punishment. Continuous reinforcement is recommended for new behavior and intermittent reinforcement for established behavior.

Terms to Understand

Influence	Behavior modification (B. Mod.)
Power	Antecedent
Leadership	Positive reinforcement
Formal leadership	Negative reinforcement
Informal leadership	Extinction
Mentor	Punishment
Behaviorism	Continuous reinforcement
Operant conditioning	Intermittent reinforcement

Questions for Discussion

1. What tactics do you usually use to influence your parents, instructors, or supervisor? Would it be better to rely on other tactics? Explain.
2. Which explanation in Figure 13.1 is the most practical from a managerial standpoint? Why?

3. Which base(s) of power do you suppose that first-line supervisors rely on the most? Explain.
4. Do you agree with the notion that power is a neutral tool, not inherently good or bad? Explain your reasoning.
5. Think of the best leader that you have personally ever known. In terms of traits, style, and situational factors, why was that person a good leader?
6. Do you agree with the situational leadership theorists' claim that there is no "one best" style of leadership? Why or why not?
7. What are the advantages and disadvantages of a mentor for a new manager?
8. What antecedents could you rearrange to improve your study (or work) behavior?
9. From a B. Mod. standpoint, what is wrong with a punitive management style? What is your personal experience in this area?
10. It has been pointed out by experts in the field that children and pets are the world's best behavior modifiers. In A → B → C terms, why is this probably true?

Back to the Opening Case

Now that you have read Chapter 13, you should be able to answer the following questions about the Parsons Pine Products case:

1. What base or bases of power is James W. Parsons, the owner, relying on? Is he using his power responsibly?
2. How well does Mr. Parsons match Bennis's contemporary trait profile of a successful leader? Explain your position in terms of the four competencies (or traits) that Bennis identified in his research.
3. Where on Blake and Mouton's Managerial Grid® would you plot Mr. Parsons's leadership style? Explain your reasoning.
4. Is Mr. Parsons doing a good job of following the guidelines for successful behavior modification outlined in this Chapter? Explain why or why not.
5. Explain in A → B → C terms how Parsons has modified unsafe behavior.

Closing Case 13.2

Keeping Up with Gould's Switch to High-Tech*

With high-tech concerns springing up in bunches, the companies of tomorrow are turning to the companies of yesterday for managerial talent. "There just aren't enough good managers in high technology," complains David Powell, who runs an executive-search firm in California's Silicon Valley. [Here is the story of one manager's struggle to make the switch from a sunset industry to a sunrise industry.]

For years, Harry Caunter managed battery and electrical-products businesses for Gould Inc. In recent times, however, the suburban-Chicago company has dumped many of its older businesses and gone full-bore into electronics. Mr. Caunter faced a choice: Go high-tech or go elsewhere. He stayed and began his difficult ascent up the learning curve.

"I used to be able to look at financials and figure out problems and solutions," he says, somewhat wistfully. Now, he says, there is little time for such reflection: "It's all marketing and products. . . . It [the market] just goes south, and you're out." He cites a device the company introduced a few years ago to test computer logic. The product was oversophisticated, and Gould's market share sank like a stone within a few months. Things didn't happen that quickly in batteries, Mr. Caunter observes.

The 49-year-old executive has felt keenly his lack of technical knowledge, he says. One of the company's four executive vice presidents, Mr. Caunter says he is only now settling in—after 23 months on the job.

To bone up, he has spent hours studying technical trade journals. He also confers frequently with knowledgeable colleagues, and he has hired more consultants than he used to. He is making progress, he believes. But he will still dispatch a technically proficient underling on an important call to neighboring Motorola Inc. rather than make the visit himself. He acknowledges that he lacks the knowledge to talk up the product, but he insists: "As time passes, I'll correct that."

Mr. Caunter has also had to change his management style considerably. A self-described introvert, he used to rely on what he calls a "fear-respect" relationship with subordinates. "I don't need anyone," he says. "That may be terrible to say, but it's made me a good manager." Now, however, he talks of keeping things "warm and toasty" for technological wizards with sensitive psyches and an abundance of job offers.

In the last year and a half, 16 of the top 20 people at Mr. Caunter's Santa Clara, Calif., design and test systems division have been lured elsewhere. "In Silicon Valley, they have no work ethic. If they get frustrated, they go

*Excerpted from John Bussey, "Smokestack Managers Moving to High Tech Find the Going Tough," by permission of *The Wall Street Journal,* © Dow Jones & Company, Inc. 1985. All rights reserved.

get another job or sit in their hot tubs or something," Mr. Caunter says. "These are different people, this electronics bunch."

Gould gambled on Mr. Caunter because of his trouble-shooting skills and his ability to get the best out of his subordinates. So far, things seem to be working out, but he and the company have hedged their bet just the same. Gould recently hired two veteran high-tech executives to serve just below Mr. Caunter, and even he says he wouldn't hire a manager without technical knowledge to run one of his electronics lines. "No way," he says, laughing. "Life's too short."

For Discussion

1. How is Mr. Caunter changing his primary power base? Is this change for better or for worse? Explain.
2. With reference to the three classic styles of leadership (Table 13.1), what sort of switch has Mr. Caunter made? How can you tell?
3. Where would you place Mr. Caunter's new leadership style on Blake and Mouton's Managerial Grid®? His old style? Explain your rationale.
4. Relative to the path-goal leadership theory, what style or combination of styles would you employ if you were in Mr. Caunter's position? Is he headed in the right direction? Explain.
5. Assume Mr. Caunter has to make a decision about whether or not to design a complicated new product. Given his present lack of technical knowledge, what decision-making style (see Figure 13.7) would the Vroom-Yetton model (see Figure 13.8) recommend?

References

Opening Quotation: B. F. Skinner, *Beyond Freedom and Dignity* (New York: Bantam, 1971), p. 206.

Opening Case: "How to Earn 'Well Pay,' " *Business Week* No. 2538 (June 12, 1978): 143, 146.

Closing Case: Excerpted from John Bussey, "Smokestack Managers Moving to High Tech Find the Going Tough," *The Wall Street Journal* 112 (January 10, 1985): 1, 20.

1. Based on David Kipnis, Stuart M. Schmidt, and Ian Wilkinson, "Intraorganizational Influence Tactics: Explorations in Getting One's Way," *Journal of Applied Psychology* 65, no. 4 (1980): 440–452.
2. For complete details, see Kipnis, Schmidt, and Wilkinson, "Intraorganizational Influence Tactics."

3. Louis Kraar, "Putting Pan Am Back Together Again," *Fortune* 104 (December 28, 1981): 42.

4. Michael Korda, *Power! How to Get It, How to Use It* (New York: Ballantine, 1975), p. 17.

5. Dean Tjosvold, "The Dynamics of Positive Power," *Training and Development Journal* 38 (June 1984): 72.

6. Morgan McCall, Jr., *Power, Influence, and Authority: The Hazards of Carrying a Sword,* Technical Report 10 (Greensboro, N.C.: Center for Creative Leadership, 1978), p. 5.

7. For more on these three effects of power, see Anthony T. Cobb, "An Episodic Model of Power: Toward an Integration of Theory and Research," *Academy of Management Review* 9 (July 1984): 482–493. A comprehensive discussion of power coalitions both inside and outside the organization may be found in Henry Mintzberg, "Power and Organization Life Cycles," *Academy of Management Review* 9 (April 1984): 207–224.

8. See John R. P. French, Jr., and Bertram Raven, "The Bases of Social Power," in *Studies in Social Power,* ed. Dorwin Cartwright (Ann Arbor: University of Michigan Press, 1959), pp. 150–167. A list of twelve power bases may be found in William Dyer, "Caring and Power," *California Management Review* 21 (Summer 1979): 84–89.

9. John P. Kotter, "Power, Dependence, and Effective Management," *Harvard Business Review* 55 (July-August 1977): 128.

10. David C. McClelland, *Power: The Inner Experience* (New York: Irvington, 1975), p. 269.

11. See Jonathan E. Smith, Kenneth P. Carson, and Ralph A. Alexander, "Leadership: It Can Make a Difference," *Academy of Management Journal* 27 (December 1984): 765–776.

12. Chester A. Schriesheim, James M. Tolliver, and Orlando C. Behling, "Leadership Theory: Some Implications for Managers," *MSU Business Topics* 26 (Summer 1978): 35.

13. Fred Luthans, *Organizational Behavior,* 3rd ed. (New York: McGraw-Hill, 1981), p. 419.

14. Ralph M. Stogdill, "Personal Factors Associated with Leadership: A Survey of the Literature," *Journal of Psychology* 25 (1948): 63.

15. Based on discussion in Warren Bennis, "The 4 Competencies of Leadership," *Training and Development Journal* 38 (August 1984): 14–19.

16. For details, see Kurt Lewin, Ronald Lippitt, and Ralph K. White, "Patterns of Aggressive Behavior in Experimentally Created 'Social Climates,' " *Journal of Social Psychology* 10 (May 1939): 271–299.

17. For an informative summary of this research, see Edwin A. Fleishman, "Twenty Years of Consideration and Structure," in Edwin A. Fleishman and James G. Hunt, *Current Developments in the Study of Leadership* (Carbondale, Ill.: Southern Illinois University, 1973), pp. 1–40.

18. Three popular extensions of the Ohio State leadership studies may be found in Robert R. Blake and Jane S. Mouton, *The Managerial Grid*® (Houston: Gulf Publishing, 1964); William J. Reddin, *Managerial Effectiveness* (New York: McGraw-Hill, 1970); and Paul Hersey and Kenneth H. Blanchard, *Management of Organizational Behavior: Utilizing Human Resources,* 3rd ed. (Englewood Cliffs, N.J.: Prentice-Hall, 1977), p. 164.

19. See Abraham K. Korman, "Consideration, 'Initiating Structure,' and Organizational Criteria—A Review," *Personnel Psychology* 19 (Winter 1966): 349–361.

20. See Robert R. Blake and Jane Srygley Mouton, *The Managerial Grid III* (Houston: Gulf Publishing, 1985), p. 12.

21. For details of this study, see Robert R. Blake and Jane S. Mouton, "Management by Grid® Principles or Situationalism: Which?" *Group & Organization Studies* 6 (December 1981): 439–455.

22. Fred E. Fiedler, "Job Engineering for Effective Leadership: A New Approach," *Management Review* 66 (September 1977): 29.

23. For an excellent comprehensive validation study of Fiedler's leadership model, see Michael J. Strube and Joseph E. Garcia, "A Meta-Analytic Investigation of Fiedler's Contingency Model of Leadership Effectiveness," *Psychological Bulletin* 90 (September 1981): 307–321.

24. Fred E. Fiedler and Martin M. Chemers, *Leadership and Effective Management* (Glenview, Ill.: Scott, Foresman, 1974), p. 91.

25. Robert J. House and Terence R. Mitchell, "Path-Goal Theory of Leadership," *Journal of Contemporary Business* 3 (Autumn 1974): 85. The entire Autumn 1974 issue is devoted to an instructive review of contrasting theories of leadership.

26. Adapted from House and Mitchell, "Path-Goal Theory of Leadership," p. 83.

27. See Victor H. Vroom and Philip W. Yetton, *Leadership and Decision-Making* (Pittsburgh: University of Pittsburgh Press, 1973); and Victor H. Vroom, "A New Look at Managerial Decision Making," *Organizational Dynamics* 1 (Spring 1973): 66–80.

28. For more on mentoring, see Gerard R. Roche, "Much Ado About Mentors," *Harvard Business Review* 57 (January-February 1979): 14–28; and David Marshall Hunt and Carol Michael, "Mentorship: A Career Training and Development Tool," *Academy of Management Review* 8 (July 1983): 475–485.

29. Abraham Zaleznik, "Managers and Leaders: Are They Different?" *Harvard Business Review* 55 (May-June 1977): 76. For more on mentorship, see the Woodlands Group, "Management Development Roles: Coach, Sponsor, and Mentor," *Personnel Journal* 59 (November 1980): 918–921.

30. See "Mentoring Process Works Best When It Is Kept Informal, Finds Study," *Management Review* 73 (June 1984): 55.

31. For more, see Kathy E. Kram, "Phases of the Mentor Relationship," *Academy of Management Journal* 26 (December 1983): 608–625.

32. A good discussion of cross-gender mentoring can be found in James G. Clawson and Kathy E. Kram, "Managing Cross-Gender Mentoring," *Business Horizons* 27 (May-June 1984): 22–32.

33. See Edward L. Thorndike, *Educational Psychology: The Psychology of Learning* (New York: Columbia University Press, 1913), II, 4.

34. For an instructive account of operant conditioning applied to human behavior, see B. F. Skinner, *Science and Human Behavior* (New York: Free Press, 1953), pp. 62–66.

35. Thomas K. Connellan, *How to Improve Human Performance: Behaviorism in Business and Industry* (New York: Harper & Row, 1978), p. 30. (Emphasis added.)

36. Kenneth Blanchard and Spencer Johnson, *The One Minute Manager* (New York: Berkley, 1982), p. 45. (Emphasis added.) Also see Kenneth Blanchard and Robert Lorber, *Putting the One Minute Manager to Work* (New York: Berkley, 1984).

37. Robert Kreitner, "PM—A New Method of Behavior Change," *Business Horizons* 18 (December 1975): 84–85.

38. For more detailed accounts of the Emery Air Freight program, see "At Emery Air Freight: Positive Reinforcement Boosts Performance," *Organizational Dynamics* 1 (Winter 1973): 41–50; and W. Clay Hamner and Ellen P. Hamner, "Behavior Modification on the Bottom Line," *Organizational Dynamics* 4 (Spring 1976): 3–21.

39. Adapted from Fred Luthans and Robert Kreitner, *Organizational Behavior Modification* (Glenview, Ill.: Scott, Foresman, 1975), pp. 117–123.

Chapter 14

Change and Organization Development

The art of progress is to preserve order amid change and to preserve change amid order.
Alfred North Whitehead

Chapter Objectives

When you finish studying this chapter, you should be able to

- Define, in your own words, the term *organization development* (OD).
- List at least six reasons why employees resist change and discuss what management can do about resistance to change.
- Explain what the term *genuine participation* means.
- Describe how the unfreezing-change-refreezing analogy applies to OD.
- Identify a strength and a weakness for each of the four major diagnostic tools.
- Explain how OD interventions can be aimed at individuals, groups, or entire organizations.

Opening Case 14.1

How Ebasco Makes the Matrix Method Work*

Matrix management, a system that adds horizontal reporting requirements to the traditional vertical chain of command, has become increasingly popular at companies that manage complex construction projects. Under a matrix system an engineer, for example, may have to satisfy several bosses. For the construction manager, he must design

*Reprinted from the June 15, 1981 issue of *Business Week* by special permission, © 1981 by McGraw-Hill, Inc.

products that perform well. For the project manager, he must consider scheduling necessities, components costs, and other bottom-line factors. Reconciling the obvious clashes that erupt from such conflicting priorities is a formidable task. Indeed, many companies have abandoned matrix management for that reason.

But Andrew O. Manzini, vice-president for human resources for Ebasco Services Inc., Enserch Corp's energy-oriented engineering and consulting arm, has developed an approach to minimize the confusion. Three years ago an extensive internal study turned up mounting friction caused by the matrix system at Ebasco's nuclear sites. Since then, Manzini and his organizational development (OD) staff have been implementing a veritable laundry list of training and troubleshooting programs to lessen the chaos. And while follow-up surveys of Ebasco managers show that matrix-caused problems have by no means been eradicated, they also show that tensions at the project sites have been reduced dramatically.

That is no mean feat in light of the problems peculiar to nuclear power-plant projects. Most such projects take more than a decade from start to finish, and changing government regulations and roadblocks can throw schedules awry at any point. Moreover, reporting requirements constantly change as the project moves from one stage to another. For example, project engineers, construction supervisors, and the like can find themselves responsible to the reactor building manager while they are working on that section of the project, and to the manager of another physical area the following month. To compound the confusion, Ebasco's employees must also interrelate with the client's employees at every step along the way.

Defusing Conflicts

Although these multiple pressures make cooperation essential, team members tend to be protective of their specialties and can be resentful and suspicious of colleagues with different priorities. Much of Manzini's effort has gone to defusing the emotional side of the conflicts, paving the way for the basic issues to be resolved.

Although dollar-and-cents results of Manzini's programs remain almost impossible to quantify, accolades from Ebasco insiders and outsiders alike clearly show that he has been on the right track. Ebasco's new 45-hour supervisory development course has so impressed the New York State Board of Regents that "graduates" receive college credit. The success of the company's "facilitators" in smoothing relations among Ebasco personnel has led clients to ask Manzini to intervene in their own staff conflicts. Indeed, President and Chief Executive Officer William Wallace III is using organizational development people to run some of his own meetings.

The OD-sponsored programs have been as diverse as the problems they were developed to solve. Since the original study highlighted the misunderstandings both from and about matrix systems, the OD staff has held more than 100 formal seminars to explain that structure to employees. It has put in a dual-performance evaluation program to ensure that employees who report to two bosses are evaluated by both. That way the employee cannot be penalized by a supervisor who says he has been recalcitrant in following orders, for example, when in fact he was given conflicting instructions by another supervisor.

Employees are also receiving a measure of reassurance from a complex computerized career tracking program in which their skills are matched against Ebasco's projected staffing needs. The program will give Ebasco early warning of manpower shortages. And it will give employees the comfort of knowing that their strengths are on record in a skills bank, ready to be tapped as promotions become available.

The Hands-on Way

While most of these programs are easily directed from Manzini's New York office, the OD staff is also taking a hands-on approach to solving problems in the field. The group has conducted some 60 "team-building interventions" in which an OD facilitator meets with project personnel who are in conflict. He asks each person for his or her perception of the cause of conflict and then leads a meeting in which those conflicts are resolved. Manzini notes that more than once facilitators have been called in to resolve "personality conflicts" between construction and project managers—and found that the trouble stemmed from faulty scheduling of materials. In those cases, the facilitator helps the managers work out a new scheduling system.

Of course, attitudes and behavior sometimes are the source of trouble. And when this kind of problem is brewing, Ebasco managers are increasingly calling facilitators in as preventive medicine. Robert K. Stemple, project manager for a nuclear power plant Ebasco is building for Louisiana Power & Light Co. in New Orleans, had been directing the project from New York, leaving the on-site management to the construction manager in New Orleans. Then the construction manager resigned, and LP&L requested that Stemple move down to the site. "Project managers are rarely on-site, and I knew the construction people would consider my presence a threat," he recalls.

Stemple's solution was to involve the project's top 15 people in a two-day team-building session with Manzini. "He started off the meeting by giving us one of those brain-teaser questions that nobody could solve," Stemple recalls. "With all of us feeling dumb, a non-threatening atmosphere was established." In that atmosphere, both sides relaxed and were able to exorcise some of their prior resentments and fears. The net result made Stemple more comfortable with the move.

Following the Example

David B. Lester, LP&L's project manager at the plant, also has used Ebasco's OD people to facilitate meetings. "Not only can outside facilitators keep a meeting on track, but when there is friction, the participants can get angry at the facilitator, not at each other," he says.

Indeed, Ebasco's top echelon has started to use a team-building approach of its own. As part of an "executive development program," OD facilitators periodically interview Wallace and some 12 members of his senior staff to ask about areas in Ebasco that need improvement, then coordinate a two-day meeting to discuss what actions can be taken on problems that had been pinpointed during the interviews. Although this program was originally meant to be a vehicle to "educate top executives on personnel issues," Wallace recalls, it has so far concentrated more on getting regional offices involved in long-range planning and other strategic areas. "We will eventually look at matters of motivation, but for now we can't really let personnel development take priority over discussions on how to proceed in synfuels and the like," he explains.

The Benefits

Few Ebasco managers are complaining that personnel development is suffering from neglect, however. The new supervisory development program is getting high marks from graduates, for example. It combines lectures on planning, delegating, communicating, and other people-oriented aspects of management with self-scored tests that help supervisors learn to handle hypothetical management problems. Graduates say they gain a better understanding of how their management styles affect their employees.

For example, Merrill W. Grogel, an expediting supervisor, notes that during the course he was able to analyze the persistent conflicts he had been having with one of his subordinates. He came to realize that he had been looking over the man's shoulder constantly and that this was the cause for the antagonism. "I thought I was giving him the benefit of my knowledge, but he thought I was belittling him," Grogel admits. Since then, Grogel says, he has given the subordinate a longer leash and now has a smoother running department.

Still, none of the new programs has proved to be a panacea for resolving all conflicts, and the matrix system remains not only a fuzzy concept but also a thorny one to many employees. "Technical employees still feel a good technical job is most important, and engineers feel they're spending too much time reporting, planning, scheduling, and budgeting," admits Wallace. Indeed, even Stemple, an obvious OD enthusiast, notes that "you lose enthusiasm with time. The problem is keeping up everyone's commitment to [cooperation]."

Manzini and the OD staff have a long way to go before their human-resource innovations can make all aspects of the matrix system trouble-free. But it is clear that even if the trouble-free point is never reached, the OD programs have made the system significantly less trouble-prone.

(Discussion questions linking this case with the material you are about to read can be found at the end of this chapter.)

When introducing change in their organizations, whether at Ebasco or elsewhere, managers are often surprised and dismayed that things don't turn out as planned. For example, consider the fate of a training program at American Telephone and Telegraph (AT&T):

> AT&T set up a school to teach managers to coordinate the design and manufacture of data products for customized sales. But when managers completed the course, they found that the traditional way of operating—making non-customized mass sales—[was] what counted in the company. They were given neither the time to analyze individual customers' needs nor rewards commensurate with such efforts. The result was that 85% of the graduates quit, and AT&T disbanded the school.[1]

This attempt to redirect AT&T's marketing efforts failed primarily because the company's culture, in regard to goals, norms, and rewards, did not support the change. Like a fish on land, AT&T's ill-fated change died for lack of a supportive climate. Because of the accelerating rate of change both inside and outside the organization, managers need to be skilled at managing change if they are to succeed. In this chapter we consider how organizational changes can be introduced more systematically and more effectively through organization development (OD).

What Is OD?

Although relatively new, OD has become a convenient label for a whole host of techniques and processes aimed at making sick organizations healthy and healthy organizations healthier. As one proponent has noted, "It is a synthesis of many different disciplines that have never been brought together in any integrated way. There is a little bit of this and a little bit of that. It is sort of like goulash without much seasoning."[2]

A more serious definition comes from a researcher who sees **organization development** as "a planned, managed, systematic process to change the culture, systems, and behavior of an organization, in order to improve the organization's effectiveness in solving its problems and achieving its objectives."[3] In short, OD centers on planned change, as opposed to the haphazard change that organizations usually experience. Although planned change can conceivably involve technical, administrative, or behavioral subsystems, the behavioral subsystem historically has received the most attention, since most OD specialists have been behavioral scientists. More recently, according to an expert in the field, the focus of OD has broadened: "The central value of OD today is that we should work to jointly optimize social and technical subsystems."[4]

The Development of OD

Like other approaches to management, OD has evolved over a period of years.[5] Since the 1960s it has developed into an amalgam of many different behavioral science techniques. Two techniques influenced OD significantly in its early years, though they are no longer the only techniques used.[6] The first, laboratory training, is popularly referred to as sensitivity training, or T-group (T stands for "training"). The second technique is survey research and feedback. After examining each of these in some detail, it will be easier to understand OD's origins and appreciate its development.

Laboratory Training In brief, **laboratory training** aims at emotional rather than intellectual learning by exposing a group of individuals to an ambiguous and sometimes anxiety-producing situation (for example, confrontation over racial or sex-role stereotyping). The result, often enough, is that the participants develop sensitivity to others' opinions, acquire a more realistic self-image, and are better able to deal openly and effectively with others.

Emotional Learning Outside consultants are usually brought into the organization to set up the sessions and to provide trained leadership. Group members may or may not know each other (if they do, they are called a family group; if they do not, they are called a stranger group). The training sessions may last from only one day to as long as two weeks. Very often there is no formal agenda, no structured activity, and sometimes no visible leader. In the unstructured situation that results, members eventually confront each other with their opinions and feelings. They often find that their favorite defenses against criticism and long-held assumptions about others do not stand up under public scrutiny. The trainer's role is mainly to focus attention on here-and-now group processes, rather than on back-home problems, and to encourage a supportive and caring atmosphere.

After a prolonged period of free exchange, the participants' attitudes tend to change in the direction of greater self-awareness and greater sensitivity to the feelings and opinions of others. They learn that these attitudes actually facilitate group interaction. But, when they return to their normal work environments, especially after experience in a group of strangers, they often discover that their coworkers are not responsive to their new attitude of openness, and they are unable to interact with them unless they fall back on their old behavior patterns. The two results that typified most early laboratory training were (1) frequent success in developing greater awareness and openness in individuals and (2) relatively poor carry-over to organizations, especially from groups of strangers.

Pros and Cons   OD specialists today are split over the issue of laboratory training. Some use it with reportedly good results, both for individuals and for the organization. Others, because of its potential for ego-shattering confrontation among participants, question its ultimate value. Proponents maintain, however, that frank and open interaction can lead to a clearer self-image and greater sensitivity to interpersonal differences. With careful screening and orientation of participants, the option to withdraw at any time, a qualified group leader-facilitator, and supportive follow-up in the work environment, laboratory training can be a powerful technique for changing behavior.[7]

Aside from various arguments for and against laboratory training, it has taught OD specialists a great deal about how people act, react, and interact. It has also helped clarify the differences between effective and ineffective group interaction. In an effective group, as discussed in Chapter 12, socially mature individuals communicate well by exchanging relevant information, constructive feedback, sincere feelings, and trust. Members of an ineffective group, on the other hand, withhold needed information and feedback, guard their feelings, and withhold or betray trust. From an OD standpoint, the processes of group interaction are as important as what the group accomplishes.

Survey Research and Feedback   While one group of behavioral scientists was experimenting with laboratory training during the 1940s and 1950s, another was discovering the practical benefits of gathering and analyzing information and then feeding it back to the people who originally provided it. This process was called **survey research and feedback.** Attitude surveys proved to be particularly useful in this regard.

Letting People Know Where They Stand   As a working example, outside consultants might devise a written questionnaire to allow employees to indicate their attitudes toward their jobs, the company, their supervisors, their coworkers, the atmosphere in the organization, and so on. This anonymously gathered information, once it is properly tabulated, tells top management a great deal about employee attitudes and values while at the same time preserving individual privacy. One department's attitude profile can be compared with that of another, or the attitudes of shop supervisors can be compared with those of clerical employees. In this manner, trouble spots that otherwise would remain undetected or ill defined are pinpointed.

A more important function of the survey approach occurs when the information is fed back to the employees who filled out the questionnaire. Feedback lets employees know where they stand without threatening their egos in the process. This end is usually accomplished by having employees compare their own attitude and opinion survey results (fed back privately with the aid of personal code words for matching purposes) with those for the entire department or organization (fed back publicly).

Change Based on Feedback Change based on feedback enables the individual to confront his or her personal shortcomings without social embarrassment. Moreover, the individual is likely to respond to appeals to change, develop, and improve. The most valuable lesson learned from experience with survey research and feedback is that many people welcome feedback and will make a good-faith effort to change when they are able to compare themselves objectively with other people.

OD as a Diagnosis-Prescription Cycle

As the field of OD began to evolve during the 1960s, it became evident to observers that both laboratory training and survey research and feedback could make valuable contributions. A marriage between these two proven techniques became possible once OD came to be viewed as a cycle that diagnosed an organization's ills and prescribed a cure for them.

The first step, diagnosis, helps an organization define its current situation. Two OD specialists have emphasized the importance of good diagnosis, asserting that "just as a good physician will diagnose the patient's particular symptoms before determining which remedy to prescribe, so the manager must diagnose the organization's symptoms before prescribing the appropriate corrective techniques."[8] Survey research in the form of attitude and opinion questionnaires is a convenient and effective diagnostic tool.

Once specific problem areas have been diagnosed, then survey feedback and group development exercises can be prescribed as the situation warrants. By interpreting the results of the diagnosis and, later, by evaluating the effects of the prescription, OD can be viewed as a complete **diagnosis-prescription cycle,** as shown in Figure 14.1. Note that the diagnosis serves two purposes. First, it provides a clear picture of how things actually are. Second, it offers a measuring stick for evaluating the success of the prescribed techniques. We shall explore the details of these processes later in this chapter.

Figure 14.1 OD as a Diagnosis-Prescription Cycle

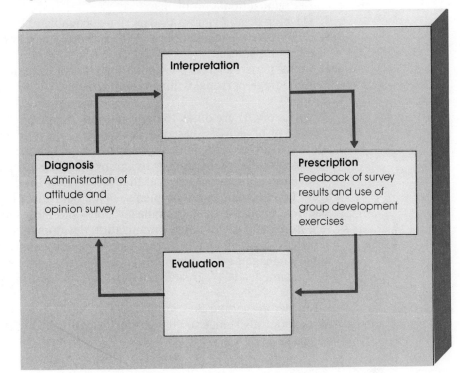

The Objectives of OD

OD programs vary because they are based, at least in part, on diagnosis of the situation. What is appropriate for one organization may be totally out of place in another. In spite of this, however, certain objectives are found in most OD programs. In general, OD programs develop social processes such as trust, problem solving, communication, and cooperation to facilitate organizational change and enhance personal and organizational effectiveness. More specifically, the typical OD program tries to achieve the following seven objectives:

1. Deepen the sense of organizational purpose (or vision) and align individuals with that purpose.
2. Strengthen interpersonal trust, communication, cooperation, and support.

3. Encourage a problem-solving rather than problem-avoiding approach to organizational problems.
4. Develop a satisfying work experience capable of building enthusiasm.
5. Supplement formal authority with authority based on personal knowledge and skill.
6. Increase personal responsibility for planning and implementing.
7. Encourage personal willingness to change.[9]

Critics of OD are quick to point out that there is nothing really new in this list of objectives. Directly or indirectly, each of these objectives is addressed by one or another general management technique. OD advocates respond to such criticism by noting that general management lacks a systematic approach. They feel that the usual practice of teaching managers how to plan, solve problems, make decisions, organize, motivate, lead, and control leads to a haphazard, bits-and-pieces management style. According to OD thinking, organization development gives managers a vehicle for systematically introducing change by applying a broad selection of management techniques as a unified and consistent package. This, they claim, leads to greater personal, group, and organizational effectiveness.

But before getting into more detail about OD, we need to say something about resistance to change, because it is the archenemy of any OD program.

Overcoming Resistance to Change

Organizational change comes in all sizes and shapes. It may be new and unfamiliar equipment such as personal computers, reorganization, a merger, a new pay plan, or perhaps a new performance appraisal program. Whatever the change, it is like a stone tossed into a still pond. The initial change causes ripples of change to radiate in all directions, often with unpredictable consequences. A common consequence of change in organizations is resistance from those whose jobs are directly affected. Both rational and irrational resistance to change can bring the wheels of progress to a halt. Management faces the challenge of foreseeing and neutralizing resistance to change. The question is, how?

The Traditional Prescription: Participation

Because of a widely cited human relations study conducted by Lester Coch and John R. P. French in 1948, participation by those directly affected has long been the prescribed technique for overcoming resistance to change. Briefly, Coch and French had the managers in a clothing factory introduce a new work procedure in three different ways to separate work groups. One group, called the "no participation" group, was simply told what the new procedure would be. A second group, the "representative" group, was introduced to the change by employee representatives who had seen a presentation of the new procedure. All members of two additional groups, referred to as "total participation" groups, were given a dramatic demonstration of how the new procedure could achieve a needed cost reduction. Employees in the total participation groups discussed the possibility for improvement until general agreement was reached.

Results varied significantly. Specifically, a steep and lasting drop in output for the no participation group was accompanied by high turnover and numerous grievances. In contrast, the total participation groups, after a slight but brief drop in output, exceeded their previous output levels. Moreover, there was no turnover or hostility toward the new work procedure among those in the total participation groups. Mixed results were recorded for the representative group. And so it was concluded that employees would not resist a change if they were given the opportunity to participate *personally* in bringing it about.[10]

Recent practical experience seems to reinforce Coch and French's findings. For example, "when Digital Equipment Corp. recently computerized a production line for making wire harnesses, it allowed some 70 workers and supervisors to participate. In the first 90 days the new line was in operation, productivity improved 25% and work-in-process inventory was reduced by one-half."[11] The key, in the cases of both Coch and French's factory and Digital, was genuine participation instead of token participation. **Genuine participation** means not only tapping the creative ideas of all relevant parties but also integrating those ideas into the nature and timing of the change.[12] Also, as Honeywell has learned through practical experience (see Table 14.1), genuine participation helps good ideas "percolate up" from lower organizational levels. With token participation, key decisions are already made before soliciting employee inputs. Token participation tends to foster alienation rather than enthusiasm and personal commitment.

Why Do Employees Resist Change?

Employees resist change for many reasons.[13] Among the most common reasons are:

- **Surprise.** Significant changes that are introduced on the spur of the moment or with no warning can create a threatening sense of imbalance in the work place. Regarding this problem, an executive task force at J. C. Penney Co., the well-known retailer, recommended: "Schedule changes in measurable, comfortable stages. Too much, too soon can be counter-productive."[14]
- **Inertia.** Many members of the typical organization desire to maintain a safe, secure, and predictable status quo. The byword of this group is:

Table 14.1 Genuine Participation Helps Reduce Resistance to Personal Computers at Honeywell

At a major Honeywell facility in Clearwater, Florida, a group of employees interested in personal computers hatched a plan. They said, "Personal computers have come of age, and our company needs a large computer-literate workforce to help us remain competitive. If Honeywell would underwrite loans by paying the interest, we bet many employees would buy computers, learn how to use them, and start finding innovative ways to use them at work." After a trial in Florida, the Honeywell Home Computer Purchase Plan was opened up throughout the company.

Many employees in the Clearweater facility have taken advantage of the purchase program, from factory workers to executive staff. They are applying their home computers and the knowledge they have gained to the job in a variety of imaginative ways. The proportion of the work force that welcomes rather than resents the arrival of computers in the work place has substantially increased, and we have created new bonds of company appreciation and loyalty at very little cost.

SOURCE: Richard J. Boyle, "Designing the Energetic Organization," *Management Review* 72 (August 1983): 24.

"But we don't do things that way here." Supervisors and middle managers who fall victim to this problem can effectively kill change programs.

- **Misunderstanding/Ignorance/Lack of skills.** Without adequate introductory or remedial training, an otherwise positive change may be perceived in a negative light.
- **Emotional side effects.** Those who are forced to accept on-the-job changes commonly experience a sense of loss over past ways of doing things. For example, consider what one AT&T employee said following the government-forced divestiture in 1984: "I felt like I had gone through a divorce that neither my wife nor my children wanted. ... It was like waking up in familiar surroundings, but your family and all that you held dear were missing."[15]
- **Lack of trust.** Promises of improvement are likely to fall on deaf ears when employees do not trust management. Conversely, managers are unlikely to permit necessary participation if they do not trust their people.
- **Fear of failure.** Just as most college freshmen have doubts about their chances of ever graduating, challenges presented by significant on-the-job changes also can be intimidating.
- **Personality conflicts.** Managers who are disliked by their people are poor conduits for change.
- **Poor timing.** In every work setting, internal and/or external events can conspire to create resentment about a particular change. For example, Intel's across-the-board salary cut, in response to the electronics industry slump of 1981–82, generated greater than expected resentment

because "the salary cuts were timed to come just as taxes for Social Security were reimposed."[16]

- **Lack of tact.** As we all know, it is not necessarily what is said that shapes our attitude toward people and events. *How* it is said is often more important. Tactful and sensitive handling of changes is essential.
- **Threat to job status/security.** Because employment fulfills basic needs, employees can be expected to resist changes with real or imaginary impacts on job status or job security.
- **Breakup of work group.** Significant changes can tear the fabric of on-the-job social relationships. Accordingly, members of cohesive work groups often exert peer pressure on one another to resist changes that threaten to break up the group.[17]

These reasons for resisting change help demonstrate that participation is not a panacea. For example, imagine the futility of trying to gain the enthusiastic support of a team of auto assembly-line welders for a robot that will eventually take over their jobs. Each reason for resisting change, in extreme form, can become an insurmountable barrier to genuine participation. Therefore, from an OD perspective, managers need a broader array of methods for dealing with resistance to change.

Strategies for Overcoming Resistance to Change

Only recently have management theorists begun to give serious attention to alternative ways of overcoming resistance to change. According to two Harvard researchers, there are at least six options, including participation, available to management in this area:

1. **Education and communication.** This particular strategy is appealing because it advocates prevention rather than cure. The idea here is to help employees understand the true need for a change as well as the logic behind it. Various media may be used, including face-to-face discussions, formal group presentations, or special reports or publications.
2. **Participation and involvement.** Once again, personal involvement through participation tends to defuse both rational and irrational fears about a workplace change. By participating in both the design and implementation of a change, one acquires a personal stake in its success.
3. **Facilitation and support.** When fear and anxiety are responsible for resistance to doing things in a new and different way, support from management in the form of special training, listening, job stress counseling, and compensatory time off can be helpful.
4. **Negotiation and agreement.** Sometimes management can neutralize potential or actual resistance by exchanging something of value for cooperation. For instance, an hourly clerical employee may be put on

salary in return for learning how to operate a new computerized word processor.

5. **Manipulation and co-optation.** Manipulation occurs when managers selectively withhold or dispense information and consciously arrange events to increase the chance that a change will be successful. Co-optation normally involves token participation. Those who are co-opted with token participation cannot claim that they have not been consulted; yet the ultimate impact of their input is negligible.

6. **Explicit and implicit coercion.** Managers who cannot or will not invest the time required for the other strategies can force employees to go along with a change by threatening them with termination, loss of pay raises or promotions, transfer, and the like.

As shown in Table 14.2, each of these strategies for overcoming resistance to change has advantages and drawbacks. Situational appropriateness is the key to success.

The OD Process

Even though OD programs are often tailor-made and hence each is slightly different, it is possible to outline a general model. Probably the best way to introduce the three major components of the model is to use a simple analogy.

Suppose someone hands you a coffee cup filled with clear, solid ice. You look down through the ice and see a penny lying tails up on the bottom of the cup. Now, suppose for some reason you want the penny to be frozen in place in a heads-up position. What can you do? There is really only one practical solution. You let the ice in the cup thaw, reach in and flip the penny over, and then refreeze the cup of water. This is precisely how the esteemed social psychologist Kurt Lewin recommended that change be handled in social systems. Specifically, Lewin recommended that change agents unfreeze, change, and refreeze social systems.

Unfreezing prepares the members of a social system for change and then helps neutralize initial resistance. Sudden, unexpected change, according to Lewin, is socially disruptive. Once the change has been introduced, **refreezing** is necessary to follow up on problems, complaints, unanticipated side effects, and any lingering resistance. This seemingly simple approach to change spells the difference between systematic and haphazard change.

The OD model introduced here is based on Lewin's approach to handling change (see Figure 14.2). It is similar to the diagnosis-prescription cycle illustrated in Figure 14.1, but it is expanded to include new concepts.

Table 14.2 Dealing with Resistance to Change

Approach	Commonly Used in Situations
1. **Education + communication**	Where there is a lack of information or inaccurate information and analysis
2. **Participation + involvement**	Where the initiators do not have all the information they need to design the change, and where others have considerable power to resist
3. **Facilitation + support**	Where people are resisting because of adjustment problems
4. **Negotiation + agreement**	Where someone or some group will clearly lose out in a change, and where that group has considerable power to resist
5. **Manipulation + co-optation**	Where other tactics will not work or are too expensive
6. **Explicit + implicit coercion**	Where speed is essential, and the change initiators possess considerable power

Advantages	Drawbacks
1. Once persuaded, people will often help with the implementation of the change	Can be very time-consuming if lots of people are involved
2. People who participate will be committed to implementing change, and any relevant information they have will be integrated into the change plan	Can be very time-consuming if participators design an inappropriate change
3. No other approach works as well with adjustment problems	Can be time-consuming, expensive, and still fail
4. Sometimes it is a relatively easy way to avoid major resistance	Can be too expensive in many cases if it alerts others to negotiate for compliance
5. It can be a relatively quick and inexpensive solution to resistance problems	Can lead to future problems if people feel manipulated
6. It is speedy, and can overcome any kind of resistance	Can be risky if it leaves people mad at the initiators

SOURCE: Reprinted by permission of the *Harvard Business Review*. An exhibit from "Choosing Strategies for Change," by John P. Kotter and Leonard A. Schlesinger (March-April 1979), p. 111. Copyright © 1979 by the President and Fellows of Harvard College; all rights reserved.

Figure 14.2 A General Model of OD

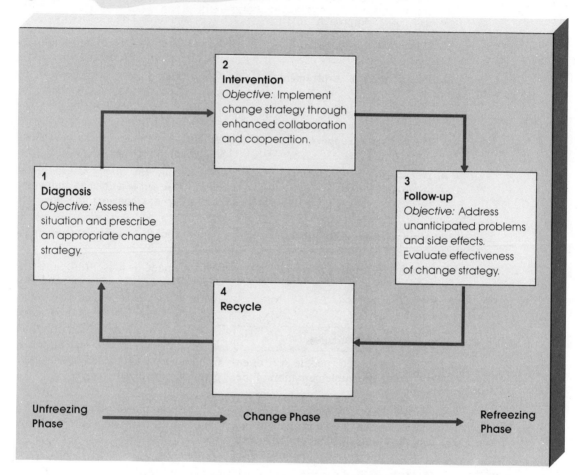

Diagnosis is carried out during the unfreezing stage. Change is then carefully introduced through tailor-made intervention. Finally, a systematic follow-up refreezes the situation. Each step is critical to successful organizational change and development. Still, it takes continual recycling through this three-step sequence to make OD an ongoing system of planned change.

Diagnosis   When approaching the diagnostic phase of OD, management has two important decisions to make. First, it needs to decide if it is capable of conducting its own diagnosis. If it does not have the time or talent to conduct an adequate diagnosis of the situation, then it will have to turn to an outside consultant. But management should be careful when hiring the services of any outside consultant.[18] A bit of shopping around for someone who is willing to do a thorough diagnosis is advisable. As one writer has observed, "There is always the temptation to respond favorably to slickly packaged programs and effective sales presentations. In most cases these are solutions looking for a problem to solve. ... "[19] Outside consultants who insist they have all the answers the minute they walk in the door should be politely dismissed.

The second important decision to be made by management before entering the diagnostic phase is precisely what areas to probe. Because of the expense of conducting a diagnosis, specific problem areas or subunits that deserve close examination need to be identified at the outset. Diagnoses that are overly comprehensive or carelessly directed are a waste of time and money.

Once these decisions have been made, management (or the outside consultants) can turn to three important aspects of the diagnostic phase: (1) unfreezing the situation, (2) designing the diagnostic strategy, and (3) interpreting the diagnostic data.

Unfreezing the Situation   Although most of us like surprises when it comes to gifts and parties, we tend to fear surprises that affect our work. An organization development program should not come as a surprise. Some unfreezing, which is usually done by making announcements, holding meetings, and launching a promotional campaign in the organization's newsletter and on bulletin boards can help start things going. All these unfreezing activities help make the following message clear: "We can improve the effectiveness of our organization while increasing our personal satisfaction if we all cooperate in a comprehensive program of finding out *where we are, where we want to go,* and *how we can get there*." A message of this type prepares people for interviewers, questionnaires, unfamiliar consultants, and group activities that could be very threatening if they came as surprises. One word of caution is in order, however. During the unfreezing phase, care should be taken to avoid creating unrealistic expectations. OD is designed to introduce change, not miracles![20] Employees who are encouraged to expect miracles are bound to come away disappointed.

Designing the Diagnostic Strategy   Those about to tackle an OD diagnosis will find it helpful to view the typical organization as an iceberg. Figure 14.3 shows that just as most of an iceberg lies beneath the surface of the water, a great proportion of an organization's activities and information is also hidden from view. OD diagnosis is difficult because hidden as well as visible information must be brought to the surface. Naturally a complete diagnosis of every feature listed in Figure 14.3 would be prohib-

Figure 14.3 The Organizational Iceberg: Hidden Features Are Also Important

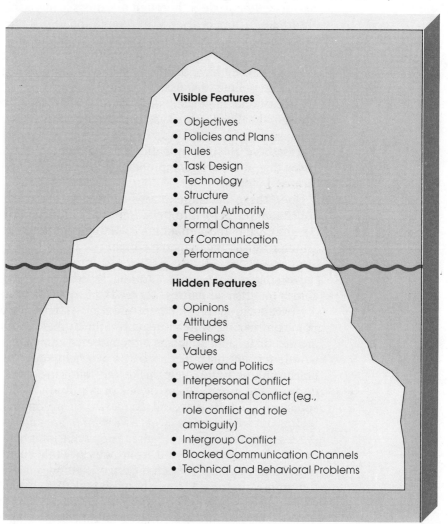

itively expensive and time consuming, and so it is important to select the right diagnostic strategy for the information sought. Four widely used approaches are:

1. **Review of records.** Largely in response to the government's increased demand for reports, today's organizations possess a wealth of recorded information and data. When change agents have the time and patience to carry out a thorough records search, they are often rewarded with valuable information about the relative health or sickness of the organi-

zation. Much can be learned by reviewing personnel records for signs of excessive absenteeism and turnover or for patterns of grievances. Similarly, a study of financial records can yield telling signs of cost overruns and other financial problems.

2. **Interviews.** By using a carefully compiled list of specific questions (requiring yes or no answers) and general, open-ended questions (requiring detailed explanations), a skilled interviewer can discover a great deal about both individuals and the organization at large.

3. **Survey questionnaires.** Survey questionnaires are the most widely used diagnostic strategy today. Questionnaires may be administered to people assembled in groups, or they may be mailed individually. They may be constructed in-house or purchased.[21] Some of the more sophisticated published survey questionnaires include scoring and statistical analysis in the purchase price.

4. **Direct observation.** It is well known that people tend to say one thing and do another. When this kind of discrepancy is likely to be a problem, then management may choose to have a neutral third party (usually an outside consultant) directly observe organizational members at work.

Each of these strategies has its appropriate place in OD diagnosis. By balancing the respective strengths and weaknesses of the various approaches (see Table 14.3), it is possible to develop a diagnostic strategy based on two or more approaches. For example, a carefully structured interview could be used to supplement the results of a records review or to fill in the gaps left by a prepackaged survey questionnaire. The overall objective, of course, is to obtain as much useful information as possible at a reasonable cost.

Interpreting Diagnostic Data   Careful interpretation of the data collected during diagnosis paves the way for effective OD intervention. But an extremely important point should be made here. It is a serious mistake to wait until the diagnosis has been completed before thinking about the interpretation phase. Diagnostic strategies need to be selected with ease of interpretation in mind. Furthermore, as one OD expert has pointed out, "Data should be collected for a reason, not just 'because it's there,' and analysis should be done with direction and purpose, not as a fishing expedition to 'see what we come up with.' "[22]

Comparisons are helpful. If a similar diagnosis has been conducted in the past, then comparing past results with present results can show how things have changed. Comparisons among departments and other organizational subunits also can be revealing. For instance, a comparatively strong negative attitude toward supervision in one department may signal the need to train or replace a particular supervisor.

Careful interpretation of diagnostic data is the key to selecting an

Table 14.3 Strengths and Weaknesses of Various Diagnostic Approaches

Diagnostic Approach	Major Strengths	Major Weaknesses
Review of records	Provides historical perspective over extended period.	Time consuming.
	Facts and figures confirm or refute employees' intentions and/or perceptions.	Faulty record keeping can be disruptive.
Interviews	Face-to-face contact is revealing (for example, body language).	Repondents often try to look good in the interviewer's eyes.
	Questions can be inserted on the spot to probe promising areas.	Time consuming and costly if a large sample is required.
Survey questionnaires	Appropriate for large samples.	Prepackaged questionnaires may ask the wrong questions.
	Administration is time and cost efficient.	Preparation and interpretation of in-house questionnaires can be time consuming and costly.
Direct observation	Behavior speaks for itself ("actions speak louder than words").	Presence of observer often causes people to behave abnormally.
	Previously unrecognized problems may be spotted by trained outside observer.	Time consuming and costly if a large sample is required.

appropriate change or intervention strategy. Inaccurate or sloppy diagnosis will doom even the best-designed and most well-intentioned OD intervention.

Intervention   Once the organization or target group has been unfrozen and the diagnosis is complete, the wheels of change can be set in motion. An **intervention,** in OD terms, is a systematic attempt to correct an organizational deficiency uncovered through diagnosis. Management teams, working either alone or in collaboration with an outside consultant, are responsible for selecting appropriate OD interventions.[23] However, the wheels of failure will be set in motion at this critical juncture if management is uninformed about alternative interventions, withholds its full support, or has unrealistic expectations. (See Table 14.4 for OD success factors that researchers have

Table 14.4 OD Success Factors

A nationwide sample of 245 OD consultants responded to a questionnaire asking about their successes and failures. "Fifty-three percent of the projects reported were successful, 47 percent unsuccessful." Among the factors found to be associated with *successful* OD programs were:

- Client system was *ready for change*.
- OD consultant's principal contact person was a *powerful* member of the organization.
- Top management *supported* and *accepted responsibility* for the OD program.
- Both inside and outside OD consultants had a *high degree of access* to client organization's resources (such as information and people).
- A high degree of consultant/client *collaboration* existed.
- Successful consultants used *multiple interventions*.

SOURCE: Adapted from W. Warner Burke, Lawrence P. Clark, and Cheryl Koopman, "Improve Your OD Project's Chances for Success," *Training and Development Journal* 38 (September 1984): 62–68.

uncovered.) Every year new OD techniques emerge—some have great potential, but others promise more than they can deliver.

In this section, we examine six popular OD interventions designed to increase effectiveness at three different organizational levels (see Figure 14.4). *Life and career planning* and *skill development* focus on the individual; *role analysis* and *team building* are aimed at the group; and *survey feedback* and *Grid® OD* target the entire organization. These particular interventions have been chosen for two reasons: they are representative of what is available among OD interventions, and they complement one another. Conceivably, all six interventions could be included in a single, comprehensive OD program.

Life and Career Planning   Many employees today have no clear plan for their life and their career; things just happen. (See Appendix A for more on career management.) But individuals can be challenged to take greater responsibility for the direction of their lives. Just as challenging objectives can stimulate organizational productivity, so life and career objectives can enhance personal effectiveness and satisfaction. Life and career planning, as an OD intervention, gives the individual an opportunity to sit down and do a thorough self-analysis. Part of this self-analysis is listing personal strengths and weaknesses. Discussion with a career counselor follows, with an eye toward taking greater advantage of one's strengths and eliminating or minimizing the weaknesses. If lack of formal education is a barrier, then a plan is formulated for going back to school. Perhaps a long-lost dream to master a second language, or play a musical instrument, or learn computer programming can be rekindled.

The overall objective of life and career planning is to get individuals to

Figure 14.4 OD Interventions for Different Levels

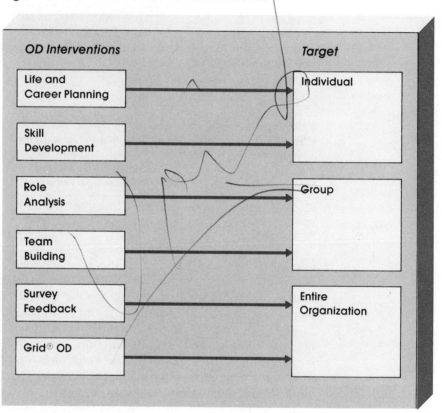

define their personal goals for growth and development and to plan ways to achieve them. Underlying all this is the assumption that organizational growth and development is a function of individual growth and development.

Skill Development   This second kind of intervention also focuses mainly on the individual. When carried out alone (rather than as part of a comprehensive OD program), it is generally considered part of management training and development. Unlike most OD interventions, skill development pertains to content rather than process. For example, when an OD diagnosis uncovers the inability of a group of engineers in the research and development department to write objectives and formulate plans, the deficiency can be corrected through appropriate training. Similarly, managers at all levels can be trained to polish their skills in areas such as delegation, problem solving, conflict resolution, and leading. Emphasis in skill development clearly is on learning "how to do it."

Role Analysis A role, once again, is a prescribed way of behaving. In an unhealthy organization, many people do not know what their roles are or should be, and if they do know, their roles typically are in direct conflict with those of their coworkers. In a healthy organization, behavioral scientists tell us, everyone knows his or her role, and those roles are meshed in a way that encourages cooperation and reduces dysfunctional conflict. For this reason many OD programs call for some sort of **role analysis,** which is the systematic clarification of interdependent modes of behavior.

The Diamond Shamrock Corporation, a large chemical and petroleum firm, had occasion to call on a team of OD consultants to deal with the rivalry, suspicion, and conflict that stemmed from a recent merger. Everyone seemed to be headed in a different direction. One part of the OD program was role negotiation. A neutral observer from *Fortune* magazine explained this technique:

> In the course of role negotiation, managers frankly discuss what they want from each other and explain why. Then they bargain. Nobody gets anything without promising something in return. For example, the head of a department might say to his plant manager, "If you give me production reports daily instead of weekly, I'll agree to review the salaries of your staff on a regular, annual basis." If they agree, they sign a contract and usually specify a penalty to be imposed if either party breaches the agreement.[24]

Although role negotiation alone did not turn Diamond Shamrock around overnight, it helped the firm's managers sort out their respective roles in a cooperative and constructive fashion.

Team Building As an OD process for developing work group maturity and effectiveness, **team building** has become very popular in recent years.[25] It takes many forms, from intensive laboratory training (T-group and sensitivity training) to structured exercises (such as the formulation of strategic plans by a team of executives). Team building is viewed by many as "pure" OD because it emphasizes interactive group processes, the "how" of effective group behavior. A noted OD specialist has ranked the purposes of team building as follows:

1. To set goals and/or priorities.
2. To analyze or allocate the way work is performed.
3. To examine the way a group is working, its processes (such as norms, decision making, communications).
4. To examine relationships among the people doing the work.[26]

It is important for the group itself to achieve these purposes by relying on its own leadership to solve real-life problems. The consultant-facilitator merely gets things headed in the right direction, quietly coaches as necessary along the way, periodically summarizes what has taken place, and selectively points out the impact of group processes such as communicating, problem solving, conflict resolution, and decision making.[27] Ideally, managers come away from a team-building session with a greater appreciation of how they as individuals can contribute effectively to group activity.

Survey Feedback   We discussed earlier the general nature of survey feedback. Data gathered through personal interviews and/or survey questionnaires is analyzed, tabulated into understandable form, and shared with those who first supplied the information. Once again, the main purpose of survey feedback is to let people know where they stand in relation to others on important organizational issues so that constructive problem solving can take place. Eight criteria for effective feedback, according to one authority, are as follows:

1. **Relevant.** Only information that is meaningful to the recipients should be fed back.
2. **Understandable.** To ensure clear communication, language and symbols should be familiar to the recipients.
3. **Descriptive.** Data should be in the form of real-life examples with which the recipients can identify.
4. **Verifiable.** The form of presentation should allow recipients to test the validity and accuracy of the data fed back to them.
5. **Limited.** Too much feedback causes an information overload, and so only significant highlights should be presented.
6. **Impactable.** Recipients should be given information on situations that they can directly control.
7. **Comparative.** Comparative data let recipients know where they stand in relation to others.
8. **Unfinalized.** Recipients must see feedback information as a beginning and a stimulus for action rather than as a final statement.[28]

Feedback that meets these criteria should be fed back to organizational subgroups, as the situation allows, until all employees have had a chance to see where and how they fit. At that point, various OD interventions such as life and career planning, skill development, team building, and role analysis can be introduced as needed.

In a sense, as Figure 14.5 indicates, feedback is only the beginning. It can have either positive or negative consequences. Careful follow-up ensures that positive results, such as personal growth, outweigh negative aspects, such as emotional conflict.

Figure 14.5 Possible Effects of Feedback

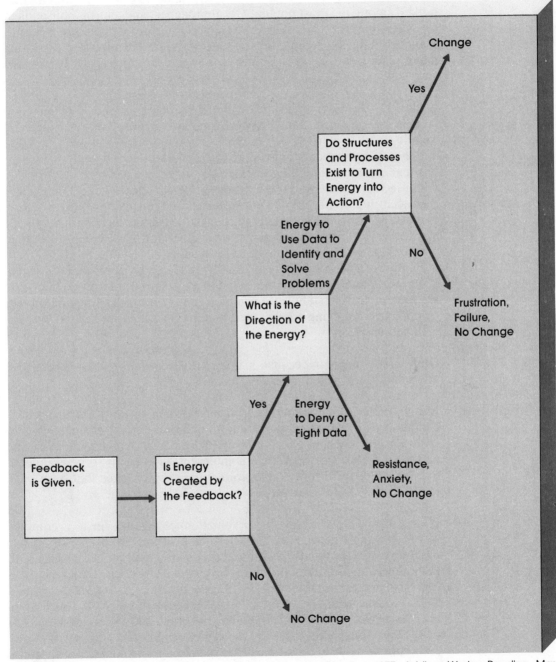

SOURCE: David A. Nadler, *Feedback and Organization Development*, © 1977, Addison Wesley, Reading, Massachusetts. P. 146, Fig. 8.1. Reprinted with permission.

Grid® OD The Grid® approach is an OD program based on Blake and Mouton's Managerial Grid.® Since the mid-1960s it has consistently ranked among the most popular OD approaches, and tens of thousands of managers have received Grid® training. Grid® proponents are quick to point out that it is a comprehensive kind of OD intervention because its six major phases unfold over a period of four, five, or more years. Briefly, the six phases are:

- **Phase 1.** During a week-long seminar, participants have their management style diagnosed and discuss how they can move toward an ideal 9,9 style (see Chapter 13).
- **Phase 2.** Participants learn how to be more effective contributors by attending a team-building workshop.
- **Phase 3.** Working from the skills developed in phases 1 and 2, managers concentrate on developing *intergroup* problem-solving ability.
- **Phase 4.** Management teams (starting at the top and filtering down) work together to devise an organizational blueprint. This blueprint details where the organization ought to be headed.
- **Phase 5.** This action phase usually takes years to complete as the organizational blueprint conceived in phase 4 is put into practice.
- **Phase 6.** In this stabilization period, newly acquired ways of solving problems, resolving conflict, and making decisions are refined for continued use.[29]

Grid® OD is popular because it is a package encompassing several OD interventions arranged in orderly fashion.

Follow-up Effective OD programs do not end abruptly when the intervention phase is completed but, rather, require a carefully monitored refreezing period to ensure lasting change. This follow-up phase has two objectives. First, the impact or effectiveness of the OD intervention(s) needs to be evaluated. Second, steps need to be taken to maintain the changes that have been introduced. We now look more closely at these two objectives.

Evaluating the OD Program Evaluation of changes in any complex social system is never easy.[30] Nevertheless, those in charge of an OD program owe it to themselves, the target group, and top management to determine whether or not they have really done any good. To date, evaluation has been the weakest link in OD practice.[31]

Two researchers who studied 160 assessments of OD programs carried out over a period of 15 years concluded that organization development "has produced relatively little systematic evidence about its efficacy."[32] If any evaluation is made at all, it usually takes the form of subjective appraisal

Figure 14.6 Measuring the Success of OD Intervention

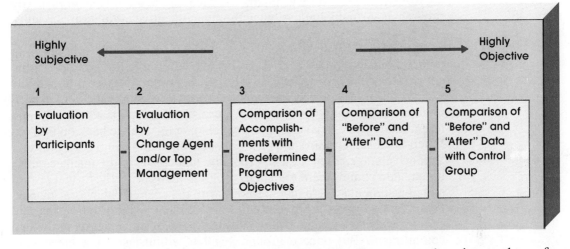

(see boxes 1 and 2 in Figure 14.6). Needless to say, there is a tendency for participants to tell change agents what they want to hear and for change agents to perceive only positive aspects. Subjective evaluations, although easy and inexpensive to obtain, offer change agents little hard evidence of the success or failure of their programs.[33]

At the very least, a moderately objective evaluation can be made by comparing the actual accomplishments of the program with the predetermined objectives. Not only should the objectives be defined at the beginning of the OD program, they also should be spelled out in clear operational terms. For example, the somewhat vague objective "to get engineering and production to work together" could be sharpened to read "to establish weekly problem-solving meetings between engineering and production." Of course, a more refined objective would then be required to help evaluate the quality of problem solving during these meetings. As has been noted several times in this book, measurable objectives are a cornerstone of effective management.

Ideally, users of OD techniques attempt to evaluate their programs in hard, factual terms. (Boxes 4 and 5 in Figure 14.6, for example, suggest comparing "before" data with "after" data and comparing both of these with sets of data from a control group.) Attitude questionnaire results as well as absentee, turnover, grievance, and financial data can be gathered before the OD program to serve as a base line against which parallel data can be compared later. The use of a control group strengthens the evaluation by helping rule out circumstantial changes that might otherwise be attributed to the OD intervention(s). From a strictly scientific perspective, objective evaluations should be a part of every OD program, even though they are difficult, time consuming, expensive, and hence largely unappealing from an administrative standpoint. Meaningful improvement in an OD program is virtually impossible without an objective evaluation of results.

Maintaining Positive Changes The purpose of any OD program is to induce organizational members to behave differently (for example, more cooperatively, more collaboratively, more productively). Although the various OD interventions are designed to persuade individuals to experiment with new modes of behavior, permanent behavior change is a different matter. The key is a supportive climate for change back on the job. When the formal reward and punishment system and peer group pressure support change, then it will probably take place. Top management's unqualified commitment to the OD program helps bring the formal reward and punishment system into harmony with the desired behavioral change. Peer group support is the difficult part. It takes skillful unfreezing and exciting, relevant, and innovative OD interventions to generate individual commitment. But once a ground swell of enthusiasm is achieved, no barrier to change is too great to be overcome.

Summary

Organization development (OD) is a systematic approach to planned organizational change. From early work in the areas of laboratory training and survey research and feedback, OD has evolved into a comprehensive diagnosis-prescription cycle. The principal objectives of OD are increased trust, better problem solving, more effective communication, improved cooperation, and greater willingness to change.

Inevitable resistance to change must be overcome if an OD program is to succeed. Because of early human relations research evidence, the traditional prescription for overcoming resistance to change has been participation. But unfortunately, participation is not always appropriate, because people resist change for many reasons. Modern managers facing resistance to change can select from several strategies, including education and communication, participation and involvement, facilitation and support, negotiation and agreement, manipulation and co-optation, and explicit and implicit coercion.

The typical OD program is a three-phase process that continuously recycles. During the unfreezing phase the diagnosis is completed. During the change phase selected interventions are carried out to improve personal, group, and organizational effectiveness. Finally, during the refreezing phase the OD program is evaluated, and steps are taken to maintain the changes that have been introduced. The process then repeats itself as part of an ongoing commitment to planned change.

After deciding whether or not the services of an outside consultant are required and pinpointing likely trouble spots, management's attention turns to unfreezing the situation, making a diagnosis, and interpreting the diagnostic data. A great deal of valuable diagnostic information can be obtained by balancing the strengths and weaknesses of various techniques. Among these techniques are record reviews, interviews, survey questionnaires, and direct observation. Careful interpretation of diagnostic data helps change agents select an appropriate intervention.

OD interventions can be designed to bring about systematic change at the individual, group, or organizational level. Life and career planning and skill development enhance individual potential. Role analysis and team building are popular OD techniques for improving the problem-solving ability of work groups. Survey feedback and Grid® OD have proved useful for improving overall organizational functioning. Because these interventions complement one another, they can be used in various combinations in accordance with the demands of the situation.

The third and final phase of OD, follow-up, is the evaluation of program effectiveness and the maintenance of newly introduced changes. Everything considered, the purpose of OD is to get people to behave in more productive and supportive ways with benefits accruing to both the individual and the organization.

Terms to Understand

Organization development (OD)	Unfreezing
Laboratory training	Refreezing
Survey research and feedback	Intervention
Diagnosis-prescription cycle	Role analysis
Genuine participation	Team building

Questions for Discussion

1. What are the roots of OD?
2. What is the practical value of a diagnosis-prescription cycle in OD?
3. Drawing on your own experience, can you describe the circumstances of an organization that needs OD?

4. In your view, which of the seven objectives of OD is the most important? Why?
5. What kinds of resistance to change have you observed recently? How could they have been overcome?
6. Why does an OD intervention without proper "unfreezing" have only limited chances of success?
7. Why are role analysis and team building useful OD interventions?
8. Which elements of effective feedback do you believe are the most important? Why?
9. Why is "refreezing" an important part of successful OD?
10. What can management do to keep evaluation from being the weak link in an OD program?

Back to the Opening Case

Now that you have read Chapter 14, you should be able to answer the following questions about the Ebasco case:

1. Using Figure 14.4 as a reference, how many different OD interventions can you identify in the Ebasco case? Cite specific instances.
2. What strategies for overcoming resistance to change are evident in this case?
3. What advantages do OD facilitators have over line managers in resolving conflict?
4. How could Ebasco do a more thorough job of evaluating its OD programs? What kind of opposition would there probably be to objective evaluation?

Closing Case 14.2

Change at Motorola: An Insider's View*

[*The following account is an "insider's" view of participation and change at Motorola, the electronics giant, contributed by Earl S. Gomersall, vice president and corporate director of operational support.*]

Several years ago, Motorola formalized its tradition of providing engi-

*Reprinted, by permission of the publisher, from *Management Review*, "AMA Forum," September 1983 © 1983 AMA Membership Publications Division, American Management Associations, New York. All rights reserved.

neers and support employees with the latest and best tools for their job *when the need was brought to management's attention.*

We concluded that, unless there was a Motorola "culture" to force employees to seek every possible new or improved "tool" to do his job, productivity would wane and quality suffer. And so the term "Tool Management Culture," or TMC as we call it, came into being. TMC has two sides: one is management's commitment to spend its available resources on new and advanced equipment chosen carefully to improve productivity and quality; the other side is the willingness of each employee to seek and/ or suggest new tools, learn new methods, and present their ideas and plans coherently to management.

These concepts are not quite as easy to accept as they seem. Getting employees to adopt new ideas, new techniques, new tools, automatic equipment, or new systems is often difficult. Retraining may be involved, and there are always these fears: not being able to make the grade, becoming too productive, denying a job to another person, automatic equipment breaking up the "gang"; being transferred to a place you don't like; losing your job and the jobs of those who work with you.

With tool management culture, however, changes will be planned and continuous. New assignments, if any, will be thought out in advance and dislocation will be minimal.

Our TMC program is intended to provide employees with a "can do" change-oriented attitude.

Here is what we try to get across: Retraining will give you a new skill and increase your value. The more productive you become, the fewer jobs go to competition and the more opportunities are created at Motorola. While automated equipment will disperse your current work group, you can still see one another at lunch, breaks, and after hours.

Every transfer is an opportunity to learn new skills, meet new people, and improve your overall background. Every new skill you possess increases your value to the company and helps insure job security. The last "worry"—that of losing your own job to "new tools" or "automation"—is the least worry of all for growth companies.

Participative Management

Our TMC program is closely linked with our Participative Management Program (PMP), which is designed to get the individual worker more involved, responsible, informed and, therefore, more productive.

Under PMP, a worker can suggest anything about how to improve a job, and management is required to give it serious consideration. Every worker is actively encouraged to define problems and suggest solutions.

Employees frequently meet in teams to tackle problems; some of the teams meet daily. Employee recommendations are posted on prominent bulletin boards and must be answered by management within 72 hours—

not just with words, but with changes in tools, procedures, or policies whenever this is humanly possible.

The results have been dramatic: Quality, output, and customer service levels are way up; costs are down; our jobs are more satisfying. Some employees are receiving incentive bonuses for their suggestions of as much as 30 percent of their base pay.

For Discussion

1. Is Motorola doing a good job of making sure that employee participation is *genuine*, and not token? Explain.
2. Acting as an OD consultant, would you tell Motorola's top managers to be on the lookout for any sources of resistance to change that were not specifically mentioned in this case? Which ones? Explain your reasoning.
3. Although Motorola does not refer to its TMC or PMP programs as organization development (OD), do those programs effectively accomplish what OD programs typically seek to accomplish? Explain. (*Tip:* Consider the seven objectives of OD that are discussed in this chapter.)
4. Do you see any "holes" or potential weak spots in Motorola's approach?

References

Opening Quotation: Laurence J. Peter, *Peter's Quotations* (New York: Bantam, 1977), p. 75

Opening Case: "How Ebasco Makes the Matrix Method Work," *Business Week* No. 2692: 126, 131. Reprinted from the June 15, 1981 issue of *Business Week* by special permission, © 1981 by McGraw-Hill, Inc., New York, NY 10020. All rights reserved.

Closing Case: Earl S. Gomersall, "How Motorola Manages to Introduce Change," *Management Review* 72 (September 1983): 29, 32.

1. "Corporate Culture," *Business Week* No. 2660 (October 27, 1980): 149–150.
2. "Bennis: Practice Versus Theory," *International Management* 30 (October 1975): 42.
3. Harold M. F. Rush, *Organization Development: A Reconnaissance,* Report 605 (New York: The Conference Board, 1973), p. 2. Also see Len Nadler, "Defining the Field—Is It HRD or OD, or ... ?" *Training and Development Journal* 34 (December 1980): 66–68.
4. C. Edward Kur, "OD: Perspectives, Processes and Prospects," *Training and*

Development Journal 35 (April 1981): 28–34. The April 1981 issue contains several good articles on OD.

5. For an informative practitioner's view of the OD field, see Mark Bieler, "Toward Value-Free OD," *Human Resource Management* 19 (Summer 1980): 28–31.

6. The following historical interpretation is based in part on that found in Wendell L. French and Cecil H. Bell, *Organization Development* (Englewood Cliffs, N.J.: Prentice-Hall, 1973), chap. 3.

7. For a more extensive discussion, see Robert J. House, "T-Group Training: Good or Bad?" *Business Horizons* 12 (December 1969): 69–77.

8. H. Kent Baker and Ronald H. Gorman, "Diagnosis: Key to O.D. Effectiveness," *Personnel Journal* 55 (October 1976): 506.

9. This list is based on material found in Wendell French, "Organization Development Objectives, Assumptions, and Strategies," *California Management Review* 12 (Winter 1969): 23–34; and Charles Kiefer and Peter Stroh, "A New Paradigm for Organization Development," *Training and Development Journal* 37 (April 1983): 26–35.

10. For a complete report of this study, see Lester Coch and John R. P. French, Jr., "Overcoming Resistance to Change," *Human Relations* 1 (1948): 512–532.

11. "Changing 45 Million Jobs," *Business Week* No. 2699 (August 3, 1981): 67.

12. For a good discussion of participation and resistance to change, see Paul R. Lawrence, "How to Deal with Resistance to Change," *Harvard Business Review* 47 (January-February 1969): 4–12, 166–176. This is a reprint of a classic 1954 article with an added retrospective commentary.

13. For a general typology of "change resisters," see George S. Odiorne, "The Change Resisters," *Personnel Administrator* 26 (January 1981): 57–62.

14. J. Alan Ofner, "Managing Change," *Personnel Administrator* 29 (September 1984): 20.

15. Jeremy Main, "Waking Up AT&T: There's Life After Culture Shock," *Fortune* 110 (December 24, 1984): 67.

16. "Why They're Jumping Ship at Intel," *Business Week* No. 2777 (February 14, 1983): 108.

17. This list is based in part on material found in John P. Kotter and Leonard A. Schlesinger, "Choosing Strategies for Change," *Harvard Business Review* 57 (March-April 1979): 106–114; and Joseph Stanislao and Bettie C. Stanislao, "Dealing with Resistance to Change," *Business Horizons* 26 (July-August 1983): 74–78.

18. For an interesting roundtable discussion about consultants, see Martin Lasden, "Managing Consultants: Get Your Money's Worth," *Computer Decisions* 16 (July 1984): 104–112, 197–198.

19. James Ross Warren, "Diagnosis of the Potential for Organizational Improvement," *Personnel Journal* 56 (June 1977): 302–304.

20. See Elizabeth S. Gorovitz, "Looking Beyond the OD Mystique," *Training and Development Journal* 37 (April 1983): 12–14.

21. One useful collection of ninety-two instruments, many with diagnostic potential, is J. William Pfeiffer, Richard Heslin, and John E. Jones, *Instrumentation in Human Relations Training,* 2nd ed. (1976). This book and other relevant OD materials are published by University Associates, Inc.; 8517 Production Ave., P.O. Box 26240; San Diego, CA 92126.

22. David Nadler, *Feedback and Organization Development: Using Data-Based Methods* (Reading, Mass.: Addison-Wesley, 1977), p. 143.

23. Good advice on handling the inevitable organizational politics surrounding OD can be found in Newton Margulies and Anthony P. Raia, "The Politics of Organization Development," *Training and Development Journal* 38 (August 1984): 20–23.

24. Arthur M. Louis, "They're Striking Some Strange Bargains at Diamond Shamrock," *Fortune* 93 (January 1976): 143.

25. For more information on team building, see William G. Dyer, *Team Building: Issues and Alternatives* (Reading, Mass.: Addison-Wesley, 1977); and H. Kent Baker, "The Hows and Whys of Team Building," *Personnel Journal* 58 (June 1979): 367–370.

26. Richard Beckhard, "Optimizing Team-Building Efforts," *Journal of Contemporary Business* 1 (Summer 1972): 24. The entire Summer 1972 issue is devoted to an informative overview of organization development.

27. For an interesting "insider's" view of team building, see Henry Marksbury, "Managerial Team Building: Casting Light on What Makes Us Tick," *Management Review* 68 (September 1979): 8–14; and Henry Marksbury, "A Manager's Trip Through the Hall of Mirrors of the Psyche," *Management Review* 68 (October 1979): 53–57.

28. This list is adapted from Nadler, *Feedback and Organization Development: Using Data-Based Methods,* pp. 147–148.

29. For more extensive discussion, see Robert R. Blake and Jane Srygley Mouton, "An Overview of the Grid®," *Training and Development Journal* 29 (May 1975): 29–37.

30. For an interesting and thought-provoking discussion of evaluation, see Henry W. Reicken, "Memorandum on Program Evaluation," in *Organization Development: Theory, Practice, and Research,* ed. Wendell L. French, Cecil H. Bell, Jr., and Robert A. Zawacki (Dallas: Business Publications, 1978), pp. 413–423.

31. An excellent review of OD evaluation problems may be found in David E. Terpstra, "The Organization Development Evaluation Process: Some Problems and Proposals," *Human Resource Management* 20 (Spring 1981): 24–29.

32. Jerry I. Porras and P. O. Berg, "The Impact of Organization Development," *Academy of Management Review* 3 (April 1978): 263.

33. For a concise but informative discussion of OD evaluation issues, see Bernard M. Bass, "Issues Involved in Relations Between Methodological Rigor and Reported Outcomes in Evaluations of Organizational Development," *Journal of Applied Psychology* 68 (February 1983): 197–199.

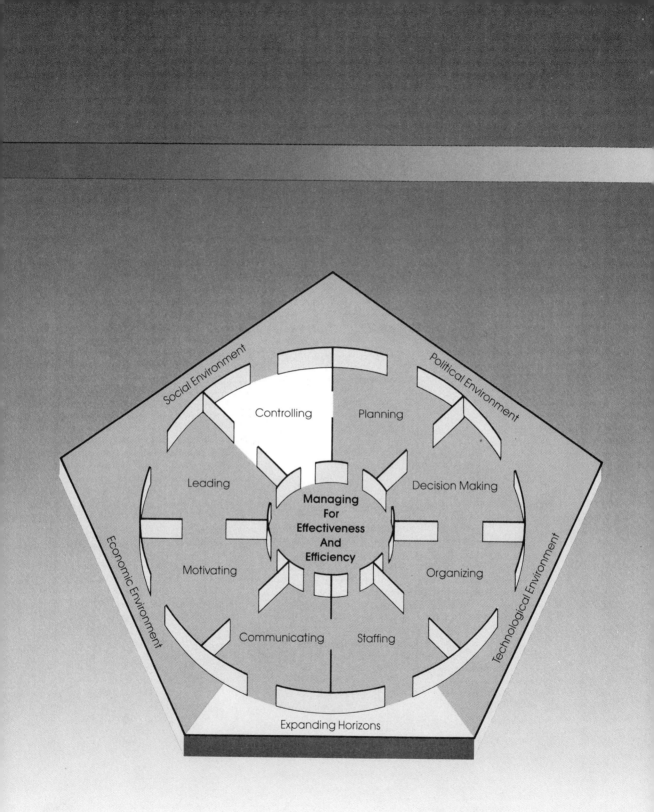

PART FIVE

Controlling

Part Five examines the vital role that the control function plays in good management. Control involves monitoring organizational performance so that plans are carried out as intended and corrective action is taken when necessary. Within the context of organizational effectiveness, Chapter 15 introduces basic control concepts and examines the control of financial performance and human resource problems. In Chapter 16, information is discussed as a vital resource and the lifeblood of organizations. Special attention is devoted to harnessing the power of personal computers. Operations management, which involves the systematic management of production processes, is examined in Chapter 17. Successful Japanese operations-management philosophies, including just-in-time production and total quality control, are explored.

Chapter 15

The Control Function

When the objectives of [an organization] are reasonably coherent and consistent, it is feasible to develop a control system that will reinforce the objectives by measuring the level of accomplishment and its cost.
  William H. Sihler

Chapter Objectives

When you finish studying this chapter, you should be able to

- Explain the time dimension of organizational effectiveness.
- Distinguish between feedforward and feedback control.
- Identify and briefly describe two ways that a control system can become misguided.
- Explain what budget variances are and when management should take steps to correct them.
- Discuss how financial ratios and cash management can enhance financial control.
- Explain the role of "constructive coercion" in dealing with employee alcohol/drug abuse.

Opening Case 15.1

A Firm Hand Gets Results at Allied Corporation

In the mid-1970s, Allied Chemical Corporation lumbered along with no real strategic direction. Then, in 1979, with the aim of redeploying assets more productively, emphasizing the bottom line more, and growing through wise acquisitions, Allied's board hired Edward L. Hennessy, Jr., as chief executive. Hennessy, characterized as an impatient hard-driver, did not lose any time in living up to the board's expectations. By dropping the word *Chemical* from the firm's name, Hennessy made it clear to insiders and outsiders alike that he intended to broaden Allied's strategic base. Toward that end, he acquired over two dozen companies in a diverse range of businesses during his first four years at the helm. Allied's most notable acquisition was the purchase in 1982 of Bendix Corp., an auto-motive parts and aerospace manufacturer, for $1.8 billion. As might be expected, Hennessy's "bigger is better" philosophy has opened him to criticism that he is simply seeking growth for its own sake. However, Allied's impressive results during Hennessy's early years have served to silence his critics. Comparing the first nine months of 1981 with the same period for 1978, revenues more than doubled to a figure of $4.7 billion, debt dropped from 40 percent of equity to 25 percent, and earnings took a threefold jump to $289 million.

By early 1985, thanks in part to the Bendix acquisition, Allied's sales revenues had mushroomed to $12 billion a year. Perhaps more impor-tantly, Hennessy has ensured Allied's survival by transforming the stodgy chemical supplier into an aggressive high-tech player in diverse markets including aerospace and health care.

Centralized Control with Decentralized Decision Making

Guided by a commitment to improve return on assets, Hennessy has locked all of his managers into measurable short- and long-term objec-tives. This management-by-objectives approach allows Hennessy to strike a workable balance between maintaining strategic control over operations while allowing subordinate managers to assume more responsibility. For example, the head of the oil-drilling operation formerly had to abide by a $1 million spending ceiling and live with bureaucratic delays while several layers of corporate staff passed judgment on expen-ditures above that limit. Under Hennessy's system, that same manager was given a $6 million discretionary spending limit. In return for this kind of added decision-making responsibility, Hennessy insists that objectives be met with no excuses.

Admitting that he is a "return-on-assets nut" because of his back-ground in accounting and finance, Hennessy recently told an interviewer how he and his managers work together:

> "We have budgets, against which we report monthly. When we have devia-tions, we ask why. And we have forecasts halfway through the month. Are they going to achieve those budgets? If not, why? For the month. Also rolling out [looking farther into the future]. We have quarterly reviews in which we discuss markets, products, technology, human resource problems, and then we also get together once a month here, and this is where we exchange what the problems are. We try to operate as a team, not as a one-man band."[1]

Pay for Performance

Aside from raising discretionary spending limits, Hennessy backed up his tough results-oriented program with changes in the corporate structure and reward system. Hennessy's predecessor was isolated from day-to-day operations, preferring to work through multiple layers of specialized corporate staff. By cutting out 1300 corporate-level staff jobs in a series of swift and deep cuts, Hennessy not only reduced annual overhead by $30 million but also effectively forced decision-making responsibility back down upon line managers. In regard to rewards, Hennessy delivered on his promise that bonuses would be tied to results. When his operating chiefs responded to his order in 1980 to trim inventories and weed out aged receivables, thus freeing up $150 million in working capital, Hennessy handed out $1.5 million in bonuses.

Keep It Simple, Stupid

A trademark of Hennessy's style is his fondness for the KISS principle, standing for "keep it simple, stupid." This, in addition to his strict emphasis on bottom-line results, has caused some observers to claim that such a climate is not conducive to the risk taking and freedom to fail that Hennessy supposedly seeks. But although some chafe under Hennessy's tough style, most of Allied's executives reportedly welcome the combination of added responsibility and precise profitability guidelines. In fact, in spite of Hennessy's reliance on measurable objectives and strict performance standards, his managers perceive that their autonomy has actually increased. Hennessy proudly points out that turnover among Allied's managers has dropped since he took charge.

(Discussion questions linking this case with the material you are about to read can be found at the end of this chapter.)

The separation of planning and control is more a conceptual convenience than a reflection of actual managerial practice. But from the standpoint of studying management, a working knowledge of all the other management functions helps one better appreciate the nature and significance of the control function. Planning and control are cornerstones of the management process; managers rely on planning to plot their future courses of action. Unfortunately, even the most carefully prepared plan is no guarantee of success, since unexpected events can and do cause plans to go astray. According to the so-called Murphy's Law, "If anything can go wrong, it will!" True, Murphy's Law is overly pessimistic, but it drives home the point that things don't always turn out as planned.

Steps need to be taken to keep things on course. This is where the control function enters the picture, as at Allied Corporation. Control complements planning by introducing corrective action as events unfold.

Because the principal rationale for control is to increase organizational effectiveness, we need to bring the latter into sharper focus.

Organizational Effectiveness

Management, once again, challenges managers to be both effective and efficient. Effectiveness pertains to whether or not organizational objectives are accomplished. Efficiency, on the other hand, is the relationship between inputs and outputs. Only monopolies can get away with being effective but not efficient. Moreover, in an era of diminishing resources and increasing concern about civil rights, society is reluctant to label any organization "effective" that wastes scarce resources or tramples on civil rights. And so management's definition of organizational effectiveness needs to be refined.

No Ultimate Criterion

According to one management scholar, "there is no ultimate criterion of effectiveness. Complex organizations pursue multiple goals. Real effectiveness can only be measured relative to a particular set of derived or prescribed goals."[2] More and more, these goals are being prescribed by society in the form of vocalized expectations, regulations, and laws. In the private sector, profitability is no longer the sole criterion of effectiveness. Major oil companies were highly profitable during the early 1980s, for example; yet many members of society weren't particularly happy about it. Despite the Reagan administration's battle against unnecessary regulation, today's managers remain caught up in an enormous web of laws and regulations covering employment practices, working conditions, job safety, pensions, product safety, pollution, and competitive practices. To be truly effective, today's productive organizations need to strike a generally acceptable balance between organizational and societal goals. Direct conflicts, such as higher wages for employees and lower prices for customers, are inevitable. Therefore, the process of determining the proper weighting of organizational effectiveness criteria is an endless one requiring frequent review and updating.[3]

A Time Dimension

In order to "flesh out" a workable definition of organizational effectiveness, we shall introduce a time dimension. As indicated in Figure 15.1, the organization needs to be effective in the near future, the intermediate future, and the distant future. Consequently, **organizational effectiveness** can be defined as meeting organizational objectives and prevailing societal expectations in the near future, adapting and developing in the intermediate future, and surviving in the distant future.

Most people think only of the near future. It is in the near future that the organization has to produce goods or render services, use resources efficiently, and satisfy both insiders and outsiders with its functioning. But this is just the beginning, not the end. If the organization fails to adapt to new environmental demands and does not mature and learn in the intermediate future (two to four years), its effectiveness will diminish. If it does

Figure 15.1   The Time Dimension of Organizational Effectiveness

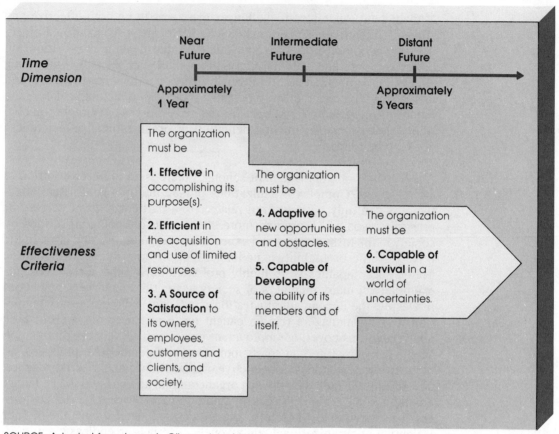

SOURCE: Adapted from James L. Gibson, John M. Ivancevich, and James H. Donnelly, Jr., *Organizations: Behavior, Structure, Processes,* 4th ed. (Plano, TX: Business Publications, Inc., 1982), p. 31.

adapt and develop, it will probably grow. Above all, in a long-run perspective, the truly effective organization survives. Without survival there can be no subsequent near or intermediate futures. An organization must be effective through all these time dimensions if it is to survive, and this can happen only when carefully conceived plans are followed up by judicious control.

Dimensions of Control

The mere mention of the word *control* brings to mind actions involving the checking, testing, regulation, verification, or adjustment of something. As a management function, **control** is the process of taking the necessary corrective action to ensure that organizational objectives are accomplished as effectively and efficiently as possible. Objectives are yardsticks against which actual performance can be measured. If actual performance is consistent with the appropriate objective, then things will proceed as planned. If not, then changes need to be made. Just as a driver controls a car by detecting and steering around potential hazards, successful managers detect deviations from desirable standards and make appropriate adjustments. Those adjustments can range from ordering more raw materials to overhauling a production line; from discarding an unnecessary procedure to hiring additional personnel; from counseling an alcoholic employee to firing a defrauder. Although the possible adjustments exercised as part of the control function are countless, the purpose of the control function is always the same: *get the job done despite environmental, organizational, and behavioral obstacles and uncertainties* (see Table 15.1).

Developing a Positive Orientation Toward Control

Control is an idea that provokes more than its fair share of controversy. Purposeful, premeditated control tends to have a negative connotation in relation to human behavior. Often, and justifiably so, it is viewed as manipulative or repressive. On the other hand, control of machines is viewed favorably (for example, learning how to type or play a musical instrument). Thus managers who are responsible for controlling human-machine systems have a dilemma on their hands. How can management control organizational contributors without being tagged as manipulative or repressive? A leading expert on the subject has suggested that control be viewed in a positive and constructive manner. Four assumptions underlie this positive orientation:

1. **Control is a normal, pervasive, and positive force.** Evaluation of results accomplished and feedback of this information to those who can influence future results is a natural phenomenon. ...

   The news may be good or bad, and the "corrective action" may be encouragement or restraint. Assuming a purpose or goal, each person and manager needs to know what progress he is making. There is nothing sinister nor dictatorial about such controlling. Rather, it is a normal aid to achieving results.

2. **Managerial control is effective only when it guides someone's behavior.** Behavior, not measurements and reports, is the essence of control. We often become so involved with the mechanics of control that we lose sight of its purpose. Unless one or more persons act differently than they otherwise would, the control reports have no impact. Consequently, when we think about designing and implementing control, we must always ask ourselves, "Who is going to behave differently, and what will be the nature of the response?"

3. **Successful control is future-oriented and dynamic.** Long before the Apollo spacecraft reached the moon, control adjustments had been

Table 15.1 Keeping Things Under Control at Marriott

Marriott Corporation, the nation's largest hotel chain with over 140 hotels in 94 cities worldwide, was selected by *Dun's Business Month* as one of the five best-managed companies of 1984. J. Willard (Bill) Marriott, the firm's president and chief executive, keeps things under control in the following manner:

> ... detail is the hallmark of Marriott's management style. "This is a penny business," Bill Marriott maintains. "We hold no patents; all we have is our name. So we watch our expenses."
>
> Marriott watches its pennies by strict control of every phase of the business, from the prescribed 66 steps that chambermaids must follow in making up a room to the 6,000 recipes that dictate food portions and preparation right down to the placement of a sprig of parsley. Bill Marriott and the four executive vice presidents who help him oversee the business spend about half the year on the road visiting company facilities and even take their turns learning to cook in a company kitchen.
>
> Marriott keeps constant tabs on operations through daily reports and frequent meetings with company managers. He also keeps a private loose-leaf notebook in which he lists "all the things I have asked people to do." In his view, "To make the right decisions, you have to have a thorough understanding of your business, products, and people. Lacking that, you make bad decisions." Whatever the secret, Marriott's hotel occupancy rate is consistently 10% above the industry average and runs as high as 80%.

SOURCE: "Marriott: The Fearless Host," *Dun's Business Month* 124 (December 1984), pp. 36–37. Extract reprinted with the permission of *Dun's Business Month*, December 1984, Copyright © 1984, Dun & Bradstreet Publications Corporation.

made. Similarly, we don't wait until next year's sales are recorded to make adjustments in packaging or pricing that are necessary to achieve the goal; instead, we use early measurements to predict where our present course is leading, and modify inputs to keep us on target. ...

4. **Control relates to all sorts of human endeavors.** The need for evaluation and feedback is just as pressing in charitable organizations as in profit-seeking corporations. Each is concerned with attaining its goals and each has limited resources.[4]*

Positive control of people at work is possible if management makes appropriate use of the motivation and influence techniques discussed in Chapters 11 and 13.

Types of Control

Every open system processes inputs from the surrounding environment to produce a unique set of outputs. Natural open systems such as the human body are kept in life-sustaining balance through automatic feedback mech-

*Adapted from William H. Newman, *Constructive Control: Design and Use of Control Systems,* © 1975, pp. 3–5, by permission of Prentice-Hall, Inc., Englewood Cliffs, N.J.

Figure 15.2 Feedforward and Feedback Control

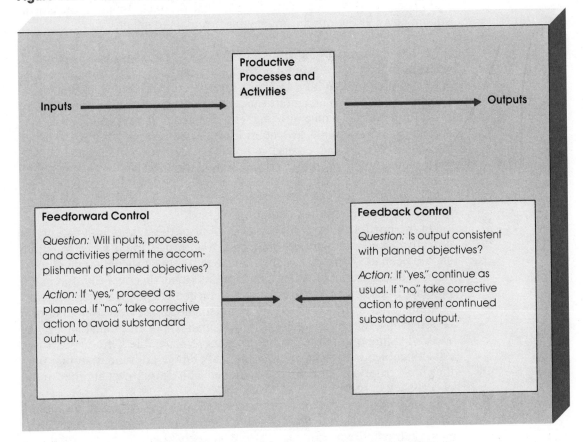

anisms. Artificial open systems such as organizations, in contrast, do not have automatic controls. They require constant monitoring and adjustment to control for deviations from the standard. Figure 15.2 illustrates the control function. Notice that there are two types of control, feedforward control and feedback control.

Feedforward Control   According to two early proponents of feedforward control, "the only way [managers] can exercise control effectively is to see the problems coming in time to do something about them."[5] **Feedforward control** is the active anticipation of problems and their timely solution, rather than after-the-fact reaction. For example, if the purchasing manager in a home appliance–manufacturing company alerts the production and marketing managers to a delay in the receipt of an important subcomponent, corrective steps can be taken to avoid costly delays. The production manager can reschedule the workload, and the marketing manager can negotiate a new delivery date for the final product. Imagine the downstream havoc if the purchasing manager remained silent.

Feedback Control **Feedback control** is gathering information about a completed activity, evaluating that information, and taking steps to improve similar activities in the future. Feedback control is beneficial because it permits managers to use information on past performance to bring future performance into line with planned objectives and acceptable standards. For example, by monitoring the complaints from discharged patients about billing errors, a hospital's comptroller learns that the performance of its billing clerks requires attention. Critics of feedback control complain that it is like closing the gate after the horse is gone. Because corrective action is taken after the fact, costs tend to pile up quickly, and problems and deviations persist.

On the positive side, feedback control tests the quality and validity of objectives and standards. Objectives that prove impossible to attain should be made more reasonable. Those that prove too lenient need to be bolstered. For example, a bank's loan officer may discover that too much potentially profitable business is being turned away because the credit-granting criteria are too strict. By exercising feedback control in the form of loosening the credit standards that loan applicants must meet, the bank's lending operation can be made more profitable. Of course, if this adjustment leads to a default rate that eats up the additional profits, then the credit criteria will have to be tightened a bit through yet another round of feedback control.

In summary, it is necessary to exercise both types of control in today's complex organizations. Feedforward control helps managers avoid mistakes in the first place; feedback control keeps them from repeating past mistakes. A workable balance between feedforward and feedback control is desirable.

Components of Organizational Control Systems

The owner-manager of a small business such as a dry cleaning establishment can keep things under control by personally overseeing operations and making necessary adjustments. An electrician can be called in to fix a broken pressing machine, poor workmanship can be improved through coaching, a customer's complaint can be handled, or a shortage of change in the cash register can be remedied. A small organization directed by a single, highly motivated individual with expert knowledge of all aspects of the operation represents the ideal control situation. Unfortunately, the sheer size and complexity of most productive organizations have made firsthand control by a single person obsolete. Consequently, multilevel, multidimensional organizational control systems have evolved.

A recent study of nine large companies in different industries sheds some needed light on the mechanics of complex organizational control systems.[6] After interviewing dozens of key managers, the researchers identified six distinct control subsystems:

1. **Strategic plans.** Qualitative analyses of the company's position within the industry.
2. **Long-range plans.** Typically five-year financial projections.
3. **Annual operating budgets.** Annual estimates of profit, expenses, and financial indicators.
4. **Statistical reports.** Quarterly, monthly, or weekly nonfinancial statistical summaries of key indicators such as orders received and personnel surpluses/shortages.
5. **Performance appraisals.** Formal evaluation of all employees through the use of management by objectives (MBO) or rating scales.
6. **Policies and procedures.** Organizational and departmental standard operating procedures referred to on an as-needed basis.

According to the researchers, use of the first two control subsystems was restricted to top management. The remaining four were used throughout the managerial ranks.

Complex organizational control systems such as those explored in the foregoing research study help keep things on the right track because they embrace three basic components. These three basic components of all organizational control systems are objectives, standards, and an evaluation-reward system.[7]

Objectives   In Chapter 4, we defined an objective as a target signifying what should be accomplished and when. Objectives are an indispensable part of a control system because they provide measurable reference points for corrective action. For example, consider the actions of Bennett A. Brown shortly after taking over the reins of the ailing Citizens & Southern National Bank in Georgia:

> In July 1978, Brown promoted Willard A. Alexander, a 30-year C&S veteran, to general vice president and gave him clear-cut marching orders: Unload bad loans as quickly as possible, and reduce nonperforming assets by 20% annually. ... He [Alexander] formed a 30-member staff that for two years concentrated solely on combing out bad loans. The result was that nonperforming assets were slashed by 25% in 1978, 38% in 1979, and 31% last year [1980]—vastly exceeding Brown's hopes.[8]

By using Brown's objective as a reference point, Alexander's efforts to bring the bank's loan portfolio under control had specific purpose and direction.

Standards   Whereas objectives serve as measurable targets, standards serve as the guideposts on the way to reaching those targets. Standards provide feedforward control by warning people when they are off the track. Golfers use par as a standard for gauging the quality of their game. When a golfer whose objective is to shoot par exceeds par on a hole, he or she is warned to improve on later holes to achieve the objective. Universities exercise a degree of feedforward control over student performance by establishing and following admission standards for grades and test scores. Businesses rely on many different kinds of standards, including purchasing standards, engineering standards, time standards, safety standards, accounting standards, and quality standards.

An Evaluation-Reward System Considering that not all employees perform equally, some sort of performance evaluation is required to find out who has done what. (Recall our discussion of performance appraisal in Chapter 9.) Subsequently, extrinsic rewards can be distributed in an equitable manner. A carefully conceived and clearly communicated evaluation-reward scheme can shape favorable effort-reward expectancies, hence motivating better performance.

When integrated systematically, objectives, standards, and an equitable evaluation-reward system provide management with a framework for steering contributors in the right direction.

Strategic Control In recent years, largely in response to Japan's striking success in world markets, managers in the United States and Western Europe have been criticized for being shortsighted.[9] A sign of improvement in this area has been the growth of strategic management. However, as one study of 52 companies in Great Britain, France, and West Germany revealed, an emphasis on short-term control persists in spite of the trend toward longer-range strategic planning. Control was found to be almost exclusively focused on operations and short-term financial performance. After warning that such a lopsided planning/control cycle could prevent long-term strategic success, the researcher explained how one British electronics company built a control program around a critical strategic variable:

> Whereas usual performance (i.e., financial results) is only reported every quarter, top management closely monitors—daily if needed—customer satisfaction, explicitly defined to be its major strategic strength: no equipment sold to a customer shall be down for more than 12 hours. To check this, every morning and afternoon the chief executive is warned when equipment has been down for more than 12 hours and corrective action is taken at the highest level to replace or send a part or equipment to the customer. A systematic procedure has been set up whereby a service man unable to repair equipment within 2 hours notifies his superior, who in turn notifies his superior after 2 more hours (and so on up to the chief executive) in order to allow close control over what has been defined as a distinctive competence by the company: no down time whatever the costs.[10]

In a similar fashion, strategic control could focus on other competitive advantages such as research and development, quality, or product delivery time. Managers who fail to complement their strategic planning with strategic control, as recommended in Chapter 5, will find themselves winning some battles but losing the war.

Diagnosing Control Problems

Control problems have a way of quietly snowballing into overwhelming proportions. In sheer magnitude, the U.S. Defense Department probably holds the record for losing control of an operation. It was discovered in 1978 that the Pentagon had

> ... lost track of up to $30 billion in undelivered foreign orders for weapons, equipment, and U.S. support services. What they do not know, because their books are so fouled up, is whether the unaccounted-for money is the result of a series of ghastly accounting errors, whether they have spent a lot of it for something else, or whether they have been undercharging foreign customers— or a combination of all three.[11]

There are constructive steps that foresighted managers can take to keep from getting entangled in this type of colossal mess. Specifically, an internal audit can diagnose weak spots and problems in the organizational control system.

Internal Audits

There are two general types of auditing, external and internal. External auditing, generally performed by certified public accountants (CPAs), is the verification of an organization's financial records and reports. In the United States, the protection of stockholders' interests is the primary rationale for objective external audits. Of course, the Internal Revenue Service (IRS) and the Securities and Exchange Commission (SEC) also benefit from external auditors' watchdog function. That is, external auditors help keep organizations honest by double checking to see if reported financial results are derived through generally accepted accounting principles and are based on material fact, not fiction.

Internal auditing differs from external auditing in a number of ways. First, and most obviously, it is performed by an organization's staff rather than by outsiders. Second, internal auditing is intended to serve the interests of the organization as a whole. Also, as the following definition illustrates, internal auditing tends to be more encompassing than the external variety: "**Internal auditing** is the independent appraisal of the various operations and systems of control within an organization to determine whether acceptable policies and procedures are followed, established standards are met, resources are used efficiently and economically, planned missions are accomplished effectively, and the organization's objectives are being achieved."[12]

The product of internal auditing is called a *process audit* by some and a *management audit* by others.[13] To strengthen the objectivity of internal auditing, experts recommend that internal auditors report directly to the top person in the organization. In OD terms, some "unfreezing" needs to be done to neutralize the common complaint that internal auditing is a top management ploy for snooping and meddling.

Symptoms of Inadequate Control

When comprehensive internal auditing is not available, a general check list of symptoms of inadequate control can be a useful diagnostic tool. Recognizing that every situation has some unusual problems, common symptoms include:

- An unexplained decline in revenues or profits.
- A degradation of service (customer complaints).
- Employee dissatisfaction (complaints, grievances, turnover).
- Working capital shortages caused by bloated inventories and/or delinquent accounts receivable.
- Idle facilities and/or personnel.
- Disorganized operations (work flow bottlenecks, excessive paperwork).
- Excessive costs.
- Evidence of waste and inefficiency (scrap, rework).[14]

Problems in one or more of these areas may signal that things are getting out of control. For example, in 1978 the then chairman of Greyhound Corporation, Gerald H. Trautman, launched a major overhaul of the firm's bus line on the basis of the following symptoms:

> He came across an internal memo, written by an angry employee who had just completed an unpleasant cross-country bus trip; it set forth a host of customer-service problems, including filthy conditions and poor security at terminals. After also reading some of the increasingly numerous letters of complaint from passengers and maintenance reports that showed a sharp increase in breakdowns, Trautman knew he had real trouble on his hands.[15]

Because of Trautman's timely diagnosis and response, passenger revenues at Greyhound improved significantly the following year.

Signs of Misguided Control Systems

Control systems breed their own special problems, two of which are goal displacement and "measurementship."[16] Goal displacement occurs when the means become more important than the ends. For example, bureaucratic paperwork may take precedence over health care when an emergency room nurse shows greater concern for gathering insignificant information than for relieving pain and suffering. **Measurementship,** on the other hand, is political maneuvering motivated by a desire to "look good" and "play the numbers game," even if it means manipulating reports and control data. Both of these problems, which erode rather than enhance control, are usually caused by managers who emphasize the secondary aspects of performance and foster a do-or-die atmosphere in which employees are afraid to fail. The wrong kind of control or too much control can turn out to be as bad as no control.

Financial Control

The ultimate survival of organizations in both the public and private sectors is dictated largely by how proficiently funds are acquired and managed. Dollars (or other units of currency) are handy measuring sticks for assessing organizational performance. Are the necessary resources available? Have resources been properly allocated? Are resources being wasted? How can available resources be more efficiently used? These are just a few of the many important questions answered by means of financial control. In this section, we consider three significant aspects of financial control: (1) budget variance, (2) financial ratios, and (3) cash management.

Budget Variance as a Control Tool

A **budget** is a formally prepared financial projection. Because all types of budgets are projections or plans of future events, they provide managers with standards for control. Control occurs when actual figures are compared with budgeted figures (see the information stage of the operating budget process illustrated in Figure 15.3). Some refer to this process as "management by exception." The difference between the actual figures and the budgeted ones is called **budget variance.** "Variances should be evaluated, however, only when the benefits of doing so outweigh the costs to investigate and correct."[17]

A look at the operating budget in Table 15.2 shows that things do not always work out favorably. Whether or not variances are favorable, a great deal can be learned by studying them. For instance, the $11,000 unfavorable variance in direct labor expense in Table 15.2 should prompt management to search for the cause. Perhaps too much was spent on costly overtime, thus suggesting a staffing deficiency. Favorable variances should trigger control action in the form of adjusting future budget figures. Following up on both favorable and unfavorable budget variances is a practical expression of feedback control.

Financial management experts recommend that managers consider four factors when deciding whether or not to take action on a favorable or unfavorable budget variance. Corrective action in the form of feedback

Figure 15.3   The Operating Budget Process

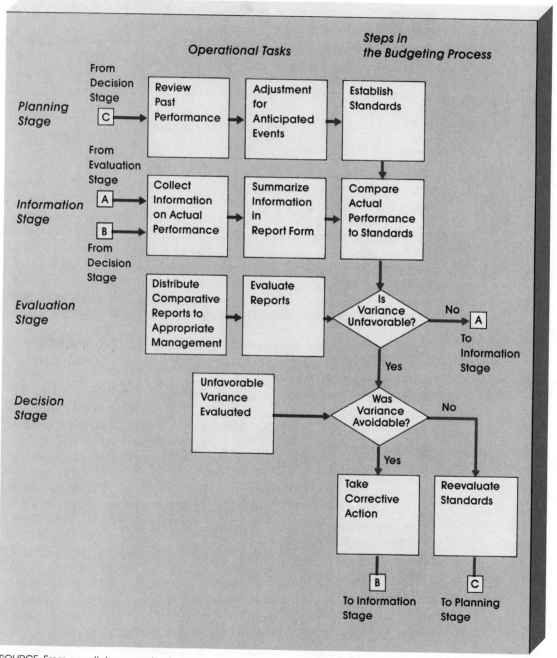

SOURCE: From an article appearing in *Cost and Management* by Ralph L. Benke, Jr. and Timothy O'Keefe, July/August 1980 issue, by permission of The Society of Management Accountants of Canada.

Table 15.2 Budget Variances Tell an Important Story

| | | | Variance | |
	Budget	**Actual**	**Favorable**	**Unfavorable**
XYZ Company Operating budget for the year _____				
Revenue	$325,000	$329,350	$4,350	
Expenses				
Direct labor	195,000	206,000		$11,000
Materials	70,000	67,200	2,800	
Overhead	35,000	33,700	1,300	
	300,000	306,900		
Pretax profit	$ 25,000	$ 22,450		$ 2,550

control is needed when a budget variance is *costly, consistent, controllable,* and *vital* to the success of the organization or unit.[18]

Making Budgets Flexible One shortcoming of the standard type of budget illustrated in Table 15.2 is that it limits managers to feedback control. It permits managers to assess financial performance only *after* the fact. A **flexible budget** is a technique using standardized costs that allows managers to exercise feedforward control over the expenditure of funds.

In a flexible budget, standard costs are calculated from past records or on the basis of informed judgment. These standard costs are tied to revenue. For example, assume that the standard cost for direct labor is $1 for every $2 of revenue, or a ratio of 1 to 2. Suppose that after three months $95,000 has been spent for direct labor while $142,500 has been received in revenue. Because the ratio of direct labor cost to revenue is now 1.33 to 2, management is warned that something must be done to limit spending on direct labor during the next nine months. Flexible budgets based on standard costs allow managers to keep a running tab on financial performance so that they can take corrective action immediately instead of waiting until the entire budget period has elapsed.[19]

Adjusting for Inflation During an inflationary period, comparing actual figures with budgeted ones can be tantamount to comparing oranges and apples. Students facing the task of trying to make this spring's expenses fit last summer's budget are well aware of this problem. One expert on financial control has gone so far as to say that recurrent inflation has rendered obsolete all traditional budgetary and cost accounting methods.[20] The recommended solution is **indexed standard costing,** in which standard costs are adjusted for inflation monthly rather than yearly. Appropriate inflation indexes dictate the magnitude of the monthly adjustments.

This approach has enabled Brazilian firms to maintain meaningful budgetary control despite annual inflation rates that have soared above 200 percent. To date, U.S. companies have largely ignored the need to modify their budgeting and cost-accounting techniques to cope with the impact of inflation.

Financial Ratios

Medical doctors would not think of recommending further tests or offering a diagnosis without first monitoring the patient's vital signs. By comparing the patient's pulse, temperature, and blood pressure with accepted standards, the doctor is in a much better position to take constructive corrective action. Similarly, managers require a convenient way to check the vital signs of their organizations. **Financial ratios,** measures of an organization's financial status that can be compared with industry standards, are a convenient way of gauging an organization's financial health. In fact, after reviewing six empirical studies of the relationship between financial ratios and corporate bankruptcies, one researcher concluded "that financial ratios have predictive power as to whether a business will survive or not."[21] Financial ratios are generally categorized into four main types:

1. **Liquidity ratios,** which measure the firm's ability to meet its maturing short-term obligations.
2. **Leverage ratios,** which measure the extent to which the firm has been financed by debt.
3. **Activity ratios,** which measure how effectively the firm is using its resources.
4. **Profitability ratios,** which measure management's overall effectiveness as shown by the returns generated on sales and investment.[22]

TURNOVER RATE →

By calculating the various ratios in each area, as shown in Table 15.3, and then comparing them with industry standards compiled and published by firms such as Dun & Bradstreet, managers can make the financial diagnosis they need in order to exercise feedforward and feedback financial control.

As with other types of control, financial ratios are not restricted to use by profit-making businesses. They may be used quite effectively to assess the financial health of not-for-profit organizations as well.[23]

Cash Management

Periodic inflation and stubbornly high interest rates in recent years have underscored the importance of managing cash as an especially valuable resource. A few percentage points in interest rates can cause a firm to gain or lose significant sums of money in just a few days when hundreds of thousands or even millions of dollars are involved.

For example, a large real estate developer recently discovered that an office in one part of the country was borrowing funds at the same time that another office

Table 15.3 Financial Ratios

Ratio	Formula for Calculation	Calculation	Industry Average	Evaluation
Liquidity				
Current	$\dfrac{\text{Current assets}}{\text{Current liabilities}}$	$\dfrac{\$700,000}{\$300,000} = 2.3$ times	2.5 times	Satisfactory
Quick ratio or acid test	$\dfrac{\text{Current assets} - \text{inventory}}{\text{Current liabilities}}$	$\dfrac{\$400,000}{\$300,000} = 1.3$ times	1 time	Good
Leverage				
Debt to total assets	$\dfrac{\text{Total debt}}{\text{Total assets}}$	$\dfrac{\$1,000,000}{\$2,000,000} = 50$ percent	33 percent	Poor
Times interest earned	$\dfrac{\text{EBIT}}{\text{Interest charges}}$	$\dfrac{\$270,000}{\$70,000} = 3.9$ times	8 times	Poor
Fixed charge coverage	$\dfrac{\text{EBIT plus other fixed charges}}{\text{Fixed charges}}$	$\dfrac{\$298,000}{\$98,000} = 3.04$ times	5.5 times	Poor
Cash flow coverage	$\dfrac{\text{Cash inflows}}{\text{Fixed charges} + (\text{other cash outflows})/(1-T)}$	$\dfrac{\$398,000}{\$188,000} = 2.1$	2	Fair
Activity				
Inventory turnover	$\dfrac{\text{Sales}}{\text{Inventory}}$	$\dfrac{\$3,000,000}{\$300,000} = 10$ times	9 times	Satisfactory
Average collection period	$\dfrac{\text{Receivables}}{\text{Sales per day}}$	$\dfrac{\$200,000}{\$8,333} = 24$ days	20 days	Satisfactory
Fixed assets turnover	$\dfrac{\text{Sales}}{\text{Fixed assets}}$	$\dfrac{\$3,000,000}{\$1,300,000} = 2.3$ times	5 times	Poor
Total assets turnover	$\dfrac{\text{Sales}}{\text{Total assets}}$	$\dfrac{\$3,000,000}{\$2,000,000} = 1.5$ times	2 times	Poor
Profitability				
Profit margin on sales	$\dfrac{\text{Net income}}{\text{Sales}}$	$\dfrac{\$120,000}{\$3,000,000} = 4$ percent	5 percent	Fair
Return on total assets	$\dfrac{\text{Net income}}{\text{Total assets}}$	$\dfrac{\$120,000}{\$2,000,000} = 6$ percent	10 percent	Poor
Return on net worth	$\dfrac{\text{Net income}}{\text{Net worth}}$	$\dfrac{\$120,000}{\$1,000,000} = 12$ percent	15 percent	Fair

SOURCE: From *Managerial Finance*, Seventh Edition, by J. Fred Weston and Eugene F. Brigham. Copyright © 1981 by The Dryden Press. Copyright © 1962, 1966, 1969, 1972, 1977, 1978 by Holt, Rinehart and Winston. Reprinted by permission of CBS College Publishing.

was investing for the short-term. The lost interest spread was close to 3 per cent on $50 million for an overlap period of 30 days, representing an interest penalty of about $120,000.[24]

One of the outstanding features of a cash management program is that, with proper training, existing staff can reap impressive profits with relatively little front-end investment.

According to one cash management expert, an effective communication and information system is the key to cost-effective cash management (see Figure 15.4). Six tips for wringing additional profits from an organization's cash resources are:

- **Keep cash moving.** The faster cash moves from customer to bank and into appropriate short-term investments, the better.
- **Coordinate cash flow among organizational units.** As in the example cited above, one unit's cash surplus can fulfill another's needs. Cash management specialists can effect economies by maintaining an information clearinghouse on an organization's cash availability and needs.
- **Shop around for banking services.** Healthy competition can be created among banks by comparing services, yields, and costs.
- **Diversify short-term investment portfolio.** This will help achieve a better match between investment terms and cash-flow requirements.
- **Take advantage of foreign exchange differentials.** Avoid weaker currencies and seek out stronger currencies as market conditions and organizational transactions permit.
- **Broaden the borrowing base.** Although effective cash management will usually reduce the need to borrow, necessary borrowing should take advantage of favorable terms and foreign currency exchange rates.[25]

Inflation quickly erodes idle cash. Consequently, an important aspect of financial control is to place cash where it will earn the best return without unreasonable risk.

Controlling Human Resource Problems

Financial controls are appropriate for monitoring the performance of the overall organization, subunits, and higher-level managers. But what about contributors farther down the line who have a more indirect impact on key financial barometers? Managers and nonmanagers alike need to be held accountable for fulfilling their responsibilities because, collectively, they can make or break the organization. Nonfinancial controls help management exercise feedforward and feedback control over performance problems at all levels. In this section we look at three contemporary human

Figure 15.4   The Cash Management System

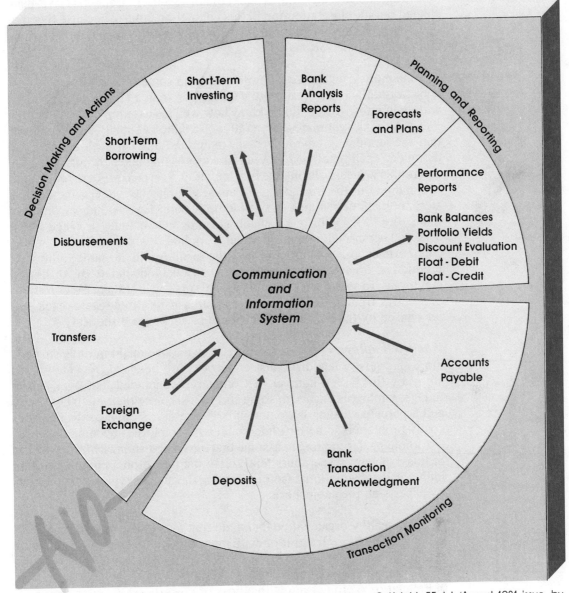

SOURCE: From an article appearing in *Cost and Management* by Henry C. Knight, 55 July/August 1981 issue, by permission of The Society of Management Accountants of Canada.

resource problems—employee theft, cardiovascular disease, and alcohol and drug abuse. These particular human resource problems have been singled out for close attention in this chapter on control because together they represent a tremendous drain on the productive capacity of our public and private organizations.

Controlling Employee Theft

The infamous gangster Al Capone once said something to the effect that "one accountant can steal more with his pen than a hundred robbers can with their guns." Little did he know how well his assessment would fit the 1980s. Although estimates vary ($40 to $75 billion annually), experts agree that the amount of company cash, materials, and services pilfered and defrauded each year by employees far exceeds that taken through burglary and robbery. In fact, during the first half of 1979, armed robbers took about $23 million out the front door of banks, whereas defrauders and embezzlers took about $80 million out the back door. Losses due to computer fraud, the vast majority of which go undetected, today average about $500,000 per crime.[26] Whatever label is applied, "employee theft," "white-collar crime," or "computer crime," the result is still the same: otherwise productive organizational assets are seriously depleted by dishonest employees. In some cases, organizational survival is at stake. According to one study, 30 percent of the business failures in the United States each year are caused by the burdensome expense of employee dishonesty.[27]

Why Do Employees Steal?   Contrary to what one might initially suspect, more than just a few dishonest employees are involved. A widely cited study by the U.S. Chamber of Commerce concluded that over half of today's employees engage in some sort of workplace theft, with between 5 and 8 percent stealing large amounts.[28] The first step in controlling this costly problem is to better understand why employees become thieves.

Although it is tempting to assume that inherent dishonesty is at the heart of this problem, researchers tend to lay the blame on a complex web of individual and situational factors. Among the factors typically mentioned by experts on the subject are:

- An unhealthy organizational climate that alienates employees.
- Personal anger or frustration with management, the organization, or an impersonal "they."
- Ego satisfaction (outsmarting "the system").
- Retaliation (getting even with a boss or coworkers).
- Response to perceived inequity ("they owe it to me").
- Compensate for a feeling of powerlessness.[29]

The complexity of employee theft necessitates a comprehensive feedforward control mechanism.

Table 15.4 Tips for Preventing Employee Theft and Fraud

Reducing Situational Pressures

- Avoid setting unrealistically high performance expectations.
- Remove unnecessary obstacles, such as insufficient working capital, excess capacity, and obsolete equipment or inventory, that block effective performance.
- Offer personal counseling to help employees with financial problems.
- Establish fair and uniform personnel policies.

Reducing Opportunities

- Carefully monitor the business transactions and interpersonal relationships of suppliers, buyers, purchasing agents, sales representatives and others who interface in the transactions among financial units.
- Maintain accurate and complete internal accounting records.
- Establish a physical security system to secure company assets, including finished goods, cash, equipment, tools, and other items of worth.
- Do not rely solely on one individual to perform an important function [such as ringing up sales on a cash register as well as tallying the day's receipts].
- Maintain accurate personnel records regarding employees' previous backgrounds and current financial activities.
- Develop strong leadership and cohesive work groups.

Strengthening Personal Integrity

- Research suggests that induction [teaching and explaining] and modeling are effective techniques for developing moral behavior.
- Honest and dishonest behaviors should be defined.
- Select honest employees to occupy positions of trust.
- Build an organizational climate that emphasizes the importance of honesty.
- The consequences of violating the rules and the punishment of fraud perpetrators should be made public.

SOURCE: Adapted from David J. Cherrington, W. Steve Albrecht, and Marshall B. Romney, "The Role of Management in Reducing Fraud," *Financial Executive* 49 (March 1981): 31–34.

Three-pronged Prevention A team of experts has suggested a three-pronged attack on employee fraud: "In short, fraud is reduced by eliminating the pressures and opportunities to commit fraud and by increasing personal integrity."[30] The suggestions in Table 15.4 can be used for the feedforward control of virtually all forms of employee theft or fraud.

Controlling Cardiovascular Disease   The human heart has a big job. During one's entire lifetime, the heart must pump approximately 100,000 times per day to circulate the equivalent of 4300 gallons of blood through 60,000 miles of blood vessels.[31] Like any other complex system, the human circulatory system weakens and eventually breaks down. The most common circulatory failure is **cardiovascular disease,** hardening of the arteries that leads to heart attack and stroke.

A Costly Epidemic   Heart attack and stroke have reached epidemic proportions in industrialized countries. Today, cardiovascular disease kills more Americans, Canadians, and Western Europeans than all other causes combined (including cancer and accidents). To make matters worse, heart attack and stroke are not exclusively associated with old age. Each year in the United States over 175,000 current or future members of the labor force—people under the age of sixty-five—die of cardiovascular disease. And for every fatal heart attack, there are two nonfatal but disabling attacks. Cardiovascular disease accounts for about 29 million lost workdays in the United States each year, thus reducing annual earnings by $2 billion.[32] Controlling this costly cardiovascular disease epidemic is essential because it is a prime contributor to soaring health care costs. Employee health care costs add more than $500 to the price of each new American-made automobile (more than any other single cost component such as steel, glass, or rubber).

Risk Factors   A "that's too bad" attitude toward cardiovascular disease is clearly inappropriate. This epidemic can be controlled if employers and employees work together.[33] Much of the battle needs to be fought on an educational front to promote healthier lifestyles. (See the lifestyle questionnaire in Table 15.5.) Most heart attacks and strokes are caused by bad habits that can be changed (for example, smoking, eating fatty foods, and not exercising). Factors such as cigarette smoking, high blood cholesterol, high blood pressure, obesity, and stress all significantly increase the risk of cardiovascular disease. By identifying and correcting these risk factors, the cardiovascular disease epidemic can be checked, with economic benefits in the form of lower health care costs and reduced disability expenditures accruing to the organization.

Company Fitness Programs   Company-sponsored screening programs have proved effective in identifying employees who are at abnormally high risk of having a heart attack or stroke.[34] Additionally, the company-sponsored diet and quit-smoking clinics and exercise and fitness programs that have become very popular in recent years promise to help curb cardiovascular disease among employees.[35] The alternative—an overfed, underexercised, and less than fully productive labor force—is unacceptable for both economic and humanitarian reasons.

Controlling Alcohol and Drug Abuse   Alcoholism affects approximately 8 percent of the labor force in the United States.[36] Although it was long believed to be a character disorder, **alcoholism** is now considered a disease in which an individual's normal social and economic roles are disrupted by the consumption of alcohol (see Table 15.6). Very few alcoholics are actually the skid-row-bum type; the vast majority are average citizens. Alcoholism cuts across all age brackets,

"You've been to business meetings and business lunches—believe me, you'll get used to business jogs!"
SOURCE: © 1985 by Sidney Harris. Management Review.

both sexes, and all racial and ethnic categories. Experts say that one needs only to look in the mirror to see what the average alcoholic looks like. Compared to nonalcoholics, alcoholic employees are 16 times more likely to be absent and nearly three times more likely to have an accident. Along with generally impaired productivity, these alcohol-related problems are costing American businesses an estimated $10 billion annually.[37]

Close on the heels of employee alcoholism is workplace drug abuse.

> Although alcohol is the nation's most abused drug, an increasingly greater number of Americans are also abusing mood-altering drug substances apart from, and in addition to, the usage of alcohol. These other drug substances can be described as "illegal"—heroin, cocaine, marijuana, morphine, and so on—or "legal"—prescription drugs such as amphetamines, tranquilizers, and barbiturates.[38]

In terms of lost productivity due to absenteeism, accidents, shoddy work, and sick leave, employee drug abuse is costing the U.S. economy nearly $5 billion a year.[39] Moreover, there is indirect evidence that employee drug

Table 15.5   How Healthy Is Your Lifestyle? A Self-test

All of us want good health. But many of us do not know how to be as healthy as possible. Health experts now describe *lifestyle* as one of the most important factors affecting health. In fact, it is estimated that as many as seven of the ten leading causes of death could be reduced through common-sense changes in lifestyle. That's what this brief test, developed by the Public Health Service, is all about. Its purpose is simply to tell you how well you are doing to stay healthy. The behaviors covered in the test are recommended for most Americans. Some of them may not apply to persons with certain chronic diseases or handicaps, or to pregnant women. Such persons may require special instructions from their physicians. [Note: 2 = Almost Always; 1 = Sometimes; 0 = Almost Never.]

Cigarette Smoking

If you never smoke, enter a score of 10 for this section and go to the next section on *Alcohol and Drugs*.

1. I avoid smoking cigarettes.   2 1 0
2. I smoke only low tar and nicotine cigarettes *or* I smoke a pipe or cigars.   2 1 0

Smoking Score: ___10___

Alcohol and Drugs

1. I avoid drinking alcoholic beverages *or* I drink no more than 1 or 2 drinks a day.   (4) 1 0
2. I avoid using alcohol or other drugs (especially illegal drugs) as a way of handling stressful situations or the problems in my life.   (2) 1 0
3. I am careful not to drink alcohol when taking certain medicines (for example, medicine for sleeping, pain, colds, and allergies), or when pregnant.   (2) 1 0
4. I read and follow the label directions when using prescribed and over-the-counter drugs.   (2) 1 0

Alcohol and Drugs Score: ___10___

Eating Habits

1. I eat a variety of foods each day, such as fruits and vegetables, whole grain breads and cereals, lean meats, dairy products, dry peas and beans, and nuts and seeds.   2 (1) 0
2. I limit the amount of fat, saturated fat, and cholesterol I eat (including fat on meats, eggs, butter, cream, shortenings, and organ meats such as liver).   2 1 (0)
3. I limit the amount of salt I eat by cooking with only small amounts, not adding salt at the table, and avoiding salty snacks.   (2) 1 0
4. I avoid eating too much sugar (especially frequent snacks of sticky candy or soft drinks).   2 (1) 0

Eating Habits Score: ___4___

Exercise/Fitness

1. I maintain a desired weight, avoiding overweight and underweight.   3 1 (0)
2. I do vigorous exercises for 15–30 minutes at least 3 times a week (examples include running, swimming, brisk walking).   3 (1) 0

3. I do exercises that enhance my muscle tone for 15–30 minutes at least 3 times a week (examples include yoga and calisthenics).   2 (1) 0

4. I use part of my leisure time participating in individual, family, or team activities that increase my level of fitness (such as gardening, bowling, golf, and baseball).   2 (1) 0

Exercise/Fitness Score: _____

Stress Control

1. I have a job or do other work that I enjoy.   2 (1) 0

2. I find it easy to relax and express my feelings freely.   2 (1) 0

3. I recognize early, and prepare for, events or situations likely to be stressful for me.   2 (1) 0

4. I have close friends, relatives, or others whom I can talk to about personal matters and call on for help when needed.   2 (1) 0

5. I participate in group activities (such as church and community organizations) or hobbies that I enjoy.   2 (1) 0

Stress Control Score: ___5___

Safety

1. I wear a seat belt while riding in a car.   2 (1) 0

2. I avoid driving while under the influence of alcohol and other drugs.   2 (1) 0

3. I obey traffic rules and the speed limit when driving.   2 (1) 0

4. I am careful when using potentially harmful products or substances (such as household cleaners, poisons, and electrical devices).   (2) 1 0

5. I avoid smoking in bed.   (2) 1 0

Safety Score: _____

Note: A scoring key can be found following the references at the end of this chapter.

SOURCE: Developed by the U.S. Public Health Service. For additional information and materials, write National Health Information Clearinghouse, P.O. Box 1133, Washington, DC 20013-1133.

abuse is playing an increasing role in workplace theft. As with cardiovascular disease, management can either do nothing about employee alcohol and drug abuse and continue to absorb a controllable expense or become actively involved. The latter option can enhance human potential and improve organizational performance.

Referral Alcoholism or drug abuse typically reveals itself to the manager in the form of increased absenteeism, tardiness, sloppy work, and complaints from coworkers. As soon as a steady decline in performance is observed, the manager should confront the individual with his or her poor performance record. Experts advise managers against making any reference to possible alcohol or drug abuse: the employee should be the one to

Table 15.6   The Legal Side of Employee Alcohol and Drug Abuse

The Vocational Rehabilitation Act of 1973, which prohibits employment discrimination by federal contractors or subcontractors against employable, handicapped workers, has been extended to include alcoholics and drug addicts. Alcoholics and drug addicts must receive the same rights as other handicapped workers who cannot be discriminated against in federally sponsored employment, education, and services. In addition, on July 5, 1977, the Department of Labor told employers who are recipients of federal contracts and subcontracts in excess of $2,500 to take affirmative action and hire alcoholics and drug addicts qualified and able to perform work.

SOURCE: Richard J. Tersine and James Hazeldine, "Alcoholism: A Productivity Hangover," *Business Horizons* 25 (November-December 1982), pp. 69–70.

admit having such a problem. If and when an employee admits having an alcohol (or drug) problem, then the manager should refer the person to appropriate sources of help. Managers are cautioned against "playing doctor" when trying to help the alcohol or drug abusing employee. If the organization has an *employee assistance program*,[40] counselors, or a company doctor, an in-house referral can be made. Counselors in General Motors' highly successful employee assistance program estimate that the company gets back $3 for every $1 spent on alcohol/drug abuse treatment.[41]

EAP

Managers in small organizations without sophisticated employee services can refer the alcoholic employee to community resources such as Alcoholics Anonymous. Similar referral agencies exist in most communities for drug abusers. The overriding objective here is to put troubled employees in touch with trained specialists as soon as possible.

A Policy of Constructive Coercion   There are no easy answers to the large and growing problem of employee substance abuse. Progress will come only from a carefully developed company policy and rigorous follow-up by individual managers. The following policy of "constructive coercion" is a step in the right direction:

1. Management must define alcoholism [and drug abuse] among its employees as a health problem requiring therapy.
2. Management must adopt a treatment attitude toward this health problem, offering assistance in securing therapy.
3. It [should] be understood that after a reasonable opportunity for progress, the employee will be dismissed unless there is noticeable improvement in work.
4. The policy [should] be communicated widely by corporate officers with their full approval.[42]

In the long run, employees, organizations, and society in general all stand to gain from management's attempts to control employee theft, cardiovascular disease, and alcohol/drug abuse.

Summary

Planning and control are complementary functions because corrective action is usually needed as plans become reality. Organizational effectiveness is the ultimate objective of the control function. Because there is no one criterion of organizational effectiveness, profit as well as not-for-profit organizations need to satisfy different effectiveness criteria in the near, intermediate, and distant future.

Control is a necessary extension of planning because of environmental, organizational, and behavioral uncertainties. Contrary to the negative connotation usually attached to the term *control,* managerial control is a pervasive, positive, and future-oriented function. Feedforward control is preventive in nature, whereas feedback control is based on the evaluation of past performance. The three basic components of organizational control systems are objectives, standards, and an evaluation-reward system. Research indicates that in spite of the growth of strategic management, strategic control is often deficient.

Timely diagnosis of control problems is important because things can quickly get out of hand. Internal auditing helps top management objectively determine whether the organization is functioning as intended. If, for some reason, comprehensive internal auditing is not carried out, weak spots in the control system can be detected by monitoring telltale symptoms. Sometimes, especially when management focuses on secondary objectives or fosters a do-or-die environment, the control system itself may breed problems, such as goal displacement and measurementship.

Financial control is vital because it monitors the organization's life-blood. Both favorable and unfavorable budget variances help management diagnose organizational ills. Managers are advised to focus their feedback control efforts on budget variances that are costly, consistent, controllable, and vital. Feedforward financial control becomes possible when flexible budgets based on standard costs are used. Indexed standard costing has been recommended for adjusting budgets for inflation. Financial ratios enable managers to gauge the financial health of their organizations in terms of liquidity, leverage, activity, and profitability. When high interest rates prevail, systematic cash management can generate handsome payoffs with relatively little additional expense.

Human resource problems can be brought under control with nonfinancial techniques. Employee theft, cardiovascular disease, and alcohol/drug abuse are three human resource problems presently sapping the productive strength of organizations and the economy. A three-pronged program involving reducing pressures, eliminating opportunities, and increasing integrity is recommended for controlling employee theft/fraud. Cardiovascular disease, a major contributor to skyrocketing health care costs, can be curbed by identifying and improving lifestyle risk factors such as smoking and lack of exercise. Employee alcohol and drug abuse cost the U.S. economy $15 billion annually. Control via a policy of constructive coercion is recommended for this difficult problem.

Terms to Understand

Organizational effectiveness	Budget variance
Control	Flexible budget
Feedforward control	Indexed standard costing
Feedback control	Financial ratios
Internal auditing	Cardiovascular disease
Measurementship	Alcoholism
Budget	

Questions for Discussion

1. How do the planning and control functions work together?
2. How is it possible that a profitable business could be considered ineffective?
3. In your opinion, which type of control—feedforward or feedback—is more desirable to an organization?
4. In regard to maintaining high quality service in a fast-food restaurant, what do you believe could be done in terms of the three components of organizational control systems?
5. What can management do to overcome resistance to internal auditing?
6. In observing firsthand an ongoing organization (for example, a factory, a restaurant, a service station, a grocery store, a bookstore, a club, or a fraternity or sorority), what symptoms of inadequate control can you detect?
7. What concerns should be raised by favorable budget variances?
8. Why is cash management especially important today?
9. In your experience, how bad is the problem of employee theft? What needs to be done to control this problem?
10. Why do you suppose experts warn against directly accusing an employee of alcohol or drug abuse?

Back to the Opening Case

Now that you have read Chapter 15, you should be able to answer the following questions about the Allied case:

1. In regard to the marriage of planning and control, what positive elements do you see in Hennessy's approach?
2. How could Hennessy's approach possibly hurt Allied's long-term (strategic) effectiveness? (See the discussion of strategic management in Chapter 5.)
3. What are the drawbacks of relying too heavily on the KISS principle?

Closing Case 15.2

The Robin Hood of Computer Criminals*

Stanley Slyngstad, the one-armed computer bandit of Thurston County, didn't worry too much about getting caught by fellow employees.

Most people just don't want to know much about computers, he said in a deposition to investigators. He went on: "When they saw that I was doing something, if anything they would turn and leave rather than say, 'Gee, that's neat, what are you doing?' They would say, 'That turkey, that technician, all he ever does is talk his buzz words, can't talk to him.' "

So Mr. Slyngstad was left alone to steal from the state of Washington, using his computer to have the state mail him and two friends vocational-rehabilitation warrants, cashable at banks. His former boss still calls him the "best damn programmer in the state of Washington."

... Stanley Slyngstad was the state employee who developed the software through which Washington's Division of Vocational Rehabilitation authorized payments to injured loggers and others requiring some form of retraining. One-armed since a childhood accident, he was nevertheless a keyboard virtuoso and, one superior says, was trusted all the more because of his own handicap.

But Mr. Slyngstad used the computer and the software he knew so well to authorize payments of nearly $17,000—to himself and two friends. By computer he prepared the records the state needed to issue the payment warrants, then erased all electronic memory of the fraud. He also capitalized on the tendency people have of ignoring little computer errors—he had the computer make the warrants out to one Stanley Lyngstad. No bank ever questioned the missing S in his last name.

*Excerpt reprinted by permission of *The Wall Street Journal*, © Dow Jones & Company, Inc. 1985. All rights reserved.

He was arrested after the daughter of one of his beneficiaries tipped police and the state to the crime. A manual search of the paper records left after the state issued its warrants turned up the name Lyngstad, and the searcher recognized Mr. Slyngstad's address. Mr. Slyngstad eventually pleaded guilty.

He claimed he never kept a dime for himself but doled the money out to friends down on their luck; he called himself the one-armed bandit and liked to think of himself as a Robin Hood, a one-man welfare agency, says Gary R. Tabor, the prosecutor in the case. The judge didn't buy it. Ignoring a pre-sentence report that recommended 60 days in jail, the judge angrily declared, "I have no vicious sheriff of Nottingham running around here" and on July 20, 1983, sentenced Mr. Slyngstad to 10 years in prison. However, the state prison board reduced that, and Mr. Slyngstad was paroled Sept. 24, [1983].

For Discussion

1. Based on the facts you have, why do you suppose Slyngstad became a computer criminal?
2. In terms of feedforward control, what could management have done to prevent this fraud?
3. In your opinion, did Slyngstad's final punishment fit the crime? What kind of signal does this case send to would-be computer criminals?

References

Opening Quotation: William H. Sihler, "Toward Better Management Control Systems," *California Management Review* 14 (Winter 1971): 34.

Opening Case: For additional information on Allied, see "The Hennessy Style May Be What Allied Needs," *Business Week* No. 2721 (January 11, 1982): 126–129; Michael A. Verespej, "Why Ed Hennessy Went on a Buying Spree," *Industry Week* 212 (February 22, 1982): 82–84; Mitchell Gordon, "The New Allied," *Barron's* 63 (June 6, 1983): 55, 58–59; and Kathy Williams, "Ed Hennessy Reshapes Allied," *Management Accounting* 66 (January 1985): 18–25.

Closing Case: Excerpted from Erik Larson, "Computers Turn Out To Be Valuable Aid in Employee Crime," *The Wall Street Journal* 112 (January 14, 1985): 1.

1. Williams, "Ed Hennessy Reshapes Allied," p. 23.
2. Bruce A. Kirchoff, "Organization Effectiveness Measurement and Policy Research," *Academy of Management Review* 2 (July 1977): 352.
3. Detailed discussions of alternative models of organizational effectiveness may be found in Frank Shipper and Charles S. White, "Linking Organizational Effectiveness and Environmental Change," *Long Range Planning* 16 (June

1983): 99–106 and Michael Keeley, "Impartiality and Participant-Interest Theories of Organizational Effectiveness," *Administrative Science Quarterly* 29
(March 1984): 1–25.

4. William H. Newman, *Constructive Control: Design and Use of Control Systems* (Englewood Cliffs, N.J.: Prentice-Hall, 1975), pp. 3–5.

5. Harold Koontz and Robert W. Bradspies, "Managing Through Feedforward
Control," *Business Horizons* 15 (June 1972): 27.

6. See Richard L. Daft and Norman B. Macintosh, "The Nature and Use of
Formal Control Systems for Management Control and Strategy Implementation," *Journal of Management* 10 (Spring 1984): 43–66.

7. Based on a more extensive discussion in Eric Flamholtz, "Organizational
Control Systems as a Managerial Tool," *California Management Review* 22
(Winter 1979): 50–59.

8. "How One Troubled Bank Turned Itself Around," *Business Week* No. 2702
(August 24, 1981): 117, 122.

9. For an interesting discussion of how Japanese students view American business schools, see "Japan Gives the B-Schools an A—For Contacts," *Business
Week* No. 2710 (October 19, 1981): 132, 136.

10. J. H. Horovitz, "Strategic Control: A New Task for Top Management," *Long
Range Planning* 12 (June 1979): 5.

11. "The Case of the Misplaced $30 Billion," *Business Week* No. 2544 (July 24,
1978): 155.

12. Lawrence B. Sawyer, "Internal Auditing: Yesterday, Today, and Tomorrow,"
The Internal Auditor 36 (December 1979): 26. (Emphasis added).

13. See Robert Louis Ellis and J. Peter Melrose, "Auditing the Management
Process," *The Internal Auditor* 37 (August 1980): 53–64.

14. This list is based in part on material found in Donald W. Murr, Harry B. Bracey,
Jr., and William K. Hill, "How to Improve Your Organization's Management
Controls," *Management Review* 69 (October 1980): 56–63.

15. John Quirt, "How Greyhound Made a U-Turn," *Fortune* 101 (March 24, 1980):
139.

16. See Flamholtz, "Organizational Control Systems as a Managerial Tool," pp.
57–58.

17. Joel G. Siegel and Mathew S. Rubin, "Corporate Planning and Control
Through Variance Analysis," *Managerial Planning* 33 (September-October
1984): 35.

18. See Ibid., p. 36.

19. For detailed discussion of flexible budgeting, see Lawrence M. Matthews,
Practical Operating Budgeting (New York: McGraw-Hill, 1977), pp. 30–34.
For a good practical example of standard costing, see Dennis M. Boll, "How
Dutch Pantry Accounts for Standard Costs," *Management Accounting* 64
(December 1982): 32–35.

20. See John Dearden, "Facing Facts with Inflation Accounting," *Harvard Business Review* 59 (July-August 1981): 8–12, 16 and John L. Grant, "Inflation's Full
Impact on the Bottom Line," *Business Week* No. 2776 (February 7, 1983): 8.

21. Donald Green, "To Predict Failure," *Management Accounting* 60 (July 1978): 45.

22. J. Fred Weston and Eugene F. Brigham, *Managerial Finance,* 7th ed. (Hinsdale, Ill.: Dryden Press, 1981), p. 138.

23. For an interesting discussion of financial ratios applied to hospital administration, see Fred Fitschen, "Look to Ratios to Measure Financial Health," *Hospital Financial Management* 6 (November 1976): 44–50.

24. Henry C. Knight, "Making Money from Money Management," *Cost and Management* 55 (July-August 1981):45.

25. This list of tips is adapted from Knight, "Making Money from Money Management." For an informative practical discussion of cash management in decentralized organizations, see Thomas E. Phillips and Mark E. Droege, "Maximizing Cash in Decentralized Organizations," *Management Accounting* 66 (August 1984): 38–42.

26. See David J. Cherrington, W. Steve Albrecht, and Marshall B. Romney, "The Role of Management in Reducing Fraud," *Financial Executive* 49 (March 1981): 28–34.

27. See Carol B. Gilmore, "To Catch a Corporate Thief," *S.A.M. Advanced Management Journal* 47 (Winter 1982): 35–39.

28. See Chamber of Commerce of the United States, *White Collar Crime* (Washington, D.C.: Chamber of Commerce, 1974).

29. For more complete discussion of the causes of employee theft, see William L. Taylor and Joseph P. Cangemi, "Employee Theft and Organizational Climate," *Personnel Journal* 58 (October 1979): 686–688, 714 and Gilmore, "To Catch a Corporate Thief." An interesting study of paper-and-pencil tests to screen out dishonest employees can be found in Paul R. Sackett and Michael M. Harris, "Honesty Testing for Personnel Selection: A Review and Critique," *Personnel Psychology* 37 (Summer 1984): 221–245.

30. Cherrington et al., "The Role of Management in Reducing Fraud," p. 31.

31. Figures are from American Heart Association, *Heart Facts 1981* (National Center, 7320 Greenville Avenue, Dallas, Texas 75231), p. 3.

32. See Robert H. Rosen, "The Picture of Health in the Work Place," *Training and Development Journal* 38 (August 1984): 24–30.

33. For more on this, see Robert Kreitner, "Employee Physical Fitness: Protecting an Investment in Human Resources," *Personnel Journal* 55 (July 1976): 340–344 and Roger W. Reed, "Is Education the Key to Lower Health Care Costs?" *Personnel Journal* 63 (January 1984): 40–46.

34. For example, see Robert Kreitner, Steven D. Wood, and Glenn M. Friedman, "Just How Fit Are Your Employees?" *Business Horizons* 22 (August 1979): 39–45.

35. For an excellent review and critique of the benefits of employee physical fitness programs, see John J. Hoffman, Jr. and Charles J. Hobson, "Physical Fitness and Employee Effectiveness," *Personnel Administrator* 29 (April 1984): 101–113, 126.

36. For an excellent account of this problem, see Kevin W. Kane, "The Corporate Responsibility in the Area of Alcoholism," *Personnel Journal* 54 (July 1975): 380–384.

37. See Robert O'Connor, "Sobering Up the Corporation," *Corporate Fitness & Recreation* 3 (February-March 1984): 16–21.

38. James A. Belohlav and Paul O. Popp, "Employee Substance Abuse: Epidemic of the Eighties," *Business Horizons* 26 (July-August 1983): 29.

39. A good overview of the employee drug abuse problem may be found in John Brecher, "Taking Drugs on the Job," *Newsweek* 101 (August 22, 1983): 52–60.

40. See, for example, Edwin J. Busch, Jr., "Developing an Employee Assistance Program," *Personnel Journal* 60 (September 1981): 708–711; Richard J. Tersine and James Hazeldine, "Alcoholism: A Productivity Hangover," *Business Horizons* 25 (November-December 1982): 68–72; and Ellen Wojahn, "How to Cut $5,000 Off the Cost of Each Employee," *Inc.* 6 (July 1984): 106–110.

41. Data drawn from Brecher, "Taking Drugs on the Job."

42. Kane, "The Corporate Responsibility in the Area of Alcoholism," p. 384.

(Scoring key for lifestyle self-test is on page 562.)

Scoring Key for Lifestyle Self-test

What Your Scores Mean to You

Scores of 8 and 10 [for each area]

Excellent! Your answers show that you are aware of the importance of this area to your health. More important, you are putting your knowledge to work for you by practicing good health habits. As long as you continue to do so, this area should not pose a serious health risk. It's likely that you are setting an example for your family and friends to follow. Since you got a very high test score on this part of the test, you may want to consider other areas where your scores indicate room for improvement.

Scores of 6 to 7

Your health practices in this area are good, but there is room for improvement. Look again at the items you answered with a "Sometimes" or "Almost Never." What changes can you make to improve your score? Even a small change can often help you achieve better health.

Scores of 3 to 5

Your health risks are showing! Would you like more information about the risks you are facing and about why it is important for you to change these behaviors? Perhaps you need help in deciding how to successfully make the changes you desire. In either case, help is available.

Scores of 0 to 2

Obviously, you were concerned enough about your health to take the test, but your answers show that you may be taking serious and unnecessary risks with your health. Perhaps you are not aware of the risks and what to do about them. You can easily get the information and help you need to improve, if you wish. The next step is up to you.

Note: Information about the various health risks in this self-test may be obtained from: National Health Information Clearinghouse, P.O. Box 1133, Washington, DC 20013-1133.

SECTION 178

Chapter 16

Managing Information

The importance of information is hard to overstate because we use informa-tion as the basis for all action. Without good information, we may blunder disastrously, but with it, we can reach our goals quickly and easily.
Edward Cornish

Chapter Objectives

When you finish studying this chapter, you should be able to

- Define the term *information* and explain why it is not an ordinary physical resource.
- Explain the role that critical success factors play in diagnosing informa-tion needs.
- Describe what a management information system (MIS) can do for managers.
- Distinguish between centralized and distributed data-processing sys-tems and compare the relative merits of each.
- Explain the steps management can take to harness the power of personal computers.
- Discuss the problem of resistance to computerized management infor-mation systems and briefly explain what management can do about it.

Opening Case 16.1

Beefing Up on Electronics Makes Hercules Leaner*

New office technologies are helping to bring dramatic changes in the way that Hercules Inc. does business. From the satellite dish on the roof to five video-conferencing rooms on various floors, the $2.6 billion chemical maker's ultramodern headquarters in downtown Wilmington, Del., could fairly be called an office building of the future.

A network of more than 400 word processing terminals and 205 per-sonal computers in the building is only the beginning of Hercules' arsenal

*Reprinted from the October 8, 1984 issue of *Business Week* by special permission, © 1984 by McGraw-Hill, Inc.

of electronic office tools. Legal drafts, news releases, and other documents are routinely produced on a three-year-old word processing system. Text can be routed electronically around the company's offices worldwide. This has resulted in a 40% reduction in secretarial work hours and has saved about $3 million a year, estimates Ross O. Watson, vice-president for information resources at Hercules.

The company has also been a pioneer in the use of voice-mail and satellite technology. Its voice mail system, installed about two years ago, has saved more than $3 million annually in employees' time, Watson says. Satellite links to plants and offices around the world—the company has leased nine earth stations—are used for, among other things, some 100 video-conferences a month. The satellite system has helped save more than $1.5 million a year in time and travel expenses.

All these new technologies have aided a major cost-cutting drive begun in the late 1970s. They have enabled Hercules to trim 1,800 jobs, or 6.6% of its work force. They have also made it possible to eliminate assistant department managers, assistant plant managers, and a level of vice-presidents that Watson terms "nonworking vice-presidents," or "the grand old men." In all, he says, half a dozen layers of management have been stripped away.

Biting the Bullet

"We believe we've embarked on a culture change, really," says Watson. With fewer managers, the new information-handling tools have become indispensable. Every top officer now has a terminal in his office, except Chairman Alexander F. Giacco, whose machine is just outside. The high-level managers—most of them in their 50s—have bitten the bullet and learned how to use the terminals effectively. For example, Arden B. Engebretsen, chief financial officer, uses his to handle text as well as to monitor the performance of the company's pension-fund investments. And Giacco can get a handy report on the company's sales performance each morning.

Such hands-on familiarity with the new systems is essential if senior managers are to understand how the new technologies can be applied to solving business problems, Watson says. Usually, office automation works its way up from the bottom. But at Hercules, some senior executives are leading the charge. Top management must "sign on and be the real leaders" of cultural change, Watson says. For if users throughout the company do not "buy in" to the plans and goals for the sophisticated new systems, "there will be no results."

(Discussion questions linking this case with the material you are about to read can be found at the end of this chapter.)

Hercules's executives take advantage of modern electronic technology to keep abreast of current, relevant information. All of us, from the time we scan the morning paper at breakfast until we click off the late-night TV show, are continuously bombarded with data. Some of this steady stream of facts, figures, names, dates, and places is useful; much is not. Isolated bits and pieces of data become useful only when they answer a personally relevant question or help us do something we want to do. For example, if we hear an advertisement on our car radio for a product we aren't interested in, while busily weaving through traffic, it will probably have little impact on our behavior. Conversely, advertisements that tell us what we need to know, when we need to know it, are more likely to affect our behavior. Useful and timely information is particularly important to managers who are responsible for making good decisions. This chapter focuses on ways to give managers the information they need, when they need it.

Technically, not every message or signal that one receives is necessarily information. Experts on the subject have offered the following clarification:

> Many messages we receive are not relevant to our interests; they are isolated facts which have no connotations in our frame of reference. For example, if we are in the catfood business, a news item about border clashes in Asia is probably not relevant to managing our business. To distinguish pertinent from irrelevant messages, we'll refer to the total set of messages we receive as data rather than information. By the term "information" we mean only those data which actively inform us about the status of some phenomenon of interest to us, like sales in the Eastern region or the terms of a recent act of Congress affecting our industry.[1]

Accordingly, in a managerial context, **information** is data organized and interpreted within a relevant frame of reference that enhances effective decision making (see Figure 16.1). It has been pointed out that information should have a "surprise effect," meaning that it should shed light on the unknown.[2] Information that does not surprise the individual is probably irrelevant or redundant (for example, last week's weather report). In recent years systematic information management has become an increasingly important part of organizational control.

Putting Information into Perspective

Today, largely as a by-product of advances in computer and telecommunications technology, information is an overriding consideration for managers. One expert on advanced technology in the workplace has

Figure 16.1 Data Versus Information

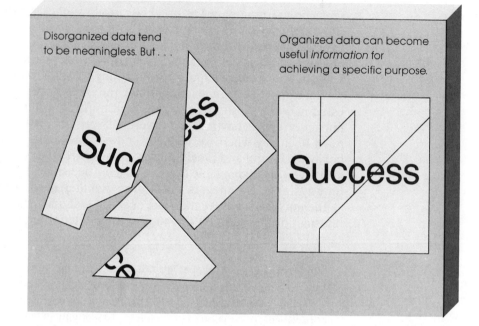

Disorganized data tend to be meaningless. But . . .

Organized data can become useful *information* for achieving a specific purpose.

asserted: "We are in the Information Age: our workforce increasingly is made up of people who work with information, we are besieged on all sides by new information sources, better information provides the competitive edge and the information industry is destined to be the dominant industry of the future."[3] Because information is the lifeblood of organized endeavor, it needs to be brought into clearer perspective. This can be accomplished by (1) realizing that information is a resource, (2) understanding the cost of information, (3) understanding common misconceptions about information, (4) being alert to the problem of information overload, and (5) appreciating the impact of new information technologies.

Information Is a Resource

Through the years, managers have generally been preoccupied with specific types of information (for example, market forecasts, production levels, and sales figures) rather than focusing more broadly on information itself. An unfortunate consequence of this tendency has been the haphazard, bits-and-pieces management of information. Costly inefficiencies due to the collection of irrelevant or redundant information have too often been the result. Information management experts have responded to this state of affairs by recommending that information be viewed as a resource.

Although experts on the subject usually agree that information is a valuable resource, they disagree over exactly what kind of resource it is. Is information a physical factor of production like land, labor, and capital? Or is it something else? According to Harlan Cleveland, a former high government official and university president, information is a unique resource:

> Unlike coal, automobiles, food, or clothing, information is *expandable* (it grows with use, enhances its value through dissemination), *diffusive* (it leaks and is therefore harder to hide), and *shareable* (if I give you food or sell you an automobile, you have it and I don't; if I give you a fact or sell you an idea, we both have it).[4]

If information is something other than a finite physical resource, then what determines the *value* of information? In response to this question, an office technology specialist has noted: "Information has no intrinsic worth as people do; its worth is entirely subjective. Information does not vary in value because of external factors, as money does; its value is in the mind of the user."[5] An example may help explain the contention that information has no intrinsic or tangible value. Suppose that you are on your way to a jeweler to get a diamond ring resized. En route, you discover that both the diamond ring and a piece of paper with the jeweler's street number on it have fallen through a hole in your pocket. To the finder, the diamond ring will have obvious value, but the piece of paper with only a number on it will be meaningless. The street number, as an informational resource, had value only to you in the context of going to get the ring resized. Purpose gives value to information. Thus, the value of information, like beauty, is in the eye of the beholder.

The Cost of Information

If information is a valuable resource, then it must cost something. But unlike a gallon of gasoline or a pound of hamburger, the cost of information is not so easy to quote in current marketplace terms. Information does not come in convenient units of measurement such as gallons or pounds. Instead, information comes in many different quantitative and qualitative dimensions. The most productive way to address the cost of information is to think in terms of contributing cost factors. The cost of organizational information is dictated by three factors—accuracy, timeliness, and reporting interval.[6] As detailed in Table 16.1, managers who demand more accurate, more prompt, and more frequent information should be prepared to pay more in terms of invested time and/or money.

Common Misconceptions About Information

Before information can be effectively managed, some common misconceptions about it need to be corrected. Six misconceptions that have proved to be especially troublesome are:

- **Computers can provide managers with all the information they need.** In view of research evidence that managers prefer verbal media for

Table 16.1   Factors That Affect the Cost of Information

Factor	Consideration	Example
Accuracy	Increased accuracy generally means increased cost. Therefore, accuracy should only be increased to the point that it still influences decisions.	At the end of each business day, bank management must decide if the books are in balance. The bank can close a couple of hours earlier by allowing its balances to be off by a few dollars. A simple adjustment entry is much less costly than spending a few hundred dollars on salaries and computer time to locate a minor mistake.
Timeliness	In general, the more quickly information is provided after the occurrence of an event, the more costly is that information. More timely information can result in earlier problem identification and resolution.	Retailers like to identify slow-moving merchandise and put it on sale to move it before it becomes even less attractive to customers. A decrease in the demand for merchandise can be determined by keeping track of inventory turnover. However, such information can usually be a few days or weeks old without serious consequences.
Reporting interval	In general, the more frequently information is updated and reported, the higher the cost. If information that affects decisions is changing quickly, the greater the need for shorter updating and reporting intervals.	An airline needs extremely short intervals for updating and reporting passenger reservations and changes in reservations to sell as many tickets as possible without overselling. However, the airline only needs to know the amount of passenger luggage to be carried once: just prior to take off.

SOURCE: Reprinted by permission from *Systems Analysis for Computer-Based Information Systems*, p. 39, by James C. Wetherbe, Copyright © 1979 by West Publishing Company. All rights reserved.

exchanging information, computers simply cannot satisfy the social dimension of information gathering. Moreover, the perceived information needs of individuals vary so widely and change so rapidly that even the most advanced computerized information system cannot satisfy every possible need.

- **More information leads to better decision making.** The unread reports that clutter many managers' offices testify to the fact that much of today's information is either irrelevant, untimely, or redundant. (Information overload is discussed in the next section.)
- **Managers actually need the information they request.** Uncertainty about decisions typically encourages managers to ask for more information than they really need and to ask for the wrong types of information.
- **Decision making will improve when managers are given the information**

they need. Information, in itself, does not guarantee good decisions. Managers need to be instructed as to how and when to use specific types of information.

- **Managers do not have to comprehend the workings of the overall information system.** Because we often fear the unknown, familiarity with information systems will produce greater acceptance. Moreover, a working knowledge of an information system's potential will encourage more sophisticated use.
- **Managers desire better information.** The term *better* implies that something was wrong in the past, which can be interpreted as personal criticism and thus resented. In addition, some individuals are threatened by new and different ways of doing things.[7]

Managers who take time to dispel these misconceptions when formulating and introducing all types of manual or computerized information systems can avoid many serious downstream problems.

The Problem of Information Overload

Thanks in large part to computer-based information systems, many of today's employees have a problem with *too much* rather than too little information. Curiously, however, information overload has unexpected consequences. Field research has shown that employees who perceive that they have too much information tend to make less accurate decisions but tend to be more satisfied than their coworkers are who have a perception of too little information.[8] This combination of outcomes suggests that information overload is a self-perpetuating problem. In other words, satisfaction creates an incentive for obtaining still more information that could further erode decision quality. Employees who must make decisions under uncertain conditions are particularly prone to information overload because an abundance of information serves to raise their confidence level. Managers need to be consciously aware of this problem if they are to break its cycle of self-perpetuation effectively. Better information, not necessarily more information, is the answer. This is where modern information technology promises to make a valuable contribution.

An Avalanche of New Information Technologies

The marriage of high-speed computers and space-age telecommunications technology has fostered exciting new ways to generate and exchange information. Hardly a day passes without some mention of an exotic new information-processing technology such as artificial intelligence or voice-activated computers. Progressive managers who tap the potential of emerging information technologies stand to gain unprecedented access to and control of information vital to organizational success. Managers who adopt a head-in-the-sand approach eventually will be at a competitive disadvantage, both personally and organizationally. Three particularly significant new information technologies are end-user computing (per-

Table 16.2   Three New Information Technologies: Promises and Potential Problems

	Promises	Potential Problems
End-user computing (personal computers)	• Provides managers and technical specialists with more timely information. • Permits tailoring of information to unique and rapidly changing needs. • User-friendly hardware and software humanizes computer technology. • Permits managers to control computerized information, rather than vice versa. • Access to personal computers can enhance status and boost morale.	• Viewed as a threat by some computer programmers and specialists who see their status eroded. • Diversity of hardware and software can create compatibility problems and fragment information system. • Creates information security problem • Can foster costly redundancy in equipment and programs. • Purchase of personal computers is often driven by "bandwagon effect" rather than by clearly defined information needs.
Teleconferencing	• Reduces travel expenses. • Cuts down unproductive travel time of high-paid managers and technical specialists. • Speeds flow of vital information and decision making. • Protects against disruptions such as airline strikes and fuel shortages. • Home office can communicate simultaneously with many widely dispersed field sites, thus eliminating redundant meetings.	• Intimidates some people who view teleconferencing as "performing." • Purchase of expensive new facilities may be used to justify unnecessary meetings. • Can disrupt the important subtleties and nuances that are so much a part of face-to-face communication. • May increase risk of electronic eavesdropping and sabotage. • Managers at field sites may resent home office intrusions.
Telecommuting	• Significantly boosts individual productivity. • Saves commuting time and travel expenses (lessens traffic congestion). • Taps broader labor pool (such as mothers with young children, handicapped and retired persons, and prison inmates). • Eliminates office distractions and politics. • Reduces employer's cost of office space.	• Fear of stagnating at home. • Lack of social contact with co-workers can foster sense of isolation. • Fear of being "out of sight, out of mind" at promotion time. • Can disrupt traditional manager-subordinate relationship. • Work may compete or interfere with family duties and foster family conflict.

Table 16.3 Personal (Micro) Computer Software Programs Can Help Managers in a Number of Different Ways

There are five generic categories of personal computer software that enable managers to do a better job of managing information:

- **Data base** programs are primarily concerned with the management of data—allowing the user to organize it easily, get at it easily, and select and review the precise data wanted. It's record-oriented and uses a structure of data from character; to field (group of related characters); to record (group of related fields); to file (group of related records).

  In simple terms, a data base program manages data according to your instructions and within the limits of the program, and it keeps track of information and the relationships between pieces of information. Depending on the sophistication of the program, it may provide menus, methods for updating information, generation of reports, and other features for actual management of information.

- **Spreadsheet** programs provide ways to manipulate data within a defined structure. They are a remarkable tool for anyone who has to crunch numbers. Programs are structured as a matrix (X Y), which allows the user to define a structure and then change the numbers within that structure to see how the change will affect other numbers. The spreadsheet also accepts formulas; i.e., column A = column D + column B. With this kind of approach, it's possible to play "what if" and to estimate changes based on different events.

- **Word processing** programs allow the user to type material on a magnetic disk. Once entered, the material can be changed, edited, revised, deleted, or printed at will. Word processing programs are loved for many of the same reasons numbers have taken to spreadsheet programs. The real strength of word processing systems shows up in multi-page documents. When revisions are needed somewhere in the middle of the text, they can be made quickly and neatly, with little additional work. There's no need to retype vast numbers of pages if there's a revision.

- **Graphics** programs make it possible to display (and often print) in graph form your findings or conclusions. These can be used for graphic presentations of financial analyses, budgets, sales projections, etc. Some sophisticated graphics software packages for micros have been developed for art, advertising, architecture, and engineering.

- **Communications** programs allow information to be passed from one terminal to another. Programs can be used for accessing information from a central computer or from outside data bases. Electronic mail falls in this category. The area of applications software promises to be the growth area of the future—especially for micros.

SOURCE: James P. Morgan, "Software Buying: A New Purchasing Frontier," *Purchasing* 97 (September 20, 1984): 71.

sonal computers), teleconferencing, and telecommuting. Together they offer a representative, though not an exhaustive, sample of how the information age is reshaping organizational life. As listed in Table 16.2, each of these new information technologies has a unique bundle of promises and potential problems.

End-user Computing   Until recently, computing was something highly trained specialists did while the typical manager watched and waited. Managers traditionally have been *consumers* of computerized information dispensed by programmers with access to large and very complex computers. Moreover, managers typically have relied on clerical and technical staff to perform duties such as preparing correspondence, scheduling meetings, collecting decision-support data, and calculating statistical summaries. Now, however, with the rapid dissemination of microcomputers (also called personal computers) in the workplace, managers are becoming "producers" of computerized information. One management consultant estimated in late 1984 that "17% of the nation's managers and 13% of top executives now have hands-on-the-keyboard access to computers."[9] Judging from the brisk sales of personal computers, these figures will climb rapidly during the next decade.

Managers with personal computers are using word processing programs to prepare letters and memos, scheduling meetings with electronic calendar networks, getting answers to "what if" questions with computer spreadsheets, referring to comprehensive computer data bases prior to making decisions, and performing their own statistical analyses (see Table 16.3). This turn of events promises to have two major impacts. First, managerial productivity should rise because a representative group of managers in one study "spent about 25% of their time on such unproductive tasks as waiting for meetings or information, expediting assigned tasks, making copies, and arranging reservations."[10] Second, end-user computing already shows signs of flattening the organizational pyramid. According to one industry observer:

> The most far-reaching effect of [personal] computers may be on the power structure of the office—flattening the hierarchy, making it more difficult to hoard authority. Managers with computers quickly notice that they delegate fewer typing chores and less statistical analysis. Secretaries and staff assistants are sometimes eliminated or moved to other positions, but more frequently they are retrained to be designers and keepers of the new computer data bases.[11]

Layers of middle managers, who have generally served as conduits of information between the operating and strategic levels, are likely to find themselves unemployed as a result of end-user computing. Of course, as discussed in Chapter 3, society's gains from managerial productivity will be partially offset by the costs of technological displacement. Meanwhile, personal computers are popping up in the workplace like spring seedlings. (More is said about the personal computer revolution later in this chapter.)

Teleconferencing   Busy managers have long complained about wasting valuable time and money on trips to field offices and plants. Although information technologists have been saying for years that a solution was just around the corner, a workable alternative is finally taking shape. It goes by the name **teleconferencing** and is defined as "interactive group communication through any electronic medium."[12] Use of the word *group* sets teleconferencing apart from the standard person-to-person telephone call. Teleconferencing technologies are numerous and growing. Communication channels for teleconferencing may vary from local and long-distance telephone lines, to in-house telephone systems, to earth station–satellite–earth station hook ups. According to experts on the subject:

> Audio and full-motion video are probably the best-known forms. Still video snapshots also can be exchanged (often called "slow-scan" or "freeze-frame" teleconferencing), as can keyboarded messages ("computer conferencing" or "electronic mail"), drawings (for example, "electronic blackboard"), or page copies ("fax").[13]

Still another teleconferencing alternative is to broadcast a live TV-quality presentation to a large audience. Questions from one or several audience sites can then be received over the phone (something like a corporate version of the Phil Donahue show).

While savings on travel are the primary motivation for installing a teleconferencing system, this new information technology is giving some companies a competitive edge.

> Boeing Co., for instance, completed development of its 757 aircraft ahead of schedule in 1982, partly because four video sites linking the company's sprawling Seattle facilities enabled hundreds of executives, technicians, and pilots to make instant design decisions. "No other aircraft maker has developed video to this extent, so the timeliness of our decisions gives us a competitive advantage," claims [a Boeing engineering manager].[14]

In addition to the possible problems listed in Table 16.2, full-motion video teleconferencing via satellite, called *videoconferencing* by some, is still quite expensive in spite of recent price cuts. "Total costs per site now average under $350,000, down 40% since 1982."[15] Smaller organizations will have to resort to less exotic forms of teleconferencing, such as audio networks, until prices drop still further.

Telecommuting   Alvin Toffler used the term "electronic cottage" to refer to the practice of working at home on a personal computer hooked, typically by telephone, to an employer's place of business. More recently, this practice has been labeled **telecommuting** because work is sent to the employee's home computer via telephone modem instead of the employee commuting to a central office. According to one business writer:

> At present, less than one percent of the labor force is telecommuting, but the figure is expected to jump to five percent within the next few years as the number of computers increases in offices and homes, sophisticated telecommunications equipment becomes less expensive and more accessible, and people continue to search for different ways to deal with social and economic changes in their lives.[16]

By 1984, an estimated 200 U.S. companies were engaged in some form of telecommuting on an experimental basis.[17] Despite some compelling advantages, as listed in Table 16.2, telecommuting has enough drawbacks to make it unsuitable for many employees as well as employers. Still, in line with our discussion of quality-of-work-life reforms in Chapter 11, telecommuting represents a significant accommodation to individual needs and circumstances. Although telecommuting is unlikely to become a predominant work mode, it is destined to be more than a passing fad.

Diagnosing Information Needs

Whether managers choose to rely on personal computers or not, organizational information needs to be handled in a systematic way so the right information gets to the right manager at the right time. Generally, managers need timely information to do five things: generate reports, monitor performance, forecast, plan, and make decisions.[18] If managers are to get the necessary information to perform these important tasks, their information needs must first be systematically diagnosed.

Roadblocks   Systems analysts, the title usually given to those responsible for diagnosing information needs, typically run into roadblocks when trying to find out precisely what information it is that managers need. First, in spite of expert job knowledge, many people have a difficult time articulating the exact details of their jobs. Second, people often wrongly assume that systems analysts already know a great deal about the job being studied. Third, some systems analysts naively think that they know more about a job than the job holder does. Fourth, mere mention of the word *computer* often brings up unrealistic expectations or prejudices that can hinder the identification of information needs. Fifth, people often mix opinion with fact when discussing their jobs, thus clouding the issue. Sixth, systems analysts have no way of knowing what significant details have been left out. Seventh, job holders often do not have the time or interest for a complete information diagnosis.[19]

With an eye toward overcoming these roadblocks, we shall now consider two approaches to diagnosing information needs more accurately. The first is appropriate for all employees, and the second is best for top-level managers who oversee more than one functional area. Whichever approach is used, the process necessarily starts at the top and works down, ensuring that the lower-level suppliers of information act in accordance with the needs of the higher-level users. When those at lower levels are free to determine what information their superiors see, top managers can end up getting too much of the wrong kind of information (for example, politically safe information that makes subordinates look good).

Conducting an Information Requirements Analysis

"**Information requirements analysis** refers to the act of identifying the meaningful data that a worker needs in order to perform a job or task."[20] One or more of the following investigative techniques is recommended when conducting an information requirements analysis:

- **Interview.** Interviews are the most widely used technique for uncovering an employee's information needs. Interviewing can be effective if the interviewer is skilled and the interviewee has had sufficient time to prepare. Closed-end questions requiring simple yes or no answers should be avoided.
- **Paper simulation.** An excellent way of diagnosing information needs is to create documents that simulate the output of a hypothetical information system. This relatively inexpensive diagnostic technique requires starting at the end rather than at the beginning.
- **Brainstorming.** A rapid-fire exchange of ideas in a nonjudgmental setting can be a productive way of stimulating creative thinking about one's information needs.
- **Protocol analysis.** The important details of an employee's information needs can be obtained by having the individual "think out loud" while working through an actual or simulated job. Insight into the user's underlying thought processes can be gained through protocol analysis.
- **Direct observation.** When the job being studied does not involve a great deal of mental processing (for example, clerical tasks), information requirements can be identified by directly observing the job being performed.
- **Questionnaires.** Questionnaires are appropriate when large numbers of people or geographically dispersed people need to be questioned. The quality of the findings will generally be a direct reflection of the quality of the survey instrument.[21]

Table 16.4   Critical Success Factors Vary from Situation to Situation

The critical success factors identified by the chief executive officer of a major oil company included:	The critical success factors identified by the division head of an electronics firm included:
1. Decentralization of the organization. 2. Improvement of the firm's liquidity position. 3. Improvement of the firm's relationships with the government. 4. Improvement of the firm's societal image. 5. Development of new ventures.	1. Better support for field sales personnel. 2. Improvement of customer relations. 3. Improvement of productivity. 4. Government support of research and development. 5. Development of new products. 6. Development of new technological capabilities. 7. Improvement of facilities.

SOURCE: Reprinted by permission of the *Harvard Business Review.* Adapted from exhibit in "Chief Executives Define Their Own Data Needs," by John F. Rockart (March-April 1979): 91. Copyright © 1979 by the President and Fellows of Harvard College; all rights reserved.

Situational time, talent, and cost constraints will determine which particular combination of these diagnostic techniques is appropriate.

Identifying Critical Success Factors

Information systems researchers at MIT have devised a practical method for getting top-level administrators to identify their *own* information needs. They call it the critical success factors (CSF) approach. **Critical success factors** have been defined as "the limited number of areas in which results, if they are satisfactory, will ensure successful competitive performance for the organization."[22] In other words, critical success factors are the strategic vital signs of organizational health (see Table 16.4).

Although critical success factors vary according to the situation, they generally are tied to four areas: (1) the nature and structure of the industry, (2) the organization's competitive position and geographic location, (3) environmental factors (for example, political climate, state of the economy, energy shortages), and (4) temporal factors (for example, loss of a key executive, a wildcat strike).[23] Temporal factors include temporary but very serious organizational problems. The benefits of the CSF approach are that it

- Focuses management's attention on key result areas.
- Forces management to measure important factors.
- Differentiates needed from unneeded information.
- Draws management's attention to data that are needed but are not normally collected.
- Emphasizes that information needs vary as time passes.
- Aids other functions such as planning and communicating.[24]

Advocates of the CSF approach recommend that critical success factors be collected in a series of two or three interviews with each top-level manager.[25] Because there generally is little overlap between traditional financial accounting data and the CSF data requested by top managers, CSF information fills important gaps.

Developing a Management Information System (MIS)

If managers are to carry out their control responsibilities in an effective and efficient manner, they require ready access to current information concerning what, when, and how things have happened in their spheres of influence. Managers who do not foresee, read, and react to changes in the organization's vital signs cannot do their jobs well, if at all. Management information systems have been developed to make sure the right manager gets the right information at the right time. A **management information system** (MIS) is a computer-based network that *integrates* the collection, processing, and transmission of information. "The purpose of an MIS is to raise the process of managing from the level of piecemeal spotty information, intuitive guesswork, and isolated problem solving to the level of systems insights, systems information, sophisticated data processing, and systems problem solving."[26] Practical experience over the last two decades has made it clear that management information systems are easier to conceptualize than to enact. In fact, MIS theory has been roundly criticized for being too idealistic. Accordingly, idealism has been responsible for most MIS failures because managers tend to go too far too fast. Successful MIS is not an all-or-nothing proposition; it is achieved step by step. We shall now explore key aspects of the MIS development process.

Levels of MIS   Every information system has two parts, one tangible, the other intangible.[27] The tangible portion consists of all storage and processing hardware and any physical data records. The intangible portion is made up of human beings and their mental and communicative abilities. These two parts are inextricably intertwined, and one cannot realistically be discussed without reference to the other. For example, the apparently simple act of a production manager's reading a quality control reject report and then telling a quality control inspector to loosen the specifications is actually a complex bit of information processing using both the tangible and the human components. Objective fact has been merged with subjective judgment in this situation. Management information systems can be classified into five levels of sophistication according to how much assistance the user receives from the tangible system.

1. **Storage of raw data only.** Manual filing systems can be used to give managers access to transaction data. Any processing that must be done, such as adding up a particular employee's sick days, is done by the user rather than the nonhuman part of the system.
2. **Selective data retrieval.** Data are both stored and screened in an elementary fashion by the system. For example, a manager may ask for a list of accounts that are overdue by at least thirty days. Computers are normally required for this level of sophistication and above.
3. **Elementary computation.** Stored data can be aggregated (totaled) for the user. For example, a manager can use aggregated data to compare this month's total sales with last month's.
4. **Advanced computations.** More advanced arithmetic computations can be performed on retrievable data. For example, statistical averages, ranges, medians, and standard deviations can provide insight into a set of data.
5. **Mathematical modeling.** Descriptive models such as PERT and break-even analysis (see Chapter 4) can be used to test the impact of pending decisions. They help answer management's "what if" questions. Prescriptive models, on the other hand, can be used to select a decision alternative.[28]

These data-processing capabilities enable computerized management information systems to perform clerical, information-provision, decision-support, and programmed decision-making functions[29] (see Figure 16.2). Thinking back to what was said earlier about the cost of information, cost increases significantly with each level of MIS. As long as the benefits continue to outweigh the costs, increased sophistication can be justified.

Enhancing an MIS with Data Base Management Systems

An MIS is only as good as the data that pass through it. A developing, yet still immature, approach to improving the quality and accessibility of MIS data goes by the name data base management systems. A **data base management system** (DBMS) is a computerized file system of organizational data that permits simultaneous access by many different users with differing information needs. *Sharing* and *comparing* of data are distinguishing characteristics of a DBMS. A financial manager might access the data base for accounts receivable to compare the percent of overdue accounts for the midwest and eastern sales regions. At the same time, a marketing manager down the hall could call up the same data to identify each region's ten largest customers to target a special product promotion. Of course, the data retrieval programs are structured in such a way that users cannot accidentally or purposefully corrupt the data base.

Experts have warned that a DBMS is prone to the "garbage in–garbage out" problem:

Figure 16.2 What a Management Information System Can Do for Managers

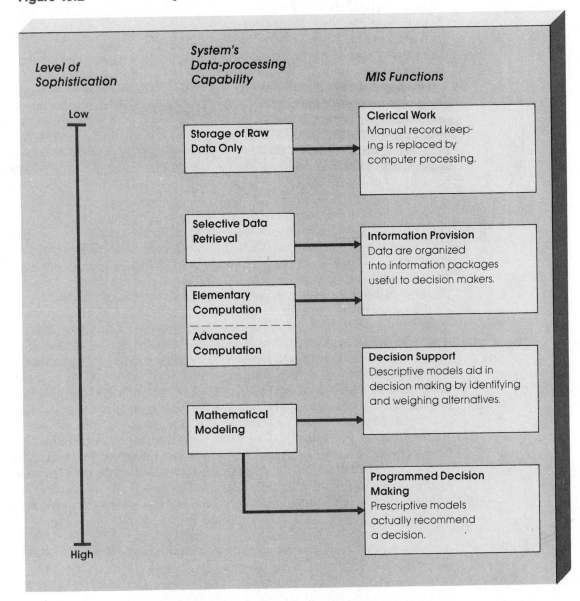

There are two distinct areas of activity in using a data base management system. These are commonly referred to as front-end and back-end data base management. The front-end activities consist of planning your data base, designing report forms, and entering data records. The back-end is the realm of the sort function: It consists of using the data you've previously stored in your data base. The back-end is the power area, but much of its power derives from how well you've done your work on the front-end.[30]

A careful diagnosis of information needs, as discussed earlier, can greatly enhance the usefulness of a DBMS.

Data base management systems will become commonplace if progress can be made in the following areas: (1) greater sophistication and standardization of DBMS software, (2) more user-friendly applications, (3) better integration of data from various organizational functions such as production, finance, and marketing, and (4) broader acceptance among managers. A DBMS can greatly enhance performance of the MIS functions listed in Figure 16.2.

Basic MIS Design

Despite variations among management information systems, they share a number of design characteristics (see Figure 16.3). First and foremost, an MIS exists to serve the decision-making manager. An MIS's ultimate effectiveness or ineffectiveness is determined by how well a particular manager's information needs are met. As illustrated in Figure 16.3, an effective MIS responds to a manager's need for information by determining if the required data are already available. If sufficient data are available in the system's data bank (or data base), they are then transformed into the type of information requested. For instance, the average age of the sales force might be calculated as a basis for projecting pending retirements.

In the event that the needed data are not in the system's data bank, then the system becomes a data-gathering device. Both auxiliary internal and external data sources are tapped if necessary. Management can gain access to a broad spectrum of general and technical information by subscribing to one or more of the many on-line data bases that are available today.[31] Newly collected, organized, and filed data are transformed into the information requested. For both existing and new information, the user has the option of having the MIS perform a decision analysis, meaning that additional analytical computations are performed to refine the resulting information.

The Developmental Process

As with all other management tools and techniques, systematic planning and execution are a fundamental part of successful MIS development. High computer hardware and software costs underscore the importance of a foresighted and rational MIS development process. Management teams that rush out and purchase a computer system and then try to figure out how to use it have clearly put the cart before the horse. Unfortunately, such has been the case time and again in recent years, especially with personal computers. Therefore the following seven-step developmental process has been recommended:

Figure 16.3   Basic MIS Design Components

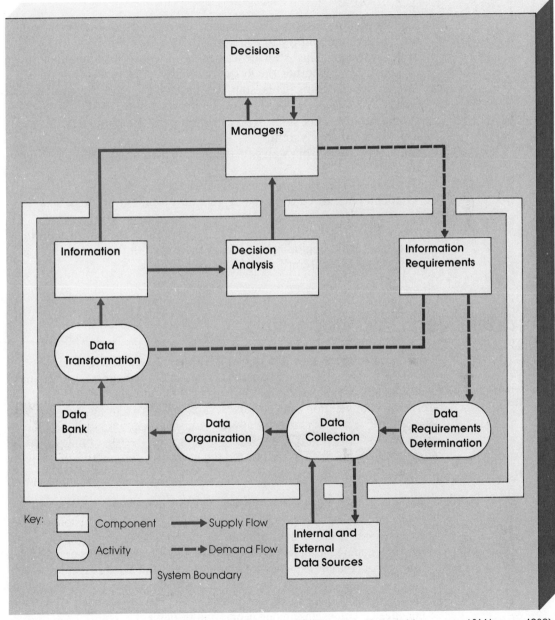

SOURCE: John C. Carter and Fred N. Silverman, "Establishing a MIS," *Journal of Systems Management* 31 (January 1980): 16. Reprinted from the *Journal of Systems Management*.

1. **System analysis.** This step documents the present system, details the system's deficiencies, and provides recommendations for improvement.
2. **Statement of objectives.** This step gives the goals (general and specific) the new system will try to accomplish.
3. **System design.** This step describes how we will accomplish those objectives and whether the system will be worth its cost.
4. **System specification.** This step details exactly how the system will work.
5. **Programming.** This step involves developing the computer programs necessary for the system.
6. **Implementation.** This step gets the new system in operation in place of the old.
7. **Evaluation.** This step analyzes how well the new system is working and what can be learned from the system development process.[32]

This developmental process has been compared to the act of painting a picture. The artist begins by sketching the rough outlines and then adds more and more detail until the picture is complete.

Computerized Data Processing

Recalling our discussion in Chapter 1, futurist Alvin Toffler believes that one of the five revolutionary sources of change for managers is occurring in what he calls the info-sphere. Toffler sees the computer as the eye of this storm of change. For our purposes, a **computer** is defined as "a data processor that can perform substantial computation, including numerous arithmetic or logic operations, without intervention by a human operator during the run."[33] Toffler has offered the following perspective of what the computer can do for us:

Because it can remember and interrelate large numbers of causal forces, the computer can help us cope with.... problems at a deeper than customary level. It can sift vast masses of data to find subtle patterns. It can help assemble "blips" into larger, more meaningful wholes. Given a set of assumptions or a model, it can trace out the consequences of alternative decisions, and do it more systematically and completely than any individual normally could. It can even suggest imaginative solutions to certain problems by identifying novel or hitherto unnoticed relationships among people and resources.

Human intelligence, imagination, and intuition will continue in the foreseeable decades to be far more important than the machine. Nevertheless, com-

Table 16.5 A Glossary of Computer Terminology for Personal Computer Users

Byte: One memory position that can usually hold one alphabetic character or two digits. Consists of eight binary digits [or bits].

Cathode ray tube (CRT): A television-like screen and keyboard used for computer input and output. Also called video display terminal or VDT [or simply the monitor].

Central processing unit (CPU): The "computer" portion of the computer system that contains the main memory, the program and data when the program is running, the logic and arithmetic circuitry, and a control unit.

Disk: A form of mass storage. [*Hard disk* units are built into or attached to the CPU; *Floppy diskettes* must be inserted into a disk drive.]

Hardware: The physical machines in a computer system.

KB: K means thousands. B is the abbreviation for "byte." 64KB, for example, refers to the size of the memory, in this case 64,000 bytes. This is relatively small as memory sizes now extend into the millions.

Megabyte (MB): 1,024,000 bytes.

Microprocessor: The "computer" portion of the microcomputer. An extremely small and low-cost component usable in many devices.

Modem (modulator/demodulator): Interface between the computer and a telephone line.

On-line: The condition in which data or information may be directly sent or received from a computer. Usually involves communications lines.

Peripheral controller: The circuit that provides the connection between the microcomputer and the peripheral device (such as a printer).

Peripheral device: Any piece of hardware in a computer system other than the CPU, e.g., printer, disk drive.

Printer: A peripheral device for printing reports.

Random access: The ability to retrieve information without regard to the sequence in which it is stored.

Real-time: Activities that take place immediately, i.e., inventory records are updated as each item is sold. There is no accumulation or batching of transactions before processing.

Software: The programs that control the operation of the computer.

SOURCE: Adapted by permission from *Business* Magazine. "Micros—Personal Computers with Power," by Ernest A. Kallman and James C. Krok, *Business*, October-December, 1982.

puters can be expected to deepen the entire culture's view of causality, heightening our understanding of the interrelatedness of things, and helping us to synthesize meaningful "wholes" out of the disconnected data whirling around us.[34]

This is a valuable perspective, from a managerial standpoint, because it emphasizes that computers will continue to be largely a decision-*aiding* tool rather than a device for actually dispensing complicated decisions. Because of the computer's predominance in today's organizational data-processing systems, we now shall examine some important considerations concerning both computer hardware and software. (See Table 16.5 for a glossary of computer terminology.)

Smaller,
Faster,
Cheaper

Experimental computers developed during the 1950s were cumbersome, unreliable, and energy inefficient. But with the development of the microprocessor (the so-called computer on a chip), today's computers are small, very fast, reliable, and highly energy efficient. Room-size hardware has shrunk to desk-top size and smaller. As computing power has skyrocketed, prices have plummeted. For instance, computing power that would have cost $15 million in 1966 became available on a quarter-inch-square microprocessor chip for $20 in 1981.[35] And things have not stopped there. In 1984 Motorola developed a 32-bit microprocessor that packs an incredible 200,000 transistors onto a silicon wafer three-eighths of an inch square. Motorola's superchip can perform 8 million tasks per second.[36] Thanks to technological leaps such as this, the price-performance ratio for computers will continue to improve. As shown by the personal computer revolution, advanced computer technology is completely reshaping the field of data processing.

From
Centralized to
Distributed
Data-
Processing
Systems

Although it is not the purpose of this chapter to probe deeply into computer technology, some background discussion of basic hardware configurations is necessary.

Centralized Data Processing   Computer data-processing hardware historically has been centralized in one location. Full-fledged departments bearing names like "data processing" or "computer services" have taken shape around very large, expensive, and sophisticated mainframe computers. These mainframe computers are segregated in costly climate-controlled facilities because of their sensitivity to heat and traffic. In this centralized arrangement, employees at work sites outside the central data-processing department enter data (for example, payments on accounts receivable) through remote "on-line" terminals (see Figure 16.4). After these data are processed on the central mainframe computer by computer specialists, statistical summaries and reports are sent back to decision-making managers.

Centralized systems employ batch and/or real-time processing. **Batch processing** means that transactions are stored up, turned into machine-readable form such as magnetic tapes, and processed all at one time. Time sheet data for hourly employees, submitted daily from remote sites, could be stored on tape and fed into the central computer every other Friday. When data files are updated immediately as each new transaction occurs, **real-time processing** is being used. Real-time centralized systems, such as those used for airline reservations, provide each remote site user with up-to-the-minute status reports that take much of the guesswork out of decision making. For example, is a seat available on a certain flight so a ticket can be sold? Real-time processing eliminates the bothersome delays associated with batch processing.

Figure 16.4 Centralized Versus Distributed Data-processing Systems

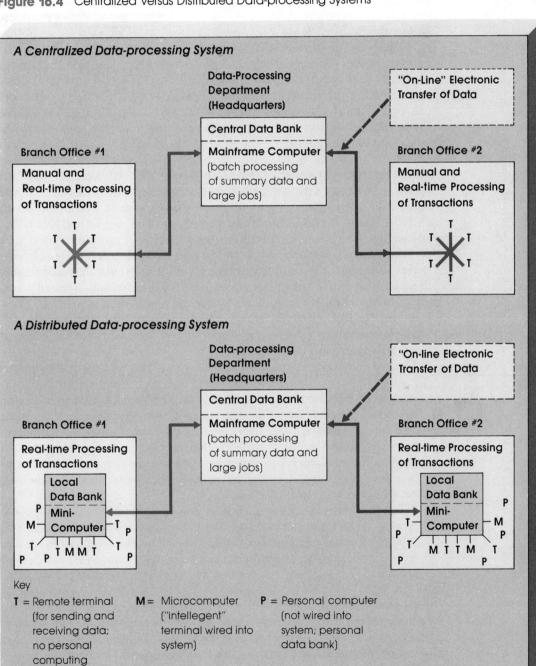

Distributed Data Processing   There has been a recent and rapidly growing trend toward more decentralized computing. **Distributed data processing** means that at least some portion of the computer logic function is performed outside a central location. Minicomputers (small, multiuser) and microcomputers (personal or desk-top) enable people outside the central computer facility to perform computing chores (see Figure 16.4). This contrasts sharply with centralized systems in which remote site personnel can only "key in" data on terminals that have no computing capability. When connected (on-line) to mainframe or minicomputers, microcomputers are called "smart" or "intelligent" terminals.

Which Approach Is Better? Lessons from the Field   Although centralized systems are giving way to distributed ones, each approach has its pros and cons. Take, for example, the contrasting experiences of Prudential Insurance Company, the largest insurance company in the world, and its smaller competitor, Travelers Corporation. Prudential is firmly committed to a centralized data-processing system. In late 1984, only 860 personal computers could be found in the insurance giant's offices. Virtually all transactions at Prudential are entered through 15,000 terminals hooked to 25 mainframe computers centralized in five regional computer centers. Travelers, on the other hand, believes in "putting power where the people are" through distributed processing. Accordingly, there are over 25,000 personal computers at Travelers.

The pros and cons of each approach have been summed up as follows:

> Prudential's mainframe orientation makes for easy access to corporate data via terminals and better ensures the data's integrity. But because of backlogs, it can take months for users to get their company's data processing professionals to tailor programs to specific applications. Managers must also rely on calculators and scratch pads for departmental budgeting and scheduling. And if mainframes or other central computers "crash," users working on terminals that are connected to the system will go down, too.
>
> Travelers' distributed approach gives individual managers quick access to computing and the ability to handle a host of applications without time-sharing delays. But a lack of coordination among the many users can lead to security problems and duplication of effort. Personal computers also have limited power and storage capacity, and they can be expensive and bothersome to maintain.[37]

This set of contrasting experiences suggests that one approach is not clearly superior to the other. Despite the fact that some have called centralized systems electronic dinosaurs, this traditional approach *does* offer one thing that distributed systems generally lack: namely, *control*. In fact, one observer has referred to the often uncoordinated influx of personal computers as "personal computer anarchy." In the final analysis, an organization's structural tradition will probably dictate the appropriateness of centralized versus distributed data-processing systems. Centralized systems will tend to work better in organizations with a tradition of centralized decision making (recall our discussion of centralization in Chapter 8). In contrast, managers who are used to wielding decentralized decision-making authority are likely to demand personal computers to enhance their autonomy.

Harnessing the Power of Personal Computers As was indicated in Table 16.2, personal computers are a mixed blessing. Proponents view them as the needed key to providing managers with more timely and relevant information. Critics maintain that giving untrained managers personal computers is like giving a child a hammer. Just as a child with a hammer soon discovers that *everything* needs hammering, novice computer users have a tendency to get carried away with inappropriate applications. While pointing out that U.S. businesses could be using as many as 13 million personal computers by 1990, *Business Week* recently observed:

> The proliferation of personal computers in the workplace led to an explosion in the use of VisiCalc, Lotus 1–2–3, and other electronic spreadsheets, and now managers can bang out models and forecasts simply and quickly. And as personal computer sales rise, the potential for error by novice operators will probably go right up with them.[38]

Adding to the problem of novice users are the problems of costly redundancy and inadequate security. According to Sperry Corporation's director of information:

> The potential for redundancy [storage and use of identical data in more than one place] is very great with end-user computing. And there is also the security question—the potential for accidental or malicious changing of data. End-user computing is the way things are definitely going, but we have to give more thought to how we are going to manage it.[39]

This section explores ways to overcome the three principal reasons why managers have yet to harness the full power of personal computers: novice users, redundancy, and security.

Computer Literacy Training Having a personal computer on one's desk and being able to use it skillfully and appropriately are two very different things. Managers who gain on-the-job access to a personal computer simply to boost their status and give them something trendy to talk about at parties can wreak havoc with organizational information resources. Novices need systematic computer literacy training to get them headed in a productive direction. Additionally, proper training can neutralize fear of computers.

Computer literacy training is a lot like a driver training course. Novice drivers are taught to operate a car, not how to build cars and tune engines. Similarly, computer literacy training teaches novices how to operate personal computers, not program and repair them. Consider the stated objectives of Allied Corporation's successful computer literacy training program:

> At the end of the program we want people to be able to: (1) distinguish between micro, mini and mainframe computers; (2) describe how a microcomputer could be applied to their own department; (3) use a set of questions and criteria to decide whether a microcomputer is appropriate for their department; and (4) use two popular software packages.[40]

This program is successful because it gives managers *hands-on* experience relative to their own job.

Some computer specialists criticize computer literacy training for being shallow. They recommend more comprehensive training in computer hardware and programming so managers can better understand the workings and potential of the organization's MIS. But computer literacy trainers respond by saying that too many managers are intimidated by arcane programming languages. They recommend "user-friendly" hardware, software, and training.

Coordinating and Integrating Personal Computers   Personal computer anarchy can be halted or prevented altogether by systematically managing the influx of personal computers into the organization. Many organizations have had problems with "back-door" personal computers, managers bringing their own machines to work. A plan such as the one displayed in Table 16.6 is required as an important first step. The in-house computer store discussed in this sample plan is a particularly promising idea for two reasons. First, it takes advantage of quantity discounts, thus saving thousands or even millions of dollars, depending upon the size of the organization's commitment to personal computers. Second, proper compatibility of hardware and software can be achieved through a coordinated purchasing effort.

Another promising way to coordinate and integrate the use of personal computers is to create a personal computing center (PCC). Grumman Corporation, an aerospace firm, has a successful PCC that effectively combines the intent of the microcomputer-management plan in Table 16.6 and computer literacy training. Here is how Grumman's PCC works:

Table 16.6 A Sample Microcomputer Management Plan

1. Select a microcomputer product for the organization.
2. Start a pilot test project using the selected microcomputer product. Involve about ten key personnel and a minioffice as testers and evaluators.
3. Develop a standard system configuration for installation organizationwide. Base the sample configuration upon the equipment tests performed in the pilot study.
4. Compile a standard program library for all organizationwide systems. This program library will expand as more programs are tested and accepted.
5. Support organizational units purchasing the standard hardware system configuration and the standard software library through an in-house computer store operated by employees. The store employees will assist with installation of the personal computers, provide training on the software packages, and answer user questions as required. This will permit negotiating the bulk purchases for the computers and the software.
6. Allow employees desiring to purchase computers for their personal use to buy them through the internal computer store at cost.

SOURCE: P. D. Moulton, "The Need for a Microcomputer-Management Plan," *SAM Advanced Management Journal* 49 (Spring 1984): 35.

First, it evaluates the latest equipment on the market. When the PCC has decided what systems are best for Grumman, the equipment is placed on display. Hardware and software demonstrations are conducted for employees who desire to implement or update their systems.

Interested employees can then sign up for a "hands-on" training program lasting anywhere from one hour to an entire day. The PCC offers whatever guidance and assistance is necessary; employees do not have to be computer-literate. They are encouraged to bring sample work with them so they can test it on a PC and determine whether a computer is the answer to their needs.[41]

Corporate software libraries also are coming into use. The alternative to this type of coordination is a leaky, redundant, and wastefully expensive distributed information system.

Reducing Personal Computer Security Risks Widely publicized accounts about computer "hackers" gaining illegal access to corporate, school, and government computer files and the movie *War Games* have made us more aware of the problem of computer security. At stake for the business community are data banks of incalculable value, trade secrets, and employee and customer privacy. The rapid spread of personal computers has magnified the problem of computer security. According to a leading computer expert, "The back-door personal computers which appeared on middle managements' desks without MIS blessing are unwittingly exposing the business community to potential loss of data and various other disasters, including corporate sabotage."[42] It would require a separate chapter to fully explore this complex topic. Consequently, we will settle for outlining the problem at this point.

There are three major types of personal computer security risks[43] that deserve management's careful attention.

- **Computer hardware security.** This covers everything from user hazards (such as spilling a soft drink onto the keyboard, damaging diskettes, or burning out the computer's circuits with a spark of static electricity) to physical theft/damage. User tidiness policies need to be passed along during training. Anti-static mats or rugs and sophisticated locking devices are readily available today.
- **Information security.** By controlling access to personal computers, stored information (on disks), applications software, and supporting documentation, management can maintain high-quality information resources. Software, back-up disk, and documentation libraries with controlled access can help reduce information security risks.
- **Network security.** The integrity of networked personal computer systems can be ensured by using impossible-to-guess passwords or coding, documenting user identification, and limiting and monitoring telephone access.

A respected computer consultant has summed up the security issue by saying: "responsibility must reside with the user under policies which will be self-enforced. Central control may work now; it won't when the number of units in existence is so large it may be impossible even to identify all of them."[44] Security policies and risks deserve high-priority attention in computer training programs.

Managerial Work-stations: Toward the "Paperless" Office

Business periodicals have bombarded their readers in recent years with countless stories of the impending *office automation* revolution. Some observers have gone so far as to predict paperless offices in which virtually all information will be handled electronically. (See Table 16.7 for a realistic description of the office of the future.) Such a revolution is eagerly awaited by management for two reasons. First, as a labor-intensive activity, the cost of processing business correspondence has climbed sharply. A single business letter that cost $1 to produce in 1940 now costs $15 to produce. Second, office productivity rose only 4 percent between 1960 and 1981, whereas factory productivity climbed 80 percent over the same period. This has put a considerable drag on the U.S. economy, considering that over half the labor force works in offices.[45] At the heart of the office of the future are managerial work-stations.

Table 16.7   A Look into the Office of the Future (1990s)

- **Human factors/ergonomics.** Human factors and ergonomic considerations will achieve ever-increasing importance in future environmental design. Awareness of their importance to office worker productivity will continue to escalate, and the environment will be restructured following human factors/ergonomic design principles.
- **Information.** Previously scattered information will be electronically consolidated, thereby reducing the clutter of the workstation. Information will be more accessible to all. Paper will not entirely disappear, however.
- **Technology.** Miniaturization of technology will continue. The bulky cathode ray tube (CRT) will be replaced by flat-panel displays offering compactness, increased mobility, and the capability of being built into the workstation. Advances in display support electronics will yield improved resolution, color, split screen capabilities, and three-dimensional perspectives. Larger displays will also be available, permitting the presentation of more information at one time.

   The typewriter-type keyboard will remain a primary human-computer interface mechanism, but touch panel displays and pointers such as the mouse and track balls (track balls are the spheres connected to terminals that are commonly used to move the cursor in computer graphics and many types of computer games) will have widespread use. Voice recognition and synthesis will be viable in a variety of applications.
- **Workstations.** Tomorrow's workstation will be smaller. Electronic information consolidation will eliminate the need for large areas to store information on paper and the materials needed for paper handling. At the same time, however, greater visual and auditory privacy will be needed. Noise created by equipment and human-voice/computer interaction will make for severe acoustical problems. Display terminals and other technologies will be incorporated within the workstation itself. The surface of the desk and workstation walls will become control and viewing surfaces. The chair may also contain fingertip controls. The office workstation and the airplane cockpit will bear some resemblance to one another.

   Comfort in working will be achieved through intelligent chairs and desks. Desk heights and angles will be modified through the touch of a button. Desired configurations will be "remembered" by the desk's electronics and changed according to the occupant's needs. The chair will configure itself to its occupant through analysis of weight distribution.
- **The office.** Office buildings as we know them will continue to operate. However, a reduction in paper and paper filing requirements and more people working at home or in satellite offices will diminish space requirements. Offices and conference rooms will also still exist, as electronic meetings are poor substitutes for a variety of communications requiring interpersonal interaction. These will be best addressed by people facing people.

   Tomorrow's office will provide a computer utility akin to that provided by the electric and telephone companies. A variety of computing services will be available at the touch of a switch.

SOURCE: Excerpted from Wilbert O. Galitz, "What the Office of the 1990s Will Be Like," *Office Administration and Automation,* © October, 1984 by Geyer-McAllister Publications, Inc., New York.

Beyond Personal Computers   **Managerial work-stations** are multifunction, on-line computer terminals connected to an organizationwide information network. They have a broader range of capabilities than personal computers alone, although personal computers can be made into managerial work-stations by wiring them into a distributed data-processing system. Among the functions of a managerial work-station are word processing,

"You know what I miss? Paper airplanes."
SOURCE: © Punch/Rothco.

electronic mail, electronic calendars, DBMS analysis and report retrieval, graphic display, dictation, and data processing.

As a sign of things to come, consider the following situation:

> Atlantic Richfield Co. of Los Angeles, the nation's eleventh largest concern, installed an elaborate $300,000 system of Xerox-designed word processors linked to a central memory bank. The system enables professionals in the corporate systems department to type and send memos among themselves as well as prepare their own reports and even store and retrieve research. Not only has this saved time and effort by file clerks and administrative assistants, but the entire department of 95 now functions smoothly with only five secretaries, a 1-to-19 ratio that compares with a 1-to-5 relationship throughout the rest of the corporate offices.[46]

Some Obstacles   Even though personal computers have seemingly taken the workplace by storm, the vast majority of managers does not yet work at a computer terminal. At this time, one can only speculate about how quickly managers will adapt to working at electronic work-stations rather than relying on clerical support for their routine information-processing needs. One observer foresees four obstacles to managerial work-stations:

- **Management resistance to new methods.** . . . The verbal communications and paper media methods may have their shortcomings, but managers may be unwilling to give them up for strange, new, computerized systems.
- **Overselling.** What has happened in the past is likely to be repeated here. Benefits will be promised that do not materialize (or at least not during the "probationary" period). The systems will turn out to be more complex to operate than expected. And some "overlooked" problems will turn out to be real challenges—such as security of the managers' information files.
- **Complex user procedures.** There are many characteristics of today's interactive computer systems that do not endear them to the casual user (which most managers are likely to be). These include log-in procedures, not only for the operating system but also perhaps for the communication network and various services. . . .
- **"Unfriendly" hardware.** The most typical terminals have typewriter-like keyboards. And many managers simply do not want to type, for a variety of reasons. Other terminals offer function keys, but these may perplex the casual user. Terminals must be "friendly" if they are to be widely used by managers.[47]

Largely because of these obstacles, the relatively "paperless" office of the future will become reality through a slow evolution rather than an overnight revolution.

The Human Side of MIS

All things considered, people are the key to MIS success. In support of this contention, a study of 122 of the 1000 largest firms in the United States found that ". . . user attitude is the most important factor affecting MIS development."[48] Even the best-designed MIS can be brought to its knees by overt and covert user resistance. Enthusiastic support, on the other hand, can greatly enhance an MIS's development and use. Managers who understand why people resist an MIS are in a better position to take preventive steps than are their counterparts who ignore the human part of the MIS equation.

The Impact of MIS on Managerial Behavior

Organizational behaviorist Chris Argyris sees a potential for conflict between MIS rationality and natural human emotions. Argyris points out that management information systems go beyond traditional attempts to make organizations more rationally effective and efficient. They do so because they affect not only formal and official dealings but also informal and unofficial interaction. For example, suppose a manager no longer gets to announce the weekly cost figures at the departmental meetings because the daily figures are now disseminated by the computerized information system. That manager may perceive a loss in personal status or influence and consequently may resist the new system. Argyris believes that overly rational management information systems will trigger stress and emotional problems:

> The managers may find themselves (1) experiencing increasing amounts of psychological failure yet system success and therefore more double binds; (2) being required to reduce interdepartmental warfare and intradepartmental politics; and (3) finding that the concept of managerial success changes its base from one of power, ambiguity, and self-fulfilling prophecy to valid information, explicitness, and technical competence.[49]

In short, Argyris is afraid that managers will be forced into a psychological corner by advanced management information systems. If such is the case, MIS will be strongly resisted.

Neutralizing Resistance to MIS

Resistance to MIS, according to two scholars, will vary from level to level in the organization,[50] as will the type of resistance. Three forms of resistance are aggression, projection, and avoidance. Aggression involves both physical and nonphysical attacks on the system. One individual may engage in outright sabotage, whereas another may resort to critical comments. Those who rely on projection will often blame, rightly or wrongly, all sorts of problems on computers and the MIS. Avoidance, as the term implies, is ignoring the system. As indicated in Table 16.8, different patterns of dysfunctional behavior can be expected from operating personnel, operating management, and top management. Technical staff are not seen as a problem area because they are the ones responsible for creating and implementing the system; hence they understand it the most and fear it the least.

Middle and lower-level managers are seen as the largest pocket of potential resistance. Their resistance may appear in different ways. With the influx of personal computers, resistance may take the form of using one's own personal computer and self-generated data bases in lieu of or in defiance of the organization's MIS. **Technostress,** "a condition resulting

Table 16.8   Different Dysfunctional Reactions to MIS

Organizational Subgroup	Relation to MIS	Probable Dysfunctional Behavior
Operating personnel		
Nonclerical	Provide system inputs	Aggression
Clerical	Particularly affected by clerical systems; job eliminated, job patterns changed	Projection
Operating management (middle management and first-line supervisors)	Controlled from above by information systems; job content modified by information-decision systems and programmed systems	Aggression, avoidance, and projection
Technical staff	Systems designers and agents of systems change	None
Top management	Generally unaffected and unconcerned with systems	Avoidance

SOURCE: G. W. Dickson and John K. Simmons, "The Behavioral Side of MIS," *Business Horizons* 13 (August 1970): 63. Copyright, 1970 by the Foundation for the School of Business at Indiana University. Reprinted by permission.

from the inability of an individual or organization to adapt to the introduction and operation of new technology,"[51] also may breed resistance to computerized systems. This is unfortunate because today's management information systems predominantly affect middle and lower-level management.

There are several constructive steps that management can take to neutralize resistance to MIS and avoid technostress:

- From the very beginning, obtain top management's support of and commitment to the MIS.
- Develop and implement the MIS with the full participation of all affected parties.
- Clearly state the MIS's purpose, characteristics, and scope. This will center discussion on facts instead of fiction.
- Humanize the information system by ensuring that users will feel that they are making a worthwhile contribution to the organization. People usually resent the idea of being controlled by machines.
- Emphasize new challenges when introducing the system.
- Update the performance evaluation and reward system so that the effective use of the MIS is encouraged rather than discouraged.
- Fit the system to the users rather than vice versa.[52]

If they are taken early in the developmental process, these steps can greatly increase the odds of the MIS's success.

Summary

Isolated and disorganized data are meaningless because they do not help us achieve some purpose. Accordingly, information is data organized and interpreted within a relevant frame of reference that enhances effective decision making. Information is unlike familiar physical resources because it is expandable, diffusive, and shareable. Some argue that information has no intrinsic value because its value is determined in the eye of the beholder. But, since information is a valuable resource, it must cost something. Three factors that determine the cost of information within organizations are accuracy, timeliness, and reporting interval. Several misconceptions about information have proved to be troublesome today because they foster unrealistic expectations. Information overload appears to be a self-perpetuating problem that can erode decision quality. Better information, not more information, is needed. Three new information technologies that are significantly reshaping the way organizational information is handled are end-user computing (personal computers), teleconferencing, and tele-commuting. Each has its own unique set of promises and problems.

A number of significant roadblocks can hamper the diagnosis of information needs. Interviews, paper simulations, brainstorming sessions, protocol analysis, direct observation, and questionnaires can be used separately or in combination when conducting an information requirements analysis. Researchers at MIT recommend that top-level managers identify their own critical success factors (CSFs) to ensure that they receive the information they need.

A management information system (MIS) is a computer-based network that integrates the collection, processing, and transmission of information. An MIS can assist the decision maker by storing raw data, selectively retrieving data, and performing computations and mathematical modeling. Four functions of management information systems are clerical, information-providing, decision-support, and programmed decision making. A data base management system (DBMS) can enhance an MIS by allowing users to share and compare vital organizational data as the need arises. An adequately designed MIS should get the right information to the right manager at the right time. Seven steps in the MIS development process are system analysis, objectives, system design, system specification, programming, implementation, and evaluation.

Computers, which have become smaller, more reliable, and less expensive in recent years, are a valuable information management tool. Traditional centralized computers are being replaced by distributed data-processing systems whose minicomputers and microcomputers share the computing chores. On-line, real-time systems, such as the kind used for airline reservations, permit managers to deal with up-to-the-minute information when making decisions. Managers are challenged to harness the power of the recent influx of personal (or micro) computers. Three responses to this challenge are computer literacy training with emphasis on hands-on experience, the systematic coordination and integration of personal computers, and containment of hardware, information, and network security risks. The "paperless" office of the future will eventually take shape around managerial work-stations, distributed on-line computer terminals capable of performing several communication and data-processing chores. "Friendly" work-stations promise to overcome managerial resistance.

Research indicates that the users' attitudes are the most important factors affecting MIS development. Chris Argyris sees an inherent conflict between the extreme rationality of management information systems and human emotions. Resistance to MIS may take the form of aggression, projection, or avoidance. Different groups in the organization typically exhibit different patterns of resistance, with middle and lower-level managers being the most resistant. The support of top management, full participation by affected parties, and a user orientation can help neutralize resistance to management information systems.

Terms to Understand

Information
Teleconferencing
Telecommuting
Information requirements analysis
Critical success factors (CSF)
Management information system
  (MIS)
Data base management system
  (DBMS)

Computer
Batch processing
Real-time processing
Distributed data processing
Managerial work-stations
Technostress

Questions for Discussion

1. What keeps much of the so-called information that you are exposed to daily from qualifying as true information?
2. Do you agree with the notion that the value of information is determined in the eye of the beholder? Provide your own reasons.
3. How do you usually respond when information overload becomes a problem?
4. What sort of experience have you had with end-user computing (per-

sonal computers)? Summarize the positive and negative aspects of this experience.

5. What critical success factors can you formulate for your present degree-seeking program (or job)?

6. How does a management information system (MIS) help the decision maker?

7. Is distributed data-processing superior to a centralized system? Explain your rationale.

8. Why is hands-on experience so important in computer literacy training?

9. What relationship does Argyris see between management information systems and human emotions?

10. Why do you suppose middle and lower-level managers tend to resist MIS more than any other group in an organization? What is the best way to overcome this resistance? (*Tip:* Refer back to Chapter 14.)

Back to the Opening Case

Now that you have read Chapter 16, you should be able to answer the following questions about the Hercules case:

1. Why might some managers at Hercules resist using the videoconferencing facilities? If you were an MIS consultant, what counter-arguments would you use?

2. How have the new information technologies at Hercules affected the structure of the organization? What are the positive and negative impacts?

3. What, in your estimation, is the primary reason for the success of Hercules's office automation program?

4. Why would "back-door" personal computers, those brought to work without the company's authorization, be a threat to Hercules's management information system?

Closing Case 16.2

Gould's Electronic Board Room

Executives in the computer age have an unprecedented amount of data at their fingertips. Unfortunately, much of it is useless for strategic decision making and control purposes because of a lopsided emphasis on more and more rather than better and better information. Gould Inc., a diversified producer of batteries and electronic components based in a Chicago suburb, launched an innovative program in the mid-1970s to provide its executives with better and more timely information. The centerpiece of this space-age program was a $300,000 electronic network that linked a $4 \times 5\frac{1}{2}$-foot screen in the firm's board room and video terminals in each senior manager's office to the company's central computer. Before installing the new information system, Gould executives controlled the firm largely on the basis of monthly reports of such things as sales, payables, and receivables. Under the new computerized system, up-to-the-minute summaries of key performance variables flashed on the video screens in full color, all at the touch of a button. Science fiction seemingly became reality as Gould's strategists mulled over "hot" information in their electronic board room.

Just Dial "Sex"

William T. Ylvisaker, Gould's chairman and chief executive officer, was the driving force behind the new information system. His background in engineering, securities analysis, and banking served him well when he and company systems experts tackled the problem of how to isolate key trends and fluctuations for the firm's executives. Dedicated to the idea of management by exception, Ylvisaker helped design a computer program that flagged all key performance measures that varied more than 10 percent from budget. Additionally, the new system also drew management's attention to any variables that were off budget for two or more months in a row and variables that moved in an unfavorable direction for three months running. All told, about 75 key indicators of company, division, and product line performance could be called up on the computer-linked video screens. Each indicator had a three-letter code that could be punched on a twelve-button box similar to a push-button telephone. By dialing "sex," Ylvisaker and his colleagues could get the latest sales figures on the board room and remote video screens. Similarly, balance sheet data could be called up by pushing "gin," and "mud" got the latest inventory figures.

Bugs and Benefits

As with any new and complex system, Gould's video information system had its share of bugs. For example, experience proved that a straightforward display of trend lines indicating actual versus planned performance was more effective than a complex, multicolor display with green lines indicating good performance, red lines indicating bad performance, orange lines indicating forecasts, and blue lines indicating budgeted figures. On the positive side, executives and board members liked the way they could call up information when interest was high. In the past, discussion often had to be tabled while needed information was gathered. When it finally arrived, attention had turned to more pressing matters.

For Discussion

1. Could Gould's computerized information system be plagued by any of the common misconceptions about information? Explain.
2. Why is the twelve-button box (and system of three-letter codes) probably a better arrangement than the usual typewriterlike video terminal?
3. Why would middle managers possibly resist the new system, even though it is not intended for their use?

References

Opening Quotation: Edward Cornish, "The Coming of an Information Society," *The Futurist* 15 (April 1981): 17.

Opening Case: "Beefing Up on Electronics Makes Hercules Leaner," *Business Week* No. 2863 (October 8, 1984): 125.

Closing Case: For additional information on Gould, see "Corporate 'War Rooms' Plug into the Computer," *Business Week* No. 2446 (August 23, 1976): 65–67; "The Exodus at the Top That Plagues Gould," *Business Week* No. 2642 (June 23, 1980): 30–31; "Bill Ylvisaker Bets His Company on Electronics," *Business Week* No. 2712 (November 2, 1981): 86–92; and Steven Anreder, "Displaying Its Old Spark: A Streamlined Gould Appears Poised for Resumption of Growth," *Barron's* 61 (November 9, 1981): 55–56.

1. John C. Carter and Fred N. Silverman, "Establishing a MIS," *Journal of Systems Management* 31 (January 1980): 15.
2. See James C. Wetherbe, *Systems Analysis for Computer-based Information Systems* (St. Paul: West, 1979), p. 36.
3. John J. Connell, "The Fallacy of Information Resource Management," *Infosystems* 28 (May 1981): 78.
4. Harlan Cleveland, "King Canute and the Information Resource," *Technology Review* 87 (January 1984): 12. (Emphasis added.)
5. Connell, "The Fallacy of Information Resource Management," pp. 81–82.
6. See Wetherbe, *Systems Analysis for Computer-based Information Systems,* pp. 37–39.
7. Adapted from more extensive discussion in Wetherbe, *Systems Analysis for Computer-based Information Systems,* pp. 42–43.
8. See Charles A. O'Reilly, III, "Individuals and Information Overload in Organ-

izations: Is More Necessarily Better?" *Academy of Management Journal* 23 (December 1980): 684–696.

9. Peter Nulty, "How Personal Computers Change Managers' Lives," *Fortune* 110 (September 3, 1984): 38.

10. "How Computers Remake the Manager's Job," *Business Week* No. 2787 (April 25, 1983): 69.

11. Nulty, "How Personal Computers Change Managers' Lives," pp. 44, 48.

12. Robert Johansen and Christine Bullen, "What to Expect from Teleconferencing," *Harvard Business Review* 62 (March-April 1984): 164.

13. Ibid.

14. "Videoconferencing: No Longer Just a Sideshow," *Business Week* No. 2868 (November 12, 1984): 117. Also see David Green and Kathleen J. Hansell, "Videoconferencing," *Business Horizons* 27 (November-December 1984): 57–61.

15. "Videoconferencing: No Longer Just a Sideshow," p. 116.

16. Dorothy Kroll, "Telecommuting: A Revealing Peek Inside Some of Industry's First Electronic Cottages," *Management Review* 73 (November 1984): 18.

17. "It's Rush Hour for 'Telecommuting,' " *Business Week* No. 2825 (January 23, 1984): 99, 102.

18. See Carter and Silverman, "Establishing a MIS," pp. 17–18.

19. Based on discussion in Albert L. Lederer, "Information Requirements Analysis," *Journal of Systems Management* 32 (December 1981): 15–19.

20. Ibid., p. 15. (Emphasis added)

21. Adapted from a longer list in Lederer, "Information Requirements Analysis."

22. John F. Rockart, "Chief Executives Define Their Own Data Needs," *Harvard Business Review* 57 (March-April 1979): 85.

23. Adapted from Rockart, "Chief Executives Define Their Own Data Needs," pp. 86–87.

24. Adapted from Rockart, "Chief Executives Define Their Own Data Needs," p. 88.

25. Instructive updates on the CSF technique may be found in "As Information Proliferates, So Does Use of CSF Technique," *Management Review* 73 (August 1984): 4–5 and Roger Dickinson, Charles Ferguson, and Sumit Sircar, "Setting Priorities with CSFs," *Business* 35 (April-June 1985): 44–47.

26. Robert G. Murdick and Joel E. Ross, *Introduction to Management Information Systems* (Englewood Cliffs, N.J.: Prentice-Hall, 1977), p. 8.

27. See R. Clifton "Dick" Young, "A Strategic Overview of Business Information Systems," *Managerial Planning* 29 (March-April 1981): 28–37.

28. Adapted from Carter and Silverman, "Establishing a MIS," pp. 20–21.

29. This list of MIS functions comes from G. W. Dickson and John K. Simmons, "The Behavioral Side of MIS," *Business Horizons* 13 (August 1970): 59–71.

30. Charles A. Miller, "The Best Sorts for Data Bases," *Personal Computing* 8 (September 1984): 130. Another good overview of DBMSs may be found in Jan Snyders, "Let's Talk DBMS," *Infosystems* 31 (December 1984): 36–44.

31. See Daniel Seligman, "Life Will Be Different When We're All On-Line," *Fortune* 111 (February 4, 1985): 68–72.

32. John R. Page and H. Paul Hooper, "Basics of Information Systems Development," *Journal of Systems Management* 30 (August 1979): 12.

33. William S. Davis, *Information Processing Systems: An Introduction to Modern, Computer-based Information Systems* (Reading, Mass.: Addison-Wesley, 1978), p. 428.

34. Alvin Toffler, *The Third Wave* (New York: Bantam, 1980), pp. 174–175.

35. See W. David Gardner and Joseph Kelly, "Technology: A Price/Performance Game," *Dun's Review* 118 (August 1981): 66–68.

36. See David E. Sanger, "The Great War Over Superchips," *The New York Times* 133 (September 9, 1984): F-1, F-27.

37. "Managing Information: Two Insurance Giants Forge Divergent Paths," *Business Week* No. 2863 (October 8, 1984): 121.

38. "How Personal Computers Can Trip Up Executives," *Business Week* No. 2861 (September 24, 1984): 94.

39. William Pat Patterson, "Corporations in Crisis: Coming to Grips with the Information Age," *Industry Week* 220 (March 5, 1984): 60, 62.

40. Dan McElwreath, "Computer Literacy Training," *Personnel Administrator* 29 (October 1984): 39. Also see Eric Vogt, "PC Education: Which Road to Take?" *Personnel Administrator* 30 (February 1985): 59–63.

41. "Grumman's Personal Computing Center Gives 'Personal' Service to Employees," *Management Review* 73 (November 1984): 42.

42. "Micros Vulnerable to Data Loss," *Data Management* 22 (July 1984): 39.

43. For a complete discussion of personal computer security, see Peter J. Haigh, "Assuring Security with Distributed Micros," *Small Systems World* 12 (July 1984): 40–44.

44. Ibid., p. 41.

45. Data adapted from Marty Robertson Seaward, "Awakening to Office Automation," *Management World* 12 (May 1983): 26–29. For additional information on office automation, see Zane Quible and Jane N. Hammer, "Office Automation's Impact on Personnel," *Personnel Administrator* 29 (September 1984): 25–32; Linda L. Willenborg and Carl H. Poedtke, Jr., "Survey Finds That Office Automation Is Different in Large and Small Firms," *Small Systems World* 12 (December 1984): 18–20, 58.

46. Christopher Byron, "Fighting the Paper Chase," *Time* 118 (November 23, 1981): 66.

47. Richard G. Canning, "What Information Do Managers Need?" *EDP Analyzer* 17 (June 1979): 11–12. For interesting reading on "friendly" computers, see Lee Smith, "Computers for Klutzes," *Fortune* 104 (November 2, 1981): 125–131. An excellent discussion of how and why executive computer terminals may be resisted may be found in "How to Conquer Fear of Computers," *Business Week* No. 2732 (March 29, 1982): 176–178.

48. Michael J. Cerullo, "Information Systems Success Factors," *Journal of Systems Management* 31 (December 1980): 11.

49. Chris Argyris, "Management Information Systems: The Challenge to Rationality and Emotionality," *Management Science* 17 (February 1971): B-281.

50. See Dickson and Simmons, "The Behavioral Side of MIS," pp. 61–63.

51. Craig Brod, "Managing Technostress: Optimizing the Use of Computer Technology," *Personnel Journal* 61 (October 1982): 754 and Craig Brod, "How to Deal with 'Technostress,' " *Office Administration and Automation* 45 (August 1984): 28, 30, 46–47.

52. This list is adapted from Dickson and Simmons, "The Behavioral Side of MIS," pp. 67–71.

Chapter 17

Operations Management

Fortunately, quality and productivity are two sides of the same coin. Everything you do for quality improves your productivity.
Lee Iacocca

Chapter Objectives

When you finish studying this chapter, you should be able to

- Define the term *operations management,* explain what the term *product* means, and discuss what American operations managers have learned from the Japanese.
- Identify and discuss three characteristics of the "factory of the future."
- Explain why product design requires open-system thinking.
- Identify and briefly describe the six criteria of vendor selection.
- Outline the arguments for and against small inventories and briefly explain how Toyota's *kanban* system minimizes work-in-process inventories.
- Differentiate between product and process work flow layouts.
- Describe the nature of feedforward quality control and discuss how quality control circles can enhance product quality.

Opening Case 17.1

How GM's Saturn Could Run Rings Around Old-style Carmakers*

Nowhere was the impact of the assembly line as profound as in the manufacture of automobiles. For nearly a century, those creeping conveyor belts that Henry Ford borrowed from the meatpacking industry have symbolized Detroit. But that technology may be reaching the end of the

*Reprinted from the January 28, 1985 issue of *Business Week* by special permission, © 1985 by McGraw-Hill, Inc.

road. Just as Ford Motor Co.'s assembly line became the mainstay of U.S. industry, General Motors Corp.'s new Saturn Corp. subsidiary may pave the way for the elusive "factory of the future."

GM's Saturn subsidiary is a $5 billion bid to do nothing short of revolutionizing automobile manufacturing. The details are still being ironed out, but GM is trying to pull together the most advanced manufacturing technology possible. By replacing the assembly line with a fully computerized production system that extends from the dealer to the factory floor, GM is betting that it can close the estimated $2,000-per-unit gap between its production costs and those of its Japanese competitors.

'Paperless' Plants

"It's an exciting approach that transcends just labor costs," says John H. Hammond Jr., director of automotive services at Data Resources Inc. "They can wipe out all of the inertia of the U.S. auto industry with one stroke."

Saturn will change nearly every aspect of auto-making operations. "It really severed all connections to the existing corporate culture," says David E. Cole, a University of Michigan professor who heads the school's automotive transportation program. GM Chairman Roger B. Smith wants his new subsidiary to have its own labor contracts with the United Auto Workers. But most significant, Saturn will tie together GM's collection of advanced technology in robots, machine vision, and computers, which the company has assembled over the past few years. A big part of that integration job will be done by Electronic Data Systems Corp. (EDS), the Texas computer services company that GM acquired for $2.5 billion last year.

Saturn's goal is to drive down costs on all fronts. Direct labor for major power-train components, stamping, and final assembly will be cut to as low as 21 hours per car, down from 55 hours today and nearly 80 hours just five years ago. "Anything in the 25 to 30 hours-per-car range is leading-edge performance in the auto industry today," says Thomas G. Gunn, an Arthur D. Little Inc. vice president who manages the company's computer-integrated manufacturing section.

GM's EDS has also been directed to make Saturn as nearly "paperless" as possible—minimizing nonproduction staffs and cutting indirect labor costs. The goal is to reduce indirect labor to 30% of the total man-hours needed to build an automobile, considerably less than the 40% average for durable-goods manufacturing.

EDS faces a monumental software engineering task in trying to forge Saturn into what will be the most highly computerized system in basic manufacturing. Computer hardware and software are expected to make up 40% of Saturn's total cost.

GM, which has long been frustrated in trying to get its myriad computer systems to communicate, has already taken a leadership position in developing the procedures that will enable all of its computers to exchange data. EDS is building a network that will hook together computers working in such diverse areas as design, engineering, and purchasing—even hooking up with individual dealers. "We envision all these links going out to engineering offices, so if a process isn't working right, you can link right to the engineer who designed it," says W. John Eichler, program director for plant network systems on GM's advanced product and manufacturing engineering staff.

'Just in Time'

Saturn's major departure from traditional auto making will be in bringing component production and assembly together on one site. To cut down on transportation and warehousing costs, the Saturn complex will include at least a half-dozen component manufacturing plants and an assembly plant. This setup will make it possible to create a fully integrated line that could, for example, cast engine blocks, machine them, and assemble the engine.

Such integration will enable Saturn to break new ground in so-called just-in-time parts production, where one day's requirement is delivered directly to the factory floor rather than produced in large quantities for inventory. Observers expect that parts suppliers—some of whom may even set up plants within the Saturn complex—will be linked directly to the central computer to keep closer tabs on production. And to make it possible to make faster design changes, many parts will be produced on machines that can quickly switch from one type of component to another. Parts will also be tested automatically and moved to assembly sites by automatic carts or conveyors as needed.

Robot Revolution

Instead of putting together a car piece-by-piece on a traditional moving assembly line, separate teams of workers will put together each of the major Saturn modules. For example, one group will handle the engine and transmission, another will fit together the dashboard with all the gauges and controls, and one will assemble the bumper, grill, radiator, and headlamps into a front-end unit. After testing, these modules will be delivered by computer-controlled vehicles to a final assembly line that combines the modules into finished cars.

Robots will play a far greater role in the process than ever before. Saturn "is going to advance significantly the state of the art in automated assembly," says Jimmy L. Haugen, vice president for automotive assembly systems at GMFANUC Robotics Corp., the joint venture of GM and Fanuc Ltd., a Japanese robot maker. "It will be the most robotized of any GM plant—and probably any plant in the world."

Robots with limited functions are widely used now in auto assembly plants for such repetitive tasks as welding and painting, but GM plans to take advantage of robots that "see," employing them in a far broader range of tasks on the factory floor. Saturn is expected to use robots to position the sheet metal for car roofs so that other robots can weld them. Robots will also install windshields and possibly rear windows. GMFANUC is working with Saturn on a robot with machine vision that will install car doors. Robots will probably put on the wheels, install the seats, and eventually install the modules in the car.

When the Saturn production lines are up and running in 1988 or 1989, GM expects to be able to manufacture and deliver one of the new compact cars just days after it is ordered. A dealer ordering a car today typically must wait six to eight weeks.

Top to Bottom

Can GM make it all work? The final proof will not be the technology that Saturn uses but the quality of the car it builds. "If they turn out a dog of a car, it won't matter what they've done with manufacturing systems," says Arthur D. Little's Gunn. However, many observers are convinced that the auto maker has gotten on the right track. "I think GM has really made a very profound decision. What it is doing is top-to-bottom computer-integrated manufacturing," comments Daniel Roos, a professor at Massachusetts Institute of Technology and the co-author of *The Future of the Automobile*.

Even if Saturn doesn't succeed in completely closing the cost gap with the Japanese, the manufacturing technology that it is pioneering seems certain to take U.S. industrial productivity a giant step forward.

(Discussion questions linking this case with the material you are about to read can be found at the end of this chapter.)

General Motors's bold new Saturn project is the direct result of greater strategic attention to the firm's manufacturing operations. In order to keep up with domestic and foreign competitors, many large and small companies in the United States can be expected to imitate GM's renewed emphasis on operations management. This will require managers to think creatively and in open-systems terms.

Unfortunately, through the years, our conceptual thinking about complex organizations has often been like the tale of the three blind men and the elephant. It seems that each man came up with an entirely different version of what elephants resembled. One, clutching the trunk, said an elephant was like a vine. Another, feeling only a leg, confidently stated that elephants were like tree trunks. The third, touching the elephant's stomach, argued that elephants were round like boulders.

So, too, the study of organizations has suffered from selective perception. Some experts have focused on human behavior, others on organization structure, and still others on technology. Although something of value has been learned from each of these restricted perspectives, the big picture has all too often been ignored. This is particularly true regarding the actual production of goods and services.

Thanks to modern systems thinking, strictly analytical treatments of organizations are being supplemented by more encompassing synthetic approaches. Operations management, which concentrates on the processes involved in producing goods and services, is one such systematic approach. This chapter takes a look at operations management concepts, processes, and techniques that enable management to turn raw materials into marketable goods and services.

What Does Operations Management Involve?

Operations management is the process of designing, operating, and controlling a productive system capable of transforming physical resources and human talent into needed goods and services. Although some prefer the label production/operations management, the more global term operations management is used here to emphasize that productive systems generate intangible services as well as tangible products.

According to two experts, there are four reasons why it is important to know something about operations management:

1. Production is a core organizational function.
2. The production function commands the flow of resources through the organization.
3. Society depends heavily on the outputs of productive organizations.
4. The production function is tied closely to many serious societal problems such as resource scarcity, [periodic] inflation, and declining productivity.[1]

The following perspectives of operations management and the factory of the future are intended to serve as a backdrop for what lies ahead.

A Special Point of View   Operations managers view organizations as productive systems complete with inputs, a transformation process, and outputs. As illustrated in Figure 17.1, this view conforms to the open-system model of organizations introduced in Chapter 7. The transformation process consists of interrelated

Figure 17.1   Viewing Organizations as a Productive Transformation System

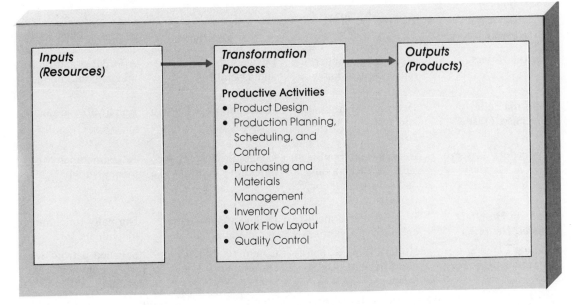

Inputs (Resources)	Transformation Process	Outputs (Products)
	Productive Activities • Product Design • Production Planning, Scheduling, and Control • Purchasing and Materials Management • Inventory Control • Work Flow Layout • Quality Control	

parts, each dependent on the others. Among the important parts of productive systems are six activities: product design; production planning, scheduling, and control; purchasing and materials management; inventory control; work flow layout; and quality control. Together, these activities enable managers to carry out their economic function of transforming resources into useful goods and services.

Goods and Services as Products

Those in the field of operations management use the term *product* as a generic label for the output of a productive system. A product does not necessarily have to be a physical object such as a drill press, a typewriter, or a television set. According to operations managers, a product may be anything from health care to an enjoyable meal in a restaurant (see Table 17.1). By viewing both goods and services as products, operations management can be generalized to manufacturing and nonmanufacturing operations alike. Today, operations management techniques are being used in hospitals, restaurants, stores, government offices, schools and universities, military operations, and a host of other nonfactory organizations.

The distinction between organizations that produce goods and those that produce services is not as clear-cut as one might first believe. In fact, most productive organizations turn out a "package" of tangible goods and intangible services. For example, McDonald's formula for success includes exacting specifications for not only how the customer's food is prepared but also how that food is served:

Table 17.1 Productive Systems Come in Many Sizes and Shapes

Typical Productive Organization	→ Primary Inputs	→ General Transformation Activity	→ Primary Output
General Motors	Steel, glass, rubber, and technical know-how	Design, fabrication, and assembly	Affordable and fuel-efficient automobiles
California State University, Fresno	High school graduates and academic knowledge	Academic instruction	Employable graduates
U.S. Federal Reserve	Information about state of the economy and economic theory/models	Economic strategy formulation	Adjustments in the money supply
Clarkson Hospital, Omaha, Nebraska	Ill patients and medical science expertise	Diagnostic and remedial medical care	Normally functioning individuals
Mamma Leone's restaurant, New York City	Hungry tourists, ingredients, and tested recipes	Commercial food preparation and service	Satisfied patrons who will recommend restaurant

McDonald's may not be everyone's idea of the best place in town to dine, but at its level McDonald's provides a quality of service that is the envy of the industry. Whether you go to the McDonald's on Queens Boulevard in New York or the one in Elk Grove Village near Chicago's O'Hare Airport, you know exactly what you'll get. They all go by the same book. Cooks must turn, never flip, hamburgers, one, never two, at a time. If they haven't been purchased, Big Macs must be discarded ten minutes after being cooked and French fries in seven minutes. Cashiers must make eye contact with and smile at every customer.[2]

McDonald's is highly successful because its integrated package of goods and services is received well in the marketplace. Throughout the balance of this chapter, the term product will refer to the package of goods and services created by a productive system.

Lessons from Japan As Japan has gained a decisive competitive edge in world automobile and consumer electronics markets, managers from the United States have taken to studying Japanese factories firsthand in an effort to discover their "secrets" of success. But observers have found that Japanese manufacturers have no magic formulas, only a steadfast devotion to *elimination of waste* and *constant improvement*.[3] Underlying these two goals are management philosophies that go by the names just-in-time production and total quality control. Many Westerners confuse just-in-time production and total quality control with specific techniques such as *kanban* and quality control circles, both of which are discussed later. But they actually are general guiding philosophies or ideals about producing better products at competitive prices. Just-in-time production and total quality control are introduced here to provide an inspiring philosophical base for operations management.

Just-in-time Production Formally defined, **just-in-time production** (JIT) is "a philosophy that focuses attention on eliminating waste by purchasing or manufacturing just enough of the right items just in time."[4] Observers have called JIT a hand-to-mouth approach to production. While it is true that JIT attacks the problem of bloated inventories that typically hamper American productivity, it involves much more. In pursuit of the JIT ideal, managers do varying combinations of the following:

- Purchase and produce goods in smaller but higher quality lots.
- Design more efficient work flows by eliminating costly bottlenecks.
- Reduce scrap and rework.
- Prevent disruptive machine breakdowns.
- Enhance employee motivation through genuine participation.

Because of JIT, Japanese production operations are lean and flexible. Leanness is achieved by keeping work-in-process inventories to a minimum. Flexibility is achieved by reducing machine setup times so that single units or small batches of different products can be produced in rapid succession. Furthermore, JIT places more emphasis on feedforward control than typically found in American companies. For instance, preventive maintenance is the *personal* responsibility of machine operators in Japanese factories pursuing the JIT ideal.

Total Quality Control According to a management scholar who has studied Japanese factories firsthand, **total quality control** (TQC) is a strongly held belief "that errors, if any, should be caught and corrected at the source, i.e., where the work is performed."[5] Under TQC, each employee firmly believes in the idea: "If I don't do it, it won't get done." This is in sharp contrast to the traditional American production operation where quality control is something done by others at the end of the line. Not surprisingly, the large quality-control departments one finds in the United States are practically nonexistent in Japan. Under TQC, *every* employee, from the president to the janitor, is a quality control inspector. One observer has offered the following perspective:

Table 17.2 Taking Advantage of Lessons from Japan

[Nissan's top executives in Japan] questioned whether Americans, especially those who had never worked in the industry before, could turn out trucks approaching the quality of trucks made in Japan.

Nissan's Smyrna [Tennessee] plant has surprised—and somewhat humiliated—the Japanese. Although many managers there are refugees from Detroit—the plant is managed entirely by Americans—80% of the work force had no experience building automobiles. Yet only a year after the plant opened, pickup trucks built in Smyrna are measurably better than their Japanese counterparts, according to customer surveys. Customers in Tennessee now demand Smyrna-made trucks from dealers rather than the imports.

SOURCE: Gene Bylinsky, "America's Best-Managed Factories," *Fortune* 109 (May 28, 1984): 24.

In many U.S. companies a "we against them" attitude prevails between production workers and quality inspectors. As a result, workers keep potential problems hidden and shunt off defects to be reworked, and the pressure to meet delivery deadlines makes quality inspectors reluctant to delay delivery because of minor quality problems.

In Japanese companies "we" is everybody, and "them" are defects.[6]

The closest thing to a magic formula in Japanese industry today is an unwavering organizational and personal commitment to reducing waste and improving product quality. Fortunately, recent experience demonstrates that these ideals translate readily to other cultures (see Table 17.2).

The Factory of the Future Has Arrived

Stiff foreign competition and sluggish productivity growth are prompting revolutionary changes in the way goods are being manufactured in the United States. Production setups that would have been categorized as science fiction just ten years ago are becoming commonplace in a wide range of industries. Unlike the office of the future, which is still largely an unfulfilled dream, the factory of the future has arrived. For example, consider the following description of Apple Computer's new Macintosh computer factory just prior to its opening in 1984:

[The $20 million] plant will be able to produce a Macintosh, with its 450 parts, every 27 seconds, or 500,000 a year. All of this will be done by just 300 workers, only 200 of them in production; labor accounts for 1% of the cost of making the computer. One of the keys to the increased productivity is cutting the time spent handling materials. Parts arriving at the factory are placed on conveyor belts that carry them to storage. Then, when they are needed for assembly, an operator has only to push a button to transfer them to the work station, either by moving belts or by vehicles guided by wires embedded in the floor. In some cases, robots attach parts to circuit boards.[7]

Although push-button control and robots, as discussed earlier in Chapter 3, are dramatic evidence of the factory of the future, operations managers need a more fundamental understanding. Three fundamental characteristics of the factory of the future are flexible automation, computerized information and control, and integrated functions and systems.[8]

Flexible Automation For many years, a guiding principle among U.S. manufacturers called for long, uninterrupted production runs of highly standardized products. This approach was epitomized by Henry Ford's often-quoted declaration: "They can have any color as long as it's black." Economic theory about economies of scale lent support to this perspective by pointing out that mass production of identical products tends to lower per-unit production costs. For example, the 1000th piece of office furniture is cheaper to produce than the first piece because of such factors as the spreading of fixed costs, quantity discounts on purchased subcomponents, and learning from experience. Change has long been regarded as the enemy of the economies of scale approach to production. Recently, however, stiff global competition has made rapid response to changing consumer tastes a matter of survival. American managers are questioning the practical value of ever larger economies of scale. Unsold stockpiles of poor quality, look-alike goods guarantee bankruptcy.

Thanks to the flexibility of modern automated equipment, economies of scale are giving way to economies of *scope*. **Economies of scope** are achieved when flexible automation makes it economical to produce small batches of a variety of products with the same machines. "With flexible automation, custom products can be produced at close to mass production costs."[9] Whereas the traditional economies of scale avoided change, the newer economies of scope accommodate change. Diablo Systems, Inc., a Xerox subsidiary that manufactures computer printers in Fremont, California, has staved off foreign competition with modern flexible automation:

> Although a major portion of Fremont's production line is devoted to models 620 and 630 daisywheel printers, it is designed to turn out almost any kind of printer. ... [The operations manager] recounts receiving on a Saturday a multimillion dollar order that required an interface change and new paint and logo. The first printer was completed on Tuesday and Diablo was shipping products by the end of the week.[10]

This type of quick turnaround on a custom order would have been virtually impossible with a traditional high-speed assembly line. Conventional assembly lines suffer from inflexibility. In fact, prior to the 1970s, American automobile manufacturers had to shut down their assembly lines for two weeks during the annual model changeover. Such costly set-up/retooling delays are being sharply curtailed or eliminated altogether in factories of the future using flexible automation.

Computerized Information and Control   As discussed in Chapter 3, CAD (computer-aided design) and CAM (computer-aided manufacturing) are cornerstones of the factory of the future. (CAD is explored later in this chapter.) CAM involves the computerized control of manufacturing equipment and machines. For example, here is how one new computer-aided manufacturing program works:

> A machine-tool operator can select, and combine from a color graphics screen, the geometric shapes that match the shape in which the metal is to be cut, and provide the location and dimensions of the cut. Conventional machine tools, by contrast, require every single machine-tool movement to be specially plotted. By eliminating programming steps, the system makes it easier to get a machine tool to perform new tasks.[11]

CAM is the heart and soul of flexible automation. Machine set-up time, once a costly part of manufacturing, is reduced practically to zero with CAM.

One of the more exciting developments in operations management in recent years has been the marriage of CAD and CAM to create computer-integrated manufacturing (CIM). This CAD/CAM marriage has been called closing the loop. According to one CIM specialist:

> **Computer-integrated manufacturing** (CIM) is CAD and CAM linked in a system that manages data flow while directing the movement and processing of material. With CIM, all manufacturing tasks and processes can be put on software. This in turn means that the actual physical production of goods will be integrated with the company's information and control systems. CIM makes manufacturing a system. Manufacturing will no longer be independent: It will be inextricably linked to the operations of the entire organization.[12]

Robots with sensory capabilities promise to extend the scope of CIM even further. They will provide instantaneous feedback to the information system so that programmed adjustments can be made.[13]

One notable consequence of CIM is a higher break-even point. (Recall our discussion of break-even analysis in Chapter 4.) The high cost of designing and installing CIM drives up fixed costs that have to be offset by greater volume. Manufacturing flexibility has its price.

Integrated Functions and Systems   Along with flexibility, *integration* is a key distinguishing characteristic of the factory of the future. "The factory of the future is highly integrated. Production processes are integrated within themselves and with other business operations. Manufacturing is tightly linked with design and marketing to maximize flexibility and responsiveness—the key features a firm uses to compete successfully."[14] This means that interdepartmental competition, conflict, and politics are pushed aside in favor of active project-oriented communication and problem solving. Referring to the distinction we made in Chapter 8 between mechanistic and organic organization structures, the factory of the future is forcing businesses to become more organic (fluid and flexible). For example, in factories of the future, engineers design products by working hand-in-hand with market research and manufacturing specialists.

Too often in the past, engineers designed products and then told manufacturing "See if you can build this thing without fouling up our great design." Having struggled with producing the product, manufacturing then told marketing "See if anybody will buy this thing." Sadly, this sequence is the exact reverse of the formula for business success: discover customer's need → design product → produce product → satisfy customer's need. Factories of the future restore the proper sequence by emphasizing integration.

Product Design

The end product itself is the logical focal point of a productive system. Generally, a good product increases but does not guarantee the probability of organizational survival. A poorly designed product, on the other hand, can destroy an organization. Marketing researchers tell us that satisfied customers typically tell three others whereas dissatisfied customers tell *eleven* others.[15] Costly product recalls are often rooted in poorly designed products. A case in point is Ford Motor Company's discovery in 1978 that 2.7 million of its four- and six-cylinder engines had a "small" design flaw. According to *Business Week,* the engines in question "were more susceptible to wearing out in cold climates because of a cost-savings move that eliminated two oil holes that normally would have been drilled into the piston connecting rods."[16] The estimated cost of *correcting* this design flaw in 56,000 recalls was approximately $250 per car, a total of $14 million. Needless to say, it would have been considerably less expensive to drill the holes in the first place. Seemingly insignificant product design decisions can have enormous long-term consequences.

Open-system Thinking Required   **Product design** may be defined as the process of creating a set of product specifications appropriate to the demands of the situation. Translation of demand into product design specifications requires a great deal of open-system thinking because of the complex combination of individual and

Figure 17.2 The Product Design Process

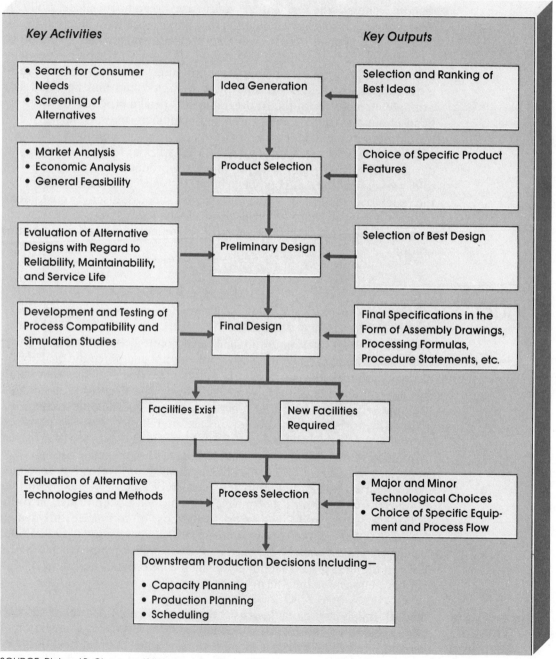

SOURCE: Richard B. Chase and Nicholas J. Aquilano, *Production and Operations Management: A Life Cycle Approach,* 4th ed. (Homewood, Ill.: Richard D. Irwin, Inc., © 1985), p. 29.

Table 17.3 Computer-aided Product Design in Action

The heart of any CAD/CAM system is the CRT (cathode ray tube), a TV screen that allows an engineer to produce a blueprint without ever lifting a pencil.

The engineer "draws" on the CRT with an input device. This can be a light-pen, which looks just like a pen with a wire connecting it to the CRT, or he can type in the information on a keyboard. There are other input devices as well, including voice command.

Once the designer gets his basic outline on the CRT he can instantly rotate it to view from any angle, stretch it, change the scale or add depth to produce a 3-D version. Recent software developments permit the use of color, shading, and solid geometric forms.

The engineer can also call up reference drawings that have been preprogrammed into the system's memory and incorporate them into the emerging design. If he wants to redesign just a corner or section, he merely has to fit the redesigned piece into the overall drawing. This eliminates redoing the entire design.

Mistakes can be detected instantly and corrections made immediately. And at the touch of a button he can have the system's printer produce a hard-copy version of the design that he can take to his boss.

SOURCE: John McElroy, "CAD/CAM Comes of Age," *Automotive Industries* 161 (July 1981): 36.

societal demands on today's organizations. Modern products must satisfy not only individual functional needs but societal demands as well. Meeting society's demands for safer products, a cleaner environment, and safer working conditions necessarily begins at the product design stage. The cost-quality tradeoff that trapped Ford in the case cited above is an example of the difficult decisions that need to be made when designing products. Production costs need to be kept as low as possible without threatening the quality needed to satisfy individual and societal demands. There are many hurdles along the path from an idea to a finished product, each requiring problem solving and important decisions (see Figure 17.2).

Computer-aided Design

As discussed earlier, CAD/CAM (computer-aided design/computer-aided manufacturing) is helping shape the factory of the future. Computer-aided design permits an engineer to develop new designs in approximately half the time required by the traditional pencil-and-paper method. Design changes can be executed in about one-quarter of the usual time (see Table 17.3). According to one observer:

> Computers take the drudgery out of design. Instead of laboriously drawing and redrawing blueprints, engineers create designs electronically and alter them at the push of a few buttons. Some computer programs also analyze the designs to see how well they handle stress or changes in temperature. Manufacturers say that encourages experimentation, yields better quality goods and helps them introduce products more quickly.[17]

One of the ultimate goals of computer-integrated manufacturing, with a CAD component, is to allow customers to phone in their particular product specifications for prompt translation into a design and then into a finished product. In effect, the phone call would trigger appropriate design and production process changes, thanks to computer-integrated manufacturing.

Computer-aided design has at least three drawbacks, according to its users. First, entrenched employees tend to resist the complex new design technology. Second, because of their complexity, CAD systems break down frequently. One researcher estimates that CAD systems are up and running about 70 percent of the time. The other 30 percent is unproductive down time. Third, the powerful CAD systems can put a burdensome drain on a company's mainframe computer. Consequently, some users are restricted to using CAD at night, when mainframe computers are under less demand.[18]

Production Planning, Scheduling, and Control

Production planning is the process of formulating a resource transformation system that will effectively and efficiently meet the forecasted demand for goods and services. Productive resources include facilities and space, equipment, skilled and unskilled employees, and raw materials. As illustrated in Figure 17.3, scheduling and control are integral parts of the production-planning process. There is a dynamic relationship between production planning and the productive process. Production planning guides the productive process, which in turn affects future planning. For example, if a vacuum cleaner manufacturer starts getting many complaints of poor quality from dealers and customers, that information is fed back into the production-planning process and translated into the necessary changes in standards, facilities, personnel, and so forth.

Needed: A Stronger Strategic Emphasis

For many years, Wickham Skinner of Harvard University and others have been urging top managers to pay more attention to the production function when formulating strategic plans. Skinner believes that too many important production decisions are left to middle and lower-level managers. He believes that production should be managed from the top down, not from the bottom up, as it too frequently is. According to Skinner:

> This approach starts with the company and its competitive strategy; its goal is to define manufacturing policy. Its presumption is that only when basic manufacturing policies are defined can the technical experts, industrial and manu-

Figure 17.3   The Production Planning, Scheduling, and Control Process

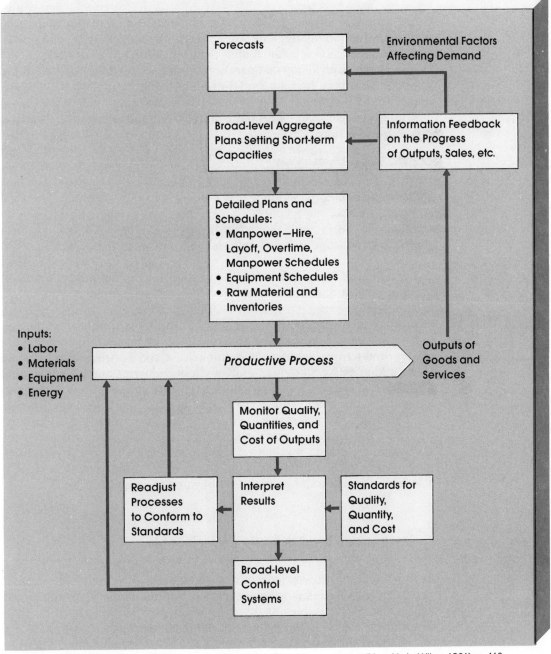

SOURCE: Elwood S. Buffa, *Elements of Production/Operations Management* (New York: Wiley, 1981), p. 113.

facturing engineers, labor relations specialists, and computer experts have the necessary guidance to do their work.[19]

Though some top managers have heeded the call for more strategic attention to production, many have not. In fact, a recent survey by one operations management scholar found that "only about a quarter of the businesses have an adequate operations strategy."[20] Worse yet, half of the firms in the survey had no formal production/operations strategy whatsoever.

At the strategic level, production planning should answer the following important questions:

- What shall we produce?
- What shall we make and what shall we buy?
- How much shall we produce?
- Where shall we produce it?
- What technology shall we use to produce it?
- Where shall we get needed material and human resources?

The production function tends to be uncoordinated and inefficient when these important questions are ignored by strategic planners.

The Master Production Schedule   Coordination of productive activities becomes both more difficult and more important as product lines and facilities are added. This is when the master production schedule comes into play. A **master production schedule** is "an authoritative statement of how many end items are to be produced and when."[21] It includes the procurement of raw materials and subcomponents, fabrication, and subassembly production.[22] In a manner of speaking, operations managers use the master production schedule in the same way that a tour guide uses an itinerary. Because it tells what will take place and when, the master production schedule is the prime source document for activities such as purchasing, inventory control, and quality control. It also provides a rational basis for staffing and training decisions.

Purchasing and Materials Management

It is not uncommon today for purchased materials to account for more than 50 percent of a product's wholesale price. Automobiles, for example, are rolling off assembly lines at this very moment with tires, mirrors, windows, electrical wire, headlights, spark plugs, microprocessors, nuts and bolts, and even entire engines purchased from other firms. When an organization decides to buy rather than make a portion of its product(s), purchasing becomes an important link in the productive system. In addition to goods, organizations purchase a broad range of services, including insurance coverage, consulting expertise, and housekeeping assistance. As the term is used here, **purchasing** refers to the procurement of raw materials, subcomponents, equipment, and services required to accomplish organizational objectives.

Coordinating the Purchasing Function

Given today's magnitude of purchasing expenditures, experts recommend the establishment of an adequately staffed purchasing/materials management department and the enforcement of clear-cut purchasing policies:

- Purchasing should do all of the prime buying for every item or service the company purchases.
- Buyers should have the knowledge, willingness, and the authority to challenge engineering specs [design specifications] when, for example, they create unnecessary sourcing problems. [For instance, a purchasing manager may convince a firm's design engineers to use a more economical brand of electric motor readily available from a single, reliable supplier.]
- The organization of the purchasing function—centralized versus various degrees of decentralization—should vary according to the item being bought. [Centralized purchasing is recommended for high-volume and/or high-priced items.]
- All suppliers should deal exclusively with purchasing, or with others under purchasing's supervision.[23]

Variations in product or service quality and periodic inflation make intelligent buying a must. The day when purchasing was little more than a spur-of-the-moment shopping spree has long since passed.[24]

Vendor Selection

Purchasing managers typically agree that *whom* you buy from is just as important as *what* you buy from them. The process of selecting suppliers or vendors should be characterized by systematic analysis, not haphazard guesswork. It is helpful to screen each potential vendor on the basis of the following six criteria:

Price Shopping around and negotiating for the lowest possible price is nearly always an essential step in deciding on a vendor. Even seemingly insignificant differences in price deserve careful consideration. For example, a large manufacturing firm that quarterly purchases five tons of copper wire can save $1200 per year by taking advantage of a small, 3-cent-per-pound price difference. Also, quantity discounts can offer great savings.

Quality In accordance with the well-known computer principle, "garbage in—garbage out," substandard and shoddy raw materials and subcomponents mean a substandard finished product. Purchasing specialists are constantly challenged to find the best possible product at the lowest possible price. Here is when product design and purchasing come together. Product design specifications are the basis for purchasing specifications. Naturally, all incoming orders need to be checked for quality according to purchasing specifications. By refusing to accept a shipment, the purchasing manager sends the vendor a clear signal that substandard performance will not be tolerated.

Reliability A favorable balance between price and quality means little if the vendor cannot reliably serve the buyer's needs. Taking time to check out a particular vendor's track record with other buyers can pay off handsomely in the long run. Vendors may fail to meet their obligations for a number of reasons, among which are inadequate financing, raw material shortages, strikes and other labor problems, unreliable transportation, and overcommitment.

Service Vendor follow-up becomes an important criterion in regard to the purchase of complex capital equipment. For example, personal computer and photocopy machine breakdowns can paralyze the flow of work in an office. Similarly, a construction company loses money when heavy equipment stands idle because it cannot be repaired promptly. Purchasers are advised to investigate the vendor's reputation for service and follow-up.

Credit Does the vendor demand immediate payment, or are liberal credit terms available? By working in concert with financial managers, purchasing personnel can effect measurable savings by negotiating favorable credit terms. Furthermore, it is possible to save money by taking advantage of cash discounts. For example, if a vendor's contract calls for terms of 2/10 net 30, it means that the buyer will receive a 2 percent discount if the account is paid within ten days. Otherwise, the entire amount is due in thirty days.

Shipping Costs Although it often receives inadequate attention, the cost of getting the purchased goods from the point of manufacture or storage to the point of use is an important consideration in vendor selection. Otherwise favorable price and credit economies can be wiped out by shipping costs. When the buyer has to pay shipping costs, it sometimes makes sense to purchase from a higher-priced yet geographically closer vendor. Also, shipping costs can be kept in line by placing large orders well enough in advance of use to allow shipment by relatively less expensive forms of transportation (for example, by rail rather than air freight).

Material Requirements Planning

The need to combat costly inefficiencies due to piecemeal handling of the various production functions (such as production planning, scheduling, purchasing, and inventory control) is being met in a growing number of organizations by a promising new technique. It is called material requirements planning, or simply MRP. **Material requirements planning** is a systematic and comprehensive manufacturing planning and control technique designed to increase the efficiency of material handling and inventory control. A practitioner explains:

> Say you're making tape recorders and you decide to change to a new speaker. Does your present system tell you what the consequences will be in terms of how many old speakers now in stock must be disposed of? Does it make sure that you don't have machines busily turning out brackets to support that old speaker, that won't fit the new one? And how about the fasteners?
>   A good MRP system answers such questions and greatly reduces the havoc that engineering changes can otherwise create.[25]

Mature "closed-loop" MRP systems keep the production process on track by sensing and responding to feedback (see Figure 17.4). MRP systems are computerized because of the massive data processing involved. A computerized MRP system performs millions of calculations based on forecasted sales and bills of material (lists of all the parts in finished products). This enables management to make data-based decisions regarding what, when, and where materials are needed. A variety of MRP packages are now available from computer hardware and software vendors.[26] But like management by objectives and management information systems, MRP requires careful planning and implementation and is not an automatic cure-all.

Benefits of MRP   As the use of MRP is becoming more widespread, the benefits promised by its proponents are becoming evident. In regard to materials management and inventory control in manufacturing operations, advocates of MRP claim that the following benefits can be realized:

- Inventory investment can be held to a minimum.
- An MRP system is change-sensitive, reactive.
- The system provides a look into the future, on an item-by-item basis.
- Under material requirements planning, inventory control is action-oriented rather than clerical bookkeeping-oriented.
- Order quantities are related to requirements.
- The *timing* of requirements, coverage, and order actions is emphasized.[27]

Figure 17.4 MRP Keeps the Production Process on Track

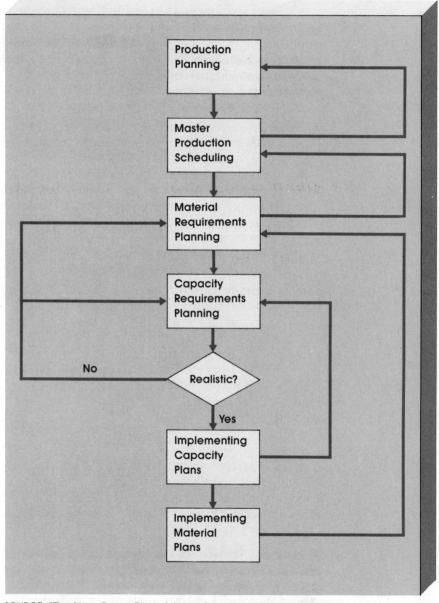

SOURCE: "The New Game Plan: A Huge Potential Is There to be Won," *Modern Materials Handling* 36 (January 6, 1981), p. 68. Copyright 1981 by Cahners Publishing Company. Division of Reed Holdings, Inc.

In terms of actual experience, a survey of over 430 MRP users uncovered the following cost-benefit data:

> Installation costs ranged from less than $100,000 for small companies to more than $1 million for large ones. But the average increase in annual inventory turnover was an astounding 50.3%. For the typical company with $65 million in annual sales, that made possible an inventory reduction of about $8 million, and a saving of $1.8 million per year in carrying costs calculated at recent interest rates. Some companies reported that MRP had enabled them to cut in half the amount of money tied up in inventories for each dollar of sales. The new system also improved service to customers: the average lead time for deliveries declined 18%.[28]

MRP II   A recent extension of MRP is *manufacturing resource planning* (MRP II). The primary distinction between MRP and MRP II is that the latter is organizationwide in scope. According to an expert on the subject:

> MRP II involves *all* departments, not just Materials Management. Engineering must maintain bills of material, Sales/Marketing must keep sales plans up to date, Purchasing and the shop floor must meet due dates. . . . MRP II provides a single, common set of reliable resource plans expressed in units, hours and dollars for everyone in the company to use. . . . MRP II focuses on the fundamental manufacturing questions—what are you going to make (production plans and master schedules), what does it take to make it (bills of material and routings), what do you have (inventory status), and, what do you need to make (planned orders)?[29]

Because MRP is a subset of MRP II, it is good practice to start with the former and grow into the latter. Like other areas of management, experience is the best teacher.

Inventory Control

In regard to raw materials, subcomponents, and supplies, purchasing/materials management and inventory control go hand in hand. Because these inputs are not used the minute they arrive, except in just-in-time (JIT) operations, they need to be kept on hand for varying periods of time. But inventory control is more than just stockpiling purchased items. Partially completed products and finished goods waiting to be sold enlarge the scope of inventory control. Considering all types of inventory as a whole, manufacturing firms like General Electric typically tie up one-fourth of their invested capital in inventories.

During 1975 General Electric sold $13.5 billion worth of products and at the end of the year owned $2.1 billion worth of inventories—stocks of materials and products. General Foods sold $3.7 billion worth of products and ended the year owning $580 million in inventories. RCA sold $4.6 billion worth of products and services and finished the year owning an inventory of $600 million.[30]

Because inventories quickly add up to staggering investments, they are a major contributor to an organization's success or failure. At General Electric, for instance, a seemingly insignificant 5 percent increase in inventories would tie up an additional $105 million in working capital. A financial burden of this magnitude can spell disaster for a firm, even one as large as General Electric, because funds locked up in inventory cannot be used elsewhere. Consequently, **inventory control,** the process of establishing and maintaining appropriate levels of reserve stocks of goods, is an important managerial concern.

Types of Inventory

There are four categories of inventory: (1) raw materials and purchased subcomponents, (2) work in process, (3) supplies, and (4) finished goods. The first category, raw materials and subcomponents, feeds the productive system. Ideally, it is a steady and reliable source of inputs. Work-in-process inventories are necessary because the transformation process usually consists of a number of consecutive subprocesses requiring different lengths of time to complete. For example, when the JIT philosophy is not being followed, automobile seats are made and stockpiled for eventual mounting during the general assembly process. Supplies such as paper, typewriter ribbons, lubricating oil, and cleansing agents, which are consumed during the transformation process, also require stockpiling for use as needed. Finally, a finished products inventory is necessitated by fluctuating demand.[31]

In spite of subtle differences in the management of these various categories of inventory, all are subject to the same set of conflicting demands. There are reasons both for maintaining large inventories and for keeping inventories as small as possible. These competing demands are outlined in Table 17.4.

The factors favoring large inventories generally are the product of conservatism and fear of the unknown. Demands for small inventories are based primarily on cost considerations. But neither side is altogether right or wrong, as both sets of factors have merit. Operations managers are challenged to balance both sides of the equation so that inventoried items are available when needed without incurring unreasonable expenses in the process. (The formula for calculating economical order quantities is discussed in Appendix B.) MRP, MRP II, and a JIT technique called *kanban* can help managers keep inventories in check.

Table 17.4   Conflicting Demands in Regard to the Size of Inventories

Factors favoring large inventories	Factors favoring small inventories
• Fear of running out of stock. • Anticipation of possible jumps in demand. • Desire to keep ordering, shipping, and production costs low. • Desire to take advantage of favorable prices and quantity discounts. • Desire to have a hedge against inflation. • Fear of unexpected events such as strikes, embargoes, and natural disasters.	• Desire to minimize working capital tied up in inventory. • Desire to minimize storage costs. • Limitations on storage capacity. • Desire to keep insurance and tax expenses down. • Fear of obsolescence. • Danger of spoilage.

Managing the Inventory Cycle

Part of determining the best inventory size is viewing inventory management as a cyclical process (see Figure 17.5). The heart of this cyclical process amounts to deciding how much to order and when. Assuming that demand for inventoried goods is relatively predictable, these two decisions are made on a regular, cyclical basis.

Before exploring the details of the inventory cycle in Figure 17.5, we should insert a qualification. The cycle in Figure 17.5 is somewhat idealistic because demand for inventoried items tends to fluctuate. For example, approximately 60 to 70 percent of each year's toy sales are made during the six weeks before Christmas. Consequently, vigorous toy production early in the year requires large raw materials inventories that gradually taper off as Christmas nears and production slows. This type of seasonal fluctuation also affects finished goods inventories. Nevertheless, even though there are seasonal fluctuations, the basic points in Figure 17.5 remain valid.

Note that the inventory cycle has two dimensions, quantity and time. In this example, inventory on hand ranges from zero to 200 units. A safety stock of 40 units has been created to reduce the danger of running out. Safety stock levels are based on prior experience and usage patterns and are used as insurance against running out and being unable to meet demand. Of course, proponents of just-in-time production reject the idea of anything more than very small safety stocks. Advocates of safety stocks point out that exhaustion of raw materials inventory can bring the entire production process to a halt—for example, a shipment of roller skates cannot leave the factory until the wheels have been mounted. Running out of finished goods can be equally disruptive. "Selling from an empty wagon" means that time-consuming back orders must be processed later or, worse, that dissatisfied customers may be lost to competitors.

Figure 17.5   The Basic Inventory Cycle

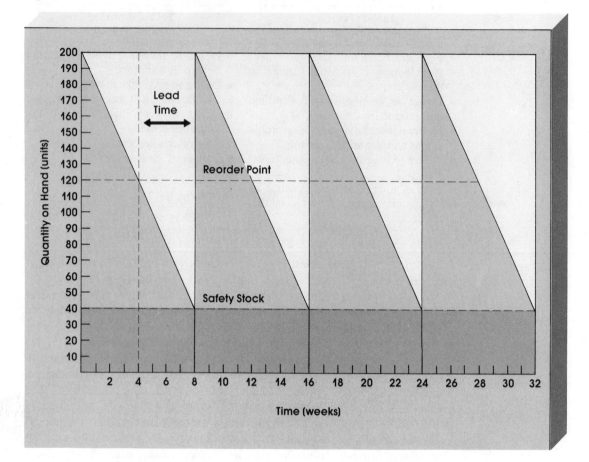

Once safety stock levels have been determined, attention then turns to ordering the right amount at the right time. Referring once again to Figure 17.5, assume that experience has shown that 160 units are used every eight weeks, or 20 units a week on the average. The order quantity would then be fixed at 160 units. Next, the timing of the order should be determined. Suppose that experience has proved that it takes about four weeks from the time the order goes out to the time the goods are received. This means that orders have to be placed at least four weeks before the inventory level reaches the safety threshold of 40 units. This four-week period is referred to as the *lead time*. Consequently, when the inventory level reaches the reorder point of 120 units, which is 40 units of safety stock plus 80 units (four times the weekly average), management knows that it is time to reorder. Four weeks later, when the inventory stands at 40 units, 160 units are received, and thus the inventory is back to 200 units. In this saw-tooth fashion, the inventory cycle repeats itself over and over again.

Kanban: A Just-in-Time Inventory Control Technique

In recent years, U.S. manufacturers have relied increasingly on what experts call *push* systems of inventory control in an attempt to balance the cost factors in Table 17.4 economically. The most common inventory push systems are computerized MRP and MRP II. Inventory push systems operate in the following manner:

> A push system in reality is simply a schedule-based system. That is, a multi-period schedule of future demands for the company's products (called a master production schedule) is prepared, and the computer breaks that schedule down into detailed schedules for making or buying the component parts. It is a push system in that the schedule pushes the production people into making the required parts and then pushing the parts out and onward.[32]

In a sense, this push approach is a Western (non-Japanese) version of just-in-time inventory management. All too often, unfortunately, the push approach gets bogged down with excess inventory because of inaccurate demand estimates and work-flow bottlenecks.

Kanban (pronounced kahn bahn), a manual inventory control technique developed by Toyota, stands in sharp contrast to computerized push systems. It relies on the "pull" of orders received (actual demand) rather than the "push" of anticipated orders (estimated demand). **Kanban** may be defined as a manual inventory control "procedure that uses cards to keep inventory status highly visible and that manages production so that necessary units are made in the necessary quantities at the necessary time."[33] *Kanban* is a Japanese word roughly translated to mean "card."

How the Kanban System Works   Aside from the inventory control cards inscribed with part numbers and lot size, a central feature of the *kanban* system is the use of standardized containers to shuttle identical (small) quantities of parts from work station to work station. By switching cards (*kanban*) from containers of unprocessed parts to containers of processed parts and keeping tallies, a work station operator (such as a milling machine operator) *pulls* inventory through the production system on a just-in-time basis. An upstream container of parts is not processed until the *kanban* of the downstream container signals the go-ahead. Hence, as illustrated in Figure 17.6 (on pp. 630–631), unanticipated work flow stoppages do not cause work-in-process inventories to stack up as is typically the case.

Managers can fine tune the flow of work by adding or removing containers of parts with attached *kanban* from the production cycle. These vital decisions are made on the basis of actual demand, not projected demand as is the case with computerized push systems such as MRP.

Figure 17.6 *Kanban* Keeps Work-in-Process Inventories Lean

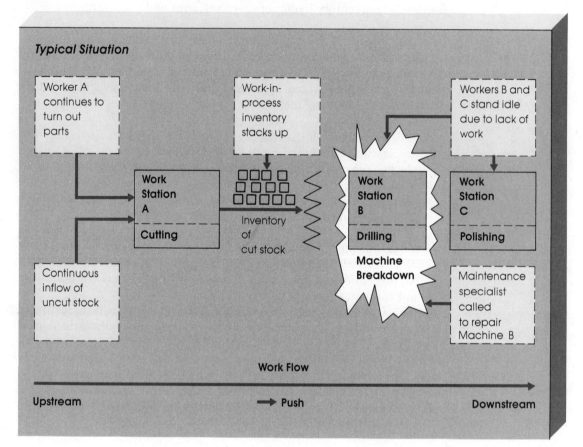

Despite the apparent primitiveness of manually switching inventory cards in the midst of the computer age, Toyota and other *kanban* users have boosted their productivity significantly by keeping work-in-process inventories to the barest minimum.

Kanban Requires a Supportive Situation Proponents of *kanban* say it works because it is simple and easy to use. But it is restricted to use in highly repetitive manufacturing operations such as auto making. Moreover, *kanban* inventory control will not work unless used in concert with just-in-time production. Since *kanban* is necessarily linked with JIT, it is plagued by what critics claim is JIT's main vulnerability: work stoppages. For example, Chrysler's Lee Iacocca related the following incident in his

Figure 17.6 (cont.)

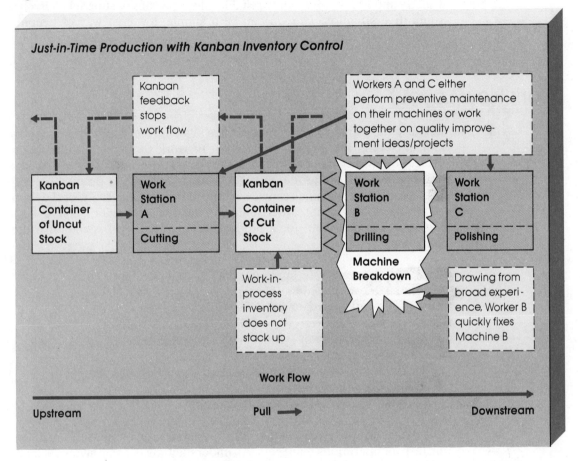

Just-in-Time Production with Kanban Inventory Control

recent autobiography: "our just-in-time system became so efficient that when our Detroit engine plant staged a wildcat strike, our assembly plant in Windsor ran out of engines four hours later!"[34]

No wonder Japanese auto makers are eroding Detroit's market shares. Because of intensive management-labor cooperation, wildcat strikes are not a problem at Toyota. In fact, Toyota employees do such a good job of *preventing* machine breakdowns that the situation just above in Figure 17.6 rarely occurs. If it does, *kanban* feedback prevents the buildup of costly work-in-process inventories. In the event of a rare prolonged stoppage, Toyota employees do not stand around wasting time, in accordance with their commitment to the JIT and total quality control philosophies, they turn to constructive activities such as preventive maintenance on their own machines. In addition to requiring labor peace and cooperation, *kanban* and JIT require highly reliable, close proximity suppliers. Given a supportive situation, *kanban* can be a simple, low-cost way of keeping inventories in check.

Work Flow Layout

Because the transformation process is a system, every part of it is important, including the physical movement of work through the production cycle. This aspect of operations management is called **work flow layout,** the process of determining the physical arrangement of the productive system. People and machines can be scattered about haphazardly, or they can be arranged in a logical, orderly, and cost-effective manner. Experts suggest that a good layout for a production operation will accomplish the following:

1. Minimize investment in equipment.
2. Minimize overall production time.
3. Utilize existing space most effectively.
4. Provide for employee convenience, safety, and comfort.
5. Maintain flexibility of arrangement and operation.
6. Minimize material-handling cost.
7. Minimize variation in types of material-handling equipment.
8. Facilitate the manufacturing process.
9. Facilitate the organizational structure.[35]

Balancing these often conflicting considerations is an immensely challenging task for operations managers. An understanding of basic layout formats and process flow charting helps.

Layout Formats   Although a manager can go out and find innumerable production layout configurations, there are three basic formats: the product layout, the process layout, and the fixed-position layout. Others are simply variations or hybrid combinations of the basic three. The three layouts are defined as follows:

- A **product layout** is one in which the components are arranged according to the progressive steps by which the product is made. Conceptually, the flow is an unbroken line from raw material input to finished goods. This type of layout is exemplified in automobile assembly, food processing, and furniture manufacture.
- A **process (or functional) layout** is one in which the components are

grouped according to the general function they perform, without regard to any particular product. Custom job shops, department stores, and hospitals are generally arranged in this manner.

- A **fixed-position layout** is one in which the product, by virtue of its bulk or weight, remains at one location. The equipment required for product manufacture is moved to the product rather than vice versa. Sound stages on a movie lot, aircraft assembly shops, and shipyards typify this mode of layout.[36]

Product Layout   If a high volume of standardized products needs to be produced, the product layout format illustrated in Figure 17.7 is most appropriate. This type of setup was referred to in Chapter 7 as long-linked technology. Typically, some sort of conveyor arrangement is used to carry work in process past fixed work-stations.

Product layouts have both advantages and disadvantages. On the plus side, relatively unskilled employees are able to perform clearly defined tasks, and a single supervisor can easily oversee the work of many people. Inflexibility is the major disadvantage. A major design change may trigger a costly restructuring of the entire assembly line, and so, for example, auto manufacturers normally shut down completely for annual retooling. Continuous assembly line operations also tend to be vulnerable to stoppages because they are only as strong as their weakest link. For instance, if operator A in Figure 17.7 runs out of windshields, operators B and C will have nothing to do, and the entire operation will grind to a costly halt. Another problem is that in recent years, large numbers of better-educated employees have begun to rebel against the monotony and boredom of doing the same highly fragmented job hundreds of times a day.

Process Layout   Although process layouts such as the one in Figure 17.7 cannot duplicate the speed of product layouts, they usually are more flexible. For example, a welding machine breakdown on an assembly line (product layout) will tie up all downstream work. But in a process layout in which all welding jobs are conducted in the same department, back-up welding machines are conveniently available. Process layouts also have the advantage of being suitable for the custom processing of diverse products. On the minus side, work scheduling is much more difficult in process layouts than in product layouts, in which the production sequence is fixed. Care must be taken not to overload one department and let others sit idle. In addition, expensively large work-in-process inventories tend to accumulate in custom process operations.

Fixed-position Layout   Normally, operations managers have little choice in their reliance on fixed-position layouts. Huge ships that are three football fields long cannot be moved around on conveyors or transported from

Figure 17.7 Basic Production Layout Formats

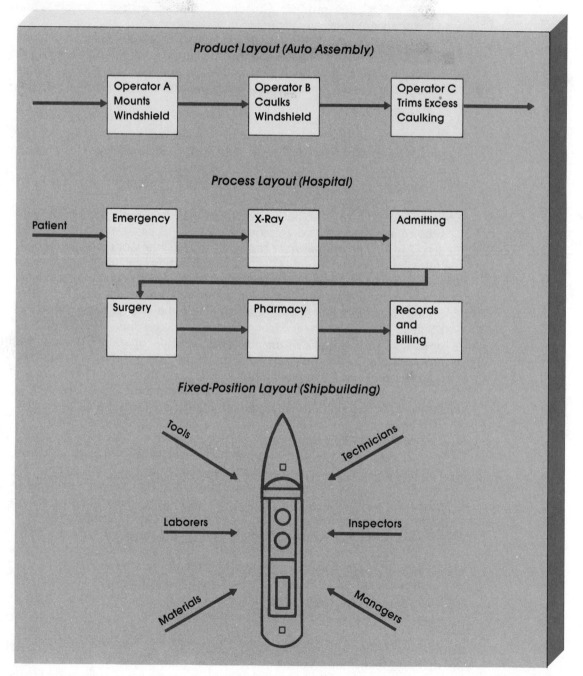

Figure 17.8 Process Flow Charting in Action

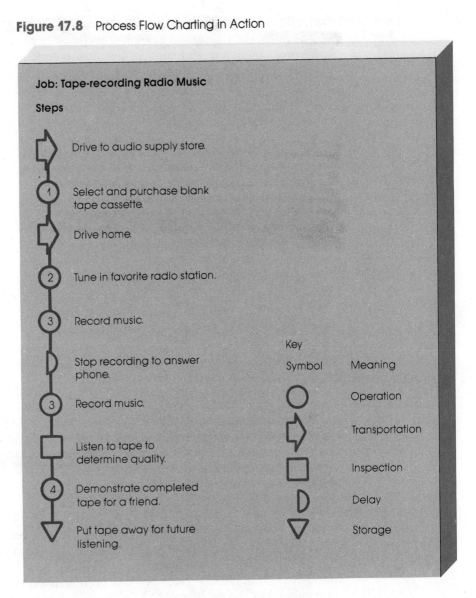

Job: Tape-recording Radio Music

Steps

Drive to audio supply store.

1 Select and purchase blank tape cassette.

Drive home.

2 Tune in favorite radio station.

3 Record music.

Stop recording to answer phone.

3 Record music.

Listen to tape to determine quality.

4 Demonstrate completed tape for a friend.

Put tape away for future listening.

Key

Symbol	Meaning
○	Operation
⇨	Transportation
□	Inspection
D	Delay
▽	Storage

department to department by lift trucks. Everything, including raw materials, supplies, and equipment, must be carried to the construction site. This type of layout is costly because of the duplication of talent and tools when more than one project is in progress at once. But it usually is popular among employees, who are able to move about freely rather than being restricted to a single work station.

Process Flow Charting   Formally defined, a **process flow chart** is "a tool for recording an operation or process in the sequence in which it occurs."[37] Process flow charts are a convenient modeling technique whose value depends partly on the fact that they employ a set of standard symbols developed by the American Society of Mechanical Engineers (see Figure 17.8). Creating a process flow chart of either proposed or existing production processes offers the following advantages:

1. It breaks down complex processes into key steps.
2. It provides a handy visual aid of the production process.
3. It helps determine equipment and labor needs.
4. It helps pinpoint bottlenecks.
5. It helps identify overlooked or missing steps.
6. It helps discover redundant or unnecessary steps.
7. It helps isolate unsafe arrangements.

Process flow charts can be even more valuable if they record the time required for each step and the distance traveled during each transportation step. The shorter the time required and the distance to be traveled are, the more cost effective the operation will be.[38]

Quality Control

Is the resource transformation system producing what it is supposed to? This deceptively simple question can be answered only through a comprehensive quality control program. **Quality control** is the process of ensuring that goods and services actually conform to the design specifications. Managers in the United States are under pressure from two fronts to do a better job of controlling quality.

First, customers who are injured or sustain a loss because of a faulty product are turning more and more to the courts. According to *Business Week*: "An estimated 110,000 product [liability] cases are filed each year in the United States. In the federal courts ... filings have increased from 1579 in 1974 to 9221 in 1983."[39] Not only have product liability lawsuits increased in number, but the dollar value of settlements has mushroomed as well.[40] Settlements topping $1 million are common today. In response to the dramatic rise in product liability insurance premiums, "many big corporations are spending vast sums on rigorous programs of product inspection and quality control in order to lessen their risks of being sued."[41]

Stiffer competition from abroad, particularly Japan, has also caused management to make quality improvement a top priority for the 1980s and beyond.

Building assiduously for 30 years on a foundation of theories developed in the U.S., the Japanese have made quality the weapon that wins the world's markets. A few bald facts show how well they have done: A new American car is almost twice as likely to have a problem as a Japanese model. An American color TV needs repair half again as often as a Japanese set. U.S.-made computer-memory chips were judged in one test . . . [in 1980] to be three times as likely to fail as Japanese chips.[42]

American manufacturers are learning that quality needs to be a concern throughout the entire productive process, from design to market. While reviewing recent productivity accomplishments in the United States, *Fortune* magazine noted that managers now realize that quality improvement "is a way to drive costs down by slashing scrappage and repair costs, as well as a strategic marketing and product-planning tool."[43]

Feedforward and Feedback Quality Control

In Chapter 15, feedforward control was discussed in regard to foreseeing problems and avoiding mistakes before they occur. Feedback control, on the other hand, was defined as the process of making sure that past mistakes are not repeated. Figure 17.9 shows the nature of feedforward and feedback *quality* control. Feedforward quality control is making sure that both productive inputs and work in process satisfy acceptable standards so as to avoid substandard output. As discussed earlier, the philosophy of total quality control (TQC), where every employee is a quality inspector, takes shape around feedforward quality control. An ounce of prevention can be worth a pound of cure when it comes to quality control. For example:

[A manager from a computer company] describes the damage a faulty 2-cent resistor can do. If you catch the resistor before it is used and throw it away, you lose 2 cents. If you don't find it until it has been soldered into a computer component, it may cost $10 to repair the part. If you don't catch the component until it is in a computer user's hands, the repair will cost hundreds of dollars. Indeed, if a $5,000 computer has to be repaired in the field, the expense may exceed the manufacturing cost.[44]

Although the inspection of inputs is relatively straightforward, the inspection of work in process can cause problems.

The Quality Control Dilemma Managers face a cost dilemma when inspecting work in process for quality. Too many inspections can eat into profits because of wasteful redundancy. But too few inspections can drive up costs through increased scrap and rework and can ultimately reduce sales because of customer dissatisfaction. Consequently, care must be taken to inspect work in process at the right time and place. Two recog-

Figure 17.9   Feedforward and Feedback Quality Control

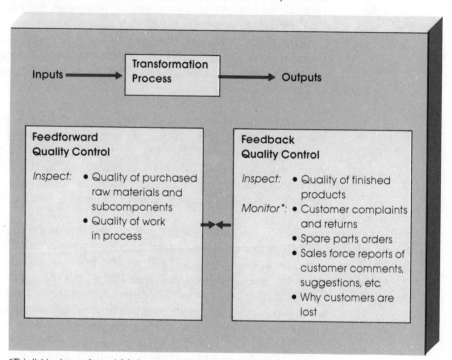

*This list is drawn from J. M. Juran and Frank M. Gryna, Jr., *Quality Planning and Analysis* (New York: McGraw-Hill, 1970), p. 559.

nized authorities on operations management have suggested the following rules for inspecting work in process:

1. Inspect *after* operations that are likely to produce faulty items so that no more work will be done on bad items.
2. Inspect *before* costly operations so that these operations will not be performed on items that are already defective.
3. Inspect *before* operations in which faulty products might break or jam the machines.
4. Inspect *before* operations that can cover up defects (such as electro-plating, painting, or assembly).
5. Inspect *before* assembly operations that cannot be undone (such as welding parts or mixing paint).
6. On automatic and semiautomatic machines, inspect the first and last pieces, but only occasionally the in-between pieces.
7. Inspect *before* storage (including purchased items).[45]

Adhering to these practical rules and conducting statistical analyses of

Table 17.5   W. Edwards Deming: The American Behind Japan's Quality
Revolution

When Japan launched a national drive to improve industrial quality in 1950, an
American statistician by the name of W. Edwards Deming was invited to Japan to
present his unconventional ideas on quality control. His ideas spread through
Japanese industry like wildfire, igniting a commitment to quality that has made
Japan a world leader in product quality. In recognition of his contribution, Japan's
most prestigious award for quality achievements carries Deming's name. The
award has been likened to the Nobel Prize of Japanese quality control. Japanese
companies compete vigorously for it. Curiously, Deming, now in his mid-80s, only
recently has captured the attention of managers in the United States. The thrust of
Deming's approach to quality control has been summed up as follows:

> Deming insists there's little use exhorting workers to improve quality because
> most of the things that contribute to quality are out of their hands—having the
> right tools, the right materials, good training, a workable production process.
> To get at the system-induced 94% of failures, Deming tells his clients and
> seminar students to adopt his 14 points and drive out his five deadly diseases.
> For example, the classic way of achieving quality control is to inspect finished
> products and throw out the bad ones. "Criminal," says Deming. Getting rid of
> defective products costs money and doesn't improve the process. Quit mass
> inspections, he urges, and instead control and improve the process so that each
> item comes out right (Point 3).
>   The heart of Deming's method for achieving high quality is statistical. Every
> process, whether it be on the factory floor or in the office, has variations from
> the ideal. Deming shows clients a systematic method for measuring these
> variations, finding out what causes them, reducing them, and so steadily
> improving the process and thereby the product. He divides the causes of
> variations into special causes, which result in 6% of failures, and common
> causes, which account for the rest. A special cause—a bad batch of parts or a
> careless worker—creates erratic, unpredictable variations. Common causes
> are the rhythmic variations in the system—such as the slight differences in the
> dimensions of a bore produced by the same tool. Deming gets clients first to
> bring the manufacturing process under statistical control by eliminating the
> chaos of special causes, then has them work on the common causes by tinkering
> with the system and consistently measuring the effects.
>   In the typical factory, adjustments to tools are made casually—when the
> operator thinks it's about time—and with so little understanding of variations
> and sampling that the correction often makes a defect worse. For example, in
> the late 1970s Nashua Corp., an office supply and equipment company in
> Nashua, New Hampshire, was having trouble laying a consistent coating on its
> carbonless paper. At the end of the run of each 40,000-foot roll of paper a
> technician would take some of the paper and make copies with it. If the copies
> were too faint he would increase the flow of coating, and if too dark, decrease it.
> Not having been taught about variations, the technician didn't realize that any
> specific test he made could measure the coating when it was at one limit or the
> other of its variation—either as thick as it could get or as thin. To make a proper

Table 17.5 (cont.)

adjustment, he would need an average based on several readings and a measure of the spread of variations. Without this information, the technician could end up increasing the flow when it didn't need adjustment or even when it needed to be reduced. Deming figures that in fact the Nashua technicians were doubling the variation, and so increasing costs and reducing quality.

Nashua's chairman, William E. Conway, came back from visits to Japan impressed with the feats of his Japanese competitors and Deming's fame over there. He called Deming one Monday in 1979 and had him up in Nashua by Thursday. For the next three years Deming visited Nashua every month or so.

Deming first persuaded Nashua to drop plans to buy a new $700,000 coating head and instead to let the existing machine run without the operator's erratic adjustments. Variations immediately decreased and quality improved. Then Nashua went to work on the system. A supplier was persuaded to furnish a more consistent chemical, bearings were tightened, the drying process was adjusted. By April 1980, eight months after the statistical controls were established, the amount of coating had been reduced 22%, saving $800,000 a year. Other processes responded equally well to the Deming treatment. "It was like a miracle," says Conway.

SOURCE: Jeremy Main, "The Curmudgeon Who Talks Tough on Quality." *Fortune* 109 (June 25, 1984): 119. Reprinted by permission.

quality variations (see Table 17.5 on pp. 639–640) can help management deal effectively with the cost dilemma of work-in-process quality control.

Monitoring Output for Quality   Feedback quality control occurs when finished goods are inspected and tested to see if they satisfy original design specifications. Items that fail must be reworked, if possible, or scrapped. At this point, the prudent manager remembers that the organization's reputation is shipped with every product. A bad product means a dissatisfied customer, and a dissatisfied customer is a target for the competition. In addition to checking finished goods, attentive monitoring of feedback from the field is necessary. For example, orders of spare parts for the company's products, normally viewed only as a source of additional revenue, may pinpoint problems in product design or quality control.

Quality Control Circles   Any discussion of modern quality control techniques would be incomplete without mentioning quality control circles. Developed in Japan during the early 1960s, this quality control innovation took the U.S. industrial scene by storm during the late 1970s. Today, thousands of quality control circles can be found in hundreds of American companies. **Quality control circles,** commonly referred to as QC circles or simply quality circles, are voluntary problem-solving groups of five to ten employees from the same work area who meet regularly to discuss quality improvement.[46] A weekly one-hour meeting, during company time, is common practice. By relying on voluntary participation, QC circles attempt to tap the creative potential that every employee possesses. Although QC circles do not work in every situation, benefits such as direct cost savings, improved worker-management relations, and greater individual commitment have been reported.[47]

An Evolutionary Process Following the Japanese model, QC circles should be introduced in evolutionary fashion rather than by management edict. As the following description of Northrop Corporation's successful QC circle program illustrates, training, supportive supervision, and team building all are part of this evolutionary development:

> In a well-managed program like Northrop's, team members are given a good dose of training in the basic techniques of problem solving. They learn to gather and analyze data, weed out trivial issues to focus on major ones, generate innovative ideas in brainstorming sessions, forge consensus decisions, and communicate effectively. At least one team member—usually though not always the supervisor—gets extra training in leadership. And any well-run program has one or more people trained as "facilitators," who help the leader organize groups and get people who were accustomed to performing isolated jobs on an assembly line to begin thinking, talking, listening, and caring as members of a team.[48]

The idea is to give those who work day in and day out at a specific job the tools, group support, and opportunity to nip quality problems in the bud. Each QC circle is responsible not only for recommending solutions but also for actually implementing and evaluating solutions. According to one organizational behaviorist, "The invisible force behind the success of QC's [quality circles] is its ability to bring the psychological principles of Maslow, McGregor and Herzberg into the work place through a structured process."[49]

Making the Cultural Translation As we stated in Chapter 1, it is naive to expect every successful Japanese management technique to work automatically in the United States and other Western nations. Japan's homogeneous culture, in which consensus is highly valued, does not have a parallel among Western nations. Consequently, the following adaptations have been recommended to ensure that the QC circle concept fits U.S. cultural constraints:

1. Full union-management cooperation is necessary if the QC circle concept is to work in the United States. Unions are generally left out of the picture in Japan, with no major ill effects.
2. QC circles have proved to be a poor union-avoidance tool in the United States.

3. Monetary incentives for voluntary contributions are generally more important to American employees than to Japanese employees. Group members can be allowed to share equally in cost-saving awards.
4. Formal recognition of QC circle achievements (for example, formal presentations to management by members) will help stifle the notion among U.S. employees that management is trying to get something for nothing.
5. Because the lack of middle-management support has been found to be a major barrier to QC circle success in the United States, middle managers should be fully involved in the development and implementation process. Otherwise, they will be threatened by the prospect of lower-level employees uncovering problems that will make middle management look bad.[50]

With proper cultural translation, participative quality control can and does work in Western organizations.

Summary

Operations management is the design, operation, and control of resource transformation systems. Raw materials and human talent are transformed into needed goods and services. Most resource transformation systems produce a package of tangible goods and intangible services. Study of highly efficient Japanese factories has revealed lean and flexible just-in-time production operations and personal commitment to total quality control, rather than "secret" techniques. Three characteristics of the factory of the future are flexible automation, computerized information and control, and integrated functions and systems. CIM (computer-integrated manufacturing) = CAD + CAM.

Product design, the process of creating a set of product specifications, should be responsive to both individual and societal demands. Poorly designed products can come back to haunt a company through costly rework, scrap, or product recalls. Computer-aided design (CAD) allows engineers to cut in half new product design time.

Production planning is needed to ensure that forecasted demand for goods and services is met effectively and efficiently. Experts recommend that top management devote more of their attention to the production function. Production tends to be uncoordinated and inefficient when important production decisions are ignored by strategic planners. The master production schedule is a key source document for operations managers because it tells what will be produced and when.

Because purchased materials often account for more than half of a product's wholesale price, systematic purchasing is a fundamental part of effective operations management. Today, an adequately staffed purchasing/materials management department and clear-cut purchasing policies are recommended for most organizations. Six criteria to be considered when selecting vendors are price, quality, reliability, service, credit, and shipping costs. Computerized material requirements planning (MRP) and manufacturing resource planning (MRP II) help operations managers make data-based decisions regarding the timing and levels of material and inventory transactions. MRP II is organizationwide in scope, whereas MRP is tied more narrowly to the production function.

Organizational success often hinges on how effectively the four categories of inventory are managed. Successful management of the inventory cycle involves balancing conflicting demands. There is both the demand for large inventories in order to meet unexpected circumstances and the demand for small inventories in order to minimize investment and carrying costs. *Kanban,* a just-in-time inventory control technique developed by Toyota, keeps work-in-process inventory lean by "pulling" containers of parts through the production process with a manual card-switching procedure. *Kanban* must be used in conjunction with just-in-time production and is suitable only for highly repetitive manufacturing situations.

Logical and orderly work flow layouts greatly improve cost effectiveness. Three basic work flow formats are product layout, process layout, and fixed-position layout. Each has inherent advantages and disadvantages. Process flow charting is a standardized tool for either planning future layout arrangements or assessing existing ones.

A production operation is only as good as its output. Both feedforward and feedback quality control are necessary to ensure that goods and services conform to design specifications. There should be a balance between inspecting too often and not often enough. Quality control circles are a Japanese innovation using the voluntary participation of work groups to identify and implement quality-related solutions. Care needs to be taken to make the appropriate cultural translation when implementing QC circles in Western countries.

Terms to Understand

Operations management	Inventory control
Just-in-time production (JIT)	*Kanban*
Total quality control (TQC)	Work flow layout

Economies of scope
Computer-integrated manufacturing (CIM)
Product design
Production planning
Master production schedule
Purchasing
Material requirements planning (MRP)

Product layout
Process layout
Fixed-position layout
Process flow chart
Quality control
Quality control circles

Questions for Discussion

1. How does the notion of a resource transformation system help one appreciate the importance of operations management?
2. How could the philosophy of total quality control (TQC) be used to improve your life (relative to your studies, job, etc.)?
3. In your opinion, which fundamental characteristic of the factory of the future is the overriding one? Explain your reasoning.
4. How do product design and quality control complement each other?
5. How would the six criteria of vendor selection help you buy an expensive item (for example, sound system, car, or bicycle)?
6. What functional group in a typical business organization would argue for large inventories? Why?
7. Why do operations producing customized products tend to rely on process layouts? Give examples.
8. What would a process flow chart of your preparing a meal look like?
9. Why are both feedforward and feedback quality control important?
10. In your view, what could cause a QC circle program to fail?

Back to the Opening Case

Now that you have read Chapter 17, you should be able to answer the following questions about the General Motors case:

1. What evidence of the "factory of the future" can you find in this case?
2. If you were a labor negotiator for GM, what would you ask the United Auto Workers Union to do in order to ensure the success of Saturn?
3. What problems could plague GM's proposed just-in-time production system?
4. Why is product design so critical to the success of Saturn?

Closing Case 17.2

What's Cooking at Pizza Hut?

Things looked bright for the pizza business in 1977 when PepsiCo, Inc. bought Pizza Hut for $340 million. Pizza Hut had tripled its size between 1972 and 1977 to over 3000 outlets, making it the nation's largest pizza chain. But PepsiCo got more than it bargained for in the Pizza Hut acquisition. Rapid growth coupled with inadequate controls caused the quality of Pizza Hut's food and service to decline, and customers were lost to local pizzerias. An attempt to bolster sagging profit margins by raising prices backfired. Despite an increase in sales from $386 to $532 million between 1977 and 1979, operating profits declined from $52 to $22.4 million for the same period. Decisive steps had to be taken to protect PepsiCo's investment. PepsiCo hired Donald N. Smith, the driving force behind such notable fast-food innovations as McDonald's breakfasts and Burger King's sandwiches, to serve as food service division head. Smith hired a new president for the Pizza Hut chain in 1980, and together they launched a $100 million campaign to get things back on track.

Operational Problems

It soon became clear that more than a bigger advertising budget was needed. By putting on an apron and actually cooking pizza and serving customers in selected Pizza Hut outlets, Smith confirmed reports of dirty facilities, slow service, and poor management. Moreover, he found that low pay and excessive reporting paperwork were largely responsible for an extraordinarily high 80 percent annual turnover rate among outlet managers. An increase in managerial salaries and a streamlined bookkeeping system helped reduce the turnover rate to 50 percent. Smith's firsthand observation of operations proved so successful that all of the top managers at the firm's Wichita, Kansas, headquarters were ordered to put in some time at local outlets.

A Whole New Strategy

Smith's turnaround strategy attacked the problem of declining profits on several fronts. An overriding strategic goal was to move from fast food to family dining. Franchisees were told to double their advertising expenditures. Pizza Hut's ad campaign was shifted from general image building, popular among fast-food companies, to a specific product emphasis. Kitchen operations, based on a 20-year-old design, were improved by installing new ovens that cut in half the baking time for pizza. A new deep-dish, thick-crust offering called Pan Pizza was introduced in 1980. This new product was a marked success. In fact, half of the 126 million pizzas the firm sold in 1981 were Pan Pizzas. By resisting the trend among competitors toward coin-operated video games and entertainment, Pizza Hut retained its competitive emphasis on quality food. Another significant shift in strategy was to focus on 25 to 34 year-olds, rather than teen-agers, as the prime target customers. A program was also launched to redecorate the company-owned stores in more cozy and family-dining-oriented wood tones.

By the end of 1981, the Pizza Hut chain, which had grown to 4000 outlets (half of them company owned, half franchised), was headed in a profitable direction. Revenues for that year topped $1 billion, and sales increased 20 percent. Annual sales per store, less than $250,000 in 1979, had climbed to $300,000 in 1981.

For Discussion

1. What is Pizza Hut's "product"?
2. Did Smith do a good job of focusing strategic attention on the production function? Explain.
3. What do you think about the practice of having top managers periodically work in production-level jobs?

References

Opening Quotation: Lee Iacocca, *Iacocca: An Autobiography* (New York: Bantam, 1984), p. 176.

Opening Case: David Whiteside, Richard Brandt, Zachary Schiller, and Andrea Gabor, "How GM's Saturn Could Run Rings Around Old-Style Carmakers," *Business Week* No. 2878 (January 28, 1985): 126, 128.

Closing Case: For additional information on Pizza Hut, see "Turnaround Updates: Pizza Hut," *Restaurant Business* 80 (January 1, 1981): 104; Peter Berlinski, "Pizza Hut's Turnaround Strategists," *Restaurant Business* 81 (January 1, 1982): 117–133; and "Pizza Hut Tries a New Recipe For Success," *Business Week* No. 2722 (January 18, 1982): 87–88.

1. Adapted from Charles G. Andrew and George A. Johnson, "The Crucial Importance of Production and Operations Management," *Academy of Management Review* 7 (January 1982): 143–147.
2. Jeremy Main, "Toward Service Without a Snarl," *Fortune* 103 (March 23, 1981): 66.
3. See Andrew Weiss, "Simple Truths of Japanese Manufacturing," *Harvard Business Review* 62 (July-August 1984): 119–125.
4. R. Dave Garwood, "Explaining JIT, MRP II, Kanban," *P&IM Review and APICS News* 4 (October 1984): 66.

5. Richard J. Schonberger, *Japanese Manufacturing Techniques: Nine Hidden Lessons in Simplicity* (New York: The Free Press, 1982), p. 35.

6. Robert H. Hayes, "Why Japanese Factories Work," *Harvard Business Review* 59 (July-August 1981): 62.

7. John S. DeMott, "Manufacturing Is in Flower," *Time* 123 (March 26, 1984): 50–51.

8. Adapted in part from discussion in Mariann Jelinek and Joel D. Goldhar, "The Strategic Implications of the Factory of the Future," *Sloan Management Review* 25 (Summer 1984): 29–37.

9. Ibid., p. 32.

10. William F. Arnold, "The Question: Automate, Emigrate, or Evaporate," *Electronic Business* 10 (February 1984): 178, 183.

11. "IBM's Big Leap onto the Factory Floor," *Business Week* No. 2860 (September 17, 1984): 50.

12. Harry B. Thompson, "CAD/CAM and the Factory of the Future," *Management Review* 72 (May 1983): 28. (Emphasis added).

13. See Michele J. Gengler and Richard J. Tersine, "Robots—Coming to Work in America," *Business* 33 (April-June 1983): 3–12.

14. Jelinek and Goldhar, "The Strategic Implications of the Factory of the Future," p. 34.

15. See "Making Service a Potent Marketing Tool," *Business Week* No. 2846 (June 11, 1984): 164–170.

16. "What Clouds Ford's Future," *Business Week* 2545 (July 31, 1978): 73.

17. Bob Davis, "Computers Speed the Design of More Workaday Products," *The Wall Street Journal* 112 (January 18, 1985): 19.

18. See Ibid.

19. Wickham Skinner, "Manufacturing—Missing Link in Corporate Strategy," *Harvard Business Review* 47 (May-June 1969): 145. Also see Robert H. Hayes and Steven C. Wheelwright, "Link Manufacturing Process and Product Life Cycles," *Harvard Business Review* 57 (January-February 1979): 133–140 and Elwood S. Buffa, *Meeting the Competitive Challenge* (Homewood, Ill.: Dow Jones-Irwin, 1984).

20. Roger Schroeder, "Operations Strategy: Missing Link in Corporate Planning?" *Management Review* 73 (August 1984): 20.

21. Joseph Orlicky, *Material Requirements Planning* (New York: McGraw-Hill, 1975), p. 38.

22. See ibid., p. 235.

23. Thomas R. Temin, "Purchasing Audit Helps Uncover Ways to Save," *Purchasing* 90 (May 28, 1981): 65.

24. An excellent overview of industrial purchasing can be found in I. Robert Parket and Joseph Eisenberg, "The Industrial Purchaser: New Star on the Organization Chart," *Business* 32 (January-March 1982): 27–32. Also see Somerby Dowst, "How the Purchasing Job Is Changing," *Purchasing* 98 (January 31, 1985): 98–107.

25. "The New Game Plan: A Huge Potential Is There to Be Won," *Modern Materials Handling* 36 (January 6, 1981): 68. There is a special series of articles on MRP application in this issue.

26. See "Computers and Software: Your Reference Sources," *Modern Materials Handling* 36 (January 6, 1981): 83–87 and Gary Stix, "Manufacturing-Resource Planning Keeps You On Time, On Target," *Computer Decisions* 16 (October 1984): 142–164.

27. Orlicky, *Material Requirements Planning*, p. 47.

28. Lewis Beman, "A Big Payoff from Inventory Controls," *Fortune* 104 (July 27, 1981): 78–79. A more recent survey of MRP users may be found in Darryl Landvater, "How Do You Compare to 1,000 Other Companies?" *Infosystems* 32 (January 1985): 86.

29. Garwood, "Explaining JIT, MRP II, Kanban," pp. 66, 68.

30. Franklin G. Moore and Thomas E. Hendrick, *Production/Operations Management*, 7th ed. (Homewood, Ill.: Irwin, 1977), p. 424.

31. For an instructive discussion of inventory control techniques, see Vincent G. Reuter, "ABC Method to Inventory Control," *Journal of Systems Management* 27 (November 1976): 26–33; and John M. Brennan, "Up Your Inventory Control," *Journal of Systems Management* 28 (January 1977): 39–45.

32. Schonberger, *Japanese Manufacturing Techniques: Nine Hidden Lessons in Simplicity*, p. 220.

33. Stephen Moss, "A Systems Approach to Productivity," *National Productivity Review* 1 (Summer 1982): 277.

34. Lee Iacocca, *Iacocca: An Autobiography* (New York: Bantam, 1984), p. 187.

35. Richard L. Francis and John A. White, *Facility Layout and Location: An Analytical Approach* (Englewood Cliffs, N.J.: Prentice-Hall, 1974), pp. 33–34.

36. Richard B. Chase and Nicholas J. Aquilano, *Production and Operations Management: A Life Cycle Approach*, 3rd ed. (Homewood, Ill.: Richard D. Irwin, 1981): p. 216.

37. Guy C. Close, Jr., *Work Improvement* (New York: John Wiley, 1960), p. 117.

38. For an interesting discussion of *office* layout, see Richard Muther and Lee Hales, "Six Steps to Making Office Layout," *The Office* 85 (March 1977): 28–36.

39. "Unsafe Products: The Great Debate Over Blame and Punishment," *Business Week* No. 2840 (April 30, 1984): 96.

40. See "More Punitive Damage Awards," *Business Week* 2670 (January 12, 1981): 86.

41. "The Dilemma of Product Liability," *Dun's Review* 109 (January 1977): 48.

42. Jeremy Main, "The Battle for Quality Begins," *Fortune* 102 (December 29, 1980): 28.

43. Sylvia Nasar, "Good News Ahead For Productivity," *Fortune* 110 (December 10, 1984): 43.

44. Main, "The Battle for Quality Begins," p. 33.

45. Condensed from Moore and Hendrick, *Production/Operations Management*, p. 676.

46. For a good introduction to QC circles, see Ed Yager, "Examining the Quality Control Circle," *Personnel Journal* 58 (October 1979): 682–684, 708.

47. For a discussion of QC circle benefits, see "Quality Circles Survey Shows Significant Change in Participants' Attitudes," *Management Review* 70 (June 1981): 29, 35; and Perry Pascarella, "Humanagement at Honeywell," *Industry Week* 210 (July 27, 1981): 33–36. Negative experiences with QC circles are discussed in Jeremy Main, "The Trouble with Managing Japanese-Style," *Fortune* 109 (April 2, 1984): 50–56.

48. Charles G. Burck, "What Happens When Workers Manage Themselves," *Fortune* 104 (July 27, 1981): 64.

49. Frank Shipper, "Tapping Creativity," *Quality Circles Journal* 4 (August 1981): 12.

50. Adapted from an excellent discussion in Robert E. Cole, "Will QC Circles Work in the U.S.?" *Quality Progress* 13 (July 1980): 30–33. Also see Merle O'Donnell and Robert J. O'Donnell, "Quality Circles—The Latest Fad or a Real Winner?" *Business Horizons* 27 (May-June 1984): 48–52 and John D. Blair and Carlton J. Whitehead, "Can Quality Circles Survive in the United States?" *Business Horizons* 27 (September-October 1984): 17–23.

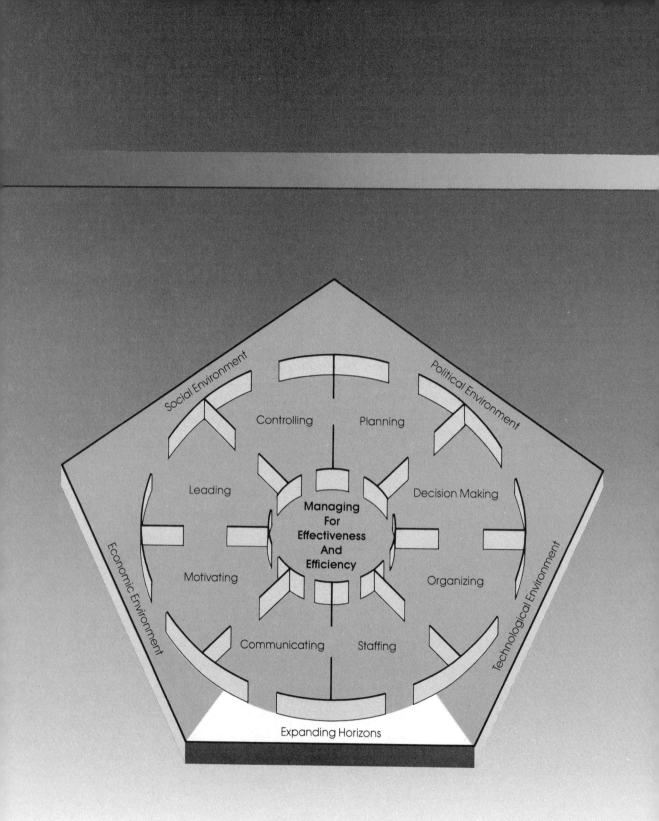

PART SIX

Expanding Horizons in Management

Part Six discusses how management's agenda has been broadened in recent years by social, ethical, and international responsibilities. Inherent in these new responsibilities is a complex web of problems and opportunities. Chapter 18 defines corporate social responsibility and outlines alternative strategies for dealing with it. The topic of business ethics is discussed relative to alternative business philosophies and ways to encourage ethical conduct are explored. Chapter 19 introduces the concept of the multinational corporation as a backdrop for exploring problems unique to international operations, such as expropriation, bribery, and cultural sensitivity.

Chapter 18

Social Responsibility and Business Ethics

While most observers concur that businesses have social responsibilities, considerably fewer are in agreement as to the nature of these responsibilities.

Sandra L. Holmes

Chapter Objectives

When you finish studying this chapter, you should be able to

- Define corporate social responsibility and summarize the arguments for and against it.
- Identify and describe the four social responsibility strategies.
- Explain the role of enlightened self-interest in social responsibility.
- Discuss the current state of social auditing.
- Summarize the research evidence on business ethics.
- Explain how management can improve business ethics.

Opening Case 18.1

Eberhard Faber's Ethical Dilemma

In 1976, an important ethical question unexpectedly cropped up at the April board of directors' meeting at Eberhard Faber, Inc. At the time, the family-owned producer of pencils, pens, markers, and other stationery supplies had annual sales approaching $30 million. According to Eberhard Faber, the firm's chief executive officer, this is what took place at the meeting.

A Very Promising Venture*
As the April meeting began, ... I was feeling quite pleased with myself.

*The rest of this case is excerpted from Eberhard Faber, "How I Lost Our Great Debate About Corporate Ethics," *Fortune,* © 1976 Time Inc. All rights reserved.

Preparations had gone smoothly, and the audited results for 1975, while not as good as we had hoped for at the beginning of that year, were far better than we had thought they would be at the previous meeting; I was sure that they would represent a pleasant surprise for the directors. True, the first quarter of 1976 had gone poorly—in the writing-instrument business, the recession was by no means over—but the outlook was now improving. In addition, I had this new and profitable-looking overseas venture in my pocket.

Several years earlier, the board had said it favored further expansion by Eberhard Faber into foreign markets. Since then we had undertaken a substantial contract with the Syrian government, under which we would provide know-how for a factory to make Eberhard Faber products. We had also settled on a similar deal for the expansion of our Brazilian licensee. This new venture promised to continue the trend.

The venture was to be in a Third World country, which, for reasons that will soon be apparent, I cannot name. I had been working on the deal for two years, and had personally visited the country a couple of months earlier. During that visit, I had reached an agreement in principle under which we would supply the know-how to enable a pencil company there to expand and improve its operations and to use our name. In return, we would be given a substantial equity position—about 30 or 40 percent—in the company.

This equity would not give us control of the operation, but it would significantly increase this year's profit and book value; in addition, it could be expected to contribute a reasonable dividend income in the years ahead. The deal also envisaged that we would supply equipment for the expanded venture over a five-year period, again at a pretty good profit. The sweetest part of the deal was that we would have to put up no cash.

In the two years of working on this negotiation, several other executives and I had done considerable traveling and incurred a fair bit of expense. I myself had contracted amoebic dysentery during these travels, and endured six months of misery thereafter, but it all seemed worthwhile that day last April.

An Unexpected Objection

There was, in fact, only one problem about the deal. The management of the pencil company had cheerfully confessed to me that they were paying off the government of their country in order to do business. I knew that this would not sit particularly well with our board—indeed, it didn't with me—and yet I saw no reason to anticipate any real problems at the meeting. After, all, Eberhard Faber would be only a minority shareholder in the venture. There seemed to be no moral exposure. From the standpoint of ethics, I viewed the proposal as a straight exchange of know-how and our name for stock in a company that needed to conserve its cash for expansion. The ethical practices of the company's management seemed to me to be as irrelevant as they would if it was simply buying merchandise from us. Besides, although the laws of the country in question prohibit bribery, it is common and accepted practice there.

My good humor had worn a bit thin by the time we got to the new venture. It was midafternoon, we were running behind schedule, and some directors were asking more questions than usual, particularly about our long-range plans—a subject that was to be taken up at a separate meeting in June and that I had not planned to discuss extensively at this meeting. A few directors were already starting to peer surreptitiously at their watches.

I introduced the proposal with a ten-minute summary of the conditions of the deal, and went on to explain that it would increase this year's budgeted profit by more than one-quarter. I also mentioned the payoff complication. Then I asked for a motion for approval, i.e., to place the proposal formally before the board. The motion was made and seconded. The discussion began with a couple of questions about the business risks, which I was able to answer satisfactorily. But then something unexpected happened.

Tony Carey [a lawyer and Faber's former college roommate] began to talk about the ethical problems involved in taking an equity position in a company that was paying off the government; he argued forcefully that the deal would set a very bad precedent for us. His position seemed to me to be a strange kind of guilt-by-association argument. I didn't (and still don't) see why we would become unethical ourselves just by virtue of owning stock in an unethical company. At first, I did not realize that Tony was actually going to oppose the deal; after all, the board had known for more than a year that we were pursuing it. I thought at first that Tony was merely dwelling on the negative aspects of a deal that he could still support on balance.

Then some other board members began to register similar concerns. At first, they did not seem to be flatly against the deal—merely hopeful that we could swing it without getting enmeshed in the payoff problem. As time wore on, however, I could sense, with mounting frustration, a growing hostility to the whole thing.

Henry Parker [an insurance executive specializing in international operations] was among those who tried to find a way to eliminate the payoffs. "We must stop them before an equity position is taken," he said. "Isn't that possible?" I had to explain that it wasn't: too much of the business depended on the payoffs. In any case, we wouldn't have control over the company.

A number of directors, including Fred Jorgensen [a retired financial adviser], pressed me on whether we couldn't be paid cash instead of stock. That distinction seemed ethically irrelevant to me, but in any case, there was no chance of our negotiating this aspect of the deal. The company would need all its cash for the expansion it contemplated. In addition, it needed government money, and the government was committed to the idea of our having an equity position, which would ensure our continued interest in and help for the venture.

Tony Carey asked: "Couldn't we forget the know-how deal and just sell them the equipment?" Unfortunately, I had to reply, that didn't work either. "Without the expansion there's no need for the equipment, and the expansion is impossible without the know-how. Anyway, the government financing depends on our participation."

At some point, one director raised the possibility of a new sales company being set up to handle the payoffs, leaving us free to participate in the manufacturing company—which would be clean. There was a chorus of noes to this idea, which would obviously be just passing the buck.

A Worsening Climate

As the afternoon wore on, Carey pursued his objections calmly but relentlessly. "I don't care whether there's any legal exposure or not," he said finally. "There are ethical considerations here which go far beyond legal exposures. I don't want Eberhard Faber Inc. to participate in a company that's paying off its government, and that's that. Besides, the climate in the U.S. is getting worse and worse for such things—there may be no legal exposure today, but how about tomorrow? If this company ever went public [sold its stock to the public], how would you like to have to disclose to the SEC [Securities and Exchange Commission] and the world at large that you have an interest in a company that's paying off the government?"

I argued that I would have no qualms whatever about such disclosure (except for the possibility of causing the principals of the foreign company trouble at home). Aside from the rights and wrongs of payoffs in countries where they are common practice, our own company would be doing no paying off, and we could not hope to change the practices of another company in which we held only a minority stock interest. In any case, we had no immediate plans to go public, and if we ever did, and the issue became a problem, we could always divest ourselves of the stock at that time.

Finally, I fired off one last shot. "Don't you realize that if we adopt this type of policy, we'll be shut out of half the world? Don't you realize that our competition in Europe, if not the U.S., won't have any such ethical qualms and will take over this opportunity in a flash, shutting us out of this market permanently? What ever happened to our policy of international expansion?"

But the momentum of the meeting was against me. It was obvious that I was beaten and I didn't even bother to ask for a vote.

(Discussion questions linking this case with the material you are about to read can be found at the end of this chapter.)

As the social, political, economic, and technological environments of management have changed, the practice of management itself has changed. This is especially true for managers in the private business sector, as we have seen in the case of Eberhard Faber, Inc. It is far less popular today than it was in the past for someone in business to stand before the public and declare that his or her only job is to make as much profit as possible. In an era in which the public is wary of the abuse of power and the betrayal of trust, business managers are expected to make a wide variety of economic and social contributions. The purpose of this chapter is to examine management's social and ethical responsibilities.

Social Responsibility: Definition and Perspectives

When John D. Rockefeller was at the zenith of his power as the founder of Standard Oil Company, he handed out dimes to rows of eager children who lined the street. Rockefeller did this on the advice of a public relations expert who believed the dime campaign would counteract his widespread reputation as a monopolist who had ruthlessly eliminated his competitors in the oil industry. The dime campaign was not a complete success, however, because Standard Oil was broken up under the Sherman Antitrust Act of 1890. Conceivably, Rockefeller believed he was fulfilling some sort of social responsibility by passing out dimes to hungry children. Since Rockefeller's time, the concept of social responsibility has grown and matured to the point at which many of today's companies are intimately involved in social programs that have no direct connection with the bottom line. These programs include everything from support of the arts and urban renewal to environmental protection. But like all other aspects of management, social responsibility needs to be carried out in an effective and efficient manner.

What Does Social Responsibility Involve?

Social responsibility, as defined in this section, is a relatively new concern of the business community. To a large extent, social responsibility is a product of the 1960s. The following account describes the historical backdrop for modern corporate social responsibility:

The Eisenhower era of the 1950s was, by and large, an era of good feeling between business and the American public.

But beginning in the 1960s, an adverse tide of public opinion began to rise against business. A more affluent, better-educated, more critical public began to question the value of ever-increasing production, the resulting pollution and environmental decay, and the defective products and services being produced; and they began to protest the public's seeming inability to influence the behavior of the business system. Frustration over the Vietnam War added fuel to the fires of discontent. Suddenly, consumerism, stockholderism, racial equalitarianism, antimilitarism, environmentalism, and feminism became forces to be reckoned with by corporate managements.[1]

Events during the 1970s, such as Watergate and corporate bribery scandals, only reinforced the public's demand for greater social responsibility in the business sector. By the time the political pendulum in the United States swung toward a more probusiness administration with the election of Ronald Reagan, the notion of corporate social responsibility had become firmly rooted. However, there remains wide-ranging disagreement over the exact nature and scope of management's social responsibilities.

Voluntary Action   One expert in the field has defined **corporate social responsibility** as "the notion that corporations have an obligation to constituent groups in society other than stockholders and beyond that prescribed by law or union contract."[2] A central feature of this particular definition is that an action must be *voluntary* for it to qualify as a socially responsible action. For example, less than two months after a chemical leak at a Union Carbide plant in Bhopal, India, claimed the lives of more than 2000 nearby residents, Monsanto took unprecedented steps to address the fears of people living near *its* chemical plants. At the time, *Business Week* observed:

> ... in late January [1985], Monsanto Co., the nation's fourth-largest chemical producer, surprised critics by announcing a voluntary right-to-know program designed to distribute information about possible hazards and precautions to residents near its 53 plants.[3]

According to our definition and the ten commandments listed in Table 18.1, Monsanto's action was socially responsible because it: (1) was anticipatory and (2) was carried out voluntarily without government coercion. Meanwhile, Union Carbide was busily trying to pin the blame for the Bhopal disaster on the managers of its Indian subsidiary.[4]

When laws must be passed or court orders issued before a company will

Table 18.1   Ten Commandments of Corporate Social Responsibility

I. Thou Shall Take Corrective Action Before It Is Required.
II. Thou Shall Work With Affected Constituents to Resolve Mutual Problems.
III. Thou Shall Work to Establish Industrywide Standards and Self-Regulation.
IV. Thou Shall Publicly Admit Your Mistakes.
V. Thou Shall Get Involved in Appropriate Social Programs.
VI. Thou Shall Help Correct Environmental Problems.
VII. Thou Shall Monitor the Changing Social Environment.
VIII. Thou Shall Establish and Enforce a Corporate Code of Conduct.
IX. Thou Shall Take Needed Public Stands on Social Issues.
X. Thou Shall Strive to Make Profits on an Ongoing Basis.

SOURCE: Excerpted from Larry D. Alexander and William F. Matthews, "The Ten Commandments of Corporate Social Responsibility," *Business and Society Review* No. 50 (Summer 1984): 62–66.

respond to societal needs, that company is not being socially responsible. A prime example of this type of foot-dragging behavior was the manner in which the Ford Motor Company responded to claims that the gas tanks in its Pinto cars were a fire hazard.[5] Endless court battles and reluctant compliance fall outside the realm of social responsibility.

An Emphasis on Means, Not Ends   Another key feature of this definition of corporate social responsibility is its emphasis on means rather than ends:

> Corporate behavior should not, in most cases, be judged by the decisions actually reached, but by the process by which they were reached. Broadly stated, corporations need to analyze the social consequences of their decisions before they make them and take steps to minimize the social costs of these decisions when appropriate. The appropriate demand to be made of those who govern large corporations is that they incorporate into their decision-making process means by which broader social concerns are given full consideration. This is corporate social responsibility as a means, not as a set of ends.[6]

Unfortunately, social consequences are too often shortchanged in the heat of competitive battle.

Underlying Philosophical Debate   Much of the disagreement over what social responsibility is can be traced to a philosophical debate about the exact purpose of a corporation. Is the corporation an economic entity solely dedicated to making a profit for its stockholders? Or is the corporation a socioeconomic entity obligated to make both economic and social contributions to society?[7] Depending on which philosophy one prefers (see Table 18.2), social responsibility can be interpreted in opposite ways.

Table 18.2 Contrasting Models of Business

Economic Model: Primary Emphasis on	Socioeconomic Model: Primary Emphasis on
Production	Quality of life
Exploitation of resources	Conservation of resources and harmony with nature
Market decisions	Some community controls on market decisions
Economic return on resources	Balanced economic and social return on resources
Individual interests	Community interests: people working in system interdependence that requires cooperation
Business as primarily a closed system	Business as primarily an open system
Minor role for government	Active government involvement

SOURCE: From *Business and Society: Concepts and Policy Issues,* 4th ed. By Keith Davis, William C. Frederick, and Robert L. Blomstrom. Copyright © 1980 by McGraw-Hill Book Company, p. 9. Used with permission of McGraw-Hill Book Company.

The Classical Economic Model The classical economic model can be traced back to the eighteenth century, when businesses were owned largely by entrepreneurs or owner-managers. Competition was vigorous among small operations, and short-run profits were the overriding concern of these early entrepreneurs. Of course, the key to attaining short-run profits was to provide society with needed goods and services. According to Adam Smith, the father of the classical economic model, an "invisible hand" promoted the public welfare. Smith believed that the efforts of competing entrepreneurs had a natural tendency to promote the public interest when each tried to maximize short-run profits. In other words, Smith believed that the public interest was served by individuals pursuing their own interests.

This model has survived into modern times. The well-known economist Milton Friedman has no doubts about the role of business in society. According to Friedman, "Few trends could so thoroughly undermine the very foundations of our free society as the acceptance by corporate officials of a social responsibility other than to make as much money for their stockholders as possible."[8] Thus, according to the classical economic model of the corporation, short-run profitability and social responsibility are one and the same thing.

The Socioeconomic Model Reflecting society's broader expectations for business (for example, safe and meaningful jobs, clean air and water, safe products), many think the time has come to revamp what they believe to be an obsolete classical economic model. Oligopolistic industries such as autos, rubber, and brewing, in which a handful of corporate giants dominate the market, are cited as evidence that the classical economic model is outdated. In its place its opponents recommend a socioeconomic model. This alternative model characterizes a business as one subsystem among many in a highly interdependent society. Proponents of the socioeconomic model point out that many groups in society beside stockholders have a stake in corporate affairs. Creditors, current and retired employees, customers, suppliers, competitors, all levels of government, the community, and society in general all have expectations, often conflicting ones, for management.[9] According to the socioeconomic view, business has an obligation to enhance the general quality of life while pursuing a profit.[10]

Arguments For and Against Corporate Social Responsibility

As one might suspect, the foregoing philosophical debate has spawned many specific arguments both for and against corporate social responsibility.[11] A sample of four major arguments on each side reveals the principal issues.

Arguments For Convinced that the corporation should be more than simply a profit machine, proponents of social responsibility have offered the following arguments:

1. **Business is unavoidably involved in social issues.** As social activists like to say, business is either part of the solution or part of the problem. There is no denying that private business shares responsibility for societal problems including unemployment, inflation, and pollution. Like everyone else, corporate citizens must balance their rights and responsibilities.
2. **Business has the resources to tackle today's complex societal problems.** With its rich stock of technical, financial, and managerial resources, the private business sector can tip the scale in favor of solving society's more troublesome problems. After all, it is argued, without the support of society, business could not have built its resource base in the first place.
3. **A better society means a better environment for doing business.** Business can enhance its long-run profitability by making an investment in society today. In other words, today's problems can turn into tomorrow's profits.
4. **Corporate social action will prevent government intervention.** As evidenced by waves of antitrust, equal employment opportunity, and pollution control legislation, the government will force business to do what it fails to do voluntarily.

These arguments give business a broad socioeconomic agenda.

Arguments Against   Remaining faithful to the classical economic model, opponents of corporate social responsibility rely on the first two arguments below. The third and fourth arguments have been voiced by those who feel that business is already too big and too powerful.

1. **Profit maximization ensures the efficient use of society's resources.** By buying goods and services, consumers collectively dictate where assets should be deployed. Social expenditures amount to theft of stockholders' equity.
2. **As an economic institution, business lacks the ability to pursue social goals.** Gross inefficiencies can be expected if managers are forced to divert their attention from their pursuit of economic goals.
3. **Business already has enough power.** Considering that business exercises powerful influence over where and how we work and live, what we buy, and what we value, additional concentration of social power in the hands of business is undesirable.
4. **Since managers are not elected, they are not directly accountable to the people.** Corporate social programs can easily become misguided. The market system effectively controls business's economic performance, but it is a poor mechanism for controlling business's social performance.

These arguments are based on the assumption that business should stick to what it does best, that is, pursuing profit by producing marketable goods and services. Social goals should be handled by other institutions such as the family, school, church, or government.

Toward Greater Social Responsibility

Is it inevitable that management must assume greater social responsibility? Some management scholars believe that it is. It has been said that business is bound by an iron law of responsibility. This **iron law of responsibility** states that "in the long run, those who do not use power in a way that society considers responsible will tend to lose it."[12] This is an important concept, considering that antibusiness sentiment runs high today, in spite of a more conservative political climate. In fact, in a 1980 national Roper survey, 68 percent judged the statement that "American business and industry is far too often not honest with the public" as "largely true."[13] Moreover, "a 1981 poll ranking twelve occupations on their 'contributions

Figure 18.1 A Continuum of Social Responsibility Strategies

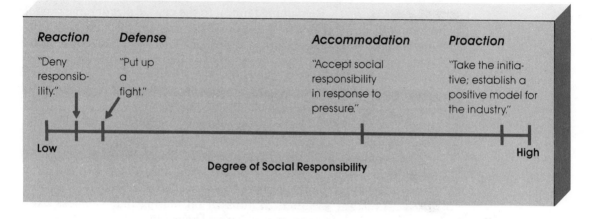

to the general good of society' listed business leaders in ninth place, behind judges, lawyers, and funeral directors."[14] The challenge for business to act more responsibly is unmistakable. And if this challenge is not met voluntarily, then government reform legislation will probably force business to meet it. In this section we look at four alternative social responsibility strategies and some contrasting expressions of corporate social responsibility.

Social Responsibility Strategies

Similar to management's political response continuum, as discussed in Chapter 3, is its social responsibility continuum (see Figure 18.1). The four strategies along this continuum are reaction, defense, accommodation, and proaction.[15] Each involves a distinctly different approach to demands for greater social responsibility.

- **Reaction.** When a business follows a reactive strategy, it will deny responsibility while building its case for maintaining the status quo.
- **Defense.** This strategy uses legal maneuvering and/or a public relations campaign to keep from having to assume additional responsibilities.
- **Accommodation.** The organization agrees to assume additional responsibilities when it follows the accommodation strategy. Some sort of outside stimulus, such as pressure from a special-interest group or threatened government action, is normally required to trigger an accommodation strategy.
- **Proaction.** A proactive strategy aggressively formulates a social responsibility program that serves as a model for the industry. Proaction clearly means taking the initiative.

Table 18.3 An Anatomy of Proactive Social Responsibility: Procter & Gamble's Response to the Toxic Shock Problem

Phase	Action
Reaction	Collected information from state health boards
	Conducted laboratory testing with suspected bacteria
	Assembled a group of outside scientific advisers
Defense	Set up military-type command post
	Refuted and/or questioned several aspects of CDC study
	Prepared news releases
Accommodation	Proposed warning label
	Voluntarily halted production
	Pulled back products from store shelves
Proaction	Offered to buy back all unused products including free promotion samples
	Pledged research expertise for further study
	Agreed to finance and direct an educational program
	Issued a warning to women not to use Rely

SOURCE: Elizabeth Gatewood and Archie B. Carroll, "The Anatomy of Corporate Social Response: The Rely, Firestone 500, and Pinto Cases," *Business Horizons* 24 (September-October 1981): 13. Copyright, 1981, by the Foundation for the School of Business at Indiana University. Reprinted by permission.

Proponents of social responsibility would like to see reactive strategies evolve into proactive ones. The manner in which Procter & Gamble responded to claims that one of its most successful products was the cause of a deadly health problem is an excellent case in point.

Procter & Gamble: A Case of Proactive Social Responsibility[16]

In mid-1980, Atlanta's Center for Disease Control notified Procter & Gamble (P&G) and other tampon manufacturers of a positive correlation between the potentially fatal toxic shock syndrome and tampon use.[17] Subsequent studies by a couple of state research centers pinpointed P&G's highly successful Rely tampons as the probable (but not certain) culprit. P&G initially reacted to this assault on its newly launched product by denying responsibility. Rely tampons were the result of twenty years of research costing millions of dollars. However, just three months after P&G learned of the possible link between its Rely tampons and toxic shock, it took unprecedented steps to prevent further use of Rely tampons. In a manner of speaking, P&G decided to aggressively "demarket" Rely tampons, just in case they were the cause of toxic shock. P&G's share of the U.S. tampon market dropped from over 17 percent to zero practically overnight. As detailed in Table 18.3, this dramatic turnaround by Procter &

Gamble involved an exemplary evolution of social responsibility strategies.

Who Benefits from Social Responsibility?

Is social responsibility like the old theory of home medicine, "It has to taste bad to be good"? In other words, does social responsibility have to be a hardship for the organization? Those who answer yes to these questions believe that social responsibility should be motivated by **altruism, an unselfish devotion to the interests of others.** This implies that businesses that are not socially responsible are motivated strictly by self-interest. In short-run economic terms, Manville's bankruptcy ploy (as will be discussed in case 18.2) has saved it millions of dollars, whereas Procter & Gamble's actions with Rely tampons *cost* it millions of dollars. On the basis of these facts alone, one would be hard pressed to say that social responsibility pays. In taking the long-run view, however, the notion of enlightened self-interest comes into play.

Enlightened Self-interest   **Enlightened self-interest,** the realization that business ultimately helps itself by helping to solve societal problems, involves a balancing of short-run costs and long-run benefits. Advocates of enlightened self-interest contend that social responsibility expenditures are profit motivated. Recent research of **corporate philanthropy,** the charitable donation of company resources, supports this contention. After analyzing Internal Revenue Service statistics for firms in 36 industries, researchers concluded that corporate giving is a form of profit-motivated advertising. They went on to observe that ". . . it would seem ill-advised to use philanthropy data to measure altruistic responses of corporations."[18] Thus, as demonstrated in Table 18.4, the answer to the question "Who benefits from social responsibility?" appears to be "Both business itself and society in general."

An Array of Benefits to the Organization   In addition to the advertising effect, other possible long-run benefits for the socially responsible organization include:

- Tax-free incentives to employees (for example, buying orchestra tickets and giving them to deserving employees).
- Retention of talented managers by satisfying their altruistic motives.
- Help in recruiting talented and socially conscious personnel.
- Swaying public opinion against government intervention.
- Improved community living standards for employees.
- Attracting socially conscious investors.
- A nontaxable employee benefit for executives by donating company funds to their favorite causes.

Table 18.4 Enlightened Self-interest: American Express Helps Itself by Helping Others

With deep gratitude, the Statue of Liberty-Ellis Island Foundation recently accepted two special traveler's checks totaling more than $1.7 million from American Express Co.

The gift, along with contributions from others, meant the grande dame of New York Harbor could be restored to past glory, Americans could gaze upon it with renewed pride and the donor could be hailed a corporate patriot.

Moreover, by doing good, American Express managed to do well. It generated the gift money by promising in a national ad campaign in last year's [1983] fourth quarter to donate a penny to the statue for each use of its charge card and a dollar for most new cards issued in the U.S. The result: Card usage increased 28% during the quarter over the same period in 1982; before the campaign was devised, the company had forecast a card-usage increase of 18% for last year's fourth quarter. New card holders rose more than 45% during the campaign, and the company's card business had its best fourth quarter ever.

SOURCE: Wendy L. Wall, "Companies Change the Ways They Make Charitable Donations," *The Wall Street Journal* 110 (June 21, 1984): 1. Reprinted by permission of *The Wall Street Journal*, © Dow Jones & Company, Inc. 1984. All rights reserved.

These benefits make it clear that social responsibility can be a "win-win" proposition, meaning that both society and the socially responsible organization can win in the long run.

Social Responsibility in Action

In earlier chapters, we emphasized that the success of organizational programs and changes hinges on the support of top management. Proactive social responsibility is no exception. A recent survey of 116 corporate chief executive officers sought to determine the strength of top management's support for some fundamental social responsibility assumptions.[19] As shown in Figure 18.2, the researchers found broad support for social responsibility among top management. Accordingly, businesses are becoming socially involved in many creative ways. As the examples in this section illustrate, opportunity is limited only by management's imagination and desire to make the world a better place in which to live, work, and do business.

Corporate Philanthropy Philanthropic contributions may take the form of money, goods, or services. U.S. tax law clearly encourages corporate giving, as charitable contributions of up to 5 percent of pretax income are allowable tax deduc-

Figure 18.2 Top Management Support for Social Responsibility

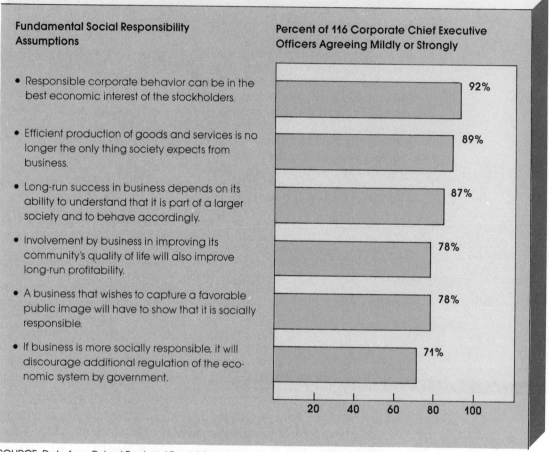

Fundamental Social Responsibility Assumptions

Percent of 116 Corporate Chief Executive Officers Agreeing Mildly or Strongly

- Responsible corporate behavior can be in the best economic interest of the stockholders. — 92%

- Efficient production of goods and services is no longer the only thing society expects from business. — 89%

- Long-run success in business depends on its ability to understand that it is part of a larger society and to behave accordingly. — 87%

- Involvement by business in improving its community's quality of life will also improve long-run profitability. — 78%

- A business that wishes to capture a favorable public image will have to show that it is socially responsible. — 78%

- If business is more socially responsible, it will discourage additional regulation of the economic system by government. — 71%

SOURCE: Data from Robert Ford and Frank McLaughlin, "Perceptions of Socially Responsible Activities and Attitudes: A Comparison of Business School Deans and Corporate Chief Executives," *Academy of Management Journal* 27 (September 1984): 670.

tions for corporations. But, as those who question the generosity of corporations like to point out, records of the last 20 years indicate that U.S. corporate giving has hovered around 1 percent of pretax income (about $2.6 billion in 1980). Tax records tend to understate corporate giving, however, because not all gifts are filed as charitable deductions. "Charity means different things to different companies. Exxon listed the $2.8 million it paid ... [in 1980] to underwrite *Great Performances* on public television as a charitable contribution, while Mobil called the $1.9 million it paid for *Masterpiece Theater* public relations."[20]

Research has uncovered another surprising fact about corporate giving. Contrary to normal expectations, there is no positive relationship between philanthropy and corporate size.[21] The biggest do not give proportionately the most. A reasonable explanation is that smaller corporations generally are one-plant operations. Consequently, their philanthropy can have strong local impact, with direct benefits for the company and its employees. Another reason is the financial reality that it takes time and talent to give away large sums of money.

> At 5%, AT&T would be laying out $500 million a year—or more than five times as much as the Ford Foundation, the largest independent foundation. The company would have to hire a huge staff of philanthropoids, as they are called in the trade. (According to one estimate, it takes one philanthropoid to give away $1 million prudently.)[22]

As government spending cuts continue to take their toll, the private business sector will be increasingly pressured to dig deeper and give more. Forty-five firms in the Minneapolis–St. Paul area that belong to the Five Percent Club have shown that business is capable of meeting the challenge.[23] One member of the Five Percent Club, H. B. Fuller Company, a maker of glues and sealants, lets its 1650 employees decide how and where the firm's charitable donations are spent.

> Each plant elects a local community affairs council to disperse a proportional amount of the total within its area. For the past few years, the chairpersons of the local councils (who meet yearly in St. Paul) have decided to put a special emphasis on battered women and child abuse.[24]

Community Service
An exciting alternative to simply giving cash grants was inaugurated in 1972 by Xerox Corporation. That year Xerox granted paid leave to 21 employees who spent from six months to one year working on community service programs of their choice. (Applications were screened by an employee board.) Since then, participants in Xerox's Social Service Leave program have contributed their time and talent, at company expense, to a wide variety of programs for the inner city, prisons, and the handicapped. Although much of the success of this program is due to the enthusiastic support of its participants, it has also been firmly supported by top management, which assures candidates that they can go on leave if their application is accepted. Moreover, top management guarantees that the same job or at least an equivalent one will be waiting when the employee returns. Xerox feels that by lending its employees to worthwhile community programs, it is donating its most valuable asset, its people.[25]

Urban Renewal Rather than fleeing to the suburbs along with many of its customers, Brooklyn Union Gas decided to remain in the center city and strive to make it a good place to live and do business. Its approach was fairly simple. Old, dilapidated, and abandoned brownstone houses were purchased and fixed up. A few were reserved as models to interest others in this form of grass-roots urban renewal. But most of the refurbished houses were sold. Soon other business as well as individuals caught on, and a wave of restoration hit surrounding decayed neighborhoods. Portions of Brooklyn that had been given up as a lost cause got a new lease on life. Over a ten-year period, Brooklyn Union Gas spent $400,000 on its urban renewal program.[26]

Aid to the Disadvantaged In observance of the International Year of Disabled Persons in 1981, Safeway, the nation's largest supermarket chain, teamed up with the Association for Retarded Citizens (ARC). Safeway helped educate its employees and customers about mental retardation in several ways. Special messages about mental retardation were put on milk cartons, shelf cards, and bags in all of Safeway's nearly two thousand stores across the United States. Banners and posters urged customers to donate ten dollars to ARC. Safeway's advertising managers helped ARC place public service messages about mental retardation on local television and radio stations. Safeway also donated cash to ARC.[27]

Energy Conservation As energy prices soared during the early 1980s, Pacific Gas & Electric, a utility company in northern California, introduced its innovative Zero Interest Plan (ZIP). ZIP was designed to help PG&E customers save energy. More specifically, the utility provided interest-free loans to its customers for energy-saving home improvements. Homeowners and renters were allowed to borrow up to $3500 and take up to 100 months to repay the loans via their utility bills.[28]

Career Development Bristol-Myers's Clairol division has responded to the greater role women are playing in the work force with scholarships for women over 30. According to *Business and Society Review*:

> The Clairol Loving Care Scholarship awards up to $1,000 to women [over 30] who want to learn a profession or skill. Over the past decade the company has given away $500,000 to 1,000 women—and now [in 1984] it has increased this funding program by 50 percent.[29]

This unique scholarship program is administered by the Business and Professional Women's Foundation in Washington, D.C.[30]

Keeping Score with the Social Audit

To ensure that investors and the general public get an accurate picture of a publicly held corporation's financial status, the law requires periodic audits. This general concept of the financial audit has prompted social responsibility experts to suggest the development and use of social audits.

Formally defined, a **social audit** is "a commitment to systematic assessment of and reporting on some meaningful, definable domain of a company's activities that have social impact."[31] In short, proponents of social audits feel that the time has come for objective accountability in the area of social responsibility. Investors and the public have begun to demand to know what is being done in the name of social responsibility.

Unfortunately, social auditing has been plagued by a number of problems. One expert on the subject has listed the following difficulties:

- Overall objectives for social programs (within our society or within a company) may not have been set.
- Criteria or units of measurement may not exist.
- The effect of an action—or an inaction—may be difficult to pinpoint, especially when measurements are sought on a "before and after" basis.
- Control points, or measurement techniques, may not have been built into the facility or system.
- Data collection, accuracy, objectivity, and completeness pose difficulties.[32]

These problems need to be kept in mind when developing a social audit.

Developing a Social Audit

Because the direct costs and benefits of social programs are not readily apparent, social audits are much more primitive than traditional financial audits. For example, imagine the difficulty of assessing the long-run economic benefits of an industrial pollution control program intended to reduce the risk of cancer in a large metropolitan area. Measuring this kind of payoff is much more difficult than assessing the direct economic benefits of, say, a new drill press. This is true because cancer might not show up for 20 years. In view of this measurability problem, social auditors have to begin in general terms and proceed toward more specific terms. They can do this by following five basic steps:

1. List all programs with social impact. See Table 18.5 for a representative listing.
2. Explain the rationale behind each program. This portion of the social audit should answer the question "Why is the organization involved in this area?"

Table 18.5   Social Responsibility Takes Many Forms

Environment	Pollution control Restoration or protection of environment Conservation of natural resources Recycling efforts
Energy	Conservation of energy in production and marketing operations Efforts to increase energy efficiency of products Other energy-saving programs (e.g., company-sponsored car pools)
Fair business practices	Employment and advancement of women and minorities Employment and advancement of disadvantaged individuals (e.g., handicapped, Vietnam veterans, ex-offenders, former drug addicts, mentally retarded, and hard-core unemployed) Support for minority-owned businesses
Human resources	Promotion of employee health and safety Employee training and development Remedial education programs for disadvantaged employees Alcohol and drug counseling programs Career counseling Child day care facilities for working parents Employee physical fitness and stress management programs
Community involvement	Donations of cash, products, services, or employee time Sponsorship of public health projects Support of education and the arts Support of community recreation programs Cooperation in community projects (e.g., recycling centers, disaster assistance, and urban renewal)
Products	Enhancement of product safety Sponsorship of product safety education programs Reduction of polluting potential of products Improvement in nutritional value of products Improvements in packaging and labeling

SOURCE: Adapted with permission from *Social Responsibility Disclosure: 1977 Survey of Fortune 500 Annual Reports,* Ernst & Ernst, 1300 Union Commerce Building, Cleveland, Ohio 44115, pp. 27–33.

3. State the objective(s) of each program.
4. Outline the progress of each program to date. The measurability problem can be avoided during this step by offering a descriptive account, in nonquantitative terms, of what has been accomplished.

5. As much as possible, quantify and match the direct costs and benefits of each program.[33]

The Future of Social Audits

Some observers contend that social audits will become a relic of the early 1970s. Research indicates that significant new approaches to social auditing are not being developed and that existing approaches are not being widely adopted.[34] It appears that social auditing is still in the early stages of development. But the slow adoption of social auditing does not necessarily signal its death. Like other significantly new concepts, social auditing is growing sporadically, with many companies watching and waiting to see how it works out for early adopters. But despite slow progress in social auditing, the general idea of reporting social contributions appears to be alive and well. For example, a 1977 survey of the annual reports of the 500 largest companies in the United States uncovered social responsibility disclosures in 91.2 percent of them.[35] Vigorous activity in the overall area of social responsibility assures that social audits will continue their development and that they will be around for a long time. In the final analysis, the public's demand for greater responsibility and accountability among managers will prevail.

The Ethical Dimension of Management

Because of highly publicized accounts of corporate misconduct in recent years, the subject of ethics is receiving renewed attention in management circles. **Ethics** is the study of moral obligation involving the separation of right from wrong. Business ethics, sometimes referred to as management ethics or organizational ethics, simply narrows the search for right and wrong to productive organizations.[36] One writer has framed the moral agenda for management as follows:

1. To provide goods and services that are socially valuable.
2. To promote economic and social well-being through effective and efficient operation.
3. To enhance the freedom, dignity, and general well-being of individuals both inside and outside the organization.[37]

With these moral obligations in mind, we turn to a discussion of business ethics research, personal philosophies of management, and steps that management can take to foster ethical business behavior.

Table 18.6 An Ethics Test

Many situations in day-to-day business are not simple right-or-wrong questions, but rather fall into a gray area. To demonstrate the perplexing array of moral dilemmas faced by 20th-century Americans, here is a "nonscientific" test for slippage.... Don't expect to score high. That is not the purpose. But give it a try, and see how you stack up.

Put your value system to the test in the following situations:

Scoring Code: Strongly Agree = SA   Disagree = D
Agree = A   Strongly Disagree = SD

	SA	A	D	SD
1. Employees should not be expected to inform on their peers for wrong-doings.	__	__	__	__
2. There are times when a manager must overlook contract and safety violations in order to get on with the job.	__	__	__	__
3. It is not always possible to keep accurate expense account records; therefore, it is sometimes necessary to give approximate figures.	__	__	__	__
4. There are times when it is necessary to withhold embarrassing information from one's superior.	__	__	__	__
5. We should do what our managers suggest, though we may have doubts about its being the right thing to do.	__	__	__	__
6. It is sometimes necessary to conduct personal business on company time.	__	__	__	__
7. Sometimes it is good psychology to set goals somewhat above normal if it will help to obtain a greater effort from the sales force.	__	__	__	__
8. I would quote a "hopeful" shipping date in order to get the order.	__	__	__	__
9. It is proper to use the company WATS line for personal calls as long as it's not in company use.	__	__	__	__
10. Management must be goal-oriented; therefore, the end usually justifies the means.	__	__	__	__
11. If it takes heavy entertainment and twisting a bit of company policy to win a large contract, I would authorize it.	__	__	__	__
12. Exceptions to company policy and procedures are a way of life.	__	__	__	__
13. Inventory controls should be designed to report "underages" rather than "overages" in goods received. [The ethical issue here is the same as that faced by someone who receives too much change from a store cashier.]	__	__	__	__
14. Occasional use of the company's copier for personal or community activities is acceptable.	__	__	__	__
15. Taking home company property (pencils, paper, tape, etc.) for personal use is an accepted fringe benefit.	__	__	__	__

Score Key: (0) for Strongly Disagree (1) for Disagree (2) for Agree (3) for Strongly Agree

If your score is:

0 Prepare for canonization ceremony	**11–15 Good ethical values**	**36–44 Slipping fast**
1– 5 Bishop material	**16–25 Average ethical values**	**45 Leave valuables**
6–10 High ethical values	**26–35 Need moral development**	**with warden**

SOURCE: "Is Your (Ethical) Slippage Showing?" by Lowell G. Rein, copyright September 1980. Reprinted with the permission of *Personnel Journal*, Costa Mesa, California; all rights reserved.

**Business
Ethics
Research
Findings**
Empirical research is always welcomed in a socially relevant and important area such as business ethics. It permits us to probe beyond mere intuition and speculation to determine more precisely who, what, and why. On-the-job research of business ethics has revealed three ethical pressure points for managers: (1) difficulty with pressure from above, (2) self-versus-others perceptual disparity, and (3) discomfort with ambiguity.

Pressure from Above   A number of studies have uncovered the problem of perceived pressure for results. As discussed in Chapter 12, pressure from superiors can lead to blind conformity. For example, after surveying 1227 *Harvard Business Review* readers, researchers noted that "respondents frequently complained of superiors' pressure to support incorrect viewpoints, sign false documents, overlook superiors' wrongdoing, and do business with superiors' friends."[38] And a study of public-sector managers led another researcher to conclude that "... some managers feel so much pressure to achieve results that they need to compromise their integrity."[39] By being aware of this problem of pressure from above, managers can decide where they want to draw the line.

A Perceptual Trap   What is the relationship between managers' perceptions of their own ethical conduct and that of their peers? Studies have discovered that managers consistently view themselves as being more ethical than their peers. After reviewing the implications of their survey results, one team of researchers concluded, "If managers believe ... that they are more ethical than their peers, they may easily justify some indiscretions on the basis of 'everybody is doing it,' or 'it is not as bad as what others are doing.' "[40] One hopes that when present and future managers are made aware of this perceptual trap, they will not deceive themselves when faced with an ethical question.

Ambiguous Situations   Surveys of purchasing managers and field sales personnel have uncovered discomfort with ambiguous situations in which there are no clear-cut ethical guidelines (take a moment now to complete the exercise in Table 18.6). One result of this kind of research is the following statement: "A striking aspect of the responses to the questionnaire is the degree to which the purchasing managers desire a stated policy."[41] In other words, those who often face ethically ambiguous situations want formal guidelines to help sort things out. Ethical codes, discussed later, can satisfy this need.

A Call for Action   Corporate misconduct and the foregoing research findings underscore the importance of the following call to action from Max Ways of *Fortune* magazine:

External pressures and internal needs require that management develop a conscious, analytical, systematic interest in ethical questions. Schools of business administration should respond seriously to the promptings of many students and alumni who recognize that the art of management cannot cut itself off from concern with the difference between right and wrong. Ethical constraints and ethical motivations will have to be brought into much clearer relation with economic constraints and economic motivations.[42]

Interestingly, a recent survey of 2856 college students from 28 schools across the United States revealed that female students were more concerned about business ethics than were their male counterparts.[43] In view of the proportional growth in female managers in recent years, this finding could foretell a needed boost for business ethics. Managers, female or male, who engage in objective philosophical reflection are better equipped to confront tough ethical questions.

Philosophies of Management

As we found in Chapter 6 in regard to decision making, people tend to perceive things differently because their instrumental and terminal values are different. So it is with ethics. For example, one person might see nothing ethically wrong with falsely calling in sick, but another individual might view the same act as unethical. Behind these two different responses are different values or, more fundamentally, different operative philosophies. An **operative philosophy** is a system of values inferred from one's actual behavior, but not necessarily from one's stated intentions. Managers are guided by their operative philosophies whether or not they consciously think about them. A business ethics scholar has observed:

> The choice is not between operating or not operating according to a given business philosophy and morality. The question is rather whether you go about your moral life with eyes open and well aware of your operative philosophy or with eyes shut, unconscious of the assumptions and moral consequences of your decisions.[44]

The eight alternative business philosophies summarized in Table 18.7 are a helpful framework for clarifying one's operative management philosophy. Of course, most of us rely on a combination of these pure types.

Each of the alternative business philosophies in Table 18.7 bases the distinction between right and wrong on a different consideration. And each raises unresolved ethical dilemmas for managers. The following questions should be kept in mind when translating these business philosophies into a personal philosophy of management: Assuming that managers have economic and social power, (1) how should that power be used, and (2) how should that power be regulated?

Table 18.7 Alternative Business Philosophies

Business Philosophy	Key Theme	Major Assumptions	Unresolved Ethical Dilemmas for Managers
Social Darwinism (named for Charles Darwin's theory of natural selection)	"Survival of the fittest."	• Natural selection, when left unimpeded, guarantees improvement in human character.	"Won't unethical managers and organizations have an unfair advantage?"
Machiavellianism (named for the fifteenth-century philosopher, Niccolo Machiavelli)	"Do whatever is necessary to get the job done."	• Business decision making is essentially amoral. • Morality is a private matter; economic necessity and expediency prevail in public business life. • Ends justify means.	"Won't destructive competition end up hurting everyone involved?"
Ethical relativism	"When in Rome, do as the Romans do."	• Morality is defined by the relevant community's responsible expectations, not by self-interest. • Social approval should be our social norm ("How would my action look on TV?") • View your actions as a disinterested observer.	"When managers are sent overseas, whose laws and ethics should they follow?"
Pure legalism	"Laws are not morally binding."	• Law is a bothersome hurdle, not a moral guide. • "Good versus bad" is an ethical question, not a legal one.	"Won't managers be encouraged to use moral justifications for breaking the law?"
Moral legalism	"Moral people follow the letter of the law."	• Law commands moral respect because it constrains the anarchical side of human nature. • Rules are needed in a dog-eat-dog world.	"Doesn't this encourage managers to follow the letter but not the *spirit* of the law?" (continued on next page)

Table 18.7 Alternative Business Philosophies (cont.)

Business Philosophy	Key Theme	Major Assumptions	Unresolved Ethical Dilemmas for Managers
● *Social responsibility*	"Voluntarily take the initiative."	● Business is capable of cleaning its own house through socially responsible self-regulation. ● A natural by-product of self-regulation is less need for outside interference in internal business matters.	"Doesn't this make it easy for some managers and organizations to do less than their fair share?"
● *Social accountability*	"Take the initiative because someone is watching."	● Objective outside observers must police organizational decisions/actions to ensure social responsibility.	"Won't this erode management's decision-making prerogatives?"
● *Pragmatism*	"Follow the most rational course of action."	● As an inherently rational matter, ethics, like science, is basically a problem-solving process. ● Specific actions, like the specific facts of a situation, speak louder than words or ideals. ● Moral and social progress result from autonomous scientific choice within a framework of free-enterprise capitalism.	"Aren't emotional considerations often left out of rational scientific analyses?"

SOURCE: Philosophies and assumptions abstracted from Edward Stevens, *Business Ethics* (New York: Paulist Press, © 1979).

"Whose idea was this?"

"It stinks!"

SOURCE: Reprinted with permission from The Saturday
Evening Post Society, a division of BFL & MS, Inc. © 1985.

**Encouraging
Ethical
Conduct**

Simply telling managers and other employees to be good will not work. Both research evidence and practical experience tell us that words need to be supported by concrete action. Three specific ways to encourage ethical conduct within the organization are ethical advocates, ethical codes, and whistle-blowing.

Ethical Advocates An **ethical advocate** is a business ethics specialist who sits as a full-fledged member of the board of directors and acts as the board's social conscience.[45] This individual may also be asked to sit in on top management decision deliberations. The idea is to assign someone the specific role of critical questioner (see Table 18.8 for recommended questions). Groupthink and blind conformity are less likely when an ethical advocate "tests" management's thinking about ethical implications during the decision-making process.

Codes of Ethics Experience in recent years has shown codes of ethics to be a step in the right direction, but not a cure-all.[46] Formal codes of ethics for organization members must satisfy two requirements if they are to

Table 18.8 Twelve Questions for Examining the Ethics of a Business Decision

1. Have you defined the problem accurately?
2. How would you define the problem if you stood on the other side of the fence?
3. How did this situation occur in the first place?
4. To whom and to what do you give your loyalty as a person and as a member of the corporation?
5. What is your intention in making this decision?
6. How does this intention compare with the probable results?
7. Whom could your decision or action injure?
8. Can you discuss the problem with the affected parties before you make your decision?
9. Are you confident that your position will be as valid over a long period of time as it seems now?
10. Could you disclose without qualm your decision or action to your boss, your CEO, the board of directors, your family, society as a whole?
11. What is the symbolic potential of your action if understood? if misunderstood?
12. Under what conditions would you allow exceptions to your stand?

SOURCE: Reprinted by permission of the *Harvard Business Review.* Exhibit from "Ethics Without the Sermon," by Laura L. Nash (November-December 1981). Copyright © 1981 by the President and Fellows of Harvard College; all rights reserved.

encourage ethical conduct. First, they should refer to specific practices such as kickbacks, payoffs, receiving gifts, record falsification, and misleading claims about products. For example, Xerox's fifteen-page ethical code says: "We're honest with our customers. No deals, no bribes, no secrets, no fooling around with prices. A kickback in any form kicks anybody out. Anybody."[47] General platitudes about good business practice or professional conduct are not effective because they don't provide specific guides and because they offer too many tempting loopholes.

Second, organizational codes of ethics should be firmly supported by top management and equitably enforced through the reward-and-punishment system. Spotty enforcement is the quickest way to kill the effectiveness of an ethical code.

Whistle-Blowing Detailed ethical codes help managers deal swiftly and effectively with subordinate misconduct. But what should a manager do when a superior or the entire organization is engaged in misconduct? Yielding to the realities of organizational politics, many managers will simply turn their backs or claim that they were "just following orders." (Nazi war criminals who based their defense at the Nuremberg trials on the argument that they were following orders ended up with ropes around their necks.) More activist managers may attempt to work within the organizational system for positive change. Still others will take the boldest step of all, whistle-blowing. **Whistle-blowing** is the practice of reporting perceived unethical practices to outsiders such as the press, government agencies, or public interest groups.[48]

Not surprisingly, whistle-blowing is a highly controversial topic among managers. Many managers believe that whistle-blowing erodes their authority and decision-making prerogatives. But according to consumer advocate Ralph Nader, "the willingness and ability of insiders to blow the whistle is the last line of defense ordinary citizens have against the denial of their rights and the destruction of their interests by secretive and powerful institutions."[49] On the other hand, considering that loyalty to the organization is a cherished value in many quarters, whistle-blowing is criticized as the epitome of disloyalty. (For example, recall Karen Silkwood's experience, as vividly portrayed in the popular movie *Silkwood*.) Whistle-blowing generally means putting one's job and/or career on the line, even though over 20 states have passed whistle-blower protection acts.[50] The challenge for today's management is to create an organizational climate in which the need to blow the whistle is reduced. An expert on the subject suggests that the organization should

- Encourage the free expression of controversial and dissenting viewpoints.
- Streamline the organization's grievance procedure so that problems receive a prompt and fair hearing.
- Find out what employees think about the organization's social responsibility policies and make appropriate changes.
- Let employees know that management respects and is sensitive to their individual consciences.
- Recognize that the harsh treatment of a whistle-blower will probably lead to adverse public opinion.[51]

These steps help management exercise feedforward control over whistle-blowing.

If one's conscience should dictate blowing the whistle on an unethical practice at work, a lawyer has recommended four rules:

1. Focus on the disclosure itself, not on personalities.
2. Use "channels" before going public.
3. Anticipate and document retaliation.
4. Know when to give up.[52]

In the final analysis, it is individual behavior that makes organizations ethical or unethical. But organizational forces can help bring out the best in people by clearly stating and rewarding ethical conduct.

Summary

Corporate social responsibility is the idea that management has broader responsibilities than just to make a profit. A strict interpretation holds that an action must be voluntary in order for it to qualify as socially responsible. Accordingly, reluctant submission to court orders or government coercion falls outside the realm of social responsibility. A vigorous debate about social responsibility has arisen between those with differing philosophies of what the purpose of the corporation is. Those who embrace the classical economic model contend that business's social responsibility is to maximize profits for stockholders. Proponents of the socioeconomic model disagree, saying that business has a responsibility to improve the general quality of life, above and beyond making a profit. This philosophical disagreement has inspired specific arguments for and against social responsibility.

Management scholars who advocate greater corporate social responsibility cite the iron law of responsibility. This law implies that if business does not use its socioeconomic power responsibly, society will take away that power. A continuum of social responsibility includes four strategies: reaction, defense, accommodation, and proaction. Many companies fail to make it past the reactive/defensive end of the continuum. Procter & Gamble's action in the Rely tampon case clearly illustrates how a large firm can quickly move from reaction to proaction. In the short run, proactive social responsibility usually costs the firm money. But, according to the notion of enlightened self-interest, both society and the company will gain in the long run. Research indicates that corporate philanthropy actually is a profit-motivated form of advertising.

Researchers have found broad support among top managers for the assumptions underlying social responsibility. Although U.S. tax law permits corporations to deduct charitable contributions equaling as much as 5 percent of pretax income, actual corporate giving has remained around 1 percent in recent years. Imaginative expressions of corporate social responsibility include Xerox's Social Service Leave Program, Brooklyn Union Gas's urban renewal program, Safeway's educational program on mental retardation, Pacific Gas & Electric's interest-free loans for energy-saving home improvements, and Clairol's scholarships for women over 30.

Experts recommend social audits for greater accountability in the area of social responsibility. Although social auditing is plagued by a measurability problem, it can be overcome through the use of program objectives and descriptive accounts of progress. The willingness of companies to publish their socially responsible activities in their annual reports suggests that social auditing will continue its slow development.

Corporate misconduct in recent years has focused attention on business ethics, the systematic consideration of right versus wrong in an organizational context. Three ethical pressure points for managers are (1) perceived pressure from above, (2) the tendency to see others as less ethical than oneself, and (3) a desire for clear ethical standards in ambiguous situations. Considering that there are conflicting operative business philosophies, management can encourage ethical conduct in the following three ways: use ethical advocates in high-level decision making; formulate and disseminate specific codes of ethics; and create an open climate for dissent in which whistle-blowing becomes unnecessary.

Terms to Understand

Corporate social responsibility	Social audit
Iron law of responsibility	Ethics
Altruism	Operative philosophy
Enlightened self-interest	Ethical advocate
Corporate philanthropy	Whistle-blowing

Questions for Discussion

1. Why is it important for an action to be voluntary before labeling it socially responsible?
2. Which model of business—classical economic or socioeconomic—appeals more to you? Why?
3. Considering the arguments for and against corporate social responsibility, which side seems to present the more convincing case? Why?
4. What evidence can you cite to validate the iron law of responsibility?
5. From an organizational standpoint, what are the principal advantages and disadvantages of each of the four social responsibility strategies?
6. What role does enlightened self-interest play in your life?
7. Why do you suppose that management has been slow in adopting full-fledged social auditing?
8. How can management successfully cope with the measurability problem that plagues social auditing?
9. How would you characterize the general state of business ethics today?
10. What is your operative management philosophy? How does it affect your general attitude toward social responsibility?

Back to the Opening Case

Now that you have read Chapter 18, you should be able to answer the following questions about the Eberhard Faber case:

1. Judging from the available evidence, what are Faber's and Carey's operative business philosophies? Why is a certain amount of conflict inevitable between these two people? Is that conflict good or bad for Eberhard Faber, Inc.? Explain.
2. If you were on the board of directors, whose side would you have taken in this case? Why?
3. What could have been done to avoid this sudden ethical uncertainty?

Closing Case 18.2

Manville: A Profitable "Bankrupt" Company

August 26, 1982 was a fateful day for Manville Corporation (formerly Johns-Manville). On that day, the firm's chief executive officer, John A. McKinney, announced that the giant Denver-based building materials company had filed for reorganization under Chapter 11 of the Federal Bankruptcy code. To the casual observer, this was probably just another mismanaged company biting the dust during hard economic times. More astute observers, however, were absolutely shocked. First, Manville was a very profitable business with annual sales in excess of $2 billion and a net worth of $1.1 billion. Second, Manville was not just another company; it was 181st on the *Fortune* 500 and one of the 30 corporations making up the Dow Jones industrial average (the closely watched barometer of U.S. industrial strength).

When announcing that his otherwise healthy company was declaring bankruptcy, McKinney pinned the blame on *asbestos*. As the world's largest producer of asbestos products, Manville was being inundated with lawsuits claiming that asbestos was the cause of an emphysema-like lung disease called asbestosis and a fatal form of lung cancer. Manville had spent approximately $50 million settling 3500 asbestos claims through mid-1982. Although those expenses were manageable, a more ominous threat emerged in a company-sponsored study predicting $2 billion in personal injury lawsuits by the year 2000. At the time of the bankruptcy announcement, Manville was saddled with 17,000 asbestos lawsuits. That number had grown to 20,000 by early 1984. Meanwhile, Manville recorded $60 million in profits in 1983. This prompted critics to lash out at the firm for taking unethical advantage of bankruptcy protection and exhibiting callous disregard for victims of horrible asbestos-related diseases. McKinney claimed he found the tactic personally distasteful but was forced to yield to the wishes of the board of directors who felt the company had no other choice.

A Cruel Irony

Asbestos has turned out to be a cruel irony for Manville. The mineral that helped the company become an industrial giant has brought Manville to its knees. For decades, the firm recorded handsome sales and profits from more than 3000 products featuring the corrosion- and fire-resistent characteristics of asbestos. Unfortunately, the razor-sharp microscopic fibers of this natural mineral have long been a suspected cause of lung disease and cancer. But since asbestos-related diseases have a latency of 10 to 40 years, the asbestos epidemic is a rather recent phenomenon. Critics claim that Manville's top management had to have known about the potential cancer risks of asbestos for miners, naval shipyard workers, and construction workers who handled either raw asbestos or products containing asbestos. They believe Manville was negligent for not taking necessary and prudent precautionary steps to prevent asbestosis and lung cancer.

Emotional and vivid accounts of the Manville case in the media have swayed public opinion strongly against the company. Schools and other public buildings have been purged of asbestos insulation amid full television coverage. Ironically, although the name Manville is synonymous with asbestos, the company sold the last of its Canadian mines in 1983 and is no longer in the asbestos business. Manville's future is staked to fiberglass, which accounted for 40 percent of the company's sales by 1984.

Manville's Side of the Story

Manville's bankruptcy announcement had a sledgehammer effect on the firm. Its stock dropped from a 1981 high of $26 per share to $4.25 following the announcement in 1982. Many of its customers jumped ship and sales dropped. Even the $60 million in profits in 1983, that critics so loudly decried, were artificially inflated by the fact that a Chapter 11 company is forbidden to pay creditors, service the interest on debt, pay dividends to stockholders, or pay legal settlements (including those for asbestos).

Although the media have not picked up on the point, Manville's top managers say that accepted accounting rules and reluctant insurance companies left Manville with no other option than Chapter 11. According to accepted accounting practice, Manville should have set up a contingency reserve account for anticipated asbestos settlements. But given the potential liability of $2 billion, far in excess of the company's net worth, Manville would have had to default on its loans (thereby becoming involuntarily bankrupt). In addition, Manville's insurance underwriters backed away from covering the company's losses when asbestos claims began to mushroom in 1982. Manville subsequently sued its 27 insurance companies to get them to cover the outstanding claims and pay punitive damages of $5 billion. The matter was still tied up in the courts in early 1985.

Another target for a Manville counterattack was the U.S. government. According to *Dun's Business Month*:

> In six separate suits, it is claiming that the government carries a substantial responsibility to asbestos victims, many of whom were exposed to asbestos while working at Naval shipyards in the 1940s and 1950s. Thus far, the government has refused to share any of the liability. ... [53]

Some observers claim that Manville is simply looking for a government bailout.

As far as Manville is concerned, the keys to its survival are its Chapter 11 reorganization plan and a comprehensive settlement plan for asbestos victims. Since these two plans must be acceptable to all relevant parties, years of legal maneuvering are inevitable. Considering that the 37 law firms representing Manville had billed the company for $25 million through mid-1984, the lawyers are likely to fare better than the asbestos victims, creditors, and stockholders for the foreseeable future. Meanwhile, according to one observer:

> Manville officials insist that filing for bankruptcy was unavoidable and in the best interest of its stockholders, employees, and creditors. Moreover, they feel that in the long run their decision will better benefit the victims of asbestos related diseases.[54]

For Discussion

1. How would you characterize Manville's social responsibility strategy? Does it involve enlightened self-interest? Explain.
2. Which of the alternative business philosophies in Table 18.7 seems to be guiding Manville's top management? What shortcomings does this philosophy have?
3. How do the business ethics research findings discussed in this chapter help explain McKinney's decision to go along with the board's recommendation to declare bankruptcy?
4. Putting yourself in the place of a manager at Manville, would you have supported the decision to seek bankruptcy protection? Justify the ethics of your decision.

References

Opening Quotation: Sandra L. Holmes, "Executive Perceptions of Corporate Social Responsibility," *Business Horizons* 19 (June 1976): 34.

Opening Case: Excerpted from Eberhard Faber, "How I Lost Our Great Debate About Corporate Ethics," *Fortune* 94 (November 1976): 180–188.

Closing Case: For additional information on Manville, see "Manville's Reorganization Plan Resolves Nothing," *Business Week* No. 2819 (December 5, 1983): 72–73; A. R. Gini, "MANVILLE: The Ethics of Economic Efficiency?" *Journal of Business Ethics* 3 (February 1984): 63–69; Eleanor Johnson Tracy, "How to Milk Money from a Bankrupt," *Fortune* 109 (May 14, 1984): 130; Robert Barker, "Where's the Equity?" *Barron's* 64 (July 23, 1984): 6–7; and Pat Wechsler Keefe, "Manville: What Price Chapter 11?" *Dun's Business Month* 124 (August 1984): 50–51, 53.

1. Neil H. Jacoby, *Corporate Power and Social Responsibility* (New York: Macmillan, 1973), p. 6.

2. Thomas M. Jones, "Corporate Social Responsibility Revisited, Redefined," *California Management Review* 22 (Spring 1980): 59–60. For an excellent conceptual treatment of social responsibility, see Archie B. Carroll, "A Three-Dimensional Conceptual Model of Corporate Performance," *Academy of Management Review* 4 (October 1979): 497–505. An informative call for greater corporate social responsibility may be found in Henry Mintzberg, "The Case for Corporate Social Responsibility," *The Journal of Business Strategy* 4 (Fall 1983): 3–15.

3. Maria Recio and Vicky Cahan, "Bhopal Has Americans Demanding the 'Right to Know,' " *Business Week* No. 2881 (February 18, 1985): 36.

4. Details of the Bhopal disaster may be found in Pico Iyer, "India's Night of Death," *Time* 124 (December 17, 1984): 22–31; Judith H. Dobrzynski, William B. Glaberson, Resa W. King, William J. Powell Jr., and Leslie Helm, "Union Carbide Fights for Its Life," *Business Week* No. 2874 (December 24, 1984): 52–56; and Richard I. Kirkland Jr., "Union Carbide: Coping with Catastrophe," *Fortune* 111 (January 7, 1985): 50–53.

5. See Mark Dowei, "How Ford Put Two Million Firetraps on Wheels," *Business and Society Review* No. 23 (Fall 1977): 26–55.

6. Jones, "Corporate Social Responsibility Revisited," p. 65.

7. This distinction between the economic and the socioeconomic models is based partly on discussion in Courtney C. Brown, *Beyond the Bottom Line* (New York: Macmillan, 1979), pp. 82–83.

8. Milton Friedman, *Capitalism and Freedom* (Chicago: University of Chicago Press, 1962), p. 133.

9. This list of stakeholders is based on discussion in R. H. Anderson, "Social Responsibility Performance: Measurement and How?" *Cost and Management* 53 (September-October 1979): 12–16.

10. For an interesting critique of the profit motive itself, see Kenneth J. Arrow, "The Limitations of the Profit Motive," *Challenge* 22 (September-October 1979): 23–27.

11. These arguments have been adapted in part from Jones, "Corporate Social Responsibility Revisited," p. 61; and Keith Davis and William C. Frederick, *Business and Society: Management, Public Policy, and Ethics,* 5th ed. (New York: McGraw-Hill, 1984), pp. 28–41.

12. Davis and Frederick, *Business and Society,* p. 34.

13. "Opinion Roundup," *Public Opinion* 3, no. 2 (1980): 24.

14. James W. Hathaway, "Has Social Responsibility Cleaned Up the Corporate Image?" *Business and Society Review* No. 51 (Fall 1984): 56.

15. Drawn from Ian Wilson, "What One Company Is Doing About Today's Demands on Business," in *Changing Business-Society Interrelationships,* ed. George A. Steiner (Los Angeles: UCLA Graduate School of Management, 1975).

16. This section was inspired by Elizabeth Gatewood and Archie B. Carroll, "The Anatomy of Corporate Social Response: The Rely, Firestone 500, and Pinto Cases," *Business Horizons* 24 (September-October 1981): 9–16.

17. For additional reading on this case, see Dean Rotbart and John A. Prestbo, "Killing a Product," *The Wall Street Journal,* November 3, 1980, p. 21; Pamela Sherrid, "Tampons After the Shock Wave," *Fortune* 104 (August 10, 1981): 114–129; and Susan Bartlett Foote, "Corporate Responsibility in a Changing Legal Environment," *California Management Review* 26 (Spring 1984): 217–228.

18. Louis W. Fry, Gerald D. Keim, and Roger E. Meiners, "Corporate Contributions: Altruistic or For-Profit?" *Academy of Management Journal* 25 (March 1982): 105.

19. See Robert Ford and Frank McLaughlin, "Perceptions of Socially Responsible Activities and Attitudes: A Comparison of Business School Deans and Corporate Chief Executives," *Academy of Management Journal* 27 (September 1984): 666–674.

20. Lee Smith, "The Unsentimental Corporate Giver," *Fortune* 104 (September 21, 1981): 121–122.

21. See Gerald D. Keim, "Managerial Behavior and the Social Responsibility Debate: Goals Versus Constraints," *Academy of Management Journal* 21 (March 1978): 57–68.

22. Smith, "The Unsentimental Corporate Giver," p. 123.

23. For complete details, see "The Minneapolis Story: A Primer in Social Concern," *Industry Week* 210 (August 10, 1981): 59–61.

24. Robert Levering, Milton Moskowitz, and Michael Katz, *The 100 Best Com-*

panies to Work for in America (Reading, Mass.: Addison-Wesley, 1984): 112.

25. For an interesting summary, see "Social Service Leave: Five Years Old and Looking Good," *Xerox World* No. 24 (April 1976).

26. See Vernon Louviere, "How a Business Fights Housing Blight," *Nation's Business* 65 (June 1977): 59.

27. Milton R. Moskowitz, "Company Performance Roundup," *Business and Society Review* No. 38 (Summer 1981): 75.

28. Milton R. Moskowitz, "Company Performance Roundup," *Business and Society Review* No. 37 (Spring 1980–81): 72.

29. Milton R. Moskowitz, "Company Performance Roundup," *Business and Society Review* No. 52 (Winter 1985): 68.

30. The Clairol Loving Care Scholarships for women over 30 are administered by the Business and Professional Women's Foundation, 2012 Massachusetts Avenue, NW, Washington, D.C. 20036. See Marilyn Hoffman, "Clairol Scholarships Aid Women Over 30 in Reaching Career Goals," *The Christian Science Monitor* 76 (October 5, 1984): 30.

31. Raymond A. Bauer and Dan H. Fenn, Jr., "What *Is* a Corporate Social Audit?" *Harvard Business Review* 51 (January-February 1973): 38.

32. Felix Pomeranz, "Social Measurement Revisited," *Journal of Accountancy* 150 (August 1980): 70.

33. Based in part on the following sources: David F. Fetyko, "The Company Social Audit," *Management Accounting* 56 (April 1975): 31–34; and Raymond A. Bauer, L. Terry Cauthorn, and Ranne P. Warner, "Auditing the Management Process for Social Performance," *Business and Society Review* No. 15 (Fall 1975): 39–45.

34. For additional discussion, see "Social Accounting: A Puff of Smoke?" *Management Review* 66 (November 1977): 4. For an interesting discussion of a company's unique approach to auditing the quality of its employees' work life, see Edward E. Lawler, Philip H. Mirvis, William M. H. Clarkson, and Lyman Randall, "How Graphic Controls Assesses the Human Side of the Corporation," *Management Review* 70 (October 1981): 54–63.

35. Drawn from *Social Responsibility Disclosure: 1977 Survey of Fortune 500 Annual Reports,* Ernst & Ernst, 1300 Union Commerce Building, Cleveland, Ohio 44115.

36. An excellent resource on ethics is a one-dollar booklet entitled "Common Sense and Everyday Ethics," available from the Ethics Resource Center, 1730 Rhode Island Ave. N.W., Washington, D.C. 20036; telephone (202) 223–3411. Also see Gene Laczniak, "Business Ethics: A Manager's Primer," *Business* 33 (January-March 1983): 23–29; Mark Pastin, "Ethics as an Integrating Force in Management," *Journal of Business Ethics* 3 (November 1984): 293–304; and Mark Pastin, "Business Ethics, by the Book," *Business Horizons* 28 (January-February 1985): 2–6.

37. Abstracted from Darrell J. Fasching, "A Case for Corporate and Management

Ethics," *California Management Review* 23 (Summer 1981): 72.

38. Steven N. Brenner and Earl A. Molander, "Is the Ethics of Business Changing?" *Harvard Business Review* 55 (January-February 1977): 60.

39. James S. Bowman, "Managerial Ethics in Business and Government," *Business Horizons* 19 (October 1976): 53. This study is a replication of one by Archie B. Carroll, "Managerial Ethics: A Post-Watergate View," *Business Horizons* 18 (April 1975): 75–80.

40. John W. Newstrom and William A. Ruch, "The Ethics of Management and the Management of Ethics," *MSU Business Topics* 23 (Winter 1975): 36. Also see O. C. Ferrell and K. Mark Weaver, "Ethical Beliefs of Marketing Managers," *Journal of Marketing* 42 (July 1978): 69–73.

41. William Rudelius and Rogene A. Buchholz, "Ethical Problems of Purchasing Managers," *Harvard Business Review* 57 (March-April 1979): 12. Also see Alan J. Dubinsky, Eric N. Berkowitz, and William Rudelius, "Ethical Problems of Field Sales Personnel," *MSU Business Topics* 28 (Summer 1980): 11–16.

42. Max Ways, "Business Faces Growing Pressures to Behave Better," *Fortune* 89 (May 1974): 194.

43. For details, see Richard F. Beltramini, Robert A. Peterson, and George Kozmetsky, "Concerns of College Students Regarding Business Ethics," *Journal of Business Ethics* 3 (August 1984): 195–200.

44. Edward Stevens, *Business Ethics* (New York: Paulist Press, 1979), p. 8.

45. For informative reading on ethical advocates, see Theodore V. Purcell, "Electing an 'Angel's Advocate' to the Board," *Management Review* 65 (May 1976): 4–11; and Theodore V. Purcell, "Institutionalizing Ethics into Top Management Decisions," *Public Relations Quarterly* 22 (Summer 1977): 15–20.

46. For an instructive content analysis of 281 corporate ethical codes, see Robert Chatov, "What Corporate Ethics Statements Say," *California Management Review* 22 (Summer 1980): 20–29. Another content analysis of 39 corporate codes of ethics may be found in Glen R. Sanderson and Iris I. Varner, "What's Wrong with Corporate Codes of Conduct?" *Management Accounting* 66 (July 1984): 28–31, 35.

47. "Business' Big Morality Play," *Dun's Review* 116 (August 1980): 56.

48. An interesting study of the characteristics of whistle-blowers among a random sample of 8587 U.S. government employees can be found in Marcia Parmerlee Miceli and Janet P. Near, "The Relationships Among Beliefs, Organizational Position, and Whistle-Blowing Status: A Discriminant Analysis," *Academy of Management Journal* 27 (December 1984): 687–705.

49. Ralph Nader, "An Anatomy of Whistle Blowing," in *Whistle Blowing,* ed. Ralph Nader, Peter Petkas, and Kate Blackwell (New York: Bantam, 1972), p. 7. For interesting case studies of whistle-blowers, see William McGowan, "The Whistleblowers Hall of Fame," *Business and Society Review* No. 52 (Winter 1985): 31–36.

50. For discussion of Michigan's Whistleblower's Protection Act that "makes it illegal for a Michigan employer to discharge, threaten, or discriminate against an employee who 'reports or is about to report' a suspected violation of federal, state, or local law to a public body," see Daniel D. Cook, "Whistle Blowers: Friend or Foe?" *Industry Week* 211 (October 5, 1981): 50–56.

51. Adapted from Kenneth D. Walters, "Your Employees' Right to Blow the Whistle," *Harvard Business Review* 53 (July-August 1975): 26–34, 161–162.

52. Peter Raven-Hansen, "Dos and Don'ts for Whistleblowers: Planning for Trouble," *Technology Review* 82 (May 1980): 34–44.

53. Keefe, "Manville: What Price Chapter 11?" p. 53.

54. Gini, "MANVILLE: The Ethics of Economic Efficiency?" p. 68.

Chapter 19

International Management

It is becoming more apparent that international competence is needed as a prerequisite for all future managers, whether or not they work abroad.
H. J. Zoffer

Chapter Objectives

When you finish studying this chapter, you should be able to

- Explain what a multinational corporation (MNC) is and describe the six-step internationalization process.
- Contrast ethnocentric, polycentric, and geocentric attitudes toward foreign operations.
- Define comparative management and discuss the applicability of American management theories abroad.
- Summarize the controversy surrounding MNCs.
- Define political risk assessment and explain why it is especially important today.
- Discuss the importance of cultural sensitivity in international management.

Opening Case 19.1

An American Takes Over at Porsche*

Many European executives have crossed the Atlantic to land top posts in U.S. companies. But few Americans have gone the opposite route, and none has lit on a more prestigious or exposed perch than Peter W. Schutz, 51. A former vice president for marketing and service at Cummins Engine, Schutz was thrust into sudden prominence in December 1980 when he

*Pages 690–692 and page 693, paragraph one, are excerpted from David B. Tinnin, "The American at the Wheel of Porsche," published in *Fortune* magazine. © 1982 Time Inc. All rights reserved.

was named president of Porsche, the Stuttgart-based maker of sophisticated sports cars whose performance and price are equally breath-
taking.

The appointment provoked astonishment and misgivings in West Germany. *GASTARBEITER* (foreign worker) *IN THE PRESIDENT'S CHAIR*,
exclaimed one nonplussed German business magazine. Porsche does
not loom large in Germany's economy—owned solely by the descen-
dants of its brilliant and inventive founder, Professor Ferdinand Porsche,
the company sold just 32,000 cars … [in 1981], compared with 351,000 for
BMW and 441,000 for Mercedes-Benz. But it is a national institution: in
German eyes its cars are a bellwether for the future competitiveness of
German technology. …

Born in Berlin, Schutz fled Germany with his Jewish parents in 1939 at
age 8 and grew up in the Midwest, where he received a bachelor's degree
in engineering from Illinois Institute of Technology. After Army service he
worked as an engineer for Caterpillar and then for Cummins at the home
office in Columbus, Indiana, where he rose to become a vice president for
marketing and service. In 1978 the big West German industrial combine
of Klöckner-Humbolt-Deutz, searching for an engineer with sales experience to run its engine business, lured Schutz to its headquarters in
Cologne. Since he had not spoken German since childhood, Schutz had
lost command of the language. His trademark at KHD was a thick
dictionary he lugged around. …

Selling More Than a Car

… Schutz began his tenure [at Porsche] by subjecting the company to its
first thorough appraisal, beginning with a fundamental question: "What
business are we in?" After poring over Porsche sales records and customer research, he soon decided the company was not really in the auto
business but was a leisure-time enterprise. Says he: "If you ask a Porsche
driver, 'Is that your car?' the answer would be, 'Yes, in a way it is. But it is
also my summer home and the yacht for which I don't have time.' In that
sense," reasons Schutz, "the price of a Porsche is not viewed in comparison with a regular utility auto, because you are not selling just a car."

He also found management in need of overhaul. Apart from its morale
problems, Porsche suffered from a particularly severe case of the hierarchical rigidity and uncommunicativeness that often afflicts German
corporations. …

[A Modified American Model]

… [In 1981] Schutz hired Heiko Lange away from his post as a personnel
director at ITT's European headquarters in Brussels. The two men are
staging a series of "information fairs"—exercises in group thinking and
decision-making—designed to make Porsche a more open company in

which information circulates freely and policy matters get thoroughly discussed before a final decision is handed down.

Porsche has been highly compartmentalized, with each department chief operating pretty much on his own. Schutz is trying to change to a modified American model. Executive-board members—roughly equivalent to group vice presidents—will operate as a team, presenting their ideas and proposals for group discussion so that Schutz can present Porsche's directors with consensual decisions. And several key department heads who previously reported to the president now answer directly to the executives in whose jurisdiction they logically belong. Styling, for instance, has been moved from the president's fiefdom and reports to the chief of engineering and development.

Schutz is making slow headway, however, in convincing his colleagues to delegate day-to-day administrative burdens and think strategically. They complain that while Schutz asks good questions, his technique is *unbequem*—uncomfortable, in essence. "We have to spend so much effort replying to him that we hardly have enough time to get our real work done," says one.

The Absence of Achtung

Both sides contribute to a communications gap. Schutz's business style is very American and thoroughly at odds with German manners and customs. In interviews German reporters often quote one of Schutz's best one-liners: "I may be able to accomplish a lot at Porsche, but I will never get people to call me Peter." In his dealings with Porsche executives, Schutz puts forward matters he would like to see tackled in an informal, almost tentative way. To German ears, Schutz's phrases lack the unmistakable ring of "*Achtung,* this is authority speaking." Such a misunderstanding can lead to Schutz's having to repeat himself several times, as he did in a recent conference when his voice took on a bit of an edge. The other executive, suddenly aware he was on the wrong wavelength, looked smitten. "You will just have to give us time, Herr Schutz," he said, "you will have to give us time."

Schutz will also have to give himself time. Working effectively in a foreign language and culture is extremely difficult. Schutz makes a point of speaking German with everyone at Porsche, even though many of its executives are completely proficient in English. The dictionary is gone; his command of technical German is impressive ("There are some subjects I can only adequately discuss in German," he laughs). And his conversational German has become fluent and grammatically flawless, though his midwestern accent rings through. But Schutz admits he lacks the knowledge of the literature and history that might enable him to divine nuances. "Some things may go past me," he concedes.

Schutz's most valued tutor in the essential graces is his wife, Sheila, also an American, whom he calls "my seeing-eye dog." Vivacious and perceptive, Sheila pointed out recently that Schutz, garrulous by nature, was wearing out everyone at parties by staying too late: German etiquette forbids others to leave a party before the highest-ranking guest departs. "So I can't close the bar anymore," quips Schutz. Seriously, he adds, "I hate all this formality, but there is absolutely nothing I can do about it."

[Things Seem to Be Working Out for the "Gastarbeiter"]
According to a recent update in *Fortune* magazine, Schultz has steered Porsche in a profitable direction.

> In 1983 Porsche sold 21,800 cars in the U.S., vs. 11,200 in 1981. The end of the oil shortage and the revival of Americans' lust for fast cars get part of the credit for that record. But a larger share goes to Porsche's popular 944. When it was introduced in mid-1982, Schutz gave it an enticing $18,450 sticker price—well below the average of about $33,000 for other Porsches. ... Porsche now gets half its worldwide sales from the U.S. ... [1]

In fiscal 1983, Porsche made a profit of $28.1 million on sales of $841 million.

(Discussion questions linking this case with the material you are about to read can be found at the end of this chapter.)

Air travel and modern telecommunications are turning the world into a global community. Key executives like Peter Schutz move more freely than ever before from one country to another. As information and even people move from place to place with amazing speed and frequency, the world seems to be growing smaller and its inhabitants more similar to each other. In addition to these technological factors, a third globe-shrinking force has been quietly gaining momentum. In many respects, this third force promises to contribute the most to a smaller world in which similarities prevail, because it is creating a global marketplace. This third force is corporate multinationalism.

Because of the dramatic growth in multinational corporations since World War II, people, technology, capital (see Figure 19.1), and goods are crossing international borders as never before. For example, many who consider the IBM PC (personal computer) to be as American as apple pie would no doubt be surprised to learn that $625 (or 73 percent) of an IBM PC's manufacturing cost of $860 goes for imported components. If you buy an IBM PC, you will likely be getting a video monitor from Korea, floppy disk drives from Singapore, and semiconductors, power supply unit, keyboard, and printer from Japan.[2]

Like any other productive enterprise, the multinational corporation needs to be effectively and efficiently managed. Consequently, **interna-**

tional management, the pursuit of organizational objectives in an international and intercultural setting, has emerged as an important discipline in recent years. The purpose of this chapter is to define and discuss the multinational corporation, stimulate international thinking, explore comparative management, examine the controversy surrounding multinational corporations, and address special problems that challenge international managers.

What Is a Multinational Corporation?

The multinational label has been attached to a growing number of privately owned corporations over the last two decades. These multinational corporations (MNCs) have many characteristics in common. They tend to be quite large in terms of assets they directly or indirectly control; they tend to wield a great deal of social, political, and economic power on a global scale; and they tend to be the subject of controversy and criticism. One authority has defined the **multinational corporation** as

> ... a number of affiliated business establishments that function as productive enterprises in different countries simultaneously. To have such capacity the firm must possess host-country-based production units such as factories, mines, retail stores, insurance offices, banking houses, or whatever operating facility is characteristic to its business.[3]

Thus true multinationalism involves more than the export of goods from a producer country to a consumer country. In a mature MNC, capital, technology, goods and services, information, and managerial talent flow freely from one country to another as business conditions dictate. Profit potential rather than national boundaries determines the multinational manager's strategies. For example, the gasoline you buy the next time you fill up could very well come from the floor of the North Sea via an intricate global network involving Dutch capital, Norwegian leasing, German engineering, British facilities and management, and American shipping and marketing. The rationale for such a multinational conglomeration is profit. This kind of multinational interdependence fairly explodes with managerial opportunities and obstacles.

The Evolution of an MNC Full-fledged multinationalism does not occur overnight. Instead it is the result of an evolutionary "internationalization" process with six identifiable stages. Since companies may choose to skip steps when pursuing foreign markets, the following sequence needs to be viewed in relative rather than lockstep terms.

Figure 19.1 Growth of Direct Foreign Investment Inside and Outside the United States, 1970–1981

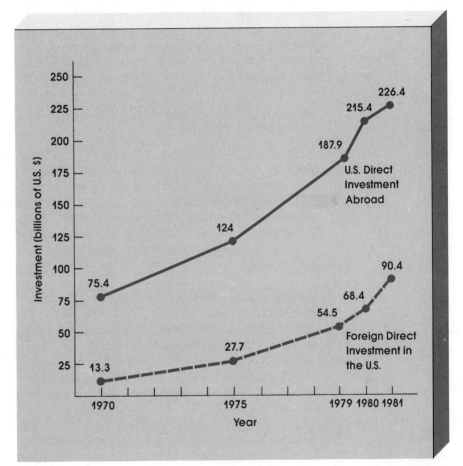

SOURCE: Data from U.S. Bureau of Census, *Statistical Abstract of the United States: 1984*, pp. 822, 824.

Stage 1. Licensing. Companies in foreign countries are authorized to produce and/or market a given product within a specified territory in return for a fee.

Stage 2. Exporting. Goods are produced in one country and sold for use or resale to one or more companies in foreign countries.

Stage 3. Local warehousing and selling. Goods that are produced in one country are shipped to the parent company's storage and marketing facilities located in one or more foreign countries.

Stage 4. Local assembly and packaging. Components rather than finished

Table 19.1 International Joint Ventures Can Be a Win-Win Situation

In the United States, GM and Toyota of Japan have formed a manufacturing joint venture, limited to a duration of up to 12 years, to produce a new, American-made small car at a former GM assembly plant in Fremont, California, for sale in North America. The joint venture (New United Motor Manufacturing, Inc.) will result in an estimated 12,000 jobs for American workers. About one-half of each car's content will be of U.S. origin. Production is scheduled to begin in the 1985 model year.

SOURCE: *1984 General Motors Public Interest Report*, April 30, 1984, General Motors Corporation, Detroit, Mich. 48202, p. 25.

products are shipped to company-owned assembly facilities in one or more foreign countries for final assembly and sales.

Stage 5. Joint venture. A company in one country pools resources with one or more companies in a foreign country to produce, store, transport, and market products with resulting profits/losses shared appropriately. Joint ventures have become very popular in recent years for the following reasons:

In environments of scarce resources, rapid rates of technological change and massive capital requirements, ... joint ventures may be the best way for some underdog firms to attain better positions in global industries which they consider to be important. Joint ventures may be used as pre-emptive maneuvers to ensure that access to distribution channels, suppliers, and technology in promising industries are not foreclosed to them because they ventured too late. They are also a way of ensuring that potential entrants do not team up with more dangerous opponents.[4]

General Motors, for example, has attempted to ensure its long-term survival in the automobile business by becoming involved in more than 20 joint ventures worldwide (see Table 19.1).

Stage 6. Direct foreign investment. A company in one country produces and markets products through wholly owned subsidiaries in foreign countries.[5] As mentioned in Chapter 17, Nissan, a Japanese firm, produces trucks in a company-owned facility in Tennessee and markets them throughout the United States.[6] A manufacturing company, according to our earlier definition of a multinational corporation, must have direct foreign investments in the form of production facilities before it can qualify as a true MNC.

According to traditional international management theory, each successive stage in this internationalization process increases the parent firm's political and economic risks. However, from a strictly economic standpoint, one writer believes that licensing is more risky than either exporting or direct foreign investment. The argument is that "there is an ever present danger of the firm's information monopoly being compromised by the licensee. ... Once the firm's knowledge advantage is lost it becomes impossible for the firm to receive a fair return for its previous investment in research and development."[7] Consequently, direct foreign investment, or multinationalism, is recommended as the way to protect the firm's technology and competitive knowledge advantage, because management can directly oversee and control its application.

The Scale of Multination-alism

When one appreciates the huge scale of multinationalism, the growing importance of international management becomes all the more apparent. The direct foreign investment trends shown in Figure 19.1 are a reliable benchmark of increased multinational activity. Although some critics see this dramatic rise as evidence of neocolonialism designed to exploit cheap foreign labor, and export pollution, and strip less developed countries of their natural resources, others see it as a progressive sign. For example, with regard to oil-producing nations, one observer has pointed out:

> The host country profits from the public income generation by royalties and taxes, from the private income derived from wage payments and other expenses in the local economy, and, above all, by the acquisition of modern technology and management skills.[8]

Another way of gauging the scale of multinationalism is to examine the annual reports of major U.S. corporations for evidence of foreign sales. As Table 19.2 indicates, the figures are often surprisingly large. The effects of growing multinationalism are seen in other ways as well. For example, in 1976, fewer than half of Ford Motor Company's employees worked in the United States. Americans traveling abroad are struck by the extent of multinational operations when they encounter familiar names like Mobil, Coca-Cola, McDonald's, Burger King, and Ford.

Thinking Internationally

Americans in general and American business students and managers in particular have long been criticized as too isolationist for the global stage. Boris Yavitz, dean of Columbia University's Graduate School of Business, has commented, "Unlike European and Asian managers, who grow up expecting to see international service, U.S. executives are required to prepare only for domestic experience, with English as their only language."[9] Business is becoming increasingly internationalized and, as dis-

Table 19.2 A Look at Selected Multinationals

Company	Principal Products	1984* Sales Outside the U.S.
Mobil	Petroleum and chemical products	62%
Colgate-Palmolive	Household and personal care products	55%
Merck & Co.	Pharmaceutical products	43%
Xerox	Photocopiers and office equipment	36%
Champion Spark Plug Co.	Spark plugs and automotive products	34%
Du Pont	Oil, chemical, and plastic products	31%
Goodyear	Tires; rubber and chemical products	31%
Borg-Warner	Air conditioning, automotive, and chemical products	30%
Honeywell	Computer and control system products	26%
Safeway	Supermarkets and grocery products	24%

*Figures for Mobil, Colgate-Palmolive, and Safeway are for 1983; all others are 1984.

cussed in Chapter 1, a global economy is emerging. Some rather curious and unanticipated cause-and-effect relationships have resulted from our global economy. For example, in the winter of 1984–85, a coal strike in Britain caused gasoline prices to *drop* in the United States. *Business Week* explains:

> ... refineries worldwide were working overtime to meet Britain's emergency demand for heavy industrial fuel oil because of a coal strike there, leaving as much as 250,000 bbl. [barrels] a day of gasoline as an unwanted byproduct. Some of this poured into the U.S., bringing the price of a gallon of regular leaded gas as low as 85¢.[10]

In order to cope with a dynamic global economy better, present and future managers need to begin thinking internationally. Improvement is needed both in attitudes and in management strategy.

**Contrasting
Attitudes
Toward
International
Operations**

Can a firm's degree of multinationality be measured in a concrete way? Some observers claim that a true MNC has subsidiaries in at least six nations. Others say that a firm must have a certain percentage of its capital or operations overseas in order to qualify as an MNC. Insisting that these measurable guidelines tell only part of the story, Howard Perlmutter has suggested it is management's *attitude* toward its foreign operations that really counts.

> The more one penetrates into the living reality of an international firm, the more one finds it is necessary to give serious weight to the way executives think about doing business around the world. The orientation toward "foreign people, ideas, resources," in headquarters and subsidiaries, and in host and home environments, becomes crucial in estimating the multinationality of a firm.[11]

Perlmutter has identified three managerial attitudes toward international operations. He has labeled them ethnocentric, polycentric, and geocentric. Each attitude is presented here in its pure form, but all three are likely to be found in a single MNC. The key question is, "Which particular attitude predominates?"

Ethnocentric Attitude   Managers with an **ethnocentric attitude** are home-country oriented. Home-country personnel, ideas, and practices are viewed as inherently superior to those from abroad. Foreign nationals are not trusted with key decisions or technology. Home-country procedures and evaluation criteria are applied worldwide without variation. Proponents of ethnocentrism say that it makes for a simpler and more tightly controlled organization. Critics believe this attitude makes for poor planning and ineffective operations because of inadequate feedback, high turnover of subsidiary managers, reduced innovation, inflexibility, and social and political backlash.

The backfiring of Revlon's aggressive marketing tactics in Japan points up one of the problems with ethnocentrism. As a Japanese management analyst told *Business Week,* "The Revlon headquarters in the U.S. doesn't know the Japanese market so well. They think all they need to do to improve sales is change the Japanese president. But that only disturbs trust in the company among Japanese retailers."[12]

Polycentric Attitude   This host-country orientation is based on the assumption that local managers know what is best for their operations because cultures are so different. A **polycentric attitude** leads to a loose confederation of comparatively independent subsidiaries rather than to a highly integrated structure. Since foreign operations are measured in terms

Table 19.3 Three Different Attitudes Toward International Operations

Organization Design	Ethnocentric	Polycentric	Geocentric
Complexity of organization	Complex in home country; simple in subsidiaries.	Varied and independent.	Increasingly complex and interdependent.
Authority; decision making	High in headquarters.	Relatively low in headquarters.	Aim for a collaborative approach between headquarters and subsidiaries.
Evaluation and control	Home standards applied for persons and performance.	Determined locally.	Find standards which are universal and local.
Rewards and punishments; incentives	High in headquarters; low in subsidiaries.	Wide variation; can be high or low rewards for subsidiary performance.	International and local executives rewarded for reaching local and worldwide objectives.
Communication; information flow	High volume to subsidiaries; orders, commands, advice.	Little to and from headquarters: little between subsidiaries.	Both ways and between subsidiaries; heads of subsidiaries part of management team.
Identification	Nationality of owner.	Nationality of host country.	Truly international company but identifying with national interests.
Perpetuation (recruiting, staffing, development)	Recruit and develop people of home country for key positions everywhere in the world.	Develop people of local nationality for key positions in their own country.	Develop best people everywhere in the world for key positions everywhere in the world.

SOURCE: Howard V. Perlmutter, "The Tortuous Evolution of the Multinational Corporation," *Columbia Journal of World Business* 4 (January-February 1969): 12.

of ends (instead of means), methods, incentives, and training procedures vary widely from location to location.

On the negative side, wasteful duplication of effort can erode the efficiency of polycentric organizations. Moreover, global objectives may be undermined by excessive concern for local traditions and success. "The main advantages are an intensive exploitation of local markets, better sales since local management is often better informed, more local initiative for new products, more host-government support, and good local managers with high morale."[13]

Geocentric Attitude Managers with a **geocentric attitude** are world-oriented. Skill rather than nationality determines who gets promoted or transferred to key positions around the globe. Local and worldwide objectives are balanced in all aspects of operation. Collaboration between headquarters and subsidiaries is high, but an effort is made to maintain a balance between global standards and local discretion. According to Perlmutter, geocentric organizations have the following combination of costs and payoffs:

> Geocentrism's costs are largely related to communication and travel expenses, educational costs at all levels, time spent in decision-making because consensus seeking among more people is required, and an international headquarters bureaucracy. Risks include those due to too wide a distribution of power, personnel problems, and those of re-entry of international executives. The payoffs are a more powerful total company throughout, a better quality of products and service, worldwide utilization of best resources, improvement of local company management, a greater sense of commitment to worldwide objectives, and last, but not least, more profit.[14]

A geocentric attitude (see Table 19.3) can help management take a long step toward success in today's vigorously competitive international marketplace.

Strategic Considerations for International Operations

As discussed in Chapter 5, effective strategic planning/implementation/control is the backbone of good management. Strategic management becomes doubly important in MNCs because geographically dispersed operations exaggerate the forces of organizational differentiation and weaken the forces of integration or coordination. (As one might expect in such circumstances, matrix organization design is common in MNCs.)[15] Cultural variations, political uncertainties, and demands from host governments and joint venture partners place further strain on top management's task of coordinating international operations.

Experts have identified six strategic questions that headquarters must address when dealing with foreign subsidiaries. They are:

1. What technology should the subsidiary employ?
2. How should the subsidiary's product market(s) be defined?
3. What relative emphasis should be placed on the subsidiary's different product lines?
4. What resources should be allocated to the subsidiary?
5. How broadly should the subsidiary be allowed to expand or diversify?
6. How much should each subsidiary participate in a global network of product flows?[16]

Figure 19.2 Competing Forces of Convergence and Divergence

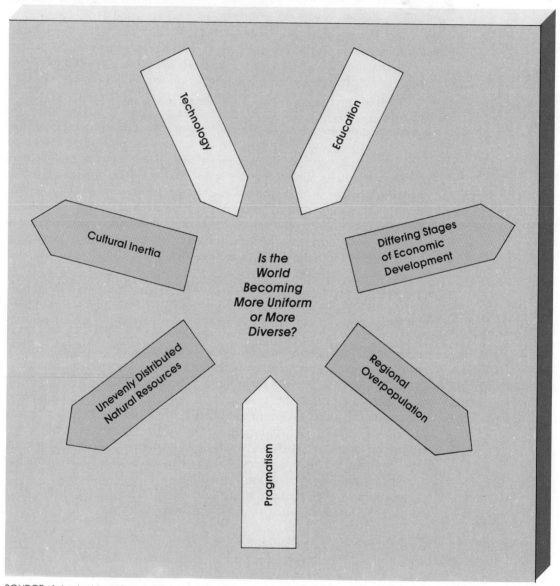

Technology

Education

Cultural Inertia

Differing Stages
of Economic
Development

*Is the
World
Becoming
More Uniform
or More
Diverse?*

Unevenly Distributed
Natural Resources

Regional
Overpopulation

Pragmatism

SOURCE: Adapted from Ross A. Webber, "Convergence or Divergence?" *Columbia Journal of World Business* 4 (May-June 1969): 81.

In geocentric organizations, these strategic questions are addressed cooperatively by both headquarters and subsidiary managers.

Comparative Management

What impact do cultural differences have on the successful practice of management? Questions like this one have been addressed in recent years by scholars in a young but growing subfield of management theory called comparative management. **Comparative management** is the study of how management practices compare across different cultures. As in other new fields, there is little agreement about research methodologies and findings. The purpose of this section is to focus on (1) two philosophies of international management, (2) research problems in comparative management, and (3) the applicability of American management theories in other cultures.

Convergence Versus Divergence

Underlying philosophical differences are responsible for much of the disagreement among comparative management scholars. On one side are those who embrace a philosophy of **convergence,** the view that the world is becoming more uniform because of forces such as technology, education, and pragmatism.[17] Other scholars are influenced by a philosophy of **divergence,** a belief that forces such as cultural inertia, differing stages of economic development, unevenly distributed resources, and regional overpopulation guarantee global diversity.[18] Figure 19.2 shows convergent forces drawing the peoples of the world together while divergent forces are pulling them apart. Applying philosophical labels, "convergents" emphasize similarities between nations and cultures, whereas "divergents" stress the differences.

These contrasting philosophies have immense implications for international management. Those who believe in a convergent world claim that management practices have universal applicability. MBO, for example, will work as well in Paris and Tokyo as it does in Los Angeles. On the other hand, managers who believe in a divergent world claim that management practices need to be adapted culturally if they are to succeed. The challenge for comparative management scholars is to determine, through research, what techniques will work where and with how much cultural adaptation, if any.

Research Difficulties

According to two comparative management researchers, their quest for "the linkage between culture and managerial attitudes, behavior, and effectiveness"[19] is frustrated by four research problems:

1. Inconsistent and vague definitions of the term *culture*.
2. Inaccurate translation of key terminology (see Table 19.4).
3. Difficulty in obtaining representative samples.
4. Difficulty in isolating cultural differences amid national economic and political realities.[20]

Table 19.4 Some Concepts Do Not Translate Well from One Culture to Another

The concept most difficult to translate to different culture [is] ... the multidimensional concept of achievement. In most work outside of America, Great Britain, and other Anglo-American societies, this word has been refined to mean autonomy and/or creativity. Similarly, the value-laden concept of "success," which in American literature appears to mean individual success, is not readily transferable to Japanese or Asian cultures. The successful man in Thailand may be one who looks after his extended family. The successful person in North American writings achieves through education, the accumulation of assets, and corporate ladder climbing. The "high achiever" (if such translation were possible) in parts of Asia succeeds primarily in his relationships and in disowning attachment to possessions; corporate ladder climbing has much lower significance. Further, for the Hindu manager in India, uncertainty is not an issue, simply because his whole life is predetermined and certain. By contrast, one's lot is clearly uncertain in Christian societies.

SOURCE: John W. Hunt, "Applying American Behavioral Science: Some Cross-Cultural Problems," *Organizational Dynamics,* Summer 1981 (New York: AMACOM, a division of American Management Associations, 1981), p. 58.

Taken together, these problems appear to be an insurmountable barrier to the formulation of empirical principles of comparative management. Nonetheless, as discussed below, recent research has shown promising progress.

Applying American Management Theories Abroad

The results of a unique survey of 116,000 IBM employees in 40 different countries by Geert Hofstede, a Dutch organizational behaviorist, question the assumption that management theories are universally applicable.[21] Hofstede classified each of his 40 national samples according to four different cultural dimensions: power distance, uncertainty avoidance, individualism-collectivism, and masculinity. Each variable probed an important question about the prevailing culture.

- **Power distance.** How readily do individuals accept the unequal distribution of power in organizations and institutions?
- **Uncertainty avoidance.** How threatening are uncertain and ambiguous situations, and how important are rules, conformity, and absolute truths?
- **Individualism-collectivism.** Are people responsible for their own welfare within a loosely knit social framework, or does the group look out for individuals in exchange for loyalty?
- **Masculinity.** How important are masculine attitudes (assertiveness, money and possessions, performance) versus feminine attitudes (concern for people, the quality of life, and the environment)?

Table 19.5 Research Indicates That Top-ranking Needs Vary from Country to Country

Security	Security and Social	Social	Self-actualization
Switzerland	Iran	Singapore	Hong Kong
West Germany	Thailand	Denmark	Great Britain
Austria	Taiwan	Sweden	India
Italy	Brazil	Norway	United States
Venezuela	Israel	Netherlands	Philippines
Mexico	France	Finland	Canada
Colombia	Spain		New Zealand
Argentina	Turkey		Australia
Belgium	Peru		South Africa
Japan	Chile		Ireland
Greece	Yugoslavia		
Pakistan	Portugal		

SOURCE: Paraphrased with permission from Geert Hofstede, "Motivation, Leadership, and Organization: Do American Theories Apply Abroad?" in *Organizational Dynamics*, vol. 9, no. 1 (Summer 1980): 54–56. This article summarizes Dr. Hofstede's reseach published in the book *Culture's Consequences: International Differences in Work-Related Values* (Beverly Hills, Calif.: Sage Publications, 1980).

Hofstede scored all 40 countries in his sample from low to high on each of the four cultural dimensions. Interestingly, the United States ranked moderately low (15 out of 40) on power distance, low (9 out of 40) on uncertainty avoidance, very high (40 out of 40) on individualism, and moderately high (28 out of 40) on masculinity.

Because of marked cultural differences among the 40 countries studied, Hofstede believes that it is more practical to adapt American management theories to local cultures than vice versa. But they do need to be adapted. He contends that because David McClelland, Abraham Maslow, Frederick Herzberg, and Victor Vroom developed their achievement, need, two-factor, and expectancy theories, respectively, within the U.S. cultural context, it is naive to expect those theories to apply automatically in significantly different cultures. For example, American-made management theories that reflect Americans' preoccupation with individualism are out of place in countries where individualism is discouraged (such as Mexico, Brazil, and Japan). Moreover, as Hofstede discovered, different needs rank the highest in different cultures (see Table 19.5).

Hofstede's research falls far short of telling international managers how to apply various management techniques in different cultures.[22] However, it does provide a useful cultural typology and presents a convincing case for the cultural adaptation of American management theory and practice.

The Controversy Surrounding MNCs

As mentioned earlier, multinational corporations have stirred a good deal of controversy. Proponents cheer MNCs as the first step toward a peaceful and prosperous global community in which national identification and arbitrary boundaries will play a secondary role. According to one financial executive:

> It should be contended up front that the MNC can have a positive effect on the world, promoting social change for the good, acting as a catalyst for encouraging social and cultural interface among nations, and demonstrating, in a more powerful voice than any government, that the Babel of languages is not an impediment to understanding among people.[23]

Critics, meanwhile, attribute to MNCs such diverse problems as the growing gap between rich and poor nations, worldwide inflation, political corruption, uncontrolled urbanization and pollution, and military hardware proliferation.[24]

Obviously, since thousands of firms can be described as MNCs, it is unrealistic to label them all as good or bad. MNCs, taken all together, have engaged in a wide variety of honorable and disgraceful practices. The purpose here is to discuss three specific sources of controversy about MNCs—labor exportation, national sovereignty, and bribery—from which you can draw your own conclusions.

Do MNCs Export Jobs? The AFL-CIO and other voices of the American labor movement are convinced that MNCs that transfer their production processes from a location inside the United States to a foreign subsidiary are, in effect, exporting jobs. Consider the huge proportion of electronic and photographic equipment, for example, that is produced overseas for U.S. companies. Not too many years ago, virtually all the electronic and photographic equipment purchased by Americans was made by Americans. There is no question that production-level jobs have been exported when one finds, for instance, a "made in Japan" label on the back of a Sears TV.

MNCs see things differently. They take a long-run view. In the long run, they say, more jobs are created than are lost, and employment statistics seem to support their argument. For example, between 1966 and 1970 the number of American employees of a sample of 298 MNCs grew at an annual rate of 2.7 percent, compared with 1.8 percent for all U.S. firms.[25]

How can we reconcile these two seemingly valid positions, one for and one against MNCs? The key is short run versus long run. When Zenith reluctantly decided to follow its competitors by moving its television production facilities overseas to take advantage of cheaper labor rates, it was criticized for exporting jobs. In the short run, it did exactly that. But in the long run, industrywide, the firm may have created more jobs than it exported.

Taking the long-run perspective, lower labor costs translate into competitive prices that stimulate sales and enable the company to grow. As it grows, it creates additional administrative and sales positions for U.S. employees. So, in the long run, the net employment picture works out favorably. Unfortunately, relatively well-paid but semiskilled employees get lost in the shuffle between the short and long run as the MNCs employ more educated specialists. Both business and government are left with the costly and time-consuming task of retraining displaced individuals for employment in upgraded jobs.

Do MNCs Threaten National Sovereignty?

National sovereignty means that a nation, within its own borders, is the supreme power and final authority. This principle is the key to our present world order. Wars have been fought and countless lives lost because the principle of national sovereignty has been trampled by aggressive nations. Today, MNCs are seen by some as a serious threat to national sovereignty because, in the pursuit of profit, they may disrupt a host nation's economy or politics. Such disruption is especially likely, critics argue, when the economic power of MNCs exceeds that of smaller host countries, as it often does.

The most damaging evidence presented by MNC critics is the infamous International Telephone and Telegraph (ITT) case. As revealed by ITT management during testimony before a Senate Foreign Relations subcommittee in early 1973, the giant multinational tampered with the internal affairs of Chile for its own purposes. In 1970 ITT, according to a *Business Week* commentary, "tried to enlist the Central Intelligence Agency and other government agencies in schemes to prevent the election of Marxist Salvador Allende as Chile's president, and to disrupt the country's economy. Their goal: To avert the expropriation of ITT's Chilean subsidiary."[26] Exactly how much damage ITT's action did to Chile will probably never be known. But the ITT case left one haunting question: Just how extensive is the MNC threat to national sovereignty?

When it comes to MNC behavior in host countries, is ITT's escapade the rule or the exception? According to a Conference Board study of U.S.-controlled MNCs operating in Canada and Italy, the ITT case seems to be an exception.

In general, when it comes to such matters as industrial relations, information disclosure, and general adherence to the laws of the host country, American companies are described as exemplars. These companies are recognized as having introduced higher wages, advanced developments in industrial safety, a wide range of amenities in the work place, and as operating with scrupulous adherence to fiscal, financial, commercial and industrial laws.[27]

Although the study touched on only two host countries, the evidence is encouraging. Nevertheless, MNCs need to take special steps to ensure that they do not erode the national sovereignty of host countries, particularly in small, poor countries with relatively unstable governments.

What About Those Bribes and Payoffs?
In 1974, when the Securities and Exchange Commission (SEC) was looking into illegal corporate contributions to Richard Nixon's 1972 reelection campaign, a curious discovery was made. Little by little, the SEC investigators learned that a number of well-known U.S. multinational corporations had relied on bribery and payoffs when doing business overseas. These initial revelations turned out to be only the tip of an iceberg of corruption. By 1978, in response to SEC promises of leniency for firms disclosing information voluntarily, over 400 U.S. corporations had admitted to making $800 million in questionable payments abroad. Public reaction to these "confessions" was indignant, to say the least. According to one observer at the time: "To the increasingly vociferous critics of the multinational corporation, payoffs to foreign officials or political parties strengthens the demand for stringent regulations."[28] MNC supporters, on the other hand, have defended payoffs as a necessary aspect of doing business in countries where such behavior is not only tolerated but an unavoidable fact of life.

Lubrication Versus Whitemail Bribery Payoffs and bribes are commonplace in many countries around the globe. Two kinds of payoffs and bribes have been identified, lubrication bribes and whitemail bribes.[29] **Lubrication bribes** involve relatively small amounts of money that grease the wheels of bureaucratic progress. A firm doing business in Italy, for example, may find that a *bustarella* (an envelope stuffed with lire notes) gets a particular license clerk to do his job. Or *la mordida* ("the bite") passed along to a Mexican building inspector may help ensure that he does *not* do his job. Although the name may vary from country to country, the purpose of lubrication bribes is always the same, to make sure that things move along smoothly. Lubrication bribery is so deeply entrenched in parts of Asia, Africa, the Middle East, and Latin America that even the critics of MNC conduct admit that it is very difficult to do business without it.

Whitemail bribery is an entirely different matter. Rather than going to the little guy, as in the case of lubrication bribes, **whitemail bribes** are large sums of money used to buy influence in high places. Because large amounts of money are involved, whitemail bribery funds must be "laundered" by keeping them in secret accounts or slush funds and passing them through unofficial channels. In 1975 Lockheed, the aerospace giant, admitted to having paid out at least $22 million to officials and politicians in a number of foreign countries during the previous five years.

During the same period, it [Lockheed] had obligated itself to pay consultants—legitimately or illegitimately retained to expand foreign sales—a mindboggling $202 million. Moreover, Lockheed conceded, it had maintained a secret fund of some $750,000 from which it had paid $290,000 in commissions and "other payments."[30]

Two heads of state, a Japanese prime minister in 1974 and an Italian president in 1978, were forced to resign after being accused of receiving payoffs in excess of $1 million from Lockheed.[31] Because of the huge amounts of money involved, whitemail bribes have been criticized by the SEC because public investors are not informed about them, by the Internal Revenue Service because they are illegal tax deductions, and by others who claim they are immoral and unethical. Meanwhile, the supporting argument remains the same: payoffs and bribes are a necessary part of doing business abroad.

The Case Against Bribery   A study of 65 major U.S. corporations, 40 of which admitted to making questionable payments abroad, has put the foreign bribery issue into clearer perspective. "Where questionable payments were effective, they often seem to have transferred orders from one American company to another. If both companies had followed the same ethical standards that govern competition in the home market, no payments would have been necessary."[32] This finding weakens the argument that payoffs and bribes are an unavoidable part of doing business overseas.

An even stronger argument against foreign payoffs and bribes is the Foreign Corrupt Practices Act. This act, passed in late 1977 in response to public outcry over the SEC's findings, made it illegal for U.S. companies to knowingly corrupt a foreign official (although lubrication bribes are not expressly outlawed). Guilty companies can be fined up to $1 million, and guilty individuals can be fined up to $10,000 and/or jailed for up to five years. The Act also requires detailed record keeping and strict accounting controls.

As one might suspect, the Foreign Corrupt Practices Act is not very popular among corporate leaders. In fact, in a 1983 survey of 1200 high-level U.S. executives, 69 percent gave the Foreign Corrupt Practices Act a negative rating. Sixty-eight percent wanted the record-keeping requirements reduced. Sixty-four percent wanted the Act to draw a more specific distinction between legal and illegal payments. Significantly, however, although 78 percent of the executives surveyed believed that the Act makes it difficult to compete in countries where bribery is common, only 20 percent said they had lost business because of the Foreign Corrupt Practices Act.[33]

In view of the present law, one expert has summed up the foreign payoffs and bribery issue with the following advice: "Improper payments, it therefore appears, are literally a losing game. They may bring short-term benefits, but they involve enormous risks in the form of scandal and even prosecution. To protect itself and its managers, a corporation operating overseas should have a comprehensive, integrated system for preventing questionable payments."[34] In short, an MNC needs a clearly defined set of ethical standards for conduct overseas and top management's unwavering support for those standards.

International Management Challenges

International managers, like all other managers, need to be effective and efficient problem solvers when it comes to the basic functions of planning, decision making, organizing, leading, and control. However, unlike the typical manager, international managers encounter significant new challenges upon leaving their home country. Heading the list of these challenges are political instability and cultural diversity. Both deserve a closer look.

Political Instability

Citizens of established democracies such as the United States and Canada take political stability for granted. They do so because the transfer of power from one political party to another occurs in an orderly fashion without general bloodshed or political upheaval. Unfortunately, in most nations political instability is a constant fact of life. But as a former U.S. State Department official told *Fortune* magazine: "Stability per se is irrelevant. ... One-third of the world's governments change every year, often not by normal or democratic processes. The question for a corporation is whether it can identify the nascent scenarios and cope profitably—and ethically— with them."[35] Managers of MNCs doing business in politically unstable countries need to keep abreast of geopolitical realities and struggles for power. Systematic political risk assessment is a step in the right direction.

Political Risk Assessment An expert on the subject has defined **political risk assessment** as "the systematic means of assessing and managing the political risks of foreign direct investment or international business."[36] The three major political risks are revolution, expropriation, and government regulation (expropriation is given special attention in the next section). While these political risks have been a fact of life for MNCs for many years, it took the Iranian revolution to awaken the international management community to the need for some sort of systematic assessment of political risk. The fact that U.S. companies lost over one billion dollars in

Iran because of a largely unexpected revolution underscored the importance of knowing what is "really happening" in host countries. Three of the most popular responses to date have been (1) hiring former government foreign relations experts as special consultants, (2) buying political-risk insurance, and (3) employing fulltime political analysts.[37] Whichever approach is used, the overriding objective should be geocentric strategies that avoid unreasonable political risks.

The Threat of Expropriation   As demonstrated by the Iranian revolution, political winds can shift with dramatic speed and impact. Consider Dow Chemical's experience in Chile. In 1966, the Christian Democratic government in Chile invited Dow Chemical Company to build a plastics plant in Concepción, Chile. Construction began, and Dow's partnership agreement with the Chilean government was hailed as a model throughout South America. Four years later, just three months before production began at the new plant, the Socialist-Communist candidate, Salvador Allende, won an upset victory and became president despite ITT's interference. In the new political climate, Dow fared poorly. The government asked for a majority share of the plastics plant in 1971, and in 1972 Allende's government seized the entire Dow operation outright and ordered its foreign managers to leave the country. The political tide turned once again in 1973 when a military coup toppled the Allende government. By 1974, Dow was back in Chile by invitation of the new government.[38]

The most amazing aspect of Dow's experience in Chile is that similar scenes have been repeated over and over again with other firms in other host countries. Technically, a takeover of a company by the host government is referred to as **expropriation,** or nationalization. The most sweeping expropriation of U.S. property occurred in 1960, when Fidel Castro overthrew the Batista dictatorship in Cuba. To date, the United States has not received one penny of compensation for this $1.5 billion takeover of hundreds of private American business interests. Expropriations have increased in both frequency and geographic dispersion since 1960.[39] In fact, 76 nations have expropriated more than 1535 companies since 1960.[40] This disturbing trend makes political risk assessment all the more important today.

Toward Multinational Reciprocity   Since MNCs cannot legally dictate what the political climate in a particular host country will be, the best thing is to learn to live with those in power. One author has highlighted the philosophy behind such peaceful coexistence.

Most host governments accept the need for foreign investment. Many realize that they need the resources, technology, management skills, capital, and foreign exchange that foreign investment can bring. But governments increasingly want foreign investment on terms that maximize the contribution to national goals and minimize the threat to national sovereignty.[41]

In other words, **multinational reciprocity,** a mutual exchange of benefits between a foreign-owned company and a host country, is replacing the lopsided colonial exploitation of the past. Host governments are beginning to screen investments by foreigners more carefully and are insisting on a greater degree of local participation in capital investment, employment, and profit distribution. Mexico, for example, requires at least 51 percent local control of foreign business ventures within its borders.[42]

Cultural Diversity   Culture is the unique system of perceptions, beliefs, and language symbols that influences the behavior of a given population. It is difficult to distinguish the individual from his or her cultural context. In a manner of speaking, you are your culture and your culture is you. Consequently, people tend to be very protective of their cultural identity. Careless defiance of cultural traditions by outsiders often has the impact of personal insult. International managers who want to profit from favorable relationships with people of differing cultures cannot afford to run roughshod over cultural diversity. They need to be sensitive to the fact that others see and do things differently—not better, not worse—just differently.

Understanding the Cultural Barriers to Female Managers   A very important issue, with regard to cultural diversity, centers around the role of women in international business. In a recent study, it was discovered that only *three percent* of a sample of over 13,000 American and Canadian managers working overseas were women. According to 686 personnel managers questioned in the same study, foreigners' prejudice was the number one barrier to North American female managers working overseas (see Figure 19.3). The researcher, Nancy Adler, a respected Canadian management scholar, interpreted this barrier in the following manner:

> A wide range of countries (including Japan, Korea, Saudi Arabia, Italy, Greece, Australia, France, etc.) were seen as limiting the role of women in business, considering women as second class citizens, restricting women's mobility, or excluding women altogether from the world of work. ... Out of respect for the integrity of the foreign culture and the difficulty in changing fundamental beliefs and values, most companies believed foreigners' prejudice to be a serious, and often insurmountable, barrier confronting North American women's successful pursuit of international careers.[43]

In spite of limited opportunities, selection bias, and increased cultural risks, the respondents in Adler's study predicted substantial growth in female expatriate managers during the coming decade.

Figure 19.3 Managers Perceive Greater Barriers to Women in International Versus Domestic Management

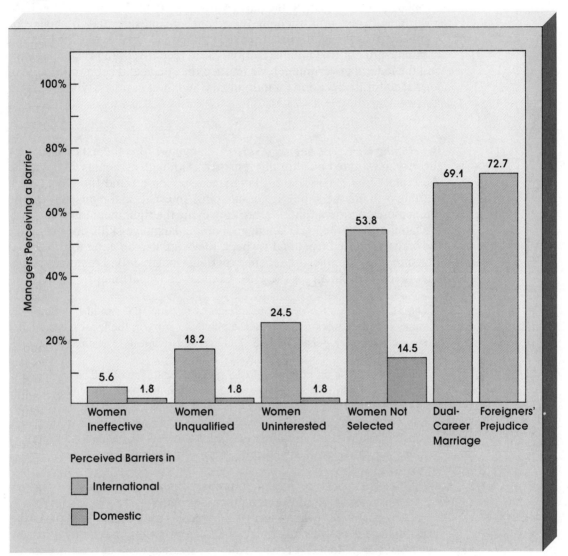

SOURCE: Nancy J. Adler, "Expecting International Success: Female Managers Overseas," *Columbia Journal of World Business* 19 (Fall 1984): 81. Permission granted by *Columbia Journal of World Business*.

Developing Cultural Sensitivity Cultural sensitivity, a sincere attempt to recognize and honor someone else's cultural values and traditions, can be learned. Unfortunately, in the past, American business firms and the U.S. government did not adequately prepare managers and officials for exposure to foreign cultures. The "ugly American" image was the product of haphazard cultural familiarization. More recently, both private industry and the federal government have learned the social and economic value of formal cultural education for individuals (and their families) who are slated for overseas duty.[44]

Developing Foreign Language Skills Language tops the list of assets for those who want to be culturally sensitive. Although estimates vary widely, there are some 3000 different languages spoken around the globe, each with its own unique subtleties of meaning. International managers can be much more confident that they are conveying the right meaning when they are familiar with the local language. Foreign language skills not only pave the way for mutual trust and respect, they can also be good for business. Consider, for example, the recent experience of Clyde V. Prestowitz, chief negotiator with Japan for the U.S. Commerce Department:

> During talks over the degree of foreign ownership that would be allowed in value-added networks, the Japanese planted a story in the local press, claiming—erroneously—that the U.S. had agreed to limit its participation to one-third.
>
> Prestowitz, the first high-level U.S. negotiator to speak and read Japanese, saw the story in a Saturday paper and counterattacked. He called a press conference and flatly denied the communication ministry's claim. After his remarks were printed, Prestowitz was invited to a special caucus of the ruling Liberal-Democratic Party—and the law was rewritten to allow 100% foreign ownership in value-added networks.[45]

MNCs have a special obligation to prepare their managers with appropriate language skills before sending them abroad.[46]

Formal language training also has a secondary benefit. It imparts the perceptual and behavioral aspects of a culture while introducing a new language. For instance, a clock "runs" in English while it (literally translated) "walks" in Spanish. This difference may lie behind the fact that English-speaking people often seem to be in a hurry to Spanish-speaking people. As indicated in Table 19.6, international managers may encounter huge differences in perception, behavior, and symbolism in different cultures. Their effectiveness depends to a large extent on their sensitivity to these cultural differences.

Table 19.6 Cultural Sensitivity: A Study in Contrasts

Characteristic	United States	Japan
Personal emphasis	Individualism (I, me); "lone wolf" personality	Groupism (part of we); "band wagon" personality
Interpersonal relationships	Independence encouraged	Mutual dependence encouraged
Worker participation	Less competition; elitism	More collaboration; egalitarianism
Competence	Ability (talent); specialist preferred	Total personality; generalist preferred
Decision making	Top-down; quick; individualistic	Bottom- or middle-up; slow; consensual
Conflict	To be confronted and surfaced; emphasis on conflict management	To be avoided or "melted" through *nemawashi**; emphasis on agreement management
Communication	Verbal and written	Nonverbal and implied
Sense of belonging (loyalty)	Low	High
Nature of change	Abrupt; complete; surgical	Evolutionary; renew or repair; massage not surgery
Basis of employment and promotion	On merit	Life-long employment; seniority

*There does not appear to be an English word that is equivalent to *nemawashi*. Literally, this Japanese term means "going around the roots." In other words, when transplanting a tree one must be careful to dig deeply so that the roots will not be severed or unduly damaged. Regarding organization behavior, the Japanese individual who wishes to sell an idea and/or make a change will work behind the scenes ("around the roots") to sound or feel out, test with, and gently persuade those he needs to convince for the idea to be adopted or the change to be made. He will not allow conflict to occur. He may have to compromise his plan somewhat, but he patiently and steadfastly sticks with his effort of convincing the other persons. Later when the idea or change is proposed officially, the consideration and adoption of the proposal is largely ceremonial.

SOURCE: Reprinted with permission from: Maurie K. Kobayashi and W. Warner Burke, "Organization Development in Japan," *Columbia Journal of World Business* 11 (Summer 1976): 113–123. Copyright © 1976 by the Trustees of Columbia University in the City of New York.

Summary

The discipline of international management has become more important in recent years because of the growing influence of multinational corporations (MNCs). Profit potential rather than international boundaries determines where and how an MNC does business. True multinationalism is associated with the final stage of a six-stage internationalization process. The six stages are licensing, exporting, local warehousing and selling, local assembly and packaging, joint venture, and direct foreign investment.

Experts, who complain that American managers are prepared only for domestic service, recommend that present and future managers begin to think internationally. According to Howard Perlmutter, management may have any of three general attitudes about international operations. They are an ethnocentric attitude (home-country oriented), a polycentric attitude (host-country oriented), and a geocentric attitude (world oriented). Perlmutter claims that a geocentric attitude will lead to better product quality, improved resource utilization, better local management, and more profit than the other attitudes. Strategic management is especially important in international firms, because geographically dispersed operations exaggerate differences.

Comparative management is a fledgling field of study concerned with how management practices compare across cultures. Much of the disagreement among comparative management scholars about the universality of management theory and practice traces to conflicting philosophies of convergence and divergence. "Convergents" emphasize global similarities; they believe that management practices apply equally well around the world. "Divergents," on the other hand, emphasize the need to adapt management theory and practice to fit different cultures. Comparative management research is hampered by terminological and representative sampling problems. A unique study by Geert Hofstede of 116,000 IBM employees in 40 nations classified each country by its prevailing attitude toward power distance, uncertainty avoidance, individualism-collectivism, and masculinity. In view of significant international differences on these cultural dimensions, Hofstede suggests that American management theory and practice be adapted to local cultures rather than imposed on them.

MNCs have stirred a good deal of controversy. Supporters point to the growth of peaceful prosperity stemming from the vigorous movement of people, capital, technology, and goods and services across international boundaries. Among a number of criticisms, MNCs have been accused of exporting jobs, threatening the national sovereignty of host countries, and operating in a corrupt atmosphere of bribery and payoffs. Research suggests that these accusations, while justified in some cases, do not characterize the typical MNC.

The task of international management is made difficult by political instability and cultural diversity. Alarmed by the sudden loss of over $1 billion in property in the Iranian revolution, U.S. companies are in-

creasingly turning to systematic assessment of political risk. Expropriation, which has increased in both frequency and geographic dispersion
over the last two decades, is a particularly serious political risk for MNCs.
Despite significant cultural barriers, North American women are expected
to gain greater access to overseas managerial positions in the coming
decade. Managers can cope successfully with cultural diversity, which is
simply a difficulty rather than an outright risk, through cultural sensitivity
and foreign language skills.

Terms to Understand

International management
Multinational corporation (MNC)
Ethnocentric attitude
Polycentric attitude
Geocentric attitude
Comparative management
Convergence (philosophy of)

Divergence (philosophy of)
Lubrication bribe
Whitemail bribe
Political risk assessment
Expropriation
Multinational reciprocity

Questions for Discussion

1. Why would the effective management of a multinational corporation
   be more difficult than managing a company with only domestic operations?
2. In your opinion, which of the six stages of internationalization is most
   risky? Explain.
3. What are the advantages of thinking geocentrically even if your company is not a multinational?
4. Why is strategic management particularly important in multinational
   organizations?
5. Which philosophy of international management—convergence or
   divergence—appeals more to you? Why?
6. Should management theories and techniques developed by Americans
   be applied without modification in foreign cultures? Explain your
   position.
7. Why is a long-run view helpful in refuting the claim that U.S. MNCs
   export jobs?
8. What is your position on paying off or bribing foreign officials in the
   course of doing business overseas?
9. In view of research evidence that only about half of America's major

MNCs engage in systematic political risk assessment, what would you say to nonusers?
10. Why is cultural sensitivity a vital aspect of successful international management?

Back to the Opening Case

Now that you have read Chapter 19, you should be able to answer the following questions about the Porsche case:

1. What evidence of geocentrism can you find in this case? What are its benefits and costs?
2. Based on what you know about Hofstede's research, do you think Schutz's approach to building an effective management team will succeed? Explain.
3. How would you rate Schutz on cultural sensitivity? Cite specific evidence in support of your position.

Closing Case 19.2

IBM Japan Has a Case of the 'Blues'*

The world over, Big Blue means IBM. To Japanese IBMers, blue means something more: They call their non-Japanese colleagues "blue eyes." More than 220 "blue eyes" landed in Tokyo last year as part of a massive reorganization of International Business Machines Corp.'s Far East operations. The invasion nearly quadruples the number of non-Japanese IBMers in the Japanese headquarters and raises a real question about IBM's proud commitment to hiring locals in its overseas operations. Explains Chief Executive John F. Akers: "We're more involved by far in Japan because the problems there are bigger."

The reorganization created a new central organization in the region, the IBM Asia/Pacific Group. Its explicit mission: overseeing operations in 17 Far East nations, including Japan and China, in a region that IBM sees as its most important growth market in the world. But observers think there was more going on. They suspect the brass in Armonk, N.Y., had had enough after watching IBM Japan Ltd. lose the lead in its home market five

*Reprinted from the February 18, 1985 issue of *Business Week* by special permission, © 1985 by McGraw-Hill, Inc.

years ago and then languish as No. 2 behind Fujitsu Ltd. in recent years. And warning signals were pointing to even further slippage.

The 23-year company man shipped in to head the new IBM group denies the reports circulating that IBM's concerns about the Japanese market prompted the decision to set up the Tokyo-based regional headquarters. Instead, says Vice-President and Group Executive George H. Conrades, IBM's growth strategy demanded it. Running the important new group is the first overseas assignment for Conrades, 45, who had been an executive in IBM's Information Systems & Technology Group.

Invasion

The growth potential of the Asian and Pacific Basin markets certainly warrants IBM's increased attention: The Japanese market is the second largest in the world, after the U.S. And vast China, awakening from decades of technological slumber, beckons from across the East China Sea.

But the invasion of U.S. staff doesn't sit well in Tokyo. Japanese inside the company and non-Japanese observers maintain that IBM Japan has taken a severe blow to its pride. "It's a loss of face," says a Tokyo industry analyst. "They spent all this effort to create an image as a Japanese company, and now the Americans move in."

Conrades is quick to play down rumors of dissension over the changes within IBM Japan. He insists "IBM Japan is one of our best company organizations." But "IBM needs to understand more about the Japanese market, and you can't get Japan experience sitting in New York. We decentralized and gave the new body authority to act."

Conrades admits strategies haven't yet gelled. And the speed of IBM's move is proof to many that faulty communications between IBM Japan and headquarters forced the change.

Tomio Tamamura, a sales promotion manager who quit IBM Japan last year after working there 23 years, calls it "an overcomputerized company," whose "do-it-by-the-manual" approach to management offends Japanese IBMers—especially when the manual is written in Armonk. "Now we have these foreigners in Tokyo, most of whom do not speak Japanese and know little or nothing about the Japanese market," says Tamamura.

Takeo Shiina, president of IBM Japan since 1975, made 10 trips to Armonk in 1983. Insiders say the visits were necessary because U.S. managers were uneasy about IBM Japan's direction. And even a high-level home office executive shuttling back and forth as a liaison couldn't narrow the gap. Shiina admits to communication snags: "Our growth made it inevitable."

There were other causes for concern. Total sales under Shiina improved from single- to doublt-digit growth, and revenues grew 20%, to $3.2 billion in 1984. But exports exceeded domestic sales last year. IBM Japan slipped to second place in the overall computer market in Japan in 1979 and is at best treading water. In midsize mainframes, for example, seven of Fujitsu's 11 new customers in the first nine months of 1984 switched from IBM gear, according to one Japanese market survey. Sales of IBM's Japanese-language PC, according to industry analysts, failed to reach the company's annual goal of 120,000 units. Industry sources also point out that third-ranked NEC Corp. is fast moving up in the local rankings.

Even so, Big Blue remains a formidable player in Japan. Says a Tokyo-based executive of a non-Japanese rival: "Those three little initials still persuade people to buy." And IBM Japan's employees seem to be moving past what Shiina concedes was "fear and anxiety" about the reorganization.

Nonetheless, Japan "is a tough, tough market," says Shiina. "The language requirements alone make it a unique challenge." IBM's rivals are banking on that. Declares a Fujitsu executive who requests anonymity: "We'll survive against IBM in our home market because of the cultural factor."

For Discussion

1. Are IBM's executives at the firm's Armonk, N.Y. headquarters "ethnocentric"? Cite specific evidence to build your case for or against this claim.
2. Referring to Table 19.5, should the different need profiles Hofstede identified for Japan and the United States be taken into consideration by the new team of American managers in Japan? Explain your rationale.
3. How serious a problem is it that most of the Americans working for IBM Japan do not speak Japanese? Explain.
4. How does the cultural contrast between the United States and Japan in Table 19.6 help explain why Tomio Tamamura, the former sales promotion manager, believes IBM's "do-it-by-the-manual" approach is offensive to Japanese employees?

References

Opening Quotation: H. J. Zoffer, "Restructuring Management Education," *Management Review* 70 (April 1981): 39.

Opening Case: Excerpted from David B. Tinnin, "The American at the Wheel of Porsche," *Fortune* 105 (April 5, 1982): 78–87. For additional information on Porsche, see Jan P. Norbye, "Porsche Recalls His Car's Origins," *Automotive News* No. 4775 (September 24, 1979): 56; Richard Feast, "High Product Hopes for

Low-Volume Porsche," *Automotive News* No. 4883 (October 5, 1981): 9–10; and "The Ups and Downs of Porsche Sales," *Automotive News* No. 4883 (October 5, 1981): 10.

Closing Case: Michael Berger, "IBM Japan Has a Case of the 'Blues,' " *Business Week* No. 2881 (February 18, 1985): 98.

1. Eleanor Johnson Tracy, "Porsche is Doing Great—So Changes Course," *Fortune* 109 (March 5, 1984): 59. Also see David B. Tinnin, "Porsche's Civil War with Its Dealers," *Fortune* 109 (April 16, 1984): 63–64, 68.

2. See John W. Wilson, "America's High-Tech Crisis," *Business Week* No. 2883 (March 11, 1985): 56–62, 67.

3. E. J. Kolde, *The Multinational Company* (Lexington, Mass.: D. C. Heath, 1974), p. 5.

4. Kathryn Rudie Harrigan, "Joint Ventures and Global Strategies," *Columbia Journal of World Business* 19 (Summer 1984): 13.

5. This six-step sequence is based on Alan M. Rugman, "A New Theory of the Multinational Enterprise: Internationalization Versus Internalization," *Columbia Journal of World Business* 15 (Spring 1980): 23–29.

6. See Gene Bylinsky, "America's Best-Managed Factories," *Fortune* 109 (May 28, 1984): 16–24. (Also see Table 17.2 in Chapter 17.)

7. Rugman, "A New Theory of the Multinational Enterprise," p. 27.

8. Neil H. Jacoby, "The Multinational Corporation," *The Center Magazine* III (May 1970) as reprinted in A. Kapoor and Phillip D. Grub, eds., *The Multinational Enterprise in Transition* (Princeton, N.J.: Darwin Press, 1972), p. 39.

9. "Amidst Stiffer International Competition, U.S. Managers Need a Broader Perspective," *Management Review* 69 (March 1980): 34.

10. William Glasgall, "It Costs More to 'Fill 'Er Up'—But Not for Long," *Business Week* No. 2889 (April 8, 1985): 35.

11. Howard V. Perlmutter, "The Tortuous Evolution of the Multinational Corporation," *Columbia Journal of World Business* 4 (January-February 1969): 11.

12. "Revlon: A Painful Case of Slow Growth and Fading Glamour," *Business Week* No. 2734 (April 12, 1982): 118.

13. Perlmutter, "The Tortuous Evolution of the Multinational Corporation," p. 16.

14. Ibid.

15. For an excellent discussion, see Rodman L. Drake and Lee M. Caudill, "Management of the Large Multinational: Trends and Future Challenges," *Business Horizons* 24 (May-June 1981): 83–91.

16. This list is derived from C. K. Prahalad and Yves L. Doz, "An Approach to Strategic Control in MNCs," *Sloan Management Review* 22 (Summer 1981): 5–13.

17. See Ross A. Webber, "Convergence or Divergence?" *Columbia Journal of World Business* 4 (May-June 1969): 75–83.

18. See George S. Vozikis and Timothy S. Mescon, "Convergence or Divergence?

A Vital Managerial Quest Revisited," *Columbia Journal of World Business* 16 (Summer 1981): 79–87.

19. Lane Kelley and Reginald Worthley, "The Role of Culture in Comparative Management: A Cross-Cultural Perspective," *Academy of Management Journal* 24 (March 1981): 165.

20. Adapted from Kelley and Worthley, "The Role of Culture in Comparative Management." For an interesting comparative management study that "refutes the widespread belief that Japanese workers are more committed to the organizations that employ them than are their U.S. counterparts," see Fred Luthans, Harriette S. McCaul, and Nancy G. Dodd, "Organizational Commitment: A Comparison of American, Japanese, and Korean Employees," *Academy of Management Journal* 28 (March 1985): 213–219. An informative critique of cross-cultural studies may be found in Nancy Adler, "Cross-Cultural Management Research: The Ostrich and the Trend," *Academy of Management Review* 8 (April 1983): 226–232.

21. See Geert Hofstede, "Motivation, Leadership, and Organization: Do American Theories Apply Abroad?" *Organizational Dynamics* 9 (Summer 1980): 42–63. Also see Geert Hofstede, "The Cultural Relativity of Organizational Practices and Theories," *Journal of International Business Studies* 14 (Fall 1983): 75–89.

22. For an interesting and informative discussion of Hofstede's article see the articles by Leonard D. Goodstein, John W. Hunt, and Geert Hofstede in *Organizational Dynamics* 10 (Summer 1981): 49–68.

23. Sam R. Goodman, "Opinion: Speaking Out For Multinationals," *Financial Executive* 47 (November 1979): 22.

24. For a landmark critique on MNCs, see Richard J. Barnet and Ronald E. Müller, *Global Reach: The Power of the Multinational Corporations* (New York: Simon and Schuster, 1974).

25. See Dominic Sorrentino, "Employment and Payroll Costs of U.S. Multinational Companies," *Monthly Labor Review* 97 (January 1974): 66–67.

26. "The Questions the ITT Case Raises," *Business Week* No. 2273 (March 31, 1973): 42. For an interesting follow-up report, see Michael H. Crosby, "ITT's Chile Confession: A Definite 'Maybe,' " *Business and Society Review* No. 18 (Summer 1976): 66–67.

27. Joseph LaPalombara, "Myths of the Multinationals," *Across the Board* 13 (October 1976): 41.

28. Peter Nehemkis, "Business Payoffs Abroad: Rhetoric and Reality," *California Management Review* 18 (Winter 1975): 6.

29. Ibid., p. 7.

30. Morton Mintz and Jerry S. Cohen, *Power, Inc.* (New York: Bantam, 1976), p. 169.

31. See Martin C. Schnitzer, Marilyn L. Liebrenz, and Konrad W. Kubin, *International Business* (Cincinnati: South-Western, 1985), chap. 10.

32. Barry Richman, "Stopping Payments Under the Table," *Business Week* No. 2535 (May 22, 1978): 18.

33. For more details, see "The Antibribery Act Splits Executives," *Business Week* No. 2808 (September 19, 1983): 16.

34. Richman, "Stopping Payments Under the Table," p. 18.

35. Louis Kraar, "The Multinationals Get Smarter About Political Risks," *Fortune* 101 (March 24, 1980): 98.

36. Joseph V. Micallef, "Political Risk Assessment," *Columbia Journal of World Business* 16 (Summer 1981): 47. Also see Warnock Davies, "Beyond the Earthquake Allegory: Managing Political Risk Vulnerability," *Business Horizons* 24 (July-August 1981): 39–43 and Mark Fitzpatrick, "The Definition and Assessment of Political Risk in International Business: A Review of the Literature," *Academy of Management Review* 8 (April 1983): 249–254.

37. Drawn from Kraar, "The Multinationals Get Smarter About Political Risks," p. 87. Another good source is Thomas W. Shreeve, "Be Prepared for Political Changes Abroad," *Harvard Business Review* 62 (July-August 1984): 111–118.

38. Drawn from Herbert E. Meyer, "Dow Picks Up the Pieces in Chile," *Fortune* 89 (April 1974): 140–152.

39. See James K. Weekly, "Expropriation of U.S. Multinational Investments," *MSU Business Topics* 25 (Winter 1977): 27–36.

40. For complete discussion of expropriation trends, see David A. Jodice, "Sources of Change in Third World Regimes for Foreign Direct Investment, 1968–1976," *International Organization* 34 (Spring 1980): 177–206.

41. Vern Terpstra, *The Cultural Environment of International Business* (Cincinnati: South-Western, 1978), pp. 240–241.

42. See Alan M. Field, "Protecting the Rich," *Forbes* 135 (March 25, 1985): 42–43.

43. Nancy J. Adler, "Expecting International Success: Female Managers Overseas," *Columbia Journal of World Business* 19 (Fall 1984): 82.

44. See Abdulhamied AlRomaithy, "How to Take the ACHE Out of International Training," *Training* 18 (June 1981): 34, 36, 39. For useful information about how to repatriate managers working overseas, see Cecil G. Howard, "How Best to Integrate Expatriate Managers in the Domestic Organization," *Personnel Administrator* 27 (July 1982): 27–33.

45. Michael Berger, "Phone Market: Japan Keeps Hanging Up on the U.S.," *Business Week* No. 2883 (March 11, 1985): 67.

46. For informative discussion, see "How to Learn a Foreign Language," *Business Week* No. 2656 (September 29, 1980): 132–134.

Appendix A

Career and Stress Management

Throughout this book, we have focused on the management of organizational resources. You have been challenged to manage human, material, and financial resources in an effective and efficient manner. Now, realizing that each of us is a valuable resource both as an individual and as an integral part of organized endeavor, we turn to self-management. Two important dimensions of self-management are career management and stress management. Some practical guidelines on effective career and stress management are therefore offered here.

Adopting a Career Perspective

Someone once said that the difference between a job and a career is about 20 hours a week. Although it is generally true that a career-oriented person attacks his or her job with above-average vigor, something more fundamental is involved. Specifically, those with a career perspective tend to see their job as a key link in a chain rather than as an isolated experience. As illustrated in Figure A.1, the typical organizational career is made up of identifiable stages.[1] Each stage has its own distinctive combination of challenges. Those who understand this evolutionary process and prepare themselves for each successive stage will do much better than those with a purely here-and-now perspective. The self-doubt that strikes many otherwise successful managers at midcareer, for example, is not as traumatic when one recognizes it as a natural way station in a long career.[2] A career perspective helps one mentally prepare for future stages.[3]

Figure A.1   The Career Cycle

Stage	Growth, Fantasy, Exploration 1	Passage into an Organization or Occupation ⟶ Entry into World of Work 2	Basic Training 3	Full Membership in Early Career 4	Full Membership, Midcareer 5
Age Range	0-21	16-25	16-25	17-30	25+
Roles	Student, aspirant, applicant	Recruit, entrant	Trainee, novice	New but full member	Full member, tenured member, life member, supervisor, manager (person may remain in this stage)

SOURCE: Edgar H. Schein, *Career Dynamics,* © 1978, Addison-Wesley, Reading, Massachusetts. Adapted from pp. 40–46. (Table 4.1). Reprinted with permission.

Dual Career Couples

As more and more women enter the labor force on a full-time basis, the traditional arrangement where the man is the sole breadwinner and the woman is the housewife/mother is undergoing significant change. **Dual career couples,** in which both partners pursue professional careers full time, have become commonplace. However, they must often cope with unresolved issues regarding housekeeping and child rearing. Another source of potential conflict is the question of whose career, the man's or the woman's, takes precedence relative to relocation and commuting distance. The first step toward resolving these role conflicts is to recognize different kinds of dual career marriages.

According to researchers, there are four categories of dual career relationships: traditional, neotraditional, matriarchal, and egalitarian.[4] The roles of husband and wife vary from category to category.

● **Traditional.** In the traditional dual career marriage the wife both works full time and assumes full responsibility for the home. The husband's career clearly takes precedence over the wife's. Some have referred to

Figure A.1 The Career Cycle (cont.)

Stage	Midcareer Crisis 6	Late Career in Nonleadership Role 7A	Late Career in Leadership Role 7B	Decline and Disengagement 8	Retirement 9
Age Range	35-45	40 to Retirement	May Begin Early but Persists	40 to Retirement	50+
Roles		Key member, member of management, good contributor or dead wood (many people stay in this stage)	General manager, officer, senior partner, internal entrepreneur, senior staff	(Different people start decline at different ages)	

Passage Out of the Organization or Occupation →

this arrangement as the "super mom" or "super wife" syndrome. Needless to say, the pressures and stress on the overloaded female partner can strain the marriage.

- **Neotraditional.** In this type of dual career marriage, the husband recognizes the wife's career as important, perhaps equally important to his. Since the husband is supportive of the wife's career, he may assume some of the household chores. "Embodied deeply is the idea of permission to work—the husband is allowing his wife to work and is helping her do this by taking on a few of her duties in the home."[5]

- **Matriarchal.** In a matriarchal relationship, the traditional male-female roles are reversed. Both the couple themselves and acquaintances fully recognize that the wife's career comes first. Male artists, writers, and others who can conveniently ply their trade at home while assuming housekeeping chores have found the "househusband" role workable.

- **Egalitarian.** Elimination of traditional gender-specific housekeeping

Table A.1 Thirteen Career Tips for Young Managers

- Remember that good performance that pleases your superiors is the basic foundation of success, but recognize that not all good performance is easily measured. Determine the real criteria by which you are evaluated and be rigorously honest in evaluating your own performance against these criteria.

- Manage your career; be active in influencing decisions, because pure effort is not necessarily rewarded.

- Strive for positions that have high visibility and exposure where you can be a hero observed by higher officials. Check to see that the organization has a formal system of keeping track of young people. Remember that high-risk line jobs tend to offer more visibility than staff positions like corporate planning or personnel, but also that visibility can sometimes be achieved by off-job community activities.

- Develop relations with a mobile senior executive who can be your sponsor. Become a complementary crucial subordinate with different skills than your superior.

- Learn your job as quickly as possible and train a replacement so you can be available to move and broaden your background in different functions.

- Nominate yourself for other positions: modesty is not necessarily a virtue. However, change jobs for more power and influence, not primarily for status or pay. The latter could be a substitute for real opportunity to make things happen.

- Before taking a position, rigorously assess your strengths and weaknesses, what you like and don't like. Don't accept a promotion if it draws on your weaknesses and entails mainly activities that you don't like.

- Leave at your convenience, but on good terms without parting criticism of the organization. Do not stay under an immobile superior who is not promoted in three to five years.

- Don't be trapped by formal, narrow job descriptions. Move outside them and probe the limits of your influence.

- Accept that responsibility will always somewhat exceed authority and that organizational politics are inevitable. Establish alliances and fight necessary battles, minimizing upward ones to very important issues.

- Get out of management if you can't stand being dependent on others and having them dependent on you.

- Recognize that you will face ethical dilemmas no matter how moral you try to be. No evidence exists that unethical managers are more successful than ethical ones, but it may well be that those who move faster are less socially conscious. Therefore, from time to time you must examine your personal values and question how much you will sacrifice for the organization.

- Don't automatically accept all tales of managerial perversity that you hear. Attributing others' success to unethical behavior is often an excuse for one's own personal inadequacies. Most of all, don't commit an act which you know to be wrong in the hope that your supervisor will see it as loyalty and reward you for it. Sometimes he will, but he may also sacrifice you when the organization is criticized.

SOURCE: © 1976 by the Regents of the University of California. Reprinted from Ross A. Webber, "Career Problems of Young Managers," *California Management Review* 18 (Summer 1976):29 by permission of the Regents.

roles is the key to an egalitarian dual career marriage. Both partners have equally important careers and both contribute equally to keeping house and rearing children. However, sex-role stereotyping and cultural conditioning are formidable barriers to a true egalitarian relationship.

Each of the foregoing arrangements has its own set of advantages and disadvantages. Couples who are committed to making their marriage work need to discuss their mutual expectations frankly, explore alternatives, select a mutually agreeable course of action, and periodically reevaluate the situation. (The conflict resolution techniques discussed in Chapter 12 can be a big help.) Since dual career couples generally enjoy above-average income, hiring a part-time housekeeper can help relieve domestic pressures. As with management, it takes commitment and creative problem solving to keep a dual career marriage on track.

Career Tips for New Managers

By being proactive rather than reactive, a new manager can anticipate and overcome adjustment problems.[6] Ross A. Webber, of the University of Pennsylvania's Wharton School, has formulated an excellent list of thirteen career tips for young managers (see Table A.1). Webber's list is particularly useful because it deals frankly and realistically with organizational politics (see the discussion in Chapter 12) and business ethics (recall our discussion in Chapter 18).

Managing Stress

When our prehistoric ancestors were faced with a charging beast, they had two choices. They could stand and fight the beast, or they could run away from it. Their bodies were mobilized for this fight-or-flight response by a complex change in body chemistry that we have come to call stress. This stress response helped our prehistoric ancestors survive by fighting harder or running faster than normal. Times have changed, however, and stress has become more of a health hazard than a survival mechanism. Today's employees do not face charging beasts; instead they have to deal with work overload, unreasonable deadlines, angry superiors, financial worries, and domestic difficulties. Those who respond to these modern problems as if each were a charging beast tend to suffer from the undesirable side effects of stress, such as headaches, lower back pain, indigestion and ulcers, loss of sleep, nervous tension, heart attack, and stroke. Managers need to learn more about stress and how to deal with it, both in themselves and in their coworkers.

What Does Stress Involve?

Formally defined, **stress** is "an adaptive response, mediated by individual characteristics and/or psychological processes, that is a consequence of any external action, situation, or event that places special physical and/or psychological demands upon a person."[7] This definition aptly focuses our attention on three major components of stress: (1) situational demands that force one to adapt (called *stressors*), (2) one's perception of those demands and one's ability to cope with them, and (3) the biochemical stress response. All three components must be properly interrelated if stress is to be meaningfully discussed.

Regarding the first component, typical organizational stressors include role overload, role conflict, role ambiguity (not knowing what is expected), interpersonal conflict and competition, deadlines, high risk, job dissatisfaction, and unrealized status/career aspirations. It is the second component—perception and coping ability—that accounts for the fact that two people may react very differently to a given stressor.[8] Accordingly, perceptual screening and coping ability are the keys to effectively managing the two faces of stress.

The Two Faces of Stress

According to Hans Selye, the father of the modern concept of stress, "Complete freedom from stress is death."[9] Stress is inevitable. Fortunately, not all stress is bad. Stress has two faces, an energizing face and a destructive face. The challenge, then, is not to totally avoid or eliminate all stress; rather it is to take advantage of energizing stress and minimize destructive stress. As illustrated in Figure A.2, too little stress, or understimulation, can lead to "rustout," a condition familiar to anyone who has known the boredom associated with an unchallenging job. At the other end of the stress scale is "burnout," caused by overstimulation.[10]

The trick to managing stress is to experience moderate *energizing* stress that enhances one's personal productivity. For example, a deadline might prompt a student to "burn the midnight oil" to finish a term paper. Or a new project might challenge a manager to create new approaches to a situation. But, with the onset of destructive stress, diminishing returns set in and productivity decreases.

The thin line between energizing and destructive stress is highly personal. Typically, symptoms such as unexplained irritability, sleeplessness, excessive alcohol and/or drug use, apathy, and vague but persistent anxiety signal an underlying problem with destructive stress. When the scale tips toward destructive stress, it is time to back off and reevaluate your circumstances.

Coping with Stress

In recent years, there has been an avalanche of advice on how best to deal with stress. But one thing stands clear: there is no panacea or quick fix. Individual differences are simply too great to make one coping technique

Figure A.2 The Two Faces of Stress

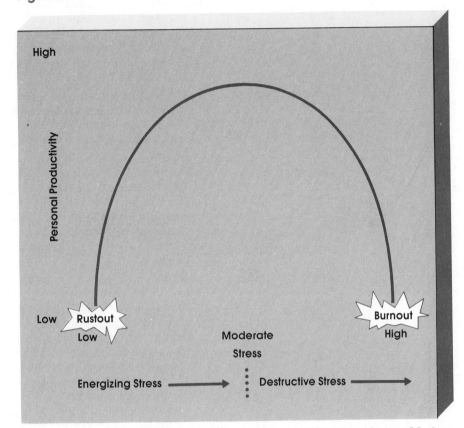

SOURCE: Adapted from Robert Kreitner, "Personal Wellness: It's Just Good Business," *Business Horizons* 25 (May/June 1982): 32. Copyright 1982 by the Foundation for the School of Business at Indiana University. Reprinted with permission.

useful for all. A comprehensive approach spelling out the word *cope*, however, has helped many deal constructively with stress.

Control the situation.
Open up to others.
Pace yourself.
Exercise and relax.[11]

An expanded version of these coping guidelines is presented in Table A.2. Those who learn to manage stress constructively, rather than depending on alcohol, barbiturates ("downers"), and other destructive habits, can look forward to a healthier, happier, and more productive career.

Table A.2 Coping with Stress

Control the situation	• Avoid unrealistic deadlines. • Do your best, but know your limits. You cannot be everything to everyone. • Learn to identify and limit your exposure to stressful situations and people.
Open up to others	• Freely discuss your problems, frustrations, and sources of uptightness with those who care about you. • When faced with a tough situation, smile! A *sincere* smile often can defuse emotion and build a bridge of goodwill.
Pace yourself	• Plan your day on a flexible basis • Don't try to do two or more things at the same time. • Counter unproductive haste by forcing yourself to slow down (stop to smell the roses along the way). • Think before reacting. • Live on a day-to-day basis rather than on a minute-by-minute basis

Exercise and relax	• Engage in regular noncompetitive physical activity (e.g., take a ten- to twenty-minute walk each day). Those who are in good physical condition can stay in shape by jogging, swimming, riding a bike, or playing tennis, handball, or racquetball on a regular basis (three or four times a week). See your doctor when in doubt about your physical condition.
	• When feeling uptight, relax for a few minutes by following these simple steps:
	  1. Sit comfortably with eyes closed in a quiet location.
	  2. Slowly repeat a peaceful word or phrase over and over to yourself in your mind. (A mental picture of a peaceful scene also works.)
	  3. Avoid distracting thoughts by keeping a passive mental attitude.

References

1. For a four-stage model of professional careers, see Gene W. Dalton, Paul H. Thompson, and Raymond L. Price, "The Four Stages of Professional Careers—A New Look at Performance by Professionals," *Organizational Dynamics* 6 (Summer 1977): 19–42. A very good collection of readings on career management may be found in Marilyn A. Morgan, ed., *Managing Career Development* (New York: Van Nostrand, 1980).

2. For useful information on the problem of mid-career crisis, see Joe Thomas, "Mid-Career Crisis and the Organization," *Business Horizons* 25 (November-December 1982): 73–78.

3. Recent theory and research in the area of careers may be found in Manuel London, "Toward a Theory of Career Motivation," *Academy of Management Review* 8 (October 1983): 620–630 and John F. Veiga, "Mobility Influences During Managerial Career Stages," *Academy of Management Journal* 26 (March 1983): 64–85.

4. For an excellent discussion, see Nancy Lee, "The Dual Career Couple: Benefits and Pitfalls," *Management Review* 70 (January 1981): 46–52.

5. Ibid., p. 49.

6. *Business Week's Guide to Careers,* in its six issues a year, is packed with good tips on succeeding in the job market. For subscription information, write: *Business Week's Guide to Careers,* Att: Patricia Quinn—Suite 4084, 1221 Avenue of the Americas, New York, NY 10020.

7. John M. Ivancevich and Michael T. Matteson, *Stress and Work: A Managerial Perspective* (Glenview, Ill.: Scott, Foresman, 1980), pp. 8–9.

8. Research evidence demonstrating that Type A (stress-prone) personality traits influence the effects of stress can be found in John M. Ivancevich, Michael T. Matteson, and Cynthia Preston, "Occupational Stress, Type A Behavior, and Physical Well Being," *Academy of Management Journal* 25 (June 1982): 373–391.

9. Hans Selye, *Stress Without Distress* (Philadelphia: Lippincott, 1974), p. 32.

10. See Donald P. Rogers, "Helping Employees Cope with Burnout," *Business* 34 (October-December 1984): 3–7.

11. These guidelines have been adapted from Meyer Friedman and Ray H. Rosenman, *Type A Behavior and Your Heart* (Greenwich, Conn.: Fawcett, 1974); Herbert Benson, *The Relaxation Response* (New York: William Morrow, 1975); "Executive's Guide to Living with Stress," *Business Week* No. 2446 (August 23, 1976): 75–80; and John W. Farquhar, *The American Way of Life Need Not Be Hazardous to Your Health* (New York: W. W. Norton, 1978).

Appendix B

Quantitative and Graphic Management Tools

As managers face increasingly complex situations and problems, ever more sophisticated techniques are pressed into service. Strategic management has helped managers cope with growing competition and limited resources. Matrix organization design has helped management coordinate complex projects. Behavior modification has helped management deal with difficult behavior problems. And computerized management information systems have helped management cope with the information explosion. The list of innovative management techniques is long and growing, and to it must be added quantitative and graphic techniques. Pictographic displays often communicate more effectively than words; indeed, a picture sometimes is better than a thousand words. Likewise, the logic and precision of mathematics can be more effective than intuitive guesswork. This appendix presents several quantitative and graphic techniques that can enhance managerial planning, problem solving, and decision making.

Zero-base Budgeting: A Cost-Benefit Planning Tool

Zero-base budgeting (ZBB) has been defined by its originator as "an operating, planning, and budgeting process which requires each manager to justify his entire budget request in detail from scratch (hence zero base) and shifts the burden of proof to each manager to justify why he should spend any money at all."[1]

This idea of reviewing proposed expenditures for ongoing activities, in addition to those for new activities, is a significant departure from tradi-

Table B.1 An Advocate's View of the Benefits of Zero-base Budgeting

Former President Jimmy Carter:

From my experience in government as well as the experiences of corporations in the business world, a number of clear-cut benefits from an effective zero-base budgeting effort can be cited. These benefits include:

- Focusing the management process on analysis and decision-making rather than simply on numbers—in other words, the what, why, and how issues as well as how much.
- Combining planning, budgeting, and operational decision-making into one process.
- Forcing managers to evaluate in detail the cost-effectiveness of their operations. This includes specific programs—both new and old—all of which are clearly identified rather than functionally buried.
- Providing a system to trade off between long-term and short-term needs during the budgeting period, as well as a follow-up tool on cost and performance during the year.
- Allowing for quick budget adjustments or resource shifts during the year, if necessary when revenue falls short. In so doing, zero-base budgeting offers the capability to quickly and rationally modify goals and expectations to correspond to a realistic and affordable plan of operation.
- Identifying similar functions among different departments for comparison and evaluation.
- And most important to me, broadly expanding managment participation and training in the planning, budgeting, and decision-making process.

SOURCE: Jimmy Carter, "Jimmy Carter Tells Why He Will Use Zero-Base Budgeting," reprinted from *Nation's Business* 65 (January 1977): 26, published by the Chamber of Commerce of the United States, January 1977.

tional incremental budgeting. Under incremental budgeting, past levels of expenditure are automatically assumed to be still valid; only proposed expenditures above the previous year's level require justification. One can readily see the weakness of the traditional incremental approach: it can hide wasteful spending on obsolete activities and unproductive personnel. Zero-base budgeting annually requires every budgeted activity to stand on its own cost-benefit merit rather than on tradition or the protection of special interests.

Zero-base budgeting has an interesting history. It was conceived during the late 1960s by Peter A. Pyhrr and a team of researchers at Texas Instruments. Published reports of Pyhrr's work caught the attention of Jimmy Carter, at that time governor of Georgia, who quickly became a strong supporter of ZBB (see Table B.1). At Carter's request, Pyhrr left Texas Instruments to help install zero-base budgeting in Georgia. Subsequently, Carter's executive budget recommendation for the entire state government for fiscal year 1973 was based on zero-base budgeting.[2]

Figure B.1 The Basic Zero-base Budgeting Process

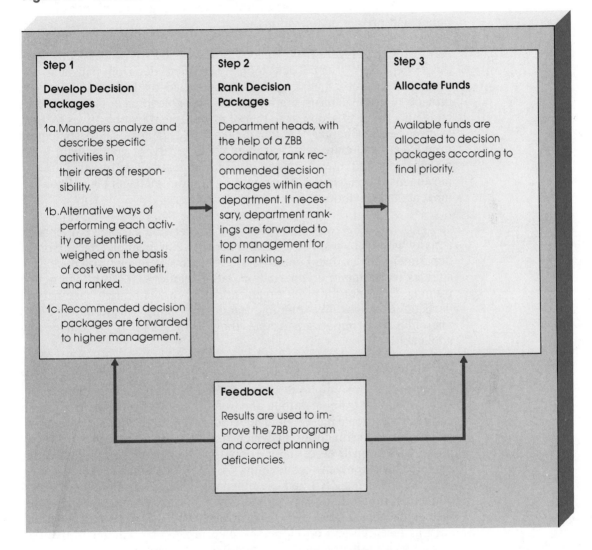

Georgia's apparent success with ZBB prompted a wave of ZBB programs in both private and public organizations. In fact, one of Carter's first moves after being elected president was to initiate a ZBB program in the federal government. But Ronald Reagan promptly dissolved the federal ZBB program soon after taking over the Oval Office from Carter. According to the Reagan Administration, the ZBB program was too expensive and cumbersome to administer. In retrospect, it is unfortunate that ZBB became a political football at the highly visible federal level. A properly administered ZBB program can curb wasteful budgeting practices in both public and private organizations.

The Zero-base Budgeting Process

As illustrated in Figure B.1 (on page B3), the basic ZBB process consists of three steps and a feedback loop.[3] So-called decision packages are developed by area managers and then ranked by higher managers to provide a rational basis for allocating available funds. This zero-base budgeting process is similar to that of management by objectives (MBO), as discussed in Chapter 4, in that it calls for a high degree of participation from lower-level managers. But unlike MBO, ZBB originates with lower management and moves upward. ZBB proponents claim that this upward movement effectively taps the creativity of lower managers who know the most about actual operations.

Step 1: Develop Decision Packages   A **ZBB decision package** is a separate activity with its own set of costs and benefits. For example, the personnel department in a business could be divided into several decision packages, such as recruitment, compensation, labor relations, job evaluation, and training. Even not-for-profit organizations such as libraries have natural decision packages like binding, cataloging, filing, subscriptions, and microfilm. It is important to note, though, that ZBB is not universally applicable.

According to experts, ZBB is better suited for use in service functions that have no tangible units of output or standardized (per unit) costs. ZBB is appropriate for employee training, for example, because there is no standard unit of training output, and training costs vary from job to job. In contrast, traditional incremental budgets are recommended for production and direct sales functions in which budget allocations can be directly linked with given levels of volume or output. Recent research supports this contingency approach to budgeting. A study of three service computer centers, one using ZBB and the other two using traditional incremental budgeting, found that client satisfaction with the services was higher for the center using ZBB.[4] ZBB is particularly well suited to staff functions such as research and development, data processing, administrative and office services, maintenance, accounting, and personnel.

Once the decision packages have been identified, ZBB's creative phase begins. Teams consisting of the decision package manager, one or two subordinates, and usually a few of the manager's peers brainstorm alternative ways of performing the activity in question (for example, see section 1 in Table B.2). Each alternative is spelled out and weighed in terms of identified costs versus benefits. Finally, the various alternatives are ranked, with the highest being forwarded to the department head as a recommended decision package. A breakdown of the decision package

Table B.2 A Sample Zero-base Budgeting Decision Package with Three Possible Levels of Performance

Situation. The Air Quality Laboratory tests air samples collected by field engineers throughout Georgia. It identifies and evaluates pollutants by type and volume, then provides reports and analyses to the field engineers. The manager involved made the typical two-part analysis.

1. **Different ways of performing the same function.**
   a) **Recommended decision package.** Use a centralized laboratory in Atlanta to conduct all tests (cost—$246,000). This expenditure would allow 75,000 tests and would determine the air quality for 90% of the population (leaving unsampled only rural areas with little or no pollution problem).
   b) **Alternatives not recommended.**
      - Contract testing to Georgia Tech (cost—$450,000). The $6 per test charged by Georgia Tech exceeds the $246,000 cost for doing the same work in the Air Quality Laboratory, and the quality of the testing is equal.
      - Conduct all testing at regional locations (cost—$590,000). Cost $590,000 the first year due to setup cost and purchase of duplicate equipment, with a $425,000 running rate in subsequent years. Many labs would be staffed at a minimum level, with less than full utilization of people and equipment.
      - Conduct tests in Central Laboratory for special pollutants only, which require special qualifications for people and equipment, and conduct routine tests in regional centers (cost—$400,000). This higher cost is created because regional centers have less than full workloads for people and equipment.

2. **Different levels of effort of performing the function.**
   a) **Air Quality Laboratory (1 of 3), cost—$140,000.** Minimum package: Test 37,300 samples, determining air quality for only five urban areas with the worst pollution (covering 70% of the population).
   b) **Air Quality Laboratory (2 of 3), cost—$61,000.** Test 17,700 additional samples (totaling 55,000, which is the current level), determining air quality for five additional problem urban areas plus eight counties chosen on the basis of worst pollution covering 80% of the population).
   c) **Air Quality Laboratory (3 of 3), cost—$45,000.** Test 20,000 additional samples (totaling 75,000), determining air quality for 90% of the population, and leaving only rural areas with little or no pollution problems unsampled.

SOURCE: Peter A. Pyhrr, *Zero-Base Budgeting* (New York: Wiley, 1973), pp. 38–39.

into component levels is also forwarded to give higher management a rational basis for making any necessary budget cuts (note in Table B.2 that the three dollar figures in section 2 add up to the decision package cost of $246,000 in section 1).

Step 2: Rank Decision Packages After receiving the decision package recommendations for all departmental activities, the department head, usually two other department heads, and a ZBB coordinator team up to rank them. Overlapping or redundant activities are merged or weeded out at the start of the ranking process. Even if a quantitative ranking model is used, subjective judgments are unavoidably made. Sometimes the ZBB coordinator is asked to mediate value conflicts. The resulting ranking of decision packages, according to ZBB advocates, gives upper management a rational basis for determining which organizational activities can earn their keep and which cannot.

Ranking does not have to stop at the departmental level. It can continue to the highest executive level. But, especially in larger organizations, the sheer volume of decision packages can hopelessly overload top management. If management chooses to take ZBB to the very top, computerization of specially coded decision packages will be necessary to streamline the process.

Step 3: Allocation of Funds   All organizations, whatever their nature or purpose, face the problem of limited funds. Businesses generate funds by selling stock, borrowing, and selling goods and services. Not-for-profit service organizations typically rely on grants, donations, and fees. Government agencies require legislated appropriations. Regardless of the source, the more intelligently that funds are allocated, the more effective the organization. Supporters of ZBB contend that this is where their cost-benefit approach to budgeting truly pays off. Only those decision packages that emerge from successive rounds of ranking with a high priority are funded. This overturns the traditional practice of allocating funds to activities that have outlived their usefulness.

Feedback   As with any planning aid, managers learn a great deal about ZBB by experiencing successes and failures while developing and implementing it. Systematically collected and interpreted feedback on the ZBB process itself provides the basis for future improvement. Moreover, general planning deficiencies, such as vague objectives, that hinder the implementation of ZBB can be targeted for corrective action during the next planning cycle.

ZBB's Track Record

As with MBO, on-the-job research evidence of ZBB's effectiveness is sparse. Fortunately, researchers evaluated the U.S. Government's ZBB program.[5] One year after the Office of Management and Budget had implemented ZBB in ten federal departments and six agencies representing 74 percent of the federal budget, a follow-up questionnaire was completed by a representative of each department and agency. Each respondent rated his or her organization's experience with ZBB on the basis of eleven criteria. Three major areas covered by the 11 criteria were achievement of agency objectives, effectiveness of resource allocation,

Table B.3 Positive and Negative Aspects of U.S. Government's ZBB Program

Positives
1. Effective tool for allocating limited resources.
2. Helpful in setting priorities.
3. Greater participation of management in decision making.
4. Participation leading to improved budget quality.

Negatives
1. No significant cost savings (though not an intended objective of the federal ZBB program).
2. Excessive expenditures of time and effort required.
3. Difficulty in defining minimum-level decision packages.
4. Difficulty in ranking both dissimilar and interrelated decision packages.

SOURCE: Reprinted by permission of Virendra S. Sherlekar and Burton V. Dean, "An Evaluation of the Initial Year of Zero-Base Budgeting in the Federal Government," *Management Science*, Volume 26, Number 8, (August 1980): 750–772. Copyright 1980 The Institute of Management Sciences.

and quality of budgets. Although the overall rating of ZBB was slightly on the positive side (six on a scale of one to ten), a revealing combination of positive and negative factors emerged (see Table B.3).

After reviewing the findings of the foregoing study, one management writer noted that the benefits attributed to the government's ZBB program were intangibles such as better communication, better understanding, and increased participation. He then offered a somewhat pessimistic conclusion about ZBB:

> In principle, it is a tool that allows a more searching examination of the budget than traditional incremental budgeting can ever hope to produce, and at the very least it can provide planners with some indication of the excess cost of a current operation compared with an idealized model, unencumbered with constraints and commitments that have accumulated with the passage of time. In reality, however, it can achieve much less than its promoters claim, largely because its success relies on the cooperation of human beings, whose first natural instinctive reaction is self-preservation and self-interest.[6]

The pushing aside of organizational interests by self-interests is not a problem unique to ZBB; it is an ever-present challenge for managers. Careful implementation of ZBB through skill training, reduction of opposition to change with give-and-take group discussions, ongoing technical assistance, and rewards for sincere effort can all help enhance ZBB's value as a planning aid. The organizational climate necessary for successful ZBB is precisely the same as that outlined in Chapter 4 for management by objectives.

EOQ: A Quantitative Inventory Control Tool

Since World War II, precise statistical inventory control techniques have been developed to replace crude rules of thumb. One such technique is the economical order quantity (EOQ) model. This useful tool was developed to help managers achieve an economical balance between two important inventory control variables, acquisition costs and carrying costs. It costs money not only to acquire inventory but also to keep it on hand. The EOQ model offers managers a rational way of determining *how much* to order each time an order is placed.

The basic EOQ formula is

$$EOQ = \sqrt{\frac{2FU}{CP}}$$

with the variables defined as follows:

EOQ = the most economical quantity to order each time an order is placed
  F = fixed costs incurred in placing and receiving a single order (acquisition costs)
  U = units of the item used per year
  C = carrying costs (storage, insurance, taxes, spoilage, and so on) expressed as a percentage of inventory value
  P = purchase price per unit of inventory.[7]

To demonstrate the use of this model, assume that a manager calculates the following values:

$$F = \$10$$
$$U = 100 \text{ units}$$
$$C = 20 \text{ percent}$$
$$P = \$1$$

These values can then be worked into the model as follows:

$$EOQ = \sqrt{\frac{2FU}{CP}}$$

$$EOQ = \sqrt{\frac{2 \times 10 \times 100}{0.2 \times 1}} = \sqrt{\frac{2,000}{0.2}} = \sqrt{10,000} = 100 \text{ units}$$

Considering the acquisition and carrying costs, an order of 100 units is the most economical quantity for this item. Smaller orders will drive up acquisition costs, but larger orders will inflate carrying costs. The EOQ model helps management balance these two costs.

Quantitative Decision-making Tools

Management scientists have devised various techniques to help managers make better decisions. In this section we introduce seven quantitative decision-making tools: payoff tables, decision trees, histograms, linear programming, queuing theory, simulation, and gaming. The first three are explained in detail and accompanied by working examples, but the last four are discussed only briefly to broaden the reader's familiarity with such techniques. Payoff tables, decision trees, and histograms have been selected for detailed examination because each is a particularly useful quantitative decision-making aid that does not require any knowledge of advanced mathematics or access to sophisticated computers. They can be used by managers in large and small organizations alike.

Payoff Tables Even under the most predictable and stable conditions, selecting from among a number of alternative courses of action can be a difficult task. Conditions of risk and uncertainty further complicate decision making. And more often than not, managers are faced with two or more decision alternatives and a number of environmental possibilities. This is where payoff tables can help sort out things. A **payoff table** lists decision alternatives and environmental conditions, and it gives the potential monetary payoff for each possible combination of variables.

It is important to remember when working with payoff tables that they deal in *net* amounts. For instance, net profit for a particular product is the result of subtracting all related expenses from the sales revenue for that product. In these terms, it is evident that net profit will be higher if expenses are kept as low as possible and/or sales revenue is as high as possible.

Conditional Payoffs Two types of payoff tables are shown in Table B.4, one for conditional payoff and the other for expected payoff. Assume that the payoff tables have been generated by managers in an automobile manufacturing company to help them decide how many electric minicars the firm should produce for the coming year. Demand could vary, because these cars are a radically new form of family transportation. The conditional payoffs for each combination of environmental condition and decision alternative are listed in Table A. This is how the conditional payoff table got its name; it is simply an "if-then" table. If management is confident that demand will be high, then production should be set at 6

Table B.4 Payoff Tables in Action

Table A Conditional Profits from Electric Minicar Sales			
Environmental Conditions (Demand for electric minicars)	**Decision Alternatives** (Production capacity devoted to electric minicars)		
	2%	4%	6%
High	$8,500,000	$11,000,000	$14,000,000
Moderate	8,000,000	8,000,000	7,000,000*
Low	7,000,000	5,500,000*	1,500,000*

*Reflects the added expense of unsold car inventory.

Table B Expected Profits from Electric Minicar Sales				
Environmental Conditions (Demand for electric minicars)	**Probability of** **Occurrence**	**Decision Alternatives** (Production capacity devoted to electric minicars)		
		2%	4%	6%
High	0.25	$2,125,000	$2,750,000	$3,500,000
Moderate	0.55	4,400,000	4,400,000	3,850,000
Low	0.20	1,400,000	1,100,000	300,000
		$7,925,000	$8,250,000	$7,650,000

percent because that would provide the highest payoff ($14 million) for that particular environmental condition. Accordingly, either 2 percent or 4 percent of capacity is appropriate for moderate demand, because they have equally high payoffs ($8 million). Finally, if management is reasonably certain that demand will be low, then production should be set at 2 percent to achieve the highest payoff possible ($7 million) under that condition.

Expected Payoffs   What if management is not certain about demand? This is when *expected* payoff tables become useful decision-making aids. Notice in Table B that probabilities have been introduced to reflect management's uncertainty about demand. The chance of high demand is estimated to be 0.25 (or 25 percent). Moderate demand is given a 0.55 probability, and low demand is assigned a 0.20 probability. The expected payoff for each set of variables in Table B is calculated by multiplying each conditional payoff in Table A by the probability assigned to each of the various environmental conditions. For example, the $8,500,000 figure in the upper-left corner of Table A yields, when multiplied by 0.25, the expected payoff of $2,125,000 found in the upper-left corner of Table B.

Expected payoff tables also vary from conditional tables in the way the decision alternative is selected. Instead of selecting the highest payoff for each condition, as was done in Table A, the decision alternative based on the highest *total* payoff is selected. In Table B, 4 percent production is recommended because it is associated with the highest total payoff ($8,250,000). This means that the *combination* of payoffs associated with 4 percent production is the best available, given uncertain demand and the relative probabilities assigned. In other words, the law of averages favors 4 percent production in this case.

Positive and Negative Aspects   Payoff tables have two advantages. First, they force managers to define decision alternatives and possible environmental conditions. Second, payoff tables require decision makers to balance expenses against revenue. In addition, *expected* payoff tables are realistic in that they define probabilities of occurrence. These probabilities may be objective if reliable historical data are available. But even in the absence of hard data, judgmental or subjective probabilities can be estimated.

On the negative side, the main disadvantage of payoff tables is that they may encourage unwarranted confidence because they involve the calculation of exact values. People tend to place a great deal of faith in precise-sounding numbers, but they often fail to consider how the numbers were derived in the first place. Payoff tables are simply an aid for decision makers. As such, they should supplement rather than replace sound managerial judgment.

Decision Trees

Payoff tables are convenient when a single decision needs to be made. But what tool can the decision maker use when a *series* of decisions must be made? Decision trees satisfy this more complex need. A **decision tree** is "a network representation of sequences of action-event combinations that are available to the decision maker. Each possible sequence of decisions and consequences is shown by a different path through the tree."[8] To a limited extent, decision trees have something in common with PERT, as discussed in Chapter 4. Both techniques force managers to define future courses of action. Unlike PERT, however, decision trees contain sequences or branches that will be abandoned once key decisions are made, whereas all branches in a PERT network represent desired action.

A sample decision tree is given in Figure B.2. The working example behind this particular illustration is a pair of decisions facing the management team of ABC Company. The company has designed two promising products, X and Y, but unfortunately it cannot afford to introduce both at once. Ideally, if one is introduced successfully, it will provide the funds

Figure B.2 A Sample Decision Tree

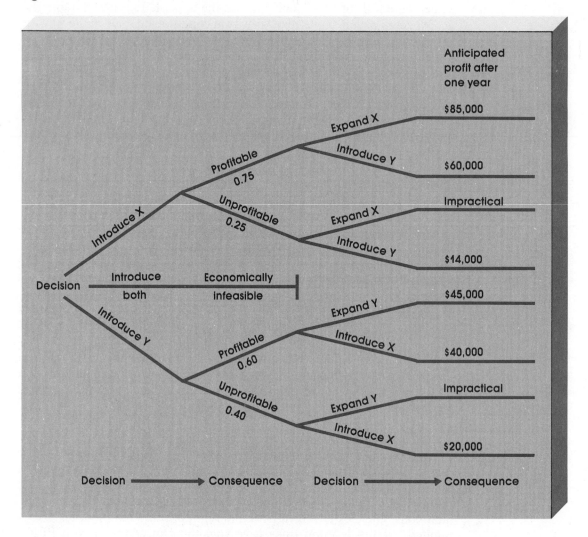

needed either to (1) expand the production and marketing efforts for that product or (2) permit the introduction of the second product. The alternative sequences for these two decisions are traced out in Figure B.2, along with the estimated probabilities and eventual profit potential for each feasible alternative.

According to this decision tree, the most profitable sequence of decisions would be to introduce product X and later expand the production and marketing of that same product. The next best sequence would be to introduce X and then Y. Notice that the estimated probabilities enhance the precision of the decision-making process. A decision tree provides a convenient visual layout of the possible choices in making a sequence of decisions, along with their probable results.

Although the decision tree in Figure B.2 is relatively simple, the technique also is suitable for more complex situations. Success with decision trees largely depends on the identification of all relevant decisions and the assignment of realistic probabilities. Actual construction of the tree is comparatively straightforward.

Histograms   Decision makers faced with conditions of risk or uncertainty may find histograms useful. Although histograms have been around for a long time, their application to managerial decision making is relatively new. Histograms have the advantage of encouraging managers to identify the various possible outcomes of a contemplated decision and to attach a subjective probability to each. As a visual aid to decision making under conditions of risk or uncertainty, a **histogram** graphically profiles the subjective probability of each outcome.

As an example, assume that the home office of an insurance company is considering the purchase of a new computerized word processor. Because of a large number of mass mailings each year, the company needs a fast and reliable way to produce attractive letters. The particular system being considered costs $45,000. One of the key decision points is the *payback period*. In other words, in how many years will the word processor pay for itself? Generally, the shorter the payback period is, the better. As a first step toward pinning down the payback period, three managers in the finance department have constructed the three histograms illustrated in Figure B.3.

What do these three histograms tell us? First, as one proponent of histograms explained, "From observing the width of the range of outcomes and the chance associated with each, a reader of the histogram is able to assess how confident the histogram maker feels about his judgments."[9] It seems that manager B is the *most* confident because the range of B's histogram is only two years, and each has a high probability. Manager C is the *least* confident because of the wide range of years and relatively low probabilities assigned to each. Manager A falls between B and C in terms of confidence. As a technical point, notice that the probabilities in each histogram add up to 100 percent.

The three histograms narrow the expected payback period to a range of two to seven years, and by calculating an average probability for each expected payback year, a *group* opinion can be obtained. For example, the average of the three estimates for a three-year payback is 33.3 percent (50 percent plus 45 percent plus 5 percent divided by 3). But 33.3 percent is not as high as the 36.6 percent for the four-year payback (30 percent plus 55 percent plus 25 percent divided by 3). The group choice, therefore, is four

Figure B.3 Histograms as a Decision-making Aid

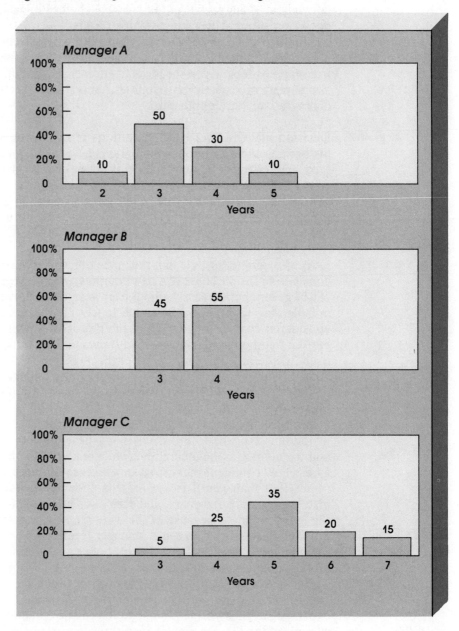

years. If a four-year payback is acceptable to management, then the decision will be to purchase the new word processor.

Histograms are suitable for any decision in which conditions of risk or uncertainty prevail and a range of identifiable outcomes can be described. They may be used in either profit-making or not-for-profit organizations, large or small, or by a single manager or groups of managers. However, since each manager develops only one histogram for a particular decision, two or more heads generally are better than one; multiple histograms permit useful comparisons. Histograms are extremely versatile.

Linear Programming

Managers often are called on to be maximizers and/or minimizers. Business managers want to maximize revenues and profits as the situation will allow, and managers of government agencies and other not-for-profit organizations want to maximize their budget allocations or operating funds. But regardless of the type of organization, expense minimization is a continuing concern, with resource allocation as the overriding problem. Prior to the development of linear programming, managers had to rely largely on subjective, hit-or-miss judgment when allocating scarce resources. Now, with the power of linear programming and the speed of computers, this aspect of decision making has become much more precise.

Linear programming is a process of identifying variables that compete for the same resources and working them into either a graphical representation or a set of algebraic formulas.[10] Linear programming techniques allow the manager to identify the best possible combination of resources. Here the term *best* means "Maximum profit or minimum expense." For example, the management of a brewery that uses the same facilities to produce both a popular-priced brand of beer and a premium-priced brand must decide exactly how much of each brand to produce. Since only one brand can be brewed at a given time, the two brands are in effect competing for the same resource (the brewing facilities). By considering the profit margins and the brewing times of the two brands, a linear programming model will give management an idea of the most profitable production mix.

Other applications of linear programming are the minimization of warehousing, transportation, raw material, energy, and personnel costs. Naturally, as with all other quantitative decision-making tools, solutions produced through linear programming are only as good as the underlying assumptions. Linear programming supplements rather than replaces sound judgment.

Queuing Theory

Waiting lines are a source of frustration to the average consumer. To the management scientist, however, a waiting line is a queue to be managed systematically. There are obvious and not so obvious queues that affect our lives. Among the obvious ones are waiting lines in supermarkets, gas stations, class registration centers, airline ticket counters, fast-food restaurants, and theater box offices. Not so obvious but nonetheless important queues can be found in assembly-line operations, truck depots, supply and toolroom check-out counters, and airport runways. The common denominator of all queues is the time and money it costs to wait in line. Thus the purpose of queuing theory is to minimize costs by identifying the relevant costs of waiting and balancing them against the costs of expanding facilities that would cut down on waiting.

Queuing theory enables the manager to achieve favorable tradeoffs among relevant costs. For example, if a supermarket manager kept every check-out counter staffed all the time, few customers would have to wait in line. Staffing only one check-out counter no matter how many customers were waiting represents the other extreme. Both options are unworkable because labor costs would erode the profit margin in the first instance, and lost customers would reduce sales revenue in the second. Queuing theory can help supermarket management determine the most profitable staffing schedule for the check-out counters. Even though queuing theory is not widely used by general managers, it has great practical potential because of its broad applicability.

Simulation and Gaming

Exciting new decision aids have emerged since the development of high-speed computers. Complex calculations that would take weeks, months, or possibly years to complete by hand can be processed by computer in a matter of minutes. Greater accuracy of calculation is a second by-product of computer technology. Two of the most promising new developments in this area are simulation and gaming.

Simulation in Action   A computer simulation is a mathematical model of the key aspects of the system under study. Obviously, when the system under study is a large company or a huge government agency, it would be virtually impossible to include all conceivable relevant variables in the mathematical model. Therefore, a simulation represents, in a manner of speaking, the system's skeleton. It is a simplified representation of reality.

Cerro de Pasco, a multinational firm specializing in primary metals such as zinc, is a good case in point. The mining and metals business is highly uncertain. Wide price swings and political turmoil in developing countries where the ore is mined are serious threats to effective planning and decision making. Cerro de Pasco's management has responded to the challenge by building a sophisticated computer simulation of its business. Data on metals prices and costs related to labor, transportation, raw materials, and capital are fed into the computer along with resource limitations and other constraints. All told, the model contains approximately 370 variables and relies on more than 150 algebraic equations. Timely manual processing would be virtually impossible. The final result is a simplified, easy-to-understand computer print-out that recommends certain decisions. As new situations and problems arise, they are worked into the simulation to test their impact on prices and profits. Hypothetical decisions are handled in a similar manner. Computer-assisted simulation helped the firm improve its profit picture. However, as the users of this approach told *Business Week,* "It is no automatic system, but rather a management tool that must be used in connection with a hefty dose of human judgment."[11]

Gaming   Computerized gaming is useful in a win-lose or competitive situation. In competitive situations, intercompany strategies are dynamically related. When one competitor makes a move, a price cut, for example, then the adversary makes a countermove, typically a larger price reduction. Price cutting, in turn, affects profit margins. Competitive relationships are constantly fluctuating, and every action has one or more reactions: only a computer can keep track of all the variables and interactions among them. Hand calculation would be difficult and time consuming, if not impossible. Like simulation, gaming is still in the developmental stage. But as the state of the art improves, gaming will be increasingly important in helping managers predict and promptly respond to competitors' actions.

References

1. Peter A. Pyhrr, unpublished speech, as cited in Stanton C. Lindquist and R. Bryant Mills, "Whatever Happened to Zero-base Budgeting?" *Managerial Planning* 29 (January-February 1981): 31.

2. See Peter A. Pyhrr, *Zero-Base Budgeting* (New York: Wiley, 1973), p. xi.

3. For a clear and concise overview of zero-base budgeting, see the five-part series by Norman H. Wright, Jr., in *Management World* (October 1976, December 1976, February 1977, April 1977, and June 1977).

4. See James C. Wetherbe and John R. Montanari, "Zero Based Budgeting in the Planning Process," *Strategic Management Journal* 2 (January/March 1981): 1–14.

5. Virendra S. Sherlekar and Burton V. Dean, "An Evaluation of the Initial Year of Zero-Base Budgeting in the Federal Government," *Management Science* 26 (August 1980): 750–772.

6. Samuel Eilon, "ZBB—Promise or Illusion?" *Omega* 9, No. 2 (1981): 112.

7. Drawn from J. Fred Weston and Eugene F. Brigham, *Managerial Finance,* 6th ed. (Hinsdale, Ill.: Dryden Press, 1978), pp. 190–195.

8. Rodney D. Johnson and Bernard R. Siskin, *Quantitative Techniques for Business Decisions* (Englewood Cliffs, N.J.: Prentice-Hall, 1976), p. 69.

9. Irwin Kabus, "You Can Bank on Uncertainty," *Harvard Business Review* 54 (May-June 1976): 97.

10. For a good introductory discussion of linear programming, see Stanley Letchford, "Linear Programming I," *The Accountant* 182 (June 5, 1980):

852–854; Stanley Letchford, "Linear Programming II," *The Accountant* 182 (June 26, 1980): 986–987; and Stanley Letchford, "Linear Programming III," *The Accountant* 183 (July 3, 1980): 36–37.

11. "A Computer Model to Upgrade Zinc Profits," *Business Week* No. 2243 (August 26, 1972): 76.

Glossary

Acceptance theory of authority Chester I. Barnard's belief that a leader's authority is determined by his or her subordinates' willingness to comply. (Ch. 7)

Advocacy advertising The controversial practice of promoting a point of view along with a product or service. (Ch. 3)

Affirmative action program (AAP) A plan for actively seeking out, employing, and developing the talents of those groups traditionally discriminated against in employment. (Ch. 9)

Alcoholism A disease in which an individual's normal social and economic roles are disrupted by the consumption of alcohol. (Ch. 15)

Altruism An unselfish devotion to the interests of others. (Ch. 18)

Antecedent An environmental cue that prompts an individual to behave in a given manner. (Ch. 13)

Authority The right to direct the actions of others. (Ch. 7)

Batch processing A data processing procedure whereby transactions are stored up, turned into machine-readable form such as magnetic tapes, and processed all at one time. (Ch. 16)

Behavior modification (B. Mod.) The practical application of Skinnerian operant conditioning techniques to everyday behavior problems. (Ch. 13)

Behaviorally anchored rating scales (BARS) Job performance rating scales divided into increments of observable job behavior determined through job analysis. (Ch. 9)

Behaviorism A philosophy that holds that observable behavior is more important than hypothetical inner states such as needs, motives, or expectancies. (Ch. 13)

Body language Nonverbal communication in the form of facial expressions and body movements. (Ch. 10)

Boredom and alienation barrier The point at which behavioral problems such as the absen-teeism and turnover caused by overspecialized jobs drive up the cost of producing each unit of output. (Ch. 11)

Break-even point The level of sales at which the firm neither suffers a loss nor realizes a profit. (Ch. 4)

Budget variance The difference between the actual figures and the budgeted ones. (Ch. 15)

Budget A formally prepared financial projection. (Ch. 15)

Bureaucracy Max Weber's model for the most rationally efficient organization characterized by (1) division of labor, (2) hierarchy of authority, (3) a framework of rules, and (4) impersonality. (Ch. 7)

Business cycle The up and down movement of an economy's ability to generate wealth (predictable sequence but variable timing). (Ch. 3)

Cafeteria compensation A plan for allowing each employee to determine the make-up of his or her employee benefit package. (Ch. 11)

Cardiovascular disease A largely preventable disease involving hardening of the arteries, which often leads to heart attack or stroke; the number one killer in industrialized nations. (Ch. 15)

Causes (of problems) Variables that, because of their presence or absence from the situation, are primarily responsible for the difference between actual and desired conditions. (Ch. 6)

Centralization Top management retains a relatively high degree of decision-making authority. (Ch. 8)

Closed system A self-sufficient entity. (Ch. 2)

Cohesiveness The tendency of group members to follow the group and resist outside influences. (Ch. 12)

Commonweal organization An organization that offers standardized services to all members of a given population. (Ch. 7)

Communication The transfer of information and understanding from one person to another person. (Ch. 10)

Comparative management The study of how management practices compare across different cultures. (Ch. 19)

Computer A data processor that can perform substantial computation, including numerous arithmetic or logic operations, without intervention by a human operator during the run. (Ch. 16)

Computer-integrated manufacturing (CIM) Computer-aided design (CAD) and computer-aided manufacturing (CAM) linked in a system that manages data flow while directing the movement and processing of material. (Ch. 17)

Condition of certainty A decision-making situation in which there is no doubt about the factual basis of a particular decision and its outcome can be predicted accurately. (Ch. 6)

Condition of risk A decision-making situation in which a decision must be made on the basis of incomplete but reliable factual information. (Ch. 6)

Condition of uncertainty A decision-making situation in which there is little or no reliable factual information available. (Ch. 6)

Conflict All kinds of opposition or antagonistic interaction; based on scarcity of power, resources or social position, and differing value structures. (Ch. 12)

Conflict trigger A circumstance that increases the chances of intergroup or interpersonal conflict. (Ch. 12)

Conformity Complying with the role expectations and norms perceived by the majority to be associated with a particular situation. (Ch. 12)

Contingency approach An effort to determine through research which managerial practices and techniques are appropriate in specific situations. (Ch. 2)

Contingency design The process of determining the degree of environmental uncertainty and adapting the organization and its subunits to that environment. (Ch. 8)

Contingent time off (CTO) Establishing a challenging yet fair daily performance standard or quota, and letting employees go home when it is reached. (Ch. 11)

Continuous reinforcement Reinforcement of every instance of a desired behavior. (Ch. 13)

Contribution margin The portion of the unit selling price above and beyond the variable costs that can be applied to fixed costs. (Ch. 4)

Control The process of taking the necessary corrective action to ensure that organizational objectives are accomplished as effectively and efficiently as possible. (Ch. 15)

Convergence The philosophical view that the world is becoming more uniform because of forces such as technology, education, and pragmatism. (Ch. 19)

Corporate philanthropy The charitable donation of company resources. (Ch. 18)

Corporate social responsibility The notion that corporations have an obligation to constituent groups in society other than stockholders and beyond that prescribed by law or union contract. (Ch. 18)

Creativity The reorganization of experience into new configurations. (Ch. 6)

Critical path The most time-consuming chain of activities and events in a PERT network. (Ch. 4)

Critical success factors The limited number of areas in which results, if they are satisfactory, will ensure successful competitive performance for the organization. (Ch. 16)

Data base management system (DBMS) A computerized file system of organizational data that permits simultaneous access by many different users with differing information needs. (Ch. 16)

Decentralization An organization design alternative in which top management delegates a relatively high degree of decision-making authority to lower-level managers. (Ch. 8)

Decision making The process of identifying and choosing alternative courses of action in a manner appropriate to the demands of the situation. (Ch. 6)

Decision rule A statement that identifies the situation in which a decision is required and specifies how the decision will be made. (Ch. 6)

Decision tree A network representation of sequences of action-event combinations that are available to the decision maker. (App. B)

Delegation The process of assigning various degrees of decision-making authority to subordinates. (Ch. 8)

Departmentalization The grouping of related jobs, activities, or processes into major organizational subunits. (Ch. 8)

Diagnosis-prescription cycle The basic organization development (OD) process in which specific problem areas are diagnosed and appropriate interventions are prescribed. (Ch. 14)

Differentiation A structural force involving the tendency among specialists to think and act differently. (Ch. 8)

Distributed data processing A decentralized configuration in which some portion of the computing function is performed outside a centralized location. (Ch. 16)

Divergence A philosophical belief that forces such as cultural inertia, differing stages of economic development, unevenly distributed resources, and regional overpopulation guarantee global diversity. (Ch. 19)

Dual career couples A relationship in which both partners pursue professional careers full time. (App. A)

Dynamic equilibrium In open systems, the process of maintaining the internal balance necessary for survival by importing needed resources from the environment. (Ch. 7)

Economics The study of how scarce resources are used to create wealth and how that wealth is distributed. (Ch. 3)

Economies of scope The opposite of economies of scale that are achieved when flexible automation makes it economical to produce small batches of a variety of products with the same machines. (Ch. 17)

Effectiveness The achievement of a stated objective. (Ch. 1)

Efficiency The resources required to achieve an objective are weighed against what was actually accomplished. (Ch. 1)

Egalitarianism A social philosophy that advocates social, political, and economic equality. (Ch. 3)

Employment selection test Any procedure used as a basis for an employment decision. (Ch. 9)

Enlightened self-interest The realization that business ultimately helps itself by helping to solve societal problems. (Ch. 18)

Equifinality Reaching the same result by different means in open systems. (Ch. 7)

Ethical advocate A business ethics specialist who sits as a full-fledged member of the board of directors and acts as the board's social conscience. (Ch. 18)

Ethics The study of moral obligation involving the separation of right from wrong. (Ch. 18)

Ethnocentric attitude An attitude among international managers in which home-country personnel, ideas, and practices are viewed as inherently superior to those from abroad. (Ch. 19)

Expectancy The subjective probability that one thing will lead to another. (Ch. 11)

Expectancy theory A motivation model based on the assumption that motivational strength is determined by perceived probabilities of success. (Ch. 11)

Expropriation The takeover or nationalization of a company by the host government. (Ch. 19)

Extinction The discouragement of a specific behavior by ignoring it. (Ch. 13)

Extrinsic rewards Payoffs granted to the individual by other people. (Ch. 11)

Feedback control The process of gathering information about a completed activity, evaluating that information, and taking steps to improve similar activities in the future. (Ch. 15)

Feedforward control The active anticipation of problems and their timely solution, rather than after-the-fact reaction. (Ch. 15)

Financial ratios Measures of an organization's financial status that can be compared with industry standards to gauge the organization's financial health. (Ch. 15)

Fixed costs Contractual costs that must be

paid regardless of the level of output or sales. (Ch. 4)

Fixed-position layout   A work flow layout in which the product, by virtue of its bulk or weight, remains at one location. (Ch. 17)

Flexible budget   A budgeting technique using standardized costs that allows managers to exercise feedforward control over the expenditure of funds. (Ch. 15)

Flexitime   A work-scheduling plan that allows employees to determine their own arrival and departure times within specified limits. (Ch. 11)

Flow chart   A graphical device for sequencing significant events and yes-or-no decisions. (Ch. 4)

Forecasts   Predictions, projections, or estimates of future events or conditions in the environment in which the organization operates. (Ch. 5)

Formal group   A group created for the purpose of doing productive work. (Ch. 12)

Formal leadership   Influencing relevant others to pursue official organizational objectives. (Ch. 13)

Functional authority   An organic design alternative that gives staff personnel temporary, limited line authority for specified tasks. (Ch. 8)

Gainsharing plan   The practice of sharing the responsibility and rewards for organizational improvements among all employees. (Ch. 11)

Gantt chart   A graphical scheduling technique named for Henry L. Gantt that is typically applied to production operations. (Ch. 4)

General systems theory   An interdisciplinary area of study based on the assumption that everything is part of a larger, interdependent arrangement. (Ch. 2)

Genuine participation   The practice of not only tapping the creative ideas of all relevant parties but also integrating those ideas into the nature and timing of the change. (Ch. 14)

Geocentric attitude   A world-oriented attitude among international managers whereby skill rather than nationality determines who gets promoted or transferred to key positions around the globe. (Ch. 19)

Grand strategy   A general explanation of how the organization's mission is to be accomplished. (Ch. 5)

Grapevine   The unofficial and informal communication system. (Ch. 10)

Group   Two or more freely interacting individuals who share a common identity and purpose. (Ch. 12)

Groupthink   A mode of thinking that people engage in when they are deeply involved in a cohesive in-group, when the members' strivings for unanimity override their motivation to realistically appraise alternative courses of action. (Ch. 12)

Histogram   A visual aid to decision making under conditions of risk or uncertainty that graphically profiles the subjective probability of each outcome. (App. B)

Human relations movement   A concerted effort among theorists and practitioners to make managers more sensitive to their employees' needs. (Ch. 2)

Human resource planning   The development of a comprehensive staffing strategy for meeting the organization's future human resource needs. (Ch. 9)

Idealize   Dissolving a problem by actually changing the nature of the system in which it resides. (Ch. 6)

Incongruency thesis   Chris Argyris's contention that the demands of the typical organization are incongruent with the psychological needs of the individual. (Ch. 9)

Indexed standard costing   A budgeting procedure whereby standard costs are adjusted for inflation monthly rather than yearly. (Ch. 15)

Influence   Any attempt by an employee to change the behavior of superiors, peers, or subordinates. (Ch. 13)

Informal group   A group in which the principal reason for belonging is friendship. (Ch. 12)

Informal leadership   Influencing others to pursue unofficial objectives that may or may not serve the organization's interests. (Ch. 13)

Information   Data organized and interpreted within a relevant frame of reference that enhances effective decision making. (Ch. 16)

Information requirements analysis   The act of identifying the meaningful data that a worker needs in order to perform a job or task. (Ch. 16)

Innovation lag   The time it takes for a new idea to be translated into satisfied demand for a good or service. (Ch. 3)

Innovation process   The systematic development and practical application of a new idea. (Ch. 3)

Instrumental value   An enduring belief that a certain way of behaving is appropriate in all situations. (Ch. 6)

Integration   A structural force involving the collaboration among specialists that is needed to achieve a common purpose. (Ch. 8)

Intensive technology   A custom technology capable of creating products or services that fit each customer's particular set of needs. (Ch. 7)

Intermediate planning   The process of determining the contributions that subunits can make with allocated resources. (Ch. 4)

Intermittent reinforcement   Reinforcement of some, rather than all, instances of a desired behavior. (Ch. 13)

Internal auditing   The independent appraisal of the various operations and systems of control within an organization to determine whether acceptable policies and procedures are followed, established standards are met, resources are used efficiently and economically, planned missions are accomplished effectively, and the organization's objectives are being achieved. (Ch. 15)

International management   The pursuit of organizational objectives in an international and intercultural setting. (Ch. 19)

Intervention   A systematic attempt in organization development (OD) to correct an organizational deficiency uncovered through diagnosis. (Ch. 14)

Intrinsic rewards   Self-granted and internally experienced payoffs. (Ch. 11)

Inventory control   The process of establishing and maintaining appropriate levels of reserve stocks of goods. (Ch. 17)

Iron law of responsibility   The belief that, in the long run, those who do not use power in a way that society considers responsible will tend to lose it. (Ch. 18)

Job analysis   The process of determining the fundamental elements of jobs through systematic observation and analysis. (Ch. 9)

Job description   A clear and concise summary of the duties of a specific job and the qualifications for holding it. (Ch. 9)

Job design   The delineation of task responsibilities as dictated by organizational strategy, technology, and structure. (Ch. 11)

Job enlargement   The process of combining two or more specialized tasks in a work flow sequence into a single job. (Ch. 11)

Job enrichment   Redesigning a job to increase its motivating potential. (Ch. 11)

Job rotation   Periodically moving people from one specialized job to another to prevent stagnation. (Ch. 11)

Just-in-time production (JIT)   A philosophy that focuses attention on eliminating waste by purchasing or manufacturing just enough of the right items just in time. (Ch. 17)

Kanban   (A Japanese word.) A manual inventory control procedure developed by Toyota that uses cards to keep inventory status highly visible and that manages production so that necessary units are made in the necessary quantities at the necessary time. (Ch. 17)

Laboratory training   A group development process that aims at emotional rather than intellectual learning by exposing a group of individuals to an ambiguous and somewhat anxiety-producing situation. (Ch. 14)

Leadership   A social influence process in which the leader seeks the voluntary participation of subordinates in an effort to reach organizational objectives. (Ch. 13)

Line and staff organization   An organization in which a distinction is made between line positions, those in the formal chain of command, and staff positions, those serving in an advisory capacity outside the formal chain of command. (Ch. 8)

Logical incrementalism   A process that top management strategists use to sell the long-range goals that they evolve in a logical but somewhat disjointed fashion. (Ch. 5)

Long-linked technology   Technology involving the serial interdependence of work, as in assembly lines. (Ch. 7)

Lubrication bribe   A relatively small amount of money that greases the wheels of bureaucratic progress. (Ch. 19)

Management   The process of working with and through others to achieve organizational objectives in a changing environment. Central to this process is the effective and efficient use of limited resources. (Ch. 1)

Management by objectives (MBO)   A comprehensive management system based on measurable and participatively set objectives. (Ch. 4)

Management information system (MIS)   A computer-based network that integrates the collection, processing, and transmission of information. (Ch. 16)

Managerial ability   The demonstrated capacity to achieve organizational objectives both effectively and efficiently. (Ch. 1)

Managerial functions   General administrative duties (for example, planning, decision making, organizing, staffing, communicating, motivating, leading, and controlling) carried out by managers in virtually all productive organizations. (Ch. 1)

Managerial roles   Specific categories of managerial behavior (for example, acting as a figurehead, leader, liaison, nerve center, disseminator, spokesperson, entrepreneur, disturbance handler, resource allocator, and negotiator). (Ch. 1)

Managerial work-stations   Multifunction, on-line computer terminals connected to an organizationwide information network. (Ch. 16)

Master production schedule   An authoritative statement of how many end items are to be produced and when. (Ch. 17)

Material requirements planning (MRP)   A systematic and comprehensive manufacturing planning and control technique designed to increase the efficiency of material handling and inventory control. (Ch. 17)

Matrix   An organization structure in which vertical and horizontal lines of authority are combined. (Ch. 8)

Measurementship   Political maneuvering motivated by a desire to "look good" and "play the numbers game," even if it means manipulating reports and control data. (Ch. 15)

Mechanistic organizations   Organizations that are rigid in design and have strong bureaucratic qualities. (Ch. 8)

Mediating technology   Technology that links together otherwise unassociated individuals in some mutually beneficial fashion. (Ch. 7)

Mentor   An individual who systematically develops a subordinate's abilities through intensive tutoring, coaching, and guidance. (Ch. 13)

Motivation   The psychological process that gives behavior purpose and direction. (Ch. 11)

Multinational corporation   A number of affiliated business establishments that function as productive enterprises in different countries simultaneously. (Ch. 19)

Multinational reciprocity   A mutual exchange of benefits between a foreign-owned company and a host country. (Ch. 19)

Multivariate analysis   A research technique used to determine how a combination of variables interacts to cause a particular outcome. (Ch. 2)

Negative reinforcement   The encouragement of a specific behavior by immediately withdrawing or terminating something the individual finds displeasing. (Ch. 13)

Noise   Any interference with the normal flow of

understanding from one person to another. (Ch. 10)

Nonprogrammed decisions   Those decisions that are made in complex, important, and nonroutine situations, often under circumstances that are new and largely unfamiliar. (Ch. 6)

Norms   General standards of conduct that help individuals judge what is right or wrong or good or bad in a given social setting. (Ch. 12)

Objective   A specific commitment to achieve a measurable result within a given time frame. (Ch. 4)

Objective probabilities   Probabilities that are derived mathematically from reliable historical data. (Ch. 6)

Open system   An entity that depends on the surrounding environment for survival (for example, the human body or an organization). (Ch. 2)

Operant conditioning   The science of how behavior is controlled by the surrounding environment. (Ch. 13)

Operational approach   A production-oriented area of management dedicated to improving efficiency and cutting waste. (Ch. 2)

Operational planning   The process of determining how specific tasks can best be accomplished on time with available resources. (Ch. 4)

Operations management   A field of management encompassing the design, implementation, operation, and control of systems made up of men, materials, capital equipment, information, and money to accomplish some set of objectives. (Chs. 2 and 17)

Operative philosophy   A system of values inferred from one's actual behavior, but not necessarily from one's stated intentions. (Ch. 18)

Optimize   Solving a problem by systematically researching alternative solutions through scientific observation and quantitative measurement and selecting the one with the best combination of benefits. (Ch. 6)

Organic organizations   Organizations that tend to be quite fluid and flexible in structure. (Ch. 8)

Organization   A system of consciously coordinated activities or forces of two or more persons. (Ch. 7)

Organization chart   A diagram of an organization's official positions and formal lines of authority. (Ch. 8)

Organization development (OD)   A planned, managed, systematic process to change the culture, systems, and behavior of an organization, in order to improve the organization's effectiveness in solving its problems and achieving its objectives. (Ch. 14)

Organizational behavior   A modern approach to management that attempts to determine the causes of human work behavior and translate the results into effective management techniques. (Ch. 2)

Organizational culture   The collection of shared (stated or implied) beliefs, values, rituals, stories and legends, myths, and specialized language that foster a feeling of community among organization members. (Ch. 7)

Organizational effectiveness   Meeting organizational objectives and prevailing societal expectations in the near future, adapting and developing in the intermediate future, and surviving in the distant future. (Ch. 15)

Organizational politics   The pursuit of self-interest at work in the face of real or imagined opposition. (Ch. 12)

Organizational productivity   The ratio of an organization's total output to total input, adjusted for inflation, for a specified period of time. (Ch. 1)

Organizational socialization   The process through which outsiders are transformed into accepted insiders. (Ch. 7)

Organizing   The structuring of a coordinated system of authority relationships and task responsibilities. (Ch. 8)

Ostracism   Rejection from the group; figuratively, the capital punishment of group dynamics. (Ch. 12)

Payoff table   A decision-making tool that lists decision alternatives and environmental conditions and gives the potential monetary payoff for each possible combination of variables. (App. B)

Perception The process by which an individual gives meaning to his environment. (Ch. 10)

Perceptual defense The perceptual screening out of environmental stimuli. (Ch. 10)

Perceptual organization A perceptual process whereby otherwise meaningless and disorganized stimuli are arranged into meaningful patterns. (Ch. 10)

Perceptual set A perceptual screening-in process. (Ch. 10)

Performance appraisal The process of evaluating individual job performance as a basis for making objective personnel decisions. (Ch. 9)

PERT An acronym for Program Evaluation and Review Technique; a graphic sequencing and scheduling tool for large, complex, and nonroutine projects. (Ch. 4)

PERT activity Work in process or time-consuming jobs that begin and end with a PERT event. (Ch. 4)

PERT event A performance milestone representing the start or finish of some activity. (Ch. 4)

PERT time Estimated time for the completion of PERT activities. (Ch. 4)

Plan A specific, documented intention consisting of an objective and an action statement. (Ch. 4)

Planning The process of preparing for change and coping with uncertainty by formulating future courses of action. (Ch. 4)

Planning horizon The time that elapses between the formulation and the execution of a planned activity. (Ch. 4)

Political risk assessment The systematic means of assessing and managing the political risks of foreign direct investment or international business. (Ch. 19)

Polycentric attitude A host-country orientation based on the assumption that local managers know what is best for their operations because cultures are so different. (Ch. 19)

Positive reinforcement The encouragement of a specific behavior by immediately following it with a consequence that the individual finds pleasing. (Ch. 13)

Power The ability to marshal the human, informational, and material resources to get something done. (Ch. 13)

Priorities A ranking of goals or objectives in order of importance. (Ch. 4)

Problem The difference between an actual state of affairs and a desired state of affairs. (Ch. 6)

Problem solving The conscious process of reducing the difference between an actual situation and the desired situation. (Ch. 6)

Process flow chart A tool employing standard symbols for recording an operation or process in the sequence in which it occurs. (Ch. 17)

Process layout A work flow layout in which the components are grouped according to the general function they perform, without regard to any particular product. (Ch. 17)

Product design The process of creating a set of product specifications appropriate to the demands of the situation. (Ch. 17)

Product layout A work flow layout in which the components are arranged according to the progressive steps by which the product is made. (Ch. 17)

Product life cycle A graphic representation of the sequential rise and fall of a product's sales and profit. (Ch. 5)

Product technology The development of a working prototype (the second step in the three-step innovation process). (Ch. 3)

Production planning The process of formulating a resource transformation system that will effectively and efficiently meet the forecasted demand for goods and services. (Ch. 17)

Production technology The development of a production process that creates a profitable quantity-quality-price relationship (the third step in the three-step innovation process). (Ch. 3)

Programmed decisions Those decisions that are repetitive and routine and can be made with decision rules. (Ch. 6)

Psychological contract The reciprocal expectations that employees and employers have of one another. (Ch. 9)

Punishment The discouragement of a specific behavior by either immediately presenting an undesirable consequence or immediately removing something desirable. (Ch. 13)

Purchasing The procurement of raw materials, subcomponents, equipment, and services required to accomplish organizational objectives. (Ch. 17)

Quality control The process of ensuring that goods and services actually conform to the design specifications. (Ch. 17)

Quality control circles Voluntary problem-solving groups of five to ten employees from the same work area who meet regularly to discuss quality improvement. (Ch. 17)

Quality of work life (QWL) A process by which an organization attempts to unlock the creative potential of its people by involving them in decisions affecting their work lives. (Ch. 11)

Real-time processing Having computerized data files updated immediately so that users can obtain up-to-the-minute status reports. (Ch. 16)

Realistic job preview An honest explanation of what a job actually entails. (Ch. 11)

Refreezing The process in organization development (OD) of following up on problems, complaints, unanticipated side effects, and any lingering resistance. (Ch. 14)

Rewards The material and psychological payoffs for doing something. (Ch. 11)

Robot A reprogrammable machine capable of performing a variety of tasks requiring programmed manipulations of materials and tools. (Ch. 3)

Role A socially determined prescription for behavior in a specific position. (Ch. 12)

Role analysis The systematic clarification of interdependent modes of behavior in organization development (OD). (Ch. 14)

Satisfice Resolving a problem by settling for a solution that is good enough rather than the best possible. (Ch. 6)

Scientific management That kind of management which conducts a business or affairs by standards established by facts or truths gained through systematic observation, experiment, or reasoning. (Ch. 2)

Selectivity A sensory screening process that allows one to sort out and mentally process only certain details in one's surroundings. (Ch. 10)

Semantics The study of meaning in words. (Ch. 10)

Situational analysis A strategic management technique for matching environmental opportunities and obstacles with organizational strengths and weaknesses to determine the organization's right niche. (Ch. 5)

Small business An independently owned and managed profit-seeking enterprise employing fewer than 100 persons. (Ch. 1)

Social audit A commitment to systematic assessment of and reporting on some meaningful, definable domain of a company's activities that have social impact. (Ch. 18)

Span of control The number of people who report directly to a given manager. (Ch. 8)

Staffing Human resource planning, acquisition, and development aimed at providing the talent necessary for organizational success. (Ch. 9)

Strategic business unit (SBU) An organizational subunit that acts like an independent business in all major respects, including the formulation of its own strategic plans. (Ch. 8)

Strategic management The ongoing process of ensuring a competitively superior fit between the organization and its ever-changing environment. (Ch. 5)

Strategic planning The process of determining how to pursue the organization's long-term goals with the resources expected to be available. (Chs. 4 and 5)

Stress An adaptive response, mediated by individual characteristics and/or psychological processes, that is a consequence of any external action, situation or event that places special physical and/or psychological demands upon a person. (App. A)

Structured interview A series of job-related questions with predetermined answers that are consistently applied across all interviews for a particular job. (Ch. 9)

Subjective probabilities Probabilities that are estimated from past experience or judgment. (Ch. 6)

Survey research and feedback The practice of gathering and analyzing information and then feeding it back to the people who originally provided it. (Ch. 14)

Synergy The 2 + 2 = 5 effect wherein the whole is greater than the sum of its parts. (Ch. 5)

Synthesis perspective A view that characterizes society as the product of a constant tug of war between the forces of stability and change. (Ch. 3)

System A collection of parts that operate interdependently to achieve a common purpose. (Ch. 2)

Team building An organization development (OD) process for developing work group maturity and effectiveness. (Ch. 14)

Technological displacement The loss of jobs because of automation. (Ch. 3)

Technology All the tools and ideas available for extending the natural physical and mental reach of humankind. (Ch. 3)

Technostress A condition resulting from the inability of an individual or organization to adapt to the introduction of a new technology. (Ch. 16)

Telecommuting Work is sent to the employee's home computer via telephone modem instead of the employee commuting to a central office. (Ch. 16)

Teleconferencing Interactive group communication through any electronic medium. (Ch. 16)

Terminal value An enduring belief that a certain end-state of existence is worth striving for and attaining. (Ch. 6)

Theory Y Douglas McGregor's optimistic belief that the typical employee is an energetic and creative individual who can achieve great things if given the opportunity. (Ch. 2)

Total quality control (TQC) A strongly held belief that errors, if any, should be caught and corrected at the source (where the work is performed). (Ch. 17)

Training The process of changing employee behavior, attitudes, or opinions through some type of guided experience. (Ch. 9)

Transience Alvin Toffler's label for accelerating change. (Ch. 3)

Trend analysis The hypothetical extension of a past pattern of events or time series into the future. (Ch. 5)

Trust A belief in the integrity, character, or ability of others that is a key to group effectiveness. (Ch. 12)

Unfreezing In organization development (OD), the process of preparing the members of a social system for change and neutralizing initial resistance. (Ch. 14)

Universal process approach The oldest and one of the most popular approaches to management based on the assumption that all organizations, public or private or large or small, require the same rational process of management that can be reduced to separate functions and related principles. (Ch. 2)

Upward communication A process of systematically encouraging subordinates to share with management their feelings and ideas. (Ch. 10)

Values Abstract ideals that shape an individual's thinking and behavior. (Ch. 6)

Variable costs Costs that vary directly with the firm's production and sales. (Ch. 4)

Whistle blowing The practice of reporting perceived unethical practices to outsiders such as the press, government agencies, or public interest groups. (Ch. 18)

Whitemail bribe A large sum of money used to buy influence in high places. (Ch. 19)

Work flow layout The process of determining the physical arrangement of the productive system. (Ch. 17)

Workplace democracy Arrangements designed to increase employee self-determination. (Ch. 11)

ZBB decision package   In the zero-base budgeting process, a separate activity with its own set of costs and benefits. (App. B)

Zero-base budgeting   An operating, planning and budgeting process which requires each manager to justify his entire budget request in detail from scratch (hence zero base) and shifts the burden of proof to each manager to justify why he should spend any money at all. (App. B)

Name Index

Subject Index